Public Relations Law

PUBLIC

RELATIONS

LAW

MORTON J. SIMON

 APPLETON-CENTURY-CROFTS

EDUCATIONAL DIVISION

New York MEREDITH CORPORATION

Dedicated to . . .

Carol, my wife, for her steady flow of professional suggestions,
ideas and criticism . . . her unflagging hours of discussion and vetting of the manuscript . . . and, above all,
for her understanding patience.

Morton Jr., my son at Harvard Law School, for his help in
research and for some of the "legal thinking" in this book.

Lawrence, my son at the Temple University School of Communications, for his creative brainstorming and some
"left field" ideas which made a lot of sense.

FOREWORD

One of the criteria by which a profession is identified is the existence of a common body of knowledge. And no body of knowledge can be called complete if it lacks a competent analysis of the profession's legal aspects, bringing together in one place, so to speak, a study of the laws under which it functions, whether state or federal.

The field of public relations has never had such a compendium, valuable both for the practitioner and for the lawyers whose practice is to a greater or lesser degree concerned with the legal aspects of public relations. The need has been recognized for many years.

It has especially been recognized by the Foundation for Public Relations Research and Education which clearly bears, among other responsibilities, the duty to contribute significantly to the development of a common body of knowledge for public relations.

If anyone deserves credit for originating this project, it probably is G. Edward Pendray, who first recognized the need for a volume on the legal aspects of public relations while helping to develop the Accreditation Program of the Public Relations Society of America and who continued active participation even after he retired. Other members of the Foundation's Board of Trustees made noteworthy contributions. I should mention Dudley Parsons, Milton Fairman, George Hammond, Carroll Bateman, and Phelps Adams, although I do so with a sinking feeling that I may have missed a few others. If I have, I apologize.

A major difficulty has been the finding of a lawyer with a sufficiently complete—and sympathetic—understanding of public relations to make him want to undertake the project and to enable him to do it well. The search was long and often frustrating, for the number of lawyers with the necessary knowledge and attitude is apparently no greater than the number of public relations men with a corresponding attitude toward the law and lawyers.

But the search ended when we prevailed upon Morton J. Simon of the Philadelphia bar, long recognized as a specialist in the legal aspects of business communications, to undertake the project. An agreement

v

was quickly reached, the work proceeded expeditiously—he is a prodigious worker—and now it is in print. It is the earnest hope of both the Foundation and Mr. Simon that it will prove valuable to those on both sides, public relations men and women, and their learned counselors.

GLEN PERRY
PRESIDENT 1966–67
FOUNDATION FOR PUBLIC RELATIONS
RESEARCH AND EDUCATION

AUTHOR'S INTRODUCTION

The law and public relations really have much in common in their service orientation. Unfortunately, the similarities sometimes escape both the PR practitioner and the lawyer. It is our hope—certainly a postulate in the preparation of the manuscript—that this volume will bring into sharper focus these common interests and will serve as a tool for both.

We have sought to produce for the PR practitioner a basic book which will also guide the lawyer when he ventures into the legal sectors of public relations. More descriptive and operational materials have, therefore, been interpolated than may be customary in a "law book." This has seemed necessary as a starting point for both types of readers. To the PR man, they will help orient his legal needs. For the lawyer, they make up a factual background with which he may not be overly familiar. Of course, for the PR man, there is still no substitute for competent legal counsel—no matter how useful this volume may be.

Public relations is a "horizonal" function. It is, therefore, subject to a broad spectrum of seemingly unassociated legal regimens. Putting these variables into a single legal "mosaic" may serve to give a better appreciation of the overall perimeter of "public relations law." It may help to develop a "feeling" which will alert the PR practitioner to his legal hurdles.

From this "feeling" there has emerged—at least in our mind—the explanation for the seeming uncertainty about PR's legal involvements. The goals and achievements of PR may be largely intangible despite the practical nature of its tools. PR deals with relational problems. Many of these—legally at least—are in areas which are constantly shifting and developing.

For example, just during the preparation of this manuscript, Congressional and Supreme Court activity produced either entirely novel legislation (actual, pending or prospective) or drastically new interpretations of existing concepts. These affect such important PR/legal areas as copyright, lobbying, foreign agents, libel, obscenity, right of privacy, civil rights, etc. We must add to these the plethora of new "consumer protection" laws and enforcement methods which are coming out of Washington, the administrative agencies and the state legislatures. Many are still pending or anticipated. The end is nowhere in sight.

Thus the PR man and his legal counsel find themselves confronted with four elusive adjectives: *intangible, relational, shifting* and *developing*. None are particularly conducive to certainty.

As PR comes to be increasingly recognized in wider circles as an important tool of *management,* its legal needs will expand. The ultimate will be a complete correlation between its needs and those of the companies or activities which it serves.

Special mention must be made of the contributions of Dr. G. Edward Pendray and Glen Perry who have been our "strong right arm." Both vetted each chapter-draft as it came from the typewriter. Their comments, suggestions and criticism—forthright and detailed—have been uniquely significant. These two men have helped bring to this volume the undefinable sequelae of practical PR know-how, refined by a high degree of PR statesmanship.

Obviously however—despite our indebtedness to these many minds and careers—the final responsibility for the volume is ours. This is especially true of its errors.

Since this is a law book, it has notes. However, these have been collected at the end of each chapter where they should prove reasonably unobtrusive but still available to the interested or skeptical reader.

A real effort has been made to reduce the *number* of notes. Multiple references to the same authority have been avoided whenever possible. The legal reader may feel "short-changed." But we have long felt that the "law review approach" results in a superfluity of fine print and excessive motion of the eyeballs. In line with this concept, cross-references to other chapters or sections of the text have been inserted in the text itself instead of in the notes. In this manner, they are more likely to "flag" the reader.

Many of these notes refer to what we might call "PR materials." Most of these are readily available to the PR practitioner. It will be obvious that we have pursued to a considerable extent such sources as *Public Relations Journal, Public Relations News, Public Relations Reporter, Public Relations Quarterly* and the standard texts such as Cutlip and Center, Canfield, Stephenson, *et al.* To the lawyer who becomes involved in a "public relations case" we recommend that he marinate in this PR material when advising a client who has considerable expertise of his own.

Ever since our law school days, we have believed strongly that a book's "back materials" are extremely important. Without a good index the best book may be frustrating to the reader. Therefore, the author has prepared the index himself. This may account for its length and detail and, we hope, for its serviceability.

As Glen Perry has pointed out in his Foreword, the basic purpose of this volume is to make available in one place what may be called "public relations law." However, by the very nature of PR as a member of the communications family, PR's communications siblings may find considerable guidance in these pages.

Morton J. Simon

1701 Delancey Place
Philadelphia

ACKNOWLEDGMENTS

As this manuscript progressed, it received aid from many minds and hands. Although the full and final responsibility for these pages is mine, I want to acknowledge this assistance which has contributed in varied ways to this volume. Always fearful of inadvertent omissions, I say "Thank You," in alphabetical order, to the following:

Phelps H. Adams, Administrative Vice President—Public Relations, United States Steel, New York.

Lewis Ames, Esq., New York.

Douglas A. Anello, Esq., General Counsel, National Association of Broadcasters, Washington.

J. Carroll Bateman, President, Insurance Information Institute, New York.

Richardson Blair, Esq., Philadelphia.

Dr. Edward Brink, Wharton School, University of Pennsylvania, Philadelphia.

W. Howard Chase, Chairman, Howard Chase Associates, Inc., New York.

S. Jerry Cohen, Staff Director and Chief Counsel, Senate Subcommittee on Antitrust, Washington.

Stanley Cohen, Washington Editor, *Advertising Age*.

Hugh Collett, American Association of Advertising Agencies, New York.

Robert V. Cummins, P. R. Mallory & Co., Indianapolis.

Francis K. Decker, Esq., New York.

Paul Rand Dixon, Chairman, Federal Trade Commission, Washington.

Paschal O. Drake, Chief Packers and Stockyards Division, Department of Agriculture, Washington.

Milton Fairman, Vice President and Director of Public Relations, The Borden Company, New York.

Arthur C. Fatt, Chairman, Grey Advertising, Inc., New York.

Dr. Charles Goodman, Wharton School, University of Pennsylvania, Philadelphia.

Bert C. Goss, Chairman, Hill and Knowlton, Inc., New York.

Denny Griswold, Publisher, *Public Relations News*, New York.

George Griswold, Jr., Public Relations Manager, American Telephone and Telegraph Company, New York.

George Hammond, Chairman, Carl Byoir Associates, New York.

Howard F. Harris, Director of Public Relations, Corn Products, New York.

Quentin Harvell, Executive Director, Public Relations Society of America, New York.

Joseph Hefferman and Lucy Guereghian of the Philadelphia Bar Association Library.

William Jibb, Public Information Officer, Federal Trade Commission, Washington.

Scott Jones, Gardner, Jones & Cowell, Inc., Chicago, Ill.

Nina Kaider, Ruder & Finn, New York.

Kerryn King, Vice President, Texaco, Inc., New York.

Rudick C. Lawrence, Vice President and Director of Public Relations, New York Stock Exchange, New York.

John Mapes, former Chairman, Hill & Knowlton Co., New York.

George P. Michaely, Jr., Chief Counsel, Division of Corporation Finance, S.E.C., Washington.

Saul J. Mindel, Esq., former Associate General Counsel, Post Office Department, Washington.

John F. Moynahan, President, John Moynahan & Company, New York.

Martha Norman, National Association of Securities Dealers, Washington.

Maurice O'Reilly, Esq., The Borden Company, New York.

Dudley L. Parsons, President, Dudley L. Parsons & Company, New York.

Dr. G. Edward Pendray, Pendray & Company, Hightstown.

Glen Perry, Director of Public Relations, E. I. du Pont de Nemours & Company, Wilmington.

Lyle Perry, United Fund, Philadelphia.

Powell Pierpoint, Esq., New York.

Irving S. Shapiro, Esq., E. I. du Pont de Nemours and Company, Wilmington.

Eliot H. Sharp, Publisher, *Investment Dealers' Digest,* New York.

Rea W. Smith, Public Relations Society of America, New York.

Ward B. Stevenson, Vice President and Director of Public Relations, First National City Bank, New York.

Charles M. Stone, N.A.B., Code Authority, Washington.

George A. Strait, Esq., Assistant Librarian, Harvard Law School, Cambridge.

Dr. Frederick H. Teahan, Executive Secretary, Foundation for Public Relations, Research and Education, New York.

Craig S. Thompson, Vice President, Edward Howard Co., New York.

Simon Trevis, Esq., Counsel, Federal Home Loan Bank Board, Washington.

Gilbert H. Weil, Esq., General Counsel, Association of National Advertisers, New York.

As indicated in the Author's Introduction, particular—albeit repetitive—mention must be made, in this context, of Dr. G. Edward Pendray and Glen Perry. They labored mightily and not in vain.

In a very real sense, "credits" are also due to the many companies, PR counselors and firms, advertising agencies and media, which have given me the opportunity over the years to work on their various legal/communications problems. Such service has sparked both the interest and the experience basic to this volume.

M. J. S.

CONTENTS

Chapter 1

Public Relations, Lawyers and the Law

A. THE OVERALL PICTURE

1. Impact of the Law on Public Relations
2. Legal Areas of Interest
3. Legal Problems of Independent Practitioners
4. Interstate Activity Problems

B. RELATIONS WITH LEGAL COUNSEL

5. The "Oil and Water" Team
6. PR Criticism of Lawyers
7. Variations in Relations With Legal Counsel
8. Need for Mutual Understanding and Respect
9. Relative Areas of Responsibility
10. Some Continuing Sources of Friction
11. Suggestions and Recommendations
12. Responsibility for Legal Fees

C. PR AND LITIGATION

13. The PR Role in General
14. Types of Litigation
15. Specific Assistance to Legal Counsel
16. Need for Accuracy

D. THE PR "LEGAL LIBRARY"

17. Purposes
18. Sources and Types of Legal Materials
19. The "Legal Opinion" File

E. COMPANY LEGAL MANUALS

20. Purpose and Content
21. Preparation and Distribution
22. Manuals of PR Firms

1

Chapter 1

Public Relations, Lawyers
and the Law

A. THE OVERALL PICTURE.

1. Impact of the Law on Public Relations.

It is, of course, elementary to inquire whether the PR practitioner is *really* involved with the law and lawyers. This query is not concerned with such obvious situations as the need of a lawyer to incorporate a public relations firm but rather with the need of legal consultation in the day-to-day successful performance of the PR function.

Just how often are there legal aspects to a specific PR campaign? How much can a lawyer contribute? How important is legal advice to client or company protection? How should PR men and lawyers work together? What are some of the sources of friction between them? These are some of the matters here involved.

The purpose and scope of this chapter is to deal generally with these and similar questions. Specific legal problems and areas are discussed in the remaining chapters.

In 1956 a survey addressed to "110 PR executives" studied some of these general questions.[1] The survey laid a firm foundation for the conclusion that PR-legal cooperation is important and that legal ramifications are involved in PR efforts about half of the time although, of course, the respondents' opinions varied from "infrequently" to "all of the time." This conclusion has become more and more self-evident over the years. Almost every PR practitioner can document this from his own office files.

In 1965 Dr. G. Edward Pendray, one of the leaders in the PRSA accreditation program, wrote: [2]

> No public relations practitioner who hasn't had legal training should attempt to be his own lawyer . . . It is quite probable that public relations people almost every day violate laws or regula-

3

tions affecting the profession, without having any idea that such
laws and regulations exist. There are, of course, an enormous
number of these . . . Few public relations people have had time
or occasion to look up these laws and regulations, and not many
have more than a smattering of knowledge about them.

While the incidence of legal implications may vary, their importance
when they exist cannot be minimized. They can and have cost companies
millions of dollars. They have contributed toward litigation. They have
helped companies lose valuable trademarks. They have resulted in
charges of unfair labor practices. They have led to SEC problems. The
catalogue is almost endless. Unfortunately some company and PR people
have had to learn this through bitter experience. It is far better to accept
the historically well-documented fact that lawyers and PR men must be
"partners"—that they can serve their clients or companies jointly far better than they can independently.

An interesting example of the possible multi-million dollar involvement of lawyers and PR people is the Consolidated Edison experience
with its proposed Storm King power plant project. As of the beginning of
1967, the utility was reported to have spent $14 million for "lawyers, ex-
pert studies and an extensive advertising and public relations campaign"
even though it had not then "turned a single spadeful of dirt." [3]

Symptomatic—by no means definitive—of the ever-increasing need for
the PR man's orientation to the law are the developments referred to in
the discussion in Chapter 19 of the "consumer protection movement"
with which government is now so involved. An entirely new philosophy
of government control seems to be emerging. It is thrusting upon business
many burdens which formerly were the consumer's and the public's. Put
bluntly, *caveat emptor* has now become *caveat venditor*. This substantive
shift carries with it a correspondingly greater onus for the PR function of
business—not merely toward government but, most significantly, toward
the public.

Also indicative of the need for further PR appreciation for the legal implications of its work is the introduction of "new enforcement theories"
by antitrust policing authorities. Writing in mid-1968, John T. Loughlin
of the Chicago Bar says: [4]

Careless words, written or oral, rather than elaborate economic
presentations are often a decisive factor in antitrust cases, strongly
influencing, first, the decision of the government to file suit, and,
later, the decision of the courts on the merits. Sometimes, when
intent is a key element of the antitrust offense charged, unguarded
statements may represent substantially the entire federal case. In
many prosecutions, poorly chosen expressions vastly simplify the
government's burden of proof. The importance of wordsmanship

in antitrust is not new. . . . What *is* new at the present time is the increased emphasis upon written and oral statements in antitrust cases. . . .

After discussing several case examples, the writer goes on to point out:

These examples of new enforcement theories merely begin to illustrate the potential for conflict between a corporation's internal planning and public relations activities and its antitrust preventive responsibilities. In other words, whereas corporate antitrust review was formerly concentrated on *business practices,* it must now critically be extended to a wide variety of intracorporate reports regarding competition, acquisition, new products, business development and planning, press releases, annual reports and other communications to the shareholders, and even statements to securities analysts.

Mr. Loughlin's discussion of twelve categories of "naughty antitrust words" merits detailed study.

2. Legal Areas of Interest.

The activities about which the careful PR practitioner may need legal advice are many. At one extreme, the PR department of a large, diversified, consumer-oriented company will probably find almost every subject in this work pertinent at some time or other. On the other hand, a financial PR specialist's interest may well be limited to matters involving the SEC and similar federal or state agencies. At the risk of oversimplification, it is probably safe to estimate that almost every relationship with which the PR department or counselor is concerned will involve legal questions of some kind.

Among the specifically compartmented legal specialties, government relations and labor relations are said to be the two most frequently troublesome. This was elicited by the survey referred to in Section 1. Canfield also seems to concentrate on government (local, state and federal) relations in his comments about public relations' legal needs. His premise is the extensive growth of government controls of business.[5]

Pendray pinpoints such legal areas as "lobbying, representation of foreign governments, release of financial information, the right of privacy, the use of copyrighted material, contracts, collections, ownership of ideas, trademarks and patents, use of photographs of individuals and groups, libel and slander, and who knows what else." [6]

The above survey adds "fair trade problems, stockholder actions, contract disputes and the preparation of selected advertising copy" as among "problem areas" requiring the combined skills of PR and legal counsel.

The moment advertising copy is introduced, a veritable Pandora's box is opened. With PR people responsible for product publicity and even some types of paid advertising—including institutional—their legal needs are greatly multiplied. The PR department of an advertising agency is particularly likely to find this to be the case.

At bottom, the specific legal areas of interest to a particular PR department or counsel will depend to a large degree upon the nature of the company's or the client's business. So too will it hinge on the relative size of the company or client, the products or services involved, the marketing methods pursued, the character of the "publics" or customers being cultivated and all of the other variables which contribute to the marketing mix.

3. Legal Problems of Independent Practitioners.

All of the legal fields mentioned in the preceding section are, of course, important to the independent PR counselor, consultant or agency in serving the needs of clients. His legal interests are naturally multiplied by the fact that he may be rendering PR services to a broad spectrum of clients, each one requiring investigation into varied legal areas. However, such independent organizations have additional and specialized legal problems. We are not here discussing the routine legal matters which every business faces such as social security, leases, etc.

The independent practitioner will undoubtedly require, and should seek, legal counsel on such matters as client contracts, agreements with suppliers or media, relations with its own employees, certain unusual tax matters, and similar administrative or operational matters.

4. Interstate Activity Problems.

The PR practitioner, in serving even the smallest company or account, may find himself involved in certain interstate legal problems. This is even more likely when a company operates nationally or an independent PR firm has branch offices in more than one state. As discussed throughout this work, many PR activities are controlled by federal law—even when there is no interstate activity. Among the obvious instances are use of the mails and financial PR.

If PR activities deal with transactions or programs in several states, there may also be state implications. The PR man may find himself and his activities restricted or regulated in a variety of ways under the laws of different states. Here two of the best examples are financial PR and "hard liquor" PR. Sometimes these variations are so important, state by state, that a company or PR counselor seeks out local legal counsel.

B. RELATIONS WITH LEGAL COUNSEL.

5. The "Oil and Water" Team.

It is almost a cliché that "Law and PR don't mix." PR men are said to believe that lawyers are necessary but hobgoblin evils. Lawyers have been known to reciprocate with remarks about "brainwashing" and "Madison Avenue." In specific cases, these dubious comments may be accurate but, as generalizations, they are not. The more enlightened the PR man and the lawyer, the more likely they are to recognize the fallibility of these judgments.

Glen Perry, Director of the Du Pont Public Relations Department, has attacked these glib generalities under the expressive title "Lawyers Are a PR Man's Best Friend." Perry acknowledges the existence of certain problems in the PR-legal relationship but concludes that: [7]

> We in the Du Pont Public Relations Department have sought every appropriate opportunity over a period of years to acquaint those in the Legal Department with the broad philosophy of our work . . . *Our approach is met with cooperation rather than hostility that can so readily accompany ignorance. And things get done.* (Emphasis added.)

James J. Cassidy, Executive Vice-President of Hill and Knowlton, Inc., describes this "oil-and-water" idea as a "platitude" and insists upon its "extinction." He writes: [8]

> Platitude Nine is heard in times of corporate stress: "The company's lawyers have investigated the matter thoroughly and are preparing all the necessary communications."
> You hear less of this. And why? Simply because legal language which is commonplace to the lawyer is usually baffling to most of the population, and has a stiff, forbidding air about it. This fact, which most lawyers recognize, has led gradually to a more cordial *entente* with the public relations specialists. Conversely, it is a careless public relations man who, bearing responsibility as a company spokesman, fails to get clearance from the legal department before putting out a release that could have important legal repercussions.
> When I was a correspondent in Europe during World War II, I developed, as did other correspondents, considerable respect for those rather misunderstood people, the censors. . . . It may have been a coincidence that many of those censors, as we found out, had been lawyers in civilian life. Here and there they used a blue pencil, but always for one purpose—to prevent disclosure of specific information that could have aided the enemy. They never

tried to alter the meaning of the scripts, they never tried to be
reporters themselves. And most of us came to regard them as helpful partners.

Today's corporate lawyer is not the same as a military censor,
but there are occasions when he can and does function to protect
the company as the censor functioned to protect the troops. At his
best, he is a valued colleague who doesn't want to do your job for
you, but can spot legal dangers of which you might not be aware.

6. PR Criticism of Lawyers.

Over the centuries lawyers have been criticized for a variety of failings.
The criticism continues today in some quarters. The PR practitioner is
no exception. As a creative person, he naturally resents and tries to shake
off any hobble on the flexibility and freedom which he deems fundamental to his success. He sometimes considers the lawyer to be such a hobble.
Furthermore, he has been vocal about the restraints imposed by lawyers.
While admitting the need and usefulness of legal advice, he has voiced
his criticism of lawyers—sometimes justifiably—in language such as
this: [9]

"The lawyer is a deterrent."

"Lawyers don't understand the importance of public attitudes."

"Lawyers are too rigid."

"Lawyers tend to advise PR people on PR whereas PR people
don't advise lawyers on the law. Lawyers mostly think they know PR.
They don't."

"They can frequently wreck a program."

Oddly enough, criticism such as this is directed at the *lawyer*—not so
much at the *law*. The careful and knowledgeable PR practitioner appears to recognize more and more the impact of the law upon his activities. He knows the need for legal advice in appropriate situations. His
concern is with the individual lawyer whom he may consult.

Just as the PR practitioner is coming to appreciate the need for competent legal advice, so too are the lawyer and his bar association realizing the
need for public relations assistance. Bar Associations throughout the
country, abetted by the American Bar Association, are engaged in PR
campaigns of various kinds. The now well-recognized Law Day—May 1
of each year—is part of that program. It includes court tours for high
school children, TV programs of various kinds, local speaking engagements for lawyers arranged by the Speakers Committee of the association,
printed materials explaining the lawyer's and the law's contribution to
the community and the individual, representation of the indigent, etc.

Some of the large bar associations employ full-time PR directors or retain PR counsel. These operate at both the state and local level.

As far back as 1957 Chief Justice Gibson of the California Supreme Court told the State Bar of California that one of the basic essentials of a successful judicial reform campaign was "a competent, professionally-directed public relations program to create and maintain public interest in good judicial administration." [10] The passing years have proved the truth of his remarks.

7. Variations in Relations With Legal Counsel.

PR people operate in a variety of positions such as in the company PR department, as the independent PR counselor or consultant, in the PR department of an advertising agency, etc. The same is true of the lawyer. He may be an inside house counsel, a member of a law firm acting as general corporate counsel, an attorney retained for a specific purpose or even local counsel in a distant city, retained in connection with specific litigation or some local legal problem such as a zoning change. He may not have any company contact but be retained by the PR counselor although his services are rendered on client problems.

These organizational or functional variations are important in the PR-legal context. The most obvious are the differences in channels of communications and liaison. They even affect such fundamental matters as the frequency with which the PR practitioner becomes involved with lawyers. It has been shown, for example, that "the independent counselors—considerably more than their counterparts in industry—found their work touching upon the legal field." [11]

This same dichotomy seems to exist in the relative attitudes, critical and otherwise, toward the legal advisor. "Company PR executives" are said to be "generally less critical" of lawyers than the independent counselor.[12] This is not incompatible with the foregoing comment and is probably quite logical. The inside PR man has a considerably simpler liaison with inside legal counsel. It may mean nothing more than walking down the corridor. They may see each other frequently in company dining rooms. Both are salaried employees and use of the other's services does not involve additional fees. On occasion both functions may be concentrated in the same corporate department, as at Procter and Gamble, where all promotional claims "are passed through the Division of Public Relations, to be checked by its Legal Section . . ." [13]

8. Need for Mutual Understanding and Respect.

Every commentator who has given any thought to the PR-legal relationship agrees that the foundation of effective cooperation is mutual respect and understanding. This is nothing more than another example of one of the most important commonplaces of human conduct.

The PR man's basic philosophy, training and background are quite different from the lawyer's. Each must come to assimilate something of the other's. If PR and the law seem to butt heads, it is really quite natural. It is not because either practitioner seeks deliberately to be stubborn or carping. If the lawyer is accused of rigidity of viewpoint or a failure to understand the importance of public attitudes—charges sometimes of real substance—the reason may well be that the PR practitioner-client has not seen fit to indoctrinate him.

Each must know the thinking of the other, the results he seeks to achieve, the reasons for his position. This can come only from a conscientious effort at understanding. The lawyer must learn and appreciate the function of PR. The PR man must learn the function of the law.

There is an interesting and quite relevant analogy between this need for PR-legal understanding and that which must obtain between our courts and the press. Supreme Court Justice Brennan, when queried about the latter relationship, said: [14]

> This matter of news media coverage of decisions of the Court is surely a difficult problem. I think that the best coverage is being given by those newspapers . . . which afford reporters an opportunity for some special instruction in the work of the Court. Those reporters seem to develop a very deep interest in the Court itself and *improve their understanding through intensive self-education* in its work.
>
> *   *   *   *
>
> The news media say to us, and perhaps not without justification, that we don't help them very much, because we provide no *briefing in advance* of the handing down of a decision, . . . (Emphasis added.)

This understanding cannot be achieved in a single PR-legal conference. It is a slow and continuous process requiring the gradual creation of a rapport with which both lawyer and PR man feel comfortable. What John Hill of Hill and Knowlton, Inc. said of public relations programs generally applies here: [15]

> Confidence and trust is something that must be built up over a long period—by speaking forthrightly at all times and by creating an atmosphere in which people know what to expect of you.

There really should be no great difficulty in achieving this if both are open-minded. There are certain similarities between both callings. Thus Alfred L. Scanlan, a Washington lawyer, has said: [16]

Public relations men, as well as lawyers, are called upon to analyze problems, advise clients, and advocate their causes. Such services, too, are usually rendered in behalf of another. In short, both lawyers and public relations practitioners are experienced, as Socrates is reported to have remarked of the Sophists, "at making the lesser cause appear the better."

In addition to these mutual techniques and characteristics, both are seeking the same end: to serve the best interest of the client. Despite these similarities, however, understanding will not develop unless it is carefully nurtured. As Glen Perry has put it: [17]

> This is a long-range matter. In order to understand a public relations project, one must first understand the philosophical background against which it was conceived, the company situation that inspired it, and the practical considerations involved in formulating and implementing such proposals. It is asking quite a lot of a man, be he lawyer or researcher or executive, to expect him to judge sympathetically and intelligently a project about which he knows little or nothing except that it is being thrown at him, not only for the first time, but also in what amounts to a vacuum so far as his background information is concerned.

Corporate management has, on occasion, been accused of practicing "brinkmanship" by failing to seek PR counsel until the last moment.[18] The same can be said, as Perry points out above, of the PR practitioner in his relations with legal counsel. The PR department or practitioner must establish his communications with counsel *before* problems arise. The approach should be prophylactic and forehanded. Every effort should be made to prevent the development of a "crisis psychosis" or the need for what John Hill has called "crisis communications." [19]

9. Relative Areas of Responsibility.

Even when the need for PR-legal liaison is clearly recognized, many problems will arise from the failure to prescribe the relative areas of responsibility. Each should know his own responsibility and, above all, not impinge on the contribution of the other. This is not always the case, even in otherwise well-organized companies.

After pointing out that particular sources of internal friction for PR people can be the departments of advertising, personnel and legal counsel, Cutlip and Center go on to say: [20]

> The conflict between public relations and legal counsel is an ancient one. In the days of the Muckrakers, corporate executives

more often turned to their lawyers to "fix things" than to the emerging public relations specialist.

Some still do. Ivy Lee felt strongly about this: [21]

I have seen more situations which the public ought to understand and which the public would sympathize with, spoiled by the intervention of the lawyer than in any other way. Whenever a lawyer starts to talk to the public, he shuts out the light.

Even in this day we can expect conflict when one corporation counsel asserts:

I am prepared to defend the position that the truly competent legal counselor to the public relation division should be expected to express his opinion not only on matters of factuality which have potential legal impact, but even on matters of good taste, logic, honesty, yet even at times on the persuasiveness of your copy.[22]

This conflict, when it exists, stems undoubtedly from misconceptions about areas of responsibility and expertise. Each shoemaker must stick to his last. This does not mean that the lawyer should be merely a mechanical "screener." He should be and frequently is constructive, contributing affirmative ideas. It is the province of the PR man, however, to be the final arbiter on these ideas.

10. Some Continuing Sources of Friction.

Aside from the initial differences described in Sections 6 and 8, there are certain continuing problems which can create misunderstanding unless both sides recognize the contribution which each can make and the reasons for the positions taken by each, perhaps even quite insistently.

Basic to these problems is, of course, the acknowledgment required of the PR man that the lawyer's hands may be tied by a definite legal requirement which must be satisfied. Once this is covered in the projected program, news release, president's speech, etc., the rest would seem to be up to the PR man. The lawyer should not be permitted to dictate form and substance beyond the legal necessities.

The closer the PR-legal relationship becomes, the less likely will the lawyer be to insist upon "legalistic" devices. At the same time, under such conditions, the PR man may come a bit more under the influence of the lawyer and accept demands which are not really necessary. This obviously should be avoided. So-called "legalistic tactics" generally do not serve the PR function, especially if they are apparent and obvious.[23]

Due to lack of experience, the lawyer may be unfamiliar with the mechanics and tools of PR. He must be educated. One problem, known to be recurrent, is the handling of news releases by editors. Every PR man knows that a release will probably not be used exactly as he wrote it. It may be edited, cut, rearranged—even mangled and mutilated. The lawyer, not aware of this, may not know the importance of getting the "whole story" into the lead paragraph with its Who, What, Where, When, Why and How.

The lawyer, given to lengthy, detailed explanations, may be satisfied to have these explanations on page 3 or 4 of the release. He must be indoctrinated to understand the importance of the lead. Some releases, cleared by the legal department, have been published in emasculated and clearly legally deficient form because the "legal language" was not where it belonged—in the opening paragraphs. At the same time, the inclusion of such material in the lead can make it limp. This is another example of the need for compromise in order to do the job.

Friction between lawyer and PR man may stem from causes beyond either's control for which the lawyer should not be faulted. The PR or industrial relations departments, for example, may have overlapping and poorly defined responsibilities. As a result, the lawyer does not understand his own responsibilities. This cannot be resolved until the basic areas of control are delimited.

Then, too, the obligation of the PR man to consult counsel may be required only, for example, "as directed specifically by the president." [24] Presidential failure to act may be the *deus ex machina* in the PR-legal breakdown. This is particularly true where outside counsel are to be consulted.

Probably the most common source of conflict, however, is the inability to agree in matters of pure judgment. Sometimes this stems from as trifling and human a thing as "pride of authorship." Here it would seem that the PR man's concept should prevail. The lawyer's chore is finished when he has either screened out the dangers or prescribed the necessary inclusions.

11. Suggestions and Recommendations.

These suggestions for a smoothly cooperative PR-legal function presume the existence within a company of both a PR department and a legal department. If either or both of these functions are performed by outside counsel, there may be some necessary variations.

(a) Table of Organization.

The channels of communication must be clearly defined. Some companies have both legal and PR functions reporting to a single vice-president who is responsible for a group of staff functions. Whatever the organization, it must be well-defined.

(b) Statement of Responsibilities.

The obligation of the PR director or staff to seek legal advice should be expressly delineated. In areas in which such obligation is imposed, legal department clearance should be made a mandatory prerequisite to any PR department recommendation to management.

(c) Committees.

Legal counsel should be a member of the corporate Public Relations Committee if there is one. This permits counsel to participate in PR decisions from the outset.

(d) Personal Acquaintance.

Every effort should be made by all members of the PR-legal team to become personally familiar with each other. They should meet frequently and informally. Even social fraternization may be important.

(e) Periodic Consultation.

A fixed schedule of periodic meetings between PR and legal staff or counsel should be set up. This is valuable even if there is no pending PR effort which requires legal screening. An agenda should be prepared by both the PR and legal staffs since either may be unaware of current developments known to the other.

(f) Legal Memoranda.

The legal department should prepare and forward memoranda to the PR department from time to time, dealing with new legal developments of interest to the PR function. The PR department should receive copies of any pertinent memoranda or opinions prepared for other departments so that the PR department will be abreast of general company developments.

(g) Task Force Method.

Certain PR campaigns are of sufficient significance and continuity to merit creation of a special task force. Its members should be drawn from every corporate department, including PR and legal, which may be involved in any way in the particular campaign. Such a task force may consist of an existing Public Relations Committee supplemented by the additional personnel required for the campaign.

Not all of these recommended methods will be used in every company. Some may be mutually exclusive. One of the most important factors in adopting one or more of these arrangements will be management's over-all attitude toward public relations. The more management considers PR as a management function, the more likely will the PR-legal liaison be considered and fully implemented by management's directives.[25]

If a company does not have an inside legal department, it should instruct its PR director to consult, both periodically and specially, with the company's outside counsel. Sometimes, because of the very specialized legal problems involved in PR, special counsel will be retained exclusively for PR consultation. Mandatory legal clearance before a recommendation to management is frequently required in this situation also.

Some independent PR firms retain their own legal counsel who are consulted regularly and frequently as to the legal implications of their clients' campaigns. Apparently, in this situation, the contact with counsel seems to be taken for granted and to be a part of the routine practice of the PR firm or counsel. It is to be recommended. In this situation, however, certain questions as to responsibility for legal fees may arise. These are discussed in Section 12.

12. Responsibility for Legal Fees.

When legal consultation is furnished by inside house counsel, no question arises as to payment for such services. The same is true when outside corporate general counsel is regularly retained. However, the situation may not be too clear when an independent PR counselor consults outside legal counsel on a client's PR matters.

In some cases, the PR counsel or firm will retain its own legal counsel on a permanent basis and will absorb such fees as part of its services. Other firms will first obtain authorization from the client to consult counsel. The fees in this latter case are the responsibility of the client and not of the PR firm. Sometimes they are billed directly to the client, sometimes to the PR firm which rebills them to the client.

There is one billing situation which may arise, usually inadvertently. It is more likely to occur with PR departments of advertising agencies where the marking up of all "suppliers' bills" is routine, the markup being either 17.65 or 15 percent. Counsel fees should *never* be marked up. If the PR practitioner were to retain a portion of the attorney's fees, this would result in "splitting fees," a practice forbidden to attorneys where someone not an attorney shares the fee.[26]

A variation of this fee-splitting may occur. The fee-bill is not improperly marked up in rebilling to the client but 15 percent thereof is later retained when the firm is a conduit for payment between the client and the attorney.

C. PR AND LITIGATION.

13. The PR Role in General.

The PR man may often find his company or clients involved in litigation. Litigation is here used as a wide-spectrum word. It includes not only adversary court matters but all of that amorphous and seemingly unlimited area of the administrative process (federal, state or local) which is of more and more significance in the determination of legal rights and obligations. This would include everything from an FTC proceeding involving an important merger to a liquor license application for a local restaurant.

The PR function can be important in almost all of these situations. Quite apart from its normal purpose of providing the public with an accurate and constructive picture of the proceedings, it may sometimes make a significant contribution to the litigation itself. The closer the routine kinship between the PR and legal members of the company team, the more frequent and important is the PR contribution likely to be.

The onset of litigation requiring a reshuffling of the relative responsibilities of the team finds the lawyer no longer merely screening or recommending. He is now the leader of the team. PR men are usually alert to this and lose much of their reluctance to accept the legal mandate. Without minimizing the importance of the PR man, he has become only a member of the supporting cast who, unless he has been "through the mill before," may find himself in something of an alien atmosphere—a world with its own procedures and even standards. Yet his continuing importance cannot be minimized. See Section 16 below.

14. Types of Litigation.

There are basically four categories of company litigation in which the PR man may find himself participating.

(a) The first of these is the "big case," of great importance to the operation of the company or one of its basic activities or practices. This may be an antitrust action directed at its entire marketing program, a labor relations hearing involving thousands of employees, suits involving product liability—especially those which deal with the basic safety or acceptability of a product—minority stockholders' actions charging mismanagement or fraud, and other litigation basic to the continued success of the company.

(b) The second category is the so-called "human interest" case in which not a great deal is really involved in dollars and cents, but which has a newsworthy appeal which can land it on the front page of the newspapers. Here we may have a minor civil rights charge, a local zoning conflict, a right of privacy suit by a "glamour name," air or water pollution charges, suits against a company by a retired employee seeking a larger pension, and myriad other kinds of litigation which may concern either an individual or some community interest.

(c) The third category is the routine type of litigation with which every company must contend. These include actions for breach of contract, workmen's compensation claims, tax refund matters, etc. The need for affirmative PR action in these run-of-the-mill situations may be rare but, even here, such action may be necessary in particular instances.

(d) The fourth type is the case in which the PR man may himself be required to testify. His evidence may be needed because he participated in the company program from which the action arises. This may range from cases growing out of the preparation of the company president's statement before a Congressional committee to a $200 supplier claim for tables and chairs used at a company picnic.

As to the relative roles of the lawyer and the PR man in each of these types of situations, subject probably to the prerogatives of management, the lawyer undoubtedly should control the situation in all but the second. In the latter, it may well be PR considerations which should dominate. Perhaps the "company image" will suffer if a settlement is not made at once even though counsel may be sure he can "beat the case." This, and other questions like this, should be the decision of the PR man, not of the lawyer.

15. Specific Assistance to Legal Counsel.

Quite apart from the customary areas of PR responsibility, the PR practitioner may sometimes be of considerable assistance to the company's attorneys. This is particularly true if both have previously worked together in close concert and have come to recognize and respect each other's strengths.

In litigation which involves the necessity of locating and developing witnesses not under the control of the company—especially so-called "public witnesses"—the PR arm can be very useful. Once counsel has briefed the PR man or staff on the case, the latter may be able to develop the necessary information and witnesses in the field far more rapidly and with greater rapport than the counsel or his own staff.

In more and more cases, consumer or other types of research is being accepted by the courts as discussed in Chapter 15. The PR practitioner, working either alone or with the assistance of outside organizations, can be very useful. However, the research must first be oriented by the attorney so that it fulfills its purpose and, above all, is not eventually held to be irrelevant.

Addressing himself to "Corporation Lawyers and Public Relations Counsel," John Hill refers to several specific examples of such research which PR was able to contribute: a study of the depletion of oyster beds, a detailed history and analysis of oil operations, selection of the proper time to take an appeal in a steel strike.[27]

There have been instances in which consumer PR techniques have been employed in selecting juries, sometimes based on investigations undertaken by PR men. Such investigation is quite legitimate when properly conducted.

The affirmative PR contribution may be limited to reshaping news releases and putting them into understandable language which will produce a more desired effect than the admittedly more formal and legalistic phraseology of the lawyer.

One veteran company PR director has described as "a massive fact" that

> [I]n any legal action which is of such a nature as to command the attention of the press, there are two trials going on. There is first the action in the courtroom. But there is a second trial before the court of public opinion. No company can be satisfied if it wins only one of these actions. If it loses either, it has been damaged. As a corollary of this, it follows that the legal and the public relations people must work closely with top management to do everything possible to see that both trials are won.[28]

The same PR practitioner, a veteran of more than one "front page" company trial, then goes on to describe the PR contribution to handling one of them:

> There was a great deal of press interest and the public relations man assigned to the case had, as one of his specific duties, serving as liaison between our counsel and the press. This worked out well from a number of viewpoints. The newspaper people, congenitally suspicious of lawyers, were very appreciative of having public relations men in close touch with the lawyers. They felt, and the event confirmed this feeling, that the public relations man could get answers to their questions faster than they could and also could, when it was desirable, get the press and the lawyers together for direct consultation. With the thorough knowledge and consent of counsel, the public relations people also arranged, at the request of members of the press, for interviews with such persons as [our president] and other people in the management of the company. Obviously, those involved in such interviews could not deal with the issues of the case, but this was not what the reporters wanted in any event. They were interested in "human interest" material.

This is a detailed extrapolation and particularization of a problem about which Canfield has written: [29]

> The public often misunderstands legal action, and the public relations department should be called upon to interpret proceedings in the courts in terms that the public can understand. . . .

By and large, the PR man will find his efforts controlled by legal counsel. PR people may sit at a lawyer's elbow at the counsel table or follow the proceedings from the public side of the rail. Corridor conferences between lawyer and PR man are quite common. The PR approach can sometimes even be used to shape, but not distort, the testimony from the stand so that the press has a favorable "public record" to report.

16. Need for Accuracy.

The conscientious PR man restricts himself to the facts even when he seeks to make "hard" facts more palatable. Such need for accuracy and truthfulness is even more important in dealing with news or comment about litigation.

The *Imdrim* case [30] is an interesting example of just such a situation. This was an injunction action by the FTC alleging false advertising of "Imdrim," an arthritis remedy. The injunction was refused by the federal district court, an apparent victory for the respondent. The circuit court later reversed. While the appeal was pending, the respondent issued news releases and used paid advertising which the FTC claimed contained misleading references to the district court action. The FTC then brought a *second* action against the company based, not on any alleged irregularities in the original product advertising, but on the misrepresentation of the opinion of the district court. In other words, the company's public efforts to explain the lower court's refusal of the injunction—essentially a PR effort—was the basis for another suit, resulting in a fine under Section 14 of the FTC Act.

Obviously, not every suit or legal action involves the FTC but the same or similar action might be anticipated if the pertinent agency should be the SEC, FDA, FCC, etc.

D. THE PR "LEGAL LIBRARY."

17. Purposes.

A so-called "legal library" can be of considerable value to a PR department or firm. At the same time, even an extensive legal library can never be a satisfactory substitute for competent legal counsel. Such shelf materials should be approached and used as "alertment—not solution." The PR man may not be aware of even the existence of possible legal problems, and reference to an appropriate work will serve as prompt warning.

Some PR firms consider the maintenance and use of such materials as part of the service which they believe necessary to render to their clients. This is particularly true of firms which serve smaller companies—clients who do not have house counsel or large inside PR departments. There will be occasions when reference to such office sources may effectively answer, at least in a deterrent manner, an initial inquiry or creative false start, thus channeling the PR effort along other and legally acceptable lines.

Some of these legal materials become almost mandatory, even when close liaison with legal counsel is maintained. Thus, testimony of witnesses before Congressional investigating committees must be carefully studied by PR men before assisting in the preparation of their own clients' statements. Such materials are extremely useful even though their own clients are not to testify but are only members of the affected industry. Congressional committee reports are also necessary if they concern matters pertinent to Bills or investigations relevant to a client's or company's industry, methods or prospective programs. Government agency (federal and state) reports of investigations of various industries, practices, marketing methods, etc., are all grist for the mill, useful in planning and programming PR activities.

Probably the most important purpose of such a collection, however, is the saving permitted in the PR man's most important asset, time.

18. Sources and Types of Legal Materials.

In the following classifications, the term "legal materials" is used rather loosely. It includes "governmental" materials as well as those more commonly denominated as "legal." Once again, the usefulness of the particular book, publication or legal service will vary, largely dependent upon the nature of the practitioner's services and the companies involved. However, some are of broad interest and are likely to be of use regardless of these restrictive requirements.

(a) General Texts.
Among basic materials are certain general texts which should be useful, especially when undertaking a new campaign or serving a new client involved with the overall legal area of the text. Some texts suffer from over-particularity and excessive detail and can be confusing to the layman. On the other hand, texts confined to a single subject such as trade-

marks or copyright can give a good working knowledge of that particular field.

(b) Specialized Materials.

Specialized legal materials run from massive works to paperbound pamphlets by bar associations or trade associations having an interest in these special legal fields or contemporary legal developments. The PR practitioner may be unaware of these when they are published but his legal counsel will undoubtedly recognize them as they cross his desk and, if the PR-legal liaison is smooth, will bring them to the attention of the PR man. Most of these deal in depth with some particular facet of a broad legal subject or important recent case or statute. This should not deter the lay reader whose work may happen to involve that subject.

(c) Periodicals.

This category includes a tremendous variety of materials ranging from the so-called "learned" law reviews or journals to trade association newsletters dealing with legal subjects but written for the layman. Some of these will undoubtedly be of interest to the PR departments or PR firms having special cognizance of the subject matter involved.

(d) Government Publications.

Here again, the spectrum is very broad and includes hardbound books, pamphlets, news releases, public notices, speeches of government administrators, administrative agency rules and regulations, rulings, guides, advisory opinions, etc. Some of these are designed strictly for the lawyer but others are prepared for the layman even though they may cover the same subjects dealt with more legalistically in other publications from the same source.

These are a very fruitful source of useful information, especially for the practitioner whose services involve government activities, programs or relations. To be particularly recommended are the speeches of the government personnel at either commission or staff level even though some of these are expressly indicated to be unofficial. In the past, such speeches have sometimes been the first public indication of new government positions, investigations, etc.

Into this category also fall the printed records and reports of Congressional committees which, as discussed in Section 17 above, may be of inestimable value. It has been suggested that one of the most important uses of such materials is that they show the PR man the strengths and weaknesses of competition.

A PR practitioner should arrange to be placed on the mailing lists of any government department or agency with which he, his company or clients may be concerned. Usually such a department or agency will have a variety of periodic publications and lists and some will be of greater use than others.

(e) Privately Published Services.

There are a number of weekly or monthly services published by professional reporting organizations, usually located in Washington. Some of these are directed exclusively to lawyers, but even these are so prepared as to be of interest and use to the non-lawyer. The subscription lists of some of these services include a significant number of PR firms, advertising agencies, inside advertising and PR departments, etc. Some of the more useful and pertinent services are listed in this volume's Bibliography.

19. The "Legal Opinion" File.

Many PR departments or independent practitioners maintain so-called "legal opinion" files consisting of opinions or conference reports prepared in past matters by counsel. These can be of considerable help in future PR activities but should be used with discretion and caution. A current matter may seem to be "a repeat," yet vary significantly.

While, in theory at least, the law is reasonably consistent, certain legal areas are rather fluid and require careful and continuous attention to current developments. Interpretations change and develop and must be followed closely. This is especially true of the rulings of many federal administrative agencies with which PR may be concerned. The same is true of the new statutes, a considerable number of which currently have an effect upon PR. More and more judicial opinions are being rendered on PR matters not previously determined. See Chapter 19 generally.

It is almost mandatory that counsel be consulted in these areas and not too much reliance be put upon past opinions.

Regularly retained legal counsel will frequently take the initiative and bring to the attention of the PR practitioner new legal developments concerning PR generally or those specific matters about which he may know there is interest.

E. COMPANY LEGAL MANUALS.

20. Purpose and Content.

More and more companies are preparing so-called "legal manuals" for use by their personnel. Many PR problems are treated therein but such content will naturally vary with the company's orientation, PR and otherwise. Companies having large PR and advertising departments sometimes prepare special manuals for such departments. The same is true of advertising agencies and PR firms.

These manuals are essentially handbooks containing relatively brief instructions to the staff concerning operational matters which are likely to recur with some frequency and which may have legal implications or requirements. Prominent among such matters are the use and form of releases so as to avoid privacy suits, warnings about defamatory contents of news releases and other materials, advice about deceptive promotional copy, instructions on handling of testimonials and endorsements, rules concerning the purchase of ideas and other externally submitted materials, channels for obtaining copyright permissions, comments on some of the legal aspects of media buying and billing practices, references to industry standards and codes (communications and otherwise), etc.

These how-to manuals usually cover only the most common and simplest "legal situations." Even when prepared in the first instance by legal counsel, they are not intended as a substitute for such counsel. Many contain express caveats against undue reliance thereon and instructions to consult counsel on specific situations. Obviously such brief materials intended for use by "laymen" cannot presume to cover all situations or even too many variations of a given type of situation.

If used intelligently and as a guide, they can be useful time savers. If relied upon to the exclusion of counsel, they may contain pitfalls.

21. Preparation and Distribution.

Since these manuals are essentially legal in content, they are usually prepared by company or outside counsel. However, company PR, advertising and personnel people usually screen them—sometimes even doing considerable rewriting—before they are printed or otherwise reproduced. Such rewriting often falls to the PR staff. Usually a well-prepared manual will be the result of the joint efforts of company personnel and legal counsel with drafts and rewrites being exchanged until final form and content emerge, satisfactory to all.

Once prepared and reproduced, these manuals should be circulated to all company staff who may be charged with responsibility for any of the transactions or relationships covered therein. Instance after instance could be cited of such helpful and useful books being kept practically under lock and key in some vice-president's office instead of being properly distributed. This is especially true of multi-plant or multi-office companies which fail to get the books into the field even though field or branch personnel may need such assistance.

Some advertising, PR and promotional department manuals are pre-

pared with third-party distribution in mind. These are circulated to perhaps hundreds of outside companies and sources as indicative of company
policy. Experience proves that such distribution of a properly prepared
manual can save much correspondence, delay and expense.

22. Manuals of PR Firms.

Independent PR counsel find such manuals very helpful also—
especially if the firm is departmentalized with authority delegated to department heads or account supervisors or executives. Such manuals will
vary somewhat from "company" manuals, if only because the PR counsel
has responsibilities to a client—technically, a "third party." Common additions to the PR counsel's manual will be instructions as to client
liaison, obtaining approvals from clients, relations with suppliers, sources
and media, etc.

Problems may arise if both the client and the PR firm have independently developed their own legal manuals which are in any way inconsistent. This can easily occur without reflecting in any way on the propriety
of either. To avoid this possibility, some firms, immediately upon acquiring a new client, inquire as to the existence of a company legal manual.
If there is one, comparison is made in order to make certain that no
problems will later arise from such possible inconsistencies.

Notes

1. Blaustein & Gross, *Working with Lawyers*, P.R.Q., July, 1956, at 7.
2. Pendray, *After Accreditation—What?* P.R.J., March, 1965, at 11.
3. As reported in the N.Y. Times, Dec. 13, 1966, at 49.
4. Loughlin, *Antitrust and the Vanishing Art of Understatement*, P.R.J., May, 1968, at 12.
5. CANFIELD, PUBLIC RELATIONS, PRINCIPLES, CASES AND PROBLEMS 58–9 (3d ed. 1960).
6. Pendray, *supra* note 2.
7. Perry, *Lawyers Are a PR Man's Best Friend*, P.R.J., April, 1955, at 3.
8. Cassidy, *Public Relations Platitudes: Ten for Extinction*, P.R.J., Dec., 1966, at 8.
9. Blaustein & Gross, *supra* note 1, at 8–9.
10. Gibson, *Public Relations and Judicial Reforms*, P.R.J., July, 1957, at 25. See also *A Professional PR Program Conducted by Members of Another Profession* (Case Study No. 1007), P.R.N., April 26, 1965, at 3–4.
11. *Id.* at 7.
12. *Id.*
13. Werner, *Public Relations Thinking in Trademarks*, 44 T.M.R. 774, at 779 (1954).
14. HARVARD LAW SCHOOL, PROCEEDINGS IN HONOR OF MR. JUSTICE BRENNAN, Occasional Pamphlet No. 9, at 16 (1967).
15. Hill, *What We Learned From the Steel Negotiations*, P.R.J., Aug., 1960, at 6, 10.
16. Scanlan, *A Lawyer's View of the Professional Status of Public Relations Practitioners*, P.R.Q., Jan., 1962, at 2.
17. Perry, *supra* note 7, at 4.
18. See, *e.g.*, Konrad, *Corporate Brinkmanship*, P.R.Q., Fall, 1966, at 17.
19. Hill, *supra* note 15, at 8.
20. CUTLIP & CENTER, EFFECTIVE PUBLIC RELATIONS 212 (3d ed. 1964).
21. LEE, PUBLICITY, SOME OF THE THINGS IT IS AND IS NOT 58–9 (1924).
22. Address by William Barron, Labor Relations Counsel, General Electric Company, Annual Conference of P.R.S.A., Nov. 18, 1957.
23. For a practical discussion of the avoidance of "legalistic tactics, dodging, bluster, or science," see Pendray, *How to Get Out of Air Pollution Trouble*, P.R.J., March, 1961, at 4.
24. See example of PR responsibilities cited by Cutlip & Center, *supra* note 20, at 209.
25. *Id.* at 206–213, for a discussion of this management policy.
26. See A.B.A. Canon 34 and see generally DRINKER, LEGAL ETHICS 179–186 (1953).
27. Hill, *Corporate Lawyers and Public Relations Counsel*, 14 BUS. LAW. 587 (1959).

28. Letter to author, March, 1967, quotation from which was permitted but without specific attribution.

29. Canfield, *supra* note 5, at 59.

30. F.T.C. v. Rhodes Pharmacal Co., Inc., 191 F.2d 744 (7th Cir. 1951); 208 F.2d 382 (7th Cir. 1953), *mod'd,* 348 U.S. 940 (1954).

Chapter 2

Legal Relationships and Liabilities of Public Relations Counsel

A. LEGAL STATUS.

1. The Principal-Agent Relationship
2. Legal Status as a Factual Matter
3. Effect of Nomenclature and Nature of Services
4. Action on Behalf of Client
5. Control by Client
6. Fiduciary Obligation
7. Historical Difference From Advertising Agencies

B. CONTRACT LIABILITIES.

8. General Business Obligations
9. Importance of Written Agreements
10. Responsibility to Client
11. Liabilities to Media
12. Liability to Suppliers

C. NON-CONTRACT LIABILITIES.

13. Liability in Tort
14. Statutory and Administrative Liability
15. Criminal Liability
16. Criminal Conspiracy

D. COUNSEL-CLIENT AGREEMENTS.

17. Purpose and Contents
18. Type of Agreements
19. Compensation and Charging Methods
20. Contingent Compensation
21. Description of Services

E. FORMS.

Chapter 2

Legal Relationships and Liabilities
of Public Relations Counsel

A. LEGAL STATUS.

1. The Principal-Agent Relationship.

The client-PR counselor relationship is that of principal and agent. The client is the principal and the counselor is the agent. The relationship clearly falls within this definitive concept of the *Restatement of Agency:* [1]

> Agency is the fiduciary relation which results from the manifestation of consent by one person to another that the other shall act on his behalf and subject to his control, and consent by the other so to act.

Dissecting this definition, we find the important requirements to be:
(a)   Manifestation of consent by the principal;
(b)   Acceptance of the relationship by the agent;
(c)   The agent is to act on behalf of the principal;
(d)   The agent is subject to the control of the principal;
(e)   The relationship is fiduciary.

We may assume that both (a) and (b) above exist in every practitioner-client relationship. Such consent and acceptance are the practical *sine qua non* thereof. Furthermore, both are almost always found in even the simplest of written contracts referred to in Sections 22 to 32 below.

Requirements (c), (d) and (e) are discussed in Sections 2 to 6 below.

2. Legal Status as a Factual Matter.

The legal status of a public relations firm or counsel is essentially a factual matter. Only after their factual relationship has been determined

29

can we reach a legal conclusion as to legal status.[2] Whether a particular organization or individual is the agent of its client "must be judged by the realities of the arrangement between the parties." [3]

Since the factual relationship is controlling, the practitioner and his client cannot, by agreement between them, make their relationship something which it is not. If a legal agency exists, the parties cannot lift it out of that category by calling it something else. As one court has said: [4]

> Even though the contract between the parties prohibited the construction of the relationship as agency, it was considered agency if the facts indicated it due to the control . . . in the hands of the principal.

This rule may have a direct effect upon provisions of some retainer contracts—perhaps rendering them internally inconsistent. See Section 32 (a) below.

A leading authority on the relationship between a PR firm and its client is the *Riss* case.[5] It appears therein that Carl Byoir & Associates had been retained by the Eastern Railroads Presidents Conference (ERPC) to perform certain PR and other activities. The question was whether the Byoir firm was the agent of ERPC for the purpose of venue in the District of Columbia, where Byoir had an office and admittedly performed considerable service for ERPC. The court found that Byoir was independent in the organizational sense but that, nevertheless, it was the agent for its client within the meaning of the statute.

Using as its springboard the *Restatement* definition of "agency" quoted in Section 1 above, the court went on to examine at some length the factual relationship between ERPC and Byoir. It stressed the fact that the activities of Byoir were subject to examination and approval or rejection by ERPC and that Byoir had written to ERPC at one point: "Nothing related to the subject will be done in this office and no material will be sent out from this office without [your] prior approval . . ."

As a result of these and other facts, the court summed up the Byoir-ERPC relationship by saying:

> From a recital of these facts, it seems clear that, by mutual consent, Byoir was acting on ERPC's behalf in the field of public relations and that its work was done under the close supervision and control of ERPC. *Byoir was acting as the agent of ERPC.* (Emphasis added.)

3. Effect of Nomenclature and Nature of Services.

Public relations organizations carry a variety of descriptive names. Some call themselves public relations counsel or counselors. Some are "consultants." Others consider themselves as "public relations agencies." The latter term is, of course, also applicable when the PR function is served by a department within an advertising agency.

Nomenclature is, however, quite unimportant. By the same token, the fact that their common progenitor was the "press *agent*" has no real significance. Legal status stems from the factual relationship maintained with its clients—not from any particular generic name by which the organization is known. In the parallel situation involving advertising agencies, the agency is the legal agent of its client also but not because it is called an "agency." Such nomenclature does not, without more, make it fit into the Procrustean bed of the principal-agent relationship. The same lack of significance applies to "automobile *agency*." In the advertising agency context, the American Association of Advertising Agencies has pointed out: [6]

> "Advertising agent" does not describe any legal relationship of principal and agent; it is merely a trade name commonly used to designate a concern engaged in rendering advertising service. The name is a misnomer and a senseless survivor from the days when it meant a broker of space.

As to the relevance of the conclusions of this comment about the legal relationship, see Section 7 below.

The status of the "person or firm offering PR services"—a broad and diffuse term deliberately used at this point—is unaffected by the nature of the services which the organization may offer. The service may be confined to general advice and counseling. It may involve the actual carrying out of an entire public relations program, addressed to one or many publics. It may be a part of a larger communications service or "overall marketing service" offered by the organization. It may be limited to financial PR or product publicity. It may involve a single short-term project such as an appearance before a Congressional legislative committee, the celebration of a twenty-fifth corporate anniversary or any other "one-shot" operation or project.

Whatever the extent, nature or duration of the service being offered and rendered, "the person or firm offering the public relations service" is the agent of its client.

4. Action on Behalf of Client.

> Among many Polynesian tribes, the chief never utters a word in public; the speaking is done for him by a "talking chief" who is expert in the history of the tribe. The U.S. has adopted a similar custom on a grand scale. Here the talking chiefs are called public relations men.[7]

Here, in anthropological terms, is a 1967 tongue-in-cheek *Time* description of how the PR counsel talks "for" his client. Some sixty years before, Ivy Lee, in his 1906 "Declaration of Principles," had said: [8]

> . . . This is not an advertising agency; if you think any of our matter ought properly to go to your business office, do not use it. . . . In brief, our plan is, frankly and openly *on behalf of the business concerns and public institutions,* to supply to the press and public of the United States prompt and accurate information concerning subjects which it is of value and interest to the public to know about. (Emphasis added.)

There is no question that the PR counselor talks "for" his client or acts "on behalf of" his client. Sometimes he even physically appears in place of his client. Thus we find the relationship satisfying the *Restatement* requirement that the agent act "on behalf" of the principal—another aspect of the factual relationship.

5. Control by Client.

In a very practical sense, the relationship between PR practitioner and client is, ideally, a partnership. The practitioner works closely and intimately with the client and is at all times subject to the control of the client. The counselor may create and direct the program but it is subject to the approval and control of the client—not only as to basic concept and overall structure but also as to many details. Even if the client depends upon the ability and perception of the counselor and bows to the latter's decisions, the client still has the final right to say YES or NO, probably the most thorough indication of control which may be imagined.

In the *Riss* case discussed in Section 2 above, the court stressed the control element. The opinion describes not only the theoretical right of control enjoyed by the client but the actual exercise of that control, pointing to careful use of channels and procedures for the clearing of releases prepared by Byoir, the client's rejection of some materials as contrary to its policy, the careful control over expenses and their handling and accounting. The relationship, the court concluded, "was much closer than mere consultation." It was real control by the client.

This is the general factual relation to be appraised in the light of the following legal analysis from the *Restatement of Agency:* [9]

> Where one who works for another represents the will of the other, not only as to the result, but also as to the means by which the result is accomplished, he is not an independent contractor but an agent; and the relationship is one of agency where the employer reserves control and an interest in the performance of the work

other than the finished product, or where the contract shows a recognition of the responsibility of the employer for obligations incurred by the other party.

Some agreements between counselor and client will specifically spell out the obligation of the counselor to submit all materials for the approval of the client. Other agreements may not be quite this specific but will indicate that the program and its progress are subject to the client's control. See Section 28 below.

6. Fiduciary Obligation.

A fiduciary obligation is one which requires a party to act as a trustee for another and to accord the other a full measure of fidelity and loyalty.

The importance of the affirmative fiduciary obligation of an agent to his principal has been described in this manner: [10]

> The fact that an agent is subject to these fiduciary duties distinguishes him from other persons who have power to affect the interests of others; and the understanding that one is to act primarily for the benefit of the other is often the determinative feature in distinguishing the agency relation from others.

Any examination of the obligations of the PR practitioner to his client demonstrates clearly that such a fiduciary obligation exists. Put another way, the PR practitioner is under an obligation of loyalty to the client he serves.

The PRSA Code of Professional Standards also makes it quite clear that the PR practitioner is deemed to have a fiduciary commitment. Thus, in Section 4 thereof, the Code provides:

> A member shall not represent conflicting or competing interests without the express consent of those concerned, given after a full disclosure of the facts; nor shall he place himself in a position where his interest is or may be in conflict with his duty to his client, employer, or other member of the public, without a full disclosure of such interest to all concerned.

In at least one case presented under this Section of the Code, the PRSA enforcement panel held that a firm which represented simultaneously two political entities whose objectives were clearly in conflict—neither client being aware of the common representation—was guilty of a violation of the Code.[11]

Other provisions of the Code require protection of "the confidences of both present and former clients or employers" and a prohibition against future retainers which may "involve the disclosure or use of . . . confidences to the disadvantage or prejudice of [former] clients or employers."

Furthermore the obligation of the PR practitioner—both implicitly and explicitly covered in some agreements—to account for funds received from clients constitutes further evidence of such fiduciary obligation.

7. Historical Difference From Advertising Agencies.

The PR counselor or firm has escaped the changes in legal status which have developed historically in the case of the advertising agency.[12] From his very origin—even when he was the "press agent"—the PR counselor has been the representative of his client, the company on behalf of which he performed his services.

The modern advertising agency is the successor to the "advertising agent" who started life in the 1830s as the representative of an individual newspaper and thereafter of various newspapers for which he sold space. Subsequently he passed through several stages as a middleman or broker between the media and the advertiser. In this period he was an acknowledged independent entrepreneur and, in handling advertising space, he "bought low and sold high," owing little, if any, allegiance to either the medium or the advertiser.

As time passed, this advertising agent became more advertiser-oriented; he began to furnish services to the advertiser beyond the purchase of space; finally he became the agent of the advertiser serving all of its needs in the preparation and placement of advertising. The advertising agency is now clearly the legal agent of its principal, the advertiser.[13]

The not-always simple marketplace relationships caused legal confusion. Much of this was the result of the so-called "commission system" whereby the advertising agent—now the advertising agency—*seemed* to be paid by the medium and not by the advertiser.

The PR man, from the outset, worked *for* the client. While he worked *with* the media—the press—it was not a commercial relationship and he owed the medium nothing except honesty and fair play.

Furthermore, he was obviously paid by the client and there was never any intimation that he was being paid, directly or indirectly, by the media. Even his detractors have hammered at the fact that the PR man is paid by his client. Carl Sandburg in his attack on Ivy Lee called him a "paid liar." [14] Whatever the ethical implications of this epithet, it avoids the supposed legal consequences which distorted, for a time, the status of the advertising agency.

The reverse has been and sometimes is charged: that the PR man has "paid off" the press. For example, charges have been brought under the

PRSA Code against "a counselor who paid a magazine a so-called contribution in a substantial amount to secure the publication of an article favorable to the counselor's client." [15] See also Chapter 22, Section 6 and Chapter 20, Section 9.

Thus the position of the PR man was factually clear and his legal status was clear. He was—and is—the agent of his client.

B. CONTRACT LIABILITIES.

8. General Business Obligations.

This chapter makes no effort to discuss any of the so-called routine or general business obligations of the PR counselor—those which are essentially the same for every businessman or company. Obviously these are beyond the scope of this work.

Our concern here is with those relationships, rights and obligations which are reasonably indigenous solely to the activities and practice of public relations by the independent PR practitioner.

9. Importance of Written Agreements.

To state the obvious, every PR counsel should understand both his rights and his liabilities. The simplest and surest channel to such understanding is the written agreement. The PR counsel lives in the world of words. He makes his living through the written word. Yet he all too frequently forgets this when dealing with his financial relationships.

Many PR counselors—especially those operating smaller organizations —for some reason seem to consider written agreements an extracurricular activity. They may look upon them as annoying distractions. Some may even resent being presented with agreements by "the other side." Many do not even use purchase orders, although they are buying things day in and day out.

Mention of the need for an agreement with the client may produce raised eyebrows. Some believe them unnecessary and even trouble-producing. After all, they say, a contract means nothing; the important thing is a "happy" client.

The desirability of a written agreement still remains one of the most controversial subjects in public relations. One thing, however, is clear. If a PR counsel has once been "hurt" by his contract derelictions, he quickly becomes a "believer." Unfortunately, too many wait until they do get hurt.

Some of the reasons for avoiding the written agreement may, in certain limited or unusual cases, make sense. Yet it should be manifest that the advantages of the written agreement far outstrip the usually intangible, alleged disadvantages.

Two early cases reaching diametrically opposite results will pinpoint this conclusion. While they happen to involve advertising agencies, they apply with equal force to the PR firm since they involve a closely allied service function.

In *N.W. Ayer v. U.S. Rubber Co.*,[16] Ayer had had a written contract with its client; after they came to a parting of the ways, Ayer sued and recovered commissions on all of the advertising "placed" by it, even though it did not appear until *after* the admittedly proper three months' notice of termination had been given by the client. The case turned squarely on the language in the contract. The advertising was "placed" during the period before termination and the fact that it did not appear until afterward was not a defense.

Compare this result with the outcome of *Kastor and Sons Advertising Co., Inc. v. Grove Laboratories.*[17] There was no written contract and the plaintiff recovered only a small part of its claim. It recovered only for the services actually performed *prior* to termination and did not recover for the much larger amount of the commissions on the unused radio time. The radio time was used after termination and the plaintiff could not show that it was entitled to a commission on such charges.

Furthermore, much litigation can be aborted and incipient disputes settled—whether client, supplier, or any third party is involved—if the parties have before them a firm and understandable blueprint of their relationship.

10. Responsibility to Client.

PR counsel's responsibility to his client stems from two sources: his agreement with the client and the implications of the legal relationship between counsel and client. As to the specific contract obligations, see Sections 17 to 32 below. We are here concerned with the so-called "legal duties" of the PR counsel.

Inasmuch as the PR counsel is an agent of his client, he owes the client all of the duties arising from the fiduciary character of the relationship. These are:

(a) Absence of Conflicting Interest.

It is fundamental that the agent may not have any conflicting interest with his principal.[18] This conflict might arise in several ways. Probably the most obvious is the handling of conflicting accounts such as those of companies which are in direct competition with each other.

Here is an interesting and persuasive discussion of both the legal and ethical rationale for this rule: [19]

> Several reasons may be given for this rule. In law, as in morals, it may be stated that as a principle, no servant can serve two masters; for either he will hate the one and love the other; or else he will hold to the one and despise the other. Luke 16, 13. Unless the principal contracts for less, the agent is bound to serve him with all his skill, judgment and discretion. The agent cannot divide this duty and give part to another. Therefore, by engaging with the second, he forfeits his right to compensation from the one who first engages him. By the second engagement, if he does not in fact disable himself from rendering to the first employer the full quantum of service contracted for, he at least tempts himself not to do so. And for the same reason he cannot recover from the second employer who is ignorant of the first engagement.

This also is specifically forbidden by the PRSA Code as discussed in Section 6 above.

Ownership or interest in a supplier may also present a conflict of interest. Some PR service involves the purchase of considerable printing. If PR counsel has a particular interest in a print shop which does the work, this would represent a conflict of interest.[20]

On the other hand, almost any conflict of interest may become "legitimate" if the client has full knowledge of it at all times. The conflict of interest still continues but now the clients have approved it and therefore cannot object to it.[21]

(b) Trusteeship.

Basic to the fiduciary commitment is the obligation of the PR counsel to act as a trustee for the client on all materials, contracts, and any other property of any kind in connection with which he acts on behalf of his client. Such materials may represent a large investment over the term of the relationship and should be delivered to the client on termination thereof.

The same is true of the more intangible materials used or purchased in the course of the service. For example, PR counsel may obtain research studies for the client who pays for them. These belong to the client—not to the counsel.[22] The counsel is so far a trustee thereof that he may not use the results of such research in serving any other client after service to the original client has terminated.[23]

The same is true as to ideas or campaigns developed by counsel for client. A leading case on this is *Brown v. Mollé*.[24] The issue in the case was the ownership of the famous Mollé shaving cream jingle which had been created by an employee of Mollé's agency. It was held that as between the agency and client, the agency was the trustee of the jingle and its copyright for the benefit of Mollé, its client.

(c) Confidentiality.

The PR counsel, as a fiduciary, must treat as confidential all information obtained by it during its service to a given client. By the very nature of his function, the PR man must learn much confidential information about the client. This must be protected.[25]

Financial PR subjects PR counsel to special burdens of confidentiality. See Chapter 22, Section 3. So, too, does long-range development of new products. See Chapter 16.

This requirement continues even after termination of service.[26] Essentially the same problems exist in this situation as exist in the relationship between a PR firm and its own employees who may leave their employment, and take with them much confidential information. See Chapter 3, Sections 25 and 32.

Confidential disclosure to PR counsel may also lead to problems impinging upon marketing intelligence or industrial espionage. See Chapter 17.

(d) Accountability.

The PR firm must account accurately for any funds or property received from or on behalf of client.[27] No mark-ups or additional charges in connection with such payments are permitted unless the client has previously agreed thereto or is promptly advised about them.[28] This is often reflected in the client agreement. See Section 25 below.

There have been cases of "secret rebates" made by free-lance writers, for example, to the PR firm. Aside from the ethics of such methods, the PR firm is legally obligated to remit such rebates to its client.[29] Otherwise it secretly profits from a fiduciary relationship.

The duty to account also requires that the PR counsel open its internal books and records to examination by a client's accountants—at least insofar as the records deal with transactions relative to such client.

(e) Obedience.

It does not belittle the function or stature of the PR counsel that he is required to obey the instructions of his client. He must always act within the four corners of his authorization and, if given specific directions by his client, must obey such instructions.[30] This requirement is natural and necessary since the PR firm, acting as the client's agent, can legally bind the client to third parties. An error of the PR firm is attributable to the client.

Many client agreements specifically cover this, providing that all work shall be subject to the approval of the client. A failure to obtain such required advance approval subjects the PR firm to liability and gives the client a right to cancel the retainer. See Section 28 below.

(f) Disclosure to Client.

Any information affecting the counsel's relationship with the client which comes to the attention of the PR counsel must be promptly disclosed to the client. This is not confined to such obvious things as the counsel's possible conflicting interest. It extends to any "material facts" which may in any way affect the conduct of the business entrusted to the PR counsel.[31]

This obligation may be an onerous one. The PR firm, located in New York and/or Washington, for example, frequently acts as a "listening post" for clients located in cities or areas somewhat remote from these centers of important information and developments.

11. Liabilities to Media.

Paid advertising is not infrequently necessary as an incidental or contributing element in a particular PR or publicity program. When this occurs, the PR counselor becomes, in effect, an advertising agency— limiting this reference and status to such portion of his effort.

Canfield suggests and discusses the following uses of such paid advertising under the title of "public relations advertising": [32]

(a) To secure acceptance of an organization by the general public.
(b) To dispel wrong impressions or correct misconceptions.
(c) To secure public acceptance of an industry.
(d) To inform suppliers and gain their good will.
(e) To stimulate owner interest and gain the understanding and confidence of stockholders.
(f) To win the good will of plant neighbors.
(g) To develop a favorable attitude by legislators and government officials.
(h) To inform dealers of company policies and programs and gain their cooperation.
(i) To inform and win the good will of employees.
(j) To serve customers by giving them helpful information.
(k) To improve labor relations.
(l) To win the support of the press.
(m) To render a public service.

The respective liabilities and responsibilities of the client and the advertising agency are discussed at length by this author in *The Law for Advertising and Marketing*.[33]

In summary form, however, the following rules apply to the liability of the PR counsel *qua* advertising agency under these circumstances:

(a) At common law—unless altered by contract—the advertising agency, as the agent of its client, a disclosed principal, is not responsible for the undertakings of the principal, even though entered into by the agency.

(b) The advertising agency *may*, by written agreement, affirmatively undertake to become responsible to the media for its charges.

(c) The obligation of the agency may be either *in addition to* the client's continuing common law liability or it may be *in lieu of* the latter's liability—the alternatives depending upon the language of the agreement between the agency and the medium.

The foregoing presupposes that the PR counsel places the paid space or time. Obviously, the problem does not arise at all if the commitment is undertaken by someone else.

There are several alternative arrangements through which such "public relations advertising" may be placed.

(a) The advertising is placed by the client's own independent advertising agency. The PR firm or counsel plans—perhaps prepares—the advertising, selects the media and does all other preliminary work. However, it is the client's advertising agency which places the advertising and handles the billing and payment therefor. The PR firm's services in preparation, etc. may be compensated under its basic fee arrangement or it may receive a portion of the media commission retained by the advertising agency which places the space or time.

(b) The PR firm may itself retain an advertising agency to place the paid advertising.[34] The PR firm, once again, prepares the advertising, selects the media, etc. and then has it placed through the advertising agency. The latter appears on the space or time order and the PR firm does not appear in the matter insofar as the media are concerned.

In some cases, the advertising agency retains the entire media commission. In other cases, the commission is divided between the PR firm and the advertising agency. Billing is also handled in either of two ways: either through the PR firm as conduit or directly to the client who remits to the advertising agency directly.

(c) The PR firm may operate a subsidiary advertising agency used for just such purposes. Here the relationships are confused, although on the surface, the advertising appears to be placed by the subsidiary advertising agency. There is very little difference here—in external appearance at least—between this arrangement and that in (b) above. The principal differences are the throw-off of profit from the media commissions and ultimate liability for unpaid media charges in the event of client default for any reason.

(d) Some PR firms are themselves subsidiaries of advertising agencies—in effect the reverse of the relationship in (c) above. When this is the case, the "parent advertising agency" places the advertising.

12. Liability to Suppliers.

Some PR counsel are merely consultants and advisors. They do not carry out the programs which they develop or recommend. Others are responsible for such implementation and, in the course thereof, are likely to make purchases on behalf of the client. These purchases may include printed materials, research by independent organizations, and all of the many other graphics which are necessary to carry a program through to successful completion. We here exclude paid advertising.

Inasmuch as the counsel is the agent of the client, the counsel is not legally responsible to the supplier, since the client is always a disclosed principal. It is the client who is bound to the third party supplier or source. See Section 11 above.

The foregoing is true even when the PR campaign is carried out by the PR department of an advertising agency. No questions arise here—as might possibly occur with paid advertising purchases—because of the use of the so-called "Standard Order Blank" positing sole liability of the agency or even any alleged "customs of the trade." [35]

C. NON-CONTRACT LIABILITIES.

13. Liability in Tort.

A tort action may be roughly described as being based on the perpetration of a "wrong" as against one growing out of a contract or similar relationship.

The PR practitioner's liability for tort may vary with the exact nature and extent of his service. If he is merely a consultant who does not carry out or implement the program causing the tort, he is probably not liable —assuming that the tort was not an integral part of the consultant's recommended program. On the other hand, if he does so carry out the program, he would be responsible. The inside corporate PR employee participating actively in the tort—he ordinarily would do so—is clearly liable.

These results follow from the general rule that all who participate in or contribute to a tort are liable to the wronged person.[36]

The PR man's exposure in tort seems to fall into two loosely-described categories:

(a) Those torts occurring in the course of his "communications" activities. This would include libel and slander, right of privacy, copyright infringement, unfair competition, conspiracy, etc. His respective involvements are discussed in the several chapters dealing with each of these legal areas.

(b) Those torts involving "physical" activities directed by the PR man. This would include "accidents" during such activities as employee athletics, plant tours, etc. See Chapters 14 and 21.

14. Statutory and Administrative Liability.

The responsibility of the public relations counselor or consultant may not always be clear when governmental or administrative agency enforcement is involved. We are here dealing with such administrative or policing agencies of government as the FTC, SEC, FDA, etc. There does not appear to be very much law on the subject although parallel or analogous decisions seem to posit counselor liability.

Insofar as the FTC is involved, there appear to be no cases directly holding a PR counselor liable or responsible in deception or unfair practice cases. However, by analogy to the many cases which have held advertising agencies responsible,[37] the counselor should anticipate liability if he in fact "participated" in the legal impropriety upon which the action is grounded. This also follows from cases such as the *A. & P.* litigations in which the Justice Department, having parallel jurisdiction with the FTC in antitrust cases, successfully included a PR firm in its prosecution. See Section 16 below. This, of course, becomes a question of fact and will undoubtedly have to be determined on a case-to-case basis.

The antitrust cases referred to in Section 16 below, although criminal proceedings brought successfully by the Justice Department against PR practitioners, are clear indications that administrative proceedings by the FTC and premised on similar activities would probably be effective against them. The burden of proof in a criminal case is substantially greater than in an administrative agency action.

The exposure of a financial PR consultant or firm to action by the SEC is discussed in Chapter 22.

Responsibilities under laws enforced and administered by other federal or state agencies would seem generally to follow the same basic rule: if the PR counselor "participates" in the legal impropriety, he will probably be held responsible for it.

15. Criminal Liability.

The possible criminal liability of the PR practitioner is no greater or lesser than would be that of any other person. If he violates a law, he may anticipate prosecution—not because he is a PR man but rather because he is a lawbreaker. This is true whether he is a counselor or a corporate staff member. There is one exception to this: the PR man's exposure may be greater because of the increased possibility of a charge of conspiracy in addition to whatever other and basic criminal charges may be brought. As to this, see Section 16 below.

PR counsel or firms have been indicted or convicted on numerous charges, including perjury, bribery, price-fixing and other antitrust charges, securities manipulation, other securities law offenses, mail fraud, extortion, etc.[38]

In most cases, the defendants have been independent PR counselors but corporate PR staff personnel have also been involved.[39]

Criminal convictions of PR personnel may also lead to "judicial procedures" of the PRSA if the defendant is a member of that association. Disciplinary action and expulsion following a court conviction would be taken under Article XIII, Section 7 of the Society's By-Laws.

PRSA takes no "overt action" until the final court verdict or judgment has been rendered except in unusual situations. PRSA makes no effort— nor should it—to prejudge criminal liability. This is for the courts.

If a member is found guilty of a "felony or misdemeanor relating to the conduct of his profession or involving moral turpitude," the PRSA Board has authority, after hearing, to take immediate and independent action to expel the member. The first action under this provision is said to have occurred in 1952 when a member was expelled upon conviction of mail fraud in fund-raising.[40]

A further question under PRSA procedures arises when a corporation is convicted and a society member is, in some manner, associated with that company or its PR counsel. PRSA's action involves only individual members—not corporations. PRSA must therefore establish "that its member from that corporation or its counseling firm was aware [of the criminal acts] and participated [therein]." PRSA makes it clear that it does not subscribe to a "guilt by association" policy. Consequently, if one member of a counseling firm should be convicted of a crime, this does not reflect upon other members of that firm unless they had knowledge of what was being done by the guilty party.[41]

16. Criminal Conspiracy.

The PR practitioner or his firm may be particularly exposed to charges of conspiracy if any criminal charges are brought.[42] Whatever he does— criminal or otherwise—he usually does by reason of his retainer by his client and in concert with the client. Joint or multi-party action is therefore almost indigenous to the PR function. This is the root of the conspiracy charge.

The individual PR counselor and his firm have been held guilty of conspiracy. The leading case is the *A. & P.* litigation brought by the Justice Department under the Sherman Act.[43] Carl Byoir and Business Organizations, Inc.—described by the court as Byoir's *"alter ego"* and "organized to promote the public relations of A & P"—were among the defendants found guilty. There was no direct evidence that Byoir knew of the conspiracy but the facts indicated that he could not have been ignorant of it since he participated and cooperated to further it. The court also pointed out that he was duty-bound by the contract of his "corporate puppet" (Business Organizations, Inc.) to "counsel, guide and direct the policy making officers of his client." The court summed up Byoir's position by saying:

> There can be no doubt on this record that the defendant Byoir had full knowledge of the monopolistic purpose of A & P's overall conspiracy which it was intended to further, and such knowledge notwithstanding, took a large personal part in its formation and development.

It is doubtful whether this case, decided some 30 years ago, would have any different result today, notwithstanding the decision of the Supreme Court in the "railroads/truckers" case—discussed in Chapter 23, Section 4—in which the PR counselor was absolved in a triple-damage civil action.

Although both cases were instituted under the Sherman Act, there is a significant distinction between them. The *A. & P.* case involved price-fixing, monopoly, etc. The railroads/truckers case involved appeals to the legislature. The two cases therefore fall within the dichotomy described by the Supreme Court:

> The proscriptions of the [Sherman] Act, tailored as they are for the business world, are not at all appropriate for application in the political arena.

There are certain guidelines as to the basis of the PR counselor's liability in cases of this sort. He may well be found culpable if he:

    (a) "participates" in the illegal action;

    (b) is found "to counsel, guide and direct" the policy behind the conspiracy;

    (c) takes "a large personal part" in the conspiracy;

    (d) sets up "an organization readily useful as a propaganda agency to fight [his client's] enemies";

    (e) "cooperates to further" the conspiracy.[44]

Notwithstanding the foregoing, PR counsel does not become a member of a conspiracy "by rendering services to it" unless he knows of the conspiracy.[45] Whether he does know is a question of fact. Direct evidence of such knowledge (such as formal agreement) is not necessary. It "may be spelled out by what the defendants said and did." [46] Each case stands on its own facts.

However, there can be no doubt that PR counsel should be most cautious in any situation in which he may have any *in limine* (threshold) indication that he may be serving or "cooperating" with a client engaged in some possibly illegal activity. This is particularly true if he is intimately involved in the councils of the client or is the source of the program in question. He most certainly should seek legal advice as to his position—necessarily from his own, independent counsel, rather than relying on the advice of the client's legal counsel.

D. COUNSEL-CLIENT AGREEMENTS.

17. Purpose and Contents.

The PR counsel-client agreement is the most important single document in the client's legal portfolio. It is the one contract which assures the PR counsel of *income*. All other commitments usually deal with the counsel's obligations and *outgo* such as agreements with suppliers, freelance writers or other talent, its own staff—even the lease with its landlord.

Yet many PR firms are reluctant to insist upon a written obligation from their clients. Some are almost apologetic and shamefaced about it. The following sentence—not atypical—was taken from a letter agreement used by a well-known, moderate-sized New York PR firm:

> We don't use contracts because the basis of all enduring relationships is mutual confidence and understanding, but our attorneys ask that we exchange informal letters of agreement with new clients. If you would initial one copy of this letter and return it for our files, I'll appreciate it.

One wonders whether this sort of hesitant *mea culpa* is even good "public relations." It certainly is not good legal relations.

At the risk of immoderate repetition, we cannot stress strongly enough the need to obtain a written agreement with all clients.

Such an agreement does not presuppose that either of the parties to it is a sneaky, unreliable "chiseler"—out to take advantage of the other. Far from it. It is merely a vehicle to set down with reasonable accuracy and clarity their mutual obligations. It is—or at least, should be—a *fair* exposition of what each party may expect from the other, drafted and signed at a time when, presumably, mutual confidence is high and both sides are satisfied with their bargain. It is, in this sense, no different from any other agreement between two honest, intelligent businessmen, both of whom look forward to a reasonable profit or benefit from the transaction.

The counselor-client agreement should contain provisions in certain basic areas. These important elements are listed below, together with cross-references to later sections hereof which contain suggested clauses relative thereto.

> (a) Description of services. See Section 23 below.
> (b) Payment of fees. See Section 24 below.
> (c) Payment for staff time and expenses. See Section 25 below.
> (d) Special Projects provisions. See Section 26 below.
> (e) Duration of retainer. See Section 27 below.
> (f) Control and approval by client. See Section 28 below.
> (g) Assignment of personnel. See Section 29 below.
> (h) Maintenance of records. See Section 30 below.
> (i) Termination provisions. See Section 31 below.
> (j) Miscellaneous provisions. See Section 32 below.

18. Type of Agreements.

There are many different types of agreements, any one of which will serve if properly drafted. The exact form of the agreement may be dictated by the relationship between the parties. Examination of many such agreements indicates that there appears to be no correlation whatsoever between the type of agreement, the size of the PR firm, or the origin of the agreement itself.

(a) Oral Understanding.

A contract may be binding even though it is merely oral but it has certain weaknesses. It depends upon the memory of the parties and, all too frequently, this may be stultified by the needs of the moment. Furthermore, under the various state "Statutes of Frauds" it is safer to have a written agreement if it is intended that the agreement or relationship is to continue for more than one year.

(b) Printed Form.

Some PR firms find a printed agreement quite useful. It spells out all of the customary terms and, in effect, is a blueprint of the firm's methods of operation, billing, assignment of personnel, etc. Furthermore, some have found that such an agreement is a useful "selling tool" when initially discussing a retainer with a concern which has not theretofore employed PR counsel. By displaying the printed form to the potential client, the latter is specifically "educated" as to the basic methods in the PR counseling field. Such printed agreements have been noted in a multiplicity of lengths, forms and contents.

(c) Formal Typewritten Document.

This refers to the so-called "bluebacked" legal instrument, usually prepared by legal counsel and almost always "custom-tailored" to suit the needs of the particular retainer. Some PR firms, however, have adopted such an agreement—usually developed over a considerable period of time—and use it in essentially a single form, making very few changes therein for use with a particular client.

Agreements of this sort are likely to be more detailed and to cover elements not ordinarily found in other forms of agreement. Most of the detail stems from experience and most of the more esoteric inclusions are the result of some unfortunate prior relationship experienced by the counseling firm.

(d) Letter of Appointment.

One of the commonest forms is the "letter of appointment." Customarily, this originates with the counseling firm and is countersigned by the client. However, in some instances, the client may originate the letter after a discussion with the counseling firm. Some of the seemingly "reverse language" contained in the contract forms in Sections 23 to 32 below results from the fact that the clauses in question have been taken from appointment letters written by the client, rather than the counseling firm.

Some PR firms prefer a very brief letter of appointment supplemented by an extended description of the services to be rendered. This supplement usually is specifically developed—not a "drug store form"—as a result of negotiations with the client.

This may be done so that the plan of operations is a separate and distinct unit. As a result, staff members of the counseling firm or client PR staff may have a blueprint before them but, at the same time, not be aware of the financial aspects of the retainer. The latter is spelled out in the brief letter and is so handled as to be "for the eyes of management only."

(e) Printed "Standards of Operations."

Some firms have developed extended "standards of operation" which also serve as the major portion of the client agreement. A facing page is then added to the Standards and tied to them by cross-reference. This additional page is usually merely a brief letter giving dates, amounts of fee, and other variables. It covers very little of the normal aspects of the relationship, leaving such matters to the Standards to which it is attached.

19. Compensation and Charging Methods.

At least four different basic methods of compensation and charging have been developed by PR counsel. There may be even more variation. For example, "fee" means different things to different firms. To some, it is merely a retainer, covering overhead and profit. To others it covers these items plus top management planning, etc. To still others, it is intended to include some or all of the direct expenses such as staff salaries chargeable to servicing the particular account.[47]

George Hammond, Chairman of the Board of Carl Byoir and Associates, has described these four basic billing concepts as follows: [48]

> 1. A monthly or annual retainer charge to cover overhead and profit with all other expenses billed separately. A percentage commission may or may not be charged on these expenses.
> 2. A flat sum covering everything, either for a specific project or for an entire program or period.
> 3. A fee that includes salaries, profit and overhead—with all other expenses billed separately.
> 4. A flat hourly rate covering salaries of staff members assigned to the account. This may be a rate computed at 2 or 2½ times the actual salary per hour, a figure calculated to cover indirect salary costs, overhead, and profits. Other expenses are billed separately.

The above reference to "specific projects" introduces another complicating factor. A firm may use several of those charging methods—even with the same client at the same time. The multiplicity will usually be based upon practical factors such as whether the retainer is a long-range relationship covering all PR needs or merely for a single, one-time project or program. The "specific projects" approach may entail a series of separate programs—product publicity, financial PR, house organ preparation, etc.—each of which is the subject of a separate fee, a time plus mark-up arrangement or a mixture of the two. These multiple approaches are evident in the diverse language quoted in Sections 24 to 26 below.

Whatever the charging method or methods may be, they should be enunciated with particularity in the agreement. Experience indicates that when disputes do arise, they are rooted in diverse interpretation of the parties' understanding of "what payment covers what service." There have been instances when this difficulty arose from such a basic matter as lack of understanding of the terms "public relations" and "publicity" as used in an agreement.

This, of course, ties in inescapably with questions about scope or description of the services to be rendered, discussed in Section 21 below.

20. Contingent Compensation.

One aspect of the PR counsel's possible charging methods merits separate consideration. This is "contingent" compensation. The term has been used in two frames of reference:

(a) "Contingent" may refer to the possibility—not presently determined—of some future project being handled by the counsel, in which event, he will receive an additional fee or other compensation.

There is nothing illegal or unethical about such provisions, which are quite common. Essentially it entails "special projects" as discussed in Section 19 above. The *amount* of counsel's compensation is not contingent. The contingent element is confined to the *basis* of his compensation. In practice, this meaning of the term is not too common but is sometimes adopted by the parties.

(b) "Contingent" may refer to an arrangement whereby the amount of the compensation is premised upon the degree of effectiveness of the counsel's actual performance.

This is the context in which the term is usually used and in which its use has caused considerable concern. There does not appear to be any legal prohibition against the contingent fee *per se*. Within the limited periphery of public relations which involves lobbying, the contingent fee may be illegal. See Chapter 23, Sections 21 and 26. This absence of legal prohibition of contingent fees is reflected also, for example, in the legal and engineering professions. It is well known that attorneys may properly use contingent fee arrangements with clients, subject, in some instances, to either statutory or court-rule restrictions and limitations.[49]

Among engineers, such fees are approached from the ethical basis also, not the legal. Thus the Code of Ethics of the National Society of Professional Engineers provides: [50]

> He [the engineer] shall not solicit or accept an engineering engagement on a contingent fee basis if payment depends on a finding of economic feasibility, or other conclusions by the engineer.

The Consulting Engineers Council particularizes the unethical conditions of contingent fees as including "the successful operation of the project served; development of a product with payment contingent upon successful manufacture and sales of the product." [51]

The PRSA uses the same ethical context under its Code of Professional Standards which, on this issue, provides:

> A member shall not propose to a prospective client or employer that the amount of his fee or other compensation be contingent on or measured by the achievement of specified results; nor shall he enter into any fee agreement to the same effect.

This has been interpreted by the PRSA Board of Directors to prohibit a member from agreeing to compensation "determined or conditioned by the amount of newspaper or magazine lineage obtained for the member's company or client." It also "applies equally to radio and TV coverage, or any form of exposure of a client's message." The Interpretation goes on to hold that this Rule applies further "to any contingent fee based on increase in sales volume, increase in profit margins, increase in stock value or the attainment of specified political or legislative results." [52]

At the same time, PRSA does not divorce a PR counsel's compensation entirely from "the benefits resulting to the client . . . from the services" rendered by the counsel. This is evident from the following descriptions of factors to be used "in determining compensation for [the counsel's] services," as taken from the same Interpretation:

> a. the experience, judgment and skills required to handle the matter properly.
> b. the characteristics and difficulty of the problems involved.
> c. the time and labor required.
> d. the effect on the member's employment by other clients or potential clients.
> e. the customary or prevailing compensation for similar services.
> f. *the values involved in the matter and the benefits resulting to the client or employer from the services.*
> g. the duration and character of the employment, whether casual or for a continuing period.
> h. the equipment or personnel investment required in order to perform the function. (Emphasis added.)

21. Description of Services.

Interrelated to the compensation provisions in the agreement is the question of the scope of services to be rendered by the PR counsel. These may range from an all-encompassing reference to "all public relations services" to a strictly limited single project or closely defined type of PR activity such as financial PR.

The need for specificity increases as the compensation base becomes more narrowly constricted. Thus, if only a single flat annual fee is to be paid, the agreement should pinpoint the type or limits of the services to be rendered. On the other hand, if the basic fee is to be supplemented by time charges, mark-ups, special project charges, etc.—in effect, an "open end" arrangement—the description of the services loses something of its importance. But, even here, there should be a specific delineation of when the time charges, etc. become operative, unless, of course, they are effective at all times from the beginning of service.

As discussed in Section 11 above, the counsel's obligations as to the preparation and placement of the necessary or incidental paid advertising should be expressly defined. This frequently is omitted in the agreement because of the apparently incidental character of such advertising—it is otherwise in a corporate institutional advertising program—or because of the obvious orientation of the counsel-client relationship and thinking towards public relations rather than advertising.

Since such advertising may come to involve considerable planning and staff time and effort as well as the need for considerable funds on the part of the counsel, the counsel's billing practices should be clearly explained in the agreement.

The biggest potential problem faced by the counsel in this area is the coupling of a flat, all-inclusive fee arrangement with a subsequent request by the client for additional PR or publicity services not discussed or contemplated in the original negotiations or understanding. Logic and memory often suffer when such demands are made. This is particularly true when smaller PR firms and/or smaller clients are involved. As to the latter, an honest misunderstanding based on lack of experience by the client with public relations and PR counsel is often the cause of friction. This may be largely avoided by use of proper limiting language in describing the counsel's service. See Sections 23 to 26.

E. FORMS.

22. Introduction.

Sections 23 to 32 below contain a wide variety of clauses taken from agreements used by public relations counseling firms in many parts of the country, of a wide range in size and dealing with clients of various kinds (business, institutional or non-profit, trade association, etc.). Some were prepared by legal counsel and others by the firms themselves. Some were initiated by the client and others by the counseling firm. Some were used by advertising agencies for their PR services.

In each of the following Sections are collected clauses applicable to, and representative or explanatory of, the single subject described in the Section heading. Some thereof may be mutually exclusive and others may represent some overlapping. Not every provision will be relevant to a given agreement. They represent considerable practical experience. They appear to have served well and to have been clearly understood and followed by the parties. Insofar as the author knows, they have not led to any litigation.

At the same time, any attempt to present agreement forms and clauses —even in the alternative—should always be accompanied by a *caveat*. These suggestions, as with any so-called "drugstore" or "form book" forms, may be misapplied. They must be used intelligently and consonantly with the needs of the relationship which they are to serve. They should not be followed blindly. Advice of counsel is still necessary. Among lawyers one of the oldest adages is: "a man who represents himself has a fool for a client"—whether he be a lawyer or a PR counselor.

23. Description of Services.

(a) ABC accepts such employment and agrees to perform the services of public relations counsel, advising [client] on matters pertaining to public relations, and working with the various media of communication with the public with a view to securing greater goodwill for [client] and creating increased acceptance for its policies and services.

(b) Our organization will serve as general public relations counsel for [client]. Our duties and responsibilities are generally outlined in the attached document.

(c) It is our understanding that ABC will promptly draft a specific program covering the first six months of the activity and submit the same to us for approval.

(d) ABC will conduct two (2) public relations and publicity programs for [client] as follows:

    (1) National program. Consisting of activities with national magazines, broadcast, wire service and newspaper media and their personnel.

    (2) Local or regional programs. Involving the public relations and publicity requirements needed to aid [client's] branches or distributors. This will be performed on a preassignment basis subject to advance approval and budgets.

(e) It is agreed that ABC will provide the following services within the terms of our counseling agreement:

(1) ABC will work with [client's] public relations department to review and advise on its regular publications (such as annual reports, quarterly reports, external house organ, and so forth).

(2) ABC will review and advise the [client] public relations department on periodic written material (such as news releases, feature articles, general memoranda to management, etc.).

(3) Prior to major corporate events (such as annual stockholder meeting, important press conferences) ABC staff members, working through [client's] public relations department, will be available for specialized counseling with [client] management.

(4) As desired by [client] public relations director, ABC will assist in training and in orienting the [client] public relations staff at certain periods of the year.

(5) ABC will act as a "listening post" for [client] in the vital New York communications area.

(6) Periodically ABC will consult with [client] public relations director on the delineation of corporate public relations objectives and on the planning and execution of corporate public relations programs.

(7) ABC will maintain regular contact with the national financial and business press on behalf of [client].

(8) ABC will maintain regular contact with security analysts who specialize in areas of interest to [client]. Our objective is to develop more adequate understanding of [client] in the financial community.

(9) ABC will follow up with the New York press and the national press (located in New York) on home-office-initiated projects.

(10) ABC will develop from time to time suitable platforms for speeches by major [client] officials.

(11) Periodically, as desired by the [client] public relations director, ABC will analyze the effectiveness of [client's] communications dollars.

(f) ABC shall perform the basic program outlined in a previously submitted memorandum dated ——————, 1966 and titled, "A Comprehensive Program to Aid the Growth of [Client]." It is understood that projects listed in this memorandum are representative of work to be done under the program, but that some projects may be dropped or other projects added as we go along.

(g) We are very pleased to work with you on the promotion of [client] and its services to the business community. Our services will include the formating, writing and editing of a [client] publication, as well as supervision of all art and layout work. We will also publicize individual issues in the business press. This agreement covers [description of issues for one-year period]. In the event that we do not produce an issue you consider publishable by ——————, 1967, this agreement is cancellable upon written notice. In the event of such cancellation, [client] will have paid ABC our specified creative fee for three months and out-of-pocket expenses as specified below.

(h) An annual fee in the amount of $——————, payable in monthly installments, will be charged for services rendered by ABC's public relations department, such services to include preparation and release of publicity, preparation of [client] house organ "——————," routine employee materials, etc. Production required in this connection such as art, photography, engravings, typography, etc. will be billed to [client] at ABC's net cost plus fifteen per cent.

24. Payment of Fees.

(a) [Client] agrees to pay ABC for said services the sum of $—————— per annum, payable in equal monthly installments per month in advance. The first of such payments shall be due and payable on the date of the execution of this agreement and the subsequent monthly payments shall be due on the same date of each succeeding month during the term of this agreement.

(b) A total annual retainer fee of $—————— will be paid by [client] at the rate of $—————— per month for the term of this agreement. This fee covers the counseling and supervisory services of the firm's principals at the New York headquarters of the firm, and access to all of its services and physical facilities.

(c) Our annual fee shall be $——————, payable monthly in advance. [Client] and ABC will review the actual number of man hours at the agency's standard billing rates, devoted to servicing the [client] account for the period from ——————, 1967 to ——————, 1967. If this review demonstrates a disparity between the value of agency man hours and the agency compensation, an equitable and mutually agreeable adjustment in the annual fee shall be made for the balance of the contract period.

(d) Our fee for this program shall be $——————— per month. It is agreed that the program shall be reviewed at the end of six months, with a view toward evaluating realistically the amount of effort required by us to implement the program adequately and that the basis for continuation of the program shall be considered at that time.

(e) We will operate on the basis of a monthly fee amounting to $———————. This covers basic public relations services as indicated under point 1 on page 8 of our proposal of ———————, 1966, and is subject to review by both you and us after we have worked together long enough to establish a track record and get a more exact feel for how much activity is required to properly service your account.

(f) If, in the course of rendering its services to [client], ABC shall place for [client] any advertising space or time which is commissionable, ABC shall retain such commission in addition to the annual fee due hereunder.

25. Payment for Staff Time and Expenses.

(a) In addition to the payment of the fee for services, [client] shall pay ABC an amount equal to all of the expenses of the latter, in connection with the servicing of the account in accordance with [client's] prior approval, including all expenses for photography, printing, mat service, traveling, relocation of employees and their families, entertainment, mimeographing, stationery used for releases, telephone, telegraph, postage, artwork, etc., and including an amount equal to the allocable portion of the base salary and payroll taxes thereon paid for the time devoted to the [client] account by the account executive of ABC and any other employees designated by ABC, with the approval of [client], to devote time to the [client] account. Other parties required to devote time to the account of [client], including personnel of such departments as investor relations, business and financial news, photography, radio and television, magazine, research, production and women's interests, and of the ABC branch offices, shall keep accurate records of the time so devoted and the time will be billed by ABC for the number of hours devoted to work on behalf of [client] at the established per diem rates. These rates will be the same as those charged all other clients.

(b) Charges for services of account executives and staff assistants as may be required to carry out the program approved by [client] will be billed at the standard per diem rates covering direct salary and applicable overhead.

(c) The [client] will reimburse ABC for all reasonable out-of-pocket disbursements made in the performance of its duties under this arrangement.

(d) Out-of-pocket expenses, such as long distance telephone, reproduction, postage, printing and so forth, will be billed to [client] at net plus the standard commission of 17.65 per cent. Entertainment and traveling costs will be billed to you at net. No out-of-pocket expenses over $200 will be contracted in your behalf without prior authorization by your appointed official.

(e) We authorize necessary monthly expenses for undesignated other out-of-pocket expenses but not to exceed $_____ per month.

(f) It is understood that during the aforesaid stated ten month period a minimum of $_____ shall be available for out-of-pocket costs such as photography, mimeographing, inter-city travel, press entertainment, etc.

(g) In addition to the fee, we will bill out-of-pocket costs (for photography, editorial contact, reproduction of news releases, etc.) at our cost, as well as the cost of any specific projects such as space advertising, press conferences, seminars, etc., as we may agree upon from time to time.

26. Special Projects Provisions.

(a) *Special Projects, Market Studies, Research, etc.*—All other work, not covered in the preceding paragraphs, shall be based upon prior written approval and agency mark-up shall be 17.54% on all outside purchases and standard billing rates on staff time.

(b) In addition to the counseling and press relations, the ABC staff will be available to [client] public relations department for work in the area of special projects. The following activities will be considered to fall into this category:

    (1) The development by ABC of feature articles in periodicals and electronic media of importance to [client].

(2) The preparation by ABC staff of speeches for [client] officials.

(3) A detailed communications audit by ABC of any specified
department or division of [client].

(4) The staging of a special event, such as a press conference, in
New York or another major city.

(5) Creative development by ABC of special printed material
(such as pamphlet, booklet, film script, and so forth) upon
the specific request of [client] public relations department.

(6) Help in the creation of a proper climate for [client] prior
to its entering a new marketing area.

(7) Use of ABC personnel in conjunction with market promotion in existing [client] markets.

(8) Legislative relations or other Federal Government relations
in behalf of [client] in Washington, D.C.

(c) All specific writing assignments performed by free lance personnel shall be undertaken at [client's] approval only. All such payments
to writers shall be billed to [client] at cost together with an additional
reasonable fee responsive in amount to the time required in connection
with each such writing project.

(d) Compensation for special publicity service (product or otherwise) will be rendered on special arrangement and upon [client's] request. Fees charged therefor will depend entirely on the amount of work
necessary to carry out the program successfully. Basic to such an arrangement is a service fee, to be agreed upon in advance, covering creative
work and development of the program. Traveling, multigraphing, photographs, artwork, engraving, mats, mailing charges, etc. will be billed at
cost in addition thereto.

(e) Special projects will be handled in two ways, always, of course,
after thorough discussion with your public relations department. On relatively short-term projects, such as special feature story placements,
Washington, D.C. relations, marketing promotions, and so forth, our
charges will be $—————— per hour for staff time and $——————
per hour for secretarial time. On longer term projects, such as the development of special publications or the planning and staging of special
events, we will work out a flat fee to be determined in advance. In any
case, we will remain flexible under these arrangements to take on whatever responsibilities [client] cares to assign to us.

27. Duration of Retainer.

(a) This arrangement is to extend from ——————, 1966 with either party having the right to terminate the agreement at the end of one year by 60 days advance written notice.

(b) [Client] employs ABC as its public relations counsel for a period of one year from the date of the signing of this Agreement. [Client] agrees that if it should decide not to renew this contract upon expiration, it will so notify ABC on or before the sixtieth day prior to the expiration date and that if notice shall not have been given by that date, the contract will automatically be extended for sixty days following the expiration date.

(c) It is mutually understood that you are retaining ABC for the period beginning ——————, 1966 and ending ——————, 1966. At the end of this six-month period, the program will be evaluated from the standpoint of its potential effectiveness, and its continuance renegotiated.

(d) This agreement will continue for the initial term of one year and then be subject to cancellation by either ABC or [client] upon sixty days written notice. Unless so terminated, this agreement will renew automatically at the end of the twelve-month period for a like period thereafter, subject to mutual agreement as to the scope of activities and services rendered.

(e) There's one other point that should be covered. Unpleasant as it is to talk about at any time—and especially at the outset of a relationship—either party to this agreement is free to cancel on 60 days written notice.

28. Control and Approval by Client.

(a) This program will require advance approval by [client], as will specific actions taken within the program itself, or within any extension of it.

(b) During the period above-mentioned, ABC will consult with and advise [client], whenever called upon to do so, in matters directly or indirectly affecting public relations of [client]. ABC further agrees to be wholly guided by [client] in all questions of policy, to the end that information released to the public, to employees, to the profession, or elsewhere shall be in keeping with the policies of [client].

(c) Budgets for projects and operating activities will be cleared in advance before commitments are made.

(d) In this work ABC will report to the undersigned, or in his absence to Mr. —————, [client's] Director of Public Relations, and be governed by their decisions.

(e) All purchases or commitments to be made on your behalf by ABC are subject to your prior approval either as part of the overall budget or as specific items. This excludes purchases merely incidental to our general counseling service, and to the projects or programs specifically described in this letter.

(f) ABC acts as your agent in making purchases necessary or expedient for the fulfillment of our services. However, your approval will be obtained before committing to you such obligations as research, purchase of printing, substantial travel expense, trade shows, special events, press parties or junkets, and similar, separate undertakings of more than nominal cost.

29. Assignment of Personnel.

(a) Assigned to work with [client] will be a full-time account executive. He will report to an officer of ABC (John Doe), who will devote a substantial portion of his time to [client] affairs. The account executive and the supervisor will be directly backed up by the specialized help of six magazine-news syndicate-broadcast media experts, who will remain at all times completely conversant with [client] affairs. Other ABC staff personnel may be called upon from time to time as the need arises. In addition, the ABC officer group will assume responsibility for general creative counseling to the [client] group.

(b) ABC will assign John Doe (account executive in charge) to general corporate public relations and Richard Roe to financial public relations on your account, to be assisted by such additional staff members as are, from time to time, necessary.

(c) Changes in assigned ABC personnel will not be made without prior consultation with you.

30. Maintenance of Records.

(a) ABC will maintain accurate records of all staff time work and all out-of-pocket expenses incurred in behalf of [client], and will be prepared to supply any supporting detail required by your auditors or yourself.

(b) All ABC records upon which reimburseable expense billings are based, are subject to your accountant's examination.

(c) ABC will maintain records (including scrapbooks) concerning [client] PR and publicity but these remain ABC's property since it is known that [client's] PR department is accustomed to preserving such materials.

(d) Both ABC and [client] shall maintain records as to dates and times when taking action on financial or securities releases requiring "immediate release" handling.

31. Termination Provisions.

(a) Upon receipt of notice of termination of our relationship, ABC shall continue with and complete any projects theretofore initiated with the approval of [client] even though such completion shall extend beyond the normal termination date hereof. ABC shall continue, until such completion, to receive the basic fee referred to above and any additional fees agreed upon for such projects with the understanding that the basic fee shall not be due after normal termination date if no part thereof is properly ascribed to such projects. ABC shall also be reimbursed for all staff time and expenses, as referred to herein, incurred in connection with such additional work.

(b) Upon termination of this agreement, [client] shall be entitled to receive and ABC shall deliver to [client] all physical materials (including artwork, mats, printed materials, photography, etc.) in ABC's possession and for which [client] shall have paid, provided that [client] shall first have paid ABC all fees and reimbursement billings through the termination date. ABC agrees to submit its final reimbursement billing within thirty days after the termination date.

(c) Any and all ideas, plans, recommendations or suggestions made by ABC to [client] during our relationship but not actually incorporated into ABC's services prior to such termination shall remain the property of ABC and [client] shall, without demand from ABC, return all materials relating thereto and in its possession to ABC.

(d) If ABC shall have entered into any firm and noncancellable commitments upon [client's] behalf and with [client's] approval prior to termination and any thereof, by their terms, shall continue thereafter, [client] shall take over and become responsible for all thereafter and shall hold ABC harmless from any and all claims by reason thereof.

(e) After termination of our relation with you, ABC will use its best efforts to preserve any of your trade secrets learned by ABC during its services to you and shall use its best efforts to see to it that members of its staff maintain such confidences. However, if despite such efforts, members of ABC should be responsible for disclosing any thereof, ABC shall not be liable in any way to [client]. ABC shall, after termination, be permitted to serve the public relations requirements of any competitive account, subject to the foregoing.

32. Miscellaneous Provisions.

(a) Pursuant to our recent discussions we are retaining ABC as an independent specialist, and not in an employee status, to serve the [client] in the area of financial communications.

(b) It is understood and agreed that none of the expenditures for fee, staff time or out-of-pocket expenses covered by this agreement will be used for lobbying, nor will any of the funds, in any way, redound to the benefit of any individual directly concerned with legislation.

(c) It is our further understanding that your firm will respect any confidential data as set forth in the code of PRSA.

(d) Our firm complies at all times with all pertinent provisions of the Code of Standards of Public Relations Society of America and all present and future amendments thereto or interpretations thereof.

(e) It is understood that the counseling fee of ABC is in no way contingent upon any specific quantitative results in the form of media use or other exposure.

(f) In your presentation to us, you [ABC] have pointed out that your organization is qualified to handle with skill and legal propriety all of the segments of our overall program. While we do not expect you to "guarantee" that the program will be successful, we do expect that you will use every reasonable effort to attain the desired solution, subject to your acknowledged obligation to avoid involving [client] adversely with the government or any of its agencies.

(g) In view of your unusual requirements, ABC is to receive the above basic annual fee and, in addition thereto, the sum of $————— for each new local franchise contract obtained through our efforts, it being understood that the latter services by ABC are not to be considered as public relations counseling services.

Notes

1. RESTATEMENT (SECOND), AGENCY §1 (1958).
2. Kaden v. Moon Motor Car Co., 26 S.W.2d 812 (Mo. Ct. App. 1930).
3. S. A. Conover Co., 6 B.T.A. 679 (1927).
4. McNeil v. Electric Storage Battery Co., 109 S.C. 326, 96 S.E. 134 (1918).
5. Riss & Co., Inc., v. Ass'n of Western Railroads *et al.*, 159 F. Supp. 288, 1958 Trade Cas. ¶68959 (D.D.C. 1958).
6. American Association of Advertising Agencies, *Analysis and Criticism of a Study Entitled Advertising Agency Compensation Theory, Law and Practice,* at 46.
7. *The Arts and Uses of Public Relations,* Time, July 7, 1967, at 40.
8. Morse, *An Awakening in Wall Street,* American Magazine, Sept., 1906, at 460, cited by HIEBERT, COURTIER TO THE CROWD 48 (1966).
9. RESTATEMENT, *supra* note 1, at §14.
10. *Id.* §13.
11. Decker, *PRSA's Code: How the Practitioner and Public Are Protected,* P.R.J., March, 1967, at 26, 27.
12. For a discussion of the legal history of the advertising agency, see SIMON, THE LAW FOR ADVERTISING AND MARKETING, ch. 1, at 3–9 (1956).
13. *Id.* ch. 2, at 10–26.
14. Sandburg, *Ivy Lee—Paid Liar,* New York Call, March 7, 1915.
15. Decker, *supra* note 11, at 27.
16. 282 Pa. 404, 126 Atl. 103 (1925).
17. 58 F. Supp. 1011 (E.D. Mo. 1945).
18. SOCOLOW, LAW OF RADIO BROADCASTING 677, note 50 (1939).
19. Bell v. McConnell, 37 Ohio St. 396, 399 (1881).
20. See Hofflin v. Moss, 67 Fed. 440 (8th Cir. 1895).
21. Socolow, *supra* note 18.
22. East and West Coast Serv. Corp. v. Papahagis, 344 Pa. 183, 25 A.2d 339 (1942); Ohio Oil Co. v. Sharp, 135 F.2d 303 (10th Cir. 1943).
23. Fairchild Co. v. Cox, 50 N.Y.S.2d 643 (1944).
24. 20 F. Supp. 135 (S.D.N.Y. 1937).
25. RESTATEMENT, *supra* note 1, at §395.
26. *Id.* §396.
27. *Id.* §§382, 388, 403.
28. Craft Reupholstering Co., Inc. v. Rosenberg, 420 Pa. 43, 216 A.2d 49 (1966).
29. Hewitt & Hosier v. Lichty Mfg. Co., 147 Iowa 270, 126 N.W. 170 (1910).
30. RESTATEMENT, *supra* note 1, at §§383, 385.
31. *Id.* §381.
32. CANFIELD, PUBLIC RELATIONS 483–86 (3d ed. 1960).
33. Simon, *supra* note 12, at 53–72.
34. Elkman Advertising Co. v. Helitzer, Waring & Wayne, Inc., N.Y.L.J., June 27, 1967 (*per* Hellman, J., Sup. Ct. 1967).

35. See Simon, *supra* note 12, at 73–97, for a discussion of legal relationships with printers and suppliers and at 27–39 for a discussion of advertising usages and customs.

36. PROSSER,TORT 150 (3d ed. 1964).

37. *E.g.,* Colgate-Palmolive Co. *et al.,* v. F.T.C., 326 F.2d 517 (1st Cir. 1963), *rev'd,* 380 U.S. 374 (1965); Carter Products, Inc. *et al.,* v. F.T.C., 325 F.2d 523 (5th Cir. 1963); J. B. Williams Co., Inc. v. F.T.C., 381 F.2d 884 (6th Cir. 1967).

38. See cases and materials cited, *infra* notes 39–43.

39. Commonwealth v. Farrell *et al.,* Mass. Super. Ct. for the Transaction of Criminal Business, Suffolk County, Case Nos. 11900, 11910, 11921 (bribery, sentenced Jan. 6, 1967. Appeal pending and undisposed of). For a discussion of these cases and approximately fifty other pending indictments, see Wall St. Jour., March 1, 1967, at 1, 14.

40. Letter from Rhea Smith, P.R.S.A. Director of Member Service, to author.

41. P.R.S.A. Bull., June, 1965.

42. For a general discussion of the position of the PR counsel, see P.R.N., July 17, 1967, at 1.

43. United States v. The New York Great A. & P. Tea Co. *et al.,* 67 F. Supp. 626, *aff'd,* 173 F.2d 79 (7th Cir. 1948).

44. See also indictments in United States v. Venn *et al.,* Case No. 65.535 cr. (S.D. Fla. 1965) (under Sherman Act and presently undisposed of); United States v. Mario S. Trombone (S.D.N.Y. 1967) (under Securities Act and presently undisposed of).

45. United States v. Falcone, 311 U.S. 205 (1940); United States v. Dellaro, 99 F.2d 781 (2d Cir. 1938).

46. United States v. The New York Great A. & P. Tea Co., *supra* note 43.

47. See generally CUTLIP & CENTER, EFFECTIVE PUBLIC RELATIONS 95 (3d ed. 1964).

48. Hammond, *Public Relations Counseling,* in HANDBOOK OF PUBLIC RELATIONS 58 (Stephenson ed. 1960).

49. See DRINKER, LEGAL ETHICS 176 (1953).

50. NATIONAL SOC'Y OF PROFESSIONAL ENGINEERS, CODE OF ETHICS, N.S.P.E. Publication No. 1102, at §9d (rev. July, 1966).

51. CONSULTING ENGINEERS COUNCIL, MANUAL §9, at 13 (1965).

52. Interpretation adopted Nov. 6, 1966, by P.R.S.A. Board of Directors after recommendation by P.R.S.A. Committee on Standards of Professional Practice.

Chapter 3

Public Relations Counsel and Their Employees

A. INTRODUCTION

1. Statement of the Problem
2. The "Service" Character of Public Relations Counseling
3. Attitudes Toward Need for Protection
4. Methods of Protection
5. Incentive Plans
6. Common Law Obligations of Employees, etc.
7. The Ireland Case
8. The Duane Jones Case
9. Loss of Employees to Clients

B. RESTRICTIVE COVENANTS

10. Relative Value of Restrictive Covenants
11. General Character of Restrictive Agreements
12. Avoidance of Complications
13. The Restriction as a Restraint of Trade
14. Contexts of Permissible Restraints
15. Subject Matter and Extent of Restraint
16. Reasonableness of Time Limitation
17. Consideration for the Restrictive Agreement
18. Statutory Provisions
19. Interstate Effect of Statutes
20. Corporate By-Laws and Restrictions
21. Restrictions in Partnership Agreements
22. Restrictions and Pension Plans
23. Restrictive Covenants and Sale of Firm
24. Restrictive Covenant Exceptions
25. Protection of Client Confidences

C. ENFORCEMENT OF RESTRICTIONS

D. FORMS

Chapter 3

Public Relations Counsel
and Their Employees

A. INTRODUCTION.

1. Statement of the Problem.

Some public relations counselors or firms serving a variety of clients find the hold on individual "business," under some circumstances, subject to something more than normal attrition. This happens in a variety of ways. A trusted employee leaves and takes with him one or more accounts. A partnership is dissolved and the junior partner takes some accounts. A branch office has become unprofitable and is closed with the local manager—perhaps of necessity—taking the remaining accounts. A supposedly trustworthy employee is hired away by a client with eventual loss of that account—perhaps to another firm.

It is this variety of situations with which we are here concerned. Some of these losses do not concern the counselor. Most, however, do—even though they are to be, and frequently are, anticipated. More than one public relations counselor has asked, "What can be done about it?"

2. The "Service" Character of Public Relations Counseling.

In most cases the problem arises from the service nature of public relations. No matter what the contribution of the particular public relations firm or counsel may be, it is essentially a service function. Physical aspects thereof are unimportant. Service, advice, experience, talent—these are the wares which the public relations counselor has to "sell."

In this sense the public relations counsel is very much like the lawyer, the accountant, the engineer, or men in the other services peripheral to business. In any of these areas ability and service are the significant factors. As time passes and as the function is performed successfully, one or more individuals—it makes no difference whether he or they are the owners or staff employees—may become identified in the client's mind with that success.

It has been suggested that "a public relations firm is a useful depository of living case histories." [1] The firm itself—as a vital and continuing entity—is usually responsible for these case histories and the experience accumulated from them. On occasion, however, individual employees of the firm acquire the laurels of performance—rightly or wrongly. If these employees are not mindful of their legal and moral obligations to the firm, problems arise—particularly if the client has misconstrued the source of the service and is given to what may degenerate into conspiratorial—perhaps financially self-serving—connivance with the employee.

In public relations, personal contact with clients is important. The need for client-counselor rapport and mutual confidence is self-evident. As one respected counselor has put it: [2]

> . . . both agency and client must select the right people for day-to-day contact, and they must go even further and train them to handle the complexities of the client-agency relationship.

Not infrequently personal predilections or prejudices loom large— even when serving large corporate accounts. Service employees quickly become acquainted with—perhaps cater to—what has been called "the particular likes and dislikes of the various [clients]." [3] This may be important in retaining the account as well as permitting the cementing of strong personal relationships between individual employees and client's personnel.

Even in the larger, departmentalized public relations firm, the contribution of a particular staff member or partner may be overemphasized by the client—especially if the firm has been retained only for that one type of specialized public relations.

All of these relational situations contribute to the exposure of the public relations firm to possible account loss.

3. Attitudes Toward Need for Protection.

There is a polar difference in the attitudes of PR firm management as to the need for protection in these situations. Some are firmly convinced that restrictive agreements are necessary; others are equally sanguine that they are unnecessary, even sometimes believing that they prejudice staff relationship and performance. The dichotomy seems premised to a significant degree upon:

    (a) Relative size of the PR firm.

    (b) Actual experience in this area.

Generally, the larger PR firm maintains that it suffers but little from employee desertion—at least from the point of view of loss of accounts to ex-employees. This may be due to the use of more "team servicing" with several men working on each account. Also, it may be due to the refusal of some such firms to accept spot assignments and insist upon a long-term relation with the client. As to this, George Hammond, President of Carl Byoir & Associates, has said: [4]

> We only represent our clients on a yearly contract basis. . . . As you might expect, we are not often limited to one or more inciden-tal situations. We are part of the client's life; we are partners with his public relations staff; and we share all of the functions from planning to execution.

The smaller firm, whether working on a specific assignment or han-dling all of the client's needs, may assign only a single employee—perhaps an account executive—to each account. To a considerable degree this is also true of an advertising agency having a PR department.[5] The exposure here is probably greater although it may be minimized to a de-gree if the agency handles the client's other needs such as advertising, marketing, etc.

Public relations counsel—regardless of size—may operate in one of three ways:

(a) He may provide consultation, the execution being undertaken by others.

(b) He may advise and thereafter collaborate with the client's own staff in the execution.

(c) He may advise and also execute his recommended plan.[6]

In the first two relationships, the prestige and personal stature of the PR counsel will usually be dominant. His staff—if involved at all—remains in the background. In the third arrangement, staff is much more important and, if the service is protracted, the account executive or other staff people may assume the mantle of the counselor or firm. The exposure in such cases has proved to be greater.

Some firms—regardless of size or method of operation—have had but little account defection because of personnel departures. Others bewail their experience in this connection. Some go as far as to say, "I wish I had had a contract to protect myself." Others are more philosophical about their losses but still have "locked the stable door after the horse was stolen."

4. Methods of Protection.

Public relations firm concern over potential account loss to employees or others—among other things—has led to a variety of protective measures, some based solely on internal organization or policy and others premised on legal considerations. These are:

(a) Incentive plans of assorted kinds.

(b) Group servicing of accounts under ownership supervision.

(c) Restrictive employment, partnership or stock purchase agreements.

(d) Reliance on legally-implied fiduciary obligations. See Sections 6 to 8 below.

5. Incentive Plans.

It is not infrequently said that the strength of a PR firm lies in its "people." Although, to a degree, there is a considerable "floating population" in the PR field, the successful firm usually is one which holds its staff and promotes from within. Many factors contribute to the ability to retain employees or junior "partners."

One of the most important is the satisfaction by management of a desire for both personal and financial security. This may be offered in many ways. Among them are bonuses, profit-sharing, substantial insurance plans, pension plans, stock acquisition plans and other benefits.

Profit-sharing and pension plans may be so designed as to insure a considerable degree of "employee longevity" and the creation of an employee loyalty—if only for reasons of self-interest. Stock ownership plans provide even more of an attraction—especially if the staff is permitted to purchase voting stock over an extended period of time. Participation in growth is important as is eventual participation in management.

While such arrangements may originally be conceived as conducive merely to employee retention, they also offer significant inducements to ownership and management. They provide a method whereby the latter may withdraw a portion of its investment from the firm. They also provide for eventual managerial take-over as the present owners approach retirement age.

Unfortunately, experience proves that even a conscientious use of any —or all—of these plans may not, without more, always guarantee continuity of service and loyalty by employees. Something more may often be needed. For example, in the *Duane Jones* case, discussed in Section 8 below, both profit-sharing and pension plans were in effect. Yet a group of key employees left in concert, taking a substantial part of the agency's accounts and personnel with them.

6. Common Law Obligations of Employees, etc.

The officers, directors and employees of a PR counseling firm are subject to a fiduciary relationship to their employer. This means a continuing duty of loyalty to the employer until such time as both their services and compensation are terminated.[7] This responsibility continues until actual termination of the employee's compensation. Notice of the intention to quit does not vitiate this employee obligation. A leading case has said: [8]

> The obligation to protect his [employer's] interests lasts until the last hour of [the employee's] service. The dividing line between owing his [employer] a duty and owing him none is that imperceptible period of time between termination of his service and the moment he acquires freedom of action after his service has terminated.

Not infrequently, the injury to the former employer develops only after the employee has left his original employment. However, if the employee began to seduce his employer's accounts prior to such termination, he is responsible.[9]

It is true that an employee—whether under notice of termination or not—need not wait until he has actually finished his employment in order to seek a new connection. However, such search may not legally include the clients or business of his employer.[10]

The employee's duty is not erased by the fact that the PR firm might—even probably would—lose the account in question shortly thereafter without the employee's intervention. If the employee induces the departure of the client, he is liable.[11]

At the same time, it must be remembered that, absent a restriction against the employee, he has a right to compete with his former employer and seek out and serve the latter's accounts, provided only that he does not begin to solicit those accounts while still "on the payroll" of the employer and that he does not use any confidential information in so doing.[12]

Furthermore, an employee may not seduce other employees to leave their common employer. This duty apparently continues only until after the employee has left.[13]

7. The Ireland Case.

In *Ireland v. Ireland Advertising Agency* [14] (1911) we have probably the first litigated instance of an attempt by employees of an "advertising agency" to deprive the owner of his interest. While the business of the concern was "advertising," the firm was one of the first to render what we would today call "product publicity" services to its accounts and clients.[15]

Ireland was the owner of the business employing, among others, his wife and one Donovan. When Ireland was about to leave on a long trip, he technically transferred the business by bill of sale to his wife—the purpose being the incorporation of the business during his absence. This was done and the wife was issued all but a few of the shares of stock. She elected herself president and treasurer and then gave Donovan a contract for a substantial salary plus some of the shares.

The Pennsylvania Supreme Court impressed a trust upon all of the shares and annulled the Donovan contract as an unwarranted act by Mrs. Ireland.

8. The Duane Jones Case.

The leading case involving so-called "account piracy" is *Duane Jones Co. v. Burke et al.*,[16] decided by the New York Court of Appeals in 1954 after protracted litigation.

The Duane Jones Company, Inc., in business as an advertising and PR agency for nine years, had been billing about $9,000,000 and employing 132 people. Nine of the agency's officers, directors and employees, as the court found, solicited its principal accounts prior to and during the period when they had resigned and were completing their duties as employees. A new firm was organized by some of these men while they were still employed by the Duane Jones Company.

While this is ostensibly an "advertising agency" case, some of the personnel involved handled public relations and publicity for the accounts which—as the court found—had moved to the new firm as a result of solicitation by some of the individual defendants.

It was shown that certain of the defendants had discussed the opening of their new firm with at least some of the Jones clients while the defendants were still employed and were still, in some instances, serving as officers and directors of the Jones agency. A representative of the group made an offer to purchase Jones's controlling interest and advised him that the clients "had been 'presold' on the proposed action." This occurred after they had met and agreed to take over the business "either by purchase of the controlling interest in the corporation or by resignation en masse and the formation of a new agency."

As a result of this action, the agency also lost to the new concern 71 of its 132 employees, including key personnel, some thereof handling public relations and publicity, and the firm was compelled to resign even those accounts which the defendants did not take with them.

It was found that the various clients of the agency "were free at any time to discharge plaintiff as its agency; and similarly, plaintiff had the right at will to resign any of its accounts." Notwithstanding this, the defendants were held liable in the amount of $300,000 since the evidence showed that the loss of the accounts was the "direct result" of the defendants' activities.

The basis of the defendants' liability to their former agency was summed up in this way:

> . . . the conduct of the individuals as officers, directors or employees of the plaintiff corporation . . . fell below the standard required by the law of one acting as an agent or employee of another. Each of [them] was prohibited from acting in any manner inconsistent with his agency or trust and [was] at all times bound to exercise the utmost good faith and loyalty in the performance of his duties.
>
> . . . while employees of plaintiff corporation, [they] determined upon a course of conduct which, when subsequently carried out, resulted in benefit to themselves through destruction of the plaintiff's business, in violation of the fiduciary duties of good faith and fair dealing imposed on [them] by their close relationship with plaintiff corporation.

9. Loss of Employees to Clients.

Almost every successful PR firm, at some time or other, has a key employee leave to join a client. This is a special problem and is not usually covered in employee agreements.

Usually the firm will agree to this arrangement—if only to preserve the presumably satisfactory relationship with the client. If the client thereafter continues with the firm, no problems arise. However, there are two possible situations which are pregnant with danger for the PR firm.

(a) The firm may have developed an inside PR staff for the client and the departing employee leaves to head it up as Public Relations Director. Here the firm may be hoist on its own petard—eventually losing both the key employee and the account—through its successful prior service to the client.[17]

(b) The account and the employee may use this as a subterfuge for the employee, shortly thereafter, to leave the client's employ and open his own PR firm with the client as an account. The client may be part of this continuing conspiracy—a device which may not easily be demonstrable if it occurs.

A properly-drawn agreement with the employee should protect the PR firm against these eventualities—especially the second. Care should be taken, however, when the employee does join the client with the firm's blessing, to preserve its rights under the agreement. See Section 36 below.

B. RESTRICTIVE COVENANTS.

10. Relative Value of Restrictive Covenants.

The public relations firm has two grounds upon which to seek legal recourse for account piracy. It may rely on its common law rights against the employee or enforce the terms of the restrictive covenant in the employee's contract, assuming that the firm has been prescient enough to obtain such an obligation.[18]

Actions for breach of the common law fiduciary obligation may be successful. See Section 6 above. The restrictive covenant is a more effective legal weapon. Furthermore, firms using such restrictions have found that their mere existence has had a definite and salutary psychological effect upon the departing employee who *may* be thinking of "taking an account or two with him."

11. General Character of Restrictive Agreements.

A restrictive covenant is sometimes referred to as a "covenant not to compete." It is an agreement executed by the employee for a consideration whereby the employee agrees not to compete with his employer during the period of the employment and, after its termination, to refrain for a reasonably limited period of time from performing any acts detrimental to the employer.

In the public relations frame of reference, these acts are usually account piracy and the preservation of confidential information.

This basic arrangement may be embroidered or varied in many ways. While such agreements containing restrictive covenants are now enforceable, this is possible only if the restrictions are reasonable. What is reasonable, in what context and as to what elements are discussed in Sections 12 to 18 below.

12. Avoidance of Complications.

Restrictive covenants have many complications. Many agreements, which have been judicially interpreted, have overreached themselves—seeking protection for the employer beyond that reasonably necessary.[19] This has led to various devious techniques.

An interesting observation comes from an Ohio court which said: [20]

> The average litigant will not find adequate justice in this subject matter until someone devotes a treatise solely on it. It has grown so elephantine yet so intricate that it needs a complete, detailed

treatment for which there is no room in general treatises on such omnibus subjects as injunctions and contracts.

This was said after the court had cited two solid pages of "fine print" consisting of close-ordered references to a veritable legal storehouse of periodicals, encyclopedias, annotations, digests and cases.

Out of this welter of precedent comes a warning to the PR firm or any other service organization of similar status or needs. The restriction should not be more extensive or encompassing than is necessary fairly to protect the PR firm. This means, usually, that protection is needed against competition by ex-employees only as to the clients referred to in Section 15 below.

13. The Restriction as a Restraint of Trade.

Every restrictive covenant against an employee or other associate is, in effect, a contract in restraint of trade, no matter how limited in time or application. The judicial history of restrictive covenants in both England and this country has reflected this.

Going back as far as 1415, we find that these restrictions were void and against public policy. An attempted enforcement of a restriction against a dyer produced a court threat that the party seeking enforcement would go to prison unless he paid a fine to the King.[21]

A 1711 case—*Mitchell v. Reynolds* [22]—gave six reasons for this position:

    (a) It deprives the employee of a chance for a livelihood.

    (b) The employee's family might become public charges.

    (c) The public would be deprived of the services of the employee.

    (d) Aggressive and ambitious "corporations" seeking monopolistic privileges would abuse these restrictions.

    (e) "Masters" would be allowed to limit future competition from their apprentices.

    (f) In many cases it would not help the employer but be highly burdensome to the employee.

This rationale was announced in 1711, but each one of these six arguments—except for (d)—applies with equal effect today. These reasons have led to the basic rule that such restrictions may not be unreasonable nor of greater extent than necessary to protect the rights of the employer.[23]

An obvious example of an unreasonable restriction—unduly burdensome to the employee and not necessary to the employer—is one which would prevent the employee from working in any phase of public relations anywhere in the United States. This would drive the employee out of the principal business which he presumably knows. Yet, in view of the generally competitive nature of the public relations business, it would add very little, if anything, to the employer's security.

On the other hand, from the point of view of public relations counsel, the following critical comment is apropos: [24]

> [The post-employment restraint's] objective is not to prevent the competitive use of the unique personal qualities of the employee . . . but to prevent competitive use, for a time, of *information* or *relationships* which pertain peculiarly to the employer and which the employee acquired during the course of the employment. . . . The promise not to act in certain ways after terminating the employment is something which the employer may or may not feel to be important and worth bargaining for, depending upon the circumstances. (Emphasis added.)

Briggs v. Mason [25] is an early and interesting application of the above explanation in a case which involves "publicity" and promotion services. The plaintiff had employed the defendant and obtained from him an agreement that he would not compete with the plaintiff for a period of two years in the same activity and in any city in which the plaintiff operated. The plaintiff's business consisted of ". . . publicity and especially in putting on special advertising, weekly business review pages, book campaigns, historical and biographical promotions and other general publicity [campaigns] through leading newspapers, magazines and periodicals throughout the United States."

Four years later, claiming that he needed a vacation, the defendant left the employ and opened up his own business, rendering the same kind of service to and for a newspaper which had been a client of the plaintiff. The plaintiff obtained an injunction against the defendant's breach of his covenant.

Although this case was decided in 1926—when public relations and publicity as we know them today were relatively in their infancy—the following statement of the court seems quite contemporary.

> The business was a new and unusual one, employing special methods which constitute trade secrets. To the average person in the business world, little or nothing is known of the business, much less the methods employed therein. . . . Necessarily, years of patient and careful study and attention were necessary to organize and develop such business and bring it to a point where it would be profitable. In its nature, it could not be confined to narrow [geographical] limits, nor could it hope to have a great number of customers or clients in any city or community . . . [T]he relatively few it had would give it large contracts, requiring the services of a number of people, and yield a splendid profit or income. Such client and customer were unlike ordinary customers or clients in the commercial world who frequently buy articles or

services, but, on the contrary, are such as make but few contracts, but such as they make extend over long periods and result in large profits . . .

14. Contexts of Permissible Restraints.

We are dealing with what may be called "partial restraints of trade." The same requirement of the "reasonableness" applies to a wide variety of restrictive provisions, many of which are quite relevant to the PR counselor.

In the leading case of *U.S. v. Addyston Pipe Co.*,[26] Chief Justice Taft said:

> Covenants in partial restraint of trade are generally upheld as valid when they are agreements (1) by the seller of property or business not to compete with the buyer in such a way as to derogate from the value of the property or business sold, (2) by a retiring partner not to compete with the firm, (3) by a partner pending the partnership not to do anything to interfere, by competition or otherwise, with the business of the firm, (4) by the buyer of property not to use the same in competition with the business retained by the seller, and (5) by an assistant, servant, or agent not to compete with his master or employer after the expiration of his time of service. Before such agreements are upheld, however, the court must find that the restraints attempted thereby are reasonably necessary . . . to the enjoyment by the buyer of the property, good will, or interest in the partnership bought; or to the legitimate ends of the existing partnership; or to the prevention of possible injury to the business of the seller from use by the buyer of the thing sold; or . . . to protection from the danger of loss to the employer's business caused by the unjust use on the part of the employee of the confidential knowledge acquired in such business. . . . [I]t would certainly seem to follow from the tests laid down for determining the validity of such an agreement that no conventional restraint of trade can be enforced unless the covenant embodying it is merely ancillary to the main purpose of a lawful contract, and necessary to protect the covenantee in the enjoyment of the legitimate fruits of the contract, or to protect him from the dangers of an unjust use of those fruits by the other party.

15. Subject Matter and Extent of Restraint.

Most restrictive covenants, outside the public relations or similar service fields, involve geographical restrictions. Once again, this geographical limitation must be reasonable if it is to be enforced.

However, the PR firm is not particularly concerned with the geographical concept. Its principal interest is to protect itself against the "seduction" of its accounts, its prospective accounts and accounts which may recently have departed—perhaps through the connivance or conspiracy of the employee.

Restrictive covenants limited to accounts such as these have been widely upheld.[27] In the *Arkansas Dailies* case,[28] the restriction applied only to the clients which the employer then represented. The restriction provided:

> It is further agreed that should you leave the employ of Arkansas Dailies, Inc., you will not for a period of three years from that date, solicit the representation of any newspaper, radio station or research client that we represent or have represented during your connection with us.

The court found that this clause was "very limited" and went on to say that it did not keep the employee from pursuing his regular line of work, saying "it leaves the whole field to his endeavors except former and present customers while he was employed by [Arkansas Dailies]."

Protection of "prospects" may be quite important and should be included in the agreement. Such inclusion has been judicially approved. Thus, an engineer—under a restrictive covenant—assisted a competitive firm to prepare a bid for a government contract which his former employer was also seeking. The competitor was awarded the contract. The court found for the employer.[29]

There may be some situations in which geographical limitations could be important to a PR firm. For example, a PR firm located in a small city—remote from any concentration of competitive public relations counselors or firms—would be quite seriously affected if an ex-employee opened up his own firm in that small city or community.

Such an event would introduce a completely new element into the business life of the employer. In such a case, a reasonable geographical restriction is important. Presumably, a covenant not to compete within the county or a small cluster of counties or neighboring communities should serve the employer's needs for protection.[30]

Small PR firms have been started in newly developing and formerly rural communities because of the inflow of industrial plants and other activities. In this situation also, protection is needed against the ex-employee's solicitation and servicing of accounts which may never have been served by the employer. To permit this could vitiate the very purpose of the original establishment of the employer's office in that area. It might even destroy a considerable portion of the employer's investment in his organization and facilities.

16. Reasonableness of Time Limitation.

Even assuming (see Section 15 above) that the scope of the restriction is limited to clients of the PR firm, a second factor must be considered. This is the time element.[31]

The restriction may not continue for too long a period. Two to three years would pass muster without question. Many cases have so held.[32]

The longevity of the PR firm's accounts may well have considerable effect upon the allowable duration. If it can be shown that the PR firm has had a record of successfully holding and serving its accounts for longer periods of time, a coeval restriction would probably be enforced. This follows from cases such as the *Arkansas Dailies* case.[33] In that case, the court had before it a three-year covenant against a newspaper representative. This was upheld, the court pointing out that the employer had contracts with its accounts for periods up to five years, their average being about two and a half years. Accordingly, a three-year restriction was not at all unreasonable and was deemed necessary to protect the employer.

Some courts have stressed the fact that the limitation covers only the employer's clients and have upheld restrictions for as long as five years.[34] This is also true where the employee has close "customer contact," is particularly aware of the client's needs, has entertained the client at the employer's expense, has built up the client's confidence in him, has had access to confidential information—all the while working for the employer.[35] A few cases have even approved "lifetime" restrictions against employees such as accountants when the restriction is limited to clients of the employer.[36]

17. Consideration for the Restrictive Agreement.

The restrictive contract—like any other contract—must be supported by consideration. This is true whether the restriction runs against an employee, a partner or a stockholder. The consideration for the obligation not to compete may be any one of several things discussed in Subsections (a) to (e) below.

(a) The Original Hiring.

The original hiring of the employee is such consideration.[37] This is also probably the best time to obtain the restriction—both psychologically and legally. If the employment is for a fixed term—one year, for example—this will be sufficient. Even if the employment is without a fixed term—at the will of either party, for example—it will, generally speaking, support the promise of the employee provided there is a fixed notice period such as thirty or sixty days.[38]

The length of time during which the employee is with the public relations firm is relevant in this connection—especially in contracts which have no fixed term. If the employee has actually been employed for several years, there should be no question in connection with the enforcement of the restrictive covenant. In the *Arkansas Dailies* case, the court was concerned with this. The employer had obtained the restriction three years *after* the original employment. The employment then continued for an additional six years. The court said: [39]

> . . . We have no doubt that, if the record showed any oppression by the employer by having secured this contract and then shortly thereafter discharged the employee, the employer would have no standing in a court of equity . . .

This presents no practical problem to the public relations counselor. Someone in his employ for only a short time is most unlikely to have developed sufficient rapport with an account so that he could take it with him if he were to leave. However, the employee may—even during a relatively short period of employment—become quite familiar with certain confidential matters pertaining to either the PR firm or its clients. Therefore, the restrictive agreement referred to in Section 32 below should have good consideration and be enforceable in the event that the employee "steals" this confidential material, using it in connection with public relations or other services for third parties. It might even be an opportunity for something similar to industrial espionage. See Chapter 17.

(b) Extension of Employment.

A public relations firm which may not have used restrictive agreements in the past may decide to obtain such undertakings from their employees. Consideration for such new promise is also necessary. The extension of the employment upon a fixed term will serve.[40] Even if there has theretofore been no written employment agreement with the staff, it should now be obtained. It should spell out the specific terms and conditions of the employment, including the new restrictions.

In cases of employment extension, it is probably safer to make the extension for a fixed term and subject to a fixed notice of termination—rather than having it continue at the will of either party. However, the extension period, though fixed, need not be very long. Thirty days has been held sufficient.[41] What was said in Subsection (a) above in connection with the *Arkansas Dailies* case applies here also.

The employer should, in all of these contexts, be certain that the eventual discharge—if it occurs—is not "savored with unjustice." [42] The court may not enforce the restriction against a competing ex-employee if it appears that the extension of the employment was a mere subterfuge in order to obtain the previously nonexistent restriction and was promptly followed by the discharge of the employee.

(c) Employee Stock Purchase or Option.

A public relations counselor's employees may be granted the right to purchase stock in the firm. The restriction may be considered by some owners as more reasonable and necessary at that time than prior thereto. The right of the employee to purchase the stock or the actual purchase serves as consideration for the promise not to compete after termination of the employment.

The purchase of the stock by the employee usually is accompanied by the execution of a so-called buy-and-sell agreement. By the terms thereof, the firm usually agrees to repurchase from the employee all of his shares of stock upon the termination of his employment.

This type of repurchase promise can be important in the states which, by statute, do not permit or enforce the basic type of restrictive covenant by employee. As to this, see Sections 18 and 19 below. In one such case [43] the Michigan Supreme Court enforced a restrictive covenant notwithstanding a statute rendering such restrictions unenforceable. Even under the statute, a "seller of corporate stock may agree not to engage in a business which would compete with that of the corporation."

(d) Partnership Agreement.

Some public relations firms operate as partnerships. Normally, the formation of such an entity is evidenced by a written partnership agreement. This may be the vehicle for the restriction. The execution of the agreement—with its various cross-promises and undertakings—serves as consideration for the restrictive covenant even though such provisions run against only one or more of the partners. This would usually be the junior partner.

(e) Partnership Dissolution Agreement.

If the public relations firm is a partnership, it will be dissolved by the withdrawal of one or more of the partners. The dissolution agreement can contain and support the restrictive covenant. If the junior partner withdraws, the restriction would naturally run against him. However, the situation may be reversed. The senior partner—perhaps the founder of the firm—may be retiring. The remaining members of the firm may desire a promise from him not to compete with the continuing firm.

18. Statutory Provisions.

At least eleven states have statutes concerning restrictive covenants. They are: Alabama, California, Florida, Georgia, Louisiana, Michigan, Montana, North Dakota, Oklahoma, South Dakota, and Wisconsin.[44] Many such statutes outlaw the usual non-competition provisions against employees. However, several contain exceptions in favor of such provisions which are ancillary to the purchase of stock or other interest in a business.

The Michigan statute, for example, provides in part:

> Section 1. All agreements and contracts by which any person, co-partnership or corporation promises or agrees not to engage in any avocation, employment, pursuit, trade, profession or business, whether reasonable or unreasonable, partial or general, limited or unlimited, are hereby declared to be against public policy and illegal and void. . . .
>
> *   *   *   *
>
> Section 6. This act shall not apply to any contract mentioned in this act nor in restraint of trade where the only object of restraint imposed by the contract is to protect the vendee, or transferee, of a trade, pursuit, avocation, profession or business, or the goodwill thereof, sold and transferred for a valuable consideration and without any intent to create, build up, establish or maintain a monopoly . . .

Also, the California law excepts restrictions which relate to sales involving good will or corporate shares and to agreements not to compete in anticipation of or following a dissolution of partnership.

Basic restrictive covenants against future competition by ex-employees are unenforceable in such states. Legal relief may be obtained, however, if the restriction is tied to non-competition by the ex-employee who once owned stock in the PR firm—or was a partner—but was required to sell the stock or interest back to the principal owner when the employment was terminated.

Since "stock buy-and-sell" agreements are not at all uncommon in PR firms, this would seem to furnish the basis for protection provided, of course, that it is reasonable in extent. In this type of transaction, the courts appear to be more lenient as to what is reasonable and enforceable.[45]

Some statutes do not prohibit restrictions and go little further than to codify the existing general rules about restrictive covenants against employees. Among these are Florida and Wisconsin. The Florida statute, for example, provides that an employee may agree to refrain from carrying on or engaging in a similar business and from soliciting old customers of such employer within a reasonably limited time and area . . . so long as such employer continues to carry on a like business therein.[46]

The Wisconsin enactment provides that a covenant not to compete

within a specified time is lawful and enforceable only if the restrictions imposed are reasonably necessary for the protection of the employer or principal.

It then makes a restriction which imposes an unreasonable restraint void and unenforceable "even as to so much of the covenant or performance as would be a reasonable restraint." [47]

19. Interstate Effect of Statutes.

Public relations and public relations counseling has become such an "interstate business" that those statutes affecting restrictions may have an important impact. Generally speaking, a court will not enforce a restriction of this sort if it is invalid under the laws of that state—even though it may have been enforceable under the laws of the state in which the employment contract (with its restrictive provisions) was executed.

In one Michigan case, an Illinois company had employed the defendant at its office in Illinois in connection with the installation of sales systems and accounting methods. There was a restrictive covenant valid under Illinois law. The employee, in violation of the covenant, opened an office in Michigan, serving a former client of his Illinois employer. The Michigan court refused to enforce the restraint, saying: [48]

It is the settled law in Michigan that a contract which is void as against the public policy of the state [of Michigan] will not be enforced by its courts even though the contract was valid where made [in Illinois].

20. Corporate By-Laws and Restrictions.

If restrictive covenants are part of the fixed policy of the public relations firm, it may be advisable to incorporate such restrictions into the By-Laws of the firm. These By-Law provisions may be tied to transfers of the corporate stock. Presumably each stockholder will also be a working employee of the corporation—no matter what fraction of the stock he may own.

The restrictive By-Law would operate against all the corporate stockholders, officers and directors, on the basis of either actual or constructive notice. Inasmuch as nonstockholding third-parties—this would include other employees—are not bound by By-Laws, the restriction should be part of the employment agreement with such employees in order to bind them.

Tying these By-Law restrictions quite specifically to the buy-and-sell terms of the stock would be useful in the states which have statutes on the subject as discussed in Section 18 above.

21. Restrictions in Partnership Agreements.

Partnership agreements frequently involve restrictive covenants— whether the partners are all of equal stature or some are admittedly "junior" partners. The partners in a PR firm owe each other a high degree of fiduciary duty. Restrictions on competition by an ex-partner have been upheld.[49]

Such restrictions, as discussed in Section 17 (d) above, also require consideration. They should therefore be included in either the partnership agreement or in the dissolution or withdrawal agreement. Obtaining a restriction in the latter case may be considerably more difficult than when the partnership is first being formed. It has been held that a "naked promise" not to compete—given after the dissolution agreement has been executed and the partnership actually dissolved—is not enforceable.[50]

When a public relations firm operating as a partnership is dissolved with each partner going his own way, the best arrangement is to divide the accounts of the firm on an amicable basis. This should be possible because each of the partners will have been serving certain accounts. At the same time, the "value" of each partner's accounts may be quite disparate. In this situation, cross-payments may be necessary in order to do equal justice among them.

In order to prevent disputes, it is probably wise to incorporate into the original partnership agreement a formula to solve any prospective disparity upon dissolution. The suggestions in Section 31 below are relevant in this situation.

22. Restrictions and Pension Plans.

Public relations firms having pension plans may also use them in conjunction with restrictive covenants. Benefits may be paid to ex-employees only as long as they do not compete with the public relations firm. Such provisions have been upheld. The restrictions should be incorporated into the pension trust instrument and also into any explanatory or supplementary material distributed to the employees.

23. Restrictive Covenants and Sale of Firm.

When a public relations firm is sold, prospective competition from the seller and prior owner may be potentially dangerous. This is true of any service organization in which the reputation, ability and experience of the former owner is an important asset.

Upon such a sale, absent any specific restrictions, the seller has a right to compete generally in the same business with the buyer.[51] On the other hand, even absent such a restriction, the law implies a restriction against the seller as to solicitation of the customers or clients of the business which he has sold.[52]

The sale of a public relations firm should include protection for the buyer. Restrictive covenants of this sort have been widely upheld provided, as always, that they are reasonable in extent and duration.[53] Furthermore, some courts permit more extensive restrictions against the seller than against the employees.[54]

Depending upon circumstances, it may be necessary to bind the seller to refrain from re-entering the public relations business for a period of three to five years. It may not be sufficient to prohibit his service of existing accounts.

Not infrequently the seller agrees to serve the firm and the new owners as a consultant for a period of time after the sale. This results from a desire for continuity in identity—especially when the name of the firm is not changed after the sale. This new relationship should be incorporated into the restriction. The continuing compensation is also consideration.

24. Restrictive Covenant Exceptions.

Circumstances may dictate that one or more accounts served by a public relations firm should not be included in the restriction against a particular employee. Among them are:

(a) A so-called "vestpocket account" may move from firm to firm as a particular individual moves. In other words, there is a long-time relationship between the individual and the account. Normally such an account would be excepted from the restrictive covenant.

(b) When an account is first obtained by the public relations firm, the new client's PR Director may "come with the account." This may be the result of closing the account's inside department or its retaining a PR firm as auxiliary to the continued operation of such department but with the PR Director on the payroll of the newly-retained firm. Here again, the relationship is unusual and such an account would probably be excepted from the restriction.

(c) In the case of an absorption of one PR firm by another, the owner of the absorbed firm will usually insist upon excepting "his" accounts from any restriction. This is usually in order.

25. Protection of Client Confidences.

The public relations counselor must usually be taken into the complete confidence of the client. The client has a right to expect that such confidence will be respected. See Chapter 2, Section 10. Disclosure of confidential information may be very harmful to the client. It is therefore necessary that the counselor's staff be equally aware of this responsibility and be bound to preserve such confidence.

Personal integrity and indoctrination will do much to preserve the confidential seal but a proper provision in the employment contract should also be used. It may even be required by the client. Such a provision may also provide protection for the counseling firm and its private information or materials—quite apart from the protection of clients.

Inside public relations departments face the same disclosure dangers as do independent public relations counselors. Inside staff employees should be made subject to similar restraints.

The law imposes a restraint on the employee not to divulge any confidential matters.[55] A written agreement can cover matters not necessarily confidential, thus going beyond what the law will imply by reason of the fiduciary nature of the employment relationship. Thus Justice Holmes has said: [56]

> Whether plaintiffs have any valuable secret or not, the defendant knows the facts, whatever they are, through a special confidence that he accepted. The property may be denied, but the confidence cannot be . . . and the first thing to be made sure of is that the defendant shall not fraudulently abuse the trust reposed in him. It is the usual incident of confidential relations. If there is any disadvantage in the fact that he knew the plaintiff's secrets, he must take the burden with the good.

C. ENFORCEMENT OF RESTRICTIONS.

26. Injunctive Relief.

Normally the employer will seek injunctive relief against the employee who has violated a restrictive covenant. Such restrictions frequently refer to such relief as within the contemplation of the parties. An injunction stops a violation with reasonable immediacy and prevents future breaches. In many cases, a preliminary injunction will be granted by the court so that the default is ended at once.[57]

The restrictive provisions should permit both injunctive relief and recovery of money damages. Pursuit of one should not exclude the possibility of the other.

An injunction is particularly effective if obtained before the ex-employee has actually begun to serve a client of the employer. Immediate relief of this sort may well be the difference between retaining and losing the account in question.

27. Recovery of Damages.

Suit for recovery of money damages from the employee may be a companion cause of action to injunctive relief. Some courts have issued an injunction and also awarded damages in the same action.[58] This is particularly valuable in a case where the employee has already begun to serve one of the forbidden clients but has not yet successfully solicited any other. The injunction would be obtained against future solicitation and money damages recovered for the loss of the one account.

28. Liquidated Damage Clauses.

Absolute and specific proof of the amount of the damages suffered by the public relations firm is not necessary in such a case.[59] Nevertheless, the dangers of inadequate proof of damages may be obviated by proper draftsmanship.

A so-called "liquidated damage clause" should be included in the agreement. This spells out the exact damages which the defaulting employee is to pay. The amount of such liquidated damages must be reasonable. It must bear some reasonable relationship to the value of the accounts and the relationship between the parties. If it is excessive or unreasonable, it may be considered a "penalty" by the court and, as such, may be unenforceable.

A liquidated damage clause tied to one or two years' income to the firm from the accounts served by the employee would probably be satisfactory.[60] This would be particularly true if it could be shown that the average representation of the firm was in excess of such period.

In effect, the liquidated damage clause, if invoked by the employer, "sells" the account to the ex-employee at the discretion of the employer.

There are essentially three bases upon which a liquidated damage clause may be developed. See Sections 29 to 31 below.

29. Fixed Damage Clause.

The agreement may provide that, in the event of a breach by the employee, he will pay the employer a fixed sum. This is the simplest of such arrangements but has certain defects.

While such a figure may be quite reasonable at the time the agreement is executed, it could easily become arbitrary as time passed and, conceivably, could be rendered unenforceable. Furthermore, assuming the reasonableness of this figure at the outset, it may become relatively too low as time passes if income from the account served by the employee should increase or additional accounts are assigned to the employee. The amount of the liquidated damage clause would be palpably insufficient to indemnify the employer for its loss or losses.

30. "Breach Profits" Formula.

A satisfactory basis for a liquidated damage clause is the actual performance and profitability of the purloined account to the employee or his new association. This involves the payment by the defaulting ex-employee of a percentage of the fee and other payments made by the account—either to him or to any public relations firm with which he and the account may become associated.

The payments may be spread over the entire period of the restrictive covenant with a provision in the agreement that the two years (for example) during which payments are to be made are to begin to run from the date upon which the first fees are received by the ex-employee and not from the date of termination of his prior employment.

31. "Past Profits" Formula.

This ties the amount of the liquidated damages to the actual profit record of the employer during the year or two prior to the departure of the employee and the account. Normally this would be the amount of the fee paid the employer. Reimbursement items would presumably wash out although mark-up payments should be included in the liquidated damage base.

Some question may arise as to whether or not such fees, etc. received by the employer should be diminished by indirect expenses and overhead. This is arguable either way but it is probably more appropriate not to subtract or deduct such items.

D. FORMS.

These forms are examples of provisions which have been heretofore used in employment and other types of agreements which involve restrictions. As with any "canned" forms, they should be used with circumspection. They are not intended to cover all types of situations or even all variations of a single situation or relationship. Under each of the following section headings, several different forms will be found. Some are mutually exclusive.

32. Agreements as to Records.

(a) Employees hereby specifically acknowledge that all of employer's records, data, plans, suggestions and recommendations concerning present clients or future clients of employer used in any manner in the furtherance of employer's business are highly confidential and valuable information entitled to any protection the law may afford as trade or business secrets, and are the sole property of the employer.

(b) The employee recognizes and acknowledges that the list of the employer's clients and the handling of the clients' accounts as they may exist from time to time, are valuable, special, and unique assets of the employer's business. The employee will not, during or after the term of this Agreement, disclose any information pertaining to the employer's business and the employer's clients to any firm, person, corporation, association, or other entity for any reason or purpose whatsoever. In the event of a breach or threatened breach by the employee of the provisions of this paragraph, the employer shall be entitled to an injunction restraining the employee from using or disclosing, in whole or in part, any information pertaining to the employer's business and the employer's clients. Nothing herein shall be construed as prohibiting the employer from pursuing any other remedies available to the employer for such breach or threatened breach, including the recovery of damages from the employee.

(c) All materials, records, correspondence, etc. which you may prepare, write or use in your employment are our property and none are to be removed from the office without our prior approval.

(d) We are on a basis of strict confidence with each of our clients to keep all plans, figures and general client data relative to their business within the confines of ——————— Associates.

To perform properly as public relations counsel to our clients it is necessary that we have in our files much confidential client information. This data is supplied to us because of the trust a client must place in his public relations firm. IT IS OUR RESPONSIBILITY TO GUARD AND PROTECT THIS TRUST.

Releasing client data outside of ——————— Associates, either directly or indirectly, is a breach of contract and faith, and is cause for immediate dismissal.

(e) Employee acknowledges that his service with the firm and its clients is of a fiduciary and confidential nature and that the performance of his assigned duties requires his familiarity with, and disclosure to him of, information and materials of various kinds all of which he agrees to preserve in confidence and trust, both during and after his employment, whether or not the same be unique and/or of a character commonly described as "trade secrets."

Employee shall not, at any time during or after his employment and in connection with the property or interests of either the firm or any of its clients, do or knowingly assist in or permit the doing of, any of the following:

(1) Remove from the offices or premises of the firm any records, documents, files, correspondence, reports, memoranda or other materials or property of any kind without express prior written permission and, in the event of such removal, all thereof shall be returned to their proper files or places of safekeeping as promptly as possible after their removal shall have served its specific purpose.

(2) Make, retain, remove and/or distribute any copies of any of the above for any reason whatsoever except as may be necessary in the discharge of the employee's assigned duties.

(3) Divulge to any third person the nature of and/or contents of any of the foregoing or of any other oral or written information to which he may have access or with which for any reason he may become familiar, except as such disclosure shall be necessary in the performance of the employee's own assigned duties.

33. Acknowledgment of Account Ownership.

(a) In consideration of the execution of this agreement and of the employment of employee by employer hereunder, it is agreed and acknowledged by employee that employer is and shall continue to be the sole owner of any and all business and accounts serviced, handled, contacted or obtained by employer as of the date of this agreement or at any time hereafter, including any and all accounts which may be originated, introduced, procured, developed, closed, sold and/or serviced by employee after the date of this agreement and while in the employ of employer and that employee shall have no right, title or interest of any kind whatsoever in any of the said present or future accounts.

(b) The accounts assigned to you, as with all of the firm's accounts, are "house accounts" and you have no interest in them (regardless of their source or channel of acquisition) including those which you may be instrumental in obtaining for the firm.

(c) As a condition of your employment and notwithstanding the fact that certain references have been made above to your serving as account executive on the _____ account, it is to be definitely understood that you have no right or interest of any kind in this account or any other account and that we shall be the sole owner of the accounts.

34. Covenant Not To Compete.

(a) Employees specifically agree that in the event of the termination of this agreement for any reason whatsoever, for a period of two years after said termination, they will not approach in any manner for their own account, or for the account of any other individual, partnership, or corporation, or for any other employer, for public relations or allied purposes, any account or client of employer handled by employer during the term of this agreement, or any prospective account or client of employer to whom any type of approach was made by employer during the term of this agreement. This restriction shall apply even though the actual servicing of a prospective account or client of employer took place subsequent to the termination of this agreement, or has taken place within the said two-year period.

In the event that any provisions herein contained are violated by employees, or enforcement thereof is sought by injunction, the two-year period provided for herein shall be extended so as to continue to a date two years after the date of such breach or of the entry of a final decree of injunction, whichever shall be later.

(b) For a period of two (2) years after the termination of this Agreement the employee will not, directly or indirectly, participate in or be connected in any manner with any advertising or public relations work affecting any client, or any subsidiary or related company thereof, of the employer, whether or not handled by the employee during the term of his employment herein. It is provided, however, that in the event the employer is succeeded by others or that this Agreement is assigned to others and the successor or assignee of the employer terminates the employment of the employee, then this restrictive covenant shall not apply.

(c) Employees specifically agree that during the course of their employment and thereafter for a period of two years, they will not divert or attempt to divert any business or accounts from employer, either directly or indirectly, for their own account or for the account of any other person, firm or corporation.

(d) In the event of the termination of employee's employment with employer for any reason, with or without cause, employee shall not, without the written consent of employer, for a period of three (3) years from and after the date of such termination, contact, solicit, serve, accept, handle or in any way become associated with, directly or indirectly or as owner, partner, stockholder, employee, agent or in any other capacity, the servicing and handling of the public relations, advertising, promotional, sales or similar requirements of any client or account represented, handled or serviced by employer during the one (1) year period immediately next prior to the termination of employee's employment or of any other account or accounts to which presentations and/or solicitations, not necessarily of a formal character, may have been made by any of the personnel of employer, including employee, during the one (1) year period immediately next prior to the termination of employee's employment even though active service to such account or accounts shall not have been started prior to the date of the termination of employee's employment.

(e) In view of the broad scope and range of the normal business activities of employer, the undertaking and covenant of employee contained in this paragraph — shall be honored and performed in any and all states or foreign countries, not being confined to the cities or states in which employer now has, or may hereafter have, offices or staffs nor to cities and states in which employee has resided or performed his duties for employer prior to the termination of his employment.

(f) In the event that you should leave us for any reason, it is to be understood that you will stay away from all of our accounts and make no effort to solicit or serve them either for yourself or for any other public relations firm or organization with which you may become associated. This is to continue for a three-year period after you leave and is also to apply to any accounts not actually in the house when you leave but to which solicitations or presentations may have been made during the period of your association with us. In other words, we should understand each other that you are to make no effort, direct or indirect, during this three-year period to take any account with you or to do anything which might cause them to leave us or to "switch" public relations shops.

35. Liquidated Damages.

(a) The parties hereto being mutually desirous of avoiding litigation in the event of the employee's breach of any of the terms and conditions of paragraph 7 above, and the amount of damage resulting from a breach of the aforesaid paragraph not being ascertainable at this time and difficult to determine in any event, it is mutually agreed that in the event of a default or breach of paragraph 7 the employee shall pay to the employer, at the discretion of the employer, as liquidated damages and not as a penalty, the sum of Ten Thousand Dollars ($10,000.00) or an amount equal to that which the employee was paid by the employer in the twelve (12) months period immediately preceding the date of termination of the employee's employment herein, whichever is greater, and the payment of said sum shall constitute full and final settlement of all claims and demands by reason of said default or breach.

(b) If employee shall breach or violate the covenant herein contained, employee shall become liable for and shall, upon demand by employer, pay to employer, as liquidated damages and not as a penalty, a sum equal to the total of the following sums:

(1) a sum equal to ——————— (—%) percent of the total income produced by or derived or accrued from the accounts and business being served or represented contrary hereto during the first six (6) months of the actual service or representation of such accounts or business;

(2) a sum equal to ——————— (—%) percent of the said income during the succeeding six (6) months period thereof;

(3) a sum equal to ——————— (—%) percent of the said income during the succeeding six (6) months period thereof;

(4) a sum equal to ——————— (—%) percent of the said income during the succeeding six (6) months period thereof.

The foregoing sums shall be paid as liquidated damages, at the discretion of, and upon demand by, employer notwithstanding that the said several six (6) months periods or any of them shall extend beyond the termination of the original two (2) year term of the covenant.

Employer shall have the right to enforce and collect from employee the foregoing damages, but employer shall also have and enjoy, within its discretion, the additional and cumulative right to proceed against employee, in the event of his breach or violation of the said covenant, to enjoin such breach or violation or the continuance thereof by employee.

(c) If during the period in which employer is paying the termination payment, the employee or any public relations agency with which the employee is affiliated, either as employee, consultant or otherwise, solicits, either directly or indirectly, any accounts which were clients of employer at any time during the 12-month period immediately preceding the termination date, then employer, at its election, may terminate its obligation hereunder and from and after the date on which employer shall notify the employee of such election, employer shall not be obligated to pay any installments of the termination payment.

36. Waiver Clauses.

(a) If employer shall, at or after the termination of employee's service, waive any of its rights or remedies hereunder, such waiver shall be strictly limited by its specific terms and shall not be construed to waive or release any other rights or remedies hereunder including rights in accounts.

(b) Should we exercise our discretion and permit you to take with you any account(s) when you leave us, such approval will be limited to the individual account involved and will not be considered as giving you any rights in any other account or even additional rights in the approved account beyond those specifically given you. If we find afterwards that you have not told us the full and true story about your connection with that account, we will still have the right to enforce this agreement against you.

(c) Approval by the employer of the removal by the employee of any account at or after the termination of the employee's services hereunder, at the discretion of the employer, shall not be deemed a waiver of any other rights including, but without being limited to, employer's ownership of all other accounts, and the continuance of the foregoing restrictions upon employee as to all such accounts.

Notes

1. CUTLIP & CENTER, EFFECTIVE PUBLIC RELATIONS 103 (3d ed. 1963).
2. Goodman, *How to Get the Most Out of an Agency,* P.R.J., Aug., 1964, at 16.
3. Peerless Oakland Laundry Co. v. Hickman, 205 Cal. App. 2d 556, 23 Cal. Rep. 105 (1962).
4. Hammond, *Why the Emphasis on Service?* P.R.J., Nov., 1964, at 35.
5. As to the relative merits of the advertising agency PR department, see Chase, *Public Relations in Modern Society,* P.R.Q., Vol. 7, No. 4, at 12, 17–20 (1962); Cutlip & Center, *supra* note 1, at 99–107.
6. Cutlip & Center, *supra* note 1, at 102.
7. See, *e.g.,* A. S. Rampell, Inc. v. Hyster Co., 3 N.Y. 2d 369, 144 N.E.2d 371, 165 N.Y.S.2d 475 (1958); Claughton v. Bear-Stearns & Co., 397 Pa. 480, 156 A.2d 314 (1959); cases cited, 9 WILLISTON, CONTRACTS §1014C (3d ed. 1959–1967).
8. Robb v. Green, [1895] 2 Q.B. 1.
9. Byrne v. Barrett, 268 N.Y. 199, 206–07 (1935); Duane Jones Co. v. Burke *et al., infra* note 16.
10. Keiser v. Walsh, 118 F.2d 13 (D.C. Cir. 1941).
11. Nichols-Morris v. Morris, 174 F. Supp. 691 (D.C. 1959).
12. Denawatz v. Milch, 407 Pa. 115, 178 A.2d 701 (1962).
13. A. S. Rampell v. Hyster Co., *supra* note 7; Krause v. Gardner, 99 N.Y.S.2d 210 (1950); Duane Jones Co. v. Burke *et al., infra* note 16.
14. 232 Pa. 605, 81 Atl. 716 (1911).
15. Personal reminiscences of Charles Blum to author.
16. 381 App. Div. 622, 121 N.Y.S.2d 107 (1953), *aff'd and mod'd,* 306 N.Y. 172, 117 N.E.2d 237 (1954).
17. For an interesting description of an example of an allied situation, see Burger, *The Crucial Gap in Public Relations,* P.R.J., April, 1962.
18. See generally 5 WILLISTON, CONTRACTS §§1635–44 (3d ed. 1959–1967).
19. Kreider, *Trends in the Enforcement of Restrictive Employment Contracts,* 35 U. CINC. L. REV. 16, 18 (1966).
20. Arthur Murray Dance Studios of Cleveland v. Witter, 105 N.E.2d 685 (C.P. Ohio 1952).
21. The Dyer's Case, 2 Hen. V, pl. 26 (1415); Carpenter, *Validity of Contracts Not to Compete,* 76 U. PA. L. REV. 244 (1928).
22. I P. Wms. 181 (1711).
23. 5 WILLISTON, CONTRACTS, *supra* note 18, §1643.
24. Blake, *Employee Agreements Not to Compete,* 73 HARV. L. REV. 625, 647 (1960).
25. 217 Ky. 269, 289 S.W. 295, 52 A.L.R. 1344 (1926).
26. 86 Fed. 271, *aff'd.,* 175 U.S. 211 (1899).
27. *E.g.,* Meyer v. Wineburgh, 110 F. Supp. 957 (D.D.C. 1953); May v. Young,

infra note 37; Racine v. Bender, 141 Wash. 606, 252 P.2d 115 (1927); Ebbeskotte v. Tyler, 142 N.E. 2d 905 (Ind. App. 1957).

28. Arkansas Dailies, Inc. v. Dan, 260 S.W.2d 200 (Tenn. 1953).

29. DeLong Corp. v. Lucas, 278 F.2d 854 (2d Cir. 1960), *cert. denied,* 364 U.S. 833 (1960).

30. Annot., 43 A.L.R.2d 94, 236–321 (1955) and cases cited and discussed therein.

31. As to duration of the restriction generally, see Annot., 41 A.L.R.2d 15 (1955).

32. See cases cited and discussed, *id.* 155–207.

33. Arkansas Dailies, Inc. v. Dan, *supra* note 28.

34. Meyer v. Wineburgh, *supra* note 27.

35. Donahue v. Tatum, 134 So.2d 442 (Miss. 1961); Bates Chevrolet Corp. v. Haven Chevrolet, Inc., 13 App. Div. 2d 27, 213 N.Y.S.2d 577 (1961).

36. Ebbeskotte v. Tyler, 142 N.E.2d 905 (Ind. App. 1957); *contra,* Toulmin v. Becker, 60 Ohio L. Abs. 109, 124 N.E.2d 778 (1954).

37. May v. Young, 125 Conn. 1, 2 A.2d 385, 119 A.L.R. 1445 (1938); see cases discussed, Annot., 119 A.L.R. 1452.

38. Arkansas Dailies, Inc. v. Dan, *supra* note 28.

39. *Id.* at 264.

40. Jenkins v. King, 224 Ind. 164, 65 N.E.2d 121, 163 A.L.R. 397; Annot., 163 A.L.R. 405.

41. Arkansas Dailies, Inc. v. Dan, *supra* note 28; Elbe File & Binder Co. v. Fine, 137 Misc. 255, 242 N.Y.S. 632 (1930). See Note, 29 COLUM. L. REV. 347 (1929).

42. Economy Grocery Stores Corp. v. McMenamy, 290 Mass. 549, 195 N.E. 747 (1935).

43. Buckout v. Witwer, 157 Mich. 406, 122 N.W. 184, 22 L.R.A. (n.s.) 506 (1909).

44. Ala. Code, Tit. 9, §§22–24 (1958); Cal. Bus. & Prof. Code §§16600–02 (1964); Fla. Stat. Ann. §542.12 (2) (1953); Ga. Code Ann. §20–504 (1965); La. Stat. Ann. R.S. 23:921 (1962); Mich. Comp. Laws §§28.61–66 (1948); Mont. Rev. Codes Ann. §§13–807–09 (1947); N.D. Comp. Laws §§5928–30 (1913); Okla. Stat. Ann., Tit. 14, §§217–19 (1937); S.D. Civ. Code §§898–900 (1929); Wis. Stat. §103.465 (1957).

45. See discussion and cases cited, Williston, *supra* note 18.

46. See Atlas Travel Serv. v. Morelly, 98 So.2d 816 (Fla. App. 1957); McQuown v. Lakeland Co., 136 So.2d 370 (Fla. App. 1962).

47. See Union Century Life Ins. Co. v. Balistrieri, 19 Wis.2d 265, 120 N.W.2d 126 (1963).

48. May v. Mulligan, 36 F. Supp. 596, *aff'd,* 117 F.2d 259 (6th Cir. 1940).

49. Simons v. Fried, 277 App. Div. 1154, 101 N.Y.S.2d 325, *aff'd,* 302 N.Y. 323, 98 N.E.2d 456 (1951); see cases cited and discussed in Williston, *supra* note 18, 4615, n. 1.

50. Cleaver v. Lenhard, 182 Pa. 285, 37 Atl. 811 (1897).

51. Kristt v. Whelan, 4 App. Div. 2d 195, 164 N.Y.S.2d 239, *aff'd,* 5 N.Y.2d 807,

181 N.Y.S.2d 205 (1959); Neuffer v. Bakery & Confectioners Workers Int'l Union, 307 F.2d 671 (D.C. Cir. 1962).

52. Snyder Milk Co. v. Burton, 80 N.J. Eq. 185, 83 Atl. 907 (1912); Williams v. Farrand, 88 Mich. 473, 50 N.W. 446, 14 L.R.A. 161 (1891).

53. Lynn Trucker Sales, Inc. v. Le Blanc, 323 Mass. 721, 84 N.E.2d 127 (1949).

54. Beit v. Beit, 135 Conn. 195, 63 A.2d 161 (1948); Markson Bros. v. Redick, 164 Pa. Super. 499, 66 A.2d 218 (1949).

55. RESTATEMENT SECOND, AGENCY §395 (1958).

56. Du Pont Powder Co. v. Masland, 244 U.S. 100 (1917).

57. E. I. du Pont de Nemours Powder Co. v. Masland, 244 U.S. 100, 102 (1917).

58. Nichols-Morris Corp. v. Morris, 174 F. Supp. 691 (1959). This case also awarded damages for inducing another employee to transfer to defendant's employment.

59. Duane Jones Co. v. Burke et al., supra note 16.

60. Bynum v. McFee, 70 S.W.2d 499 (Tex. Civ. App. 1934). See Annots., 9 A.L.R. 1481, 98 A.L.R. 988.

Chapter 4

Business Communications, the Public and Censorship

A. Freedom of Speech and Press

1. Constitutional and Judicial Protection
2. Limitations
3. Protection of Business Communications

B. Censorship

4. History of Censorship
5. Nature of Censorship
6. Prepublication/Postpublication Censorship
7. Public Relations and Censorship
8. Censorship of Specific Activities
9. Public Relations Practitioners as Censors

C. Sources of Censorship

10. The Congress
11. Government Agencies Generally
12. Federal Communications Commission
13. Federal Trade Commission
14. Miscellaneous Federal Agencies
    (a) Securities and Exchange Commission
    (b) Food and Drug Administration
    (c) Other Agencies
15. Military and Space Agencies
16. Media
17. Public and Community Opinion
18. Self-Censorship

D. Media and Business Communications

19. Basic Right of Media
20. News Releases and Advertising

E. Obscenity

Chapter 4

Business Communications, the Public and Censorship

A. FREEDOM OF SPEECH AND PRESS.

1. Constitutional and Judicial Protection.

The First Amendment to the Constitution provides in part as follows:

> Congress shall make no law . . . abridging the freedom of speech, or of the press;

The rights of free speech and the press have been characterized by the Supreme Court as "fundamental personal rights and liberties," reflecting the conviction of the framers of the Constitution that their exercise "lies at the foundation of free government by free men." [1]

These rights are designed to "assure unfettered interchange of ideas for the bringing about of political and social changes desired by the people" and they are cited again and again by the Supreme Court for their essentiality "to the development and well-being of our free society" and as "indispensable to its continued growth." [2]

Neither truth, nor orthodoxy, nor public value is an essential ingredient of speech in order to qualify it for constitutional protection.[3] The constitutional protection of the exercise of free speech is not limited to the bare freedom to utter words in the silence of one's own room or to a small select group of willing listeners. Rather, it embraces the broad spectrum of activities involved in the *communication* of ideas to the public, including the right to speak in public places, to picket, to solicit, to publish and disseminate and to be free of unreasonable deterrents, either financial or psychological, in such expression or communication.[4]

The First Amendment, prohibiting federal attack, has been held applicable to the states.[5]

2. Limitations.

While enjoying a "preferred position" in our constitutional system, the freedoms of speech and press have never been regarded as absolute. The Supreme Court has consistently held that in a proper case these rights may of necessity undergo some restriction where their exercise comes into conflict with other essential public interests of the community.[6]

In making these determinations, the Supreme Court has been primarily concerned with the degree of burden on the exercise of the protected right,[7] whether the statute giving rise to the restraint was reasonable and nondiscriminatory in its objectives,[8] and whether the standards for its application were sufficiently defined.[9] Thus the constitutionality of regulatory statutes has been sustained against attack even where their impact resulted in some restraint of the exercise of constitutional freedoms.

3. Protection of Business Communications.[10]

The freedoms of speech and press are not confined to the individual. The business corporation comes within their protection. As Chief Justice Hughes has said: [11]

> The press in its historic connotation comprehends every sort of publication which affords a vehicle of information and opinion.

Unfortunately, a "casual, almost offhand" observation of the Supreme Court has cast some doubt upon the right of business—for admittedly commercial purposes—to cloak itself in the protection of the First Amendment.[12]

It seems clear that a commercial purpose does not taint an activity otherwise acceptable. We need only point to the motion picture censorship cases. The Supreme Court has held that the profit motive behind a "movie" does not remove it from the Constitutional aegis.[13] For that matter, the fact that books are published for profit and as the sole purpose of many business enterprises does not invalidate their claim to constitutional protection—even in alleged obscenity cases.[14]

In the "railroad/truckers" case, the right of these two industries to present their views to the people and the legislature was clearly protected.[15] Even though both parties in that landmark case were found to have employed methods which may not have satisfied the most ethical and may have had antitrust implications, the right of corporate and joint free speech was held to be so strong as to override these other considerations. See Chapter 23, Section 4.

The PR function of business is as much a protected area as any other form of corporate speech. Even if, for the sake of argument, it might eventually be held that paid advertising is not entirely constitutionally protected, such a rule would not militate against the public relations rights of business. Even the cases which denied tax deductibility to certain expenses incurred by business in placing before the public their statements as to their position in connection with pending legislation recognize the right of business to speak.[16]

Business communications, in the guise of publicity and PR, are subject to the same limits and restrictions as those of the individual. As to these restrictions generally, see Section 2 above. For example, an ordinance prohibiting use of sound trucks putting out sound at objectionably high levels has been sustained.[17] So, too, has been a reasonably and fairly administered law which requires a license to parade.[18] Neither of these cases involved public speech or activity by business but the outcome would have been the same in such case.

In other words, the rights of business in communicating with the public rise no higher and fall no lower than do the rights of the individual. Business can ask no more than this.

There seem to be two types of cases which have been principally responsible for the idea that business is, for some reason or other, treated differently from the individual.

(a) The antitrust cases against newspapers have held the antitrust laws applicable to such organs of speech and press.[19] The decisions, however, did not turn on the fact that the newspapers were profit-making business ventures but merely applied the same antitrust rules to them as to any other business.

(b) The *false* advertising cases dealing with First Amendment applicability appear to have cast a shadow on the rights of business. Whatever the limited validity of such purported holdings may be, they do not imply a taint on speech motivated by profit.

B. CENSORSHIP.

4. History of Censorship.

The word "censor" is derived from a similar official title in ancient Rome.[20] The censor's function was to preside over the census, the registration of Roman citizens for the purpose of determining their duties to the community. It has been suggested that the word's etymology concerns the "arbitrary assignment of burdens or duties." Gradually, from this genesis, it came to be applied more to morals than the assignment of duties, the Roman manifestation of the state control of conduct which was a not unusual feature of ancient societies.

The jurisdiction over the moral rules of the time went beyond family life and private relations and even involved breaches of political duties. *Infamia* was the name given to censor-imposed disabilities.

A curious censorial body developed in Pennsylvania and Vermont in the Revolutionary period, continuing in Vermont until as recently as 1870. This was the Council of Censors, elected once in seven years, to inquire into the workings of government, the conduct of state officials, the operation of state laws and similar matters. The Vermont Council could even call a state constitutional convention if necessary and actually did so in 1870.

These Councils were, in effect, forerunners of the European ombudsman and the growing movement in this country currently for a similar watchdog over government, its members, and its operations.

In more modern times, the word "censor" is sometimes defined generally as "one who exercises supervision over, or criticizes, the conduct of other persons." The title is an old one at the Universities of Oxford and Cambridge and is, in effect, a parietal supervision of students not attached to a particular college or hall.

Over the centuries the thrust of censorship has varied quite considerably. Through the medieval period and into the beginnings of the Enlightenment, the basic focus of censorship was heresy. Milton's *Areopagitica* of 1644—one of the truly great anti-censorship literary documents —was directed at his own prosecution for the unlicensed publication of his tracts denouncing the "priestly" prohibitions of divorce. Parliament brought him to its bar for heresy.

The church's interest and activities in censorship still continue but today, due largely to the separation of church and state, such bans are unofficial—no longer the policy of the government.[21]

Heresy was succeeded by political non-conformity as censorship's principal target. Treason and its associated anti-crown crimes then led the censorship parade. It was not until 1727 that obscenity appeared in the English law books. Only under Lord Campbell's Act in 1727 and the leading case of *Regina v. Hicklin* in 1868 did anti-obscenity censorship become important in our legal system.[22]

The interest of government in obscenity has continued down to date but whether obscenity is today the principal target of censorship may be open to considerable question. Writing in 1956, we said:[23] "At the moment, the prohibitions are directed largely to obscenity." Since that was written, the Supreme Court seems to have retreated very decisively from any restrictions on obscenity except as to "hard-core" examples thereof and, perhaps, the peripheral attack mounted under the "pandering" and "sales to minors" concepts. See Sections 26 to 31 below.

There is no question that the targets and the judicial rules for censorship have changed with the concepts, philosophy and general moral and political attitudes of the times. A changing policy which can be, over the centuries, successively anti-heresy, anti-treason, anti-obscenity, may well now have become anti-business despite the constitutional shield discussed in Sections 1 to 3 above. At the risk of prophecy, the current principal interest of censorship of all kinds—governmental or private—seems to be homing in, more and more, on business and especially on its communications functions, activities and tools. While lip service is being paid to the prohibitions against direct censorship, indirect attacks on "commercial speech" are proliferating.

5. Nature of Censorship.

Censorship has been variously defined over the centuries. All of these definitions seem to have three factors in common:

(a) Censorship is the expression—on an organized and perhaps official basis—of the scruples, morality and desires of the community, whether announced or policed by the community itself or by others (perhaps the state) presuming to speak for the community. Historically, this formulation has been by those in authority. On the other hand, the community attitudes and controls may spring directly from the grass roots of the citizenry. Today such censorship is frequently more effective than that which originates "on high," especially in the commercial frame of reference. See Section 17 below.

(b) All censorship is basically "protective" in certain aspects. It may protect the government, the military, the church or the community. The element of protection may be divorced from the source of the censorship. Not infrequently it is the "excuse" for censorship. Sometimes it serves as the popular "mask" for official restrictions which would otherwise cause resistance.

(c) Censorship always involves restrictions, limitations and prohibitions—all directed against freedom of communication or some aspect of it. We need only look back over the years to the restrictions on wartime news, limitations on the circulation of allegedly obscene books, the prohibition of the utterance of heretical doctrine. In each case, some hobble has fettered the freedom of expression and of communication.

These restrictions, in turn, have a common result. They interfere with communication. The degree of the interference may vary; the thrust of the interference may change; the ostensible purpose of the interference may vary; the practical enforcement of the interference may vacillate. But interference it is. This analysis is particularly pertinent from the point of view of the public relations practitioner, so vitally concerned as he is with communications and the untrammeled freedom to communicate.

For this reason, we have herein adopted and applied, as an encompassing definition: *censorship is any interference with the freedom of communication.*

There may be a difference of opinion as to whether this definition of censorship is too sweeping and inclusive. This is probably the result of not distinguishing between censorship and the motive or need for the censorship. Censorship is basically distasteful to the American mind. It is therefore easy to say that all censorship is bad and must be rejected. This is not true as we see it. A few examples pinpoint this.

Wartime military censorship has but rarely been criticized. See the comments of James Cassidy in Chapter 1, Section 5. A large and vocal segment of the population looks askance at the current Supreme Court position as to censorship of the obscene. See Sections 26 to 31 below. For a company to withdraw sponsorship of a documentary broadcast may be censorship as discussed in Section 9 below. At the same time, this may be justified. Probably the best example is Justice Holmes' pungent admonition that no one may shout "Fire" in a crowded theater.

To cry "censorship," therefore, is not necessarily to pass judgment on its propriety. Even under the guarantees of the First Amendment, its "gray areas" must be evaluated as part of our overall pattern of rights and obligations.

6. Prepublication/Postpublication Censorship.

In this concept of censorship, an important distinction must be kept in mind. Traditionally in the United States, "official" censorship has been largely limited to "prepublication" interference with, or control of, speech or communications. Our definition goes beyond prepublication controls and includes postpublication controls as well.[24]

This seems inevitable in view of the character of commercial communications activity. For example: a company plans an institutional advertising campaign. A series of advertisements are projected for use in local newspapers. The initial advertisement appears. Public or governmental clamor against the initial advertisement is considerable so the company immediately withdraws the balance of the campaign. This sort of thing has happened.

This is only partly prepublication censorship. The first advertisement appeared without let or hindrance. As to such advertisement, it is postpublication censorship. However, as to the rest of the campaign, it is prepublication censorship of the program even though its cancellation may have been seemingly voluntary.

7. Public Relations and Censorship.

The PR practitioner, as a company's principal communicator, is more likely to be involved in or concerned with the various kinds and sources of censorship discussed in Sections 10 to 18 below than any other company staff member or advisor. There are several reasons for this:

(a) The public is eventually the root of all censorship. See Section 17 below. The PR practitioner has the obligation of recording playback from the public for his company or client so that its activities are in step with public attitudes. This is particularly important in matters within or on the fringe of the censorial areas and not subject to overly precise definition.

Frequently the question must be faced: what can we do and how far can we go? The best answer is probably found in the PR man's interpretation, evaluation and prediction of public attitudes and response. This is the reflection, in the corporate world, of the often-quoted:

Give me liberty to *know,* to *utter,* and to argue freely according to conscience, above all other liberties. (Emphasis added.)

Thus Milton, in his *Areopagitica,* early laid the foundation for what the modern public relations man calls "the two-way street" of public relations. In Thoreau's words: "It takes two to speak the truth; one to speak and another to hear." [25]

(b) The PR man is the one who must overtly react to the results of censorship as they affect a company. It is the PR man who must advise as to company reaction to any form of censorship. It is he who prepares the company's answers and statements. It is his duty to advise on or direct the affirmative, constructive and remedial steps to be taken—not merely to confront but to reverse the censorial attitudes and results.

Steinberg has described an example of this interplay of management and public relations staff reaction to censorship: [26]

A motion picture distributing company found that one of its films was censored in a major city by the local censor board. Foolishly, the vice-president thought that this could be kept secret and, when queried about it, he disclaimed any knowledge of it. At the same time he failed to advise his public relations director of either the censor board action or his own decision. The public relations man learned about it through an inquiry from an enterprising reporter.

. . . It took considerable persuasion to convince management
. . . that such a situation could not be suppressed or denied and
that the only action was a statement of admission of fact plus a
statement of company policy attitude in the matter. In this case the
PR man suggested that the company statement point out that the
city in question was the *only one,* among several hundred, which
had insisted on censoring the film. By and large, the press carried
this statement in a most favorable manner.

(c) One of the important sources of censorship is the blue pencil
of the editor. The company public relations staff—or its member responsible for press relations—can do an important prophylactic job by creating in the editorial mind a receptive, rather than antagonistic, attitude.
Such blue pencil censorship is less likely to develop under these circumstances.

The release is less likely to be badly cut or mutilated. The headline is
more likely to follow the substance of the story. This is especially important when the editor is dealing with unfavorable company news and has
a choice of treatment or approaches. Such properly cultivated editorial
attitudes may be basic to the use of the story at all. This is not tampering
with or prostituting the communications media. It is merely laying the
foundation for a fair and truthful handling of the release or story. See
Section 16 below.

(d) The PR man is frequently involved with government—local,
state or national. This is true even though he may not be charged with
"government relations" as such. Because of this, the PR man is even more
exposed to sources of censorship, official or unofficial.

This is not to confuse regulation with censorship. It confines censorship
to business communications, excluding other business functions such as
pricing, product quality, licenses, etc. which are the subjects of a government interest more properly described as regulation. See Chapter 19.

(e) Probably the most important source of a PR man's constant
awareness of censorship is his shaping and creation of a company's informational materials. It is from these materials that the censorship questions arise. Probably the only communications of the company with
which the public relations man may not at some time be involved is its
paid product-advertising. Except for this, it is the PR man who is constantly on the censorship firing line due to the communications creativity
demanded of him. See Section 8 below.

8. Censorship of Specific Activities.

Almost every PR activity may run into some form or degree of censorship. This is true of the so-called non-communications activities as well.
Probably one of the most unexpected and esoteric was the reaction of a

local mayor of a small "plant town" who insisted that the company Public Relations Director be present at all company athletic activities to prevent the employees from using any profanity.[27]

A question may arise with the speech of a company or trade association official which is subjected to pre-presentation censorship. One obvious example was the experience of George J. Hecht, publisher of *Parents' Magazine* and then president of the Federation of the Periodical Press. Those in charge of the Federation's 1965 Rome meeting were given an advance copy of his remarks. They objected to the portion thereof dealing with birth control and the use of contraceptives. Mr. Hecht was compelled to delete this material but told his audience, ". . . the next five pages of my prepared remarks have been censored. However, I have released them to the press in this country and in the U.S." [28]

A common product publicity technique has been the use of the product on TV shows or of product plugs in radio and TV scripts or ad lib shows. Indicative of this type of censorship is the evidence presented to the Senate judiciary committee by the Columbia Broadcasting System concerning its prebroadcast editing and screening of such publicity methods: [29]

> CBS editors snatched plugs for *Life* and American Airlines from "Blue Angel" script for Oct. 5. They kept "Portia Faces Life" from giving plug to United Air Lines Mainliner Oct. 12. Then decided a bottle of Testers liquid cement with label prominently displayed could be used on "Portia Faces Life" Oct. 7.

Even some institutional or non-profit PR "stunts" may generate interest of the local "censors" if not actual interference with the event. One of the best remembered may be the ride which Marilyn Monroe, showing considerable "bosom and flesh," took in Atlantic City to publicize the recruitment activities of the Wacs.[30]

Other promotions may run into actual governmental censorship as did a promotion for "The Naked Maja." United Artists sought an injunction to prevent the Post Office Department from refusing delivery of newspapers and periodicals carrying advertisements showing the famous Goya nude. The department called this action a "publicity stunt." Three weeks later the department did seize 2000 postcards carrying the same picture as a violation of the obscenity laws. As a result both the painting and the motion picture "reaped more publicity . . . at the Post Office hearing to decide whether postcards of the painting were too obscene for the mails." [31]

Somewhat similar to the Naked Maja situation was the problem of a traveling company-sponsored art exhibit. Two of the oils in the show were considered too risqué for local school children and had to be removed under threat of immediate legal action by the county prosecutor.

Such actions, unlikely though they may seem to be, can be multiplied. These include: attempted gun-point censorship of company employment-policy statements by "white supremacists"; the militarily-enforced erection of screens around a piece of equipment during a plant tour even though similar equipment had appeared elsewhere in a parade without objection; judicial refusal to allow a tax deduction for certain institutional "editorial advertising"; [32] certain union demands that a serial story be discontinued in a house organ; insistence by a stock exchange that a certain release about a company contract be withdrawn and re-written.

9. Public Relations Practitioners as Censors.

The shoe may be on the other foot. The PR practitioner may himself be the genesis of what amounts to censorship. This may also arise against a variety of backgrounds.

Most obvious is the affirmative effort of the PR man to screen out from his releases or other communications and activities anything which may be deceptive or in bad taste. This is a common effort and may be anticipated as standard operating procedure. Other censorship activities are not as obvious and, perhaps to some, not as commendable.

In 1962, for example, considerable industry and government concern and comment were generated by the effort of a few sponsors to cancel commitments with ABC-TV because of network programming which the sponsors felt might adversely affect their "reputation."

This seems like a strictly advertising matter but is basically a public relations "headache." Not only is the PR man involved in the company's basic policy decision to withdraw the sponsorship, but he usually prepares the company's press statements explaining the decision. Such action also affects the public relations posture of the company generally. As James Badgett, advertising manager of Schick Safety Razor Co., one of the companies concerned with the ABC-TV cancellations, said at the time: [33]

> No one at Schick wants to restrict freedom. They can put anything on the air they want to. However, we reserve the right to put our *public relations* and advertising where it is going to get results. (Emphasis added.)

This company attitude and action drew a prompt reaction from Newton Minow, then FCC Chairman, who said: [34]

> Whether this particular program was in good taste is for the public to decide. The real issue transcends this particular program.

The basic issue is the freedom and responsibility of broadcast journalism. To be responsible, broadcast journalism on all the networks and stations must be free. *This means freedom not only from government censorship, but also from threatening pressure groups* and from those few fearful advertisers who seek through commercial reprisals to influence the professional judgment of broadcast newsmen. (Emphasis added.)

To industry, this withdrawal of sponsorship may not seem to be censorship at all. In a narrow sense it is not. The questioned newscast or documentary is usually still broadcast. However, it is censorship in the sense that it withdraws—perhaps at the last minute—the financial support needed by the news medium and results in a sustaining broadcast. Furthermore, it is likely to have some lasting effect upon future programming attitudes and policies of the media. In the latter configuration, it may be censorship (perhaps even prepublication censorship) though seemingly indirect and remote.

This sort of cancellation may also have considerable financial repercussions. In one such case [35] suit was brought by the network. It recovered from the cancelling sponsor the full amount of the broadcast contract price, reduced only by the amount of the proceeds realized from such resales as it could reasonably make under the circumstances. The court pointed out that "commercial minutes of time" are perishable and there is no market for them in the sense that there is a market and market value for goods and commodities. The network was not required to disrupt its business by trying to resell the time at such low prices as to assure "a complete sell-off."

It has even been suggested that use of "no comment" by the PR man is such interference with proper communications as to amount to censorship. Thus Steinberg writes: [36]

More often than not, the reporter will ferret out the answer elsewhere and confront the public relations director with the data. . . . *Frequently, the decision must be made whether to attempt discreet censorship* or allow the press to have the requested information. (Emphasis added.)

Company policy or some immediate and important circumstance or "sensitive issue" may be involved in such pseudo-censorial position. Thus Steinberg goes on to say:

Censorship of press information arises when reporters get wind of impending activities which the company is not ready to release. . . .

Although today this probably is not too prevalent, there are still instances in which a company may actively seek to suppress news. It is the

PR man who becomes the censor. Here again, we have something similar to the press relations situation discussed in Section 7 above. Most PR practitioners will not even attempt to "kill a story." Some will try—probably without too much success.

C. SOURCES OF CENSORSHIP.

10. The Congress.

The Congress generally observes the constitutional prohibition of censorship. However, its federal agency legislation often permits an agency, in effect, to censor through agency-adopted Regulations, a basic feature of the administrative agency concept. This is an almost classic example of the well-worn Washington paraphrase: "I care not who writes my nation's laws so long as I can write its Regulations."

As far as business communications are concerned, Congress and a particular agency may not always agree. Not infrequently commission chairmen find their views rather critically examined during legislative committee hearings.

11. Government Agencies Generally.

Under the federal system of regulation by administrative agencies, their power over business generally is increasing. This includes greater interdiction of business communications sometimes amounting to censorship, perhaps even of a prepublication character.

In no instance of which we are aware has an agency openly referred to its communicatory controls as "censorship." Continuing lip service is paid to the complete disavowal of censorship no matter what the direct or indirect results of agency action may be. Yet the results of some agency "regulation" are definitely censorial. This has developed notwithstanding Supreme Court prohibitions including those against "financial or psychological" deterrents to free speech.[37]

Every agency proceeding which inhibits a particular communications campaign or program in any way is a "red flag" to all other concerns, interfering prospectively with their future communications in the same area or having the same thrust. The same may be said of any "advance regulation" such as the Trade Regulation Rules of the FTC which seek to point out what the FTC will prospectively condemn. See Section 13 below, and Chapter 20, Section 17.

Probably one of the best examples of communications interference is the continuing—at times heated—dialogue between the FCC and the broadcasting industry dealing with that agency's right to regulate radio and television programming, discussed more fully in Section 12 below.

Much of the interest of the government agencies is posited on prevention of deception or unfair practices involving the public and the competitive enterprise system. See Chapter 11 generally. Its tangible effects, however, are censorial in many aspects. Their interference with communication is clear. They constitute an attrition of free speech and, since the agencies usually operate under poorly defined legislative authority, the loose perimeters of such interference seem to be expanding under the aegis of a court-protected concept of "agency expertise." [38]

12. Federal Communications Commission.

The FCC's basic requirement is that broadcasters operate "in the public interest, convenience and necessity." [39] Unfortunately, there is but little specific legislative direction given the Commission as to what these general words mean.

Section 1464 of the Federal Criminal Code punishes "obscene, indecent or profane language by means of radio communication." [40] See Section 30 below. Section 1304 of the same Act forbids the broadcast of information or advertising about lotteries. [41] Beyond this, federal law is sparse except for such matters as political broadcasts under Section 315 of the Communications Act of 1934 and the general prohibition against censorship in Section 326 of the same Act, specifically forbidding the FCC to "interfere with the right of free speech by means of radio (and television) communication." [42] The approach of the FCC must, therefore, be indirect if it seeks to accomplish such an end.

As indicated in Section 11 above, the dispute between the FCC and the broadcasters as to FCC control of programming is a continuing one. The following example is typical.

In 1965, the FCC began to explore its so-called "50-50" proposal whereby network interest in, and control of, broadcast programs would be drastically limited. [43] The two views on this proposal—squarely opposed to each other—turn clearly on censorship. The FCC position as stated by then Chairman Henry was that: [44]

[P]rogramming *per se* is not the dominant theme of this proposal. . . . Our aim is not to select or direct programming, but to promote the development of conditions that will lead to the widest possible program production and distribution.

This is the indirect approach taken to avoid the mandate against prepublication censorship which the courts have indicated is not permissible. [45]

Reacting to the 50-50 proposal on behalf of the broadcast industry, the editor of *Sponsor* wrote: [46]

No matter what the guise cloaking such proposed regulations, the ultimate objective is program control. Stymied by the danger of abridging our basic freedoms in their efforts to impose their idea of program quality, legislators and regulators are wary of decreeing that something be included or something else left out. This alternative 50-50 rule presupposes that restricting something in one direction will automatically produce a desired result in another. And it's safer. Let's keep the issue confined to quantity, not unstable and unsafe "quality." Let's first create the vacuum and something will, no doubt, be sucked into it.

Changing policies have marked the censorial posture of the FCC over the years as indicated, for example, on the "editorializing" issue. In the 1941 *Mayflower* case [47] the Commission abolished broadcast editorials. Yet later, in 1949, it recognized the broadcaster's rights to express opinions and to editorialize.[48] Its general posture as to editorializing under the fairness doctrine is: [49]

[Stations] have an affirmative duty generally to encourage and implement the broadcast of all sides of controversial public issues over their facilities, over and beyond their obligation to make available on demand opportunities for the expression of opposing views. [This] will be difficult if not impossible of achievement unless the licensee plays a conscious and positive role in bringing about balanced presentation of the opposing viewpoints.

NAB has summed up this requirement by describing as "a bedrock requirement" the "equal opportunity . . . for expression of views contrary to the station's editorial stand . . . that all sides of a controversial issue must be fairly presented." [50]

This is an important area for the consideration of the PR man whose company, client or organization may be the subject of editorializing or other adverse program content. He should be conversant with his rights under the fairness doctrine. This is particularly true since the FCC in 1967 introduced the fairness doctrine into the product advertising ambit with its requirement that broadcasters carry anti-cigarette-smoking announcements to answer the cigarette company broadcast advertising.

The problem extends far beyond station editorializing—particularly with the growth of interview and "talk" shows. The solution admittedly is a difficult one. Preserving the three-way balance among freedom of speech, fairness and the exploitation of the sensational requires a delicate hand. In 1967, for example, certain "talk and discussion programs" came under criticism because of the apparently unlimited opportunities given "bigots" to express their views under the guise of "discussion." [51]

Documentary programs also present the same question of according the "other side" the right to answer or to present their own interpretation of events. Here again the role of the PR man is an important one. Because of the fairness doctrine his position is stronger than it is with print media where he must depend upon the publisher's or editor's innate sense of fairness and integrity in opening his columns to the reply to adverse news or editorializing. See Section 22 below.

The individual, company, political party or ethnic group concerned about unfair treatment by a broadcaster does have recourse despite the FCC's apparent lack of direct and immediate control over the station's operation. Complaints to the FCC will usually cause the Commission to direct a prompt inquiry to the station. Such an inquiry is likely to be respected and probably effective. Unsatisfactory resolution of the complaint may not elicit any specific action by the Commission but it then becomes part of the station's FCC dossier and will be considered when the station's license comes up for its triennial renewal.

This renewal proceedings—always involving the possibility of a refusal to renew or to renew for one year only—is probably the FCC's greatest source of control and implied censorship. Generally, it is conducive to a conservative station attitude. See Chapter 19, Sections 30 to 33 for a discussion of the public relations and public interest aspects of renewal proceedings.

Program content has been upheld as a reason for a refusal of a renewal.[52] Some cases are reasonably clear. Thus a refusal has been based on past use of patently vulgar language over a station.[53] However, types of conduct in which the PR practitioner is likely to be interested are by no means as clear in this connection.

Censorship of the broadcast and print media differ in one important jurisdictional aspect. It is generally held that control of broadcasting, including its censorship, has been preempted by Congress under the Communications Act of 1934. Thus films shown on TV may not be censored by state boards or other non-federal authorities.[54]

13. Federal Trade Commission.

Exercise of the FTC authority over various deceptive or unfair trade practices—including business communications—may not technically be prepublication censorship. The FTC takes action normally after the impropriety has been committed. At least, this is the traditional approach as discussed in Chapter 11.

On the other hand, several techniques have been developed—some relatively recently—which may amount to prepublication censorship and constitute an increased interference with free communication.

(a) The initial appearance of an FTC investigator at a company's office is known to have immediate effects upon the promotional, advertising and other practices of that concern. In many instances the practices are promptly terminated or materially altered. This is well documented by the evidence in FTC cases which later reach the litigation stage.[55] The same is true even when the initial FTC contact with a concern is by letter only.

The immediate psychological impact of such inquiries cannot be denied. This is particularly true with smaller firms, as evidenced by a 1966 survey dealing with "Small Business Before the Federal Trade Commission." [56] This has led to many instances in which the mere threat of adjudicatory proceedings has brought the company "to its knees," seeking an "administrative disposition" of the case or a consent order—even though there may be no proof that anything illegal has been done. This is evidenced by the fact that such orders provide that entry thereof does not constitute an admission of any illegal act.[57] See Chapter 19, Section 5.

(b) The FTC may hold a public hearing into certain business practices accompanied by considerable publicity. No complaint is filed; the hearing is purely investigatory and preliminary. The thrust of such hearings may drive companies to change or end certain practices. There have been instances in which a company's entire public relations and advertising program has been stultified or altered—sometimes without any evidence of wrongdoing. This is censorship—even prepublication censorship masked by the investigatory powers of the Commission. See Chapter 19, Section 7.

(c) The FTC is said to move slowly but it can sometimes move with speed sufficient to hamstring an entire communications program. As far back as 1950, there was evidence of this in connection with the so-called "child appeal" theme used in the promotion, public relations and advertising of TV set manufacturers. Within *three days* after this campaign first broke, it was withdrawn because the Commission had announced that it had started an active investigation of the campaign.

(d) In 1963, the Commission set up its Advisory Opinions procedure. This is a form of prepublication censorship even though it is a purely voluntary procedure. The Commission will give an Advisory Opinion as to the apparent acceptability of an advertising campaign or other promotional techniques.

(e) The Commission's Trade Regulation Rule program also partakes of prepublication censorship. Beginning in 1962, the Commission has adopted a series of Rules which it considers as "law" and binding upon all members of the affected industry. The future impact of this procedure is evidenced by the fact that in 1967 the Commission announced that it would no longer adopt Fair Trade Practice Rules, a form of *voluntary* compliance going back several decades. The Commission now apparently feels that its Trade Regulation Rules have supplanted this earlier structure of regulation and with greater significance—at least from the Commission's point of view.

(f) The FTC has adopted a series of Guides—ostensibly for the instruction of the Commission staff. While, even in FTC eyes, they are not "law" or *per se* enforceable through adjudicatory action, their mere promulgation has had a direct and continuing effect on subsequent business activity and practices with which the Guides are concerned.

We thus have a series of FTC "prophylactic" programs which specifically inhibit and corrosively affect business communications. Whatever the legal posture of these programs may be—the Trade Regulation Rules program, for example, is presently untested by final court scrutiny—their practical results are clear. They contribute to prepublication censorship of the business message.

14. Miscellaneous Federal Agencies.

Other federal agencies exercise varying degrees of communications control over business and its public relations and publicity activities. Some are censorial in effect and even in purpose. Most operate under the guise of regulation.

(a) *Securities and Exchange Commission.*

Federal control of financial public relations and communications is undoubtedly one of the most detailed, drastic and demonstrable of any likely to be encountered by business or public relations. Furthermore, in many instances, they are specifically prepublication controls, requiring submissions to SEC and NASD before use, publication or distribution.

The statutes—together with the SEC Regulations adopted thereunder —specify what may be said, what may not be said or what must be said. It is difficult to postulate a more sweeping censorial structure. The detailed requirements thereunder are discussed in Chapter 22.

The same is true of state controls. For example, in the 1967 *Ling-Temco-Vought* case,[58] the Wisconsin Commissioner of Securities entered an "Order Prohibiting Solicitation" against the company, prohibiting it from "soliciting"—in effect, communicating with—Allis-Chalmers stockholders to sell their stock until certain state registrations were completed "or until further order of this office."

(b) *Food and Drug Administration.*

In addition to its controls over the formulation and other aspects of foods, drugs, cosmetics and devices, the FDA also exercises communications control over their manufacturers. Aside from regulation of their labeling and advertising, such controls appear to extend to the publicity and public relations activities of such concerns.

News releases also appear to be coming under their surveillance. For example, in May, 1967, an FDA staff member "suggested" to industry participants at a joint conference of the FDA and the Grocery Manufacturers of America that his name be placed on their mailing lists to receive copies of "public releases concerning special dietary foods, which are being distributed to news media by food manufacturers." The stated purpose was "to assist the Food and Drug Administration to keep abreast of new developments in this important area" of FDA activities.[59]

Industry sources and trade publications indicate that, from time to time, requests are made for copies of company news releases—even when their substance has appeared in the press, the apparent purpose being to go behind the edited and published story. It is said that there has been some FDA reaction to these publicity materials.

(c) Other Agencies.

From time to time other federal agencies take affirmative steps to block, censor or otherwise control company publicity.

The Civil Aeronautics Board, for example, in 1967 ordered competing bidders for the government contract for the new supersonic airliner to stop further publicity efforts because of their possible effect on the eventual award decision.[60] It has also taken action against what it considered premature or improper announcements of fare changes.[61]

The Federal Home Loan Bank Board is known to take informal steps to stop publicity or other practices by savings and loan associations, which the Board considers improper.[62]

The Federal Power Commission has instructed power companies subject to its jurisdiction as to the language to be used on certain signs displayed upon their properties dealing with uses thereof having "civil rights" implications.[63]

While these and other agencies may take only sporadic action of a censorial character, they do not appear to hesitate about doing so when they consider such action appropriate—apparently without too much concern as to the censorship implications of such action.

15. Military and Space Agencies.

At the end of World War II and the apparent "return to normalcy," the business world and its PR arm heaved a collective sigh of relief. Censorship seemed to be at an end. Yet the secrecy phobia has apparently continued in the military establishment. It may, in certain aspects, have a broader force than before.

With the growing intrusion of government into the research and development activities of business, especially those companies directly or peripherally concerned with areas relevant to the military, "Cold War" and space efforts of the country, there had come a renewed and at times seemingly excessive censorship by government of PR communications. It has been said: [64]

> The technological revolution in warfare is pushing the frontiers of knowledge; as a result much work in basic science is classified as "top secret," "secret" and "confidential." And because people, as well as documents, are classified, censorship reaches far outside the government payroll to embroil a frightening percentage of our scientific establishment in the security system.

The same author goes on to point out that evidence before the Moss Committee—a subcommittee of the House Committee on Government Operations—indicates that censorship since the outbreak of World War II has been applied to some 100,000 file drawers of classified documents in Washington and at military installations throughout the world. The Army estimates that it has some two million classified documents in its own files.

The impact of such censorship on both the scientific and business worlds cannot easily be imagined. Its very scope and volume make it difficult to picture what American business would be like should even a fraction of such materials be declassified. This release of scientific information—made available to American businesses generally since it presumably is not under copyright—would undoubtedly result in a technological revolution in American industry.

The continued enforcement of governmental and military censorship of such scope means, among other things, that research is being duplicated wastefully—without any knowledge of the repetition—by American industry as well as in tangential research in the American university structure.

However, from the point of view of the PR function, there is an additional front upon which a continuing battle must be waged. This is the right to disclose the results of corporate research and the receipt of certain government contracts.

Normally, some of this information would be subject to "immediate release" in order to satisfy the strictures of the Securities and Exchange Commission or the stock exchanges. Such work—especially when successful or culminating in contracts—is of a nature which qualifies it for such handling. The PR man must walk a tightrope. Faced by disclosure requirements on the one hand and badgered by governmental censorship restrictions on the other—plus an understandable element of patriotic restraint—the quandary of the PR man is easily understood. Even going beyond the demands of "immediate release," much is being done today by American industry which would normally be appropriately disseminated as routine publicity, beneficial to the company. A good part of this may be forbidden. Many a PR man has shed "hot tears in a cold sweat."

Fortunately, the military and space agencies may cooperate to some degree with the PR man in clearing releases. Such clearance may result in mutilation or distortion of what would otherwise be a highly acceptable story. Yet such clearance is necessary. National security, laws and Regulations require it. Some government contracts demand it.[65]

The public relations officers of the armed services face the same dilemma. Thus Navy Regulations provide: [66]

> Although the paramount consideration is that of safeguarding classified information, officers in command and others concerned with the release of information will bear in mind that undue delay in releasing information or unreasonable refusal to formally release information already generally known has an adverse effect on the Navy's public affairs effort, inconveniencing and therefore alienating individuals and organizations who otherwise might favorably support the Navy.

Due to the overall growing impact of science upon the community and the life of the American people, many newspapers and other periodicals have added so-called "science editors" to their staffs. These editors and writers—many of them highly qualified in their fields—are knocking on the doors of industry for stories which cannot be released due to government restraints.

The situation is similar to that faced when a securities analyst asks a financial PR man for certain facts and details about the plans or prospects of his company. See Chapter 22, Section 26. In both cases the PR man is faced with intelligent, reasonable and warranted inquiries. In both cases, the PR man usually has a "good story" to tell. Yet, for purely legal reasons, he cannot always give even general answers to the inquiries.

This dilemma shows no signs of being eased in the immediate future. Efforts have been made—through the Moss Committee and other channels—to declassify much of this material. These efforts have not been too successful.

The PR man has no overall objection to such secrecy when it is necessary to national security. The complaint is with the overly assiduous application of a basically sound but mishandled policy. There seems to be a built-in disinclination to apply such censorship on a selective basis. It is here that the trouble lies.

16. Media.

The censorship function of the media is well known to every PR man. There can be no question about the right of the editor to cut a release or refuse to use it at all, viewing its news value from his side of the desk. This is clearly prepublication censorship.

Actually, it is part of the same freedom of the press which is so basic to our communications structure. It applies to the advertising columns as well as the news and editorial columns of the press. This right to refuse business communications is discussed in Sections 19 to 25 below.

17. Public and Community Opinion.

In the long run, the most important source of censorship may well be the public at large. Private citizens, either as individuals or as organized sub-publics, have learned to make their wishes, demands and criticism clear to business. In the extreme case, it may be an organized boycott. It may be simply a ground swell of refusal to patronize or buy.

More commonly this public attitude or criticism may be in the form of letters to the editor, to the company president or to Congressmen and agency administrators. It may be a formal resolution from a church group, a women's club or an American Legion post.

Under the pressures of the consumer protection drive of the 1960s these communications have multiplied. Washington—from the President down —is urging the housewife to "write your Congressman." See Chapter 19, Section 25. Whatever the channel or the vehicle of communication, the thrust and threat of the criticism are usually clear and, in most cases, effective.

Largely through enlightened public relations—together with the results of its "two-way" concept—business has become quite sensitive to such public criticism. In this arena, as in the marketplace itself, business today reacts to the doctrine of *caveat venditor*. The result is change in company programs and communications, even as to those which originally may have been sincerely believed proper.

Much of this "unofficial" censorship deals with the indeterminate complex of "good taste" which is normally beyond the jurisdiction of government censorship. As far as the PR man is concerned, errors in this area are likely to be inadvertent. The playback, however, may be no less disastrous.

18. Self-Censorship.

The internal soul-searching by business about its various functions, including communications, has produced substantial self-censorship. There is no question that over the years business has become more and more aware of its public obligations. It has also become more aware of the importance of public attitudes and reactions. The result has been a great deal of self-censorship. The task of government and the community would be impossible in this area without the screening effect of self-censorship. See Chapter 20 generally.

Every code of ethics, every set of "standards" enunciated by the public relations industry is all directed toward this end. The screening of the public relations and publicity activities for truthfulness, factual information, good taste, etc. is censorship of the most salutary kind. It is censorship at the source, the point at which the built-in multipliers of communications results are most effective.

D. MEDIA AND BUSINESS COMMUNICATIONS.

19. Basic Right of Media.

Under its constitutional protection, the press is the arbiter of its own content. This applies to its news or editorial columns and to its advertising space. At the same time it may be subsequently held liable for its derelictions in doing so. This liability may be litigated in a libel, antitrust, right of privacy, copyright or other action.

This right is both affirmative and negative. Its positive indications are seen in the right to print what it will and for whatever reason it will. Negatively, it is apparent from the right to reject news or advertising according to its own conscience or policy. There is, generally speaking, little that government or business can do about this selectivity.

Various aspects and implications of this almost autocratic power are discussed in Sections 20 to 25 below.

20. News Releases and Advertising.

One of the major differences between the news release and the paid advertisement is the control which the company has over its use. The newspaper or the broadcast medium may censor both but in a vastly different manner. The difference is premised upon the fact that the advertisement is paid for; the release is not.

The PR practitioner often complains of the treatment accorded his release even when it is used. The editor can cut, rearrange, mangle or otherwise distort it. The wrong headline on the story may give the "reader who reads and runs" a completely incorrect idea of the story. All of this assumes that the editor has no personal prejudice about the subject or source of the release. It also ignores matters of position, timing and other questions of editorial judgment.

On the other hand, if an advertisement is involved, it appears precisely in the manner in which it was submitted. Of course, there is no legal requirement that the newspaper accept the advertisement at all. See Sections 23 to 25 below. If, however, the advertisement does run, it runs as it was intended to appear, without changes.

The newspaper may see fit not to accept the advertisement. This is its privilege. It may require it to be changed but the final control over such changes is in the advertiser. He has the correlative privilege of meeting the media's demands for revision or withdrawing the advertising completely. This privilege does not exist with the news release.

The newspaper may reject the news release completely. In most instances this happens. Studies show that from sixty to eighty percent of releases coming to newspapers are rejected.[67]

Among the reasons for rejection in one such study are the following: [68]

> Limited local interest,
> No reader interest at all,
> Story poorly written,
> Reasons of policy,
> Disguised advertising,
> Material obviously faked,
> Apparent inaccuracy of story,
> Duplication of release,
> Material stretched too thin.

Criticism of publicity releases was again studied in 1967. In a symposium on "Public Relations and the Media," the second most objectionable practice, according to members of the press, was "misleading angles." [69]

Some reasons stem from the medium's integrity and the protection of the public from inaccuracies. Others are mere matters of judgment or taste. Some may be the effect of deliberate and adverse policy. Nearly every newspaper is said to have a "black list."

But whatever the reason for the rejection of the release, every such rejection—even if due only to space limitations—is another example of some degree of censorship. This is not to say that such censorship is necessarily improper or evil. Yet it is censorship.

21. Treatment of Corporate News.

Quite apart from editorial handling of company-originated news releases, many PR problems may arise as a result of media's handling of corporate news which does not so originate. This may occur in connection with news reporting of such matters as government hearings, product quality litigation, labor negotiations and strikes, financial information, some "human interest" aspect of corporate operations, awards of contracts or anything else in the corporate spectrum. Feature stories, developed by the medium on its own, may also present similar problems.

The company has no control over such reporting except, perhaps, through the development of editorial understanding through a continued program of good press relations. Some recourse lies in the "letter to the editor" technique.

Statutes against even outright lying and scandal-mongering have been held unconstitutional.[70] Legal actions against the medium may be possible but are not likely to be effective in a practical sense.

In such cases the "right of reply" is probably the most effective approach as discussed in Section 22 below.

22. Right of Reply.

Responsible newspapers will ordinarily permit a right of reply by those adversely mentioned in their columns. Many papers even seek out such statements, going to considerable effort in some cases, so that the reply accompanies the original news.[71] Other media are less scrupulous about such replies. Some seem deliberately to manage the situation so as to prevent a reply or "bury" it in some later issue.

A compulsory and legally enforceable right of reply is not at all common in this country. It is quite different from statutes dealing with retractions in libel cases.[72] Retractions are not made compulsory and usually only go to mitigate damages in some degree if suit should later be brought.

This right of reply is well-recognized in French law (*droit de réponses*) and in German law (*Berichtigung*). In both legal systems, the person referred to in a news item has an absolute reply privilege in *that* publication subject to certain specific but relatively limited restrictions or exceptions.[73] However, in both England and the United States such right has not been given much recognition. In 1911 Nevada adopted such a statute [74] but its sister states have been very slow to follow suit. Only Mississippi has done so.[75]

While a right of reply has certain disadvantages, Chafee points out that it "has been shown to be the best new remedy for misstatements in the press." Writing in 1947, he felt that "it was too early to make a positive recommendation that the right of reply be established by law." However, the Commission on the Freedom of the Press unanimously believed that "[t]he right of reply should be carefully considered in the near future." [76]

The right of reply situation is different when we deal with the broadcast media. Under the fairness doctrine enforced by the FCC, a broadcaster is required to give notice to the person concerned and to permit a reply on his behalf. See Section 12 above.

23. Right to Refuse Advertising.

Closely akin to the newspaper's right to refuse to print a corporate news release or to cover some corporate activity is its right to refuse to accept paid advertising.

Generally speaking, a newspaper has the right, without liability, to refuse advertising. [77]

In other words, freedom of the press—the right to pick and choose its own contents—applies to advertising columns as much as it does to news or editorial columns.

The reason is that the newspaper is not a public utility or a hotel which must accept all customers or guests provided only that it has sufficient facilities to do so—in the case of a newspaper, sufficient unused space in which the advertising might run. The newspaper is generally held to be a private enterprise and, as such, may deal with such customers as it wishes—provided only that it does not reject a particular customer or his advertising for an otherwise illegal reason. See Section 25 below.

In *Shuck v. Carroll Daily Herald*,[78] the leading case on this subject, the court discussed the history of newspapers and their functions and dealt at great length with their relation to public utilities, public carriers, inns and hotels which are required to accept all comers. The court summed up its position in these words:

> The newspaper business is an ordinary business. It is a business essentially private in nature—as private as that of the baker, grocer or milkman, all of which perform a service on which, to a greater or less extent, the communities depend, but which bears no such relation to the public as to warrant its inclusion in the category of business charged with public use. If a newspaper were required to accept an advertisement, it could be compelled to publish a news item. . . .
>
> To us, as a newspaper is a strictly private enterprise, the publishers thereof have a right to publish whatever advertisements they desire and to refuse to publish whatever advertisements they do not wish to publish.

This rule has been frequently attacked by disgruntled advertisers but it appears that only one Ohio lower court case is contrary to the general rule.[79] This case has been widely and severely criticized and is without question the minority rule—not even followed by other courts in Ohio.[80]

24. Refusal of Deceptive Advertising.

Since a newspaper has the right to refuse any advertising, it follows that it may also refuse advertising which is false and deceptive or which is so considered by the newspaper. Normally the newspaper need give no reason at all for its refusal. Certainly a belief, even if incorrect, that the proffered advertising is deceptive—therefore illegal under the FTC Act or a state law—is a legitimate reason.

A further question may arise: *must* the newspaper refuse deceptive advertising? There does not seem to be any clear holding on this matter. However, in the *Rochester Times-Union* case,[81] a New York court posited such a duty to exist.

It would seem that the courts should not force such an obligation upon the press. This would be an unsupportable burden and would require every paper to undertake its own investigations, printing advertisements at its peril. This seems to be the position of the FTC which, so far as we are aware, has never cited a newspaper in a false advertising case.

However, the FTC has expressed its views on the *right* of a newspaper to refuse deceptive advertising, saying that it does have such a right, particularly when the newspaper is in "open competition with other newspapers in the same area, is acting in accord with the exercise of its own independent judgment and not in concert with others to reject the particular advertisement." [82]

In *Clegg v. New York Newspaper Union,*[83] decided in 1887, the court held it proper for defendant newspaper *association* to refuse advertising from the plaintiff, an "advertising agent," obtained by the plaintiff in violation of the association's rules. This case would probably be decided differently today in view of the concerted action by members of the association in the face of current antitrust law interpretation.

On the other hand, a radio or TV station probably does have a duty to refuse deceptive advertising, especially if it is known to be false.

Typical of a station's responsibility to investigate the advertising submitted to it, and its penalty for a failure to do so, is the WMPS case.[84] Radio station WMPS filed an application for a television channel in Memphis in competition with station WREC. The former's application was refused because the station had accepted what was described in the ruling as "bait and switch" advertising. The decision points out:

> Acceptance in good faith of all advertising offered unaccompanied by an investigation into the practices of the advertiser is an avoidance of the proper responsibility of the broadcaster to its listeners. . . . Had more care been exercised by the WMPS management it would have been informed of the undesirability of such advertising and have eliminated it from its programs.

Also, the FCC has advised licensees that they are responsible for familiarity with the actions of the FTC in false and deceptive advertising cases.[85]

25. Refusal of Advertising and the Antitrust Laws.

A newspaper may not refuse advertising if such refusal is actually a subterfuge to create a monopoly. This was clearly announced by the Supreme Court in *Lorain Journal v. United States*.[86]

The record indicated that the Lorain *Journal* enjoyed a "substantial monopoly" on advertising in Lorain, Ohio. A new radio station (WEOL) was started in the area. It immediately found difficulty in selling advertising time to local merchants because the *Journal* refused to accept advertising from any merchant who also purchased time on WEOL. Since the *Journal* reached 99% of the families in the area, this threat by the newspaper was effective inasmuch as the local advertisers needed the *Journal* for proper coverage of the community. The Supreme Court described the *Journal's* activity as "bold, relentless and predatory commercial behavior" and said "it was undertaken to destroy the broadcasting company." The court found that the newspaper's policy imperiled "the very existence" of the station.

The Supreme Court affirmed the issuance of an injunction against continuance of such activities. The language of the Supreme Court as to a newspaper's rights in this context is enlightening:

> The publisher claims a right as a private business concern to select its customers and to refuse to accept advertisements from whomever it pleases. We do not dispute that general right . . . The right claimed by the publisher is neither absolute nor exempt from regulation. Its exercise as a purposeful means of monopolizing interstate commerce is prohibited by the Sherman Act. The operator of the radio station, equally with the publisher, is entitled to the protection of that Act. "In the absence of any purpose to create or maintain a monopoly, the Act does not restrict the long recognized right of trader or manufacturer engaged in an entirely private business, freely to exercise his own independent discretion as to parties with whom he will deal [citing cases]."

In 1967 the Federal Trade Commission had approved a newspaper's right to refuse advertising but had made it clear that its opinion is based upon "the fact that the newspaper, which is in open competition with other newspapers in the same area, is acting in accord with the exercise of its own independent judgment and not in concert with others in proposing to reject the particular advertisement." [87] While this opinion was issued under Section 5 of the Federal Trade Commission Act relating to unfair trade practices, it is quite consonant with the holding of the Supreme Court in the *Lorain Journal* case, decided under the Sherman Act.

Undoubtedly, one of the key questions to be faced in cases of this sort is whether the refusal is a result of individual decision or of group action by all media—or part of them—in a given area. This raises interesting questions—as yet apparently unsettled—as to the anticipated legal results should it be proved that the newspapers and broadcast outlets in a given community or area agreed not to accept and publish news releases from a particular company.

This may seem, at first glance, to be a rather unlikely possibility. Newspapers generally compete actively with each other and with their broadcast competition for the news—perhaps the traditional word "scoop" is applicable in this context. However, "blackouts" of news emanating from a given corporate source have been observed from time to time. There has been no evidence that this was a matter of conspiracy or concert on the part of the news media but certain inferences seem to follow from the facts. Also, a refusal to carry such stories by even one newspaper raises certain antitrust questions when the newspaper is the only medium in a given community. With the decline in the number of daily newspapers, this question becomes more evident.

E. OBSCENITY.

26. Public Relations and Obscenity.

At first glance, it may seem that questions of obscenity are alien to the concern of the PR man. Yet it is impinging more and more on his activities.

(a) The Supreme Court now premises its opinions on the publicity and promotional aspects of the distribution of allegedly obscene materials. Since the *Ginzburg* decision of 1966 and its "pandering" approach, this has become more important—possibly even in connection with communications materials or products which would not ordinarily seem within the obscenity context. See Section 29 below.

(b) Some of the activities of the local and state anti-obscenity groups have involved types of public relations activities which have been judicially criticized. These include letter-writing campaigns addressed to judges, "packing" of courtrooms, etc.[88]

Such activities may be used by the PR man—especially in serving community or civic groups. They tie in with matters such as "lobbying" and various institutional types of appeals to government or judicial arbiters. See Chapter 23, Sections 3, 4, and 16.

(c) In the *Roth* case, one question raised as a defense was the use by postal inspectors of aliases on the defendant's mailing lists in order to follow his activities. The Supreme Court "summarily disposed" of this defense, thus validating such activities by representatives of government. It is known that this practice is fairly common with many federal agencies as sources of information upon which to premise later government action. See Section 14 (b) above.

(d) Probably the most important of all influences of the "obscenity picture" in the PR context is the guidance to be derived from the public reaction to the liberalization of the law as it has come to be currently interpreted. The Supreme Court may well be reflecting the permissive character of our current culture and the "supremacy of the individual." These are reactions not without considerable importance to the PR practitioner. In other words, the PR function is as interested as the Supreme Court in what the court calls "contemporary community standards."

27. Changing and Obscure Nature of Obscenity Concept.

The major thrust of censorship, for at least the last hundred years, has been in the area of obscenity. Generally speaking, the repressive character of this branch of censorship has gradually diminished and been diluted as time passed until, today, there are those who ask whether anything is obscene. However, the present obscenity doctrine of the Supreme Court is probably best delineated against the changing background of this continuing censorship battle.[89]

To a considerable degree attitudes about obscenity in literature generally have been paralleled by attitudes toward sex as used in commercial communications although the Supreme Court has said that sex and obscenity are not synonymous.[90]

Many books or pictures which would undoubtedly have been censored as "obscene" 50—even 20—years ago now escape such a label—perhaps being merely considered as examples of "poor taste." Even such a description may depend upon the context or occasion involved. We need only look at our advertising in the print media and, to a lesser degree, in our broadcast media, to realize that the same thing has happened in this area.

Advertisements which even a "barbershop publication" would not have carried in the past are today accepted by some of our general media. Furthermore, they produce only limited objections from the public. It would seem that the posture of the media has followed that of the readership they serve.

The emphasis of the Supreme Court in *Roth*—discussed in Section 28 below—and other cases upon the application of "contemporary community standards" in obscenity-screening is probably a strong reason for the changing judicial attitudes about obscenity as applied to specific pieces or types of literature. As community "tastes" change, so, too, do judicial thresholds of condemnation.

One thing is certain: obscenity is today a confused legal and sociological area. It is, as Chafee called it, "the most perplexing" of all mass communications subjects, adding: [91]

> If we . . . think only of publications which disturb the community, obscenity is the type of objectionable material as to which there is the strongest support for some kind of suppression. Almost everybody agrees that some line ought to be drawn which will shut out a considerable amount of indecency. And yet there are wide differences of opinion about the proper location of this line.

Writing in 1947 of "some line which ought to be drawn," Chafee perhaps intuitively but cautiously foresaw the extent to which the Supreme Court would eventually go in its obscenity decisions. Under the impact of the *Roth* test, discussed in Section 28 below, it has been suggested that the only material likely to be held as obscene is so-called "hard-core pornography." [92] This does seem to be the only aspect of obscenity about which the several justices of the Supreme Court do agree.[93]

Aside from this minimum factor, the judicial lack of agreement referred to below promises to be an important chapter in our obscenity legal primer.[94] The Supreme Court is unable to agree on a theoretical definition of obscenity and its application to specific cases. For example, in the 1959 *Lady Chatterley's Lover* case,[95] the Supreme Court was *unanimous* in holding the book not to be obscene, but it required *six* opinions to express the several views of the nine justices. In *Ginzburg*, decided in 1966, it required *five* opinions with each of the four dissenting justices writing separate opinions. See Section 29 below.

28. Obscenity Definitions and Tests.

In the landmark English case of *Regina v. Hicklin*,[96] we find the first clearly enunciated test of obscenity:

[W]hether the tendency of the matter charged as obscenity is to deprave and corrupt those whose minds are open to such immoral influences and into whose hands a publication of this sort may fall.

Material was thus considered obscene if it might corrupt only an abnormal mind—one "open to such immoral influences"—even though it would not have that effect on a normal mind or the public generally. This came to be called "the most susceptible person test." As late as 1951 an American court applied this rule.[97]

However, most American courts, even before 1951, had adopted a less restrictive definition. Obscenity, as stated by Judge Woolsey in the leading *Ulysses* case,[98] came to mean "tending to stir the sex impulses or to lead to sexually impure and lustful thoughts [of a] person with average sex instincts. . . ." These cases therefore postulated the "reasonable man" doctrine. As Judge Woolsey pointed out:

Whether a particular book would tend to incite such impulses and thoughts must be tested by the court's opinion as to its effect upon a person with average sex instincts—what the French would call *l'homme moyen sensuel*—who plays, in this branch of legal inquiry, the same role of hypothetical reagent as does the "reasonable man" in the law of torts and the man "learned in the art" on questions of invention in patent law.

With the adoption of the "reasonable man" test, the judicial doors began to open. This approach gave the courts broader scope in appraising possible obscenity. Dissents became more frequent at appellate level.

In 1957 the Supreme Court decided five cases: *Butler, Roth, Alberts, Kingsley Books* and *Adams Theater*,[99] which have had a permanent effect upon censorship of obscenity. Of these *Roth* is pre-eminent, being the source of the so-called "Roth test" of obscenity:

Whether to the average person, applying contemporary community standards, the dominant theme of the material taken as a whole, appeals to the prurient interest.

Roth also held squarely for the first time that obscenity is not a constitutionally protected form of speech because it is "utterly without redeeming social importance." [100] This latter phrase was to become part of the Roth test itself in later cases.

Roth was widely interpreted as setting up only two—not three—requirements for obscenity-screening: (a) the material must be judged as a whole and (b) it must be judged by its impact on average persons, not the weak and the susceptible, the test under the old *Hicklin* case.[101]

However, by 1966 when the Court decided the *Fanny Hill* case, discussed below, a third factor had been added to these two requirements: that the material be utterly without redeeming social importance.

Butler, involving a Michigan statute forbidding the sale to *adults* of books tending to incite *minors* to depravity or to corrupt their morals, gave us Justice Frankfurter's widely-quoted admonition not "to burn the house to roast the pig" in censorship and obscenity cases.

In the 1966 *Fanny Hill* case [102] the definition of obscenity in the *Roth* case was restated by the Supreme Court:

> Under this definition, as elaborated in subsequent cases, three elements must coalesce: it must be established that (a) the dominant theme of the material *taken as a whole appeals to a prurient interest in sex;* (b) the material is patently offensive because it *affronts contemporary community standards* relating to the description or representation of sexual matters; and (c) the material *is utterly without redeeming social value.* (Emphasis added.)

Utter lack of redeeming social value has now been added as a third necessary factor in the Roth test. In *Roth* itself, this language had been used only as a *reason* for denying constitutional protection to obscenity—not as a prerequisite *element* to the finding of obscenity. The Court's language was criticized for this reason in the separate dissents of Justices Clark and White. Also, in his dissent to *Ginzburg,* announced the same day, Justice Black considered this third element "[A]s uncertain, if not more uncertain, than is the unknown substance of the Milky Way."

It would seem clear that the Roth test has been expanded from its original reading. This additional element is probably responsible for the belief that proscribed obscenity has now been whittled down to almost nothing, except for hard core pornography and, perhaps, a more permissive court attitude toward restrictive statutes addressed to protection of minors. See Section 30 below.

The Supreme Court reversed the Massachusetts court and held that the book was not obscene because it had some redeeming social value, going on to associate its holding with that in *Ginzburg,* decided the same day. It pointed out that its ruling might well be different if the "circumstances of production, sale and *publicity"* (emphasis added) were such as to indicate that the book was "commercially exploited for the sake of prurient appeal, to the exclusion of all other values, . . ." Inasmuch as there was no evidence of such exploitation, the court did not go further into that aspect of the matter.

29. "Pandering" as an Obscenity Factor.

In the 1966 *Ginzburg* case [103]—one of the most celebrated obscenity cases since World War II—the Supreme Court pinpointed a new dimension in the law of obscenity. The Court went beyond the substance of the publications involved and, to sustain a violation of the postal obscenity statute, relied to a great extent on the salacious promotional methods of the publisher.

The Court appears to have proceeded on the assumption that "the publications themselves might not be obscene" but premised its approval of defendant's conviction upon the "defendant's conduct." The Court went on to say:

> We perceive no threat to First Amendment guarantees in thus holding that in close cases evidence of pandering may be probative with respect to the nature of the material in question and thus satisfy the Roth test.

* * * *

> . . . the fact that each of these publications was created or exploited entirely on the basis of its appeal to prurient interests strengthens the conclusion that the transactions here were sales of illicit merchandise, not sales of constitutionally protected matter.

* * * *

> . . . questionable publications are obscene in a context which brands them as obscene as that term is defined in Roth—a use inconsistent with any claim to the shelter of the First Amendment.

* * * *

> Where an exploitation of interests in titillation by pornography is shown with respect to material lending itself to such exploitation through pervasive treatment or description of sexual matters, such evidence may support the determination that the material is obscene, even though in other contexts the material would escape such condemnation.

This circumambient approach to obscenity is not entirely new. Chief Justice Warren, in his concurring opinion in *Roth*, had said: [104]

> The nature of the material is, of course, relevant as an attribute of the defendant's conduct, but the materials are thus placed in context from which they draw color and character. A wholly different result might be reached in a different setting.

The Court also relied upon the 1940 opinion of Learned Hand in the *Rebhuhn* case [105] in which the book was not hard core pornography and admittedly had a scientific purpose. However, it was advertised by a random, direct mail campaign—not confined to anthropologists, psychologists, sociologists or others having a legitimate interest therein. The Court upheld a conviction because "the circulars were no more than an

appeal to the salaciously disposed, . . . It was [the] misuse which constituted the gravamen of the crime."

Ginzburg really seems to boil down to one thing: all claims of social
value mean little if the publisher himself publicizes and promotes his
books as obscene publications. As the Court said, it "could accept his
valuation at its face value" if the purveyor's sole emphasis "is on the
sexually provocative aspects of his publications, . . ."

The real importance of *Ginzburg* may lie in the apparent willingness
of at least the majority of the Supreme Court to adopt the "variable
obscenity" concept discussed in Section 30 below. This would represent a
departure for the Court and possibly open the way to the solution of
problems which have heretofore led to continued confusion.[106]

30. Variable Obscenity.

The "pandering" factor relied upon in *Ginzburg* and *Mishkin* is part
of a larger and increasingly more important concept: variable obscenity.
Variable obscenity assumes that obscenity is not an inherent, absolute
and unchanging characteristic of a book or picture. Rather, legal obscenity or non-obscenity depends upon the audience to which it is directed
and the means of its promotion.[107] Thus, as in the *Kinsey* case,[108] even
hard core pornography directed solely to the social scientist for professional use is not considered obscene or objectionable. It also hits at the
panderer who may "pornographically" promote non-pornographic materials as though they were really pornographic.

Variable obscenity is also the genesis of the growing Supreme Court
inclination toward appraising obscenity in the adolescent frame of reference with a more relaxed attitude toward statutes controlling or prohibiting sales thereof to minors.

In the 1964 Ohio film censorship case involving "The Lovers," [109] the
Supreme Court said that the states would be better off to enact obscenity
statutes "aimed specifically at preventing distribution of objectionable
material to children, rather than at totally prohibiting its dissemination." The same intimation appeared in several cases decided in 1967.[110]
Assuming that these minor-oriented laws are not defective because of
vagueness, they may be destined for Supreme Court approval generally.

This relatively new judicial posture is indicative of an overall "variable obscenity" theory. The books are held obscene insofar as minors are
concerned but not as to adults. No single obscenity badge is hung on a
given work: much depends upon the public (minors or adults) to which
the work is directed or sold.

31. Federal Obscenity Statutes.

Federal controls of obscenity are found in §§1461-4 of the Federal Criminal Code.[111] These four sections concern respectively the use of the mails, imports into the United States or shipments between the several states, indecent displays on otherwise mailable envelopes or wrappers, and radio and TV broadcasting—all, of course, in connection with obscene matter.

All four sections are essentially similar, deriving from the basic mail section (§1461). Aside from provisions as to mailability of abortion or contraceptive devices and information—with which we are not here concerned—the pertinent portions of the mail section are:

> Every obscene, lewd, lascivious, indecent, filthy or vile article, matter, thing, device, or substance; and—
>
> *   *   *   *
>
> Every written or printed card, letter, circular, book, pamphlet, advertisement, or notice of any kind giving information, directly or indirectly, where, or how, or from whom, or by what means of such mentioned matters . . . may be obtained . . .
>
> Is declared to be nonmailable matter and shall not be conveyed in the mails or delivered from any post office or by any letter carrier.
>
> Whoever knowingly uses the mails for the mailing, carriage in the mails, or delivery of anything declared by this section to be nonmailable . . . shall be fined not more than $5000 or imprisoned not more than five years, or both, for the first such offense . . .

The radio section adds "profane" matter as among prohibited materials.

As with so many statutes, these sections do not define the terms which they use. Generally, they are construed in accordance with the common law meaning of the terms.[112] In the obscenity arena, the terms have received long and continued judicial attention and interpretation in both their theoretical and practical aspects, among them being those discussed in Sections 27 to 30 above.

There is also a cross-pollination between these various obscenity sections. Thus the *Ulysses* decision [113] involving the importation of a book is equated in precedential value with decisions such as *Roth* [114] involving use of the mails. In other words, "obscenity is obscenity," no matter what the context, and while the definition of obscenity has changed over the years—see Sections 27 and 28 above—the application of the then current definition is operationally similar regardless of context or the relevant section of the Code.

32. State Obscenity Statutes.

State obscenity statutes are presently in something of a state of flux, changing in cycles as new Supreme Court pronouncements appear. This is particularly true as to laws directed at sales to minors and bookseller liability.

Indicative was the reaction to the *Butler*[115] decision. In February, 1957 this held unduly restrictive a Michigan statute proscribing sales to *adults* of books unsuitable for *minors*. Within four months Michigan substituted a new statute.[116] Florida amended its obscenity statute only a few days after Michigan.[117] Two months later Maine fell in line, altering its applicable statute.[118] Later, after the courts had invalidated their Butler-type statutes, Rhode Island[119] and Virginia[120] changed their laws.

On the other hand, the other Butler-type states did not amend their laws to bring them into conformity with the Supreme Court holding. These are Iowa, South Carolina, Texas, Utah, Vermont and West Virginia.[121]

Not unmindful of Supreme Court comments about possible propriety of statutes directed to protection of minors from pornography,[122] states are now exploring the use of such statutes.[123]

Notes

1. Schneider v. Irvington, 308 U.S. 147, 161 (1939).
2. Roth v. United States, 354 U.S. 476 (1957); Marsh v. Alabama, 326 U.S. 501 (1946).
3. Roth v. United States, *supra* note 2, at 484.
4. Lamont v. Postmaster General, 381 U.S. 301 (1965); Freedman v. Maryland, 380 U.S. 51 (1965); Bantam Books, Inc. v. Sullivan, 372 U.S. 58 (1963); Smith v. California, 361 U.S. 147 (1959); Murdock v. Pennsylvania, 319 U.S. 105 (1943); Marin v. Struthers, 319 U.S. 141 (1943); Lovell v. Griffin, 303 U.S. 444 (1938); Grosjean v. American Press Co., 297 U.S. 233 (1936).
5. Stromberg v. California, 283 U.S. 359 (1931).
6. Adderley v. Florida, 385 U.S. 39 (1966); Sheppard v. Maxwell, 384 U.S. 333 (1966); United States v. Harriss, 347 U.S. 612 (1954); Breard v. Alexandria, 341 U.S. 622 (1951); Communications Ass'n v. Douds, 399 U.S. 382 (1950); Teamsters Union v. Hanke, 339 U.S. 470 (1950); Kovacs v. Cooper, 336 U.S. 77 (1949); Prince v. Massachusetts, 321 U.S. 158 (1944); Labor Board v. Virginia Power Co., 314 U.S. 469 (1941); Schenk v. United States, 249 U. S. 47 (1919).
7. Cox v. Louisiana, 379 U.S. 559 (1965); Kovacs v. Cooper, *supra* note 6; Cox v. New Hampshire, 312 U.S. 569 (1941); Whitney v. California, 274 U.S. 357 (1927).
8. Edwards v. South Carolina, 372 U.S. 229 (1963); Grosjean v. American Press Co., *supra* note 4; Adderley v. Florida, *supra* note 6.
9. Kevishian v. Board of Regents, 385 U.S. 589 (1967); Joseph Burstyn, Inc. v. Wilson, 343 U.S. 495 (1952); Niemotko v. Maryland, 340 U.S. 268 (1951); Terminiello v. Chicago, 337 U.S. 1 (1949); Cantwell v. Connecticut, 310 U.S. 296 (1940).
10. Associated Press v. United States, 326 U.S. 195 (1945); Associated Press v. Labor Board, 301 U.S. 103 (1937); United States v. Times-Picayune Publishing Co., 345 U.S. 594 (1953); Lorain Journal Co. v. United States, 342 U.S. 143 (1951); Indiana Farmer's Guide Publishing Co. v. Prairie Farmer Publishing Co., 293 U.S. 268 (1934).
11. Lovell v. Griffin, 303 U. S. 444 (1938).
12. Cammarano v. United States, 358 U.S. 498, 513–15 (1959) (concurring opinion of Douglas, J.).
13. Joseph Burstyn, Inc. v. Wilson, *supra* note 9; Superior Films v. Department of Educ., 346 U.S. 587 (1954).
14. Bantam Books, Inc. v. Sullivan, *supra* note 4; Joseph Burstyn, Inc. v. Wilson, *supra* note 9.
15. Eastern R.R. Pres. Conf. v. Noerr Motor Freight, Inc., 115 F. Supp. 768 (E.D. Pa. 1957), *aff'd*, 273 F.2d 218 (3d Cir. 1959), *rev'd*, 365 U.S. 127 (1961).

16. Cammarano v. United States, *supra* note 12; Strauss v. United States, 358 U.S. 493 (1959).

17. Kovacs v. Cooper, *supra* note 6.

18. Cox v. New Hampshire, *supra* note 7.

19. See cases cited, *supra* note 10.

20. See 5 ENCYCLOPÆDIA BRITANNICA 660–61 (11th ed. 1910) from which a portion of this section is drawn.

21. See remarks of Judge Curtis Bok, *Censorship and the Arts*, at Swarthmore College under the auspices of the Cooper Foundation, March 11, 1951, reprinted in 124 LEGAL INTELLIGENCER 483 (Philadelphia, April 18, 1951).

22. L.R. 3 Q.B. 360 (1868).

23. SIMON, THE LAW FOR ADVERTISING AND MARKETING 328 (1956).

24. For a discussion of this dichotomy, see CHAFEE, GOVERNMENT AND MASS COMMUNICATIONS 69–74 (1947).

25. CUTLIP & CENTER, EFFECTIVE PUBLIC RELATIONS 111–12 (3d ed. 1964).

26. STEINBERG, THE MASS COMMUNICATORS 187 (1958).

27. Author's interview with PR director of company involved; use authorized but without attribution.

28. *Censorship in Rome*, A.A., May 10, 1965, at 16.

29. *CBS V.P. Reveals Net Has Its Woes Toning Down Scripts* (quoting CBS Vice-President Merle Jones), A.A., Nov. 1, 1954, at 28.

30. *Cellu-Craft Uses Unpackaged Model in Series Promoting Package Service*, A.A., Aug. 9, 1954, at 73.

31. A.A., April 20, 1959, at 64, April 27, 1959, at 3, 110.

32. Cammarano v. United States, *supra* note 12; Strauss v. United States, *supra* note 16.

33. Frawley, *Have Right to Guard Repute*, A.A., Nov. 26, 1962, at 3.

34. Minow, *TV Must Fight All Censorship, id.*

35. American Broadcasting-Paramount Pictures, Inc. v. American Mfr. Mut. Ins. Co., 265 N.Y.S.2d 76 (Sup. Ct. 1965).

36. Steinberg, *supra* note 26, at 265. See also *How to Act When Your Company Is Under Fire*, Business Management, July, 1967, at 19.

37. See cases cited, *supra* note 4.

38. Algoma Lumber Co. v. F.T.C., 291 U.S. 67 (1934); F.T.C. v. R. F. Keppel and Bros., Inc., 291 U.S. 304 (1934).

39. Communications Act of 1934, 48 Stat. 1064, §303 *et seq.*, 47 U.S.C. §303 *et seq.*

40. 18 U.S.C. §1464.

41. *Id.* §1304.

42. 47 U.S.C. §326. For an excellent discussion of the legal background, premises and authorities involved in F.C.C. program control and censorship, see Rosenbloom, *Authority of the Federal Communications Commission*, in FREEDOM AND RESPONSIBILITY IN BROADCASTING 96–170 (Coons ed. 1961).

43. F.C.C. Proposes Rule to Foster Competition in Television Program Production and Procurement, F.C.C. Public Notice 65461, Report No. 5466, March 22, 1965.

44. Henry, *"The 50–50 Rule,"* Television Quarterly, Fall, 1965, at 9.

45. KFKB Broadcasting Ass'n, Inc. v. F.R.C., 47 F.2d 670 (D.C. Cir. 1931). For a discussion of this subject generally, see SMEAD, FREEDOM OF SPEECH BY RADIO AND TELEVISION 108–13 (1959); NATIONAL ASS'N OF BROADCASTERS, BROADCASTING AND THE BILL OF RIGHTS 1–79 (1947).

46. *Safety in Numbers,* Sponsor, Oct. 4, 1965, at 11.

47. In the Matter of the Mayflower Broadcasting Corp., 8 F.C.C. 333 (1941).

48. In the Matter of Editorializing by Licensees, Report of the Commission, 1 R.R. 91:201 (1949).

49. *Id.* 91:211.

50. NATIONAL ASS'N OF BROADCASTERS, BROADCASTING THE NEWS 16 (1966).

51. See *Talk Shows Draw Complaints on Bigots,* TV Code News, Vol. 6, No. 8, Aug., 1967, at 1.

52. KFKB Broadcasting Ass'n, Inc., v. F.R.C., *supra* note 45; Young People's Ass'n for Propagation of the Gospel, 6 F.C.C. 178 (1938).

53. *In re* WDKD, 33 F.C.C. 250 (1962), discussed in 47 MINN. L. REV. 465 (1963).

54. Dumont Laboratories, Inc. v. Carroll, 86 F. Supp. 813, *aff'd,* 184 F.2d 153 (1950).

55. Coro, Inc. v. F.T.C., 338 F.2d 149 (1st Cir. 1964), *cert. denied,* 180 U.S. 954 (1965); Carter Products, Inc. v. F.T.C., 323 F.2d 523 (5th Cir. 1963); Clinton Watch Co. v. F.T.C., 291 F.2d 838 (7th Cir. 1961), *cert. denied,* 368 U.S. 952 (1962).

56. Note, *Small Business Before the Federal Trade Commission,* 75 YALE L.J. 487 (1966).

57. See, *e.g.,* orders entered in F.T.C. Dkt. Nos. C-1287, C-1290, C-1291.

58. Wis. Com. of Sec., File No. 3.92, Order Prohibiting Solicitation, issued Aug. 17, 1967.

59. Letter from Food and Drug Administration to author, dated June 16, 1967.

60. Letter to author dated Oct. 28, 1966, *in re* telegram to airframe and engine manufacturers dated Sept. 16, 1966.

61. United States v. Eastern Airlines, 192 F. Supp. 187, 7 Av. L. REP. ¶17,538 (D.C. Fla. 1961).

62. Letter to author dated April 7, 1967.

63. Prohibition of Discrimination at Recreational Facilities at Licensed Hydroelectric Projects, F.P.C. Dkt. No. R-304, Order No. 341, F.P.C. Release No. 14894 (April 19, 1967).

64. Piel, *Science, Censorship and the Public Interest,* P.R.J., July, 1957, at 12.

65. Department of Defense Directive *Information Releases by Manufacturers,* Pub. Info. Sec. Guidance No. 16, Directive No. 5230.3, Jan. 18, 1952.

66. *U.S. Navy Public Affairs Regulations,* Office of Information, NAVSO P-1035, (Rev. 12–65) §F-1001, at 311.

67. For a discussion of various studies indicating the treatment received by news releases, see Cutlip & Center, *supra* note 25, at 288–289.

68. *Id.* at 289.

69. P.R.J., June, 1967, at 6.

70. Near v. Minnesota, 283 U.S. 697 (1931).

71. Chafee, *supra* note 24, at 173–74, note 30.

72. See Morris, *Inadvertent Newspaper Libel and Retraction,* 32 ILL. L. REV. 36 (1937); *Retraction Statutes,* 19 WASH. & LEE L. REV. 239 (1962).

73. For a discussion of such laws see Chafee, *supra* note 24, at 147–160.

74. Nev. Con. Laws, §10506 (Hillyer, 1929).

75. Miss. Code Ann. §3175 (1942).

76. Chafee, *supra* note 24, at 184. See also Barron, *Access to the Press,* 80 HARV. L. REV. 1641 (1967).

77. Mack v. Costello, 32 S.D. 511, 143 N.W. 950 (1913); Philadelphia Record Co. v. Curtis-Martin Newspapers, 305 Pa. 372, 157 Atl. 796 (1931); Com. v. Boston Transcript, 249 Mass. 477, 144 N.E. 400, 35 A.L.R. 1 (1924); Friedenburg v. Times Publishing Co., 170 La. 3, 127 So. 345 (1930); *in re* Wohl, 50 F.2d 254 (D.C.Mich. 1931). See generally *Right of Publisher of Newspaper to Refuse Advertising,* 87 A.L.R. 979; *Right to Refuse an Advertisement,* 18 MINN. L. REV. 89 (1933); Gordon v. Worcester Telegram Publishing Co., 177 N.E.2d 586 (Mass. 1961); Sky High Theatre, Inc. v. Gaumer Publishing Co., C.P. Ct., Champaign City, Ohio, No. 22820 (1964) (unreported); Bloss d/b/a Eastown Theatre v. Federated Publications, Inc., Cir. Ct., Calhoun City, Mich., No. 2-279 (1965), *aff'd,* Mich. Ct. App., Div. 3, 145 N.W.2d 800 (1966); Poughkeepsie Buying Serv., Inc. v. Poughkeepsie Newspapers, Inc., 205 Misc. 982 (N.Y. 1954); 3 BOSTON COLL. I. & C.L.J. 522 (1966); 37 NOTRE DAME LAW. 575 (1962).

78. 215 Iowa 247, 247 N.W. 813, 87 A.L.R. 979 (1933).

79. Uhlman v. Sherman, 22 Ohio N.P. (n.s.) 225 (1919). See Ohio Att'y Gen. Op. No. 771, Sept. 26, 1951, criticizing Uhlman case.

80. Sky High Theatre, Inc. v. Gaumer Publishing Co., *supra* note 77.

81. 128 Misc. 673, 219 N.Y.S. 705 (1927).

82. F.T.C. Ad. Op. Dig., No. 93, 4 TRADE REG. REP. ¶17,717 (Oct. 13, 1966).

83. 44 Hun 630 (N.Y. 1887).

84. As reported in A.A., Sept. 6, 1954, at 54.

85. Licensee Responsibility with Respect to the Broadcast of False, Misleading or Deceptive Advertising, F.C.C. 61–1316, Nov. 7, 1961.

86. 342 U.S. 143 (1951).

87. F.T.C. Ad. Op. Dig., No. 93, *supra* note 82.

88. Lockhart & McClure, *infra* note 89, at 10 and note 28.

89. Probably the best legal sources and discussions of obscenity are those of Dean William B. Lockhart and Professor Robert C. McClure, referred to by Mr. Justice Douglas in *Roth v. United States* as the "outstanding authorities on obscenity." Therefore, see Lockhart & McClure, *Literature, The Law of Obscenity and the Constitution,* 38 MINN. L. REV. 295 (1954); *Censorship of Obscenity: The Developing Constitutional Standards,* 45 MINN. L. REV. 4 (1960) [referred to *infra* as Lockhart & McClure (1960)]; *Obscenity Censorship: The Core Constitutional Issue—What Is Obscene?* 7 WASH. L. REV. 289 (1961).

90. Roth v. United States, *supra* note 2, at 487.

91. Chafee, *supra* note 24, at 200. For a later (1967) extended and informative discussion of the obscenity problem and relevant Supreme Court divisions, see KUH, FOOLISH FIGLEAVES? PORNOGRAPHY IN—AND OUT OF—COURT (1967).

92. Lockhart & McClure (1960), *supra* note 89, at 58–69. See also People v. Richmond County News, 9 N.Y.2d 578, 175 N.E.2d 681, 216 N.Y.S.2d 369 (1961); Comment, 31 ALBANY L. REV. 143 (1967).

93. Jacobellis v. Ohio, 378 U.S. 184 (1964). For descriptions of hard core pornography, see Ginzburg v. United States, *infra* note 103 (dissenting opinion of Stewart, J.) and Lockhart & McClure (1960), *supra* note 89, at 60–68.

94. This lack of Supreme Court agreement has already produced some pointed comment from state courts. Thus the Pennsylvania Supreme Court, in *Common. v. Dell Publications, Inc.* 427 Pa. 189, 36 L.W. 2219 (1967) held *Candy* not to be legally obscene but based its conclusion on the Court's "simple arithmetic" and the position of the "Black-Douglas-Stewart axis."

95. Kingsley Int'l Pictures Corp. v. Regents of the Univ. of New York, 360 U.S. 684 (1959).

96. Kingsley Int'l Pictures Corp. v. Regents of the Univ. of New York, *supra* note 95.

97. United States v. Two Obscene Books, 90 F. Supp. 760 (D.C. Cal. 1951).

98. United States v. One Book Called Ulysses, 5 F. Supp. 182, *aff'd*, 72 F.2d 705 (2d Cir. 1930).

99. Butler v. Michigan, 352 U.S. 380 (1957); Roth v. United States, *supra* note 2; Alberts v. California, 354 U.S. 476 (1957) (decided with Roth v. United States); Kingsley Books, Inc. v. Brown, 354 U.S. 436 (1957); Adams Newark Theatre Co. v. City of Newark, 354 U.S. 931 (1957).

100. See Doubleday & Co. v. New York, 335 U.S. 848 (1948) in which the question was presented to the Supreme Court but avoided in a 4–4 affirmation without opinion.

101. Lockhart & McClure (1960), *supra* note 89, at 53.

102. One Book Named "John Cleland's Memoirs of a Woman of Pleasure" *et al.*, v. Attorney General of the Commonwealth of Massachusetts, 383 U.S. 413, 34 L.W. 4236 (1966).

103. 383 U.S. 463, 34 L.W. 4255 (1966).

104. *Supra* note 2, at 495.

105. United States v. Rebhuhn, 108 F.2d 512 (2d Cir. 1940). For a discussion of the "pandering" concept of the *Ginzburg* case as a basis for stopping the advertisement of smut through the mails, see Day, *Mailing Lists and Pornography*, 52 A.B.A.J. 1103 (1966). See also United States v. Hornick, 131 F. Supp. 603 (E.D.Pa.), *aff'd*, 229 F.2d 120 (3d Cir. 1956); United States v. Perkins, 286 F.2d 150 (6th Cir. 1961); United States v. Frew, 187 F. Supp. 500 (E.D. Mich. 1960); Poss v. Christenberry, 179 F. Supp. 411 (S.D.N.Y. 1959); Manual Enterprises v. Day, 370 U.S. 478 (1962) (opinion of Harlan, J., and Stewart, J.).

106. See Graham, *Still No Clear View on Obscenity*, N.Y. Times, May 14, 1967, § E, p. 6.

107. Lockhart & McClure (1960), *supra* note 89, at 77–88.

108. United States v. Thirty-one Photographs, 156 F. Supp. 350 (S.D.N.Y. 1957); Comment, 34 IND. L.J. 426 (1959).

109. Jacobellis v. Ohio, 378 U.S. 184 (1964).

110. Redrup v. New York, Austin v. Kentucky, Gent v. Arkansas, 386 U.S. 767, 35 L.W. 4396 (1967) (cases argued and decided together).

111. 18 U.S.C. §§1461–4.

112. Knowles v. United States, 170 Fed. 409 (1909); United States v. Barlow, 56 F. Supp. 793 (D.C. Utah 1944).

113. United States v. One Book Called Ulysses, *supra* note 98.

114. Roth v. United States, *supra* note 2.

115. *Supra* note 99.

116. Mich. Stat. Ann. §28.575 (1) (Supp. 1959). For the history of the statutory reactions by the states, see Lockhart & McClure, *supra* note 89, at 17–18.

117. Fla. Stat. Ann. §847.01 (1944) amended by Fla. Laws 1957, ch. 57–779, §1, at 1103–04.

118. Me. Laws 1957, ch. 321, §1, at 276. See also Me. Rev. Stat. Ann. ch. 134, §24 (Supp. 1959).

119. R.I. Gen. Laws Ann. ch. 86, §1 (Supp. 1959).

120. Va. Code Ann. §§18.1-227–18.1-236.3 (Supp. 1960).

121. Lockhart & McClure (1960), *supra* note 89, at 18.

122. See *supra* note 109 and *supra* text Section 30.

123. See Kuh, *supra* note 91, for a discussion of such statutes.

Chapter 5

Copyright

A. INTRODUCTION

1. Caveat
2. Public Relations and Copyright
3. Copyright/Tangible Property Distinction

B. LITERARY PROPERTY AND COMMON LAW COPYRIGHT

4. Common Law Rights
5. General Publication
6. Limited Publication
7. Continuing Importance of Common Law Rights

C. STATUTORY COPYRIGHT

8. Ownership of Copyright
9. Subject Matter of Copyright
10. Works Not Subject to Copyright
11. Regulations as to Classification of Registrations
12. Errors in Classification
13. Duration of Copyright
14. Protection of Work's Components
15. Originality and Artistic Merit
16. Author's Rights Under Copyright Act
17. Fair Use
18. Business Use and Fair Use
19. Registration as Adjudication of Rights

D. COPYRIGHT PROCEDURES

20. "Published"/"Unpublished" Works Distinction
21. Published Works Checklist
22. The Statutory Notice
23. Form of the Notice

Chapter 5

Copyright

A. INTRODUCTION.

1. Caveat.

As this was written during the first half of 1968, the copyright law was in a state of statutory flux, with a complete revision working its way through Congress. The nature and thrust of the probable changes were reasonably apparent. While important changes are coming, the character of most can now be delineated with some certainty but no final or complete assurance.

Copyright protection in the United States goes back to the Constitution and the Act of 1790. Copyright laws were thereafter enacted in 1831, 1870 and 1909, the latter being currently our basic legislation.[1] References below to the "Act" are intended to refer to this Copyright Act of 1909. Several piecemeal amendments have since been adopted. Attempts at broad and general revision have also been made over the years, stemming largely from the problems and demands created by the technological advances in communications and reproduction methods.

Beginning in 1955 a serious revisionary movement developed with a comprehensive research and study program fostered by Federal funds. In 1961 came the *Report of the Register of Copyright on the General Revision of the U.S. Copyright Law*. In 1964 and 1965 revisions were introduced in Congress but progress was slow. In the 90th Congress—then in session—H. R. 2512 was introduced and was favorably reported by the House Committee on the Judiciary in March, 1967 and thereafter passed the House. The Senate did not act on its own Bill (S. 597) and the final passage of the new law cannot be projected with certainty although it has been knowledgeably described as "tantalizingly close."

Most of the changes may be extrapolated with fair certainty on the basis of the House Report of March, 1967.[2] Some of its provisions were the result of compromise on controversial issues and this controversy may continue in later debate. However the unsettled areas—such as CATV (Cable TV) and record royalties—are not of great general interest to the average company communicator.

This chapter has been written on the basis of the existing law. Appropriate references to H.R. 2512 have been inserted in *brackets* following those Sections below which are likely to be materially affected or changed by the prospective revision. This is hereafter referred to as the *Revision.* If bracketed material does not appear at any point, it may be generally assumed that the *Revision* will merely restate existing law or will not significantly alter it insofar as that Section of the text is concerned.

The reader should hereafter ascertain whether the *Revision* has, in fact, been finally adopted and also the precise language of the final provision with which he may at the moment be concerned. The bracketed material is based essentially on the above 1967 House Report.

The bill provides that at least a year is to be allowed between its enactment and its effective date to allow for the substantive, procedural and administrative changes the new law will bring. During this period after enactment, the present Act will continue in force.

2. Public Relations and Copyright.

The so-called "communications explosion" has created increasing interest in copyright law. Alan Latman, Howell's revisor, writing in 1962 and adverting to changes during the prior 20 years, has said: [3]

> This increase in interest is reflected in law school curricula, legal publications and activities of bar associations and *trade groups.* (Emphasis added.)

This deeper concern is true not only of the creative individual but also of the business community. It is particularly evident among the latter's communicators, whether they be PR practitioners, advertising people or others. This flows initially from the proliferation of existing media and the introduction of significant additional types of media. What Gutenberg initiated, Telstar has multiplied. More than this, however, it is the result of an important change in the nature of the business communication.

What was once a simple assemblage of routine language, prepared by the untrained, has developed into published sophistication and polish, much of it having considerable artistic or literary value and comparable, in some instances, to the best noncommercial effort. We see this in company house organs, company books, advertisements, industrial films, product photography, company manuals and catalogs—even in annual reports. Much of this requires protection—not only because of its cost and prospective future or repeat use—but because of the ever-increasing desire to forestall dilution of its impact through competitive use.

Beyond this, business has entered the literary and artistic marketplace as a *buyer*. A company finds itself dealing frequently with outside sources such as freelance creative people, many of whom now have the prescience to protect themselves through recourse to the copyright laws.

Thus the business communicator—whether as a maker, user or buyer of copyrightable materials—is more and more being drawn into the shifting field of copyright.

This chapter has been developed against this background. What follows is not intended as a complete text on copyright law—there are many such available [4]—but as a description of those areas thereof which are likely to be of concern to the PR practitioner and other company communicators.

3. Copyright/Tangible Property Distinction.

Ownership of the physical property—manuscript, book, painting, etc.—created by an author is distinct from the ownership of the copyright of the work or the common law literary property rights in it. Each is a separate right and may be dealt with separately.

Thus, in the well-known Mark Twain case,[5] an old manuscript of the author was rediscovered. The purchaser sought to publish it. The Clemens heirs were able to prevent such publication. In 1876 Clemens had submitted it to the *Atlantic Monthly* but it was not then or later published. The court held that the common law copyright belonged to the heirs even though the physical manuscript belonged to the purchaser. Furthermore the submission to the magazine had not destroyed the author's rights. See Section 6 below.

Section 2 of the Act recognizes and preserves this distinction.

[*Revision:* Section 202 continues to recognize this distinction. However, this section and sections 204 (a) and 301 *reverse* the presumption that an author transfers his literary property rights when he transfers ownership of the physical work unless he reserves his rights. This is the doctrine of cases such as *Pushman v. N. Y. Graphic Society*,[6] discussed at length in Chapter 9, Section 10. A specific waiver or transfer of such rights would now be required for the sale of the material object to carry with it a transfer of the copyright.]

B. LITERARY PROPERTY AND
COMMON LAW COPYRIGHT.

4. Common Law Rights.

When a person creates a tangible expression of his ideas, he has created "literary property" and acquires a so-called common law copyright in the tangible expression. These rights continue until the creator—the "author"—either dedicates his work to the public domain or surrenders this common law right in exchange for statutory copyright. This latter exchange has been described as "the legendary bargain between the public and the author." [7]

The author need not comply with any formalities to protect his rights in his unpublished efforts. These rights are exclusively his.[8] This right is really a perpetual monopoly which is defeated only by either of the acts referred to above. Section 2 of the Act specifically recognizes these common law rights.

If the author seeks to profit by his efforts, he will normally be required to submit the work to "publication," as discussed in Sections 5 to 7 below. The exact nature of such "publication" will have very material effect upon the author's common law rights.

[*Revision:* See Section 7 below.]

5. General Publication.

"Publication" is a legal word of art in copyright and has caused considerable confusion. It is not necessarily the same as "making public" or distributing the work through some form of multiple reproduction or public offering. Publication may be either general or limited. When used without adjectival modification, the word is generally taken to refer to a general publication.

Publication is not defined in the Act although collaterally referred to therein as "placed on sale, sold or publicly distributed." [9] It is any act by which the author makes the material available to the world [10] or which indicates an intention to surrender the author's rights unless, of course, the statutory procedures are followed.[11]

Certain acts are definitely held to be a general publication: selling the work publicly,[12] distributing it publicly even though no charge is made —this would include "house organs, pamphlets, handbills, and similar matter left on doorsteps or sent through the mails" [13]—distribution of several hundred copies to prospects at a convention,[14] and similar public distributions evidencing an intention to make the work available to the public generally.

A general publication throws the work into the public domain unless the work bears the required notice when so sold or distributed. The early cases of *Donaldson v. Becket* (1774) [15] and *Wheaton v. Peters* (1834) [16] laid down this rule in England and the United States respectively: the common law rights of the author cannot survive a general publication. It may, therefore, be said: there is no second chance in copyright.

This element of forfeiture has led some courts to require evidence of a more unrestricted distribution in cases involving loss of rights ("divestiture") than in cases where the issue is merely a publication to justify copyright protection ("investiture").[17]

[*Revision:* See Section 7 below.]

6. Limited Publication.

A distribution or publication for a specific, limited, restricted or private purpose will not generally be considered a general publication. Such a limited publication does not forfeit the author's rights as discussed in Section 4 above.[18]

Among the recognized forms of limited publication are: delivery of a manuscript to a publisher for possible later purchase and publication; [19] delivery of a lecture even though students are permitted to take notes; [20] the public performance of a play—even to large audiences—provided the play is not printed and copies sold; [21] exhibition of a motion picture in public provided a print thereof is not sold; [22] distribution of several thousand copies of sheet music for purposes of "plugging" only; [23] broadcasting a script over the radio; [24] deposit of copies of the work in the Copyright Office and nothing more.[25]

[*Revision:* See Section 7 below.]

7. Continuing Importance of Common Law Rights.

Overall orientation to compliance with the requirements of the Copyright Act has led some to believe that common law rights are no longer of any value. This is not true. The various situations and transactions described in Section 6 above are all examples of the continued impact of common law rights. Without such concept, many important communications dealings would be impossible or—at best—would necessarily become the subject of extensive preliminary or auxiliary agreements between the parties.

Esoteric though it may appear, the Mark Twain case discussed in Section 3 above is an example of the underlying literary property concept. Set against this episode of the last century are the quite avant garde and presently unsettled copyright ramifications of computers and their future storage of literary and other works. These involve basically the same concept.[26]

> [*Revision:* Considered "one of the bedrock provisions of the bill," common law protection for works coming within the scope of the statute would be abrogated even though they be unpublished. The concept of publication therefore loses "its all-embracing importance as a dividing line between common law and statutory protection and between both of these forms of legal protection and the public domain."
>
> The statute will apply to all works created after its effective date, whether or not they are ever published or disseminated. Works created before such effective date and therefore still under common law protection will be protected from that date on for the same period (life of the author plus 50 years) as a published work.]

C. STATUTORY COPYRIGHT.

8. Ownership of Copyright.

The Act provides that the "author . . . or his executors, administrators or assigns" of a work is entitled to copyright. Foreign authors' rights depend upon the existence of reciprocal international rights under a variety of treaties including the UNESCO Universal Copyright Convention (UCC) which became effective as to the United States in 1955.[27]

> [*Revision:* In place of "all the writing of an author," the phrase "original works of authorship" is used. This is to avoid repetition in the future of past problems of protecting works in new forms of creative expression and to prevent the freezing of protection in the present stage of communications technology.]

Corporations may obtain and own copyrights.[28] Partnerships may be authors and the copyright may be in the trade name used by the partnership.[29]

Under the Act "author" specifically includes an "employer in the case of works made for hire." This covers employees and those who created the work under contract.[30] These rights are essentially similar to those dealt with in the "photograph cases" discussed in Chapter 9, Sections 6 to 8.

Brown v. Mollé [31] is a prime example of this rule. A paid employee of an advertising agency created the well-known jingle and singing commercial used in the promotion of Mollé shaving cream. The employee later copyrighted the jingle in his own name. The court held that the employee had no rights in the material; that the employer (the agency) was the proprietor of the copyright; and that the agency, in turn, held the copyright in trust for its client, the advertiser. As to the latter element, see Chapter 2, Sections 6 and 10 (b) .

9. Subject Matter of Copyright.

The Act protects "all the writings of an author." The term "author" has been construed to go far beyond the accepted literary reference. In the leading case of *Burrow-Giles Litho. Co. v. Sarony*,[32] the Supreme Court held the term to include

> . . . all forms of writing, printing, engraving, etching, etc. by which ideas in the mind of the author are given visible expression.

"Writings" has thus been held to include a wide variety of methods of expression including photographs,[33] motion pictures,[34] applied art including three-dimensional commercial products such as lamp bases,[35] advertisements,[36] circus posters,[37] product photographs,[38] etc. The Copyright Office Rules and Regulations as to classification of copyright registrations—reproduced in Section 11 below—list many other forms of "writings" acceptable for copyright.

10. Works Not Subject to Copyright.

(a) Public Domain Materials.

The "original text" of works or materials in the public domain are not subject to copyright under the Act. However, the Act does protect "compilations or abridgements, adaptations, arrangements, dramatizations, translations, or other versions of works in the public domain." These are considered "new works." Protection as a new work does not imply exclusive rights in the original work now in the public domain and any third party is free to make his own new version thereof.

It is in this context that we have the well-known judicial stricture: [39]

> . . . if by some magic a man who has never known it, were to compose anew Keats's ode on a Grecian Urn, he would be an "author" and, if he copyrighted it, others might not copy that poem although they might, of course, copy Keats's.

(b) Obscene, Blasphemous or Immoral Works.

Works of this character are generally not proper subjects of copyright.[40] The Act does not specifically exclude them. One theory of exclusion is that they do not contribute to "the progress of science and the useful arts" which is the constitutional premise for copyright protection.[41]

The changing concepts of obscenity discussed in Chapter 4, Sections 26 to 32 are very relevant here also and the prohibition has been described as a "fluid concept." [42]

(c) Fraudulent and Misleading Matter.

Just as obscene matter is considered contrary to public policy in this connection, so too will a work, otherwise a proper subject of copyright, be refused protection if it be deceptive or fraudulent.

In *Stone & McCarrick, Inc. v. Dugan Piano Co.*[43] the plaintiff copyrighted layouts and advertising copy for the sale of pianos but the copy was deceptive. When the defendant copied and used the copyrighted material without permission, the court found for the defendant since the law would not protect matter which was a fraud upon the public.

(d) Government Publications.

Copyright may not be obtained on "any publication of the United States Government or any reprint in whole or in part, thereof." This applies to the federal government but not the state governments [44] although this latter rule has been seriously questioned.

This exemption as to government publications includes materials such as reports, circulars, or bulletins prepared and circulated by the government, whether prepared by a government employee or some other person.[45]

Difficult questions may arise when a government employee himself publishes or circulates materials developed by reason of, or relating to, his government work. It is generally held that the individual may copyright such materials provided, as was suggested in the *Rickover* case, that the work was not "commissioned or printed at the cost and direction of the United States." [46]

The Act also provides that the government's use of an author's copyrighted work does not thereby make the work a government publication nor cause the author to lose his copyright. Liability of the government for use of such work involves the doctrine of "sovereign immunity." In 1960 Congress legislatively made the government—but not its employees—liable in such instances.[47]

> [*Revision:* The prohibition against copyright in government publication is expanded to cover any published or unpublished "work of the United States Government" and the term is defined as "a work prepared by an officer or employee of the United States Government as part of his official duties."]

(e) Ideas.

An idea, as such, may not be copyrighted although its literary or pictorial expression may be. This follows from the distinctions discussed in

Chapter 6. Even ideas set forth in an otherwise properly copyrighted book are not protected—merely as ideas.[48] Ideas here include "plans, methods, systems, or devices." [49]

[*Revision:* See Subsection (g) below.]

(f) *Names and Titles.*

As indicated in Subsection (g) below, names and titles of works are non-copyrightable. However, they may be protected under other legal devices or theories.

If a title has become distinctive in the public mind as relating to the work of a specific author, protection will be granted him under the equitable doctrine of unfair competition.[50] In one of the best-known cases, the author of the "Frank Merriwell" books was able to prevent motion picture use of the name.[51] "Information Please" was protected on this theory [52] as was Hemingway's "The Fifth Column." [53]

This right is by no means certain and depends to a large extent on the public identification element. However, unfair competition is an expanding doctrine and unfairness of the use (a "free ride") seems to be now more important than actual competition between the properties of the plaintiff and the defendant. This is essentially the same change in judicial attitude as is expressed in the results of the older and more current "ideas cases" discussed in Chapter 6.

A name or title may sometimes be protected as a trademark, as discussed in Chapter 10, Section 14.

[*Revision:* See Subsection (g) below.]

(g) *Miscellaneous.*

A wide variety of miscellaneous material will not be admitted to copyright. Among them are: [54]

Words and short phrases such as names, titles, and slogans; familiar symbols or designs; mere variations of typographic ornamentation; lettering or coloring; mere listing of ingredients; works designed for recording information which do not in themselves convey information, such as time cards, graph paper, account books, diaries, bank checks, score cards, address books, report forms and the like; works consisting entirely of information that is common property containing no authorship, such as standard calendars, height and weight charts, tape measures and rulers, schedules of sporting events and lists or tables taken from public documents or other common sources.

[*Revision:* These matters are not altered by the proposed bill but the House Report points out: "These are areas of subject matter now on the fringe of literary property but not intended, solely as such, to come within the scope of the bill: typography; unfixed performances or broadcast emissions; blank forms and calculating devices; titles, slogans and similar short expressions; certain three-dimensional designs; interior decoration; ideas, plans, methods, systems, mathematical principles; formats and synopses of television series and the like; color schemes; news and factual information considered apart from its compilation or expression. Many of these kinds of works can be clothed in or combined with copyrightable subject matter and thus achieve a degree of protection for them under the bill, but any protection for them as separate copyrightable works is not here intended and will require action by a future Congress."]

11. Rules and Regulations as to Classification of Registrations.

The Act divides copyrightable material into 13 categories which are listed and more fully explained in Sections 202.4 to 202.15 of the Copyright Office Rules and Regulations:

§ *202.4 Books (Class A)*.

(a) *Subject matter and forms.* This class includes such published works as fiction and nonfiction, poems, compilations, composite works, directories, catalogs, annual publications, information in tabular form, and similar text matter, with or without illustrations, as books, either bound or in loose-leaf form, pamphlets, leaflets, cards, single pages or the like. Applications for registration of claims to copyright in published books manufactured in the United States of America are made on Form A; in books manufactured outside of the United States of America, except those subject to ad interim provisions of the copyright law, on Form A-B Foreign; and in books in the English language manufactured and first published outside the United States of America, and subject to the ad interim provisions of the copyright law, on Form A-B Ad Interim.

(b) *Ad interim registrations.* (1) An American edition of an English-language book or periodical identical in substance to that first published abroad will not be registered unless an ad interim registration is first made.

(2) When a book or periodical has been registered under the ad interim provisions, an American edition of the same work, to be registrable, must be manufactured and published in the United States within five years after the date of first publication abroad.

(3) Since by law ad interim copyright expires at the end of the ad interim term unless an American edition is published during that term, a renewal application covering a work registered only under the ad interim provisions will be rejected. Where both an ad interim and an American edition have been registered, the registrability of the renewal application is governed by the date of the first publication abroad.

§ *202.5 Periodicals (Class B)*.

This class includes such works as newspapers, magazines, reviews, bulletins, and serial publications, published at intervals of less than a year. Applications for registration of claims to copyright in published periodicals manufactured in the United States of America are made on Form B; in periodicals, or in contributions thereto, manufactured outside the United States of America, except those subject to the ad interim provisions of the copyright law, on Form A-B Foreign; and in periodicals, or in contributions thereto, in the English language manufactured and first published outside of the United States of America, and subject to the ad interim provisions of the copyright law, on Form A-B Ad Interim. Applications for registration of claims to copyright in contributions to periodicals manufactured in the United States of America are made on Form BB. Applications for registration of claims to copyright in contributions to periodicals, which contributions are prints published in connection with the sale or advertisement of an article or articles of merchandise, are made on Form KK.

§ *202.6 Lectures or similar productions prepared for oral delivery (Class C)*.

This class includes the scripts of unpublished works prepared in the first instance for oral delivery, such as lectures, sermons, addresses, monologs, panel discussions, and variety programs prepared for radio or television. The script submitted for registration in Class C should consist of the actual text of the works to be presented orally. Formats, outlines, brochures, synopses, or general descriptions of radio and television programs are not registrable in unpublished form. When published with notice as prescribed by law, such works may be considered for registration as "books" in Class A.

§ *202.7 Dramatic and dramatico-musical compositions (Class D)*.

This class includes published or unpublished works dramatic in character such as the acting version of plays for the stage, motion pictures, radio, television and the like, operas, operettas, musical comedies and similar productions, and pantomimes. Choreographic works of a dramatic character, whether the story or theme be expressed by music and action combined or by actions alone, are subject to registration in Class D. However, descriptions of dance steps and other physical gestures, including ballroom and social dances or choreographic works which do not tell a story, develop a character or emotion, or otherwise convey a dramatic concept or idea, are not subject to registration in Class D.

§ *202.8 Musical compositions (Class E)*.

(a) This class includes published or unpublished musical compositions in the form of visible notation (other than dramatico-musical compositions), with or without words, as well as new versions of musical compositions, such as adaptations or arrangements, and editing when such editing is the writing of an author. The words of a song, when unaccompanied by music, are not registrable in Class E.

(b) A phonograph record or other sound recording is not considered a "copy" of the compositions recorded on it, and is not acceptable for copyright registration. Likewise, the Copyright Office does not register claims to exclusive rights in mechanical recordings themselves, or in the performances they reproduce.

§ *202.9 Maps (Class F)* .

This class includes all published cartographic representations of area, such as terrestrial maps and atlases, marine charts, celestial maps and such three-dimensional works as globes and relief models.

§ *202.10 Works of art (Class G)* .

(a) *General.* This class includes published or unpublished works of artistic craftsmanship, insofar as their form but not their mechanical or utilitarian aspects are concerned, such as artistic jewelry, enamels, glassware, and tapestries, as well as works belonging to the fine arts, such as paintings, drawings and sculpture.

(b) In order to be acceptable as a work of art, the work must embody some creative authorship in its delineation or form. The registrability of a work of art is not affected by the intention of the author as to the use of the work, the number of copies reproduced, or the fact that it appears on a textile material or textile product. The potential availability of protection under the design patent law will not affect the registrability of a work of art, but a copyright claim in a patented design or in the drawings or photographs in a patent application will not be registered after the patent has been issued.

(c) If the sole intrinsic function of an article is its utility, the fact that the article is unique and attractively shaped will not qualify it as a work of art. However, if the shape of a utilitarian article incorporates features, such as artistic sculpture, carving, or pictorial representation, which can be identified separately and are capable of existing independently as a work of art, such features will be eligible for registration.

§ *202.11 Reproductions of works of art (Class H)* .

This class includes published reproductions of existing works of art in the same or a different medium, such as a lithograph, photoengraving, etching or drawing of a painting, sculpture or other work of art.

§ *202.12 Drawings or plastic works of a scientific or technical character* (Class I) .

(a) This class includes published or unpublished two-dimensional drawings and three-dimensional plastic works which have been designed for a scientific or technical use and which contain copyrightable graphic, pictorial, or sculptured material. Works registrable in Class I include diagrams or models illustrating scientific or technical works or formulating scientific or technical information in linear or plastic form, such as, for example: a mechanical drawing, an astronomical chart, an architect's blueprint, an anatomical model, or an engineering diagram.

(b) A work is not eligible for registration as a "plastic" work in Class I merely because it is formed from one of the commonly known synthetic chemical derivatives such as styrenes, vinyl compounds, or acrylic resins. The term "plastic work" as used in this context refers to a three-dimensional work giving the effect of that which is molded or sculptured. Examples of such works include statues of animals or plants used for scientific or educational purposes, and engineers' scale models.

(c) A claim to copyright in a scientific or technical drawing, otherwise registrable in Class I, will not be refused registration solely by reason of the fact that it is known to form a part of a pending patent application. Where the patent has been issued, however, the claim to copyright in the drawing will be denied copyright registration.

§ 202.13   Photographs (Class J).

This class includes published or unpublished photographic prints and filmstrips, slide films and individual slides. Photoengravings and other photomechanical reproductions of photographs are registered in Class K on Form K.

§ 202.14   Prints, pictorial illustrations and commercial prints or labels (Class K).

(a) This class includes prints or pictorial illustrations, greeting cards, picture postcards and similar prints, produced by means of lithography, photoengraving or other methods of reproduction. These works when published are registered on Form K.

(b) A print or label, not a trademark, containing copyrightable pictorial matter, text, or both, published in connection with the sale or advertisement of an article or articles of merchandise is also registered in this class on Form KK. In the case of a print which is published in a periodical, use Form KK if the print is used in connection with the sale or advertisement of an article of merchandise, Form BB if it is not. Multipage works are more appropriately classified in Class A than in Class K.

(c) A claim to copyright cannot be registered in a print or label consisting solely of trademark subject matter and lacking copyrightable matter. While the Copyright Office will not investigate whether the matter has been or can be registered at the Patent Office, it will register a properly filed copyright claim in a print or label that contains the requisite qualifications for copyright even though there is a trademark on it. However, registration of a claim to copyright does not give the claimant rights available by trademark registrations at the Patent Office.

§ *202.15*   *Motion pictures* (*Classes L–M*).

A single application Form L-M is available for registration of works in Classes L (Motion-picture photoplays) and M (Motion pictures other than photoplays).

(a) *Photoplays* (*Class L*). This class includes published or unpublished motion pictures that are dramatic in character and tell a connected story, such as feature films, filmed television plays, short subjects and animated cartoons having a plot.

(b) *Other than photoplays* (*Class M*). This class includes published or unpublished nondramatic films such as newsreels, travelogs, training or promotional films, nature studies, and filmed television programs having no plot.

Unless otherwise indicated above, the proper form to be used for registration is designated by the same letter as is the class.

Further information as to classification and appropriate forms will be found in Chapter 9, Section 13.

[*Revision:* "Works of Authorship" include the following *seven* categories:

"(1)   literary works;

(2)   musical works, including any accompanying words;

(3)   dramatic works, including any accompanying music;

(4)   pantomimes and choreographic works;

(5)   pictorial, graphic and sculptural works;

(6)   motion pictures and other audiovisual works;

(7)   sound recordings."

In the aggregate, these seven categories contain all works now copyrightable and, in addition, enumerate "pantomimes and choreographic works" and create the new category of "sound recordings"—to be distinguished from "phonorecords." The former is the aggregate of musical, spoken or other sounds that have been fixed in tangible form; the latter are the physical objects in which the sounds are fixed.

It is anticipated that the Register of Copyrights will issue Rules and Regulations under the *Revision* similar to those referred to above in this Section.]

12. Errors in Classification.

Under Section 5 of the Act an error in classification of the registration does not invalidate or impair the protection. Classification as a "map" of a sheet with a map on one side and guide material on the other does not work a forfeiture of rights in the guide material on the back.[55]

13. Duration of Copyright.

A copyright of a published work continues for a term of 28 years from the date of the first publication and is subject to a single renewal of 28 years.

As to unpublished works, there is no such publication date and the 28 year term begins to run from "the date upon which the work is registered." [56] The same single renewal is available.

As to renewal of copyright, see Section 31 below.

[*Revision:* Extension of the copyright term is considered, in the words of the Register of Copyright, as the "foundation of the entire bill." There will be a single term consisting of the life of the author plus 50 years. This applies to published works, unpublished works, and to works published posthumously.

Copyrights of joint works will run "for the life of the second of the authors to die and 50 years after his death"—even though there be more than two authors.

There is a special term for anonymous works, pseudonymous works and works made for hire: 75 years from publication or 100 years from creation, whichever is shorter.]

14. Protection of Work's Components.

A copyright protects all parts and components of the work which are themselves copyrightable. The proprietor has the same rights in each such component as he has in the entire work. A copyright of a catalog or manual containing many illustrations or cuts protects each thereof.[57]

Company communicators, including house organ editors, may purchase "stock art" or syndicated material. It is copyrighted as individual pieces or by copyright of a catalog of the material. The handling and reproduction of such works—many of which are intended to be cut apart and reproduced directly from the catalog or "service"—present problems discussed by this author elsewhere.[58]

[*Revision:* Protection is not affected by the removal, destruction or obliteration of the notice, without the authorization of the copyright owner, from any publicly distributed copies or phonorecords.]

Somewhat parallel questions may develop with an article or other material which *first* appears in a "periodical" but is authored by someone other than the publisher or staff of the periodical. Such periodicals—whether they are daily newspapers or house organs "published under the same distinctive title at periodic intervals of less than a year"—are the subject of whole issue copyright. If the article does not bear a separate copyright and is owned by the publisher, it is covered by the whole issue copyright under Section 3 of the Act. On the other hand, if not owned by the publisher and bearing no separate copyright, rights therein may be lost.[59]

Therefore, the article—if individual protection is desired—should bear its own and separate copyright notice in the name of the individual author and if the piece is serialized, each installment should bear a similar and appropriate notice, bearing in mind that the year date may change on installments of a lengthy series.[60] The separate copyright should then be separately registered.

Ordinarily an advertisement in a periodical is not considered a "contribution" but a "commercial print." [61] See Section 11 above.

> [*Revision:* Copyright in each contribution is separate from copyright in the whole. Absent any express transfer, it is presumed that the publisher acquires only the privilege of reproducing the work in that particular collective work. This is true even if the contribution does not bear a separate coypright in the contributor's name. Good practice still dictates the separate notice.]

15. Originality and Artistic Merit.

No great degree of originality or artistic value is necessary to admit to copyright. Even a so-called "repulsive" picture [62] or a "grotesque" work [63] will be acceptable. A book is considered original even though its components are old but the treatment and arrangement are the author's own efforts and not mere copying.[64] The work need not be "strikingly unique or novel," [65] and the courts will not act as critics in appraising the degree of originality or merit.[66] The required "slight degree of originality" seems particularly relevant to advertisements or other commercial or promotional materials.[67]

At the same time there are certain minimum requirements as to requirements of originality. This minimum is difficult to define and is best explained by examples such as brief commercial slogans and the other examples discussed in Section 10 above.

16. Author's Rights Under Copyright Act.

An author's exclusive rights in his work are only those granted by the Act which, in Section 1, describes these rights in this manner:

(a) To print, reprint, publish, copy and vend the copyrighted work;

(b) To translate the copyrighted work into other languages or dialects, or make any other version thereof, if it be a literary work; to dramatize it if it be a nondramatic work; to convert it into a novel or other nondramatic work if it be a drama; to arrange or adapt it if it be a musical work; to complete, execute, and finish it if it be a model or design for a work of art;

(c) To deliver, authorize the delivery of, read, or present the copyrighted work in public for profit if it be a lecture, sermon, address or similar production, or other nondramatic literary work; to make or procure the making of any transcription or record thereof by or from which, in whole or in part, it may in any way or by any method be exhibited, delivered, presented, produced, or reproduced; and to play or perform it in public for profit, and to exhibit, represent, or reproduce it in any manner or by any method whatsoever. . . .

(d) To perform or represent the copyrighted work in copies for sale, to vend any manuscript or any transcription or record thereof by or from which, in whole or in part, it may in any manner or by any method be exhibited, performed, represented, produced, or reproduced: and to exhibit, perform, represent, produce, or reproduce it in any manner or by any method whatsoever; and

(e) To perform the copyrighted work publicly for profit if it be a musical composition; and for the purpose of public performance for profit, and for the purposes set forth in subsection (a) hereof, to make any arrangement or setting of it or of the melody of it in any system of notation or any form of record in which the thought of an author may be recorded and from which it may be read or reproduced:
Provided . . .

[*Revision:* The author's exclusive rights continue essentially the same but are more broadly defined in Section 106 as the following:

(1) to reproduce the copyrighted work in copies or phonorecords;

(2) to prepare derivative works based upon the copyrighted work;

(3) to distribute copies or phonorecords of the copyrighted work to the public by sale or other transfer of ownership, or by rental, lease, or lending;

(4) in the case of literary, musical, dramatic, and choreographic works, pantomimes, and other audiovisual works, to perform the copyrighted work publicly;

(5) in the case of literary, musical, dramatic, and choreographic works, pantomimes and pictorial, graphic, or sculptural works, to display the copyrighted work publicly.

The structure of the *Revision* is to accord these exclusive rights in Section 106 and "to provide various limitations, qualifications, or exemptions" in Sections 107 to 116. These include various uses under such headings as fair use (see Section 17 below in the text) , reproduction in archival collections, face-to-face teaching, instruc-

tional broadcasting, religious services, certain non-profit performances, secondary broadcast transmissions including CATV,
ephemeral recordings, reproduction in useful articles, sound recordings, licenses for phonorecords, "jukebox" performances—
matters generally beyond the scope of this volume.]

17. Fair Use.

Fair use is the doctrine under which third parties may, without becoming infringers, make certain limited use of a copyrighted work without
permission of its proprietor. The rule was early recognized and was described by Drone in 1879 in these terms: [68]

> The recognition of this doctrine is essential to the growth of
> knowledge . . . The law, therefore, wisely allows a "fair use" to
> be made of every copyrighted production; and this liberty is con-
> sistent with the true purpose of the law to give to the earlier
> author adequate protection for the results of his labor. But to
> determine the extent of this license, and to draw the line between
> a fair and an unlawful use, is often one of the most difficult
> problems in the law of copyright. The question must generally be
> determined by the special facts in each case. What will be con-
> sidered a fair use in one case may amount to piracy in another.

Under this concept a critic may quote from a copyrighted work in a
review; [69] a subsequent technical or learned writer may quote relevant
copyrighted works on his subject; [70] a magazine may repeat the chorus of
a copyrighted song in an article; [71] etc.

However, wholesale copying is not permitted, even for apparently
proper purposes. Taking 10 pages from a book [72] or one-quarter of a
musical work [73] exceeds fair use. The same limitation was used as one of
the grounds for infringement in the famous "Gaslight" parody case involving a Jack Benny TV program on CBS.[74]

> [Revision: The House Report describes fair use as "one of the
> most important and well-established limitations on the exclusive
> rights of copyright" but that "no real definition of the concept has
> ever emerged" despite the courts' ruling "over and over again."
> The Revision gives statutory recognition to the judicial concept of
> "fair use" for the first time and sets forth four criteria by which
> this essentially equitable doctrine is to be judged:
>
> (1) the purpose and character of the use;
>
> (2) the nature of the copyrighted work;
>
> (3) the amount and substantiality of the portion used in rela-
> tion to the copyrighted work as a whole; and

(4) the effect of the use upon the potential market for or value of the copyrighted work.

Each instance of alleged fair use will continue to be decided on its own facts.]

18. Business Use and Fair Use.

Fair use has not been successfully applied in cases of advertising or promotional use. Such subsequent users should assume that they must first obtain permission to use even excerpts from a copyrighted work.

In a leading case, *Henry Holt & Co. v. Liggett & Myers Co.*,[75] the defendant used without permission three sentences from plaintiff's copyrighted scientific book *The Human Voice, Its Care and Development*, written by a physician. This portion, significant for defendant's promotion of its cigarettes, was about one-twentieth of the defendant's booklet. Fair use was held to be no defense even though credit had been given the author of the copyrighted work. The court pointed out that the credit to the physician-author compounded the offense since it made the infringed sentences even more valuable to the defendant and also "cast reflections upon [the author's] professional ethics."

The court also adverted to the supposed explanation of the fair use concept—the implied consent of the author to such subsequent use [76] —but refused to accept it, pointing out:

In such cases the law implies the consent of the copyright owner to a fair use of his publication for the advancement of the science or art.

This principle, however, does not excuse the defendant's infringement in this case. Its publication was not one in the field in which Dr. Felderman wrote, nor was it a scientific treatise or a work designed to advance human knowledge. On the contrary, it is clear that its pamphlet intended to advance the sale of its product— Chesterfield cigarettes—a purely commercial purpose. It cannot be implied that Dr. Felderman consented to the use of his work for such a purpose. . . . We think that the bill discloses an appropriation by the defendant of the labors of Dr. Felderman which constitutes an infringement of his copyrighted work.

19. Registration as Adjudication of Rights.

The Copyright Office does not carefully scrutinize each work submitted for registration. Its interest is the work's technical compliance with the Act. Therefore, registration of a copyright by the Copyright Office does not adjudicate the proprietor's rights or possible rights of other persons in the work. The registration is largely an administration act. This means that a registration of a copyright should not be considered as effective as a patent with which, in many minds, it is often associated.

In *Sheldon v. Metro-Goldwyn Pictures Corp.*,[77] this distinction and its importance were discussed in these words:

> The Copyright Office does not, when a book is offered for copyright, study any prior art, as does the Patent Office when a patent is sought. It grants the copyright, thus putting the protection of the law not only over the copyrighted book as an entirety, but over the original content of the book. It is then left to the courts, if litigation ensues, to say what the original content is, and to define the zone in which the copyright owner is protected.

D. COPYRIGHT PROCEDURES.

20. "Published"/"Unpublished" Works Distinction.

There are two procedures for obtaining copyright protection. The choice arises from the nature of the work involved. One deals with "works published in the first instance"—referred to as "published works"—and the other deals with "works not reproduced for sale"—referred to as "unpublished works." The following Sections 21 to 31 deal with "published works," except for Section 29.

21. Published Works Checklist.

The following four steps are involved in acquiring statutory copyright protection for published works:

(a) Publication of the work with the proper notice affixed. See Sections 22 to 26 below.

(b) Compliance with the "manufacturing clause." See Section 27 below.

(c) Deposit of copies of the work in the Copyright Office. See Section 28 below.

(d) Claim of copyright and filing of application for registration of the claim. See Section 23 below.

Protection attaches as soon as steps (a) and (b) have been followed. Steps (c) and (d) are supplementary but should always be taken since, among other reasons, they are necessary to the institution of an infringement action.

22. The Statutory Notice.

Section 10 of the Act provides that copyright is secured by "publication with the notice required by this title." The notice must be affixed to the work when it is first published and offered for sale. Failure to affix the notice at that time means loss of rights.[78]

The notice must also be "affixed to each copy [of the work] published or offered for sale in the United States by authority of the copyright proprietor."

> [*Revision:* Outright omission of the notice does not automatically forfeit protection, whether omission was intentional or unintentional, provided either (1) the omission was on "no more than a relatively small number" of the copies, or (2) if registration is made within five years after the publication without notice, and a reasonable effort is made to add the notice to copies distributed after the omission is discovered. Innocent infringers are protected.]

23. Form of the Notice.

Section 19 of the Act provides:

> The notice of copyright . . . shall consist either of the word "Copyright" or the abbreviation "Copr.," or the symbol ©, accompanied by the name of the copyright proprietor, and if the work be a printed literary, musical, or dramatic work, the notice shall include also the year in which the copyright was secured by publication. In the case, however, of copies of works, specified in subsections (f) to (k), inclusive, of Section 5 of this title, the notice may consist of the letter C enclosed within a circle, thus ©, accompanied by the initials, monogram, mark, or symbol of the copyright proprietor: Provided, that on some accessible portion of such copies or of the margin, back, permanent base, or pedestal, or of the substance on which such copies shall be mounted, his name shall appear . . .

All parts of the notice must be used although no specific internal sequence is necessary. Omission of either the date or the name of the proprietor is fatal, except under the short form allowed under Section 10 of the Act.[79] Strict compliance with the notice requirements is important [80] even though the courts have accepted certain limited variations. See Sections 24 to 27 below.

24. The Copyright Claim.

The copyright claim is made by use in the notice of "Copyright," the abbreviation "Copr." or the symbol ©. Unless one of these three is used, the notice is defective.[81]

"All Rights Reserved," without more, is insufficient.[82] So is "Registered." [83] However, "Copyrighted" is acceptable since it is only a slight variation and gives notice of the claim.

25. Form of Proprietor's Name.

Good practice suggests the full legal name of the copyright proprietor but some variance is tolerated. The test seems to be that his or its identification be clear.[84]

Use of fictitious or assumed business names, trade names, partnership names, subsidiary or division names or styles, etc. is acceptable provided the proprietor is generally known by that name.[85] Use of initials, without the surname or corporate name may well be bad.[86]

When a company takes an assignment of a copyright and the assignment is recorded in the Copyright Office, the name of the assignee (the new proprietor) may be substituted for the original proprietor but rights may be lost if the substitution is made before the actual recording.[87] If an assignment is not recorded, there can be no such substitution.[88]

If the copyright proprietor legally changes his or its name, the change can be recorded in the Copyright Office and if so recorded, it would appear that the new name may be used in the notice.[89]

> [*Revision:* An error in the name does not affect the validity or ownership of the copyright. An infringer is completely protected by a purported transfer or license from the person named in the notice provided registration had not been made in the name of the true owner before the infringement began.]

26. The Year Date.

The year of publication should appear in all notices except those in Classes F through K, generally considered the graphic and artistic works. However, if the additional U.C.C. protection is desired, the year date must appear even on works in these classes.[90]

The proper year date is the year in which copies are first placed on sale, sold or publicly distributed. However, if the work was previously registered as an unpublished work, the notice should contain the year date of its registration. As to the addition of new copyrightable material to the previously unpublished work, see Subsection (c) below.

> [*Revision:* If the copy "contains no name or no date that could reasonably be considered a part of the notice," the result is the same as though the notice had been omitted completely.]

(a) Antedated Notices.

If the year in the notice is earlier than the date of actual publication, the copyright is not invalid but the protection is shortened by the number of years' difference.[91] The copyright term is then computed from the last day of the year in the notice, rather than from the date of actual publication.[92] This is important in determination of the proper time to apply for renewal of the copyright. See Section 31 below.

Antedated notices usually result from publishing plans which call for publication late in a given year but actual publication occurs—for whatever the reason—early in the following year.

(b) Postdated Notices.

If the notice contains a year date later than the year of actual publication, this defect has usually been considered fatal to the copyright.[93] The reason has been that this represents an attempt at the extension of the protection to the detriment of the public. However, in 1959, the Copyright Office amended its policy so that registration would be considered "as a doubtful case" if the actual publication was "not more than one year earlier than the year date in the notice." [94] This new policy resulted from the "philosophy" of the decision in *Advisers, Inc. v. Wiesenhart, Inc.*[95] wherein it was said that "useless technicalities are not to be allowed to cut down the benefits conferred."

> [*Revision:* Where the year date is more than one year later than the year in which the publication first occurred, the work is considered to have been published without any notice. See Section 26 above.]

(c) New Editions and New Matter.

When a new edition of a copyrighted work is published, it should carry the original year date if the edition is merely a reprint.[96] Otherwise, it may be considered a postdated notice and invalidate protection entirely.

If the new edition is a new version or has new matter added to the original edition, the new year date may be used. It is probably safer to use both the original and the new year date in the notice: *e.g.* "© 1960, 1965 John Doe." [97]

If the work contains material originally copyrighted in unpublished form, and now published for the first time, the proper year date depends upon whether or not the original work has been changed. If both are essentially the same, the year date of the original registration should be used. If there have been substantial changes or additions, the later year date should be used. Once again, it is preferable to use both of the year dates.[98]

27. Position of Notice.

Under Section 20 of the Act, the copyright notice should be located as follows: [99]

(a) On books and other printed publications: on the title page or the page immediately following, the latter normally being the reverse side of the page bearing the title.

(b) On periodicals: on the title page, on the first page of text, or under the title heading.

(c) On contributions to periodicals: on the contribution itself. If the contribution is a literary, dramatic or musical work, the notice should appear on the first page (the title page) of the contribution.

(d) On musical works: on the title page or on the first page of music.

(e) On motion pictures: on the title frame or near it.

These provisions are mandatory under the "explicit provision of the statute" and therefore, "a notice on any other page, no matter how prominent, is ineffective." [100] If it is printed on the last page of a book or on the back cover of a pamphlet, it is insufficient.[101]

A notice on the title page of a book is not invalidated merely because that page is not the first page in the book, being preceded by several pages of advertising.[102]

[*Revision:* The notice shall be affixed to all copies "in such manner and located as to give reasonable notice of the claim of copyright." The Register of Copyrights will prescribe by regulation, as examples, specific methods of affixation and position of the notice but such specifications shall not be considered exhaustive.]

28. The "Manufacturing Clause."

To be admissible to copyright, it is required under Section 16 of the Act that all books or periodicals printed in the English language be printed from type set or plates made in the United States. If reproduction is by lithography or photoengraving, such process must be performed in the United States.

Under Section 17 of the Act an affidavit as to compliance with Section 16 as above must be taken by the applicant or the printer of the work. This affidavit is incorporated into the application forms for registration of the classes so affected.

[*Revision:* The manufacturing clause is retained but considerably limited in application. Its details are probably not of concern to the company communicator.

Compliance with the clause no longer is a condition of copyright protection but provides for the possible loss of certain rights against infringers.]

29. Deposit of Copies of Work.

Section 13 of the Act requires that "after copyright has been secured by publication of the work with the notice of copyright" there shall be "promptly deposited with the Register of Copyrights, . . . two complete copies of the best edition" of the work. Certain options are permissible with the registration of published three-dimensional works of art.

The law requires that this deposit shall be made "promptly." This is a loose term and in *Washingtonian Publishing Co. v. Pearson*,[103] it was held that a delay of fourteen months was not sufficient to "cause forfeiture of the right theretofore distinctly granted."

Good practice dictates the immediate deposit of the necessary copies. The Registrar of Copyrights may, under Section 14 of the Act, demand the deposit of the copies and if not so deposited within three months, the copyright proprietor is liable to a $100 fine and other charges and forfeiture of the copyright.

> [*Revision:* Within three months after publication with notice affixed, two copies of the work must be deposited with the Copyright Office. Deposit is not a condition of copyright protection. The Register of Copyrights may, by regulation, exempt any categories of material from the deposit requirements. At any time after publication, the Register of Copyrights may make demand for the deposit. If not complied with within three months thereafter, the persons upon whom demand was made is subject to a fine of not more than $250 and the total retail price of the copies demanded. However, such failure will no longer result in loss of copyright.]

30. "Unpublished Works."

Section 12 of the Act provides for statutory protection for "unpublished works"—works "of which copies are not reproduced for sale":

> Copyright may also be had of the works of an author, of which copies are not reproduced for sale, by the deposit, with claim of copyright, of one complete copy of such work, if it be a lecture or similar production or a dramatic, musical, or dramatico-musical composition; of a title and description, with one print taken from each scene or act, if the work be a motion-picture photoplay; of a photographic print if the work be a photograph; of a title and description, with not less than two prints taken from different sections of a complete motion picture, if the work be a motion picture other than a photoplay; or of a photograph or other identifying reproduction thereof, if it be a work of art or a plastic work

or drawing. But the privilege of registration secured hereunder shall not exempt the copyright proprietor from the deposit of copies, under sections 13 and 14 of this title, where the work is reproduced in copies for sale.

If such registered but unpublished works are later generally published and sold, the deposit provision—discussed in Section 29 above—must be followed.

The term of such a copyright is the same as for that of a published work but the term begins to run from the date of original deposit in the unpublished state.[104] If such an unpublished work is later revised so as to qualify as a new version or edition and then published, it may be registered as such at the time of publication and the term begins to run on the new version or edition from that time.

> [*Revision:* Unpublished works will come under essentially the same statutory protective system as published works. Protection will attach and the term begin to run when the work is "created"—defined as "fixed in a copy or phonorecord for the first time." See also Section 7 [*Revision*] above.]

31. Renewal of Copyright.

A single 28-year renewal is available after the expiration of the original 28-year term. The application therefor must be filed on form R during the last year of the original term, measured from the *exact* date on which the original copyright began.

Renewal copyright may be claimed only *seriatim* by the author (if alive); by the widow (widower) of the author and/or the child (children) of a deceased author; absent such survivors, by the executors of a deceased author; and, absent executors, by the next of kin of the deceased author. This order must be followed even if the author, during his lifetime, had assigned the copyright and the right to renew. The assignment is effective only if the author survives into the 28th year. The renewal is then taken in his name and assigned to the original assignee.[105]

The devolution of the renewal right has caused much confusion, particularly as it concerns widow and children. If one such survivor makes the application, it is the act of all and the applicant holds the renewal in trust for all.[106]

In cases of works prepared for hire, the renewal may be filed by the employer as proprietor.[107]

> [*Revision:* As to new works, there will be only a single, longer term under the new law and no renewal thereof will be either necessary or permissible. See Section 13 [*Revision*] above.
>
> As to subsisting first-term copyrights, the *Revision* requires es-

sentially the same renewal procedure during its 28th year but the renewal will run for 47 years.

As to copyrights, the renewal term of which would have expired during the pendency of the *Revision* legislation, Congress adopted independent interim legislation, to extend and preserve such renewal terms.[108] The *Revision* further extends such subsisting renewal terms for 75 years from the date copyright was *originally* secured.]

32. Assignment of Copyright.

A copyright may be assigned, encumbered, or bequeathed by will under Section 28 of the Act. The assignment, etc. must be in writing and signed by the proprietor. This is not true of a license. The assignment must be recorded in the Copyright Office "within three months after its execution" under Section 30 of the Act; otherwise it is void against a subsequent purchaser for a valuable consideration.

Even if not recorded, the assignment is still binding as between the assignor and the assignee.[109] However, such recording is necessary before the assignee may use his own name in the copyright notice. See Section 25 above.

As to assignment of renewal rights, see Section 31 above.

Licenses need not be recorded but more and more such instruments— together with "contracts covering specific rights embraced in copyright" —are being recorded nevertheless. The effect of such unprescribed recording is open to question.[110] However, it is recommended if important rights are involved.

[*Revision:* Unlimited alienability of copyrights is recognized and continued and exclusive licenses are included as subject to "transfer of copyright ownership." For the first time, divisibility of copyright is recognized and therefore there may be a transfer of a specific right without transfer of all rights in the copyright. The owner of a particular right then has all the rights—as to that particular right—enjoyed by a copyright owner.]

Notes

1. Copyright Act of March 4, 1909, 35 Stat. 1075–88, 17 U.S.C. (1965).
2. *House Comm. on the Judiciary, Copyright Law Revision*, H. R. Rep. No. 83, 90th Cong., 1st Sess. (1967).
3. LATMAN, HOWELL'S COPYRIGHT LAW vii (rev. ed. 1962).
4. Latman, *supra* note 3; AMDUR, COPYRIGHT LAW AND PRACTICE (1936); BALL, LAW OF COPYRIGHT AND LITERARY PROPERTY (1944); DRONE, LAW OF PROPERTY IN INTELLECTUAL PRODUCTIONS IN GREAT BRITAIN AND THE UNITED STATES (1879).
5. Chamberlain v. Feldman, 300 N.Y. 135, 89 N.E.2d 863 (1949).
6. 287 N.Y. 302, 39 N.E.2d 249 (1942).
7. Latman, *supra* note 3, at 61, citing Donaldson v. Becket, 4 Burr. 2408, 98 Eng. Rep. 257 (1774).
8. Atlas Mfg. Co. v. Street & Smith, 204 Fed. 398, 47 L.R.A. (n.s.) 1002 (1913), *cert. denied*, 231 U.S. 755 (1913).
9. Copyright Act, *supra* note 1, at §26.
10. Atlantic Monthly v. Post Publishing Co., 27 F.2d 556 (D. Mass. 1928).
11. National Comics Publications, Inc. v. Fawcett Publishing Co., 191 F.2d 594 (2d Cir. 1951).
12. Atlantic Monthly v. Post Publishing Co., *supra* note 10.
13. Latman, *supra* note 3, at 64.
14. American Visuals Corp. v. Holland, 239 F.2d 740 (2d Cir. 1957).
15. Latman, *supra* note 3.
16. Wheaton v. Peters, 33 U.S. 591 (1834).
17. See cases cited and discussed, Latman, *supra* note 3, at 62, 64–65.
18. See cases cited, 17 U.S.C.A. §2, notes 71–80.
19. Dieckhaus v. Twentieth Century-Fox Film Corp., 74 F. Supp. 425 (D. Mo. 1944), *rev'd on other grounds*, 153 F.2d 893 (7th Cir. 1944).
20. Nutt v. National Inst. 31 F.2d 236 (2d Cir. 1929).
21. Frohman v. Ferris, 238 Ill. 430, 87 N.E. 327, 43 L.R.A. (n.s.) 639 (1909).
22. Univ. Film Mfg. Co. v. Copperman, 212 Fed. 301 (S.D.N.Y. 1914), *aff'd*, 218 F. 573 (2d Cir. 1914).
23. Hirshon v. United Artists Corp., 243 F.2d 640 (D.C. Cir. 1957).
24. Uproar Co. v. N.B.C., 8 F. Supp. 358 (D. Mass. 1934), *mod'd*, 81 F.2d 373 (1st Cir. 1936).
25. Mittenthal v. Berlin, 291 Fed. 714 (S.D.N.Y. 1923).
26. Lieb, *The Computer and Copyright the Next Five Years*, A.B.A. Section on Patent, Trademark and Copyright, Summary of Proceedings, at 132 (1967).
27. As to such treaties, see Latman, *supra* note 3, at 185–90.
28. Mutual Advertising Co. v. Refo, 76 Fed. 961 (C.C.S.C. 1896); Vitaphone Corp. v. Hutchinson Co., 28 F. Supp. 526 (D. Mass. 1939).
29. Campbell v. Wireback, 269 Fed. 372 (4th Cir. 1920).
30. Yardley v. Houghton Mifflin Co., 108 F.2d 28 (2d Cir. 1939); Shapiro,

Bernstein & Co. v. Jerry Vogel Music Co., 115 F. Supp. 754 (S.D.N.Y. 1953), *rev'd on other grounds,* 221 F.2d 569 (2d Cir. 1955).

31. 20 F. Supp. 135 (S.D.N.Y. 1937).

32. 111 U.S. 53, at 58 (1884).

33. Burrow-Giles Lithographing v. Sarony, *supra* note 32.

34. American Mutascope, etc. v. Edison, 137 Fed. 262 (C.C.N.J. 1905).

35. Mazer v. Stein, 347 U.S. 201 (1954).

36. Ansehl v. Puritan Pharmacal Co., 61 F.2d 131 (8th Cir. 1932).

37. Bleistein v. Donaldson Lithographing Co., 188 U.S. 239 (1903).

38. Westerman v. Dispatch Printing Co., 249 U.S. 100 (1919).

39. Sheldon v. Metro-Goldwyn Pictures Corp., 81 F.2d 49, at 54 (2d Cir. 1936).

40. Hoffman v. Le Traunik, 209 Fed. 375 (N.D.N.Y. 1913); Richardson v. Miller, 20 F. Cas. 722 (Case No. 11,791) (C.C. Mass. 1877).

41. Barnes v. Miner, 122 Fed. 480 (C.C.S.D.N.Y. 1903).

42. Latman, *supra* note 3, at 45–46.

43. 210 Fed. 399 (E.D. La. 1914), *aff'd,* 220 Fed. 837 (5th Cir. 1915).

44. Wheaton v. Peters, *supra* note 16.

45. DuPuy v. Post Telegram, 210 Fed. 883 (3d Cir. 1914).

46. Public Affairs Associates, Inc. v. Rickover, 284 F.2d 262 (D.C. Cir. 1960), *cert. granted,* 365 U.S. 841 (1961). See also United States v. First Trust Co. of St. Paul, 251 F.2d 686 (8th Cir. 1958).

47. For a discussion of this problem and its legislative solution, see Latman, *supra* note 3, at 47–48.

48. Dymow v. Bolton, 11 F.2d 690 (3d Cir. 1936); Bordon v. General Motors Corp., 28 F. Supp. 330 (S.D.N.Y. 1939).

49. Copyright Office Regulations, §202.1 (1966).

50. Becker v. Loew's, Inc., 133 F.2d 889 (7th Cir. 1943).

51. Patten v. Superior Talking Pictures, Inc., 8 F. Supp. 196 (S.D.N.Y. 1934).

52. Golenpaul v. Rosett, 174 Misc. 114, 18 N.Y.S.2d 889 (N.Y. Sup. Ct. 1940).

53. Hemingway v. Film Alliance, 174 Misc. 725, 21 N.Y.S.2d 827 (N.Y. Sup. Ct. 1940).

54. This list is taken *seriatim* from Copyright Office Regulations, §202.1 (a), (c) and (d).

55. Freedman v. Milnag Leasing Corp., 20 F. Supp. 802 (S.D.N.Y. 1937).

56. Marx v. United States, 96 F.2d 204 (9th Cir. 1938).

57. Basevi v. O'Toole Co., 26 F. Supp. 39 (S.D.N.Y. 1937); Jewelers' Circular Publishing Co. v. Keystone Publishing Co., 274 Fed. 932 (S.D.N.Y. 1921), *aff'd,* 281 Fed. 83, 26 L.R.A. 571 (2d Cir. 1922), *cert. denied,* 259 U.S. 581 (1922).

58. SIMON, THE LAW FOR ADVERTISING AND MARKETING 190–93 (1956).

59. Dam v. Kirke LaShelle Co., 175 Fed. 902 (2d Cir. 1910); Morse v. Fields, 127 F. Supp. 63 (S.D.N.Y. 1954).

60. Copyright Office Circular No. 43 (1966).

61. 39 OP. ATT'Y GEN. 498 (1940); Copyright Office Circular No. 43 (1966).

62. Stuff v. La Budde Feed, etc., 42 F. Supp. 493 (E.D. Wis. 1941).

63. Dieckhaus v. Twentieth Century-Fox Film Corp., *supra* note 19.

64. Jones v. Underkoffler, 16 F. Supp. 729 (D.C. Pa. 1936).

65. Alfred Bell & Co. v. Catalda Fine Arts, 191 F.2d 99 (2d Cir. 1951).
66. Henderson v. Tompkins, 60 Fed. 758 (C.C. Mass. 1894).
67. Laskowitz v. Marie Designer, Inc., 119 F. Supp. 541 (S.D. Cal. 1954).
68. Drone, *supra* note 4, at 386–87.
69. Mawman v. Tegg, 2 Russ. 385, 38 Eng. Rep. 380; Harper v. Shoppell, 26 Fed. 519 (C.C.S.D.N.Y. 1886).
70. Thompson v. Gernsback, 94 F. Supp. 453 (S.D.N.Y. 1950); Drone, *supra* note 4, at 386.
71. Karll v. Curtis Publishing Co., 39 F. Supp. 836 (E.D. Wis. 1941); Shapiro, Bernstein & Co. v. P. F. Collier & Son, 26 U.S.P.Q. 40 (S.D.N.Y. 1934).
72. Farmer v. Elstner, 33 Fed. 494 (C.C.E.D. Mich. 1888).
73. Associated Music Publishers, Inc. v. Debs Memorial Radio Fund, 46 F. Supp. 829 (S.D.N.Y. 1942), *aff'd*, 141 F.2d 852 (2d Cir. 1944).
74. Loew's, Inc. v. C.B.S., 131 F. Supp. 165 (S.D. Cal. 1955), *aff'd*, 239 F.2d 532 (9th Cir. 1956), *aff'd*, 356 U.S. 43 (1958).
75. 23 F. Supp. 302 (E.D. Pa. 1938). See also Eliot v. Geare-Marston, Inc., 30 F. Supp. 301 (E.D. Pa. 1939); Robertson v. Batten, Barton, Durstine & Osborne, 146 F. Supp. 795 (S.D. Cal. 1956); Farmer v. Elstner, *supra* note 72.
76. Latman, *supra* note 3, at 153–54.
77. Sheldon v. Metro-Goldwyn Pictures Corp., *supra* note 39.
78. Wheaton v. Peters, *supra* note 16.
79. Buck v. Liederkranz, 34 F. Supp. 1006 (E.D. Pa. 1940); Thompson v. Hubbard, 131 U.S. 123 (1889).
80. Mifflin v. White, 190 U.S. 260 (1903); Bentley v. Tibbals, 223 Fed. 247 (2d Cir. 1915); Moger v. WHDH, Inc., 194 F. Supp. 605 (D. Mass. 1961).
81. Kramer v. Capri Jewelry, Inc., 143 F. Supp. 120 (S.D.N.Y. 1956).
82. Osgood v. Aloe Instrument Co., 83 Fed. 470 (C.C. Mo. 1897); Falk v. Schumacker, 48 Fed. 222 (C.C.N.Y. 1891).
83. Higgins v. Keuffel, 140 U.S. 428 (1891).
84. Burrow-Giles Lithographing Co. v. Sarony, *supra* note 32.
85. Hollywood Jewelry Mfg. Co. v. Dushkin, 136 F. Supp. 738 (S.D.N.Y. 1955); National Comics Publications, Inc. v. Fawcett Publishing Co., *supra* note 11.
86. Metro Associated Services, Inc. v. Webster City Graphic, Inc., 117 F. Supp. 224 (N.D. Iowa 1953).
87. Copyright Office Circular No. 10 (1965).
88. Group Publishers, Inc. v. Winchell, 86 F. Supp. 573 (S.D.N.Y. 1949).
89. Copyright Office Circular No. 10D (1965).
90. Copyright Office Circular No. 3 (1966).
91. Callaghan v. Myers, 128 U.S. 645 (1888); Shapiro, Bernstein & Co. v. Jerry Vogel Music Co., *supra* note 30.
92. Copyright Office Circular No. 3S (1964).
93. Baker v. Taylor, 2 F. Cas. 478 (Case No. 782) (C.C.S.D.N.Y. 1848); American Code Co. v. Bensinger, 282 Fed. 829 (2d Cir. 1922).
94. Copyright Office Regulations, §202.2 (b) (6) (iii) (1966).
95. 238 F.2d 706 (6th Cir. 1956), *cert. denied,* 353 U.S. 949 (1957).
96. Wrench v. Universal Pictures, 104 F. Supp. 374 (S.D.N.Y. 1952).
97. Copyright Office Circular No. 35B (1967).

98. *Id.*

99. This resumé is taken from Copyright Office Circular No. 3 (1966).

100. Richards v. New York Post, Inc., 23 F. Supp. 619 (E.D.N.Y. 1929).

101. Krafft v. Cohen, 117 F.2d 579 (3d Cir. 1941); Deward & Rich v. Bristol Sav. & Loan Ass'n, 34 F. Supp. 345 (D. Va. 1940), *aff'd,* 120 F.2d 537 (4th Cir. 1941).

102. American Travel & Hotel Directory Co. v. Gehring Publishing Co., 4 F.2d 415 (S.D.N.Y. 1925).

103. 306 U.S. 30 (1939).

104. Marx v. United States, *supra* note 56.

105. Witmark & Sons v. Fred Fisher Music Co., 125 F.2d 949 (2d Cir. 1942), *aff'd,* 318 U.S. 643 (1943).

106. Silverman v. Sunrise Picture Corp., 290 Fed. 804 (2d Cir. 1923); Vogel v. Miller Music Co., 299 N.Y. 782 (1949); Tobani v. Carl Fischer, Inc., 98 F.2d 57 (2d Cir. 1938), *cert. denied,* 305 U.S. 650 (1938).

107. Shapiro, Bernstein & Co. v. Bryan, 123 F.2d 697 (2d Cir. 1941); Tobani v. Carl Fischer, Inc., *supra* note 106.

108. See *e.g.,* P.L. 87-668, 87th Cong. 2d Sess. (1962); P.L. 89-142, 89th Cong. 1st Sess. (1965). See also Copyright Office Circular No. 16X (1965).

109. New Fiction Publishing Co. v. Star, 220 Fed. 994 (S.D.N.Y. 1915).

110. Latman, *supra* note 3, at 56.

Chapter 6

Ideas:
Their Protection and Marketing

A. INTRODUCTION

1. Chapter Scope
2. Value of Unsolicited Ideas
3. The Public Relations Dilemma
4. Changing Judicial Attitudes

B. PROTECTION AGAINST IDEA CLAIMS

5. In General
6. Need for Basic Company Policy
7. Total Rejection Policy
8. Mandatory Release Method
9. The Borden Company Program
10. "Maximum Value" Contracts
11. Office Procedures

C. OWNERSHIP OF IDEAS

12. Basic Concepts
13. Ideas Created by PR Firms
14. Employee-Created Ideas
15. Multiple Ownership
16. Multiple Submissions

D. BASES OF LIABILITY

17. Unconditional Communication
18. Varied Legal Premises Involved
19. Express Contract
20. Implied Contract
21. Quasi Contract

Chapter 6

Ideas:

Their Protection and Marketing

A. INTRODUCTION.

1. Chapter Scope.

The purpose of this chapter is to explore in broad strokes the sale, marketing and protection of "ideas," using that term in an inclusive sense. Frequently "ideas" are considered—at least in the vernacular—as being confined to promotional, public relations, advertising, entertainment, marketing and similar concepts. However, most of the discussion herein is applicable also to technical and scientific ideas and submissions.

This appears to be the approach taken by companies which require releases or other instruments to be signed by the submitter. These instruments are usually so drawn as to cover a technical product suggestion as well as a promotional idea.

No effort is made herein to deal with the fields of copyright or patents. If the submission is susceptible to such protection, the submitter is well-advised to pursue these possibilities.

A good example of the importance of copyright in this situation was the 1967 "Paladin" case.[1] The plaintiff had called himself Paladin and had appeared publicly in costume under that name for many years. He handed out cards reading "Have Gun, Will Travel . . . Wire Paladin" and his home address. The card also carried the insigne of a chess knight. The appellate reversal of a $150,000 trial court verdict for the plaintiff was premised largely on the fact that the cards explained the entire unique nature of the Paladin concept—aside from the usual trappings of all "Westerns"—but the cards were *not* copyrighted. Therefore C.B.S. had the right to use an idea which was in the public domain.

2. Value of Unsolicited Ideas.

There is a distinct difference of corporate opinion as to the importance of, or need for, ideas submitted gratuitously by the public.[2] Many of the major companies clearly believe they are non-productive. General Foods receives about 5000 such letter submissions a year and its officers are reported as having "difficulty recalling anything useful being originated by such mail." Colgate, Standard Brands and American Tobacco Co. refuse to consider such submissions at all.

Other companies welcome this flow of ideas. For example, Parker Brothers, the game manufacturer, gets more than 2000 submissions a year but considers the "three to five" usable ones worth the expense and trouble of processing this entire volume.

The broadcasting networks are prime targets for submissions and the three major networks disagree as to their importance. One of them has reversed itself and now considers the submissions even though reported to have received "only a handful" which were useful over a period of three years.

In two 1952 studies by the *Harvard Law Review* covering 77 companies only a small fraction welcomed or would entertain unsolicited ideas.[3] This may well represent the view of a majority of business concerns. In the final analysis, however, company policy will probably depend on a mixture of many factors: the nature of the company; its products and activities; the extent of its own research and development programs; its own experience in obtaining useful material from these sources; the ingenuity of its outside PR counsel or advertising agency; the cost of handling submissions, and perhaps most important, its prior experience in the legal arena in "idea cases."

3. The Public Relations Dilemma.

One of the most perplexing PR problems may be the handling of "idea submissions." On the one hand, the PR man recognizes the need for protecting the company against future litigation by submitters. On the other, he naturally wants the submitter and his idea handled "delicately" if at all possible.

In a sense, this dual desire is akin to two legal and ethical concepts which have developed in the law of ideas. Justice Brandeis, in the landmark *Associated Press* case,[4] recognized that "to appropriate . . . ideas produced by other men, without making compensation . . . may be inconsistent with the finer sense of propriety, . . ." Yet Judge Clark of the Second Circuit also recognized that there are people who do try to take advantage of a company and he therefore wrote: [5]

To be rejected are attempts made by telegraphing or writing vague and general suggestions to business corporations and then seizing upon some later general similarity between their products and the notion propounded as a basis for damages.

This desire to maintain the PR/legal balance is evident in the attitude of American Telephone and Telegraph Co. A special department referred to as "Suggestion Studies" handles submissions. Frank Wurst, the "Engineer Manager" in charge, has pointed out that company procedures are aimed "primarily at servicing the customer, not protecting against a lawsuit" but added, "if we do our job right, we won't be sued." [6]

The situation is further complicated by the fact that submissions may be valuable and useful to a company. As with company or communications research and development, the public also has become more sophisticated. Some companies, therefore, believe that idea submissions are likely to be more worthwhile today than in the past. See Section 2 above.

The aim should be to strike a happy balance between company protection and company needs, both for new ideas and good public relations. Lawyers and law teachers have also recognized this practical need. Dean Havighurst of Northwestern University Law School, for example, has said: [7]

> The problem . . . is not only legal . . . but it is also partly one of psychology and public relations. The hopes of the submitter must be disappointed in all but a very few instances but he must be kept in as happy a frame of mind as possible. The company must steer a middle course in the matter of cordiality.

At the same time, the desire to be "polite" and "put the best company foot forward" should not be permitted to raise false hopes in the minds of the submitter nor to cloud the company's position. As one federal court has said: [8] "Frankness and candor, rather than a desire to be polite, would have saved the parties needless time and litigation."

4. Changing Judicial Attitudes.

The courts today are more receptive to plaintiff claims in idea suits. This change has not gone unnoticed by either plaintiff-submitters or company-defendants. As a result, suits have proliferated and business has become more wary.

Typical of the more relaxed judicial attitude is a comparison of two cases decided 25 years apart. In both the 1921 *Masline* case [9] and the 1946 *High* case [10] the plaintiff-submitter had an express agreement with the defendant whereby the plaintiff would be paid on a specific percentage basis if the defendant used the idea. Each defendant did use the idea and refused to pay the plaintiff. In neither case was the idea novel or original with the plaintiff.

In *Masline,* the defendant prevailed and in *High* the plaintiff won. The primary difference was that the court in *High* did not require that the idea be novel as had been the position of the court in *Masline* 25 years before.

In even more recent years some courts have departed from the novelty requirement even in cases in which the plaintiff does not claim an express agreement with the defendant but is suing on an implied agreement. For a further discussion of these cases, see Section 19 below.

From this and other examples we can only conclude that the plaintiff has a lighter burden today in idea litigation.[11] Perhaps a basic explanation is that the courts have come gradually to attune their thinking to the modern "facts of life" in a rather practical way. This is the legal philosophy expressed in a leading "idea case," *Meyer v. Liggett & Myers Tobacco Co.,* decided in 1935: [12]

> The rules of the common law are continually changing and expanding with the progress of the society in which it prevails. It does not lag behind, but adapts itself . . . so that the ends of justice may be reached.

B. PROTECTION AGAINST IDEA CLAIMS.

5. In General.

The cases dealing with a company's liability for ideas submitted to it are a changing and, at times, amorphous amalgam. A prophylactic company methodology to avoid exposure is to be preferred over reliance upon a legal position which may be tenuous and shifting—dependent, to some degree, even upon the particular jurisdiction in which the submission is made or the "idea suit" is filed.

It seems preferable, therefore, to deal with such company methods before treating the legal background and tests which such requirements seek to avoid. Sections 6 to 11 below, therefore, constitute a step by step series of recommendations—some in the alternative—whereby a company may do much to protect itself against the institution of idea litigation and also lay the groundwork for a defense if such actions are brought. It should be recognized that these preventive steps are not a subterfuge to "steal" valuable ideas from the submitter.

6. Need for Basic Company Policy.

Before the PR or legal department can establish an office procedure for handling unsolicited idea submissions, management must determine company policy. This management value judgment will undoubtedly be based upon the factors discussed in Section 2 above.

Both the PR and the legal staffs should contribute to this judgment. It should not be reached in a high-level vacuum as has sometimes been the case. Such staff personnel should also investigate the experience of other companies which have theretofore faced and resolved the question.

Once the policy has been adopted, it should be periodically reviewed and intervening company experience evaluated. Some companies have reversed themselves as time passed and a former decision proved empirically unsound. Reevaluation is especially important as a company diversifies and enters new product areas. A policy sound for one type of product may not be best for others. An industrial concern, interested only in technical or scientific matters, may reject out of hand all submissions and, later, when it enters consumer-product marketing, find that unsolicited submissions may be valuable.

7. Total Rejection Policy.

Some companies utterly refuse to consider any unsolicited submissions. See Section 2 above. Assuming this policy, a submission should be returned to the submitter at once together with an explanation of company policy. A somewhat similar letter should be used if the submitter merely indicates that he desires to make a submission and inquires as to the company's receptivity. The following form is suggested:

> Thank you for your interest in our company [client, etc.] as indicated in your letter to us. Unfortunately, we are not in a position to consider the contents of your letter.
>
> As you can easily understand, our own people are hard at work on new and useful advertising, marketing, and merchandising plans and ideas. So too are the many professional organizations whose sole function is the development of new ideas, formats, and techniques. We find that these efforts are sufficient for our purposes.
>
> Accordingly, we have adopted a permanent policy of not considering any unsolicited submissions of ideas or other suggestions.
>
> We are sure that you will realize that this policy will avoid any misunderstandings.
>
> You will, therefore, find enclosed all of the material which you were kind enough to send us.
>
> We again want to thank you for your interest.

Companies adhering to this policy seem to feel that their exposure is less than if they were to accept submissions even when accompanied by the releases referred to in Section 8 below. This is not necessarily true. Unless proper internal handling procedures are scrupulously followed, the submitter may later be able to prove—at least sufficiently to have his case go to the jury—that the company *did* use his idea notwithstanding its professed policy against acceptance of submissions.

A company may reject *some* submissions because of either (a) the non-applicability of the submission to the company's product line or marketing methods or (b) the anticipation of the submission by earlier developments either within the company or in the "art" generally. Usually the company conclusion under either (a) or (b) will be quickly reached without any investigation or search by company technical personnel.

In such cases, the following letter—here presented in an alternative form—may be used:

> Thank you for your recent letter of ——————— concerning your suggestion for (give general title, no detail).
>
> I am sorry to tell you that the matter you mention is one in which the XYZ Company is not interested. (Add reasons if desirable. Consider suggesting organizations that might be interested, particularly where the idea may be of interest to customers of ours such as fabricators and converters.)
>
> [OR]
>
> I am sorry to tell you that your suggestion has already been anticipated by (make appropriate reference to identify the anticipation).
>
> We appreciate your thinking of the XYZ Company in connection with your suggestion.

8. Mandatory Release Method.

A technique which has been described as a "middle of the road" approach is to require prior releases in connection with all idea submissions. Essentially, this involves a refusal to examine—even preliminarily—any unsolicited submission unless the submitter first signs a full release. Normally, under such a release, any payment which might be made, should the company use the idea eventually, is up to the company itself. The company does not become bound merely because it later agrees to examine the submission.

If releases are being used, it is particularly important that unsolicited submission be handled only by the "custodian" according to a strict internal office procedure as described in Section 11 below.

The custodian should photostat it and return it at once to the submitter together with a letter making clear that it has not been considered as yet and that it will not be considered unless the submitter sees fit to return it to the company together with the executed release form, forwarded with the rejection letter. The language of the covering letter may be as polite and circumspect as the PR department desires but it should not depart from or weaken its central thrust.

The release itself may be in any form considered desirable but its core meaning should be clear: that examination of the submission implies no obligation whatsoever and that the submitter's compensation, if any, in the event of use of the idea by the company, is solely within the company's discretion. The following covers these points: [13]

> You shall not in any way be responsible by virtue of your examination and appraisal of the material submitted herewith. In the event that you use this material, all decisions as to its originality and value, if any, shall lie entirely within your discretion.

Davis v. General Foods [14] dealt with release language similar to that above. The court held against the plaintiff on the ground that the discretionary power of the defendant as to the plaintiff's compensation made the agreement "too indefinite for legal performance."

On the other hand, in the later *Pillois v. Billingsley* [15] the plaintiff recovered $6,000 on an agreement that the defendant would pay the plaintiff what the defendant thought plaintiff's services were worth. The "unlimited choice" of the defendant did not make the defendant's promise "illusory."

Some companies prefer not to return the submission with the request for execution of the release. Instead it is held by the custodian until the signed release is returned.

One national company uses the following letter which is both the explanation and the release:

> Thank you for your letter of _____ suggesting a (give general title, no detail).
>
> Before I forward your suggestion to the appropriate people in the XYZ Company for study, I must ask you to agree to the conditions upon which the XYZ Company is willing to consider your suggestion. This is to avoid the chance of misunderstanding later. In the meantime, I am holding your letter in my file.
>
> When we receive suggestions we follow a procedure designed to protect both the suggester and us. We prefer to consider a suggestion only after the suggester has established his right to it and protected himself to the extent of obtaining a U. S. patent (or copyright). I assume you do not have such protection. You should consider carefully whether to seek it.
>
> If you do not now have a patent (or copyright), we are willing to review your suggestion, and tell you whether or not we are interested, only if you agree that:
>
> (1) We are under no obligation to make any payment to you and you are willing to rely completely upon our judgement as to the value of your suggestion and the amount of compensation to

be paid to you, if any, unless you obtain a patent (or copyright),
in which event we would expect to negotiate with you as to obtaining rights under the patent (or copyright) if we are interested.

(2) If you subsequently obtain a patent (or copyright), you will
rely completely upon such rights in your suggestion as the patent
(or copyright) gives you.

(3) We are not obligated to keep your suggestion secret or
handle it on a confidential basis. These conditions are necessary
because we may find out that your suggestion is already available
to us through work of our own employees, or through suggestions
made to us or published by others. Of course, you would not
expect us to enter into an arrangement that would limit any right
we already have to adopt and use your suggestion.

If you wish to accept the above conditions and to have our
people consider your suggestion, please sign and date one copy of
this letter (the other is for your file) and return it to me. I shall
then transmit your suggestion to persons in our Company who are
qualified to consider it. Otherwise, I shall keep your letter in my
file and your suggestion will not be considered by the XYZ
Company.

We appreciate your thinking of the Company in connection
with your suggestion.

The foregoing letter form is used when the suggestion has already been
received by the company. Sometimes, however, the initial letter from the
submitter merely inquires whether the company is "interested." In this
case, the same letter is used except for the following changes in the opening two paragraphs and the closing two paragraphs:

Thank you for your letter of _____ offering to disclose
your suggestion for a (give general title).

I think that we would be interested in reviewing a description
of your suggestion if you are willing to submit it on the conditions
set forth below. This is to avoid the chance of misunderstanding
later.

*   *   *   *

If you wish to accept these conditions and to have our people
consider your suggestion, please sign and date one copy of this
letter (the other is for your file) and return it to me, along with a
description of your suggestion.

Regardless of whether or not you choose to submit your idea to
us, we appreciate your thinking of the Company in connection
with your suggestion.

Some ideas are submitted by persons who have no desire for any compensation. However, the company rarely knows this initially. It may
become apparent only when the company receives a reply or release from

the submitter. If the submitter makes it clear that he anticipates no benefit or compensation from the company, the matter would seem to end there.

Sometimes the company may have trouble deciding whether the submitter is offering an idea without hope of compensation. Some submitters are masters of double talk or merely inexpert in expressing their intentions in writing. We have, for example, seen letters which read as follows:

> (a) I suppose you won't consider this suggestion of mine unless I say that you can have it for nothing but I am sure that a company as reputable as yours wants to be fair if you use somebody's brainchild.
>
> (b) I have heard that the bigger the company the more honest it is. So I'm not asking $50,000 or $10,000. You just go ahead and look this over.
>
> (c) I'm a great beliver (sic) in our American System of Business and I like to help a company make more jobs and more money. So I'm letting you look at this so we can make money together.

Whenever an ambiguous statement such as this is received, the company should return the material at once to the submitter and ask point blank whether he expects to be paid should the company use his submission. This contretemps may be avoided if *two* release forms are sent to the submitter, one for gratuitous and the other for a compensable submission. This is the technique used in the "booklet method" referred to in Section 9 below.

9. The Borden Company Program.

One of the best and most complete programs of handling idea submissions which has come to the author's attention is that of The Borden Company, here presented by permission.

The company makes it clear that it "intends to protect itself fully" but tempers this with a full explanation of its policies and the reason therefor in a 16-page booklet "Policies Concerning Submitted Ideas" which is sent to every submitter. The booklet deals with situations where compensation is not expected as well as with those for which compensation is sought.

The core of the booklet is a three-page set of "Conditions of Submission" which are individually and fully explained. These Conditions are also reprinted on the back of the printed form which the submitter is required to sign if he desires the company to consider his submission. These conditions are:

> 1. The entire subject matter of the submission must be made in writing with a complete and detailed written description of it

on or attached to the "Acceptance of Conditions" form, together with any other designs or illustrations that are identified and referred to in the written description.

2. A submitter must represent and warrant that the material submitted is the submitter's original work and that it is owned solely by the submitter.

3. Neither the submitter nor the Company assumes any contractual commitments with regard thereto, either express or implied, or any duty of any kind except as specified in its "Acceptance of Conditions" form.

4. The submitter and the Company each reserves the right to produce and rely on such evidence as may be available with regard to questions of originality, novelty, priority, ownership and availability to the Company or to the public or with regard to any similar question.

5. It is understood that no confidential relationship or fiduciary responsibility is to exist with regard to the submitted material.

6. The Company does not undertake to keep any submitted material secret or confidential and shall be in no way liable for any failure to keep such material secret or confidential.

7. Without limiting the generality of any of the conditions of submission, it is understood that the Company does not agree to pay any compensation whatsoever for its use of ideas which have not been patented.

8. The consideration by the Company of any submitted material shall not in any way limit the Company's right to contest the validity of any patent that may have been or may thereafter be obtained on it. The submitter's only remedy for such alleged infringement shall be under the applicable patent laws.

   It is understood that the Company will have complete freedom as to the type and extent of consideration to be given any submitted idea.

9. The Company shall have the ownership of, and the right to retain any material submitted to it in connection with any submitted idea.

   The Company shall not be required under any circumstances to reveal to the submitter what the Company did in considering the submission or to reveal any information regarding its activities in any fields relating to the submitted idea.

10. In instances in which the Company decides it is not interested in making any offer with regard to submitted material, the Company shall not be required to give any reasons for its so deciding.

11. If and whenever the Company negotiates for rights with regard to a submitted idea, so doing shall not constitute an admission by the Company that the idea is new or that the submitter is the first or original inventor of it.

12. Any and all prior negotiations or agreements with the Company are hereby rendered null and void and it is agreed that these conditions of submission constitute the entire agreement between the Company and the submitter with regard to the submission.

13. These conditions of submission may not be changed or supplemented in any way except by a written document duly signed on behalf of the Company by one of its officers.

14. No statement will be received in any language other than English.

The "Acceptance of Conditions"—the face of the above form—provides as follows:

Form for Use Where Compensation Is Hoped For.
Fill out—Sign—Detach—Mail

ACCEPTANCE OF CONDITIONS

The Borden Company:

I have read your pamphlet SI-64 on Policies Concerning Submitted Ideas. In consideration of the Company's being willing to examine certain ideas which I have submitted or propose to submit to it, I agree to the Conditions of Submission set forth on pages 6–8 of the pamphlet (also printed on the back of this sheet as page 16). I further agree that such Conditions shall apply to all disclosures made incidental to the original material submitted and to all information previously or hereafter disclosed or submitted relating directly or indirectly to such material. The subject matter which I am submitting relates to the following:

_____

_____

_____

_____

_____
Signature of Submitter

Date: _____   _____
Submitter's Address

_____

(If your idea is submitted with the hope of compensation, please sign the above form, filling in the subject matter, date and address, then detach it and return it in the envelope provided to The Borden Company, Law Department, 350 Madison Avenue, New York, N. Y. 10017. A duplicate of this form appears on the next-to-last sheet (page 13) of the pamphlet so that you may have a record of its contents.)

(See Reverse Side)

Two identical forms are provided for situations in which no compensation is anticipated. Only the upper portion of the dual form is here included.

Form for Use Where Compensation Is Not Expected
Fill out—Sign—Detach—Mail

The Borden Company
Law Department
350 Madison Avenue
New York, N. Y. 10017

The suggestion concerning _____

_____

which I am submitting for your consideration is submitted gratuitously and without expectation of compensation. You are free to
consider and use it without obligation to me for its consideration
or use.

_____

Signature of Submitter

Date: _____   _____

Submitter's Address

_____

It should be noted that both of the above forms are addressed to the
"Law Department" of the company as is the forwarding envelope which
is provided the submitter. This avoids the possibility of any misrouting
within the company structure. See Chapter 14, Sections 14 and 15.

The Borden Company is not alone in using the "booklet approach."
General Foods, Procter & Gamble, General Motors and others also use
it.

10. "Maximum Value" Contracts.

Another protective device is the so-called "maximum value" contract.
Under its terms the submitter agrees that even if the company admittedly
uses his suggestion, its liability will be limited to $500 or some other simi-
lar nominal sum. This has been used, for example, by one of the broadcasting networks, employing a letter essentially as follows:

We appreciate the courtesy of our listeners and professional people
who suggest material, including ideas, program formats, literary
material, and other suggestions, for our use. However, we receive
many suggestions which have been made previously either by our
own staff or by others. Likewise, we may commence using material
similar to yours which we receive after the date of your submission. It has therefore become necessary for us to adopt the policy of
refusing to consider any material unless the person submitting it
has signed the agreement appended to this statement and has
specified the maximum payment to be made to him in the event of
our use of his material. KINDLY DO NOT SUBMIT TO US
ANY MATERIAL WHICH YOU DEEM TO HAVE A VALUE

IN EXCESS OF THE LIMITS SPECIFIED IN PARAGRAPH 1 OF THE BELOW AGREEMENT BETWEEN US. (Emphasis in original.)

In effect, this means that the company may be liable for "something" but only in a limited amount. The nominal liability is similar to an insurance premium—an expenditure voluntarily undertaken as a safeguard against the possibility of a much larger loss.

11. Office Procedures.

Regardless of company policy as to unsolicited submissions, all should be handled and processed under an established office policy—faithfully followed. Its basic premise is that no one within the company who is qualified to appraise the submission should even "sight" it until the submitter has signed such releases or other agreements as the company may require.

To shortcircuit such possibility, all submissions—the moment they are recognized for what they are—should be routed to a "custodian" for handling. This custodian should be a non-technical, non-creative, non-policy-making individual. It has been facetiously suggested that a company should "get the dumbest girl you can find to handle the mail, one who obviously wouldn't know what to do with a good idea if she ever saw one." [16] The custodian may be a member of the legal or PR Department, a librarian, the comptroller, or even a special department set up just for this purpose. The identity of the custodian will naturally vary with the size and attitude of the company.

The following suggested procedure, involving the "watchdog" custodian and other company personnel, is based upon the methods used in several companies:

(a) All company personnel should be directed to route immediately all submissions to the custodian without any consideration, analysis, study—or even complete reading—thereof whatsoever. This is important because incoming submissions may be addressed to the attention of some named individual who might be qualified to analyze the submission.

(b) The custodian should mark and identify the submission carefully, thereafter logging it by number, date, name, subject matter and any other pertinent data known to the custodian, such as the name of the original addressee under (a) above and the time and method of its handling by that person.

(c) The submission should be photostated and the photostat preserved even when the original is to be returned to the submitter. This is to protect against a false claim by the submitter that his submission was different or more complete than was the fact. The submitter may not be satisfied with a "60 percent case" and later seek to make out a "100 percent case."

(d) The submission should either be returned to the submitter or filed—depending upon company policy.

(e) In all correspondence to the submitter, registered or certified mail should be used and the "red card receipt" filed and retained permanently.

(f) If and when signed releases are received from the submitter, they should be attached to the photostat of the submission.

(g) Only after receipt of releases etc. should the submission be delivered to appropriate company personnel for evaluation and possible negotiations.

(h) All of the custodian's submission files should be kept under lock and key and no one else—regardless of authority or echelon—should be permitted access to such locked files.

(i) All subsequent "back searches" of submissions should be made by the custodian. Other personnel should give the custodian a description of the later submission being checked against possible earlier submissions. It is at this point that the computer system referred to in Section 16 below becomes useful.

(j) The custodian should cross-reference all similar ideas. Many companies receive the same idea—in perhaps slightly different dress—over and over again and from a wide variety of sources.

(k) All company personnel—except clerical or secretarial—should be required to deliver a written report to the custodian promptly concerning any *oral* suggestions or submissions made to them. This should include even the most casual such as "that idea I gave you last year in the XYZ bar one night."

C. OWNERSHIP OF IDEAS.

12. Basic Concepts.

Ideas, as such, are abstractions. As far back as Seneca they were "common property." [17] More traditionally, they have been described as being "free as air." [18] "Creators" of ideas, therefore, were early held to have no property right in their concepts.[19] A New Jersey court said in 1906: [20] "It has never, in the absence of contract or statute, been held . . . that mere ideas are capable of legal ownership and protection."

The emphasis should be upon the word *mere*. *Mere* ideas may not be subject to ownership or protection but their reduction to literary, graphic or physical form will be—under appropriate circumstances. The clearest evidence of this is that an idea cannot be the subject of copyright but the expression of the idea can be.[21]

When so reduced to written form, the creator has a *common law* copyright. Having this right, the creator may (a) keep it secret and private, (b) generally "publish" the written expression of the idea under circumstances satisfying the statutory copyright requirements, (c) reveal it to certain persons under circumstances or conditions which protect the creator or reveal it generally with no effort at protection. It may even be said that the bulk of the "idea cases" are merely judicial determinations as to the legal efficacy of the various revelatory methods. These various methods and legal premises for recovery are discussed in Sections 17 to 29 below.

However, whether the creator "owns" or has a "property right" in his idea seems to be becoming relatively unimportant. From the more recent decisions it would appear that the courts are "more concerned with protecting the plaintiff than in protecting the property rights in an idea." [22] A more equitable attitude is being shown by the courts—instead of a strict application of traditional legal rules and concepts. This is a modern reverberation of the then-new ethical and equitable judgment of Justice Brandeis in the 1918 *Associated Press* case.[23] See Section 30 below.

13. Ideas Created by PR Firms.

Many valuable ideas are created by a PR firm or counsel in the course of serving clients. These ideas or concepts, which are developed in the course of such service and paid for by the client, are the property of the client.[24] This follows from the basic fiduciary relationship between the PR firm and its clients as to which see Chapter 2, Section 6.

On the other hand, it has been held that a firm soliciting a new client and revealing slogans or other plans and ideas to the prospective client who then retains another firm but uses the ideas of the first, will be compensated for such use.[25]

14. Employee-Created Ideas.

Employees of a company or of the PR firm may create the idea in question. The ideas are the "property" of the employer.[26] This is true as to both the "ideas" and the expressions thereof. Thus, an employee of a radio station was unable to stop the station from using plot ideas in future broadcasts after the ideas had been converted into scripts by other persons.[27]

Of course, if there is a contract between employer and employee as to relative rights in the output of the employee, the agreement would control.

If the source of the idea and its expression or manifestation is an independent contractor (not an employee) paid for his work, he may lose his rights if there is no reservation thereof.[28]

15. Multiple Ownership.

More than one person may "own" the idea. If more than one person collaborates and the result is the idea or the expression thereof, all such parties have rights therein as tenants in common and each is the owner of an undivided interest in the result.[29]

To transfer full title and all rights in the creation, all of the contributors should execute the transfer documents. The buyer may not know of this multiplicity of interest and one owner may not divulge the other's interest. To protect against this situation, most "idea agreements" contain warranties and representations that the seller is the sole owner and that no other person has any interest therein.

Similar ownership and transfer problems may arise if the idea is originally created by only one person but—perhaps after presentation to a possible purchaser—a second or third person "helps to work it up." The purchaser has dealt with the proper person in the first instance and may not know anything about the subsequent contribution and interest of the other.

16. Multiple Submissions.

The company's position is most ambivalent when two or more persons submit the same idea over a period of time, each claiming to be the originator and owner thereof, and the company later uses the idea. If the company can show that its own staff developed the concept or product independently without any contact with *any* of the submissions, the company's position is satisfactory.

However, the company may honestly believe that it received the idea from "X" originally and therefore negotiate with "X" for its purchase. However, in reality, the idea *first* came to the company staff from "A" but the company does not realize this.

The danger of multiple claims can probably best be met by using the warranty referred to above and a careful backcheck of company records before entering the subsequent transaction. Some companies are known to use a punchcard system or other computerized method to foreclose these dilemmas. Each submission is carefully broken down into a large number of components or elements, each of which is punched out on a card or stored in the computer. This stored information is checked against *every* later submission. The company does not rely on staff memories or a simple, one- or two-reference indexing system.

Storing the history of outside, unsolicited submissions is not enough. Staff developments—especially those not used—should also be stored. The unused contributions of the company's PR counsel, its advertising agency, consultants etc. should also go into the index or storage.

D. BASES OF LIABILITY.

17. Unconditional Communication.

If an idea is unconditionally communicated to another, the creator loses his rights—whatever they may have been before the communication —and anyone thereafter using the idea or its concrete expression is under no liability to the creator.[30] As the California Supreme Court has said: [31]

> The idea man who blurts out his idea without first having made his bargain has no one but himself to blame for the loss of his bargaining power.

This is true whether the idea is formally forwarded to the defendant in writing or idly mentioned at a social function.

Unless the disclosure is made under some form of restriction, confidential circumstances or relationship, agreement or circumstances indicating the expectation of compensation, the submitter has no claim against the user.[32]

18. Varied Legal Premises Involved.

Assuming that the creator of the idea has not unconditionally communicated it or "blurted it out" as discussed in Section 17 above, the next step is an examination of the various legal grounds upon which to seek possible protection and recovery for use of the idea. These are admittedly "legal" concepts but they have a very definite practical correlation with the method by which the idea is communicated or controlled by the plaintiff.

The various legal concepts which have received varying degrees of recognition by the courts are:

    (a) Express contract,
    (b) Implied contract,
    (c) Quasi contract,
    (d) Unjust enrichment,
    (e) Plagiarism,

    (f) Copyright infringement,

    (g) Trade custom,

    (h) Confidential relationship.

Obviously, with so many legal grounds from which to choose, it would be an unusual situation or relationship which would not posit at least a colorable foundation for a legal action. Most modern actions are based on more than one such ground. In the *Kurlan* case,[33] the suit was premised on *five*.

19. Express Contract.

  If the submitter and the company expressly agree—either orally or in writing—that the company will pay the submitter should it use the idea, the law will generally enforce such an agreement.[34]

  A common defense in an "express contract" case is that there was no "consideration" for the company's promise. This is based on the theory that an idea is not "property"; in some of the earlier cases, it was a good defense.[35] The leading case to this effect is *Masline v. New York, New Haven & Hartford R. R.*[36] in which the plaintiff had an express agreement with the defendant, revealed his idea (to sell advertising space on signs on railroad property) and the defendant promptly began to do so. The court held that since the plaintiff could not claim a property right in this concept—it was not novel—he could not recover.

  More recent cases have held otherwise. Even if the idea is not novel or original with the plaintiff, the courts find the consideration in the revelation of the idea (not otherwise required of the plaintiff) rather than in the idea itself.[37]

  A representative case is *High v. Trade Union Carrier Publ. Corp.,*[38] in which plaintiff revealed to defendant a simple tax-saving device (taken from the Internal Revenue Code) after defendant agreed to pay plaintiff 35 percent of its savings if it adopted the suggestion. The court said that "such *disclosure,* if protected by contract, is sufficient consideration for the promise to pay" (emphasis added).

  Sometimes the express promise to pay will be forthcoming *after* the plaintiff has revealed the idea. This must run the gauntlet of "past consideration" which, normally, will not create a contract nor support a promise to pay.[39]

  If the idea is merely abstract, the promise to pay should still be enforceable if the defendant uses the abstraction. The parties can agree to anything they wish. The tendency seems to be not to require concreteness in express contract cases.[40]

20. Implied Contract.

An implied contract is one which arises because of the *conduct* of the parties rather than by virtue of their *words,* oral or written.[41] It is a contract—as much as an express contract—and once the plaintiff proves appropriate conduct by both parties, the plaintiff has been held entitled to recover in idea cases.[42]

When a company receives an unsolicited submission—even with a clear indication that compensation is expected by the submitter if the submission is used—but the company does nothing to imply a promise to pay for it, the company is not liable (on this theory, at least) even though it uses the submission.[43] Also, when a company first receives an *offer* to submit an idea and then does nothing but the idea itself is later submitted, there is generally no liability.[44] California, however, appears to hold to the contrary and, in effect, requires that the company, in this situation, tell the submitter in advance that the idea is not wanted.[45]

If the defendant tells the submitter that it will consider the idea to be submitted or otherwise "solicits" the submission and later uses it, such conduct gives rise to an implied contract.[46] This result has been reached even in some cases in which it would seem that the parties understood that the idea was being submitted "gratis" or "without obligation." [47] It is these cases which seem to have cast some doubt on the use of "releases" by companies willing to consider submissions after execution of their release forms. But see Section 8 above.

21. Quasi Contract.

"Quasi contract" does not refer to a real contract. It is, rather, a legal theory which applies equitable principles and creates an obligation "for reasons of justice." [48] It is sometimes called a contract implied in law as against the "implied contract" which is a contract implied in fact. See Section 20 above.

This distinction is important even though it is not always understood or applied by the courts.[49] The contract implied in fact *is* a contract. The quasi contract action is not based on a contract of any kind but on the fact that the defendant has received a benefit from the submission and therefore should be liable as though (quasi) there had been a contract. The importance of this distinction lies in the fact that a company using the submission may be liable even though it did nothing affirmatively to give rise to either an express contract or an implied contract.

There seems to be a difference of judicial opinion as to the nature and scope of application of the quasi contract theory, some seeking to limit its application and others unduly extending it.[50]

22. Unjust Enrichment.

This is an equitable doctrine used by the courts to enforce payment by a defendant which has unjustly benefited by use of the property or service of another party. It has been applied in some idea cases. Thus in *Galanis v. Procter and Gamble Corp.*,[51] the court said:

> [Even] if the plaintiff has no property right in an idea, and . . . no contract for the sale or use . . . the defendant may be held liable in quantum meruit on the theory of unjust enrichment, where defendant utilized a concrete and novel idea submitted by the plaintiff.

This judicial approach seems to cut across the traditional rules in idea cases and simply asks, "Is it fair for the defendant to use the plaintiff's idea without paying for it?" It is akin to quasi contract discussed in Section 21 above. See Section 30 below.

23. Plagiarism.

The various legal bases for recovery heretofore discussed in Sections 19 to 22 presuppose that there has been some kind of contact or relationship between the submitter and the company. However, such a relationship may not exist. If the company has had access to the concrete expression of the plaintiff's ideas and then uses them, a claim for plagiarism may be justified.

Thus far, the legal ground has apparently been applied only in cases involving motion picture, radio or television properties which have been carefully plotted and described by the plaintiff.[52]

24. Copyright Infringement.

If a person has created something which is of such a nature as to be a proper subject of copyright, any other person or company using the material will be subject to a claim of copyright infringement. There is nothing unique about "idea claims" in this context. However, it is an unusual situation in which an "idea" is of such a nature [53] and there do not appear to be many cases applying this doctrine. In the *Kurlan* case,[54] however, copyright infringement was one of the grounds for recovery approved by the court.

Here again, there need be no relationship between the submitter and the company. In fact, there may not even be a "submitter" at all in the physical or relational sense.

As to copyright infringement generally, see Chapter 5.

25. Custom of the Trade.

There has been some judicial recognition of a "custom of the trade" whereby it is understood that if a recipient uses a submission from a professional or commercial source it must be paid for.[55] On the other hand, the New York Court of Appeals has held that evidence of such a custom "cannot create a contract where there has been no agreement by the parties . . ."[56]

For this rule to be applied, it is probably necessary for both the submitter and the company to be engaged in the same industry (The Theater, for example) and for the submitter to be a commercial source. It is unlikely to be applied if an advertising idea is submitted to a manufacturing company since the latter is not in the business of buying such ideas generally and constantly.

26. Confidential Relationship.

If an idea is revealed within the framework of a confidential relationship, the submitter usually will be protected.[57] It becomes a question of fact whether a confidential relationship exists. The employer-employee context usually creates such a relationship [58] although it may also be created under other circumstances. For example, new dress styles openly revealed at a fashion showing to a considerable group but under a prior seal of confidentiality will be protected on this basis.[59] The confidentiality must be made clear before the revelation; otherwise there will be no protection.[60]

Some cases have found a confidential relationship to exist where the creator of the idea turns it over to the defendant who is to prepare it suitably for marketing and sale[61] since, to hold otherwise, would "impede the industrial progress of the nation."[62] Other courts deny a confidential relationship in such circumstances.[63]

This concept may be important to the company approached by the "amateur" inventor or idea man who lacks sufficient "know-how" or experience to prepare the product or concept for the marketplace. It is for this reason that many of the releases or "conditions of submission" required of the submitter specifically spell out that there is no confidential relationship between the parties. See forms in Section 8 above.

27. Concreteness.

As the law of ideas developed, most courts have adverted, in some way or other, to the requirement that the submission must be "concrete" to be protectible. This stemmed from the belief that an abstraction could not be "property" but that a specific expression of the abstract idea is protectible property.[64]

The big question is how much flesh and blood must clothe the abstract idea for it to be considered "concrete." The cases vary considerably in their applications of the concreteness requirement. However, in most instances, the variable results can be justified by analyzing the idea before the court. It is probably safe to say that a submission—whether it be short or long, plain or embellished, oral or written—will be judicially "concrete" if its form is such that it can be used by the recipient without much further development, addition or change. This has been called the "immediate use" test.[65]

Probably specific examples are more instructive than extended definitions.

At one end of the scale in brevity and seeming abstraction are the "slogan cases" in which recovery has been allowed. In the *Century Brewing* case,[66] the plaintiff submitted the brief slogan "Beer of the Century." The court found for the plaintiff. At the other end of the scale are cases such as *Stanley v. C.B.S.*[67] in which the plaintiff submitted a detailed and highly polished broadcasting format which the court found to be "as concrete, definite and specific as could be devised by the use of words."

These two submissions have much in common despite their apparent contrariness. Both were as concrete and detailed as the recipient needed. The few words of the slogan constituted an effective slogan, usable by the brewery, without more, in almost any medium. The broadcasting format naturally would have to be more detailed and extensive to be usable and valuable.

This rationalization seems borne out by some of the motion picture cases which refused recovery for lack of concreteness. Thus, in *O'Brien v. R.K.O. Pictures* [68] the plaintiff submitted a suggestion that the defendant produce a picture based on the history of New York's Palace Theater. The idea was held insufficiently concrete and properly so. It needed a great deal of "work" and development to amount to anything. Furthermore, it could be developed along a number of different lines into many different kinds of picture.

Further support for the "immediate use" test is found in cases in which brief "gags" were submitted to W. C. Fields for which he was held liable,[69] and a bank was held liable as a result of a general, oral submission of a radio show format tied in with local schools.[70] So, too, was the submission held concrete in the bellwether 1935 case of *Meyer v. Liggett & Myers Tobacco Co.*[71] in which the plaintiff wrote the company the following frequently-quoted letter:

The idea consists of this. Two gentlemen, well groomed, in working clothes or in hunting togs, apparently engaged in conversation, one extending to the other a package of cigarettes saying, "Have one of these," the other replying, "No thanks; I smoke Chesterfields."

Yet there are cases in which seemingly detailed and lengthy explanations and submissions have been held not to be sufficiently concrete.[72] Despite such contrary holdings, however, the submitter would seem to be well-advised to expand his idea as much as possible. This does seem to be one situation in which it is wise to talk as much as possible—at least as far as concreteness is concerned.

28. Novelty.

Throughout most of the idea case decisions runs a rather confusing use of the terms "novelty," "original" and "novel and original" in discussing prerequisites to recovery regardless of the legal theory used by the plaintiff. "Novelty" means "new" in the sense that the idea has not been used or presented before by anyone.[73] "Original" is a less burdensome term since it means "new" with the submitter and "the result of his independent labor." [74]

But even these definitions do not cover all of the cases since certain more recent decisions have "watered down" the definition of "novelty" to mean new to the defendant—not as to the world.[75]

Certain basic concepts which are "common and general to the whole world" cannot be protected.[76] On the other hand, "old" in the sense of well-known ideas may be considered novel if they are combined together for the first time.[77] So too, a group of old ideas added to a new one will be protected.[78]

In the *Silver* case,[79] a Pennsylvania court said of this kind of situation:

[T]hey must evidence the exercise of skill, description and creative effort. It is no objection . . . [that the plaintiff] takes existing material from sources common to all writers and combines and arranges them so long as he creates a new form and gives them an application unknown before in a different manner and for different purposes resulting in a real improvement upon existing modes.

The courts seem to be paying less heed to the novelty and originality requirements, especially in the express contract and confidential disclosure cases.[80] More to the point, however, is the procedural fact that, although it is for the court in the first instance to decide whether there is *evidence* of originality to go to the jury,[81] it is then for the jury—not the court—to decide whether the submission is in fact novel, original or whatever the requirement on this score may be.[82] Once the case gets to the jury, the plaintiff is likely to have a better than even chance.

29. Liability Through Intervening Parties.

If the plaintiff communicated the idea—not to the defendant who used it—but to some third person, defendant's liability will depend on his relationship with the third person. If he is an authorized employee of the defendant, the defendant will be liable.[83] If he was not so authorized, defendant will prevail but the burden of proving lack of authority is the defendant's and this burden may be a severe one. Thus, in *Desny v. Wilder,* the employee was only a secretary but communication to her was sufficient.

If the third party was in a confidential relationship with the plaintiff and communicated the idea to defendant who used it with knowledge of the confidential relationship, defendant is liable.[84] The same results follow in trade secrets cases. See Chapter 17, Section 9.

30. Reconciliation of the Cases.

There is no doubt that some of the cases seem contradictory. This is true of even the more recent cases and although we recognize that some jurisdictions—California, for example—may have gone down a somewhat different road.

This apparent inconsistency and discontinuity may, however, be reconciled if we approach the entire field of "idea law" from an equitable point of view.[85] No matter what theories the courts may profess to apply, the judges seem to be seeking for even-handed justice and, in the words of Gilbert, "to make the punishment fit the crime." In the vernacular, despite closely-reasoned opinions, they seem to be asking, "Should we make the defendant pay the plaintiff for this idea?"

Among the various facets which the courts are likely to explore are these:

    (a) What is the basic character of the idea?

    (b) How much time, skill and effort did the plaintiff put into his submission?

    (c) How specific and detailed was the submission?

    (d) What was the relationship between the parties?

    (e) How much use did the defendant make of this idea?

    (f) Could the defendant also have obtained the plaintiff's idea from other sources?

    (g) How valuable was the idea to the defendant after he used it?

    (h) Did the defendant lead the plaintiff into a trap?

(i) Could the plaintiff have "made a deal" with someone else if the defendant did not use the idea?

(j) Will the plaintiff get a lucky "windfall"?

Based on the "pros and cons" of the answer to these questions, a court seems to get a "feeling" about the case before it. From this point it is not difficult to find appropriate legal stepping stones to a satisfactory legal answer—particularly if the court leaves critical issues to the jury.

While the courts may talk of "concreteness" or "novelty" and especially of ideas as being or not being "property," the courts seem to be veering toward what Holmes said in the *Masland* case fifty years ago: [86]

> Property in ideas is only an unanalyzed expression of certain secondary consequences of the primary fact that the law makes some rudimentary requirements of good faith.

Notes

1. C.B.S. v. De Costa, 377 F.2d 315, 153 U.S.P.Q. 649 (1st Cir. 1967). Other aspects of this case remain open as this is written and the holding should now be limited to the copyright issue.

2. For an interesting and illustrative discussion of company attitudes as to the usefulness of ideas submitted by non-company sources, see *Got Idea? Forget It!* Wall St. Jour., Nov. 25, 1966, p. 1; see also Leibman, *Problems Arising on Use of Art and Ideas by Business,* University of Chicago Conference on the Arts, Publishing and the Law, 81 (1952).

3. Note, *Corporate Protective Devices in the Acquisition of Ideas,* 65 HARV. L. REV. 673 (1952). For a report of a somewhat similar study, see Havighurst, *The Right to Compensation for an Idea,* 49 Nw. U.L. REV. 295 (1954), in LANDMARKS OF LAW 399, at 412, and notes 56–65 (Henson ed. 1960).

4. International News Service v. Associated Press, 248 U.S. 215, at 250 (1918).

5. Materese v. Moore-McCormack Lines, 158 F.2d 631 (2d Cir. 1946).

6. Wall St. Jour. *supra* note 2.

7. Havighurst, *supra* note 3.

8. Ketcham v. New York World Fair, 34 F.Supp. 657, at 661 (S.D.N.Y. 1940).

9. Masline v. New York, New Haven & Hartford R.R., *infra* note 36.

10. High v. Trade Union Courier Publishing Corp., *infra* note 38.

11. See Havighurst, *supra* note 3; Yankwich, *Legal Protection of Ideas—A Judge's Approach,* 43 VA. L. REV. 375, at 377 (1957).

12. 101 Ind. App. 420, 194 N.E. 206 (1935).

13. As quoted in Note, *supra* note 3, at 679, note 36.

14. 21 F.Supp. 445 (S.D.N.Y. 1937).

15. 179 F.2d 205 (2d Cir. 1950). For comments as to the meaning of this case, see Solinger, *Idea Piracy Claims—or Advertiser, Beware!* in 1953 COPYRIGHT PROBLEMS ANALYZED 121, at 128–32 (1953); Havighurst, *supra* note 3, at 410. See also Hampton v. La Salle Hat Co., 88 F. Supp. 153 (S.D.N.Y. 1949).

16. Wall St. Jour., *supra* note 2.

17. One of the best and most complete discussions of the law as applied to "ideas" will be found in NIMMER, THE LAW OF COPYRIGHT, ch. 15 (1963, 1965).

18. Fendler v. Morosco, 253 N.Y. 281, 171 N.E. 56 (1930).

19. Bristol v. Equitable Life Assurance Soc'y, 132 N.Y. 264, 30 N.E. 506 (1892).

20. Haskins v. Ryan, 71 N.J. Eq. 575, 64 N.E. 436 (1906).

21. Dollar v. Samuel Goldwyn, Inc., 150 F.2d 612 (2d Cir. 1945).

22. Note, *Compensation for Unsolicited Disclosure of Business Ideas,* 21 MD. L. REV. 139, at 145. See also Havighurst, *supra* note 3, at 406.

23. International News Service v. Associated Press, *supra* note 4.

24. Brown v. Mollé, 20 F. Supp. 135 (S.D.N.Y. 1937).

25. Ryan v. Century Brewing Ass'n, 185 Wash. 600, 55 P.2d 1053 (1936).

26. Phillips v. W.G.N., Inc., 307 Ill. App. 1, 29 N.E.2d 849 (1940); Von Tilzer v. Jerry Vogel Music Co., 53 F. Supp. 191 (S.D.N.Y. 1943), aff'd, 158 F.2d 516 (2d Cir. 1944).

27. Phillips v. W.G.N., Inc., supra note 26.

28. Bixby v. Dawson, 277 N.Y. 718, 14 N.E.2d 193 (1938); Grant v. Kellogg Co., 58 F. Supp. 48 (S.D.N.Y. 1944) aff'd, 154 F.2d 59 (2d Cir. 1946).

29. Carlson v. Phillips, 326 Ill. App. 594, 63 N.E.2d 193 (1945); Yardley v. Houghton Mifflin Co., 25 F. Supp. 361, aff'd, 108 F.2d 28 (2d Cir. 1939).

30. Univ. Sav. Corp. v. Morris Plan Co. of New York, 234 Fed. 382 (S.D.N.Y. 1916): Noahson v. Gunther Brewing Co., Balto. Daily Record, July 6, 1960 (Balto. Cty. Ct. 1960), discussed in Note, 21 Md. L. Rev. 139 (1961).

31. Desny v. Wilder, 46 Cal. 2d 715, 739; 299 P.2d 257, 270 (1956).

32. Havighurst, supra note 3, at 403–04.

33. Kurlan v. C.B.S., 40 Cal. 2d 799, 256 P.2d 962 (1953).

34. Desny v. Wilder, supra note 31; Weitzenkorn v. Lesser, 40 Cal. 2d 778, 256 P.2d 947 (1953): Yadkoe v. Fields, 66 Cal. App. 2d 150, 151 P.2d 906 (1944); Stone v. Goodson, 8 N.Y.2d 8, 200 N.Y.S.2d 627, 167 N.E.2d 328 (1960); Cole v. Phillip H. Lord, Inc., 262 App. Div. 11, 28 N.Y.S.2d 424 (1941); Engel v. Tom Fields, Ltd., 5 App. Div. 2d 874, 171 N.Y.S.2d 416 (1958).

35. Soule v. Bon Ami Co., 201 App. Div. 794, 195 N.Y.S. 574 (1922), aff'd, 235 N.Y. 609, 139 N.E. 754 (1923); Singer v. Karon, 162 Misc. 809, 249 N.Y.S. 566 (1937); Boop v. Ford Motor Co., 177 F. Supp. 522 (S.D. Ind. 1959), aff'd, 278 F.2d 197 (7th Cir. 1960).

36. 95 Conn. 702, 112 Atl. 639 (1921).

37. Elfenbein v. Luckenbach Terminal, Inc., 111 N.J.L. 67, 166 Atl. 91 (1933); Desny v. Wilder, supra note 31; Chandler v. Roach, 156 Cal. App. 2d 435, 319 P.2d 776 (1957); Comm. v. Affiliated Enterprises, 123 F.2d 776 (1957); Comm. v. Affiliated Enterprises, 123 F.2d 665 (10th Cir. 1941); Brunner v. Stix, etc., 352 Mo. 1225, 181 S.W.2d 643 (1944).

38. 69 N.Y.S.2d 526 (1946).

39. Gellert v. Dick, 277 N.Y. 125, 13 N.E.2d 603 (1938); contra, Desny v. Wilder, supra note 31.

40. Weitzenkorn v. Lesser, supra note 34; Kurlan v. C.B.S., supra note 33; contra, Alberts v. Remington Rand, Inc. 175 Misc. 486, 23 N.Y.S.2d 892 (1940).

41. Weitzenkorn v. Lesser, supra note 34.

42. Desny v. Wilder, supra note 31; Stanley v. C.B.S., 35 Cal. 2d 653, 221 P.2d 73, 23 A.L.R.2d 216 (1950); Kurlan v. C.B.S., supra note 33.

43. Bowen v. Yankee Network, 46 F. Supp. 62 (D.C. Mass. 1942); Grombach Productions v. Waring, 293 N.Y. 609, 59 N.E.2d 425 (1944).

44. Carneval v. William Morris Agency, 124 N.Y.S.2d 319 (Sup. Ct. 1953); Irizarry y Puente v. Harvard College, 248 F.2d 799 (1st Cir. 1957).

45. Desny v. Wilder, supra note 31.

46. Yadkoe v. Fields, supra note 34; Moore v. Ford Motor Co., 43 F.2d 685 (2d Cir. 1930); see also Nimmer, supra note 17, at notes 110–20.

47. See cases cited, supra note 37.

48. Weitzenkorn v. Lesser, *supra* note 34.

49. See discussion, Nimmer, *supra* note 17, at §168 and notes 33–37.

50. See discussion and cases cited in Nimmer, *supra* note 17, at §§168.1–2.

51. 153 F. Supp. 34 (S.D.N.Y. 1957). See also Ryan v. Century Brewing Ass'n, *supra* note 25; Healey v. R. H. Macy Co., 277 N.Y. 681, 14 N.E.2d 388 (1937).

52. Golding v. R.K.O., 35 Cal. 2d 690, 221 P.2d 95 (1950); Kovacs v. M.B.S., 221 P.2d 108 (Cal. App. 1950).

53. See Havighurst, *supra* note 3, at 400–401.

54. Kurlan v. C.B.S., *supra* note 33.

55. Kurlan v. C.B.S., *supra* note 33; Cole v. Lord, *supra* note 34.

56. Grombach Productions v. Waring, *supra* note 43, at 615. See also Bailey v. Haberle Brewing Co., 193 Misc. 723, 85 N.Y.S.2d 51 (Mun. Ct. 1948) (dictum).

57. Smith v. Petroleum Iron Works, 73 F.2d 531 (6th Cir. 1934); Bolt v. Alpine Geophysical Ass'n, 244 F. Supp. 458 (D.C.N.J. 1965); see Nimmer, *supra* note 17, at §171.

58. American Visuals Corp. v. Holland, 261 F.2d 652 (2d Cir. 1958); Radium Remedies Co. v. Weiss, 173 Minn. 342, 217 N.W. 339 (1928).

59. Dior v. Milton, 155 N.Y.S.2d 443 (1956), *aff'd,* 2 App. Div. 2d 878, 156 N.Y.S. 2d 196 (1956).

60. Cole v. Manhattan Modes, 2 App. Div. 2d 539, 157 N.Y.S. 2d 259 (1956).

61. Shellmar Products Co. v. Allen-Qualey Co., 36 F.2d 623 (7th Cir. 1930); Booth v. Stutz Motor Car Co., 56 F.2d 962 (7th Cir. 1932); Ojala v. Bohlin, 124 U.S.P.Q. 526 (1960).

62. Jones v. Ulrich, 324 Ill. App. 16, 95 N.E.2d 113 (1950).

63. Bowen v. Yankee Network, 46 F. Supp. 62 (D.C. Mass. 1942).

64. Havighurst, *supra* note 3, at 406–07.

65. Falk, *Originality or Novelty in Cases of Misappropriation of Ideas,* 33 J. Pat. Off. Soc'y 888, at 890 (1951).

66. Ryan v. Century Brewing Ass'n, 185 Wash. 600, 55 P.2d 1053 (1936). See also Healey v. R. H. Macy Co., *supra* note 51; *contra,* cases cited, *supra* note 56.

67. *Supra* note 42.

68. 68 F. Supp. 13 (S.D.N.Y. 1946).

69. Yadkoe v. Fields, *supra* note 34.

70. Belt v. Hamilton Nat'l Bank, 108 F. Supp. 689 (D.D.C. 1952).

71. *Supra* note 12.

72. See *e.g.,* Plus Promotions, Inc. v. R.C.A., 49 F. Supp. 116 (S.D.N.Y. 1943).

73 Thomas v. R. J. Reynolds Tobacco Co., 350 Pa. 262, 38 A.2d 61 (1944).

74. Golding v. R.K.O., *supra* note 52.

75. Berry v. Glidden, 92 F. Supp. 909 (S.D.N.Y. 1950); Weitzenkorn v. Lesser, *supra* note 34.

76. Soule v. Bon Ami Co., *supra* note 35.

77. Stanley v. C.B.S., *supra* note 42.

78. Kovacs v. M.B.S., *supra* note 52; Silver v. Television City, Inc., 207 Pa. Super. 150, 215 A.2d 335 (1965).

79. *Supra* note 78.

80. See Nimmer, *supra* note 17, at §173.2 and notes cited thereto.

81. Thomas v. R. J. Reynolds Tobacco Co., *supra* note 73; Silver v. Television City, Inc., *supra* note 78; Stanley v. C.B.S., *supra* note 42; Dezendorf v. Twentieth Century-Fox Film Corp., 99 F.2d 850, 39 U.S.P.Q. 467 (9th Cir. 1938) ; Yadkoe v. Fields, *supra* note 34.

82. Curtis v. United States, 168 F. Supp. 213 (Ct. Cl. 1958).

83. *Supra* note 34.

84. Carter Products v. Colgate-Palmolive Co., 130 F. Supp. 557 (D.C. Md. 1955), *aff'd,* 230 F.2d 855 (4th Cir. 1955), *cert. denied,* 352 U.S. 843 (1956).

85. See Mayer, *The Legal War of Ideas,* 5 PRAC. LAW. 17, at 23–24 (1959).

86. Du Pont Powder Co. v. Masland, 244 U.S. 100, at 102 (1917).

Chapter 7

Defamation: Libel and Slander

A. INTRODUCTION

1. The Influences of History
2. Defamation and Public Relations
3. Important Distinctions

B. DEFAMATION

4. Definition of Defamation
5. Publication
6. Standards of Language Construction
7. Techniques of Defamation
8. Subjects of Defamation
9. Colloquium
10. Inducement and Innuendo

C. LIBEL AND SLANDER

11. Definitions
12. Broadcast Defamation
13. Proof of Damage Dichotomy
14. Imputation of Crime
15. Accusation Affecting Business or Profession
16. Defamation of Public Relations Practitioners
17. Imputation of Unchastity
18. Damages: Special/General/Punitive
19. Innocent Defamation

D. DEFENSES

20. In General
21. Absolute Privilege
22. Consent to Defamation
23. Qualified Privilege

Chapter 7

Defamation: Libel and Slander

A. INTRODUCTION.

1. The Influences of History.

Much of the law of defamation may seem erratic and even ridiculous to both lawyer and layman. Prosser points out that "it must be confessed at the beginning that there is a great deal of the law of defamation which makes no sense" [1] and Pollock, the eminent English writer, has said, "No branch of the law has been more fertile of litigation than this . . . The law went wrong from the beginning." [2]

Practically every sector of the law of libel and slander has changed considerably over the years or is still changing—either through statutory adjustment or judicial interpretation. Many of its rules still suffer from a lack of uniformity with "majority" and "minority" rules abounding and the several states taking different positions on a given issue.

Some anachronistic concepts still prevail. Elsewhere more modern and persuasive applications and adaptations have developed.

Defamation law is the modern scion of a weird historical parentage— the marriage of ecclesiastic control of defamation as a spiritual "sin" and the temporal and political improvisations of the Star Chamber. The historical effects of this mating have been compounded by growing demands for freedom of the press, changing community mores, the introduction and supervention of modern communications, techniques and media, the persistence of anachronistic distinctions and the effect of the federal-state dichotomy.

It is probably safe to generalize that a "law" of libel and slander just does not exist as a viable, cohesive legal concept, premised on some fundamental and all-pervasive basic theory or approach. [3]

For these reasons, even the lawyer and the judge walk carefully when they venture into the defamation morass. Furthermore, the importance of the jury in defamation actions—its sometime waywardness of decision and its frequently unconscionable damage awards—has added to the difficulties of prophylactic advice and the reasonable resolution of defamation litigation.

2. Defamation and Public Relations.

As a prime company communicator, the PR man is constantly concerned with possible exposure—either of his company or of himself—to claims for libel or slander. Even a news release [4] or newspaper interview may open this door.[5] As company communications and statements become more competitive and aggressive, the possibilities increase.[6]

Obviously the PR man is not going to slander or libel anyone deliberately—if only because this would be "bad PR." But even innocent defamation may cause problems. It must also be kept in mind that the company communicator is probably less protected by the "privilege" which enures to the "press." [7] See Sections 21 to 27 below.

Public relations, publicity and all forms of commercial communication thrive on the use of words. Yet there is a growing feeling that some in the field do less than a brilliant job in handling words. Edwin Locke, President of Union Tank Car Company, has gone so far as to write that "verbal incompetence is threatening to become a chronic disease of the American intellect." [8]

In the hands of the PR man, such verbal incompetence, if it exists, can be an expensive mistake if it results in a libel action.

Juries have become more prodigal with the defendant's money in defamation cases. Verdicts running into hundreds of thousands of dollars have been returned with increasing frequency.[9] Inflation has hit the courtroom as well as the marketplace. Even when a court sets aside that portion of the verdict which covered punitive damages, the remaining figure may be in six figures.

The defendant—especially if it be a large company—may be "taught a lesson" by a jury. This is particularly likely to occur if the trial takes place in a jurisdiction distant from the defendant's "home town." Even at home the corporate defendant may be not too well-liked—worse yet, actively disliked—and a large verdict may be the jury's vehicle to manifest local antagonism toward the company.

In 1958 Dr. Frank Thayer, Professor of Journalism at the University of Wisconsin, published a study dealing with the spiraling verdicts in libel cases.[10] He summed up the results by saying, "Words are dangerous—and expensive." After reciting many high libel verdicts—the situation has worsened since 1958—Thayer discussed the suit of Henry Ford against the *Chicago Tribune* after the paper called Ford an anarchist. The plaintiff recovered but only a nominal, six cent verdict. However, Thayer

places "the cost of the *Tribune's* defense" at $303,968.72. This was un-
doubtedly a *cause célèbre* but defense costs do run high in libel cases—
even when the defendant prevails.

The PR man thus has a dual job: to make sure he does not open the
company to a libel action in the first place, and to do his best to create a
happy community environment so that the company "gets a fair shake" if
forced to defend such an action.

3. Important Distinctions.

Several important distinctions must be kept in mind in appraising defamation and its consequences to the parties.

(a) Because of the character of the historical development of the
subject, defamation is divided into two basic concepts: libel and slander.
These are defined in Sections 11 and 12 below.

(b) Words may be defamatory, slanderous or libelous and yet not
be actionable. This is the result of "privilege" or other defenses such as
"truth" which, under appropriate circumstances or by reason of certain
relationships, exonerate the defamer from liability. See Sections 20 to 29
below.

(c) The word "publication" is used with two meanings. One is
the normal meaning: a newspaper, magazine or other periodical circulated by a "publisher." The other is a technical meaning (a word of art)
having a special meaning: the communication of the defamation to a
third person. It need not be written or printed. It may be spoken. It may
result from an act such as shadowing the plaintiff in public.[11] The communication may be in the form of a statue.[12]

(d) The term *"per se"* is used in two ways. Basically *"per se"*
means "by or of itself." The distinction is between "defamation *per se*"
and "actionable *per se*." Prosser thus distinguishes the two uses: [13]

> A publication may be defamatory on its face; or it may carry a
> defamatory meaning only by reason of extrinsic circumstances.
> The distinction is not the same as that between defamation which
> is actionable of itself and that which requires proof of special
> damage, . . .

See Section 10 below.

B. DEFAMATION.

4. Definition of Defamation.

There does not appear to be any definition of defamation accepted by
all courts. According to Prosser: [14]

A defamatory communication usually has been defined as one which tends to hold the plaintiff up to hatred, contempt, or ridicule, or to cause him to be shunned or avoided.

Prosser goes on to explain that this may be too limited and adds:

Defamation is rather that which tends to injure "reputation" in the popular sense; to diminish the esteem, respect, goodwill or confidence in which the plaintiff is held; or to excite adverse, derogatory or unpleasant feelings or opinions against him.

The Supreme Court has defined defamation as being: [15]

An utterance tending to impugn the honesty, virtue or reputation, or publish the alleged or natural defects of a person and thereby expose him to public hatred, contempt, or ridicule.

Wittenberg, after dealing with the definitions of many courts, writes that "each of the courts . . . has added varied words and terms." He then summarizes "the judicial definitions of libel"—this applies to defamation generally—as being: [16]

False written or printed words, symbols, signs, pictures, or other methods of expression which expose or tend to expose a person to contumely, contempt, shame, disrepute, and ridicule, including words which tend to degrade the individual or lessen him in the estimation of an appreciable portion of the community, or that portion of the community which affects or may affect his personality or his business, or calling, and malicious publications tending to blacken reputations or to expose the object of the libel to public hatred, contempt and ridicule are libelous.

Inherent in every definition of defamation is the requirement that the *reputation* of the plaintiff must be adversely affected. This follows from the fact that reputation is the attribute of personality which the law of defamation seeks to protect. In the closely allied action for invasion of a person's right of privacy, the protected interest is not reputation but the feelings of the plaintiff.

See Chapter 8, Section 4 (a).

5. Publication.

As indicated in Section 3 (c) above, "publication" is a technical word in the law of defamation. It requires that the defamation must be communicated to some third party,[17] as a result of which the plaintiff's reputation suffers in some way. It is not enough to tell the plaintiff "to his face." The publication may occur by reason of a written or printed medium or any of the other means or techniques discussed in Section 7 below.

From the point of view of the corporate communicator, concerned with both internal and external communications, some question has arisen as to whether dictation by a *corporate* executive of a defamatory letter or memorandum to his stenographer is a publication. There would be no question about it except for the involvement of the corporate entity. If it is an individual (unincorporated) business, it is a publication.[18] Some courts, however, including those of New York, early held such dictation to be the "single act" of the corporation and therefore not a publication.[19]

However, in 1965 this doctrine was seriously questioned and not followed by a New York lower court in *Lux-Brill Productions, Inc. v. Remco Industries, Inc.*[20] as well as in subsequent legal commentary on this case. The court, in *Lux-Brill*, said:

> Any rule that would treat the stenographer of a corporation differently from the stenographer of a private business man, with reference to a libelous statement, would not be sound or just.

It is likely that the future will find the treatment of both situations alike—even in states which may have previously followed the questioned rule. Furthermore, apart from this, even in New York it has been held that once the dictated letter is transcribed and mailed, it is a publication binding upon the corporation.[21] The same is true of a transcribed corporate memorandum, distributed internally to corporate employees.[22]

Whoever repeats the original publication is party to a separate publication which is as actionable as the first.[23] It has been said that "talebearers are as bad as talemakers."[24] Reprinting a defamatory article in a house organ would be such a republication and open the company to a defamation claim. This is true even though permission to reprint had been obtained from the original publisher, and the source credited. Such stories or articles must be screened for defamation as carefully as an original piece, written expressly for the company organ.

6. Standards of Language Construction.

Once it has been established that allegedly defamatory words have been "published," it becomes necessary to decide whether they are, in fact, defamatory. By what semantic standard are they to be screened and tested? Must they hold the plaintiff up to disrepute with the entire community or just a segment thereof?

Justice Holmes has given us two memorable statements in this area. In *Towne v. Eisner* [25] he wrote of the meaning of words:

A word is not a crystal, transparent and unchanged; it is the skin of a living thought and may vary greatly in color and content according to the circumstances and the time in which it is used.

In *Peck v. Tribune* [26] he held:

Liability is not a matter of majority vote.

As to the meaning of the words themselves, the holdings in cases dealing with allegedly humorous remarks are instructive. A leading New York case [27] has held this to be no defense "unless it is perfectly manifest from the language employed that it could in no respect be regarded as an attack upon the reputation or business of the person to whom it related." The Colorado Supreme Court has pointed out that words are to be taken in their "natural, ordinary and commonly accepted meanings." [28]

Holmes' comment about "majority vote" is validated by cases such as *Ben-Oliel v. Press Publishing Co.,*[29] in which the plaintiff was defamed by the false attribution to him of a poorly written book even though only experts in his field would know that it was a poor book.

From these and other holdings, a statement will be considered defamatory if the plaintiff "is lowered in the esteem of any substantial and respectable group even though it may be quite a small minority" [30] provided its import is defamatory to a reasonable mind at the time and from the circumstances under which it was uttered.[31]

7. Techniques of Defamation.

Almost any method of communication, style of writing or graphic representation may render the communicator liable if the import of the words or representation is defamatory. The plaintiff is not limited to clearly defamatory words such as "thief." The defamation may occur through the use of any of the following:

(a) Alleged jest or humor. See Section 6 above.

(b) Fulsome praise uttered in an obviously ironic context or meaning.[32]

(c) Otherwise proper language becoming defamatory because of its application to the plaintiff. See Section 10 below.

(d) Cartoons and caricatures.[33]

(e) Photographs.[34]

(f) Ridicule.[35]

(g) Poetry or limericks.[36]

(h) Rumors or "whispers." [37]

(i) Advertisements.[38]

(j) Juxtaposition of plaintiff's name to animal pictures—the defamation resulting from the overall physical layout.[39]

(k) Statues or other three dimensional forms. See Section 3 (c) above.

(l) Physical acts such as hanging the plaintiff in effigy. See Section 3 (c) above.

8. Subjects of Defamation.

Any living person may be the subject of defamation.[40] Ordinarily a dead person may not be defamed.[41] However, living persons may be mentioned in connection with stories of deceased persons and, if the references to the living are defamatory, the living may recover.[42] Normally, however, relatives of the deceased cannot recover merely by virtue of their relationship.[43]

Corporations, corporate officers, partnerships and their members, non-profit groups such as benevolent, charitable and community institutions, etc. may also be defamed.[44]

Many of the allegedly defamatory statements about business corporations arise from their community relations and are intimately tied to the question of "privilege" as discussed in Sections 23 to 27 below. This has arisen in connection with a company's operation of its railroad,[45] pollution of local water supply,[46] premises' sanitation,[47] and employment practices.[48]

9. Colloquium.

For a plaintiff to succeed, he must prove that the defamatory words applied to *him*. This is known as the *colloquium*. There is no problem if the plaintiff is mentioned by name. If he is not named, he must prove that those who heard or read the defamation reasonably took it to apply to him.[49]

The greatest problem in this sector is so-called group libel—when the admittedly defamatory words are published about a group which may consist of any number from two [50] to millions. After showing that he is included in the group in question, the plaintiff must then show that he personally was defamed. If the group is a large one—such as "all lawyers," "parking lot owners in the city of Washington," [51] or "non-scheduled airlines," [52] it is generally held that neither the group nor an individual in the group has any legal recourse.

According to Prosser, the approximate numerical cut-off in these group cases is "twenty-five persons." If the group is a small one, such as an election board or the three or four members of a board of trustees or other identified group, there is probably liability at the suit of any member thereof. The same would be true of statements such as "all but one" or "some" in referring to a jury of twelve or a similarly limited group.[53]

Problems of this sort concerning libel of various ethnic, racial or religious minority groups of varying size have led to the enactment of state statutes on the subject. These are criminal in concept and there is no civil recourse for such libel.[54]

10. Inducement and Innuendo.

Words may seem quite innocent on their face but become defamatory as applied to the plaintiff by reason of facts not apparent in the publication itself. To make out his case, the plaintiff must prove these facts. This is known as the "inducement." It should not be confused with the "colloquium," discussed in Section 9 above.

Ashley cites the following hypothetical situation: [55]

> Suppose a story in print or over the air tells of the fine pitching of Jim Good at Saturday's sand-lot game. It should have said "Friday." If Jim is a leader in a church that makes Saturday the Sabbath, and forbids sports on a holy day, Jim may be libeled . . . Jim must demonstrate the defamation and prove that he suffered special harm.

The ever-present danger in a seemingly innocent situation such as this is pinpointed by the actual refusal of "Sandy" Koufax, the former star pitcher, to pitch in the World Series on a Jewish high holy day.

The plaintiff—after proving the inducement—must also prove that the words were defamatory with reference to the facts proved thereby. This additional probative step is the "innuendo." [56]

C. LIBEL AND SLANDER.

11. Definitions.

The two branches of defamation are libel and slander. Despite the fact that both have much in common, they have continued as distinct entities since their historical origins as separate wrongs. Their eventual coalescence as "defamation" did not result in unified rules.[57]

At one time *libel* was defined as *written* defamation; *slander* as *oral*. This libel definition has been expanded so that other forms of graphic defamation—in photographs,[58] cartoons and drawings,[59] motion pictures, statues—are libel. It has been suggested, therefore, that libel is defamation communicated by the sense of sight. Yet an oral interview given to a reporter—naturally intended to be printed later—is libel.[60] The sound of talking motion pictures has been called libel.[61] As to the status of broadcast sound, see Section 12 below. Chafee thus sums up the modern delineation: [62]

Libel is the principal branch of the law of defamation. The other branch is slander. Whereas in *libel* the derogatory statements are *printed or otherwise permanent,* in slander they take a *transitory form* and usually consist of *spoken words* or *insulting gestures.* . . .

*   *   *   *

As compared with libel, slander has little importance for mass communications. (Emphasis added.)

12. Broadcast Defamation.

The historically-engrafted differences between libel and slander have been compounded by the introduction of broadcasting—first radio and then television. Even now, the courts of the several states are not in agreement as to the legal character or status of such defamation. Some consider it as slander because it is oral.[63] Others consider it to be libel, largely because of the powerful impact of the media and the tremendous audiences exposed to a single defamatory broadcast.[64]

It seems agreed, however, that it is libel if the defamation is read from a written script.[65]

At least one state has considered it libel when a prepared radio speech —an "advance copy"—was sent to the newspapers shortly before it was actually broadcast.[66]

Several courts have tried to cut across the problem and have coined new terms for broadcast defamation. In the *Summit Hotel* case,[67] the Pennsylvania Supreme Court referred to it as "radio defamation," an entirely new tort, saying:

Publication by radio has physical aspects quite different from those attending the publication of a libel or slander as the law understands them. The danger of attempting to apply fixed principles of law governing either libel or slander to this new medium of communication is obvious. But the law is not so firmly and rigidly cast that it is incapable of meeting a new wrong as the demands of progress and change require.

The court then went on to say that the derogatory "ad lib" of Al Jolson about the plaintiff hotel was without the knowledge or approval of the defendant; that Jolson had not been employed by the defendant; and that the defendant had not been negligent in monitoring the broadcast. Therefore the defendant was not liable.

This "new wrong" approach was also taken by a Georgia court which coined "defamacast" to apply to broadcast defamation but then proceeded to treat the defamation as though it were libel.[68]

Some states have adopted statutes dealing with the matter and the statutory trend seems to be to consider broadcast defamation as slander. Prosser suggests that this is due to the "industrious lobbying of the broadcasting companies" and that slander is its category in most jurisdictions which have considered the matter.[69] This, of course, lightens the burden of the broadcasters. See Section 13 below.

In the absence of any statute on the subject it is likely that televised defamation is libel. This is true as to both the audio and video portions. At the same time, the video may be defamatory but the audio would not be. The reverse is also possible.

This libel categorization would certainly follow in states which have held radio defamation to be libel. Even in the other states, the tremendous impact of the visual medium should make the broadcast libel. If the show is "pretaped" and then televised, it should be libel just as the radio broadcast is considered libel if the defamation is first reduced to permanent script form as a script.

While not in the broadcast field, similar questions arise with the recording on a tape recorder of a speech—perhaps in "practice" form—intended for later public, oral delivery.

13. Proof of Damage Dichotomy.

The distinction between libel and slander, referred to in Sections 11 and 12 above, is today important largely because of its influence upon the necessity that the plaintiff prove actual damage to his reputation—or other actual damages—in a defamation case.

If the defamation is libelous on its face, no damages need be proved. They will be presumed because of the more permanent and forceful form of the defamation.[70] On the other hand, if it is "only" slander, no recovery will be allowed, generally speaking, unless damages are proved.[71]

However, as to slander, there are four generally accepted exceptions. Specific and actual damages need not be proved if the defamation:

(a) Imputes to the plaintiff the commission of a crime. See Section 14 below.

(b) Charges the plaintiff with having a "loathsome disease."

(c) Affects the plaintiff in his business, profession, calling, trade or office. See Sections 15 and 16 below.

(d) Charges a woman with being unchaste. See Section 17 below.

If a false oral accusation does not fall within any of these four exceptions, the plaintiff cannot recover for the defamation, no matter how derogatory it may be, unless he proves that he has suffered "special" damages. "Special" in this context means damages based upon specific facts and incidents, such as loss of customers or business. See Section 18 below.

Akin to the damage-requirement rule of slander (together with its four above exceptions) is the requirement in cases of "libel *per quod*." This is alleged libel which is not defamatory on its face and which, therefore, requires proof of extrinsic facts to make the statement defamatory.[72]

Most states consider libel *per quod* similar to slander and, unless the publication qualifies under one of the four exceptions, proof of damages is necessary to recovery.[73] A minority of jurisdictions, including England, hold that no special damages need be shown even in such cases, adhering to the general rule about libel.[74]

14. Imputation of Crime.

Imputing to the plaintiff the commission of a crime is actionable in slander without proving any special damages. This flows from the probable social ostracism which such a false charge would undoubtedly entail. However, under the doctrine of most states, the offense falsely charged must be one which involved "moral turpitude." Some states also require that it must be a charge which is subject to indictment or one which may lead to an "infamous punishment," generally taken to mean a sentence of imprisonment or death.[75]

The meaning and extent of "moral turpitude" are ambiguous. Usually it must involve some vile or mean action. Thus, a simple assault and battery caused by tempers at a social party probably would not involve such turpitude; a vicious or bloody assault and battery on a child or cripple would be so considered.

15. Accusation Affecting Business or Profession.

False derogatory statements affecting a person's business, profession, calling, trade or office probably constitute the most dangerous of the four exceptions in slander cases—at least insofar as communicators are concerned. In such cases probable injury to the plaintiff from a false accusation seems clear—even without proof of any specific damages.

There must be a false charge of activity which is incompatible with the plaintiff's proper behavior, conduct or ability in his business or profession. A false charge against a government official that he is a communist would be such an imputation.[76] On the other hand, in the well-known *LaGuardia* case,[77] the former New York mayor was held not liable for orally calling a lawyer "a bum in a gin mill." The court said that no special damages were shown and a charge of drunkenness did not reflect upon the plaintiff's ability as a lawyer. However, calling a lawyer "unethical" or a "shyster" would be such a reflection.[78]

The same false oral words may or may not be actionable depending upon the plaintiff's business or profession. If LaGuardia had applied the same oral epithet to a clergyman, this would have been actionable.

The false charge need not refer to a specific lapse or episode but may be generally descriptive of the plaintiff's conduct in his business or profession. Also, the same words may involve both the imputation of a crime and an adverse effect on the plaintiff's business. Thus a charge against a financial PR man that he conspired with a client to issue false financial information would involve a crime and also would affect his status in the PR business—even, perhaps, resulting in his expulsion from the PRSA. See Chapter 22, Section 8.

16. Defamation of Public Relations Practitioners.

There have been cases which have applied the rules discussed in Section 15 above as they apply to defamatory charges against PR practitioners and advertising agencies. In *Bates v. Campbell*,[79] for example, the defendant charged that the plaintiff had continued to represent herself as the publicity woman for a bar association even after her services had been terminated. This was held to reflect on the plaintiff so as to injure her in her business and was therefore actionable without proof of specific damages.

In *MacDonald v. Lord and Thomas*,[80] the plaintiff was an "advertising agent" and had a space contract with *Church and Home,* obtaining this directly from the publication. He sold the space to Vibert. However, the defendants, already a well-known agency but then operating as an "advertising concessionaire," controlled all of the space in the publication.[81] The defendants wrote to Vibert, saying they were obliged to decline the advertising but that they "would be glad to receive [the] order direct or through any responsible agency." This was held to libel the plaintiff without proof of damages because the language was "reasonably susceptible of conveying the idea that plaintiff's agency was not responsible."

These cases are the reverse of those which have held the agency liable for defamation. In *Locke v. Benton and Bowles, Inc.*,[82] for example, plaintiff was a newswriter and brought suit against the defendant agency because it mishandled plaintiff's story, as a result of which plaintiff was held up to disrepute and injured in his reputation as a writer. Plaintiff recovered.

Generally speaking, a PR firm or advertising agency will be held responsible along with its client for libel or defamation if it was "primarily involved in the transaction." [83]

17. Imputation of Unchastity.

Normally company communicators are not likely to impute a lack of chastity to a woman. However, the imputation may be indirect and proved by the "inducement." See Section 10 above.

A "personal" in a house organ announcing that John and Mary Jones have just had twins would fall within this category if John and Mary had been married only a month before, and this fact was known to their friends at the plant.[84] Many a "breezy" item in such personals may infer such unchastity and should be carefully avoided.[85]

Similar charges may be inferred from erroneous captions or photographs issued by a company to local newspapers—especially when a woman actually married to A is captioned as being "Mrs. B." Company absentee lists should also be carefully checked if any female employees are shown thereon as being on "maternity leave" when the employee is not even married.

Imputation of unchastity to a woman also may be an accusation of a crime such as fornication or adultery, depending on the marital state of the plaintiff. See Section 14 above.

18. Damages: Special/General/Punitive.

As discussed in Section 13 above, the primary importance of the libel/ slander dichotomy is its effect on damages and the need for proving them. However, when the plaintiff has proved that the defendant is liable—either because the publication was a libel or, if oral, fell within one of the four slander exceptions, the door is open to the plaintiff to recover substantial additional damages.

Even if proof of special damages may not be a basic prerequisite to liability in the particular case, the plaintiff may still prove such specific injury if he can. In one of the earliest cases (1614) the plaintiff proved that the slander caused loss of an advantageous marriage.[86] Special damages may include loss of an existing job or the refusal of new employment, loss of credit rating by a business man, loss of trade by a storekeeper, etc.

General damages compensate for such things as loss of reputation, the plaintiff's injured feelings or possible illness resulting from the defamation.[87]

Punitive damages—"smart money" as it is sometimes called—are additional assessments against the defendant as a punishment, unconnected with the plaintiff's loss or injury, in order to prevent the defendant from "doing it again." These punitive damages can mount very high.[88]

19. Innocent Defamation.

Defamation may be—often is—innocent of any intention or malice. It is still actionable. In the leading English case, *Hulton & Co. v. Jones,*[89] the House of Lords affirmed a £1,500 judgment for the plaintiff, Artemus Jones, a lawyer from North Wales. The plaintiff claimed that he was libeled by a newspaper story about "Artemus Jones"—intended to be a fictitious character—sent to the defendant by its Paris correspondent.

This is "strict liability"—a legal rule not often applied, its most common examples being the liability of those handling explosives or keeping wild animals. No negligence on the part of the defendant need be shown. Probably the only limitation on the strict liability rule for innocent defamation is that the language must be false and that it must be understood as applying to the plaintiff.[90] Of course, its innocence may be shown in an effort to avoid punitive damages against the defendant.[91]

This situation arises frequently in cases of republication by newspapers obtaining the libelous story from a reputable wire service. This is no defense.[92]

The innocent or inadvertent defamatory publication may occur through a typographical error, use of a fictitious name the same as that of the plaintiff, ignorance of even the existence of the plaintiff—as in *Hulton v. Jones*—mistake as to name or address in a story or photographic caption,[93] honest belief in existence of a privilege, etc.

Since the publisher is liable even for libel innocently published, he is also liable for defamation negligently published.

Questions of inadvertence, negligence, knowledge, malice, etc., as they affect the basic question of *publication* of defamation, should not be confused with similar questions as they affect privileges, as to which see Sections 21 to 27 below.

D. DEFENSES.

20. In General.

The defendant in a libel or slander case is not entirely unarmed. Assuming that the plaintiff has proved that the utterance was defamatory, that it was published by the defendant, applied to him, that he has suffered damage (special or general)—in other words, the plaintiff has made out a complete case—the defendant then may attempt to rely on and prove one of several defenses of which the major are:

    (a) Privilege in its various aspects. See Sections 21 to 27 below.

    (b) Truth. See Section 28 below.

    (c) Retraction. See Section 29 below.

Privilege and truth are complete defenses. If made out, the defendant is completely absolved of wrongdoing. Retraction is normally only a partial defense; it goes only to mitigate damages.

21. Absolute Privilege.

Absolute privilege is the right, regardless of motive, to be free from claims for libel or slander. Ordinarily it is limited to such persons or situations as judges and judicial proceedings, counsel, litigating parties and witnesses, legislative proceedings and legislators (both state and federal), members of the executive.[94]

Absolute privilege is of only limited interest to the communicator or publisher in the private sector. It applies largely to the statements or writings of those in various branches of government—judicial, legislative, and executive. However, because of the increasing involvement of the private sector—especially of business—with government, absolute privilege is having a greater, although still indirect, effect on the company communicator or PR man.

Almost every federal governmental officer, from the highest to within reach of the lowest,[95] enjoys an absolute privilege, provided that the defamatory statement is made within his "line of duty."

From the point of view of governmental-personnel activities and decisions and the communication thereof to the public, the 1959 Supreme Court holding in *Barr v. Matteo* [96] is of great significance. The Court first approved the doctrine of absolute privilege for federal officers and employees when performing their required duties. It then extended the privilege to the *issuance of news releases* explaining or reporting their official acts, considering such releases to be publications within the "outer perimeter" of their duties.[97] Other decisions have held, however, that state officers and officials, especially those in lower or local echelons, are not protected by an absolute privilege but only a qualified privilege.

This matter of press releases—so important to the private and business sector—is limited to situations in which the issuer is acting within the limits of his proper realm or function. Prosser describes this limitation by pointing out: [98]

> It is no part of the duties of a janitor, or a United States marshal, to issue a press release concerning what he sees and hears, or of school district trustees to issue such statements concerning the superintendent or pupils, . . . or of a mayor to act as unofficial censor of art.

As to the right of an individual or a corporation to answer or rebut such governmental news releases when they concern him or it, see Sections 23 and 26 below.

Under certain circumstances, a private individual or company may be clothed with the government's absolute privilege. Thus, in *Becker v. Philco Corp.*,[99] the defendant was required by its contract with the Defense Department to report immediately not only actual but suspected compromise of classified information. The court applied the protective doctrine of *Barr v. Matteo* to the defendant, particularly because its report about the plaintiff was made in confidence and not given any "open publication."

When an employer's representative utters a defamation at a grievance meeting with the union—in answer to a question—his statement is "unqualifiedly privileged." This is premised on the national policy of settling labor/management disputes.[100]

22. Consent to Defamation.

In most areas of tort law, consent to the tort by the person later claiming to be aggrieved is a full defense. This is also true in defamation. Thus, if a person approves an article about him, he cannot later claim that he has been libeled in the article.[101] This also arises in cases in which a person, in effect, tempts or "dares" another to publish something defamatory. A company or trade group cannot deliberately invite investigation and then sue for defamation as a result of the investigation and the publication of its results.[102]

This looms as important in advertising cases also where consent is given to use of name or photograph by a person who later claims that the advertisement libels him or violates his right of privacy. However, such consent must not be exceeded if it is to constitute a full release.

As to the application of this rule to right of privacy cases, see Chapter 8, Sections 30 to 36.

23. Qualified Privilege.

Qualified privilege excuses a defamatory publication provided it is published for a proper purpose or motive and in a proper or reasonable manner. The classic frame of reference of qualified privilege is the 1834 description by Baron Parke: [103]

> [Defamation is privileged when] fairly made by a person in the discharge of some public or private duty, whether legal or moral, or in the conduct of his own affairs, in matters where his interest is concerned.

There are many situations and relationships which give rise to a qualified privilege. Generally, they concern an interest which the defendant properly seeks to serve but which does not have the overwhelming social importance of those protected by absolute privilege.[104]

The privilege applies where the defendant is reasonably protecting some interest of his own, such as his property or his reputation; when he has a duty to warn a family member or an employee; when he serves a socially recognized purpose such as warning a prospective employer— especially one who has inquired—as to the misconduct or unreliability of a former employee of the defendant; where there is a mutual interest to be served such as communication with stockholders by a corporation's officers or among members of a group (a trade association, for example) having common interests.[105]

Other qualified privilege areas are discussed in Sections 24 to 27 below.

Since this privilege is only qualified—not absolute—the defendant loses the defense if he "goes too far." This abuse may take any one of several forms.

The substance of the statement may go beyond the permitted relevant scope. It may be published to persons or through media which are beyond those having an interest in the matter.[106] It is usually said that the privilege is lost if it is motivated by "malice" although "malice" is sometimes used here ambiguously. It has been suggested that the better rationale is that the privilege falls if there be some motive other than "the purpose of furthering the interest which is entitled to protection." [107]

A further requirement for the privilege—variously stated—is that the defendant must believe what he says, have reason or probable cause to believe the truth of his statement, or must act as a reasonable man under the circumstance. Conscious lies are not permitted. See Section 27 below.

24. Public Proceedings Reports.

Generally speaking, the public's "right to know" is the basis for the privilege of reporting publicly on legislative and judicial proceedings. This includes federal, state and municipal proceedings. It also covers reports and communications made to members of government, such as the report to a state governor by an investigating committee.[108]

This privilege is not limited to newspapers or other elements of the press. Any individual or company enjoys it. Thus it has been held that this qualified privilege bars recovery against a corporate burglary victim which issued a substantially correct news release about its pending suit against a burglary-protection company. The suit charged fraudulent misrepresentation about the effectiveness of the devices which the company had previously installed on the victim's premises.[109]

On the other hand, if a company starts a suit solely for the purpose of ruining a competitor's reputation, it may not then widely distribute copies of its complaint—or releases about the suit—and claim a privilege to do so.[110] This is in accord with the position of the *Restatement of Torts* which provides that this privilege is lost if the report is circulated or published "solely for the purpose of defaming the other and not . . . of informing the public." [111]

25. Public Interest Communications.

Members of the public—this includes the PR man, of course—have a right to communicate with members of government concerning matters which should be investigated or otherwise dealt with by such authorities. This includes information as to crimes, improper government operations, etc.[112]

The communications must be made in good faith [113] and may be made, under this qualified privilege, only to the government official who is charged with following up the complaint or communication. Assuming good faith, misstatements of fact are protected.

26. Fair Comment.

One of the most important areas of qualified privilege is "fair comment." A person may make a fair and reasonable comment upon matters of legitimate interest to the public and such comment may be published broadly.[114] The natural targets for such comment (by either the press or "anyone else") are members of government, candidates for public office, operations of various public institutions—even private companies or individuals whose activities have an impact upon the community or a substantial portion of the public. Such persons may be variously called "public officers," "public persons," "affected with a public interest," etc.[115] See Section 27 below.

However, the privilege does not extend to a defamatory discussion of every person or subject which may constitute "news." The subject must be one which affects a substantial segment of the public. Furthermore the substance and extent of the statement or comment must be "fair." This means that it must not go beyond the aspects of the matter which are of interest to the public.

The usual example is that of a theater critic or book reviewer who has a right to comment—perhaps even caustically or violently—about the book or play; yet he exceeds his privilege if he deals with the private life or personal character of the author or the playwright or there is evidence of malice underlying the otherwise proper criticism.[116] As to comment or criticism about persons in public life, the same is true. An official may not be safely defamed for something which has nothing to do with his public service.

Until 1964 there was a continuing dispute among the courts of the various states as to whether the privilege of fair comment covered misstatements of both fact and opinion.[117] However, in 1964, in *New York Times v. Sullivan,* the Supreme Court held that the privilege applied to misstatements of fact as well as opinion, as discussed more fully in Section 27 below.

This concept of privilege—with its limitations—must still be considered despite the ruling in *New York Times.* This decision has not been fully implemented as this is written and the true extent of its perimeter is not yet clear.

27. New York Times v. Sullivan.

In 1964 the Supreme Court decided *New York Times v. Sullivan,*[118] of which it has been said: "[No] case in modern jurisprudence has had any greater effect on a given field of law. . . ." [119]

A full-page paid advertisement was placed in the *New York Times* by a committee defending Dr. Martin Luther King. The advertisement was libelous of Sullivan (the plaintiff) who was the Commissioner of Public Affairs in Montgomery, Alabama. The lower courts had held for the plaintiff but the Supreme Court reversed, saying:

> [The First Amendment] prohibits a public official from recovering damages for a defamatory falsehood relating to his official conduct unless he proves that the statement was made with "actual malice" —that is, with knowledge that it was false or with reckless disregard of whether it was false or not.

The *Times* had in its "morgue" information which would have disclosed that certain matters in the advertisement were false but the Supreme Court disregarded this since, under the circumstances, the editor was not required to search through "the vast files" of the *Times.*

The Court was careful to point out that it was not deciding "how far down into the lower ranks of government the 'public official' designation would extend . . . or otherwise to specify categories of persons who would or would not be included." This cautionary comment may have been temporizing since the decision was premised, in part, on a 1909 decision [120] which had suggested that this privilege should extend to comments about private business men, the earlier decision referring to:

> the conduct of all corporate enterprises affected with a public interest—transportation, banking, insurance, and to innumerable other subjects involving the public interest.

Subsequent cases have given some indication of the extent to which this new rule will be extended. *Garrison v. Louisiana* [121] held that judges were open to criticism by a district attorney. *Washington Post Co. v. Keogh* [122] applied it to a Congressman. The Supreme Court, in *Rosenblatt v. Baer*,[123] included a *former* supervisor of a country recreational area. The Court said that it would "at the very least" apply the designation of "public official" to government employees "who have, or appear to the public to have, substantial responsibility for or control over the conduct of governmental affairs."

Dyer v. Davis [124] applied the rule to a *candidate* for public office. The court has held that General Edwin A. Walker, while not a public official, was a "public man" and therefore covered by the *Times* holding.[125]

In *Butts v. Curtis Publishing Co.*,[126] the Supreme Court extended the rule to nonofficial public figures when it affirmed a $460,000 verdict for the plaintiff, a football coach. However, the court found that the defendant had not checked its facts and sources properly and, from this, found the necessary "malice" which vitiates the privilege.

The "public figure" or "public man" test has been applied in other cases. Professor Linus Pauling, winner of both the Nobel Peace Prize and the Nobel Prize in science, was held to have no action for being erroneously referred to as a fellow traveler and as having been cited for contempt of Congress.[127] The Eighth Circuit explained that Pauling had "projected himself into the arena of public policy, public controversy and pressing public concern."

While the Alaska Supreme Court did not specifically adopt the *New York Times* rule as to a columnist, Drew Pearson, it applied the substance of the rule as to the necessity of malice as to *all* privilege and held that Pearson had no action against a publication which referred to him as "the garbageman of the Fourth Estate." [128]

The new rule has also been applied to the law partner of a mayor by the New York Court of Appeals.[129] This extension of the rule to persons incidentally defamed is in accordance with prior law.[130]

In *Time, Inc. v. Hill*,[131] the Supreme Court reversed a verdict for the plaintiff in a privacy case—not a libel case—on grounds similar to that enunciated in *New York Times*, while carefully pointing out that it was not blindly following that rule. Also, in *Julian Messner, Inc. v. Spahn*,[132] the Court summarily vacated the order of the New York Court of Appeals which had upheld a verdict for the plaintiff in a privacy case. For further discussion of the *Hill* and *Spahn* cases, see Chapter 8, Section 22.

While the scope of this rule has been growing under these Supreme Court decisions, there have been other cases which have denied its application to a lobbyist,[133] a former sports figure,[134] an entertainer,[135] an educator.[136]

However, some of these cases were decided before the latest Supreme Court decisions and conceivably would not be so decided today.

As this is written, it would appear that the *New York Times* rule will be extended to protect against claims for libel by most—if not all—persons who are public officials having some control of public affairs and defamed in their public capacity, public persons or persons in the public eye even though involuntarily, persons openly injecting themselves into public affairs or public controversy, provided that the defendant's statement, made without malice, deals with the plaintiff's public activities, as against his private life.

The cases thus far have all involved newspapers, magazines or other elements of the press such as a wire service. The question of the extension of this shield to private citizens or corporations still remains to be definitively proclaimed. However, the First Amendment rationale of the Supreme Court would appear to warrant such extension. Furthermore, the libel in *New York Times* was itself a paid advertisement and the Court held this to be immaterial. It has been suggested: [137]

> What the Court's new ruling means is that anyone with access to a printing press—the civil rights activist, Ku Klux Klansman or wealthy magazine publishers alike—has wide privilege in publishing defamatory remarks about almost anyone involved in public controversy.

At the same time, the rule does have limits. A New York court has held it not to be privileged for an allegedly defamatory paid advertisement to be published by a group of advertising men critical of the plaintiff's work on behalf of the New York Police Department's Civilian Review Board.[138]

28. Truth.

In civil suits for defamation truth is generally a defense. However, the truth of the defamatory statement must be substantially proved. Proof of partial truth is insufficient as is proof of similar but other facts.[139] It is, therefore, important to avoid an "embroidery" of the facts in making a charge. Such peripheral matters cannot later be proved as true and this inability may strike down the entire "truth defense."

Some courts have held that the failure to prove the truth of the charge after alleging such a defense, aggravates the offense. More recent cases, however, seem to have departed from this.[140]

29. Retraction.

A retraction by the defendant is not a complete defense in a libel action. On the other hand, it will do much to mitigate damages and will often result in a lesser award.[141] One of the virtues of the retraction is that it does much to negative the existence of malice and, therefore, helps to avert punitive damages.

The retraction—as with a plea of truth—must be a full retraction. It may not offer other innuendoes as in the frequently-quoted classic example of the "phony" retraction: a charge that the plaintiff "isn't fit to sleep with pigs" is not retracted by a statement that the plaintiff "is fit to sleep with pigs."

Many states have enacted statutes dealing with retractions, under which the defendant is generally protected against punitive and excessive damages.[142]

See Chapter 4, Section 22 as to the "right of reply," an additional protective device available in some jurisdictions to the plaintiff—and the defendant as well.

Notes

1. PROSSER, TORTS 754 (3d ed. 1964).
2. POLLOCK, TORT 243, 249 (13th ed. 1929).
3. For an explanation of this historical development, see Prosser, *supra* note 1, at 754, *passim;* Holdsworth, *History of Defamation,* 40 L.Q. REV. 302 (1924), 41 L.Q. REV. 13 (1925); Veeder, *History and Theory of Defamation,* 3 COLUM. L. REV. 546 (1903), 4 COLUM. L. REV. 33 (1904); 1 STREET, FOUNDATIONS OF LEGAL LIABILITY, ch. XIX (1906).
4. American Dist. Tel. Co. v. Brink's, Inc., 35 L.W. 2667 (7th Cir. 1967).
5. Valentine v. Gonzales, 190 App. Div. 490, 179 N.Y.S. 711 (Sup. Ct. 1920).
6. American Dist. Tel. Co. v. Brink's, Inc., *supra* note 4.
7. Williams v. Williams, 27 App. Div.2d 550, 275 N.Y. S.2d 425, 35 L.W. 2364 (1966).
8. Locke, *What Price Verbal Incompetence?* P.R.J., April, 1962, at 9.
9. See *e.g.,* Butts v. Curtis Publishing Co., *infra* note 126.
10. Thayer, *Libel, Privacy Costs on Inflationary Spiral,* Ed. & Publ., March 15, 1958, at 50, 52.
11. Schultz v. Frankfort, etc., Ins. Co., 151 Wis. 537, 139 N.W. 386 (1913).
12. Monson v. Toussauds, [1894] 1 Q.B. 671.
13. Prosser, *supra* note 1, at 766. See, as illustrative of the distinction, Bowie v. Evening News, 148 Md. 569, 129 Atl. 797 (1925); Woolston v. Montana Free Press, 90 Mont. 299, 2 P.2d 1020 (1931).
14. Prosser, *supra* note 1, at 756.
15. Dorr v. United States, 195 U.S. 138 (1904).
16. WITTENBERG, DANGEROUS WORDS 6 (1947).
17. Pullman v. Walter Hill & Co., [1891] 1 Q.B. 529; Gambrill v. Schooley, 93 Md. 48, 48 Atl. 730 (1901).
18. Fulton v. Atlantic Coastline R. Co., 220 S.C. 287, 67 S.E.2d 425 (1951); Cochran v. Sears, Roebuck & Co., 72 Ga. App. 458, 34 S.E.2d 296 (1945).
19. Wells v. Belstrat Hotel Corp., 212 App. Div. 366, 208 N.Y.S. 625 (Sup. Ct. 1925); Owen v. Ogilvie, 32 App. Div. 465, 53 N.Y.S. 1033 (1898); Magnolia Petroleum Co. v. Davidson, 194 Okla. 115, 148 P.2d 468 (1944); Prinz v. Holland-North American Mtg. Co., 107 Wash. 206, 181 P.2d 680 (1919).
20. 40 Misc. 697, 265 N.Y.S.2d 440, 34 L.W. 2314 (Sup. Ct. 1965). Note, 19 OKLA. L. REV. 467 (1966).
21. Ostrowe v. Lee, 256 N.Y. 36, 175 N.E. 505 (1931).
22. Kennedy v. Butler, Inc., 245 N.Y. 204, 156 N.E. 666 (1927).
23. See Painter, *Republication Problem in the Law of Defamation,* 43 VA. L. REV. 1131 (1961); Prosser, *supra* note 1, at 787–90 and notes 77–99, 1–14.
24. Cavalier v. Original Club Forest, 59 So. 2d 489 (La. App. 1952).
25. 245 U.S. 418 (1917).
26. 214 U.S. 185 (1909).

27. Triggs v. Sun Printing & Publishing Ass'n, 179 N.Y. 144 (1904).

28. Knapp v. Post Publishing, etc., Co., 111 Colo. 492, 144 P.2d 981 (1943).

29. 251 N.Y. 250, 167 N.E. 432 (1929). See also Locke v. Benton & Bowles, 165 Misc. 631, 1 N.Y.S.2d 240 (1937); Gershwin v. Ethical Publishing Co., 166 Misc. 39, 1 N.Y.S.2d 904 (1937).

30. Prosser, *supra* note 1, at 760.

31. Buckstaff v. Viall, 84 Wis. 129, 54 N.W. 111 (1893); Polakoff v. Hill, 261 App. Div. 777, 27 N.Y.S.2d 142 (1941); Grant v. New York Daily Herald, 138 App. Div. 727, 123 N.Y.S. 499 (1910); Sullivan v. Daily Mirror, 232 App. Div. 507, 250 N.Y.S. 420 (Sup. Ct. 1931).

32. Buckstaff v. Viall, *supra* note 31.

33. Tolley v. Fry & Sons, Ltd., [1931] A.C. 333, 16 B.R.C. 1031; Brown v. Harrington, 268 Mass. 600, 95 N.E. 655 (1911).

34. Burton v. Crowell Publishing Co., 82 F.2d 154 (2d Cir. 1936); Peck v. Tribune, 214 U.S. 185 (1909).

35. Dolby v. Newnes, 3 T.L.R. 393 (1887).

36. Tolley v. Fry & Sons, Ltd., *supra* note 33; Triggs v. Sun Printing & Publishing Ass'n, 179 N.Y. 144, 71 N.E. 739 (1904); Villers v. Monsley, 95 Eng. Rep. 886 (1769).

37. MacRae v. Afro-American Publishing Co., 172 F. Supp. 184 (E.D.Pa. 1959), *aff'd,* 274 F.2d 287 (3d Cir. 1960).

38. Louka v. Park, 294 Mass. 268, 1 N.E.2d 41 (1936); Myers v. Afro-American Publishing Co., 168 Misc. 429, 5 N.Y.S.2d 223, *aff'd* 255 App. Div. 838, 7 N.Y.S.2d 662 (1938).

39. Zbyszko v. New York American, 228 App. Div. 277, 239 N.Y.S. 411 (1930).

40. This includes children. See Munden v. Harris, 153 Mo. App. 652, 134 S.W. 1076 (1910)

41. Hughes v. North Eastern Newspaper Publishing Co., 312 Mass. 178, 43 N.E.2d 757 (1942). Most states have *criminal* statutes concerning defamation of the dead. This is beyond our concern in this work. See *e.g.,* N.Y. Penal Law §1340.

42. Dall v. Time, Inc., 252 App. Div. 636, 300 N.Y.S. 680 (1937), *aff'd,* 278 N.Y. 635, 16 N.E.2d 297 (1938), *rearg. denied,* 278 N.Y. 718, 17 N.E.2d 138 (1938); RESTATEMENT, TORTS §560 (1939).

43. Skrocki v. Stahl, 14 Cal. App. 1, 110 Pac. 957 (1910); Bradt v. New Nonpareil Co., 108 Iowa 449 (1899). See Armstrong, *Nothing But Good of the Dead,* 18 A.B.A.J. 5229 (1932).

44. See cases cited, Prosser, *supra* note 1, at 762, notes 3–19.

45. Crane v. Waters, 10 Fed. 619 (C.C. Mass. 1882).

46. Williams v. Standard-Examiner Publishing Co., 83 Utah 31, 27 P.2d 1 (1933).

47. South Hetten Coal Co. v. North-Eastern News Ass'n, [1894] 1 Q.B. 133.

48. Charles Parker Co. v. Silver City Crystal Co., 142 Conn. 605, 116 A.2d 440 (1955).

49. Davis v. R.K.O. Pictures, 191 F.2d 901 (8th Cir. 1951); Cosgrove Studio v.

Pane, 408 Pa. 314, 182 A.2d 751 (1962); Youssoupoff v. M-G-M Pictures, Ltd., 50 T.L.R. 581, 99 A.L.R. 864 (1934).

50. American Broadcasting-Paramount Theatres, Inc. v. Simpson, 106 Ga. App. 230, 126 S.E.2d 873 (1962).

51. Service Parking Corp. v. Washington Times Co., 92 F.2d 902 (D.C. Cir. 1937).

52. Golden North Airways v. Tanuaua Publishing Co., 218 F.2d 612 (9th Cir. 1955).

53. See Prosser, *supra* note 1, at 767–69, notes 60–74.

54. For discussions of this problem, see Scott, *Criminal Sanctions for Group Libel; Feasibility and Constitutionality,* 1 DUKE U.B.J. 218 (1951); Beth, *Group Libel and Free Speech,* 39 MINN. L. REV. 167 (1955); Tanenhaus, *Group Libel,* 35 CORNELL L.Q. 261 (1950).

55. ASHLEY, SAY IT SAFELY 18 (3d ed. 1966).

56. See cases cited, Prosser, *supra* note 1, at 766, notes 46–47.

57. For a discussion of the history, distinctions and underlying theories of the cases, see Prosser, *supra* note 1, at 769–70.

58. Burton v. Crowell Publishing Co., 82 F.2d 154 (2d Cir. 1936). See *Libel By Lens,* 52 A.B.A.J. 873 (1966).

59. Tolley v. Fry & Sons, Ltd., *supra* note 33.

60. Valentine v. Gonzales, *supra* note 5.

61. Kelley v. Loews, 76 F. Supp. 473 (D.C. Mass. 1948); Youssoupoff v. M-G-M Pictures, Ltd., 50 T.L.R. 581, 99 A.L.R. 864 (Eng. 1934).

62. CHAFEE, GOVERNMENT AND MASS COMMUNICATIONS 78–79 (1947).

63. Remington v. Bentley, 88 F. Supp. 166 (S.D.N.Y. 1949); Meldrum v. Australian Broadcasting Co., [1932] Vict. L. Rep. 425.

64. Wanamaker v. Lewis, 173 F. Supp. 126 (D.D.C. 1959); Sorenson v. Wood, 123 Neb. 348, 243 N.W. 82, 82 A.L.R. 1098 (1932); Shor v. Billingsley, 158 N.Y.S.2d 476 (Sup. Ct. 1956), *aff'd without op.,* 4 App. Div. 2d 1017, 169 N.Y.S.2d 416 (1957); Notes, 71 HARV. L. REV. 384 (1957); 10 ALA. L. REV. 10 (1957); 37 B.U.L. REV. 378 (1957); 32 TUL. L. REV. 135 (1957); 35 TEXAS L. REV. 854 (1957); 8 SYRACUSE L. REV. 296 (1957).

65. Hartmann v. Winchell, 296 N.Y. 296, 73 N.E.2d 30 (1947); Landau v. C.B.S., 205 Misc. 357, 128 N.Y.S.2d 254 (1954).

66. Weglein v. Golder, 317 Pa. 437, 177 Atl. 47 (1935).

67. Summit Hotel Co. v. N.B.C., 336 Pa. 182, 8 A.2d 302 (1939).

68. American Broadcasting-Paramount Theatres, Inc., v. Simpson, *supra* note 50. See Notes, 46 MARQ. L. REV. 397 (1962); 37 TUL. L. REV. 147 (1964); 36 TEMPLE L.Q. 240 (1963); 25 GA. B.J. 310 (1963); 9 WAYNE L. REV. 391 (1963); 16 VAND. L. REV. 472 (1963).

69. Prosser, *supra* note 1, at 772.

70. Youssoupoff v. M-G-M Pictures, Ltd., *supra* note 61.

71. RESTATEMENT SECOND, TORTS §384 (1965).

72. Green, *Relational Interests,* 31 ILL. L. REV. 35 (1936); Note, 13 VAND. L. REV. 730 (1960); Prosser, *More Libel Per Quod,* 79 HARV. L. REV. 1629 (1966); Hann, *Libel by Intrinsic Fact,* 47 CORNELL L.Q. 14 (1961).

73. Caldwell v. Crowell-Collier Publishing Co., 161 F.2d 333 (5th Cir. 1947), *cert. denied,* 332 U.S. 766, *sec. app.,* 170 F.2d 941 (5th Cir. 1949).

74. Smith v. Smith, 236 N.Y. 581, 142 N.E. 292 (1923); Herrmann v. Newark Morning Ledger, 48 N.J. Super. 420, 138 A.2d 61 (1958).

75. See cases cited, Prosser, *supra* note 1, at 773–74, notes 25–35.

76. Remington v. Bentley, *supra* note 63.

77. Weidberg v. La Guardia, 170 Misc. 374, 10 N.Y.S.2d 445 (1939).

78. Kraushaar v. Levin, 181 Misc. 508, 42 N.Y.S.2d 857 (1943).

79. 213 Cal. 438, 2 P.2d 383 (1931).

80. 27 Ill. App. 111 (1888).

81. For a discussion of advertising concessionaires and other historical functions of the advertising agent or agency, see Simon, The Law for Advertising and Marketing, ch. 1, at 3, *passim.*

82. 253 App. Div. 369, 2 N.Y.S.2d 150 (1938).

83. Spring, Risks and Rights 49 (1952); see also Socolow, Law of Radio Broadcasting §481 (1939).

84. Morrison v. Ritchie, 39 Scot. L. R. 214 (1904); Cassidy v. Daily Mirror, [1929] 2 K.B. 331, 69 A.L.R. 720.

85. See Bentley, Editing the Company Publication 54 (2d ed. 1953).

86. Matthew v. Crass, Cro. Jac. 323, 79 Eng. Rep. 276 (1614).

87. See cases cited, Prosser, *supra* note 1, at 779–80, notes 6–11.

88. Butts v. Curtis Publishing Co., *infra* note 126; Walker v. Associated Press, *infra* note 125.

89. [1909] 2 K.B. 44, *aff'd,* [1910] A.C. 20. See Smith, *Jones v. Hulton: Three Conflicting Views as to Defamation,* 60 U. Pa. L. Rev. 364 (1912); Morris, *Inadvertent Newspaper Libel and Retraction,* 32 Ill. L. Rev. 36 (1937).

90. Nebb v. Bell Syndicate, 41 F. Supp. 929 (S.D.N.Y. 1941).

91. Wood v. Constitution Publishing Co., 57 Ga. App. 123, 194 S.E. 760 (1937).

92. Carey v. Hearst Publications, 19 Wash. 2d 655, 143 P.2d 857 (1943); Wood v. Constitution Publishing Co., *supra* note 91; *contra,* Layne v. Tribune Co., 108 Fla. 177, 146 So. 234, 86 A.L.R. 466 (1933).

93. Peck v. Tribune, 214 U.S. 85 (1909).

94. See Prosser, *supra* note 1, at 796–804.

95. *E.g.,* Harwood v. McMurtry, 22 F. Supp. 572 (W.D.Ky. 1938) (internal revenue agent); Lyons v. Howard, 250 F.2d 912 (1st Cir. 1958), *aff'd,* 360 U.S. 593 (1959) (naval officer).

96. 360 U.S. 564, *reh. denied,* 361 U.S. 855 (1959).

97. To the same effect, see Matson v. Margiotti, 371 Pa. 188, 88 A.2d 892 (1952) (Attorney General); Glass v. Ickes, 117 F.2d 273, 132 A.L.R. 1328 (D.C. Cir. 1940), *cert. denied,* 311 U.S. 718 (1941) (Secretary of Interior); Ryan v. Wilson, 231 Iowa 33, 300 N.W. 707 (1941) (Governor); Lombardo v. Stroke, 18 N.Y.2d 349, 222 N.E.2d 721, 35 L.W. 2347 (1966).

98. See Prosser, *supra* note 1, at 803–04.

99. 372 F.2d 771, 35 L.W. 2498 (4th Cir. 1967), *rev. denied,* 36 L.W. 3224 (1967).

100. General Motors Corp. v. Mendicke, 367 F.2d 66, 35 L.W. 2201 (10th Cir. 1966).

101. Sharman v. C. Schmidt & Sons, 216 F. Supp. 401 (E.D. Pa. 1963); Ginsburg v. Black, 237 F.2d 790 (7th Cir. 1956), *cert. denied,* 353 U.S. 911 (1957).
102. National Disabled Soldiers League v. Haan, 4 F.2d 436 (D.C. Cir. 1925).
103. Toogood v. Spyring, [1834] 1 C.M. & R. 181, 149 Eng. Rep. 1044.
104. See Jones, *Interest and Duty in Relation to Qualified Privilege,* 22 MICH. L. REV. 437 (1924); Harper, *Privileged Defamation,* 22 VA. L. REV. 642 (1936).
105. Prosser, *supra* note 1, at 809.
106. See Hallen, *Excessive Publication in Defamation,* 16 MINN. L. REV. 160 (1932).
107. Prosser, *supra* note 1, at 822.
108. Brandon v. Gazette Co., 234 Ark. 332, 352 S.W.2d 92 (1961).
109. American Dist. Tel. Co. v. Brink's, Inc., *supra* note 4.
110. Williams v. Williams, *supra* note 7.
111. RESTATEMENT SECOND, TORTS, *supra* note 71, at §611.
112. Dempsky v. Double, 386 Pa. 542, 126 A.2d 915 (1956); Foltz v. Moore-McCormack Lines, 189 F.2d 537 (2d Cir. 1951), *cert. denied,* 342 U.S. 871 (1951).
113. Otten v. Schutt, 15 Wis.2d 497, 113 N.W.2d 152 (1962).
114. See text and cases cited, Prosser, *supra* note 1, at 812–16.
115. *Id.*
116. Taylor v. Hungerford, 205 Iowa 1146, 217 N.W. 83 (1927); Buckstaff v. Viall, *supra* note 31; Brinkley v. Fishbein, 110 F.2d 62 (5th Cir. 1940), *cert. denied,* 311 U.S. 672 (1941).
117. Titus, *Statement of Fact versus Statement of Opinion—a Spurious Dispute in Fair Comment,* 15 VAND. L. REV. 1203 (1962); Noel, *Defamation of Public Officers and Candidates,* 49 COLUM. L. REV. 875 (1949).
118. 376 U.S. 254 (1964). See Notes, 113 U. PA. L. REV. 284 (1964); 38 So. CAL. L. REV. 349 (1965); 30 Mo. L. REV. 467 (1965); 114 U. PA. L. REV. 241 (1965); 30 ALBANY L. REV. 316 (1966); 7 WM. & MARY L. REV. 215 (1966); 15 DE PAUL L. REV. 376 (1966).
119. Arthur Hanson, *The Law of Libel,* remarks made before Practicing Law Institute, New York, April 14, 1967.
120. Coleman v. MacLennan, 78 Kans. 711, 98 Pac. 281 (1909). See also cases and authorities cited in 376 U.S. 280, note 20.
121. 379 U.S. 64 (1964).
122. 365 F.2d 965 (D.C. Cir. 1966), *cert. denied,* 35 L.W. 3234 (1967).
123. 383 U.S. 75 (1966).
124. 189 So. 2d 678 (La. 1966); *contra,* Fignole v. Curtis Publishing Co., 247 F. Supp. 595, 34 L.W. 2297 (S.D.N.Y. 1965).
125. Walker v. Associated Press, 388 U.S. 130 (1967).
126. 388 U.S. 130, 35 L.W. 4636 (1967).
127. Pauling v. National Review, Inc., 269 N.Y.S.2d 11 (Sup. Ct. 1966); Pauling v. Globe–Democrat Publishing Co., 362 F.2d 188 (6th Cir. 1966). See also Rose v. Roch, 36 L.W. 2248 (Minn. 1967).

128. Pearson v. Fairbanks Publishing Co., 413 P.2d 711 (Alaska 1966).

129. Gilberg v. Goffi, 21 App. Div.2d 517, 251 N.Y.S.2d 823 (1964), *aff'd*, 15 N.Y.2d 1023, 207 N.E.2d 620 (1965).

130. See 75 YALE L.J. 642 (1966).

131. 385 U.S. 375, 35 L.W. 4108 (1967).

132. 35 L.W. 3409 (1967).

133. Clark v. Pearson, 248 F. Supp. 188 (D.D.C. 1965).

134. Dempsey v. Time, Inc., 43 Misc. 2d 759, 252 N.Y.S.2d 186 (Sup. Ct. 1964).

135. Mason v. Sullivan, 26 App. Div.2d 115, 27 N.Y.S.2d 314 (1966).

136. Harper v. National Review, Inc., 33 L.W. 2341 (Sup. Ct. 1964), *aff'd memo. op.*, 263 N.Y.S.2d 292 (Sup. Ct. 1965).

137. N.Y. Times, June 18, 1967, sec. 4, p. 6E.

138. Cole Fisher Rogow, Inc. v. Carl Ally, Inc. *et al.*, 35 L.W. 2798 (N.Y. Sup. Ct. 1967). See also report of this case including the allegedly libelous advertisement involved in the case, A.A., May 29, 1967, at 2, 92.

139. Kilian v. Doubleday & Co., 367 Pa. 117, 79 A.2d 657 (1951).

140. Domchick v. Greenbelt Consumer Serv., 200 Md. 36, 87 A.2d 831 (1952); Will v. Press Publishing Co., 309 Pa. 539, 164 Atl. 621 (1932); Las Vegas Sun, Inc. v. Franklin, 74 Nev. 282, 329 P.2d 867 (1958).

141. Morris, *Inadvertent Newspaper Libel and Retraction*, 32 ILL. L. REV. 36 (1937); Leflar, *Legal Remedies for Defamation*, 6 ARK. L. REV. 423 (1952).

142. See Morris, *supra* note 141; *Retraction Statutes*, 19 WASH. & LEE L. REV. 239 (1962); *contra*, Gersten v. Newark Ledger Co., 52 N.J. Super. 152, 145 A.2d 56 (1958).

Chapter 8

Rights of Privacy and Publicity

A. HISTORY AND DEVELOPMENT

1. Public Relations and Right of Privacy
2. Definition of "Privacy"
3. Background and Development
4. Differences From Other Rights
5. Classification of Privacy Cases
6. Jurisdictions Recognizing Privacy
7. Jurisdictions Not Recognizing Privacy
8. Privacy Statutes

B. RIGHTS AND PERSONS INVOLVED

9. Rights Protected
10. Identification Requirements
11. Persons Protected
12. "Public Figures"
13. Rights of Minors
14. Rights of Employees
15. Deceased Persons
16. Relations and Heirs of Deceased **Person**
17. Persons Liable

C. "ADVERTISING PURPOSES" AND "PURPOSES OF TRADE"

18. Importance to Business Communications
19. Confusion of the Cases
20. Paid Advertising
21. Broad Scope of the Terms
22. "Public Figure" Problems
23. Incidental Use
24. Incidental Advertising Use by Publishers
25. Collateral Use
26. Editorial Endorsement Reprints

D. RELEASE AND WAIVER OF RIGHTS

E. THE RIGHT OF PUBLICITY

Chapter 8

Rights of Privacy and Publicity

A. HISTORY AND DEVELOPMENT

1. Public Relations and Right of Privacy.

> Trude Heller booked a new rock 'n' roll combo into her Village nightclub and gave it the name "Abercrombie and the Fitches." Her aide phoned Abercrombie & Fitch, spoke to the head of the promotion department and asked if the store would cooperate for some tie-in publicity with the rock 'n' rollers. "Well, what would you like us to do," replied the store's promotion man, "sue 'em or outfit 'em?"[1]

Here, in capsulized Broadway columnist form, is the dilemma of the modern promotion or PR man when faced with the twin rights of privacy and publicity. We do not know what happened as a sequel to this telephone conversation, but the legal records reveal no lawsuit by Abercrombie & Fitch.

Public relations, by its very nature, is intimately concerned with the right of privacy—as both prospective plaintiff and defendant. Continually concerned with names, news, pictures, "publicity values" and all of the other trappings of effective corporate communications, the PR man is at the very core of situations which may give rise to "privacy problems."

2. Definition of "Privacy."

The right of privacy encompasses a broad spectrum of the human personality and activities. It is, therefore, not easily defined. Two brief definitions which early appeared are "the right to be let alone" (1888)[2] and "the right to an inviolate personality" (1890).[3] These early definitions have continued to be applied. Thus, in 1940, in reviewing fifty years of privacy law, Nizer merely elaborated on these simple meanings when he wrote:[4]

> . . . the right of an individual to live a life of seclusion and
> anonymity, free from the prying curiosity which accompanies both
> fame and notoriety. It presupposes a desire to withdraw from the
> public gaze, to be free from the insatiable interest of the great
> mass of men in one who has risen—or fallen—below the mean. It
> is the recognition of the dignity of man's free will and the power
> to mold his own destiny, of the sacred and inviolate nature of
> one's innermost self.

Such sweeping, humanistic generalizations are almost inescapable because of the flexible character of the privacy theory. Privacy is a legal
catch-all for the protection of many of the individual's rights which fall
into no other legal pigeonhole. It defends those intangible attributes of
the human personality which exist apart from his physical person and his
worldly assets.

As new cases come down, the perimeters of both privacy and publicity
seem to be continually expanding. This has led Dean Prosser to re-
mark: [5]

> This is not to say that the developments in the law of privacy are
> wrong. Undoubtedly they have been supported by genuine public
> demand and lively public feeling, and made necessary by real
> abuses on the part of the defendants who have brought it all upon
> themselves. It is to say rather that *it is high time that we realize
> what we are doing, and give some consideration to the question of
> where, if anywhere, we are to call a halt.* (Emphasis added.)

3. Background and Development.

Every legal text or law review article dealing with the right of privacy
attributes its existence to a "famous article by Samuel D. Warren and
Louis D. Brandeis" which appeared in the *Harvard Law Review* in 1890
as a result of the highly personal and embarrassing nosiness of the Boston
press in the "elaborate" social activities of Mrs. Warren in what was an
era of yellow journalism.[6]

The adulation for this article is undoubtedly merited, since it effectively synthesized what was essentially an entirely new legal category.
Earlier cases—both in England and the United States—had redressed
violations which today would be "privacy cases." They had done so,
however, within the framework of other and already well-recognized legal
concepts such as property rights, breach of contract, copyright, breach of
confidence or unfair competition.[7]

Probably the best known of these early cases (1849) involved etchings
made by Prince Albert, consort of Queen Victoria.[8] The court enjoined
their publication by the defendant who had surreptitiously obtained
them. The decision was based on property rights and breach of trust.

Even earlier (1816) Lord Byron had legally stopped the attribution to him by defendant of an inferior poem.[9]

Despite these early gropings toward a privacy concept in England, that country does not, even now, appear to apply it, either at common law or by statute. The great growth has been in the United States.

While most states today recognize the right, the trend was not always smooth. New York at first refused to admit its existence at common law in the famous *Roberson* case [10] involving advertising and labeling—a commercial use of the plaintiff's name. It required a statute to reverse this holding. The thrust of the statute is against commercial use, rather than against the yellow press "nosiness." See Section 8 below.

There is no question that today the right of privacy is a well-accepted member of the legal family in most jurisdictions although its exact application may vary from state to state. As far back as 1945 one court said: [11]

> Courts which have had occasion to pass upon the matter have pretty generally accepted the right of privacy as an established part of Tort Law. The Restatement states its existence has been established . . . Likewise have the writers in the law reviews . . .

As to the position of each of the American jurisdictions, and of the *Restatement of the Law, Torts,* see Sections 6 to 8 below.

The judicial history of privacy is marked with the footsteps of the famous and, in a few instances, the infamous.

We find poets and writers such as Byron, Pope and Swift. Royalty is represented by Emperor Franz Josef of Austria, Prince Albert, Victoria's consort, Princess Irina Alexandrovna Youssoupoff of Russia and Elizabeth II along with Prince Philip. Nobility is there in the persons of the Dukes of Rutland, Buccleuch and Queensbury, the Earl of Clarendon and Count Orsini. Vassar College is matched by President Eliot of Harvard. Serge Koussevitsky, Walter Gieseking, Mary Garden and Fred Waring and his Pennsylvanians are on hand from music and opera. Tom Edison was an early figure.

There have been athletes and figures from several sports including Ben Hogan, Cyril Tolley, Bill Sharman, Davey O'Brien, Graham McNamee, Warren Spahn and hundreds of other baseball players. Restaurateurs such as Sherman Billingsley and "Toots" Shor march through the cases. Even Al Capone and Jesse James are among those involved. Finally, but by no means least, there are some of the brightest names of Broadway and Hollywood, past and present: Walt Disney, Groucho Marx, Kirk Douglas, Shirley Booth, Fred Astaire, Charlie Chaplin, Fatty Arbuckle, Aunt Jemima, Bert Lahr, Bea Lillie and Ed Wynn.

While, of course, these "big names" can be easily matched by a horde of "little names" in the privacy cases, the big-little name dichotomy points up an ambiguous aspect of the law's development. There is a natural tendency to find big names in the "appropriation" cases referred to in Section 5 below because of their obvious commercial or "free ride" value. The little names appear more frequently in cases in the other three categories: the "intrusion," "disclosure" and "false light" cases.

Probably this distinction will disappear as more jurisdictions approve the "right of publicity" doctrine discussed in Sections 39 to 44 below. Many of the appropriation cases, especially the more recent, though decided under the privacy theory, could have been decided under the publicity theory.[12] The future is likely to bring a corrective judicial orientation whereby more courts will recognize that publicity, not privacy, is involved. Publicity or appropriation values will be compensated rather than privacy rights protected.

4. Differences From Other Rights.

As indicated in Section 3 above, the precursor cases of the right of privacy fell within different legal doctrines. Then privacy gradually became an accepted legal right and was protected as such. Subsections (a) to (f) below delineate these different rights.

(a) Defamation.

Defamation was an early basis for recoveries which, under some later cases, would probably have been based upon privacy. When privacy was first recognized, a definite effort was made to distinguish it from the libel and slander cases.

These distinctions came to be recognized. Thus Judge Yankwich has said: [13]

> In defamation, the publication must be such as to expose a person to hatred, contempt, ridicule or obloquy by imputing to him qualities which, in the minds of a segment of the population, are undesirable. But the publications which invade the right of privacy may be actionable, although the persons who see the publication may find nothing objectionable in it. The important thing is that the publication injures the feelings of the person himself, although it may not have any effect whatsoever on his reputation.

So distinctive has the difference between privacy and defamation become that many of the cases contain separate "counts," one based on privacy and the other on defamation. Furthermore, in some, the defamation count was dismissed but recovery allowed on the privacy count. This has usually occurred in cases based upon use of the plaintiff's name or likeness but in a non-derogatory manner.[14]

More and more, in the recent privacy cases, there seems to be a tendency to require that the plaintiff show some act by the defendant which reflects upon the plaintiff. Certainly, courts are not awarding substantial damages unless something akin to libel is shown—at least, in the nonappropriation cases.

(b) Contract Rights.

Contract rights are quite distinct from privacy rights. In the *Gautier* case—discussed at length in Section 40 below—the plaintiff was protected by a specific contractual provision that his act was not to be televised when he performed between the halves of a professional football game. It was so telecast, sandwiched between commercial announcements.

The New York Court of Appeals would not permit a privacy recovery under the New York statute, but did point out that Gautier might have an action for breach of contract, refusing to consider that aspect of the case because the contract claim was not then in issue.

(c) Property Rights.

The right of privacy is quite different from property rights in such things as pictures, broadcast scripts or published letters. The most common example is the model or "sitter" who poses for a picture. As the sitter, she has no rights at all in the photograph; yet she definitely has a right of privacy in connection with its potential use.[15] See Chapter 9, Section 9.

Some cases have called the right of privacy itself a property right.[16] These have usually been cases which fall into the "appropriation" category discussed in Section 5 below. These instances of appropriation or exploitation of face, name or history are more properly considered as property rights in the context of "publicity values" as Nimmer has called them.[17] Such property rights involve exploitation values which attach to an individual's personality. In a sense, they are the exact opposite of rights of privacy and are, more correctly, considered as an entirely different kind of legal attribute or right. See Sections 39 to 44 below.

(d) Copyright Interests.

There is no necessitous association between the rights of the copyright owner of a photograph and the privacy rights arising out of that same photograph. Both may reside in the same individual but, more commonly, they do not.

It is for this reason that the purchaser of a photograph from the admitted copyright owner may not, without more, assume that he is protected against privacy claims by the identifiable individual portrayed in the picture. Additional releases or waivers are necessary.

(e) Unfair Competition.

There is a practical relevance and, to a degree, resemblance between certain types of unfair competition cases and others which may be described as privacy cases.[18] At the same time, there is a distinct difference between the two. For example, a corporation may succeed in an unfair competition case based on misappropriation of its name but would lose out if the action were based on the privacy theory as discussed in Section 11 below.

Thus, in the *Madison Square Garden Corp.* case,[19] the operators of the "Garden" did not claim any injury to their "feelings" but charged misappropriation of its name by the defendant which had produced a hockey picture "Idol of the Crowds" of which the "Garden" was a part. The court found unfair competition and that the defendant had infringed on plaintiff's property rights. See Section 8 below.

Also, the FTC is more likely to move if unfair competition can be shown than if its preliminary investigation points only to a privacy violation. The former lays the groundwork for a Commission charge of "unfair trade practices" while a simple privacy background usually does not—except possibly in the fictitious testimonial cases discussed in Chapter 12, Section 6.

(f) The Right of Publicity.

Some cases have been decided on privacy grounds which should better have been considered as violations of the "right of publicity." This latter right has come to be recognized only relatively recently. If adopted broadly, it will carve out of the privacy case load a considerable and very important segment of cases which traditionally are dealt with on the privacy theory.

This difference between privacy and publicity is a basic one, although its recognition has been slow. The right of publicity is discussed at length in Sections 39 to 44 below.

5. Classification of Privacy Cases.

One of the difficulties with the right of privacy is the fact that, as Dean Prosser has pointed out: [20]

> [Privacy] is not one tort, but a complex of four. The law of privacy comprises four distinct kinds of invasion of four different interests . . . which are tied together by the common name, but otherwise have almost nothing in common except that each represents an interference with the right . . . "to be let alone."

Dean Prosser has described these four "invasions" as follows: [21]

1. Intrusion upon the plaintiff's seclusion or solitude, or into his private affairs.
2. Public disclosure of embarrassing private facts about the plaintiff.
3. Publicity which places the plaintiff in a false light in the public eye.
4. Appropriation, for the defendant's advantage, of the plaintiff's name or likeness.

These four different aspects may be generally described as "intrusion, disclosure, false light, and appropriation." Our principal concern is with "appropriation." See Section 18 below.

6. Jurisdictions Recognizing Privacy.

Not all of the states have yet ruled, one way or the other, as to the existence of a right of privacy within their jurisdiction. However, the vast majority of states ruling on the matter have approved its existence. These are: Alabama, Alaska, Arizona, Arkansas, California, Connecticut, Delaware, District of Columbia, Florida, Georgia, Illinois, Indiana, Iowa, Kansas, Kentucky, Louisiana, Maryland, Michigan, Mississippi, Missouri, Montana, Nevada, New Jersey, North Carolina, Ohio, Oregon, Pennsylvania, South Carolina, South Dakota, Tennessee, and West Virginia.[22]

Four states have not specifically approved the concept but have refrained from a direct denial of the right. These are: Colorado, Massachusetts, Minnesota, and Washington.

Typical of the action of the courts in these states is the *Frick* case in Massachusetts.[23] In this so-called "book case," the defendant had written an autobiography extolling the charitable work of a Massachusetts woman (the plaintiff) with whom the defendant-author had been associated for many years. There was no mention of any personal matters about the plaintiff. It was held that there was no invasion of privacy, assuming—but without ruling—that a right of privacy did exist in Massachusetts.

It thus may be hazarded that these states will eventually approve the right of privacy although they have not specifically recognized it thus far.[24]

7. Jurisdictions Not Recognizing Privacy.

The only states which currently appear to deny the existence of privacy at common law are Nebraska, Rhode Island, Texas and Wisconsin.[25] The Texas situation merits special attention. While holding that privacy does not exist at common law in that state,[26] Texas has allowed recovery on the basis of commercial appropriation of the plaintiff's personality.[27]

In other words, Texas does not recognize privacy *per se* but permits recovery in commercial exploitation cases without the necessity of bringing the case under the privacy umbrella. This is another example of the judicial difficulties which have arisen because of the commercial/noncommercial dichotomy in the privacy area.

Jurisdictions recognizing privacy as a statutory right are discussed in Section 8 below.

8. Privacy Statutes.

Four states have adopted statutes relative to the right of privacy. They are New York, Oklahoma, Utah and Virginia.[28] The New York statute, enacted in 1903 as §§50–51 of the Civil Rights Act, is generally considered to be the most important. Court decisions applying and interpreting it are given considerable respect in other jurisdictions. Its full text provides: [29]

> *Section 50.* A person, firm or corporation that uses for advertising purposes or for the purpose of trade, the name, portrait or picture of any living person without having first obtained the written consent of such person, or if a minor of his or her guardian, shall be guilty of a misdemeanor.
>
> *Section 51.* Any person, whose name, portrait or picture is used within this state for advertising purposes or purposes of trade without the written consent first obtained as above may maintain an equitable action in the supreme court of this state against the person, firm or corporation so using his name, portrait or picture, to prevent and restrain the use thereof; and may also sue and recover damages for any injuries sustained by reason of such use and if the defendant shall have knowingly used such person's name, portrait or picture in such manner as is forbidden and declared to be unlawful by the last section, may award exemplary damages.

It will be noted that this statute is limited in its application to use for advertising purposes or for the purpose of trade, of the name, portrait or picture of any living person unless his written consent is first obtained. Thus, the application of the privacy concept may be more circumscribed in New York than in other states which follow the so-called common law doctrine of privacy.

Although the state statutes are at least partly criminal in nature, they are only rarely, if ever, used for that purpose. There appear to be only two penal cases under the New York statute since its enactment in 1903.[30]

It has been said that a statute "defining the right has been enacted" in

Wisconsin but this refers only to an Act dealing with publication of the name of a woman who may have been raped or subjected to criminal assault. It is not really a "right of privacy statute" as are the four statutes referred to above.[31]

Other states have such statutes relative to mention of rape victims, "Peeping Toms," privacy of letters, eavesdropping, etc., and are not within the limits of this chapter.[32] The 1967 Federal statute about electronic "bugging" falls into this group.

The Federal Trademark Act gives a limited amount of protection[33] but it has seldom been invoked because of its limitations. It prevents the registration of a trademark if it "consists of or compromises a name, portrait or sign identifying a particular living individual except by his written consent, or the name, signature or portrait of a deceased President of the United States, during the life of his widow, except by the written consent of the widow."

Between 1899 and 1915, California had a privacy statute on its books. This was the earliest statute of its kind but it proved impractical and was repealed.

It has been suggested that the right of privacy is best protected by the common law process. Statutory protection has not been significantly successful.[34] This may stem from the fact that current statutory protection is limited to trade or advertising violations. This makes for considerable inflexibility even if the courts desire to expand the statute's application.[35]

In 1961, New York extended protection to non-profit groups by statute, Section (1) of which provides: [36]

> No person, firm, association or corporation shall use, *for advertising purposes or for purposes of trade,* the name, symbol, device or other identification of any non-profit corporation, association, society or organization . . . without having first obtained the written consent of such non-profit corporation, association, society or organization. Any violation of this section shall be a misdemeanor. (Emphasis added.)

Injunctive relief restraining actual or threatened violation may be granted under Subsection (3) .

This statute was tested in the effort of the University of Notre Dame to prevent the release of the motion picture "John Goldfarb, Please Come Home" which dealt with the defeat of the Notre Dame football team by a "farcical" team of Bedouins.[37] The trial court granted relief but was reversed by the Appellate Division, which held that the picture was not "trade" within this statute and, further, was not "commercial immorality."[38] There was also an intimation of unconstitutionality as a restraint on free speech even if the picture was "ugly, vulgar, and tawdry."

This decision points up, once again, the unsuccessful struggle of the New York courts "with the definition of the term 'trade.'" The statute has also been criticized as "unwarranted and unwise [39]—one more example of the unsatisfactory solution of the privacy question by statute. See Sections 18 to 26 below.

B. RIGHTS AND PERSONS INVOLVED.

9. Rights Protected.

The most common rights of personality protected by the privacy doctrines are name, portrait or picture. The four statutes discussed in Section 8 are limited to these attributes. Almost any form of the name is protected provided it is sufficient to identify the plaintiff as discussed in Section 10 below.

A first name (by itself) is protected.[40] So, too, is a woman's maiden name.[41] Although it is not entirely clear, stage names and pen names seem to fall under the privacy shield.[42] Certainly the better view supports this. As Prosser has said: [43]

> Apart from statutory language, however, it is suggested [that a stage or fictitious name should be protected]. The suggestion, for example, that Samuel L. Clemens would have a cause of action when that name was used in advertising, but not for the use of "Mark Twain," fully speaks for itself.

See also the discussion of the *Cholly Knickerbocker* case in Section 36 below.

Usually the picture involved will be a photograph or similar likeness of the plaintiff but it may also be any identifiable impersonation of the plaintiff.[44] A three-dimensional likeness or image such as a manikin or statue of the plaintiff will suffice.[45] According to the leading *Binns* case, "any representation" will suffice.[46]

This includes sketches which may be reasonably identified as the likeness of the plaintiff. In this connection, the extent of the resemblance between the sketch based on a photograph of the plaintiff is likely to be important.[47]

In the *Bert Lahr* case,[48] it was held that the well-known comic had no privacy claim for use by the defendant in a telecast commercial of the plaintiff's "style of vocal comic delivery" which had made him widely known. On the other hand, in the *Roy Rogers* case [49] the court said that Rogers "has the right to use his name, picture and *voice* in advertisements" (emphasis added) except as otherwise affected by an earlier contract between the parties.

A band leader's musical style has also been protected.[50]

Another important aspect of the individual's personality is his life history. This looms large in publishing, the theatre, radio and television.[51] However, such uses must be analyzed in the context of the plaintiff's status as a public figure (see Section 12 below) and whether the biographical use is or is not fictional.

Usually a fictionalized book or article about the plaintiff would be considered a privacy violation even if the plaintiff is an acknowledged public figure as held in the *Warren Spahn* case [52] where the New York Court of Appeals said there had been "dramatization, imagined dialogue, manipulated chronologies and fictionalization of events." However, the Supreme Court reversed and ordered a new trial under the new *New York Times* doctrine discussed in Chapter 7, Section 27. Apparently it will now be necessary for the plaintiff in such a case to prove "malice" as defined in *New York Times*.

Fictitious endorsements or testimonials also give rise to privacy actions.[53] These are usually—probably necessarily—tied to the use of the individual's name and therefore may be considered with the name cases. However, the addition of a testimonial to a simple "tie-up" undoubtedly simplifies the plaintiff's action and also gives rise to a claim under the right of publicity doctrine. As to the right of publicity, see Sections 39 to 44 below. As to testimonials generally, see Chapter 12.

10. Identification Requirements.

Mere use of a name which happens to be the same as that of the plaintiff is not sufficient basis for liability. As was said in the *Nebb* case,[54] violation of the New York statute requires

the use of a name coupled with circumstances tending to refer to the plaintiff and not a mere similarity of names.

Prosser stresses the importance of the plaintiff's name as "a symbol of the identity that is involved . . . , and not as a mere name." [55]

If defendant defends on the ground of mere coincidence of names, it becomes a question for the jury to decide.[56] Surrounding circumstances and additional references and elements in the allegedly violative publication are important in resolving this question. They may include use of biographical references to plaintiff, a facsimile of his signature, use of his coat of arms or other aspects of the plaintiff's personality which tend to show that the name used really was that of the plaintiff.[57]

Where "there was not a single parallel between him and the character depicted," it was held that the plaintiff's privacy was not invaded even though both first and family names were the same as the plaintiff's.[58] On the other hand, merely changing a name somewhat does not provide a defense as long as the character is identifiable with the plaintiff.[59] The identification "bridge" may even be extraneous to the alleged violation as occurred in *Walcher v. Loew's, Inc.*,[60] one of the cases growing out of the motion picture "They Were Expendable" made from the book of the same name. The plaintiff, a nurse in both book and picture, was not referred to by her real name in the picture but had been identified to the public as the "nurse" through the earlier book in which her name was used.

11. Persons Protected.

Both the privacy and publicity doctrines protect every living person regardless of his economic, social, political or intellectual status. It is not necessary that an individual be a hermit in a cave to enjoy the right of privacy.[61] At the same time, the degree of "privacy" accorded the individual varies with the nature of his activities and his personal exposure through such activities to the public eye. The right of privacy nonetheless exists, but its enforcement may be materially diminished by such activities. As to these public figures or "celebrities," and the alleged waiver of their rights of privacy, see Section 12 below.

A partnership or corporation has no right of privacy.[62] This is not the case, however, as to the name or portrait of an individual who is a member of a partnership or an officer of a corporation.[63] On the other hand, the business partnership or corporation is not without recourse despite this lack of privacy right. It may seek protection under the doctrines of unfair competition, libel, copyright, antitrust, etc., all of which involve different legal concepts.[64] See Section 4 above.

12. "Public Figures."

One of the truly ambivalent and confusing aspects of privacy is the so-called "public figure." It is here that the difference between the exploitation cases and the "real" privacy cases—the "right-to-be-alone" cases—becomes particularly clear.

It is sometimes said that a public figure "has no right of privacy." Other sources have spoken of an "implied waiver" of the right by the public figure because he has made himself newsworthy and of interest to the public by activities either voluntarily undertaken or forced upon him. It is for this reason that the "public figure" concept has been criticized and the "newsworthy" approach preferred.[65]

Under the latter concept, even a completely "private figure," ordinarily of no interest at all to the public and therefore having a well-recognized right of privacy, may become newsworthy through some activity or event.[66] When this happens, the press is free to comment or report factually without any liability. Of course, the "public figure" is subject to the same reportorial invasion of his so-called privacy by virtue of his activities and general interest to the public, being subject even "to the often searching beam of publicity."[67]

The problem arises from a conflict between the basic right of privacy of the individual, on the one hand, and the "right to know" of the public—the "free dissemination of thoughts, ideas, newsworthy events, and matters of public interest"—on the other hand.[68] The latter is usually served by the activities of the press and the cases seem uniform that there is no liability for such news reporting.[69]

Whether using the "public figure" or the "newsworthy" test, it is necessarily pertinent to establish and limit a definition of such person. One analysis suggests: [70]

[T]he achievement of public office, of eminence in the arts, sciences, the theatre, sports, any activity in politics, prominence in society or the slightest notoriety make a person a public figure. The occurrence of a single event . . . may catapult a person into "public figurehood." . . .

Probably the most telling language concerning the position of a public figure appears in the *Pavesich* case.[71] In this early leading case, the court said:

It would seem to us that even the President of the United States in the lofty position which he occupies has some rights in reference to matters of this kind, which he does not forfeit by aspiring to or accepting the highest office within the gift of the people of the United States.

In other words, even the best-known public figure retains certain rights whether they be called right of privacy, right of publicity, or right against commercial exploitation.

As to public figures, the protected elements most commonly are those which deal with commercial exploitation of their personality and success and distortion or fictionalization of their activities or biographies.

If commercial exploitation of the public figure is not involved, there usually is not too much difficulty in the public figure cases except for the question as to *when* an admitted "person who was prominent" ceases to be a public figure, thereby retiring from the newsworthy stage and again having an enforceable right of privacy.

In the leading *Sidis* case [72] twenty-seven years had passed between the plaintiff's admitted newsworthiness as a child prodigy and the *New Yorker* article about which he complained. The plaintiff had spent the intervening years in obscurity and claimed he was no longer a public figure. It was held that his activities in obscurity—when viewed against his prior achievements—satisfied a legitimate public interest and judgment was entered for the defendant.

Fifteen years has been held insufficient to prevent the republication without privacy liability of plaintiff's photograph when it was originally privileged because of the original newsworthy character of the plaintiff.[73] Several cases have held variously that the passage of two years, six months, "a generation" was insufficient to remove the public figure defense.[74]

On the other hand, as little as three months has been held sufficient time lapse to remove a magazine article from the news category.[75] However, the cases taking this view usually couple the time lapse with "the element of fictionalization, dramatization or sensationalism" and the courts have "alluded to the time lag as additional confirmation that the item complained of is primarily commercial in character since it is no longer newsworthy." [76]

13. Rights of Minors.

Privacy protects minors to the same extent as adults. Certain practical and procedural problems may result from the minority, however. The most important practical difference is that the minor's release is not acceptable as a waiver of the minor's rights.[77]

14. Rights of Employees.

Merely because a person is an employee does not, without more, automatically give his employer the right to use his name or picture. Mere status as an employee does not waive such rights.[78] However, the employment relationship may—under certain circumstances—serve to create an implied waiver which has been considered sufficient to foreclose privacy relief.[79]

This matter is particularly relevant in connection with use of employees' names and pictures in corporate house organs or other corporate PR activities. Presumably, routine use thereof in connection with some "news item" of interest to his fellow-employees should not be a privacy violation, assuming that it does not go beyond the limits of normal reporting and interest and is in good taste. However, any such use in an external house organ, distributed widely outside the "corporate family"—among a public which normally has no interest in an employee—might raise serious questions.[80] For a further discussion on this subject see Chapter 18, Section 8.

Labor unions have occasionally concerned themselves with employee-related matters which essentially are privacy situations. Two examples will suffice to illustrate such peripheral interest by the unions.

In one situation, a house organ published a story about an employee which, while perhaps not defamatory, created resentment. The employee took his grievance to the union which instructed its members not to cooperate with the house organ activities. It was only when the matter was brought to the attention of management that the former rapport was restored.[81]

In another situation, the company had used employees' pictures in its public relations and advertising activities but without releases. Thereafter a union tried to organize the plant but without much success. The union learned of the prior use of the employees' photographs. The weight of these privacy violations is said to have contributed substantially to the acquiescence of the company to the unionization drive.

15. Deceased Persons.

From its inception the right of privacy has been considered a personal right belonging to the individual, living person. When the person dies, the right dies with him.[82] This rule has been somewhat misunderstood. It has led to the assumption that the name, photograph or life history of a person may be freely used—even for non-news or commercial or promotional purposes—provided only that the person has died. This may be a mischievous assumption.

The better approach in this situation is to consider each use of the personality of a deceased person *sui generis* and to appraise the potential exposure on a case-by-case basis. It will probably be found—especially in cases of appropriation or exploitation as discussed in Section 16 below—that the only situations in which such use is "safe" are those in which the deceased person would have had no recourse even were he still living.

16. Relations and Heirs of Deceased Person.

Many privacy cases turn on the rights of a surviving spouse, child, other heir or executor of a deceased person under the privacy doctrine. This is sometimes referred to as the "relational right of privacy." [83]

It undoubtedly involves one of the most misunderstood and dangerous areas of "privacy law"—meriting particular attention, especially by those (including the PR practitioner) who are concerned with the commercial use of intangibles relating to a deceased person. Its importance is demonstrated by the opinion in the *Glenn Miller* case [84] where it was shown that the late bandleader's estate had (through approximately 1959) already received $650,000 from the exploitation of property rights relating to his "name, likeness, history and musical style."

To a degree this misunderstanding arises from the same commercial/ non-commercial distinction frequently adverted to elsewhere in this chapter.

It is generally said that relatives and survivors have no such rights.[85] This is an oversimplification. The cases are confused, go both ways, have sometimes been judicially misinterpreted and have been the victims of "legal labels" such as "personal" or "relational." [86]

The general rule goes back to three cases of the vintage of the 1890s.

In *Schuyler v. Curtis*,[87] a nephew sought to prevent the erection of a monument to his aunt's memory as a "typical woman philanthropist." The court held that the nephew "does not represent that right [of the aunt]. . . . It is the right of privacy of the living which is sought to [sic] enforce here." Judgment was entered for the defendants.

In *Atkinson v. John E. Doherty & Co.*[88] the court refused relief to a widow seeking to prevent the use of her deceased husband's picture on defendant's cigar bands. This Michigan case would have had the same result if the husband had been a "live plaintiff" because Michigan, at that time, did not recognize the right of privacy at all—whether the plaintiff was living or dead. Michigan has since recognized privacy.[89]

The third of the early cases is *Corliss v. E. W. Walker*[90] in which a widow was unsuccessful in stopping the publication of a biographical sketch and picture of her late husband, a well-known inventor. The court put the decision on the ground of privilege. Thus the case did not really turn on the death of the husband despite its subsequent citation for such principle.

Other cases seemingly following the general rule are easily explained on the ground that the deceased relative would not have had a right even if alive. For example, in *Metter v. Los Angeles Examiner*,[91] a leading case, it was held that a husband had no recourse in connection with newspaper publicity attendant upon his wife's suicide, an event obviously privileged as "legitimate news." [92]

In some cases, recovery has been allowed for violation of the relatives' own rights even though premised on circumstances relating to the deceased. This is especially true where there has been a showing of some other circumstances such as a breach of confidence or contract involving the relatives or some extreme situation such as pictures of deceased malformed children.[93] In one such case, the court said: [94]

> [T]he suit is not based on injury to the deceased child. . . . The
> right . . . began after the death of the child and is a right of
> action on the part of the parents.

It is when we turn to the "appropriation" cases that the basic distinction between suits for "injured feelings" and for exploitation of "property rights" (appropriation) becomes apparent and important. It has been pointed out: [95]

> While the decisions are conflicting, eminent authority and authors of legal articles on the subject are almost unanimous in recognizing the rights of surviving relatives, both as to their right of recovery for their own injured feelings as well as for a *property interest in some aspect of the deceased's personality which is commercialized after his death.* (Emphasis added.)

Dean Green, in reference to such cases, has pinpointed the real basis for recovery by surviving relatives as "profit making [by the defendant] from the exploitation of a deceased relative's personality." [96]

In the *Glenn Miller* case [97] the rights of the bandleader's widow and surviving children were protected—through suit by his administrator—in, among other things, his "unique style" of musical rendition. This was an exploitation case in which Miller's music was being commercialized.

In an action by the widow of "Chappie" Blackburn, one-time trainer of Joe Lewis, she sought redress, not for injured feelings but for the "appropriation and conversion of the property rights of Blackburn in his name, likeness and incidents of his life which accrued to his estate." [98] Recovery was allowed.

On the other hand, in the *Jesse James* case [99] the widow claimed a remedy for her personal feelings (privacy) because of the picturization of her husband's life even though she was not mentioned in the script. The action was not for values resulting from commercial exploitation of her husband's life story. The same result occurred in the so-called *Al Capone* case [100] in which, as the circuit court said:

> Comment, fictionalization and even distortion of a dead man's career do not invade the privacy of his offspring, relatives and friends, if they are not even mentioned therein.

The plaintiffs also claimed that they had a separate cause of action for intentional infliction of emotional harm, then recently recognized by Illinois,[101] but the court did not even discuss its application. As to this, "the law is clearly in a process of growth [and] the ultimate limits [thereof] . . . cannot be determined." [102]

Certain cases clearly indicate that merely being a descendant does not give the plaintiff enforceable rights. Thus, a group of the heirs of Robert Schumann could not recover for use of their ancestor's name in a motion picture.[103] The "line of demarcation lies in the existence, creation or reopening of a valid estate in which the next of kin make an authentic proof of heirship." [104]

An action in the name of the executor or administrator seeking to enforce the surviving property right being exploited is more likely to succeed as it did in the *Glenn Miller* case and the *Blackburn* case, in both of which action was brought by the estate. The situation has been thus summarized: [105]

> Courts have not had the same reluctance in granting relief when suit has been brought by an executor or personal representative of the spouse and next of kin, on the basis of the appropriation of a property right (where the element of injured feelings is entirely absent).

If recoveries by relatives and heirs are limited to clear cases of exploitation and commercialization, this would satisfy the judicial concern that allowing recovery by survivors generally ". . . would open the courts to persons whose only relation to the asserted wrong is that they are related to the victim of the wrongdoers and were therefore brought unwillingly into the limelight." [106]

The cumulative impact of the "exceptions" to the general rule set out at the beginning of this Section is considerable. The "no-liability" conception of using a deceased's personal attributes should be approached very carefully—especially by PR practitioners, advertising and promotion people since their activities may eventually be considered exploitation of the deceased or his activities before his death. This impact may be expected to develop further as more courts accept the property right theory and come to recognize the right of publicity discussed in Sections 39 to 44 below.

The Oklahoma, Utah and Virginia statutes specifically give certain rights to survivors, executors, etc. See Section 8 above.

17. Persons Liable.

As far back as 1613 it had been held that all parties who commit a tort are jointly responsible for it.[107] The modern rule has been stated by Prosser to be: [108]

> All those who, in pursuance of a common plan or design to commit a tortious act, actively take part in it, or further it by cooperation or request, or who lend aid or encouragement to the wrongdoer, or ratify and adopt his acts for their benefit, are equally liable with him.

This is true of actions for violation of privacy or publicity rights. In some cases, the plaintiff has brought suit against "everybody" including the sponsor, the medium (newspaper, periodical, station or network), the agency, the author, the actors involved, and all others who participated in the alleged violation.[109]

It has been held that the State of New York itself is liable under the New York privacy statute.[110]

C. "ADVERTISING PURPOSES" AND "PURPOSES OF TRADE."

18. Importance to Business Communications.

Of the four privacy categories of torts referred to in Section 5 above, only the fourth—appropriation for the benefit of another—is generally pertinent to the business communications techniques of which public relations, promotion and advertising are a part. Most of the appropriation cases have arisen under application and interpretation of the terms "advertising purposes" and "purposes of trade," whether controlled by statute or common law.

This importance is very substantial. Many aspects of such communications are involved—even those which do not patently fall into the "advertising" pigeonhole. As to these, "purposes of trade" may be more applicable. In any event, nearly every channel of business communication may involve these concepts—except, perhaps, routine correspondence. Even here such involvement may occur. Simple examples are the routine reply of a sales manager to an inquiry wherein he encloses some sales or promotional literature and the PR man who sends to an inquiring stockholder a reprint of a favorable news story about the company.

19. Confusion of the Cases.

The state of the law of privacy has been characterized as a "haystack in a hurricane." [111] Nowhere is this more apparent than in the effort to reconcile some of the cases which have dealt with "advertising" and "purposes of trade."

For example, under New York's statute which uses these terms, recovery has been permitted, since the *Binns* case [112] of 1913, for motion picture use of a person's name and impersonation. Yet, in 1954, the Utah Supreme Court refused recovery, in the *Donohue* case,[113] under a statute using these same terms and clearly patterned after the New York act. The Utah court saw fit to ignore the words "purposes of trade." It relied on *some* New York cases but not the *Binns* case.

To compound the confusion, a prior federal circuit court opinion in the same *Donohue* case [114] found such use to be "for gain or profit within the meaning of the [Utah] statute" following the criteria of the *Binns* case.[115]

20. Paid Advertising.

The use of a person's name, photograph, life history, testimonial or other attributes of personality, without permission, in *paid* advertising is clearly a violation of that person's right of privacy under both the statutes and the common law, subject to possible limited exceptions discussed in Section 23 below.

The same is true of the "public figure" as discussed in Section 12 above. Status as a public figure, a celebrity or a "VIP" does not, in and of itself, permit the exploitation of that person's personality, popularity or notoriety in paid advertising.

In the early and frequently-cited *Edison* case [116] the inventor was able to stop the exploitation of his name, likeness and "certificate" by a patent medicine manufacturer even though Edison had sold the defendant the formula and was obviously a public figure. The Court said:

> If a man's name be his own property and no less an authority than the United States Supreme Court says it is (citing cases), it is difficult to understand why the particular cast of one's features is not also one's property, and why its pecuniary value, if it has one, does not belong to its owner rather than to the person seeking to make an unauthorized use of it.

However, as communications and promotional media proliferated and new ones came into use, the "simple advertising case" acquired more complicated and sophisticated brothers. Changes in judicial attitudes and applications developed. Privacy cases spawned by these new media or promotional techniques have fallen, in many instances, into either or both the "advertising" or "trade" categories, sometimes under the label of "commercial" or "publicity."

21. Broad Scope of the Terms.

There is, in the public relations industry, the conviction that public relations is different in purpose, technique and impact from paid advertising.[117] This attitude is known to carry over sometimes into consideration of privacy problems.

Although this differentiation is generally valid, it is doubtful whether this can support the theory that public relations is not within the broader "purposes of trade" category. Should the PR practitioner go this far, he would run into the contrary judicial mandate cumulatively expressed in the cases.

The two phrases "advertising purposes" and "purposes of trade" have been given broad definition and application in the cases decided under both the statutes and the common law privacy doctrine.[118] They have come to include almost every aspect of the *commercial* use of a person's picture, name or personality. This is clear from the appropriation or exploitation cases.

Recoveries have not been limited to the paid product-advertising cases or even to "advertising" as that term may be broadly understood in the business community. The two expressions seem to include many different kinds of promotion, publicity, public relations, "stunts," merchandising, product manuals, use of reprints, etc.

Quite apart from the obvious "paid advertising" cases, referred to in Section 20 above, the following are examples of the scope of application of these terms.[119]

(a) A campaign dealing with safety in entering and alighting from street cars.

(b) Article by doctors in a learned journal.

(c) Unionization drive.

(d) Inclusion in a photographic "annual."

(e) Reprints of articles from the public press or learned journals, more fully discussed in Section 26 below.

(f) "Teaser" letters.

(g) Staged stunt involving a reenactment of a bank holdup.

(h) Promotional motion picture shown by a merchant in a local theatre.

(i) Promotional booklet sold at a sporting event.

(j) A sample picture of a woman's locket.

(k) Use in door-to-door selling.

(l) A "manual" about use of defendant's products.

(m) Inclusion of picture in boxes of popcorn.

Even though newspapers and magazines are money-making or commercial enterprises, "items of news are not treated as trade." [120] The same rule is here applied as in obscenity cases where the Supreme Court has said: [121]

> That books, newspapers and magazines are published and sold for profit does not prevent them from being a form of expression whose liberty is safeguarded by the First Amendment.

22. "Public Figure" Problems.

As discussed in Section 12 above, the "public figure" and "newsworthy" concepts have introduced exemptions into the privacy doctrine insofar as news or informational media are concerned. Also (see Section 20 above) such concepts do not exempt clearly commercial use. However, a different—certainly a more difficult—legal question is posited when the original news medium use is alleged to be tainted by promotional or commercial purposes.

This was the situation in *Time, Inc. v. Hill*,[122] decided by the Supreme Court in 1967, although, as developed below, the "promotional taint" aspects of the case are not too clear. This case will undoubtedly have a lasting impact on the liability of a publisher.

Hill, the plaintiff, brought an action against the publishers because of a 1955 illustrated story in *Life* about Hill's experience in 1952 when he and his wife had been held hostages in their Pennsylvania home by three escaped convicts. After the event, Hill had moved from Pennsylvania to Connecticut and "discouraged all efforts to keep [Hill and his family] in the public spotlight through magazine articles or appearances on television."

The *Life* story was clearly tied to a then-current play, "The Desperate Hours," which was said to have been "inspired" by the experience of Hill and his family. Actors from the play's cast posed for the photographs in the house where the original episode had occurred, the article saying that "scenes from the play are reenacted on the site of the crime."

Hill sued under the New York privacy statute (see Section 8 above), charging that the article was knowingly "false and untrue." At issue was also whether the article was a promotional piece for both the play and the magazine.

After a jury verdict in favor of the plaintiff, judgment was entered in his favor for $30,000, the lower court, *inter alia,* saying:

> Although the play was fictionalized, *Life's* article portrayed it as a reenactment of Hill's experience. It is an inescapable conclusion that this was done to advertise and attract further attention to the play, and to increase present and future magazine circulation as well. It is evident that the article cannot be characterized as a mere dissemination of news, nor even an effort to supply legitimate newsworthy information in which the public had, or might have a proper interest.

After argument and reargument, the Supreme Court reversed and remanded the case to the New York courts, "presumably . . . [for] a new trial." The Supreme Court concerned itself almost exclusively with conflicts between the privacy statute and freedom of the press, saying:

> We hold that the constitutional protections for speech and press preclude the application of the New York statute to redress false reports of matters of public interest *in the absence of proof that the defendant published the report with knowledge of its falsity or in reckless disregard of the truth.* (Emphasis added.)

This conclusion was reached by extension of the Court's position in *New York Times v. Sullivan* (a libel action by a public official discussed at length in Chapter 7, Section 27) although the Court said:

> [This standard was applied] not through blind application of [that case] . . . but only upon consideration of the factors which arise in the particular context of the application of the New York statute in cases involving private individuals.

The Court's opinion does not appear to deal definitely with the plaintiff's claim that the article was a promotion for the play. However, it does say, by way of *dictum,* that New York's statutory proscription against "advertising" or use to "promote the sale of goods" would "present different questions of violation of the constitutional protections for speech and press." The Court, in commenting on the charge of the lower court, does not appear to have criticized it insofar as it dealt with the necessity of finding—as a prerequisite to recovery—that "the article was published to advertise the play or 'for trade purposes.' . . ."

All of this leads to a reasoned conclusion that the decision does not effectively decide the liability for privacy violations when an article is deliberately "planted" to promote a product or service. Furthermore, the decision deals only with the position of the *medium*—not with the liability of the party whose product or service is being promoted.[123]

The court was badly divided in its thinking as to both theory and meaning of the court's charge to the jury. Four opinions were needed to present the views of the nine justices, three justices vigorously dissenting and one partly concurring and dissenting.

However, there can be no doubt that, in cases of allegedly newsworthy figures, the court's requirement of "actual malice—knowledge that the statements are false or in reckless disregard of the truth" will probably have a deterrent effect upon recoveries in privacy cases.

23. Incidental Use.

Public relations, publicity and paid advertising are concerned with the "incidental" use of personality. In the leading case on this subject, *Wallach v. Bacharach*,[124] the court said:

> [W]e . . . have to weigh the circumstances, the extent, degree or character of the use. It is well established that every incidental mention of some person's name in connection with advertising or trade does not constitute a violation of the [statutory] provisions . . .

The court then held that the use of plaintiff's name in a news item or commentary but reproduced in paid space and juxtaposed to advertising copy, was not actionable.

Use of plaintiff's name in a sponsored television broadcast, if it is merely incidental, "does not ipso facto constitute a use for advertising purposes. . . . [T]here must be an exploitation of the name in the commercial announcement with the product itself." [125]

Casual oral mention or visual display of the plaintiff's name in a motion picture does not warrant recovery.[126] This is also true of a single mention of a person in a novel or article.[127] A curious "incidental use" occurred in *Moglen v. Varsity Pajamas* [128] which involved a design print on clothing fabric. It included a reprint of a newspaper story in which plaintiff's name appeared. It was held not to be actionable.

24. Incidental Advertising Use by Publishers.

In 1962, in a case "substantially one of first impression" and described as "[t]he extreme limit of 'incidental' use"[129] publishers of news media and informative periodicals seem to have placed by the New York courts in a specially-protected position insofar as their own advertising or promotional use of a person's name and photograph is concerned.

In *Shirley Booth v. Curtis Publishing Co.*,[130] *Holiday* had carried the plaintiff's picture and name in a story, the use of which was admittedly privileged. Thereafter, Curtis used the same picture and plaintiff's name in its own advertising in *The New Yorker* and *Advertising Age* in a clear effort to sell advertising space in *Holiday*. The court held that this was merely incidental advertising used to "illustrate the quality and content of the publication" and entered judgment for Curtis despite a jury finding in the trial court that this was a "separate and independent use by the defendant for their own advertising purposes, not reasonably related to the original use of the photograph."

The court held for the publisher even though it specifically conceded that the subsequent use was "in motivation, sheer advertising and solicitation."

The court added a *caveat* limiting somewhat the scope of this exemption, saying:

> Further comment by way of *caveat* is merited on the distinction between collateral (discussed in Section 25 below) and incidental advertising. . . . It may well be that a news or periodical publisher is doing more than selling a news medium. *Or it may be that there is an issue whether there is involved a genuine news medium. Then a question of fact may be raised whether the advertising is incidental to the dissemination of news. Or it may*

*become clear enough, even as a matter of law, that the use was
collateral and only ill-disguised as a news medium.* (Emphasis and
parenthetical matter added.)

This involves the corporate communicator and PR man. For example,
a baseball team's roster booklet, sold to the fans, even though it contains
background stories about the players, would probably not be considered
a "genuine news medium." Nor would a self-liquidating premium book
sold by a company. Also, house organs are specifically involved. See Chapter 18, Sections 5, 6 and 11.

There was a vigorous dissent on the basis of the *Flores* case, discussed
in Section 25 below. This dissent has been considered the better view by
legal commentators.[131] The New York Court of Appeals, though affirm-
ing for the defendant, found itself split with two judges agreeing with the
lower court dissent.

The basis of the holding was the doctrine of the 1919 *Humiston*
case [132] holding that a newsreel disseminator was privileged to display
prints from the newsreel for "purposes of attracting users and selling its
product" even though newsreel dissemination may be an activity for
profit. Other cases have generally followed this rule.[133]

The court may have gone too far in this case. A magazine does two
kinds of advertising. One is directed to the public so that it will buy and
read, thus catering to the public interest; the other is directed to advertising agencies and advertisers so that they will buy space in future issues.
The court failed to make this basic distinction.

Curtis was definitely "plugging" its publication to advertising buyers—
not to the general public. Its copy included "What a provocative selling
opportunity for advertisers!" This line's implications are reinforced by its
appearance in *Advertising Age,* a trade book published for advertising
buyers—not the general public.

Whatever protection a news medium may have under the *Humiston*
doctrine is limited to advertising to the public—not to the "trade." The
facts and holding in *Humiston* are limited to attracting the public to the
current newsreel. Only advertising to the public involves the "free dissemination of thoughts, ideas, newsworthy events and matters of public
interest," [134] frequently balanced against the right of privacy—to the
detriment of the latter.

25. Collateral Use.

Collateral use of name or picture—as distinct from incidental use
thereof—involves a use of materials which may have been originally privileged but which, when subsequently used, is actionable.

The leading case on such use is *Flores v. Mosler Safe Co.*[135] in which a privileged news item about a fire (mentioning the plaintiff) was later used by the defendant "to illustrate the loss of valuable business records in the event of fire" and "as a solicitation for patronage" by the defendant, a safe manufacturer.

Such originally privileged material, whether or not it deals with a public figure, may, therefore, not be used with impunity.

The *Flores* case raises certain questions—quite apart from the *Booth* case—when compared with the *Wallach* holding, discussed in Section 23 above. Both involved "advertising" use yet seem to have been decided differently.

Perhaps they may be reconciled because the news item later commercially used in the *Flores* case was "no longer current or newsworthy," did not appear (in its commercial garb) in a news medium and was so obviously a "solicitation for patronage." On the other hand, these disparate results may be evidence of what the court in the *Booth* case described as "the delicate judicial elaboration" which the New York statute has "required and received."

As a cautionary measure, it should be assumed that any advertising or promotional use of originally privileged matter by any defendant (other than a publisher, newsreel producer or distributor) would be considered as collateral, subject to the limited context of the *Wallach* case. Even though the subsequent use may, as a practical matter, be of interest to the public as a "reprint of news," it still would be collateral if used for exploitation, commercial, solicitation or other trade purposes by the defendant in connection with "the sale of a completely unconnected product rather than the sale of the news medium" as spelled out in the *Flores* case.

This problem becomes quite relevant to institutional advertising such as that used by International Latex which consists of reprinted articles or stories apparently considered by the company as worthy of further public attention. Institutional advertising, even if not reprinting prior news stories, might—under some circumstances or by some courts, especially outside of the statutory states—be considered as collateral. This may occur—even if it promotes some "nonprofit public causes." Cutlip and Center write: [136]

> This kind of advertising has been found rewarding by many sponsors. The Sinclair Oil Company's advertising to promote and preserve the national parks and shrines brought that company much favorable public reaction *and increased its business, too.* (Emphasis added.)

26. Editorial Endorsement Reprints.

The use of editorial or news item reprints as "advertising" is undoubtedly a useful method of direct product promotion and selling. David Finn has said: [137]

> In many types of sales programs, public relations achievements can be merchandised to the customer directly. It is in this way that public relations come closest to "paying off" in sales results that can be measured . . . The most common form of this type of public relations merchandising is the use of *publicity in advertising*. Many producers of drug products, cigarettes, household supplies, have based entire advertising campaigns on editorial endorsement by leading magazines. This is particularly effective in competitive fields, where editorial endorsement seems to confirm a claim for superior quality by the advertiser.

Such reprints are also extremely effective in direct mail advertising as appeared to be the channel in the *Flores* case. Once again, a public relations tool and its implementation are used to generate what some would call "advertising" but which, in reality, is an extension of the PR arm of the company. The same author has pointed out:

> This has proven to be particularly true with service business . . . One fleet-leasing company, for instance, developed its entire direct mail advertising program around a series of reprints of articles in trade publications, reporting the many advantages of its service to industry . . . Other types of firms which have used public relations results in direct mail are management consulting firms, suppliers of office equipment and systems, architectural firms, etc.

Whatever may be the legal sequelae flowing from the original public relations activity, there can be no question that the use of reprints thereof are usually a purely commercial activity aimed at product sales.[138]

D. RELEASE AND WAIVER OF RIGHTS.

27. Need for Releases.

In their original 1890 article, Warren and Brandeis wrote: [139]

> The right to privacy ceases upon the publication of the facts by the individual or with his consent.

Despite the generally wide recognition of this basic rule when dealing with paid advertising, other corporate commercial communications are more loosely and informally managed. Proper releases are sometimes neither sought nor obtained. The company may later be forced to depend on "implied" consent or waiver which has received varying treatment by the courts.

In the common law states, a written consent is not necessary and it has been held that an oral understanding will suffice.[140] However, in the four statutory states (see Section 8 above), written consent is expressly required and oral consent will not suffice.[141]

Some cases have held that oral consent, while not a full defense, nevertheless mitigates or reduces damages. This appears to be the result of the application of general equitable principles.[142] See also Section 39 below.

There is some indication that the statutory written consent may be given by an authorized agent.[143] However, this "remote" consent should not be relied upon. In the case of minors, the authorization to the agent is generally unenforceable because of the subject's minority.[144] Also, the statutes require "the written consent of such person" as in the New York statute.

For example, releases issued by the publicity department of motion picture studios—though signed by some studio official—usually do carry an approval signed by the film personality involved. The same is true of the many sports personalities who are represented by agents. See discussion of *Sharman* case in Section 38 below.

It is undoubtedly preferable to require the signature of the subject involved and not to rely on that of an alleged agent, no matter how clear the latter's authority may appear to be.

On the other hand, such approval by the representative or agent would probably go to mitigate damages.

28. Structure of Release.

Among the requirements for a valid release are the following:

(a) In Writing.
See Section 27 above.

(b) Proper Parties.
Ordinarily, there is no problem about execution of the release by the proper parties. This will be the person whose name, picture or other attribute of personality is involved. If such a person is a minor, see Section 29 below. Although the minor's signature may be of no effect during minority, it may become significant once such minor has attained majority.

With some minor "professionals" a further question may arise if there is a court-appointed guardian who must act for the minor in place of the natural parents. This occurs more often if the minor is a theatrical personality whose income is substantial.

(c) Consideration.

Consideration is usually recited formally in the release. A mere recital may be valid but it is preferable to make an actual payment and have such payment acknowledged in the release itself. If anything more than nominal consideration is actually paid, the exact amount should be indicated.[145]

In the case of minors, it is better practice to make two separate payments so that there is a clear indication that the parent or guardian has received a certain sum on behalf of the minor and the minor's rights and another sum for his own rights. This latter may be necessary since a minor is, under the laws of many states, theoretically required to turn over all the proceeds of his services to his parents unless he has been legally "emancipated."

(d) Scope.

The question of the "scope" of a release and the dangers of limited releases have been discussed in Sections 30 to 36 below. The release should therefore be carefully examined to ascertain that it is broad enough to permit the usage contemplated or required.

The language of the release in this connection will vary rather widely with the circumstances, use or other relationships or transactions involved and no definitive generalizations can, or should, be made except to point out that the broader the release, the more protection it gives.

(e) Duration of Release.

As indicated in Section 34 below, it has been held that releases should not be relied upon as "perpetual" in duration. The release should include a specific term of years or a terminal date for the privilege granted by the release. Five years should be considered reasonable.

The inclusion of a time limit has another practical effect: it alerts the custodian of the photographic/art control file described in Chapter 9, Section 4 to the need for a new release. In any event, it prevents the use of photographs covered by "stale" releases.

(f) Other Inducements.

The release should clearly state that no other inducements, statements or promises have been made to the signer. This helps to avoid the operation of the so-called "parole evidence rule," preventing, in most cases, the raising of future questions as to oral limitations.

(g) *Binding Effect on Personal Representatives.*

The release should be made binding upon the heirs of the subject as well as any other person who may succeed to the rights of the subject. This may accord greater protection under some of the privacy statutes which grant heirs and family members certain interests and rights. It may also give some protection under so-called "survival of action" statutes.

(h) *Reference to Contract Rights.*

Not infrequently a release may be merely one part of an agreement between the parties as discussed in Section 37 below. If this is the case, the agreement should be so drawn as to tie the release elements thereof to the other terms and to render the release irrevocable.

29. Releases by Minors.

A release by a minor (a person under twenty-one) is not sufficient. Such an instrument, as is generally true, conveys or extinguishes no rights. Since a minor has a right of privacy as much as an adult, something more is needed. This means that the minor's rights—whatever they may be— must be dealt with and released by his parents, guardian or the person *in loco parentis,* as the case may be.

Ordinarily, an agreement signed by a minor is not void but only void-able by the minor after reaching majority.[146] Thus, it would seem that a privacy release signed by the minor only should be effective if the minor, after attaining twenty-one, does not within a reasonable time, take affirm-ative steps to disavow the earlier release.

In at least one New York case [147] it was held that a plaintiff, just under twenty years old, was bound by her release in connection with her appearance in a motion picture. The plaintiff had assured the defendant that she was of age and signed a release. Some question later arose as to the agreed method of exhibition of the film and the plaintiff then claimed a privacy violation. Her claim was dismissed, the court adverting to the "infancy" factor by saying that "factors . . . such as plaintiff's infancy and the invalidity of the release . . . are immaterial. The point is that resort to the statute under these circumstances perverts its pur-pose."

Because of the circumstances involved in this case, it is doubtful whether it should be relied upon in dealing with minors. The releases of parents, etc. should be obtained in any case in which there is doubt as to majority of the subject.

30. Limited and Restricted Releases.

A continuing problem—likely to become more frequent and acute as publicity-minded persons become more sophisticated—is the nature and effect of the limited release. It has long been judicially recognized that a privacy release may be less than total. The leading 1905 *Pavesich* case [148] pointed out:

> This waiver may be express or implied but the acceptance of the waiver carries with it the right to an invasion of privacy only to such an extent as may be legitimately necessary and proper in dealing with the matter which has brought about the waiver. It may be waived for one purpose and still asserted for another; it may be waived in behalf of one class and retained as against another class; it may be waived as to one individual and retained as against all other persons.

The limitations or restrictions, express or implied, may relate to any one of several aspects of the use. Principal among them are the following:

Restrictions as to purpose. See Section 31 below.

Use only with certain products, services or campaigns. See Section 31 below.

Releases in favor of certain parties only. See Section 32 below.

Restrictions on substance or subject matter permitted to be used. See Section 33 below.

Limitation of duration of permitted use. See Section 34 below.

Requirements as to subsequent approval. See Section 35 below.

Miscellaneous restrictions. See Section 36 below.

When categorized in this manner, the several restrictions may appear to be separate and isolated from each other. However, several will be found to overlap or supplement each other in particular instances.

All deal with what may be called the "scope" of the release. If the user exceeds the permissible scope—regardless of the aspect involved—the subject probably has a legally enforceable right against the user, either at law for damages or in equity for an injunction.

31. Limitations as to Purposes.

Use of a person's name or photograph may be limited to a particular purpose either expressly in the release, or by implication from the parties' relationship. Express limitations in the release are usually the result of negotiations, frequently being keyed to the amount of consideration paid for the release. Any use beyond the permitted use is an invasion. Thus in the *Glenn Miller* case, discussed in Section 16 above, there was a lengthy agreement between the parties with releases given as to certain uses, not including the use of soundtrack scores on phonograph records. The court held this to be an invasion and entered judgment for the plaintiff.

The limitation may be shown under an oral understanding. Thus, in the leading case of *Myers v. Afro-American Publishing Co.*,[149] the plaintiff was both a dancer and professional artist's model and "as a dancer . . . had never exhibited herself wholly or partly in the nude, but as an artist's model . . . had posed in the nude or semi-nude, but only for artistic representations."

The defendant published an article about the plaintiff as a dancer and accompanied it with her semi-nude model photographs. It had previously been orally agreed that "the semi-nudity would be appropriately covered and that proofs of any such pictures would be submitted to [the plaintiff] for approval before publication." This was not done. The court found for the plaintiff on the ground that use of the photographs had been expressly granted by the plaintiff only for limited purposes, subject to an understanding which had been breached.

The limitation may refer to the medium in which the name or picture is to be used or to the product with which it may be used. Once again, this limitation may be either express or implied.

It was held in the *Ettore* case [150] that the defendant had no right to use the plaintiff's name and photograph in telecasting old fight films. The prior express permission was held to be limited to the media in existence during the thirties when the grant was made. There are also some cases going the other way. Thus it has been held that permission to use a name in "circulars" also includes the right to use it in general media or promotion.[151]

Product references and restrictions may be specific or general, affirmative or negative. The release may permit use only with Product X or only with products in a given category. On the other hand, the permission may be very broad and general but except therefrom use with a certain product, group of products or brand names. A common example of such exception is the so-called "delicate" or "intimate" product or one of a "very personal nature." See Chapter 9, Section 26 for examples of such restrictions.

Both the category and the "brand name" exception are likely to be the result of other and prior commitments of the subject—especially if he or she is a professional model or entertainment personality. The reverse of this is also used: the subject, under such circumstances, is "tied up" in the release so as to forbid any future work or association with competitive products, product lines or companies.

Limitation by implication from the circumstances under which the permission was originally granted—but without any specific or express limitation or consent—provides some close questions and the cases have gone both ways. In the *Reed* case,[152] discussed in Chapter 9, Section 23, the plaintiff's picture had been taken originally by the United States Army while he was in service and published as part of the war information program. When the defendant company used the same picture commercially, the implied consent of the plaintiff was held to run only as far as the original circumstances warranted. Accordingly, the use by the defendant was considered as beyond the limits of such consent.

In the so-called "employee cases," the consent, whether expressly granted by the employee or implied from the relationship and accepted by the employee during the employment, has been held to terminate with the employment.[153]

In *Manger v. Kree Institute of Electrolysis* [154] the plaintiff wrote the prize-winning letter in defendant's contest, giving the defendant express consent to publish it in defendant's house organ. However, the letter was used for advertising and testimonial purposes after it had been altered. Plaintiff brought suit and recovered $2250 under the New York statute since the consent had been exceeded and because of the alteration, discussed in Section 33 below.

32. Limitation as to Parties.

A release or consent—whether written or oral—may run in favor of certain parties only. A broad, unlimited release is to be preferred. It is mandatory, for example, in the case of the stock photography house which must have the unencumbered privilege to sell and distribute the released pictures as widely as possible. See Chapter 9, Section 26.

On the other hand, a release may be required only for a specific use, relationship or transaction. The *Kree* case referred to in Section 31 above is typical, the release or agreement resulting from the winning of a contest. See Chapter 13, Section 38.

A group of distinct—but related—corporate entities may be involved. This occurs, for example, in connection with franchising. The franchisor may obtain a release for the pictures used in its national advertising. The franchisor then makes up advertisements in mat form, using the same picture. It distributes them to its franchisees for use in their local advertising. Litigation may be invited unless the original release specifically gives the franchisor the right to distribute the picture for such use.

The same question may arise with a company which has subsidiaries, subordinate divisions or other associated but distinct activities or operations.

It is for this reason that releases frequently grant rights to assignees, transferees, subsidiaries, licensees, and a wide variety of other parties, all of whom claim under or are related to the original releasee.

This problem is particularly pertinent in connection with releases given to nonprofit organizations. This results from two different situations.

A "national headquarters" of a nonprofit association having chapters or separately organized local groups subordinate to it but operating in conjunction with it, may obtain a release. Unless properly worded, this release can pose the same questions referred to above in the franchisor-franchisee situation.

But even bypassing such problems, most nonprofit groups do not seek broad, general releases. They limit their rights to use of a name or photograph for their own nonprofit purposes. Thus, the release used by the United Fund in Philadelphia—as shown in the reproduction of the full form below—contains a consent "to the use of the photograph hereinafter described for advertising and publicity purposes by the United Fund, or their licensees, or member organizations, . . ."

PHOTOGRAPHIC RELEASE

Date:————————

I hereby agree and consent to the use of the photograph hereinafter described for advertising and publicity purposes by the United Fund, or their licensees or member organizations, and I waive all claims for any compensation for such use or for damages.

Description of photograph ————————————————————

Signature of person photographed (if adult) ————————————

Print name of above signatory ————————————————

Print name of minor photographed ————————————————

Signature of parent or guardian ————————————————
    (if signing for minor)

Print name of above signatory ————————————————

Address (print) ————————————City, State ————————

Name of Photographer (print) ————————————————

Photographer's Negative Code No. ————————————————

Separate and individual releases must be signed by each adult, and by parent or guardian of each minor appearing in a photograph.

Use space below for circumstances of picture, titles, locale, other identifying data.

Under such language, a commercial advertiser seeking to assist the United Fund solicitation would be a "licensee." However, if that picture should be used for the company's own commercial purposes, even inadvertently, the release would not be operative in favor of such commercial use.

Indicative of the effort which may be necessary to protect a company properly is the 1950 institutional advertisement of Westinghouse Electric Corporation under the headline "Who Owns Westinghouse." The full-page advertisement contained the names of 3500 Westinghouse stockholders, selected from a group of "over 23,000 stockholders who granted permission for their names to be used." [155]

Another good example is the effort of an advertising agency which found in its files an unidentified picture of a young ice skater. Apparently, it was known when and where the picture was taken. The agency advertised in the newspapers—without using the picture of the child—and identified only the place at which it was taken. Fortunately, the advertisement reached the parents of the child and they signed releases, permitting safe use of the picture. It should be noted that the agency did not reproduce the picture in its "search ad." This itself would probably have been a violation of privacy.

33. Limitations as to Photographic Changes.

There have been several cases which indicate that it may be quite dangerous to retouch or change a released photograph. Probably the best-known of these cases is *Russell v. Marboro Books*.[156] In this case a professional model had signed the following release:

> The undersigned hereby irrevocably consents to the unrestricted use by ABC Photographer, advertisers, customers, successors and assigns, of her name, portrait or picture, for advertising purposes or purposes of trade, and I waive the right to inspect or approve such completed portraits, pictures, or advertising matter in connection therewith.

The picture was properly used by Marboro Books and thereafter was sold to Spring Mills. It was retouched and substantially altered, captions described as "vulgar and salacious" were substituted and various other changes were made. When the model sued, the above release was the principal defense. The court said:

> I would hold that the original written consent would not apply and that liability would accrue where the *content* of the picture has been so changed that it is *substantially* unlike the original. In this aspect of the case I speak of content of the picture as used, not

the *purpose* or extent of its use. If, for instance, Spring had used the original picture for its advertising of bed sheets, without the attendant objectionable writing or references, the fact that the *purpose* of the advertisement was not to interest readers in books would not negate the effect of the release. (Emphasis added.)

In the *Manger* case, referred to in Section 31 above, the alteration took place in the winning letter submitted by the plaintiff in defendant's contest. Notwithstanding an express release from the defendant, substantial damages were recovered, due, in part at least, to the fact that there had been no consent to the alteration.[157]

On the other hand, in *Dahl v. Columbia Pictures Corp.*, [158] the plaintiff, a well-known motion picture actress, was under contract to make a picture for the defendant. The defendant used certain sketches in exploitation thereof, the plaintiff claiming that these sketches gave the impression that "the character portrayed was wild and sexually promiscuous." Inasmuch as the sketches were found to have been based upon actual scenes in the film itself, it was held that this was not such alteration or impropriety as to warrant recovery.

34. Limitations as to Term.

Releases usually do not contain any limitations as to their duration. Nevertheless, there are indications from the cases that this should be included. Thus, in *MacAndrew v. Roy* [159] the plaintiff consented to use by the defendant of "before and after" pictures, shot when the plaintiff was taking a physical development course. There was no time limitation on their use and the defendant used them ten years later. The court held that the original consent would not protect the defendant ten years later and that renewal thereof should have been sought. Judgment was entered for the plaintiff in the amount of $1000.

Releases used by various concerns have time limits ranging from five to 50 years. The important thing is to include some time limit so that the subject of the release will know definitely, when he signs the release, the extent of the permission and have the opportunity to object thereto. It would probably then be held that he was bound for the whole period.

35. Requirements as to Subsequent Approval.

It seems clear that it is a privacy violation if the subject is not accorded the right to examine the photograph, script or other use when such submission and approval is required by the agreement between the parties. This is particularly true if the public use proves eventually to be unacceptable to the subject. Such requirements are not unusual—especially in connection with personalities to whom the "public image" is important. This provision will be found in motion picture studio releases.

In the *Myers* case, discussed in Section 31 above, such right of final approval was expressly retained by the plaintiff when she delivered to the defendant semi-nude photographs which defendant was to retouch. The use without plaintiff's examination was important to the finding.

In order to circumvent even the implication of this right, some releases contain an express waiver of the right. See the discussion of the *Sharman* case in Section 38 below. Also, some users require the subject to execute an approval on the back of the final prints or on the final proofs before publication. See Chapter 9, Section 24.

36. Miscellaneous Restrictions.

Most of the restrictions which do not fall easily into the several categories dealt with in Sections 31 to 35 above, are the results of specific provisions in agreements between the parties of which the release may only be a part. They may vary as widely as do the ingenuity and needs of the parties to the transaction.

One troublesome case is the variation from the permitted "life story" in motion picture, radio or television scripts. Illustrative is *Kelly v. Loew's, Inc.*[160] This involved a motion picture made from the best-seller "They Were Expendable." A release had been carefully prepared with the assistance of the Office of Public Relations of the United States Navy and then signed by the plaintiff who was, at the time, a naval officer who was to be portrayed in the film. Yet Kelly later recovered $3000 because the film did not comply fully with the release, which required that the actual facts be portrayed as accurately as possible. The defendant took some "dramatic license" with its script as it involved Kelly and the suit and recovery resulted.

This requirement of adherence to fact is not uncommon in releases and must be carefully observed although it is likely that minor deviations would not vitiate the granted permission.[161]

Another type of express restriction deals with details of the copy or typography with which the released name and picture may be used. Motion picture studios may provide that the name of the actor must be in a certain size type; the actor's photograph must be of a certain size or occupy at least an indicated minimum area; it must be coupled with the title of his then current picture; the advertisement may not mention certain subjects, may not be used in conjunction with other illustrations, etc.

An interesting but apparently unlitigated example occurred in connection with an advertisement for Charter Oak bourbon.[162] The advertisement contained an endorsement from Igor Cassini who used the *nom de plume* "Cholly Knickerbocker" in his society column in the *Journal-American,* the name being "copyrighted and owned by the newspaper."

"Cholly Knickerbocker" was used in the advertisement allegedly without permission of either the newspaper or Cassini. Cassini "explained that he was represented by [an intermediary] as Igor Cassini and that he had not given permission to use the Cholly Knickerbocker name. . . ." After the advertisement had been questioned by the *Journal-American,* two other newspapers were reported to have declined to run the advertisement upon learning of the contretemps.

It is unlikely that the "malice requirement" of the Supreme Court as spelled out in *Time, Inc. v. Hill* and discussed in Section 22 above would protect the defendant in any instances of non-conformance with the release's terms discussed in Sections 30 to 36 above. Once the parties have arrived at an understanding as evidenced by the release or other agreement, they have taken themselves beyond the pale of the First Amendment and other bases of the *Time* case.

37. Revocation of Releases.

A person gratuitously giving a release of his right of privacy has the right to revoke the release.[163] This doctrine has been followed even though the party relying on the release may have expended considerable sums of money in promoting the products with which the release was concerned.

It has also been held that revocation may take place "automatically" if there is a termination of the relationship between the parties, upon which or by reason of which the release or permission was initially implied or granted.[164]

Even in Texas, where the right of privacy as such is not recognized, it has been held that a company no longer has the right to use the name of a former employee as signatory to its correspondence, once that employee is no longer with the company.[165]

On the other hand, when the release is not gratuitous but part of a contract for which consideration is involved, the release will normally not be revocable but will continue according to its terms and there is no liability for use or appropriation permitted by its terms.

In an effort to avoid the possibility of revocation, several steps may be taken:

(a) The release should contain a specific term or duration. See Section 34 above.

(b) The release may be part of an agreement containing other obligations.

(c) The release should be, by its terms, irrevocable.

(d) The release should state that the releasee will rely thereon and that its rights "are coupled with an interest."

(e) Actual consideration should be paid for the release.

38. Release Forms and Their Use.

Since most of the privacy releases likely to be used in a public relations and advertising context involve photographs, these have been collected in Chapter 9, Section 30. As with any forms, however, they should not be blindly followed but should be used with discretion and subject to the specific needs of the transaction.

One matter must be stressed: The written release should be carefully drafted. In *Sharman v. C. Schmidt & Sons, Inc.*[166] we have an example of the judicial results of carefully designed privacy releases.

Two releases were signed by the plaintiff in this case. The first ran to the photographer; the second ran to the agency representing the defendant. The photographer's release, as quoted in the court's opinion, provided:

> In consideration of $125.00, receipt whereof is acknowledged, I hereby give XYZ STUDIO, its legal representatives and assigns, and all persons or corporations acting with its permission or upon its authority, and all persons and corporations for whom XYZ STUDIO is acting, the absolute right and unrestricted permission to copyright and/or use, and/or publish photographic portraits or pictures of me, or in which I may be included in whole or in part, or composite or distorted in character, or form, in conjunction with my own or a fictitious name, or reproductions thereof, in color or otherwise, made through any media at their studios or elsewhere for purposes of art, advertising, trade, or any other lawful purpose whatsoever.

The agency release, similarly quoted, provided:

> In consideration of $125.00 to me paid, receipt of which is hereby acknowledged, I hereby grant to *** ABC AGENCY or those for whom *** ABC AGENCY are acting, the absolute right and permission to copyright, and/or use, and/or publish photographic portraits or pictures of me still, single, multiple or moving picture or in which I may be included in whole or in part, or composite, or distorted in character or form, in conjunction with my own or any other name, or reproductions thereof, in color or otherwise, made through any media at its studios or elsewhere, for art, advertising, trade or any other lawful purpose whatsoever.
>
> I hereby waive any right that I may have to inspect and approve the finished product or the advertising copy that may be used in connection therewith, or the use to which it may be applied.

> I hereby release, discharge and agree to hold harmless *** ABC
> AGENCY their nominees, or others for whom *** ABC AGENCY
> are acting, from any liability by virtue of any use whatsoever,
> whether intentional or otherwise, that may occur or be produced
> in the taking of said picture, or in any processing tending towards
> the completion of the finished product, unless it can be shown that
> said reproduction was maliciously caused, produced and published
> solely for the purpose of subjecting me to conspicuous ridicule,
> scandal, reproach, scorn and indignity.

The plaintiff, a professional basketball star, charged a privacy violation because his photograph was used in a beer advertisement, a contemplated use of which he had never been advised before or after the execution of the releases or the taking of the photograph. The photograph
showed the plaintiff—not in basketball uniform—as a bowler holding a
bowling ball.

Relying on the *Marboro* case, discussed in Section 33, the plaintiff
claimed that the use of his picture "in connection with beer and the
composite advertising containing his picture and a bowling ball, a beer-
glass and a bottle exceeded the authorization of the release" and "subjected him to conspicuous ridicule and scorn . . ."

The court rejected this argument, saying:

> [W]e conclude that Sharman's picture was not substantially al-
> tered in content. It remained a bowling picture to which was
> appended a glass and a bottle of beer. These additions supplied
> the purpose of the picture, namely: to sell beer. Having in mind,
> as we have previously stated, that Sharman did not restrict the
> commercial use of his picture before it was published in order to
> justify his position here he would have to bring himself within the
> provision of the release (relative to "ridicule, scandal, reproach,
> scorn and indignity") , which we find he cannot do. It was contem-
> plated by all parties concerned that the picture would eventually
> be used for a commercial purpose. The sale of beer is a commercial
> purpose and is not such a use as brings the facts of this case within
> those of the *Russell* case. (Parenthetical matter added.)

This opinion poses a definite distinction between the commercial *purpose* and the *content* of a photograph. Since the court did not believe
that adding the advertising elements was a change of content within the
release reservation dealing with scorn and ridicule, it held the use to be
within the terms of the release and found for the defendant.

The interpretation of the releases is particularly significant because the
court went on to say:

> We might add that we do not condone all that took place and in
> fact are forced to conclude that some economic advantage was

taken of Sharman by his own agent and the agency with which he, on Sharman's behalf, negotiated. This situation is not one for which the law provides redress in this action, even though we conclude that there may have been reprehensible conduct and an unfair advantage taken by the recipients of the picture and the release.

E. THE RIGHT OF PUBLICITY.

39. Inadequacy of the "Privacy" Concept.

As the right of privacy gradually developed and was applied or interpreted by the courts, it slowly became clear that it was inadequate as a shield for *all* rights of personality—especially as to those of the "public figure" relevant to his unauthorized commercial exploitation. This led to a series of confusing, often irreconcilable decisions, some of them obviously the result of a judicial Procrustean bed. Gordon has described this evolution and problem: [167]

> An analysis of the decided cases through the years leads to the conclusion that much of the confusion and conflict in the decisions arose because litigants chose to sue in almost every case for invasion of privacy (premised on injury to feelings), rather than for the appropriation for commercial exploitation of property rights in name, likeness, etc., in situations where injury to feelings had only secondary application. So long as privacy suits were confined (as in most of the early cases) to the advertising exploitation of private individuals plucked from obscurity against their will, to invasions by wire-tapping, or to similar indignities where injury to feelings was the principal harm, there was little difficulty. However, when the suits began to involve all types of commercial exploitations, particularly of public figures, the decisions became confused.

Not only did the decisions become confused but the entire privacy doctrine proved inadequate to meet the demands of the modern publicity-minded and promotion-oriented commercial community. There have been several reasons for this.[168]

(a) Non-offensive Publicity.

Privacy was originally designed to protect against offensive comment or use; hence its protection of the individual's sensitivities and feelings.[169] Some courts have refused redress for commercial uses which were not offensive—at least insofar as anything more than nominal damages are concerned.[170] See Section 43 below.

Most commercialization is non-offensive. Its effectiveness almost demands this.

(b) Non-assignability.

The right of privacy has been held to be non-assignable. See Sections 15 and 16 above. This may prevent effective promotion or sale by the celebrity of his publicity values. A prospective buyer of his right may not be likely to pay substantially for a privilege which may be struck down for an inherent legal weakness.

(c) Limitation to Living Human Beings.

Privacy, as a personal right, inheres only in the personality of a living human being. The economic realities demand that animals, buildings, corporations, partnerships, and other objects or entities have protectible rights.[171] Yet the privacy doctrine does not do this.

Also, the privacy rule that the right dies with the individual may mean that his heirs and family have no recourse. See Section 16 above.

40. Development of the Right of Publicity.

The inadequacy of the privacy right in the commercial context was gradually recognized, especially by legal writers. Thus, Zechariah Chafee wrote in 1947: [172]

> Seeing how society dames and damsels sell their faces for cash in connection with cosmetics, cameras and cars, one suspects that the right to publicity is more highly valued than any right of privacy.

This approaches the commercial aspects of personality squarely and recognizes the publicity value of the individual—especially those deemed by the commercial community to have public influence by virtue of their eminence, achievement or, in some cases, notoriety. Such persons do not want "to be let alone." Instead, they want publicity, but under their control and for proper compensation.

Some earlier cases had recognized as a "valuable asset" the face and figure of the well-known.[173] Privacy was noted by some cases to be different from publicity exploitation. Thus, in the *Davey O'Brien* case [174] the court held that a right of privacy did not exist at common law in Texas but Judge Holmes, in his dissent, said:

> The right of privacy is distinct from the right to use one's name or picture for purposes of commercial advertisement. The latter is a property right that belongs to everyone; it may have much or little, or only a nominal value; but it is a personal right which may not be violated with impunity.

This distinct right was again recognized and given a name in the concurring opinion of Judge Desmond in the *Gautier* case [175] when he wrote:

My difficulty is that there was no invasion of any "right of privacy." Plaintiff, a professional entertainer, gave his show before a vast audience in an athletic stadium. His grievance here is not the invasion of his "privacy"—privacy is the one thing he did not want or need in his occupation. His real complaint, and perhaps a justified one . . . is that he was not paid for the telecasting of his show.

A year later, the Second Circuit Court gave its blessing to a right of publicity—distinct from the highly personal and nonassignable right of privacy. In the *Haelan* case,[176] a bubblegum manufacturer had obtained exclusive rights from several baseball players to use their pictures in a gum promotion. The defendant later bought the pictures of the same players and used them competitively to the plaintiff. The court held that the plaintiff had such a right, by assignment from the ballplayers, as could be protected in an action against the defendant.

The plaintiff and the defendant were both bubblegum manufacturers. Only the ballplayers could have maintained a privacy action. Instead, the plaintiff invoked the right of publicity. Since the right of publicity—"publicity value"—was found to exist by the court, it was treated as assignable by the ballplayers and the senior user thereof (the plaintiff) had the right to prevent the junior user (the defendant) from infringing upon it.

In a highly practical sense, the case is of landmark importance. The plaintiff could have sued the individual ballplayers for breach of their exclusive contract with him. This would have meant little because the competitive use by the second company would have continued. However, using the right of publicity as a premise, the court gave the plaintiff a right directly against its competitor. This prevented a competitive dilution of the plaintiff's rights and gave the plaintiff what it had bought in the first place: exclusive rights in the pictures and names of the ballplayers.

Subsequent cases have recognized the right of publicity as discussed in Sections 42 to 44 below.

41. Public Relations and the Right of Publicity.

The courts have approached the right of publicity largely from the point of view of the individual involved. From the other side of the fence—where the corporate communicator, PR practitioner or advertiser stands—the new judicial view is just as pleasing and important.

The publicity concept now protects the successful buyer of a celebrity's publicity values. It permits a grant of exclusive rights and above all, it gives the publicity-minded company an enforceable right against dilution of what it has bought and paid for.

Furthermore, the newer concept gives a corporation or a nonprofit institution a basis for protecting its own "right of publicity" since it is not likely to be confined to living individuals. It creates a justifiable and easily identifiable legal basis which, in the future, should obviate the need for a court's judicial gymnastics in finding some other and perhaps incidental grounds for protection as had been necessary theretofore.[177]

It may also obviate the struggles which the New York courts have had with "purposes of trade" under the original privacy statute and its 1961 extension to nonprofit corporations as discussed in Section 8 above. Divorcing a "publicity" action entirely from the statutory "privacy" strictures should permit the courts to deal more fairly with the appropriation of corporate publicity values which may be just as meaningful and valuable as those of an individual.[178]

42. Scope of Judicial Protection of Publicity Values.

As yet not too many courts have had occasion to pass upon or apply the right of publicity—as apart from the right of privacy. However, such courts as have been faced with the question have recognized the right, several specifically enforcing it where appropriate or necessary. This has involved the following media uses and invasions: [179]

(a) Television broadcasts, whether or not conjoined closely with "commercials" or in sponsored telecasts.

(b) Books and photographs in books.

(c) "Tie-ins." This term has been defined as the use of "the name and portrait of [a] celebrity within the context of an advertisement without necessarily indicating [endorsement of] the product." [180] See Chapter 12, Section 1. It is similar to testimonial use.

(d) Marketing and packaging exploitation.

(e) Commercial use of "home movies."

At the same time, a re-examination of earlier "appropriation" or "exploitation" cases permitting recovery on other and then-recognized theories—privacy, property rights, unfair competition, etc.—indicates with some clarity that such cases would likely be decided by applying the right of publicity doctrine should they be presented anew in the future.

It appears fair to say that all of the publicity, promotional or communications uses referred to in Section 21 above [181] are candidates for future application of the right of publicity theory.[182] To add the obvious, this is also true of use in paid advertising.

43. Value of the Right.

At the turn of the century, endorsements by United States Senators were hawked for $40 and of a Representative for $15. [183] The market has changed. Some earlier cases referred generally to the values inherent in exploitation of the celebrity's name and picture but it remained for the court in the *Hogan* case [184] to spell out with particularity the "dollars and cents" implications of the right of publicity.

The court found that the famous golfer had earned approximately a million dollars as the direct and indirect result of his golfing prowess. Of this, about 25 percent were winnings on fairway and green. The balance (three times as much) resulted from the sale and use of his name in testimonials, etc. When a book appeared containing twelve pages of photographs of Hogan illustrating various shots, but without the golfer's consent, Hogan brought suit.

The court held that he had an enforceable property right growing out of the commercial value of his name and picture and that the book had misappropriated this property right—the "right of publicity." After enumerating Hogan's earnings from tournaments, books, articles, endorsements, personal appearances, motion pictures, etc., a judgment was entered for the amount of $5000.

Judgments in "publicity" cases are likely to be higher than in "privacy" cases. Publicity values can be premised upon earnings or actual payments for the same or similar publicity, appearances or uses in the past. Privacy values deal with personal humiliation or anguish—intangible elements extremely difficult to appraise and prove. Failures to prove such damages have, in some cases, resulted in nominal or "six cent" verdicts, [185] especially where oral consent (insufficient under the statute) has been given.[186]

Some courts, especially in New York, appear to take into consideration a publicity value, once a violation of the privacy right has been established.[187]

Thus, in "Toots" Shor's suit against Sherman Billingsley,[188] Shor claimed that his picture and comments about him had been used on the defendant's television show in order to increase the value of the program to the sponsor and to the telecasters. The court overruled a motion to dismiss the privacy count and said:

> If plaintiff's name and picture were used without his consent and as part of the program telecast by the defendant; and *if this was done for the purpose of increasing the value of this program to defendants,* then the jury may find that the plaintiff's right under Section 51 of the Civil Rights law have been violated. (Emphasis added.)

44. Rights After Death.

The right of publicity is properly considered a property right and therefore is as much of an asset to a man's estate as any other property right. Accordingly, it passes by will or intestacy when a person dies.[189] This is quite different from the right of privacy which is a personal right inherent in the individual, and dies with the individual as discussed in Sections 15 and 16 above.

This situation should not be confused with the privacy rights of heirs under the statutes in Oklahoma, Utah and Virginia as discussed in Section 8 above.

Notes

1. Lyons, *Best of Broadway*, Philadelphia Inquirer, Oct. 26, 1965, p. 13.
2. COOLEY, TORTS 29 (2d ed. 1888); Roberson v. Rochester Folding Bar Co., 171 N.Y. 538, 64 N.E. 442 (1902).
3. Warren and Brandeis, *infra* note 6.
4. Nizer, *The Right of Privacy*, 39 MICH. L. REV. 526, 528 (1941).
5. Prosser, *Privacy*, *infra* note 6, at 423.
6. Warren and Brandeis, *The Right of Privacy*, 4 HARV. L. REV. 193 (1890). In addition to this seminal article, other important legal materials are: PROSSER, TORTS, ch. 22, at 829–51 (3d ed. 1964). HOFSTADTER & HOROWITZ, RIGHT OF PRIVACY (1964) (dealing essentially with the New York statute); ERNST & SCHWARTZ, PRIVACY, THE RIGHT TO BE LET ALONE (1962); ZELE-MEYER, INVASION OF PRIVACY (1959) (the latter two works being intended for the layman); Prosser, *Privacy*, 48 CAL. L. REV. 383 (1960), reprinted in 1 P.E.A.L.Q. 315 (1961); Nimmer, *The Right of Publicity*, 19 LAW & CONTEMP. PROB. 203 (1954); Gordon, *Right of Property in Name, Likeness, Personality and History*, 55 NEV. U.L. REV. 553 (1960); Green, *The Right of Privacy*, 27 ILL. L. REV. 237 (1932). In 1967 there again became available a bibliography of privacy materials: LAMOREUX, THE RIGHT OF PRIVACY— A BIBLIOGRAPHY—1890–1961 (1961).
7. See cases cited, PROSSER, TORTS, *supra* note 6, at 829, notes 2, 5, 6; Hofstadter & Horowitz, *supra* note 6, at 9–16 where the concept is traced back to its beginnings in the Jewish *Mishnah* and early Roman and Greek law.
8. Prince Albert v. Strange, 2 Deg. & Sm. 652, 64 Eng. Rep. 293, *aff'd*, 1 McN. & G. & G. 23, 41 Eng. Rep. 1171 (1849).
9. Byron v. Johnston, 2 Mer. 29, 35 Eng. 851 (1816).
10. *Supra* note 2.
11. Reed v. Real Detective Publishing Co., 63 Ariz. 194, 162 P.2d 133 (1945).
12. See Sections 12, 15, 16, 39 to 44 of this chapter.
13. Yankwich, *The Right to Privacy*, 27 NOTRE DAME LAW. 499, at 506 (1952).
14. *E.g.,* Cason v. Baskin, 159 Fla. 31, 30 S.E.2d 635 (1947).
15. See the results of this distinction in Continental Optical Co. v. Reed, 119 Ind. App. 643, 86 N.E.2d 306, 14 A.L.R.2d 743 (1949).
16. See, *e.g.,* Miller v. Universal Pictures, *infra* note 97.
17. Nimmer, *supra* note 6, at 204.
18. See Gordon, *supra* note 6, at 554, 565; Nimmer, *supra* note 6, at 210–214.
19. Madison Square Garden Corp. v. Universal Pictures Co., 255 App. Div. 459, 7 N.Y.S.2d 845 (1938).
20. PROSSER, TORTS, *supra* note 6, at 832.
21. *Id.* at 832.
22. *Id.* at 831–32 and cases cited, notes 16–50.
23. Frick v. Boyd, 350 Mass. 259, 214 N.E.2d 460, 34 L.W. 2527 (1966). For discussion of the Washington cases, see Lamoreux, *supra* note 6, at VII.

24. See PROSSER, TORTS, *supra* note 6, at 32.
25. PROSSER, TORTS, *supra* note 22.
26. O'Brien v. Pabst Brewing Co., 124 F.2d 167 (5th Cir. 1942), *cert. denied,* 315 U.S. 827 (1942).
27. United States Life Ins. Co. v. Hamilton, 238 S.W.2d 289 (Tex. Cir. App. 1951).
28. See description of statutes, Gordon, *supra* note 6, at 603, notes 204–06.
29. N.Y. Civil Rights Law, §§50,51 (1948).
30. People on Complaint of Stern v. McBride, 150 Misc. 5, 268 N.Y.S. 381 (1936); People on Complaint of Maggie v. Charles Scribner's Sons, 205 Misc. 818, 130 N.Y.S. 514 (1954).
31. Yankwich, *supra* note 13.
32. For a collection of such statutes, see Hofstadter & Horowitz, *supra* note 6, at 327–341.
33. Lanham Act, §2(c), 15 U.S.C. §1052(c) (1958).
34. Ragland, *The Right of Privacy,* 17 KY. L.J. 85 (1929); Casedan, *The Right of Privacy,* 12 B.U.L.R. 353 (1937); 2 SOCOLOW, LAW OF RADIO BROADCASTING 844–5, (1939); WARNER, RADIO AND TELEVISION LAW 1189–90 (1948).
35. See discussion of the two *Donohue* cases under the Utah statute, discussed in Section 19 of the text and in Gordon, *supra* note 6, at 604.
36. N.Y. Gen. Bus. Law, §397 (1) (Supp. 1965).
37. University of Notre Dame du Lac v. Twentieth Century-Fox Film Corp., 44 Misc. 2d 808, 255 N.Y.S.2d 210 (Sup. Ct. 1964), *aff'd mem.,* 15 N.Y.2d 940, 207 N.E.2d 508, 259 N.Y.S.2d 832 (1965).
38. See Dior v. Milton, 9 Misc. 2d 425, 155 N.Y.S.2d 443 (Sup. Ct.), *aff'd mem.,* 2 App. Div. 2d 878, 156 N.Y.S.2d 996 (1956).
39. 79 HARV. L. REV. 863 (1966). See also Cornell Univ. v. Messing Bakeries, Inc., 285 App. Div. 490, 138 N.Y.S.2d 280, *aff'd,* 309 N.Y. 722, 128 N.E.2d 421 (1955) (use of university name held deceptive). *Cf.* Vassar v. Loose-Wiles Biscuit Co., 197 Fed. 982 (W.D. Mo. 1912).
40. Uproar Co. v. N.B.C., 8 F.2d 373 (1st Cir. 1936). It has also been reported that Tallulah Bankhead was able to stop the unauthorized use of "Tallulah" although this does not appear to have been litigated.
41. Bailey v. Bloomingdale Bros., 103 N.Y.L.J. 1533 (April 4, 1940).
42. Gardella v. Log Cabin Products Co., 89 F.2d 891 (2d Cir. 1937) ("Aunt Jemima"). *Contra,* Davis v. R.K.O. Radio Pictures, 16 F. Supp. 195 (S.D.N.Y. 1936) ("Cassandra"). See also Annot., 138 A.L.R. 22, at 84.
43. Prosser, *Right of Privacy, supra* note 6, at 404.
44. Binns v. Vitagraph Corp., 210 N.Y. 51, 103 N.E. 1108 (1913).
45. Young v. Greneker Studios, 175 Misc. 1027, 26 N.Y.S.2d 357 (1941). A statute was at issue in Schuyler v. Curtis, *infra* note 87, although decided for the defendant on other grounds.
46. Binns v. Vitagraph Corp., *supra* note 44.
47. Freed v. Loew's, Inc., 175 Misc. 616, 24 N.Y.S. 679 (Sup. Ct. 1940); Loftus v. Greenwich Lithographing Co., 192 App. Div. 251, 182 N.Y.S. 428 (1920).
48. Lahr v. Adell Chemical Co., 300 F.2d 256 (1st Cir. 1962).

49. Republic Pictures Corp. v. Rogers, 213 F.2d 662 (9th Cir. 1954), *petition for recall of mandate denied,* 222 F.2d 950 (1955).

50. Waring v. WDAS Station, Inc., 327 Pa. 433, 194 Atl. 631 (1937). See also Miller v. Universal Pictures, *infra* note 97.

51. Melvin v. Reid, *infra* note 82 (motion picture); Strickler v. N.B.C., 167 F. Supp. 68 (S.D. Cal. 1958) (radio); Ettore v. Philco Television Broadcasting Co., 229 F.2d 481 (3d Cir. 1956) (television); Koussevitsky v. Allen, Towne & Heath, 188 Misc. 479, 68 N.Y.2d 779 (Sup. Ct. 1946), *aff'd,* 272 App. Div. 759, 69 N.Y.S.2d 432 (1947) (book).

52. Spahn v. Julian Messner, Inc., 43 Misc.2d 219, 250 N.Y.S.2d 529 (1965), *aff'd,* 18 N.Y.2d 324, 221 N.E.2d 543 (1966), *judg. vacated and remanded,* 35 L.W. 3411 (1967).

53. See Hofstadter & Horowitz, *supra* note 6, at 220–26.

54. Nebb v. Bell Syndicate, 41 F. Supp. 929 (S.D.N.Y. 1941).

55. PROSSER, TORTS, *supra* note 6, at 840.

56. Krieger v. Popular Publications, 167 Misc. 5, 3 N.Y.S.2d 480 (Sup. Ct. 1938).

57. Mackenzie v. Soden Mineral Springs Co., 27 Abb. N.C. 402, 18 N.Y.S. 240 (Sup. Ct. 1891) (facsimile signature); Orsini v. Eastern Wine Corp., 190 Misc. 235, 73 N.Y.S.2d 426 (1947), *aff'd,* 273 App. Div. 947, 78 N.Y.S.2d 224 (1948), *appeal denied,* 273 App. Div. 996, 79 N.Y.S.2d 870 (1948) (coat of arms).

58. Swacker v. Wright, 154 Misc. 277 (1934). See also People on Complaint of Maggie v. Charles Scribner's Sons, *supra* note 30.

59. Brown v. Paramount Publix Corp., 240 App. Div. 520, 270 N.Y.S. 544 (1934).

60. 129 F. Supp. 815 (E.D. Mo. 1949). To the same result but on slightly different "bridge" facts, see Kelly v. Loew's, Inc., 76 F. Supp. 473 (D.C. Mass. 1948).

61. Nizer, *supra* note 4.

62. Vassar v. Loose-Wiles Biscuit Co., *supra* note 39; Shubert v. Columbia Pictures, 189 Misc. 734 (N.Y. 1947).

63. Maysville Transit Co. v. Ort, 296 Ky. 594, 177 S.W.2d 369 (1943).

64. See generally Derenberg, *Federal Unfair Competition Law at End of the First Decade of the Lanham Act: Prologue or Epilogue,* 32 N.Y.U.L. REV. 1029 (1957); Weil, *Protectibility of Trademark Values Against False Competitive Advertising,* 44 CAL. L. REV. 527 (1956); 77 HARV. L. REV. 890 (1964). See also Aikens v. State of Wisconsin, 195 U.S. 194 (1904) (prima facie tort); Caldwell-Clements, Inc. v. Cowan Publishing Co., 130 F. Supp. 326 (S.D.N.Y. 1955) (Sherman Act §1); Cornell Univ. v. Messing Bakeries, Inc., *supra* note 39 (deception of public).

65. Gordon, *supra* note 6, at 578–79.

66. Sidis v. F-R Publishing Co., 113 F.2d 806 (2d Cir. 1940), *cert. denied,* 61 Sup. Ct. 393 (1940).

67. Spahn v. Julian Messner, Inc., *supra* note 52. See also Goelet v. Confidential, Inc., 5 App. Div. 2d 266, 171 N.Y.S.2d 223 (Sup. Ct. 1958).

68. This "right to know" now seems to have achieved the upper hand according to the reversal of *Spahn v. Julian Messner, Inc.* by the Supreme Court on First Amendment grounds. See Spahn v. Julian Messner, Inc., *supra* note 52.

69. In the original Warren and Brandeis, *supra* note 6, this exception was recognized. See Comments, 17 WASH. & LEE L. REV. 279 (1960), 37 U. DET. L. REV. 415 (1960), 24 TENN. L. REV. 914 (1957), 9 BUFFALO L. REV. 362 (1960), 22 So. CAL. L. REV. 320 (1949).

70. Hofstadter & Horowitz, *supra* note 6, at 48 and cases cited and discussed thereat in §6.2.

71. Pavesich v. New England Life Ins. Co., 122 Ga. 190, 50 S.E. 68 (1905).

72. Sidis v. F-R Publishing Corp., *supra* note 66.

73. Estill v. Hearst Publishing Co., 186 F.2d 1017 (7th Cir. 1961).

74. Hofstadter & Horowitz, *supra* note 6, at 51 *et seq.;* Gordon, *supra* note 6, at 574 *et seq.*

75. Annerino v. Dell Publishing Co., 117 Ill. App.2d 205, 149 N.E.2d 761 (1958).

76. Gordon, *supra* note 6, at 575.

77. Semler v. Ultem Publications, 170 Misc. 551, 9 N.Y.S.2d 319 (N.Y. City Ct. 1938); Wyatt v. James McCreary Co., 126 App. Div. 650, 11 N.Y.S. 86 (1908).

78. Colgate-Palmolive Co. v. Tullos, 219 F.2d 617 (5th Cir. 1955).

79. Wendell v. Conduit Machine Co., 74 Misc. 201 (N.Y. 1911); Tanner-Brice Co. v. Sims, 174 Ga. 13, 161 S.E. 819 (1931).

80. Birmingham Broadcasting Co. v. Bell, 266 Ala. 266, 96 So.2d 263 (1957) (*Semble*); Manger v. Kree Institute of Electrolysis, 233 F.2d 8 (2d Cir. 1956).

81. P.R.J., Feb., 1967, at 4.

82. Melvin v. Reid, 112 Cal. 285, 297 Pac. 91 (1931).

83. Note, *The Relational Right of Privacy Theory—Recovery on the Basis of Conduct Directed at a Deceased or Living Relative, Friend or Associate,* 21 RUTGERS L. REV. 74, 75 (1967). This is an excellent discussion of the subject generally.

84. Miller v. Universal Pictures Co., *infra* note 97.

85. See cases cited, *infra* notes 87 to 92.

86. Note, *supra* note 83, at 83.

87. 147 N.Y. 434, 42 N.E. 22 (1895).

88. 121 Mich. 372, 80 N.W. 285 (1899).

89. Pallas v. Crowley, Milner & Co., 322 Mich. 411, 33 N.W.2d 911 (1948).

90. 57 Fed. 434 (D.C. Mass. 1893).

91. 35 Cal. App. 2d 304, 95 P.2d 491 (1939).

92. See also Bradley v. Cowles Magazines, Inc., 26 Ill. App. 331, 168 N.E.2d 64 (1960); Smith v. Doss, 251 Ala. 250, 37 So.2d 118 (1948); Waters v. Fleetwood, 212 Ga. 161, 91 S.E.2d 344 (1956); Sellers v. Henry, 329 S.W.2d 214 (1959); Kelly v. Post Publishing Co., 327 Mass. 275, 98 N.E.2d 286 (1951).

93. Douglas v. Stokes, 149 Ky. 506, 149 S.W. 849 (1912); Fitzsimmons v. Clinger Mortuary Ass'n, 91 Colo. 544, 17 P.2d 535 (1932).

94. Bazemore v. Savannah Hospital, 171 Ga. 257, 155 S.E. 194 (1930).

95. Gordon, *supra* note 6, at 598–599.

96. Green, *supra* note 6, at 249.

97. Miller v. Universal Pictures Co., 18 Misc. 2d 626, 188 N.Y.S.2d 386 (Sup. Ct. 1959).

98. Shaw v. United Artists Corp., 54 C. 290 (N.D.E.D. Ill.) (unreported but cited and discussed by Gordon, *supra* note 6, at 600).

99. James v. Screen Gems, Inc., 174 Cal. App. 650, 344 P.2d 799 (1959).

100. Maritote v. Desilu Productions, 230 F. Supp. 721 (N.D. Ill. 1964), *aff'd,* 345 F.2d 418 (7th Cir. 1965), *cert. denied,* 362 U.S. 838 (1965); Comment, 9 UTAH L. REV. 999 (1965).

101. Knierem v. Izzo, 22 Ill. 2d 73, 174 N.E.2d 157 (1961).

102. PROSSER, TORTS, *supra* note 6, at 42.

103. Schumann v. Loew's, Inc., 199 Misc. 38, 102 N.Y.S.2d 572 (Sup. Ct. 1951), *amended complaint dismissed,* 135 N.Y.S.2d 361 (Sup. Ct. 1954).

104. Gordon, *supra* note 6, at 601.

105. *Id.* at 599.

106. James v. Screen Gems, Inc., *supra* note 99, at 650, quoting from Coverstone v. Davies, 38 Cal.2d 315, 239 P.2d 876 (1952). See also Note, *supra* note 83, at 83.

107. Sir John Heydon's Case, 11 Co. Rep. 5, 77 Eng. Rep. 1150 (1613).

108. PROSSER, TORTS, *supra* note 6, at 258; see also 1 COOLEY, TORTS 276–278 (4th ed. 1932).

109. Apparently this "catch-all" type of litigation is premised, in part at least, on the theory that some one of the defendants will have insurance coverage for privacy, etc., risks.

110. Siedelman v. State, 110 N.Y.S.2d 380 (Ct. Cl. 1952); Hofstadter & Horowitz, *supra* note 6, at 32.

111. Ettore v. Philco Television Broadcasting Corp., 229 F.2d 481, 485 (3d Cir. 1956).

112. Binns v. Vitagraph Corp., *supra* note 44.

113. Donohue v. Warner Bros. Pictures, 2 Utah 2d 256, 272 P.2d 117 (1954).

114. Donohue v. Warner Bros. Pictures, 194 F.2d 6 (10th Cir. 1952).

115. Binns v. Vitagraph, *supra* note 44.

116. Edison v. Edison Polyform Mfg. Co., 73 N.J. Eq. 136, 67 Atl. 392 (1907).

117. CUTLIP & CENTER, EFFECTIVE PUBLIC RELATIONS, ch. 6 (3d ed. 1964); Weir, *How Public Relations Should Look at Advertising,* P.R.J., Oct., 1961, at 9; Rodd, *How to Establish Liaison Between Public Relations and Advertising,* P.R.J., Oct., 1961, at 21.

118. Spahn v. Julian Messner, Inc., *supra* note 52 and cases cited therein.

119. [a] Almind v. Sea Beach Ry., 157 App. Div. 230, 141 N.Y.S. 842 (1913); [b] Griffin v. Medical Society, 11 N.Y.S.2d 109 (1939); [c] Rubino v. Slaughter, 136 N.Y.S.2d 98 (1934); [d] Myers v. United States Camera Publishing Co., 9 Misc. 2d 765, 167 N.Y.S.2d 771 (1957); [e] Flores v. Mosler Safe Co., 7 N.Y.2d 276, 164 N.E.2d 853, 196 N.Y.S.2d 975 (1959); [f] Kerby v. Hal Roach Studios, Inc., 53 Cal. App. 2d 207, 127 P.2d 577 (1942); [g] Brunson v. Banks Army Store, 161 Neb. 519, 73 N.W.2d 803

(1955) (recovery refused because of denial of existence of privacy in Nebraska, a minority view); [h] Kunz v. Allen, 102 Kans. 883, 172 Pac. 532 (1918); [i] Miller v. Madison Square Garden Corp., 176 Misc. 714, 28 N.Y.S.2d 811 (Sup. Ct. 1941); [j] Lane v. Woolworth Co., 171 Misc. 66, 11 N.Y.S.2d 199 (1939); [k] Olan Mills, Inc. v. Dodd, 353 S.W.2d 22 (Ark. 1961); [l] Gelsman v. Universal Photo Books, 18 App. Div. 2d 151, 238 N.Y.S.2d 686 (1963); [m] Jansen v. Hilo Packing Co., 202 Misc. 99, 118 N.Y.S.2d 162 (1952).

120. Sutton v. Hearst Corp., 277 App. Div. 155, 98 N.Y.S.2d 233 (1950).

121. Joseph Burstyn, Inc. v. Wilson, 343 U.S. 495, 501 (1952).

122. 18 App. Div. 2d 485, 240 N.Y.S.2d 286 (Sup. Ct. 1963) (reversed as to damages only), aff'd, 15 N.Y.2d 986, 207 N.E.2d 604 (1965), probable jurisdiction noted, 382 U.S. 936 (1965), restored to docket for reargument, 384 U.S. 995 (1966), reversed and remanded, 35 L.W. 4108 (1967).

123. See also as to this issue, Brizinski v. DoAll Co. et al., 31 Ill. App. 2d 191, 175 N.E.2d 577 (1961) where the plaintiff was included "incidentally" in a product picture.

124. 192 Misc. 979, 80 N.Y.S.2d 37, aff'd, 274 App. Div. 919, 84 N.Y.S.2d 894 (1948).

125. Fleischer v. W.P.I.X., Inc., 30 Misc. 2d 17, 213 N.Y.S.2d 632 (Sup. Ct. 1961) citing Gautier v. Pro Football, Inc., infra note 175; Brizinski v. DoAll Co. et al., supra note 123.

126. Stillman v. Paramount Pictures, 1 Misc. 2d 108, 147 N.Y.S.2d 504 (Sup. Ct. 1956), mod'd, 2 App. Div. 2d 18, 153 N.Y.S.2d 190 (1956), aff'd, 5 N.Y.2d 994, 184 N.Y.S.2d 856, 157 N.E.2d 728 (oral mention); Merle v. Sociological Film Corp., 166 App. Div. 376 (1915) (visual display).

127. Damron v. Doubleday, Doran & Co., 133 Misc. 302, 231 N.Y.S. 444 (1928), aff'd, 226 App. Div. 796, 234 N.Y.S. 773 (1929) (novel); Colyer v. Fox Publishing Co., 162 App. Div. 297 (1914) (article).

128. 13 App. Div. 2d 114, 213 N.Y.S.2d 999 (1961).

129. Hofstadter & Horowitz, supra note 6, at 215.

130. 15 App. Div. 2d 343, 223 N.Y.S.2d 737 (1962), aff'd, 11 N.Y.2d 907, 182 N.E.2d 812 (1962).

131. Hofstadter & Horowitz, supra note 6, at 217; Note, 37 FORDHAM L. REV. 950 (1962).

132. 189 App. Div. 467, 178 N.Y.S. 752 (1919).

133. Dallesandro v. Holt & Co., 4 App. Div. 2d 470, 160 N.Y.S.2d 805 (1957); Oma v. Hillman Periodicals, 281 App. Div. 240, 118 N.Y.S.2d 720 (1953); Koussevitsky v. Allen, Towne & Heath, supra note 51.

134. Spahn v. Julian Messner, Inc., supra note 52 at 327. See also Time, Inc. v. Hill, supra note 122.

135. 7 N.Y.2d 276, 196 N.Y.S.2d 975, 164 N.E.2d 853 (1959).

136. Cutlip & Center, supra note 117, at 190.

137. Finn, Public Relations in Marketing, in HANDBOOK OF PUBLIC RELATIONS (Stephenson ed. 1960).

138. See Ravitch v. King, 17 Misc. 2d 683, 187 N.Y.S.2d 272 (Sup. Ct. 1955).

139. Warren and Brandeis, *supra* note 6, at 218.
140. Tanner-Brice Co. v. Sims, *supra* note 79; Jenkins v. Dell Publishing Co., 143 F. Supp. 953 (W.D. Pa. 1956), *aff'd*, 250 F.2d 447 (3d Cir. 1958).
141. Almind v. Sea Beach Ry., *supra* note 119; Wilk v. Andrea Radio Corp., 200 N.Y.S.2d 522 (1960), *mod'd*, 13 App. Div. 2d 745, 216 N.Y.S.2d 662 (1961); Lomax v. New Broadcasting Co., 18 App. Div. 2d 229, 238 N.Y.S.2d 781 (1963).
142. Roberts v. Condé Nast Publications, Inc., 286 App. Div. 729, 146 N.Y.S.2d 493 (1955).
143. Martinelli v. Wil-Low Cafeterias, Inc., 95 N.Y.L.J. 230 (April 13, 1936), cited in Hofstadter & Horowitz, *supra* note 6, at 87.
144. PROSSER, TORTS, *supra* note 6, at 1026.
145. Contracts such as those required by S.A.G. indicate the exact amount paid. As to tax treatment of such consideration, see Roosevelt, 43 T.C. 195, 33 L.W. 2217 (1964); Starrells, 35 T.C. 649, 29 L.W. 2339 (1960).
146. See 2 WILLISTON, CONTRACTS §§226–31 (3d ed. 1959).
147. Sherwood v. McGowan, 3 Misc. 2d 234, 152 N.Y.S.2d 685 (Sup. Ct., 1956).
148. Pavesich v. New England Life Ins. Co., *supra* note 71.
149. 168 Misc. 429, 5 N.Y.S.2d 225 (Sup. Ct. 1938), *aff'd*, 255 App. Div. 838, 7 N.Y.S.2d 662 (1938).
150. Ettore v. Philco Tel. Broadcasting Corp., 299 F.2d 481 (3d Cir. 1956).
151. Marek v. Zanol Products Co., 298 Mass. 1, 9 N.E.2d 393 (1937).
152. Continental Optical Co. v. Reed, *supra* note 15.
153. Colgate-Palmolive Co. v. Tullos, 219 F.2d 617 (5th Cir. 1955); United States Life Ins. Co. v. Hamilton, *supra* note 27.
154. Manger v. Kree Institute of Electrolysis, *supra* note 80.
155. A.A., May 15, 1950, at 40.
156. 18 Misc. 2d 166, 183 N.Y.S.2d 8 (1959).
157. See also Sinclair v. Postal Tel. and Cable Co., 72 N.Y.S.2d 841 (Sup. Ct. 1935).
158. 166 N.Y.S.2d 708 (Sup. Ct. 1957).
159. 131 So.2d 256 (La. App. 1961).
160. 76 F. Supp. 473 (D.C. Mass. 1948). See also the parallel case of Walcher v. Loew's, Inc., *supra* note 60.
161. Marek v. Zanol Products Co., *supra* note 151 (*semble*); Dahl v. Columbia Pictures Corp., *supra* note 158.
162. As reported in A.A., Feb. 20, 1956, at 29.
163. State *ex. rel.* La Follette v. Hinkle, 131 Wash. 86, 229 Pac. 317 (1924).
164. Lillie v. Warner Bros. Pictures, 139 Cal. App. 734, 34 P.2d 835 (1934); Long v. Decca Records, 76 N.Y.S.2d 133 (Sup. Ct. 1947); Fairbanks v. Winik, 119 Misc. 809, 108 N.Y.S. 299 (1922), *rev'd on other grounds*, 206 App. Div. 449, 201 N.Y.S. 287 (1923).
165. Colgate-Palmolive Co. v. Tullos, *supra* note 153.
166. 216 F. Supp. 401 (E.D. Pa. 1963).
167. Gordon, *supra* note 6, at 554.
168. Nimmer, *supra* note 6, is an excellent discussion of the questions dealt with in this and succeeding sections.

169. RESTATEMENT, TORTS §867 (1939) ; Yankwich, *supra* note 13, at 506.
170. Miller v. Madison Square Garden Corp., *supra* note 119; Cason v. Baskin, *supra* note 14.
171. Nimmer, *supra* note 6, at 210.
172. CHAFEE, GOVERNMENT AND MASS COMMUNICATIONS 138 (1947) .
173. Flake v. Greensboro News Co., 212 N.C. 780, 195 S.E. 55 (1938) .
174. O'Brien v. Pabst Brewing Co., *supra* note 26.
175. Gautier v. Pro Football, Inc., 278 App. Div. 431, 106 N.Y.S.2d 553, *aff'd*, 304 N.Y. 354, 107 N.E.2d 485 (1952) .
176. Haelen Laboratories v. Topps Chewing Gum, Inc., 202 F.2d 866 (2d Cir. 1953) .
177. See, *e.g.*, Lawrence v. Ylla, 184 Misc. 807, 55 N.Y.S.2d 343 (1945) (contract) ; Madison Square Garden Corp. v. Universal Pictures Co., *supra* note 19 (unfair competition) ; Cornell Univ. v. Messing Bakeries, Inc., *supra* note 39 (deception of public) .
178. Nimmer, *supra* note 6, at 216.
179. [a] Gautier v. Pro Football, Inc., *supra* note 175; Douglas v. Disney (Cal. Super. Ct. 1956) (unreported) ; [b] Hogan v. Barnes & Co., 114 U.S.P.Q. 314 (Pa. Com. Pl. Ct. 1957) ; [c] Sharman v. C. Schmidt & Sons, Inc., *supra* note 166; [d] Haelen Laboratories v. Topps Chewing Gum, Inc., *supra* note 176; Jansen v. Hilo Packing Co., *supra* note 119; [e] Douglas v. Disney.
180. Nimmer, *supra* note 6, at note 64.
181. See cases cited, *supra* note 119.
182. Gordon, *supra* note 6, at 605–13.
183. PRESBREY, HISTORY OF ADVERTISING 533 (1929).
184. Hogan v. Barnes & Co., *supra* note 179 [b].
185. Miller v. Madison Square Garden Corp., *supra* note 119; Cason v. Baskin, *supra* note 14.
186. Lane v. Woolworth Co., *supra* note 119; Harris v. Gossard Co., 194 App. Div. 688 (1921) .
187. Richmond v. Columbia Pictures Corp., 253 App. Div. 708, 1 N.Y.S.2d 643 (1937) , *aff'd*, 277 N.Y. 707, 14 N.E.2d 636 (1938) ; Foster-Milburn Co. v. Chinn, 134 Ky. 424, 120 S.W. 364 (1909); Myers v. United States Camera Publishing Co., *supra* note 119.
188. 4 Misc. 2d 857, 158 N.Y.S.2d 476 (Sup. Ct.) , *aff'd*, 4 App. Div. 2d 1017, 169 N.Y.S.2d 416 (1957) , *app. denied*, 5 App. Div.2d 768, 170 N.Y.D.2d 976 (1957) .
189. Gordon, *supra* note 6, at 598–603.

Chapter 9

Photography, Artwork and Graphics

A. INTRODUCTION

1. Scope and Purpose of Chapter
2. Public Relations Involvement
3. Applicable Legal Areas
4. Photographic/Art Control Files

B. OWNERSHIP

5. Important Distinctions
6. Photographs
7. Portrait/Commercial Photographs
8. Negatives
9. Rights of "Sitters"
10. Fine Art
11. Commercial Art

C. COPYRIGHT

12. Special Copyright Notice and Registration Procedure
13. Graphics Admissible to Copyright
14. Position of Copyright Notice
15. Product Photographs
16. Staff Artist's Work
17. Stock and Other Copyrighted Materials

D. PURCHASE METHODS

18. Rights Involved
19. Pricing Problems
20. Purchase Orders for Photographs
21. Purchase Orders for Art
22. Competitive Use of Graphics

E. PRIVACY

F. PHOTOGRAPHIC LIBEL

G. RESPONSIBILITY FOR PHOTOGRAPHIC MATERIALS

Chapter 9

Photography, Artwork and Graphics

A. INTRODUCTION.

1. Scope and Purpose of Chapter.

This is a "horizontal" chapter, cutting across a variety of important legal areas, each the subject of fuller discussion in other chapters. The use of photographs, art, artwork and graphics of various kinds is such a continuing, important aspect of various public relations activities that it merits concentrated treatment within a single focus.[1] Furthermore, the interrelation of these legal areas—as applicable to graphics—is frequently so intimate that understanding of their overall importance may be appreciably aided by this treatment.

We are, in effect, here concerned with the "bundle" of rights and obligations to be faced and resolved whenever public relations photography, etc. is involved.

The thrust of this chapter covers all forms of graphics, using the term with an inclusive connotation. It is not confined to photography or art, fine or commercial. Its sweep may be considered as including all of the matter tabulated in Section 13 below. Even that tabulation should not be taken as definitive or all-inclusive.

2. Public Relations Involvement.

Nearly every kind of graphic is in the PR man's kit. This includes a studio portrait accompanying the news release about a new corporate officer; publicity with specially-shot product pictures; cartoons in a house organ; a traveling art show sponsored by a company; charts and graphs included in annual reports; snapshots used in employee publications; motion pictures to present evidence at government hearings;[2] explanatory pictorial wall displays used during plant tours; on-the-spot disaster photographs to illustrate company-community involvement; slides for lectures or speeches to church groups. The range is limitless, dictated

only by the company's public relations activities and the imagination of
the public relations practitioner.

As public relations develops and contributes more and more to corporate activities, so too does the need increase for an ever wider variety of
photography and graphics.

This has been so evident that some public relations firms and departments maintain their own staff photographers and artists. Some firms
have even organized subsidiary companies to produce pictorial and other
PR aids. What may once have been considered merely an adjunct to press
relations has now become a full-fledged member of the public relations
family, useful in nearly every phase of its activities.

The varied use of photography, etc. in such a wide variety of activities
has naturally increased the PR man's legal exposure. While perhaps not
overly typical, *Young v. J. M. Hickerson, Inc.*[3] presents an interesting
interplay of the law and public relations as demonstrated by a public
relations use of a photograph.

This was a state-court action by a photographer against a public relations and advertising agency. In 1948 the photographer had taken an
architect's photograph for use in a portraiture exhibit. In 1950 and 1951
the architect bought several prints. Some bore the photographer's copyright notice. In 1955 the defendant "was instrumental in having published" an article in *Architectural Record,* promoting and publicizing
the use of copper in industry. The architect's picture was used with the
article after he gave releases to both the publication and the defendant.
No copyright or credit was given the photographer when using the picture. The court found against the photographer on the ground that he
had lost his common law rights, but it left open the question as to his
rights under the copyright laws.

3. Applicable Legal Areas.

There are essentially six different legal concepts or areas with which
photography, artwork or graphics may be involved. They are:

    (a) Ownership. See Sections 5 to 11 below.
    (b) Copyright. See Sections 12 to 17 below.
    (c) Purchase methods. See Sections 18 to 22 below.
    (d) Right of privacy. See Sections 23 to 30 below.
    (e) Libel. See Sections 31 to 33 below.
    (f) Responsibility for loss. See Sections 34 to 36 below.

Some of these may overlap. Such overlaps are discussed below, and also
at greater length in the relevant chapters.

4. Photographic/Art Control Files.

The multiplicity of legal exposures suggested in Section 3 above dictates purchase and handling controls if the PR practitioner or department is to avoid a multiplicity of legal claims. While even the largest and most careful companies and counselors have not always been immune, their experience proves the importance of careful handling.

The primary tool is a "photograph/art control file." This may involve extra paperwork but is strongly recommended. It brings together in one place and under the jurisdiction of one person—available for easy and frequent reference—all of the background data which should be known about a particular picture, drawing or other graphic *before* it is used.

Every acquisition—whether through routine purchase or some other method—should be "logged" in this central file and a permanent number assigned to it *immediately*. Only after this has been done should it be "passed" for use. A photographic or photostatic print of the material should be kept in this master file—even a photographic copy of an oil painting if that be involved. This copy or print should have entered on its back all pertinent information. Absence of information should also be noted so that it may later be obtained before actual use.

The information to be obtained and entered relates to the following:

(a) Source.
This data should be specific and detailed so that follow-up is possible if it becomes necessary.

(b) Extent of Rights.
This should indicate whether full rights have been acquired or merely a limited reproduction privilege or license. The name of the referrent account, program or story should be noted if rights are so limited.

(c) Copyright.
The name and address of the copyright proprietor, which may be different from the source, should be indicated. A license or assignment should be specifically detailed with a cross-reference to the instrument in question. If no copyrights are involved, this should be noted.

(d) Privacy Releases.
A simple "OK ON RELEASES" is sufficient if adequate releases have been obtained. "NO RELEASES" should be noted in red if that is the case. If no privacy releases are deemed necessary, this should also be indicated.

(e) Purchase Instruments.

Ordinarily, bills of sale or other documents of title will not be obtained in making routine purchases. Some particularly important art may be accompanied thereby. A reference should be included to the number of the purchase order used.

(f) Approval of Counsel.

If any questions on the above matters seem relevant, a red-ink stamp CLEAR WITH COUNSEL should be used. Some large firms or departments require legal approval routinely. Approval is then noted on the print.

Photographic morgues are built up from a wide variety of sources. Some are through "formal" purchases but others are obtained from as transient a source as a mailing piece crossing the PR man's desk. It may therefore be impossible to log all of the necessary information listed above. Usually, the more coincidental or accidental the acquisition, the greater the exposure in the event of use.

Organization and sedulous use of this control file is not enough. All staff members must be alerted and directed to check the file before using any graphic materials. This admonition may be included in a staff memorandum or in the "legal manual" if one is being used. See Chapter 1, Sections 20–22.

B. OWNERSHIP.

5. Important Distinctions.

In any consideration of the legal ramifications of graphics, certain important distinctions must be recognized at all times. They are:

(a) The difference between the physical graphic property and the copyright thereof is basic.

(b) Full title and ownership with unlimited rights to use and reproduce are quite different from limited and transient rights therein, frequently the subject of public relations transactions.

(c) The distinction between a finished photograph, on the one hand, and the negative, plate, proofs or other preliminary or intermediate materials required to produce the finished job, on the other hand, has long been recognized.

(d) Ownership of, or the right to use and reproduce, a picture, sketch or other graphic is separate and apart from any rights of privacy which may be involved.

6. Photographs.

The ownership of photographs—referring by that term to the finished, positive print—depends upon the relationship between the parties and the circumstances under which the pictures were originally taken. Public relations photographic transactions are so varied that they involve more than one such set of circumstances.

(a) If a photographer takes a specific picture or group of pictures at the instruction of the purchaser, the relationship between purchaser and photographer is one of employment. This is true whether the purchaser happens to be the sitter or merely some third party.[4]

The leading case is *Lumiere v. Robertson-Cole Distributing Corp.*,[5] where the court said:

> The usual contact between a photographer and his customer is one of employment. The production of the photograph is work done for the customer, not for the photographer, and the sitter is entitled to all proprietary rights therein. The work is done for the person procuring it to be done, and the negative, so far as it is a picture, or capable of reproducing pictures, of that person, and all photographs, so made from it, belong to the person. Neither the artist nor anyone else has the right to make pictures from the negative, or to copy the photographs, if not otherwise published, for anyone else . . . Where a photographer takes photographs of a person, who goes or is sent to the photographer in the usual course, and the photographer is paid for the photographs and his services in taking the photographs, the right of copyright is in the sitter, or in the person sending the sitter to be photographed, and it is not in the photographer.

The facts of the case represent a series of photographic transactions. The pictures were of Georges Carpentier, the French prizefighter. The order had been given by an American motion-picture distributor who purchased several thousand positive prints of the pictures and paid the photographer for them. The latter retained the negatives and later made additional prints therefrom, registering the copyright thereon. He then sought to enjoin the original purchaser from distributing any prints. The court, as indicated above, found in favor of the purchaser and against the photographer.

Not only could the photographer not stop the sale of the prints, but the court held that the photographer had no right to reproduce any further prints from the negatives in his possession. He was held to be, in effect, a trustee for the purchaser who had paid him for the original pictures. This is a natural result of the employment relationship. It is similar to the holding of the *Mollé* case discussed in Chapter 2, Section 6.

(b) When the photographer is not specifically employed to take a picture but does so on his own initiative without being paid, the photographs belong to the photographer. In one case, for example, the photographer took several pictures of an actress. He did not charge her and gratuitously gave her a number of prints. It was held that the photographer was the owner of the pictures and could reproduce them freely.[6]

This is the usual situation of the free-lance photographer with whom the PR man frequently deals. It is also true of the stock photography house. See Section 17 below.

(c) When a photographer is given the opportunity to photograph a group or certain activity but is not paid for his services, his compensation coming from possible sale of prints to participants or other interested parties, the photographer owns the photographs.[7] Typical is a high school class picture or a free-lance photographer who roams the floor at a banquet, taking pictures of various table groups.

If the sponsors of an event—the group which gives the photographer permission—want prints of pictures, this should be made clear to him before the permission or invitation is given. Otherwise there may be a serious question whether or not the photographer need give—rather than sell—prints to the sponsors.

This should not be confused with the arrangements made by similar sponsors who employ and pay a free-lance photographer to take pictures of an event. This relationship falls under Subsection (a) above. The photographs and the right to reproduce them belong to the sponsor. The number of prints of each shot to be delivered will depend upon the specific arrangements with the photographer.

(d) A free-lance photographer may be asked to take a series of pictures of a certain subject. The prospective purchaser is to make a selection from the group. There may be no obligation to buy even a single shot. The photographer's work is completely speculative.

This is the case, for example, when a house organ needs pictures to illustrate an article. When the purchaser makes a selection, it certainly becomes the owner of these pictures which it has specifically bought. Some question may arise as to its rights in the other and unpurchased shots.

To prevent any misunderstanding, the original request should specifically indicate that the photographer retains no rights in any of the shots —whether purchased or not—and the purchaser acquires full rights in all thereof. This may require payment of a larger consideration and, of course, depends upon the relationship and negotiations between the parties. Even if it does involve such additional payment, the additional charge is worthwhile because it prevents the photographer from selling the unpurchased shots elsewhere—a course which might have unsatisfactory competitive results.

(e) When a staff photographer—a full-time employee—takes the pictures, there is no question about the ownership of the photographs. They belong to the employer. This follows from the general rule referred to in Subsection (a) above. However, some such staff photographers may "moonlight" and desire to sell their work to outside third parties. To prevent any conflict in this situation, there should be a clear-cut written understanding as to the relative rights in such work.

7. Portrait/Commercial Photographs.

Some effort has been made by photographers to avoid the well-recognized rule as to the ownership of photographs on the basis that this rule applies only to portrait photography and not to commercial photography.

In the *Avedon* case,[8] the court rejected this alleged dichotomy and held that the same rule applied to both portraits and commercial photography, saying:

> Just as one who had his picture taken would not relish seeing it published by others, so a commercial client, attempting to attract customers to his product by means of a picture, would not relish seeing others trying to attract customers by means of the same picture. We all know that novelty and imagination are two of the most important elements of good advertising.

Furthermore, the court pointed out that a uniform rule had been applied in commercial cases in the well-known "Snap, Crackle and Pop" case,[9] discussed in Section 11 below.

8. Negatives.

There is some legal confusion as to the ownership of photographic negatives. We include in this term negatives, plates, proofs or other initial or preliminary materials from which the finished print is made.

In the earlier cases—both English and American—it had been intimated that the photographer retained the property rights in the negatives.[10] However, this was dictum—not necessary to the decision on the facts presented to the courts in these cases. On the other hand, the court in the *Lumiere* case [11] had said that ". . . the negative, so far as it is a picture, or capable of reproducing pictures . . . belongs" to the customer.

In 1947 in the *Hochstadter* case,[12] a New York court said:

> We hold, therefore, that where a customer employs a photographer to make pictures of him, the photographer in the absence of an agreement to the contrary, has the right to retain the negatives. He may not, however, make any use of the negative without the permission of the customer.

The case turned on evidence that "it has always been the custom for photographers to retain the negatives." It is this alleged custom which has complicated the situation. This court admitted evidence of the custom and the decision was largely premised on it inasmuch as there were no prior decisions squarely on the question and no agreement between the parties.

A year earlier, in the *Colten* case,[13] a similar question had come up in another New York court. The photographer sought to incorporate into the employment contract an alleged custom which "gives [a photographer] the right to own and possess the negatives of photographs made for his customer." The court refused to accept such proof and dismissed the photographer's claim. The court also ordered the photographer to deliver to the customer 422 negatives, described as "the property of the [customer]."

This case is particularly interesting because the photographer also offered as further proof of his ownership of the negatives a form of label pasted on invoices and labels which read in part: ". . . negatives are property of and in possession of Colten Photos." The court refused to rely on this because it was not shown that the purchaser had agreed to this inscription.

This case has been criticized in some legal comment, suggesting that the court should have admitted the evidence of the custom [14] as was permitted in the *Hochstadter* case a short time later.

Most photographers do take the position that they retain rights in the negatives. This stand was officially taken by the Professional Photographers Club of New York which appeared as *amicus curiae* in the *Hochstadter* case.

This represents a desire to retain a leverage position so that the customer will have to return to the photographer if he desires additional prints. This is a situation which frequent users of photography—including PR practitioners—should avoid. The purchase order for photography should make it clear that the purchaser has the rights in the negatives. See Section 20 below.

The practical result of physically obtaining the negatives was well demonstrated in the *Avedon* case.[15] The photographer did deliver the negatives to the advertising agency which had originally ordered the work. In the subsequent litigation, dealing with later use of the negatives for an allegedly uncontemplated purpose, the court found in favor of the agency.

On the other hand, even assuming that the photographer owns the negatives and has the right to retain them, the latter "may not make any use of the negative without the permission of the customer." [16] This restriction is well-recognized in other cases.[17]

The photographer and his customer are therefore faced with an anomaly: the customer does not own the negative but the photographer may make no use thereof without the consent of the customer. The customer "controls" the negative and its subsequent use but does not own it. Of course, the situation is otherwise if rights of ownership and possession have passed to the customer under the terms of a purchase order or agreement as discussed in Section 20 below.

Modern technological advances—especially in color photography—introduce some ambivalent questions. A photographer may take color shots in transparency or slide form. This is the "negative" from which the purchaser will reproduce the picture in its final form. The purchaser needs the negative—even for the initial printing—quite apart from any possible future or repeat use.

There would seem to be no question that the "negative" in this case belongs to the purchaser despite its technical character. On the other hand, situations have developed—unlitigated to the best of our knowledge—in which photographers claimed that the purchaser could use the transparency only for its originally contemplated purpose and could not thereafter use it for other purposes or in different media.

In a sense, this involves pricing problems as discussed in Section 19 below. Such questions, however, may be obviated and foreclosed by a proper purchase order. See Section 20 below.

9. Rights of "Sitters."

Apart from possible rights of privacy, a "sitter" for a photograph—whether he be the subject of a candid shot or a professional model employed for the purpose—has no rights in the picture merely because he is the subject.[18] Any rights therein which such subject has arise from other circumstances or relationships. For example, he may have ordered and paid for the pictures and owns them for that reason.

PR men may gratuitously give prints to the subjects—house organ editors do this frequently—but such gifts create no rights.[19] On the other hand, it is wise to stamp the back of such prints "This photograph is the sole property of ABC Company and is not to be reproduced without specific written permission."

10. Fine Art.

More and more fine art is being purchased for use in public relations, promotional, advertising and similar corporate activities. A distinction is sometimes sought to be made between "fine art" and "commercial art." As developed herein and in Section 11 below, there is very little legal difference.

As to ownership and various other rights in fine art, the leading *Pushman* case [20] presents both the general rule and an excellent example of how unforeseen circumstances may later develop—in this case, ten years later—which present problems better solved at the outset.

Pushman was a well-known foreign artist who sold one of his paintings to the University of Illinois. His American agent gave the university a bill of sale for the painting which retained no rights of any kind for the artist. Ten years later, the defendant obtained from the University the right to make multiple reproductions of the painting. Pushman brought suit to stop such reproductions. The court held for the defendant on the ground that the artist had sold and delivered the painting with a routine bill of sale and did not "retain or protect" any rights. If the artist wished to retain reproduction rights or any other rights, this should have been spelled out in the bill of sale. As a result, the university had the right to give the defendant reproduction rights.

This rule may present an ambivalent situation to the company buying fine art. The company may desire to acquire only the right to reproduce a painting for a one-time use. On the other hand, it may require full ownership if the painting, for example, is to be used as part of a corporate touring art show as discussed in Chapter 14, Sections 17 to 20.

In the latter case, the customary bill of sale (without retention or limitation) is proper. In the former situation, there is no need to purchase all rights at what may be a disproportionate price. A one-time reproduction right for a specific purpose should be purchased. At the same time, it must be kept in mind that the company *may* thereafter desire to use the reproduction rights more extensively because of, perhaps, the success with the initial effort with that painting. As to this, see Section 21 below.

11. Commercial Art.

The rule as to ownership and rights in commercial art is essentially as announced in the *Pushman* case discussed in Section 10. Unfortunately, however, commercial art appears to be purchased more "loosely" than is fine art.

An artist may make a few sample sketches, the company or PR man selects one and the artist then does the finished art on the basis of the selection. The entire proceeding is quite informal and there is no agreement. It is from this type of relationship that there spring many of the problems in this field.

Grant v. Kellogg Co.[21] is a good example of the need for perception in the purchase of what may seem to be casual commercial art. In 1932, Vernon Grant began what later developed into a seven-year series of drawings for the Kellogg Company. Kellogg's agency, N. W. Ayer, made the contact with the artist and continued to deal with him, the drawings being used for the advertising and other promotion of Rice Krispies. The early drawings developed into the now-famous "Snap, Crackle and Pop" characters. In 1939, Kellogg stopped buying these drawings from Grant but bought similar drawings from other artists for the same purposes.

Grant sought to stop such further use but the court decided in favor of Kellogg, applying the doctrine of the *Pushman* case. The gist of the court's opinion was:

> If in the transfer there was any limitation for the benefit of the [artist], that limitation, restriction or reservation, whatever it may be called, must have been expressed and clearly imposed. Otherwise it will not be presumed.

There had been no agreement as to the rights in the drawings as they were delivered and the artist was paid. The burden was placed by the court on the artist if he wished to retain any rights such as preventing Kellogg from reusing old drawings, using old drawings for other purposes, buying new drawings in the same style from other artists, etc.

The only agreement or document of any kind was a routine purchase order. The court may have also felt that the copyrighting of a few of the drawings in its own name by Kellogg—without any objection by Grant —reinforced Kellogg's right.

C. COPYRIGHT.

12. Special Copyright Notice and Registration Procedure.

Section 19 of the Copyright Act permits the use of a special shortened or alternative form of copyright notice on works of fine, graphic or commercial art as follows:

> . . . the notice may consist of the letter C enclosed within a circle, thus ©, accompanied by the initials, monogram, mark or symbol of the copyright proprietor: Provided, That on some accessible portion of such copies or of the margin, back, permanent base or pedestal, or of the substance on which such copy shall be mounted, his name shall appear . . .

This shorter notice permits minimum aesthetic damage. To be effective, the shortened form must always be accompanied by the full name of the copyright proprietor on the back of the photograph or artwork or on some other accessible and permanent portion thereof.

It is doubtful whether the short notice protects anything beyond the art in, for example, an advertisement which also contains copy or other matter. If this is sought to be covered, the full notice should be used. See Chapter 5, Section 23.

A special and money-saving procedure for registration of copyrights of "related photographs" is available. The Copyright Office has said: [22]

> A group of related photographs, assembled and identified as a unit, with one overall title, can be registered with one application and fee. However, any photographs first published separately, bearing notice of copyright, secure separate copyright, requiring a registration for each photograph.

13. Graphics Admissible to Copyright.

An artist is considered an "author" as that term is used in copyright law.[23] A wide variety of graphic, photographic and artistic materials and subject matter is properly admissible to copyright and copyright registration.

This subject is discussed at greater length in Chapter 5. However, the following tabulation deals with such graphic materials specifically, according to their varied natures, copyright classes and the copyright forms to be used in their registration.

TYPE OF MATERIALS	CLASSI-FICATION *	COPYRIGHT FORM **
Advertisements (if commercial print)	K	KK
Animated cartoons	L	L-M
Architectural plans	I	I
Blueprints	I	I
Brochures	A	A
Calendar illustrations	K	K
Catalogues	A	A
Ceramics	G	G
Diagrams	I	I
Drawings (if not an advertisement)	G	G
Enamels (if artistic)	G	G
Engineering diagrams	I	I

TYPE OF MATERIALS	CLASSI-FICATION *	COPYRIGHT FORM **
Film strips	J	J
Fine art (including paintings, drawings and sculpture)	G	G
Fine art embodied in a useful article	G	G
Glassware, pottery, etc. (if artistic)	G	G
Greeting cards (See below, "Prints (a)")		
Illustrations (first published as a "contribution to a periodical" but not in an advertisement)	B	BB
Jewelry (if artistic)	G	G
Labels (See below, "Prints (b)")		
Maps	F	F
Mechanical drawings	I	I
Models	I	I
Motion picture—photoplays having connected story	L	L-M
Motion picture—other than photoplays as above	M	L-M
Newsreels	M	L-M
Paintings	G	G
Photoengravings	K	K
Photographic prints	J	J
Photographs (individual)	J	J
Photographs (published in book form)	A	A
Photographs (first published with separate copyright notice in a magazine or newspaper)	B	BB
Photomechanical reproductions	K	K
Pictorial illustrations	K	K
Picture postcards (See below, "Prints (a)")		
Prints (a) produced by printing, lithography, photoengravings, etc.	K	K
Prints (b) not a trademark and used in the sale or advertising of merchandise	K	KK
Promotional films	M	L-M
Relief models	F	F
Reproduction of existing work of art in same or other medium (as lithographics, photoengravings, etchings, drawings, etc.)	H	H
Scientific or technical drawings	I	I

TYPE OF MATERIALS	CLASSI- FICATION *	COPYRIGHT FORM **
Sculpture	G	G
Slide films	J	J
Slides (individual)	J	J
Television programs on film	G	G
Textile designs (if artistic)	G	G
Textual matter (with or without illustration)	A	A
Three-dimensional works of art	G	G
Training films	M	L-M
Travelogs	M	L-M
Video tapes	L/M	L-M
Works of art generally	G	G
Works of "artistic craftsmanship"	G	G

* According to Copyright office requirements.

** Designation of official form to be used for *registration* of the copyright of the indicated graphic.

14. Position of Copyright Notice.

Except for the requirements of the Copyright Act as to position of the notice in books, periodicals and musical works there are no mandatory requirements as to position of the notice. This includes photography and art. The courts seem to be rather lenient as to the "art classes" in this connection. Probably any position which is likely to be seen by the public will be acceptable.[24]

On motion pictures and filmed or video tape television commercials and commercial films, etc. the notice should be placed in or near the title and again at the end. As to use of the short or alternative notice and its dual positional requirements, see Section 12 above.

15. Product Photographs.

Normally, all product photographs will be taken by or at the direction of the client, its public relations firm or its advertising agency. There should be no problem as to ownership thereof. However, questions as to the admissibility of such photography to copyright have occurred. This in turn involves the right to prevent a competitor from using the same pictures.

Such photographs are protectible under the copyright laws even though they are not of any particularly great artistic value. This is especially true when it is clear that there has been copying by a competitor.

In one case [25] involving the rights in photographs of cake and other baked goods, used on packaging, etc., it was held that a copyright would exist in these photographs although, as the court said:

> The pictures of the cakes used by plaintiff on its labels although possibly not achieving the quality of a Leonardo "Still Life" nevertheless have sufficient commercial artistry to entitle them to protection against obvious copying (citing cases).

Photographs of this sort will receive greater protection than will the rest of a label or other graphics which may not have any particular "artistry" about them. This follows the general rule that "familiar symbols or designs, mere variations of typographic ornamentation, lettering or coloring, and mere listings of ingredients or contents" are not sufficient to warrant copyright registration.[26]

In order to lay the groundwork for this protection, it is necessary that the product photograph carry the copyright notice at all times, regardless of the nature of use or media. This includes glossies accompanying news releases, advertisements in which the photograph appears, labels and labeling, house organ pictures, blowups for display use, tradeshow pictures, catalogues, etc.

16. Staff Artist's Work.

An employer may ordinarily copyright the work of his employees. This is true even though the employer is a corporation. However, practical questions have arisen occasionally as to this. A simple employment agreement should make it clear that all staff art or photography is the property of the employer who may copyright the same without limitation. See Section 6 (e) above.

17. Stock and Other Copyrighted Materials.

Much stock or other non-exclusive photography and artwork is used in all phases of public relations and promotion. This is acquired from a wide variety of sources [27] but most of it comes from houses specializing in such stock materials.

Such photographs and artwork are usually copyrighted by the supplier —perhaps in catalogue or sample form. The PR man should try to protect that copyright when he uses such material. Ordinarily the supplier will indicate what protection, if any, is required.

When buying stock art or photography, normally only a right to one-time use is acquired. No copyright assignment or additional rights are involved. Thus the proper copyright notice is that of the supplier—not that of the purchaser or user.

As to privacy questions arising from use of such photographs, see Section 26 below.

Institutional photographs may be freely supplied by such organizations as the National Safety Council, Red Cross, Boy Scouts of America, Red Feather Campaign, etc. Others may be obtained from the trade press. Some of this is copyrighted and such rights should be respected and the appropriate notices repeated. It may not be unusual for a house organ, for example, to carry several completely different credit lines and copyright notices on the various photographs scattered throughout a single issue. See Chapter 18, Section 20.

D. PURCHASE METHODS.

18. Rights Involved.

Preliminary to the consideration of purchase methods is the nature of the materials in question and the extent of the rights being acquired. The discussion of ownership and copyright (Sections 5 to 17 above) is the foundation of the following purchase procedures.

A considerable degree of prescience on the part of the purchaser may sometimes be necessary. It is understandably difficult for the practitioner always to anticipate the potential importance, if any, of a photograph or particular artwork. He can only guess how much repeat use may be made, whether it will be used in different media, whether it may serve as a prototype for multiple reproduction, what changes are likely to be made in it, and a wide variety of possible—presently undefined—operations or uses which may become advisable or even necessary.

It is better to obtain full rights in such materials. This obviates any of the above questions. If full rights can be obtained at an acceptable cost, this should be done—except in connection with the most casual and routine materials. Sections 18 to 22 below are premised upon this concept.

19. Pricing Problems.

An effort is being made by some artists and photographers—with some success—to tie their prices to the extent of the use to which their work will be put. It has been suggested that this has been instigated to some extent by the successful demands of actors and performers for more substantial payments. A 1967 example of this concerned use of professional models' photographs on product packages. A large New York model agency announced that, unless a special arrangement were to be made, "it would refuse any photographic assignments which are intended for package use." Its models were to be instructed "to exclude package use on all releases where there is no special agreement." Believing that such use excluded the models from competitive assignments as long as the package carried the photograph, the agency required "a substantial initial bonus plus an annual fee as long as the picture . . . is used on the package."

Creative people or their agents may have become better bargainers but the practical solutions have become no easier. As pointed out in Section 18 above, no matter how fair-minded the buyer may try to be, he usually must "guess" as to possible future reuse. These day-to-day difficulties with pricing were clearly and pithily described by Robert J. Burton, counsel for Broadcast Music, Inc. when he wrote in 1952: [28]

> There is no field in which it is more difficult to fix a price than in the purchase of commercial art work. For example: The customary practice is for an agency to call someone in and say: "This is what we want for such and such a campaign." The artist says: "Fine, I will give you some sketches and they will be $50 apiece or $100 apiece, and if you accept one of them my fee will be $500 or $1000." Prices are not high; as a matter of fact, a Saturday Evening Post cover at best won't earn the artist over several thousand dollars. Yet, by the very nature of the advertising trademark significance of some oft-repeated commercial art, the ultimate value to the advertiser may be enormous. I don't know whether the man who drew Elsie the Cow should go on and on and on sharing in Elsie's success. Probably the Borden people paid him the normal price for his work, which would be somewhere in the hundreds, infrequently in the thousands. The only way you can fix a price so as to tie the subject of your invoice to the realities of the case is by stating that the drawing is intended for use in the Sheepherder's Gazette, one time only, and the fee for that use is so much and then, if it is going to be used again, you open it up for negotiation. Well, an artist won't sell much of his work that way. Then you can try the other way, which is to tie the sale expressly to the campaign on a sort of percentage of the gross. If the company spends a million dollars on Elsie, the artist would receive a percentage of the million; that is the basis on which the advertising agency receives its income—a percentage of the expenditure.

A specific example of this was before the court in *Otten v. Curtis Publishing Co.*[29] A designer had sold Curtis a design for an ash tray intended for use as a promotional piece. Much later—apparently without any prior intention—Curtis used the same design on a magazine cover.

The designer sued for additional compensation, claiming that such subsequent reuse was contrary to the parties' understanding as well as contrary to a custom of the trade. The court found for Curtis since there had been no reservation of rights by the designer. Thus the doctrine of the *Pushman* and *Grant* cases (discussed in Sections 10 and 11 above) was conclusive in this commercial context.

It has been suggested that the pricing of these materials—as with literary purchases—is "more in the field of ethics" than law or copyright.[30] This may be true but the legal perimeters must also be observed.

20. Purchase Orders for Photographs.

It is important that the purchaser retain control of a photograph (including its negatives, proofs, etc.). Having paid therefor, he should be forehanded enough to obviate, among other things, the legal anomaly referred to in Section 8 above. It is therefore suggested that the following language be included in a purchase order for photography:

> All film, plates, negatives, proofs and similar materials made, processed or used in connection with the photographs ordered hereby shall be at all times our property and shall be delivered to us upon request and without any additional charge. If requested by us, a general bill of sale in the usual form will be executed and delivered to us by you.

This provision gives the purchaser the right to demand possession. Usually, such right will not be exercised. However, its exercise may save considerable money.

Similar but more complicated problems arise with motion picture films, whether they be made as "commercials" or as industrial or public service films. Due to the nature of their filming, production and editing, the final master negative is almost always merely a residue of a much larger amount of "shooting." Much ends up "on the cutting room floor." Yet that rejected portion may have considerable value—especially for possible future use. The purchaser should be careful to retain his rights in all of it and to demand its delivery—immediately or at some later date.

Purchase orders for such films, therefore, should require the producer to store all such material and deliver it on demand to the purchaser. Usually this storage requirement will be limited to some period such as a year. Even after the year has passed, the producer should not have the right to destroy any such rejected material without first giving notice to the purchaser so that the latter may claim it.

21. Purchase Orders for Art.

Art is often bought on an informal, personal basis. The purchase should be confirmed in writing. Some PR practitioners and departments have developed special forms for art purchase orders. Whatever its form, it should relate to the following matters:

(a) The artist's work is to be done to the satisfaction of the purchaser—either the client or the PR firm. Such satisfaction should be evidenced only by a written acceptance of the work (routinely unlikely), use thereof or payment therefor.

(b) All right, title and interest in the work (together with the unlimited right to use, reproduce and vend) should pass to the purchaser upon delivery. This should include all preliminary sketches, layouts, designs or any other materials, all thereof to be delivered to the purchaser upon request.

(c) The price should be fixed and firm.

(d) If the artist has copyrighted the work, he is to license or assign the copyright in such manner as may be necessary to permit unlimited use thereof.

(e) Delivery date should be stated to be "of the essence." Failure to deliver should give the purchaser the right, at its discretion, to accept or refuse the work.

(f) The purchaser should have the right to use the artist's name—not only on the work—but also in any public relations, promotional, publicity or other use of the work or reference thereto.

(g) The artist is to be responsible for the loss of any materials delivered to him by the purchaser. This usually involves only photographs, models or other materials intended to aid the artist in his work.

(h) If the artist is represented by an agent, the artist alone is to be responsible for the agent's commissions. The purchaser should have the right to pay the agent as the representative of the artist.

(i) If the finished work identifiably portrays any living person—whether or not that person sat or modeled for the artist and with or without compensation—the artist should obtain and deliver to the purchaser proper releases from the sitter. This should not be required, however, if the artist merely worked with photographs supplied by the purchaser.

(j) Purchase order terms prevail over any inconsistent provisions in the artist's invoices.

(k) The artist's acceptance of the purchase order and the commencement of work pursuant thereto are acceptance of all terms and provisions thereof.

(l) The artist should warrant that he has not produced and sold nor will he produce or sell any work in any medium reasonably similar to the subject work.

(m) Any inconsistent provisions in any Code of Standards or alleged customs of the trade shall be subject to this agreement and shall not bind the purchaser.

22. Competitive Use of Graphics.

Unless full rights are obtained, the purchaser must anticipate the possibility of competitive use of the material. This is true of the particular purchase and of other and similar materials created by the same artist.

A particular style or subject matter created by the artist may become identified with a particular company or product. This was the situation in the "Snap, Crackle and Pop" case discussed in Section 11 above. The artist has the right to make other—although similar—depictions in the same style for others, perhaps for competitors, if there is no provision to the contrary.[31]

If the artist has been engaged and paid to do a series of similar works in a given style and there is no overreaching by the purchaser, a restrictive covenant binding the artist should be upheld. As discussed at length in Chapter 2, the restrictive covenants should not be unreasonable in extent and no more exclusionary than is necessary to protect the purchaser. The restriction should cover character names, if any, as well as representational or graphic features.

The purchaser *may* have another channel of protection even if the restriction is not obtained. This would be under the doctrine of unfair competition if a competitor should use the same artistic style or characters—especially if produced by the same artist. However, this legal ground may not be too secure unless the style, etc. has achieved a real "secondary meaning" in association with the purchaser. See Chapter 10, Section 12.

E. PRIVACY.

23. Privacy/Ownership Dichotomy.

There is an important legal difference between the right of ownership in a photograph (or of its copyright) and the right of privacy of a person identifiably portrayed therein. This, of course, presupposes that the picture is being used for some purpose of commerce or trade such as public relations, publicity or promotion. As to this matter generally, see Chapter 8, Section 4.

A striking example of this occurred in *Continental Optical Co. v. Reed*.[32] Reed, the plaintiff, had been an optical lens grinder prior to World War II and resumed his commercial work thereafter. During the war he had been attached to a mobile optical unit in France. An Army photographer took his picture at work and it was published as a "news" item in St. Paul, Reed's home town. The defendant later used the picture in its advertising. Reed sued and recovered $20,000 at trial. On appeal, Reed's verdict was reduced to $1,000 but the court recognized Reed's right of privacy and its violation by the defendant. Reed had also claimed special damages, claiming his own business use of the picture had been destroyed by the defendant's use thereof. As to this, the court said:

> The evidence shows, without dispute, that the negative involved belongs to the United States Army and there is nothing in the record indicating that [Reed] had any right to use prints therefrom for advertising his own private business . . . [W]hen [Reed] seeks special damage based solely on the theory that another has used that particular photograph without his consent and thereby destroyed its value to him for a similar use, he must show a right to such use himself. When a person sits voluntarily for a photograph and his picture is taken by the photographer gratuitously for his or his principal's sole use and benefit, the sitter, simply because the picture is of himself, acquires no greater property right therein than does a stranger.

In other words, Reed—having an admitted and recognized right of privacy—still had no right in the photograph itself.

24. Professional Models.

Professional models ordinarily present fewer privacy questions than almost any subject of a commercial photograph. Their work and payment are completely under the control of the photographer or the PR man supervising the shots. Obtaining proper releases presents no problem. Releases referred to in Section 30 below may be used.

It is also recommended that the model sign the back of the finished print so that no later question may arise by reason of the specific photographic result. The following language is suggested:

> My signature hereon identifies my photograph on the face hereof as having been taken on __(date)__ for full and valid consideration and I confirm my full release for all commercial and trade purposes.

This legend is usually applied to the back of the print by a rubber stamp. The signed photograph should then be handled in accordance with the procedures suggested in Section 4 above.

25. Nonprofessional Subjects.

Public relations uses many photographs of so-called nonprofessional subjects. A few examples will pinpoint this. Publicity in connection with a corporate contest may use pictures of contest winners. Some contest rules provide that winners must agree in advance to the use of their pictures in exploitation or promotion. This should not be relied upon and signed releases should be obtained. Pictures of a company's employees at work or of other persons in "case history" publicity fall into this category also.

Every PR organization or house organ editor develops a "morgue" of photographic and other art materials. These "swipes" rarely are accompanied by releases. Perhaps years later one or more of such pictures may be found useful. It is sometimes impossible to get releases. Even the source of the photograph might not be known—even less the identity of the person shown therein.[33]

Some relief from this situation will be found in proper logging of each photograph in accordance with the suggestions in Section 4 above.

Corporate PR or personnel departments usually maintain files of photographs of company employees for use from time to time. If possible, releases should be obtained from each such employee at the time the photograph is taken. As to privacy questions involving employees generally, see Chapter 21, Section 14.

Handling of other types of nonprofessional subjects is discussed in Sections 27–29 below.

26. Stock Photographs.

By the nature of the transaction, the purchaser of stock photography is remote from its subjects. This may present a privacy question if the photograph portrays an identifiable living person. Usually the supplier protects the purchaser with the assurance that releases have been obtained.

This may be merely a stamp on the back of the print reading "Model released" or it may be a fuller legend of which the two following, taken from different sources, are reasonably typical: [34]

> We hold legal releases of recognizable models appearing in these photographs. Obviously, crowds and street scenes are not so released. In fairness to our models we must except products of an intimate nature or copy which might prove embarrassing to them. When in doubt we ask that you check with us in advance. Our

viewpoint will be found very liberal, taking exception only when absolutely necessary.

. . . . . .

Recognizable persons, singly and in groups, appearing in this catalog are covered by legal advertising releases. Crowds and general street scenes are not so released. If any photo is doubtful, your inquiry is invited. Restrictions are imposed on the use of the photos for feminine hygiene, testimonials and subjects of a very personal nature, except with special releases which necessarily have to be obtained in advance of such use.

It will be noted that there are certain exceptions to these assurances. Each stock photograph purchased should be carefully scanned to ascertain whether such exceptions are pertinent.

In some instances, the supplier of the photograph may not have releases or, perhaps, releases of a scope sufficient to protect the purchaser. In at least one lower court case,[35] it has been suggested that good faith on the part of the purchaser and inquiry as to releases will protect the purchaser—even if the supplier is at fault and proper releases have not been obtained.

If the purchaser has any questions as to its position, it is recommended that the following language be included in photography purchase orders:

This order is placed with the understanding and only on the condition that the seller has in its possession such valid and presently effective written releases, waivers, and consents as may be necessary for the use of the said photography for all purposes of publishing, promotion, advertising and trade, executed by each person portrayed identifiably in the said photographs, or their proper legal representatives, as the case may be. The seller agrees by the acceptance of this order to defend at its own expense any actions against the purchaser or its client for violation of any right of privacy, libel or copyright infringement, and to pay in full any sums finally adjudged to be due by reason thereof by either the purchaser or client.

In a sense, news photographs present some of the same questions as stock photographs—being perhaps even more dangerous. Such news photographs may not be used for commercial use under the doctrine of the *Flores* case, discussed in Chapter 8, Section 25, unless releases are first obtained. Even if they are used for later feature stories, their use may be improper. See Section 12 in Chapter 8.

The method of procurement of such photographs was well described in *Hull v. Curtis Publishing Co.*[36] where the court said:

The defendant purchased the pictures from the Acme News Agency in New York. With it the agency sent an explanation of the circumstances surrounding the taking of the photograph and the names of the plaintiffs. The photograph was selected by members of the defendant's staff from 76 different pictures obtained from several news agencies. The particular photograph was chosen because defendant felt it most effectively illustrated the articles with which it was published.

Although the plaintiff did not succeed in the action, this result stemmed only from the technical application of the Statute of Limitations.

27. Pictures From Institutional Sources.

Various organizations—national, regional or local—freely cooperate with a PR man in supplying photographs for use in company publications or for other company PR activities, especially if promoting the institution's functions. The institutional source usually has releases but such releases are limited to the contemplated institutional use or promotion.

If the company is using the picture merely in support of such activity, there probably is no exposure. However, such pictures may sometimes be used for the interests of the company. If the company use is for any purpose other than institutional, the releases should be first examined. If not found adequate for company use, new releases should be obtained.

28. Government Pictures.

Even though there is no copyright in pictures taken by or belonging to the United States government, they may not be used commercially in any way unless normal right of privacy releases are first obtained. If the company use relates directly and exclusively to the promotion or support of some government activity, the use is not commercial even though sponsored by a commercial concern.

However, if there is any deviation from this toward the purely commercial, releases should be obtained as a matter of course.[37]

29. Armed Forces Photographs.

Pictures of members of the various branches of the Armed Forces may not be used in public relations or commercial activities with impunity. This is clear from the *Reed* case discussed in Section 23 above.

Releases should be obtained in routine fashion unless the use being made of such photographs is in support of some official military promotion. Anything tinged with a commercial aspect may be considered tainted.

This subject is discussed at greater length in Chapter 12, Section 19.

30. Photography Release Forms.

A wide variety of photography release forms is used, dependent upon the circumstances and the subject matter involved. All of them, however, are directed toward the same end: protection against future claims for privacy violations. These forms [38] are intended to cover the various needs of the PR practitioner but, with slight change, they may also be used for parallel purposes such as promotion or advertising.

Provisions for execution, witnesses, dating, etc. have been omitted in these forms except as to (d) and (j). Such provisions should, of course, be added.

(a) Adult Release.

This is a general consent by an adult for use of his name and/or photograph in company publicity:

> In consideration of One Dollar and other valuable consideration, paid to me, which I have received, I, the undersigned, —————, being over 21 years of age, authorize The ABC Company, its successors, subsidiaries and other agents, to use, at any time in connection with internal or external publicity, (strike out in ink the following item that does *not* apply) :
>
> Photographs taken this date showing me, but not to identify me by name, address or otherwise.
>
> Photographs taken this date showing me, and to identify me by name, address or otherwise.

(b) Adult Release—Alternative Form.

This is a general form also, not limited to any particular photograph.

> IN CONSIDERATION of one dollar and of other good and valuable considerations, receipt of which is hereby acknowledged, the undersigned hereby gives his written consent to ABC Company, its successors and assigns, to use for a period of fifty years, the name, portrait and picture of the undersigned for publicity and advertising purposes.

(c) Adult Release—Short Form.

This one-sentence consent is sometimes used for essentially one-time publication in a house organ or news release.

> This is my irrevocable consent to ABC Co. to use my name and photograph for publicity, publication, news or trade purposes.

(d) Adult Release—Limited Form.

This may be used if the photographs are to be used only in connection with a specific story or subject. It is useful also for gratuitously submitted pictures or unsolicited pictures, sometimes accompanied by textual matter such as an article. If this form is used, the control file should indicate that the release is specifically limited. See Section 4 above.

> For good and valuable consideration received, I, ——————————,
> hereby grant my full and irrevocable consent to ABC Co. or its assigns for commercial, publication and/or art purposes of the photograph or photographs described below:
>
> *Story or Subject:*
> Date: ————————————   Signed ———————————— (SEAL)
> Witness ————————————

(e) Minor's Release.

If the subject is a minor, a release should be signed by the minor as well as his parent or guardian.

> For good and valuable consideration paid to me personally, the undersigned, a minor born on ————————————, 19—, grants full and irrevocable consent to use and publication by ABC Co., its assigns or successors for all commercial and other purposes, of the photographs taken of me on or about this date.

This form, especially if used with a professional model, may be expanded in accordance with Forms (f) and (g) below.

Also, the parent's or guardian's consent (Form (l) below) should be appended.

(f) Professional Model Release Including Name and Testimonial.

The professional model release may be somewhat more detailed. Permission to use name and testimonial may be deleted if not pertinent.

> For good and valuable consideration received and being over 21 years of age, I hereby grant my full and irrevocable consent to ABC Co., its licensees, subsidiaries, successors and assigns, to copyright, renew copyright, use, reuse, reproduce, and license for commercial and art purposes, in any medium of communication, publication, promotion or publicity, whether domestic or foreign, alone or in conjunction with the photographs of other persons, objects or text matter or translations, and either with or without my name or accompanying quotation or testimonial, the photograph and other material attached hereto, it being understood that such grant expressly includes the right to make such alterations thereto as the said Company may desire.

(g) Professional Model Release—Alternative Form.

It is directed to the public relations firm and its client. By its terms, there is a time limit to the authorization.

> In consideration of the payment of $——————— to me, receipt of which is acknowledged as full compensation for my services, the undersigned, being of full and legal age, hereby authorizes ABC Co., its client, and their several legal representatives, successors, subsidiaries, agents, assigns or licensees, to use and reuse, publish and republish, copyright, sell and otherwise distribute for any and all purposes including public relations, promotion, publicity, news, publication and all purposes of commerce and trade, without limitation, for a period of five (5) years from date, the photographs (in original or altered form) of me taken on or about this date by ——————— (photographer). No other oral or written representations have been made to me.

(h) Photographer's Release.

This "broad form" photographer's release has initialed proofs attached. It permits wide use and sale by the photographer. It should not be used if exclusive use of the photographs is desired unless it is supplemented by a restrictive agreement with the photographer, possibly included in the company's purchase order.

> For value received, I hereby consent to the use of the photographs of me (proofs thereof approved and initialed by me are attached) taken by ABC Photographers on or about this date, or any reproductions thereof in the same or similar form and in all media, by ABC Photographers, its assigns and licensees for purposes of news, publicity, promotion, illustration, syndication, advertising or for any other purpose of business or trade and in any other form or manner.

(i) Photographer's Release.—Long Form.

This form waives the right to inspect the finished pictures or printed matter in which they are used.

> For and in consideration of my engagement as a model by ———————, hereafter referred to as the photographer, on terms or fee hereinafter stated, I hereby give the photographer, his legal representatives and assigns, those for whom the photographer is acting, and those acting with his permission, or his employees, the right and permission to copyright and/or use, reuse and/or publish, and republish photographic pictures or portraits of me, or in which I may be distorted in character, or form, in conjunction with my own or a fictitious name, on reproductions thereof in color, or black and white made through any media by the photographer at his studio or elsewhere, for any purpose whatsoever; including the use of any printed matter in conjunction therewith.
>
> I hereby waive any right to inspect or approve the finished

photograph or advertising copy or printed matter that may be used in conjunction therewith or to the eventual use that it might be applied.

I hereby release, discharge and agree to save harmless the photographer, his representatives, assigns, employees or any person or persons, corporation or corporations, acting under his permission or authority, or any person, persons, corporation or corporations, for whom he might be acting, including any firm publishing and/or distributing the finished product, in whole or in part, from and against any liability as a result of any distortion, blurring, or alteration, optical illusion, or use in composite forms, either intentionally or otherwise, that may occur or be produced in the taking, processing or reproduction of the same, even should the same subject me to ridicule, reproach, scorn or indignity.

I hereby warrant that I am $\dfrac{\text{under}}{\text{over}}$ twenty-one years of age, and competent to contract in my own name insofar as the above is concerned.

I am to be compensated as follows: _____

I have read the foregoing release, authorization and agreement, before affixing my signature below, and warrant that I fully understand the contents thereof.

(j) Full-cast Talent Release.

Promotional, publicity, training or other forms of commercial film usually use more than a single actor. This multiple release form may be used by the producing firm. It also protects the purchaser and sponsor of the film. The introductory caveat to Form (h) above applies here also.

For good and sufficient consideration, the receipt of which is hereby acknowledged, each of the undersigned, representing to be over twenty-one years of age, grants irrevocable permission to ABC Productions, Inc., its clients, assignees and licensees, to use his name and likeness in portraits, pictures, photographs, motion pictures and television and all reproductions thereof, in any form whatsoever, and to record, amplify and reproduce his voice and/or instrument, completely or in part for any publication, publicity, promotion, informative, advertising, commercial or other purpose whatsoever.

Legal Signature	Name Printed	Part Portrayed

Witness:_____ Date:_____

(k) Talent Agreement.

This more elaborate release may be used when the talent in a film or television commercial is a member of any union or talent guild.

> In consideration of the sum of $————— paid to me by ABC Co., receipt of which is hereby acknowledged, and for other good and valuable consideration, I hereby give the said Company, its licensees, successors, agents and assigns, all rights of every kind and character in and to all work herein and heretofore done, and all poses, acts, plays, and appearances herein and heretofore made by me for it, as well as in and to the right to use without territorial restrictions my name and photographs, either still or moving, for all forms of commercial, publicity and advertising purposes including television. I further give the said company the right to reproduce in any manner whatsoever any recordations herein and heretofore made for it of my voice, and all instrumental, musical or other sound effects produced by me. The company shall also have the right to "double" or "dub" not only all poses, acts, plays and appearances herein and heretofore made by me but also my voice and all instrumental, musical and other sound effects produced by me to such extent as it may desire. I further agree upon completion of the work covered by this agreement, in the event of a retake of all or any of the scenes in which I participated; or if additional scenes are required (whether originally contemplated or not) I will return to work and render my services in such scenes at a rate of compensation to be agreed upon but not to exceed that paid me for the original taking. Finally, I give the company my unqualified and irrevocable consent to copyright and renew copyright, use and reuse copies, reproductions, translations and simulations of my likeness and my voice, with or without my name, for any and all forms of art and exhibition, illustrative, publication, commercial and trade purposes.
>
> Signed ————— (SEAL)

(l) Parent's Consent to Minor's Release.

This is intended as a "rider" to a minor's release.

> I hereby, for additional consideration, individually and as the father, mother or guardian of the above minor, consent to the foregoing.

(m) Parent's Consent to Photographer's Release.

This is affixed to the consent signed by the minor model, usually a professional.

> I hereby certify that I am the parent and/or guardian of ————, an infant under the age of twenty-one years, and in consideration of value received, the receipt of which is hereby

acknowledged, I hereby consent that any photographs which have
been, or are about to be taken by the photographer, may be used
by him for the purpose set forth in original release hereinabove,
signed by the infant model, with the same force and effect as if
executed by me.

F. PHOTOGRAPHIC LIBEL.

31. Pictorial Defamation as Libel.

One of the basic—perhaps oversimplified—differences between libel
and slander is that libel is either written, printed or somehow or other
permanent. Consequently, a defamatory photograph or drawing is always
libel—not slander. This places a heavier burden upon the use of photography because of subject's lighter onus of proof, exposure to damages, etc.
resulting from libel as against slander. As to this generally, see Chapter 7,
Section 11.

32. Types of Photographic Libel.

A photograph may be libelous in and of itself or in conjunction with
its context. This leads to a variety of different situations against which
the practitioner must be alert. The most obvious is the picture which
holds the subject up to disrepute. It needs no caption nor anything else
to make it actionable.[39]

Many otherwise innocent photographs become libelous because mis-
captioned as to name [40] or derogatorily captioned, if only by implication.[41]

A picture otherwise innocent may be libelous when used in conjunction with or illustrative of a story of some disreputable, unsavory or
criminal action or situation. By implication the pictured individual is
associated with the facts of the story which, as to him, are completely
untrue and defamatory.[42]

Undoubtedly one of the most interesting pictorial libel cases is *Burton
v. Crowell Publishing Co.*,[43] involving a Camel cigarette advertisement
for which the plaintiff had posed and had signed the customary releases.
However, due to a photographic quirk, a portion of the saddle held by
Mr. Burton (the plaintiff) appeared to be attached to his body, making
him appear guilty of indecent exposure. There was no question that this
was due exclusively to a photographic lapse—"patently an optical illusion," amounting to a photographic "caricature." Judge Learned Hand
held the photograph, though not intentional, to be actionable as a libel.
He said:

The contrast between the drawn and serious face and the accompanying fantastic and lewd deformity was so extravagant that, though utterly unfair, it in fact made of the plaintiff a preposterously ridiculous spectacle; and the obvious mistake only added to the amusement. Had such a picture been deliberately produced, surely every right-minded person would agree that he would have had a genuine grievance; and the effect is the same whether it is deliberate or not. Such a caricature affects a man's reputation, if by that is meant his position in the minds of others; the association so established may be beyond repair; he may become known indefinitely as the absurd victim of this unhappy mischance. Literally, therefore, the injury falls within the accepted rubric; it exposes the sufferer to "ridicule" and "contempt."

Experienced public relations men and house organ editors well appreciate the troubles lurking innocently in photographs. Garth Bentley, past president of the International Council of Industrial Editors, has pointedly warned—under the heading "Danger! Beware!"—of some of the "traps" with these highly practical suggestions: [44]

You must watch for other things besides quality. Never run a picture which will make anyone appear ridiculous, cause him mortification, or damage his standing. . . . [L]earn to distinguish between the deliberately posed comic picture and one that is unintentionally so. . . . Know the people concerned. . . . Above all, avoid photographs which heighten physical deformities or defects. . . . [S]hots of women should not be too revealing. . . . [A] photo in conventional dress may be very embarrassing if the camera or some accident exposes more than it should. Examine all group pictures for this offense. . . . Be careful, also, about pictures which show employees with other than their respective husbands or wives.[45] . . . If submitted by a third party . . . it is safest to ask the subject for permission to use the photograph.

Some of these lapses may not rise—or sink—to the level of actionable photographic libel, but they do nothing to enhance the appreciation of a publication or public relations effort.

In public relations practice, we may assume that there will never be an intentionally libelous use of a photograph. Yet, as is clear from the *Burton* case, even an innocent misuse of a photograph may expose the company or client to a claim for libel. The following is an example of a perhaps esoteric—certainly unusual—instance of such innocent exposure:

A national company, committed to the support of the civil rights movement, had instructed the managers of its various local plants to this effect. Later, an employee of a local plant in a Southern community was suspected of being the Klu Klux Klan leader who had led a "cross-burning." The employee had left the community. Needing a picture of the man, the police asked the cooperative plant manager, who gave them a picture from his employee files. Unfortunately, it was the picture of another and quite innocent person. The erroneously-titled picture was publicized widely in the area by the police and press.[46]

33. Cartoons and Caricatures.

Cartoons and caricatures may be as much the vehicles of libel as the photograph.[47] Photographic libel is usually innocent or accidental; the caricature or cartoon rarely is. Its "bite" is intentional.

G. RESPONSIBILITY FOR PHOTOGRAPHIC MATERIALS.

34. Generally.

Responsibility for the safekeeping of photographic, art or pictorial materials—as between photographer, artist, PR firm and client, as the case may be—follows the same general rules discussed in Chapter 2, Sections 10 (b) and 30. However, there are certain special situations involving loss of films, negatives and prints which are discussed in Sections 35 and 36 below.

35. Film and Pictures Lost in Transit.

Undeveloped film or finished photographs may be lost in transit or while in the custody or control of third parties. There does not appear to be much law on the subject. Such cases as have been decided appear to favor recovery by the photographer or the owner.

An early case involved the loss by a carrier of a box of negatives of pictures shot overseas but which had no particular market value.[48] The plaintiff recovered a verdict at trial. The court said that it could not say that the amount of the verdict was improper despite the fact that the negatives were not good ones and were not well taken. However, the jury might also consider the difficulty of obtaining these foreign photographs or the fact that they portrayed some incident "not likely to be repeated" so that even a poor representation might be of considerable value. Also to be considered was the cost of the trip in order to obtain these pictures.

In another case, a verdict of $4,000 was recovered against the carrier by a professional free-lance photographer for the loss of exposed but undeveloped film taken on a trip through the West. This is apparently a case of first instance. The film had been insured for $5,000 and this was claimed to be the actual value thereof.[49]

36. Loss of Film During Processing.

Unless a photographer does his own processing, there is always the risk that exposed but undeveloped film may be lost by the processor. Ordinarily, the receipt issued by the processor limits the liability for such loss. If this is the case, then the customer is limited by such language.[50]

An interesting example of such liability occurred in *Willard Van Dyke Productions, Inc. v. Eastman Kodak*,[51] decided by the New York Court of Appeals when it had before it for the first time the legal results of a liability limitation legend printed on film packages. The language indicated clearly that the film was sold without any warranty of any kind except for the replacement in the event that it was damaged or lost by Kodak.

The plaintiff went to Alaska to take certain photographs under contract and sent the exposed film to Kodak for processing. It was conceded that the film was in good condition when it was received by Kodak but during its development a considerable portion was damaged. As a result, the plaintiff had to go back to Alaska and take the pictures over again. He claimed his expenses in excess of $1500.

Kodak did not claim that it was not due to exercise care in processing the film. Its position was that its liability, in the event of damage or loss, was merely replacement value of the film.

The court broke the case down into two parts: sale of the film and the processing thereof. As to the former, the limitation of liability did apply but not as to the latter—the real problem in the case. Inasmuch as the cost of processing was not included in the price of the film, the court found that the limitation did not apply to processing.

The Court of Appeals was careful to point out that while such exculpatory clauses will be applied by the courts as defense in certain cases, the courts insist that it must be absolutely clear "that such was the understanding of the parties." This latter language may be very important in cases in which the liability limitation applies also to processing. It would undoubtedly have to be shown that the purchaser and user of the film ever had notice of the limitation when he bought it or had actually agreed to it. This then becomes a matter of proof which may be rather difficult.

However, if it can be shown that no such release or receipt was issued at the time the film was delivered to the processor, the photographer or owner of the film may be able to recover the full value thereof. At least one case has so held.[52]

Notes

1. As to use of photographs in public relations and publicity, see CUTLIP & CENTER, EFFECTIVE PUBLIC RELATIONS 312–313 (3d ed. 1964). See also *Public Relations Journal,* Dec., 1961, the entire issue being devoted to "Visual Communications."
2. See Carlson, *Washington Hearings Provide Opportunity for Visuals,* P.R.J., Dec., 1961, at 18.
3. 5 Misc. 2d 140, 159 N.Y.S.2d 616, *rev'd,* 9 Misc. 2d 934, 170 N.Y.S.2d 168 (1957).
4. Press Publishing Co. v. Falk, 59 Fed. 324 (C.C.N.Y. 1894); Corliss v. E. W. Walker Co., 64 Fed. 280, 31 L.R.A. 283 (C.C. Mass. 1894); Douglas v. Stokes, 149 Ky. 849, 149 S.W. 506 (1912); Moore v. Rugg, 44 Minn. 28, 46 N.W. 141, 9 L.R.A. 58 (1890); Pollard v. Photographic Co., 40 Ch. Div. 418 (Eng. 1888); White Studio v. Dreyfoos, 156 App. Div. 762 (1913).
5. 280 Fed. 550 (2d Cir. 1922), *cert. denied,* 259 U.S. 583 (1922).
6. Melville v. Mirror of Life Co., [1895] 2 Ch. 531, 11 T.L.R. 477; Press Publishing Co. v. Jack, 59 Fed. 324 (C.C.S.D. N.Y. 1894).
7. Altman v. New Haven Union Co., 254 Fed. 113 (D.C. Conn. 1918).
8. Avedon v. Exstein *et al.,* 141 F. Supp. 278 (S.D.N.Y. 1956).
9. Grant v. Kellogg Co., 58 F. Supp. 48 (S.D.N.Y. 1944), *aff'd,* 154 F.2d 59 (2d Cir. 1946).
10. Corliss v. E. W. Walker Co., *supra* note 4; Pollard v. Photographic Co., *supra* note 4.
11. *Supra* note 5.
12. Hochstadter *et al.,* v. H. Tarr, Inc., 68 N.Y.S.2d 762 (App. T., 1947).
13. Colten v. Jacques Marchais, Inc., 61 N.Y.S.2d 269 (M.C.N.Y. 1946).
14. 70 HARV. L. REV. 554 (1957).
15. Avedon v. Exstein *et al.,* *supra* note 8.
16. Hochstadter *et al.,* v. H. Tarr, Inc., *supra* note 12, at 764.
17. *E.g.,* Corliss v. E. W. Walker Co., *supra* note 4; Lumiere v. Robertson-Cole Distributing Corp., *supra* note 5; Holmes v. Underwood & Underwood, 225 App. Div. 360 (1929).
18. Reed v. Continental Optical Co., *infra* note 32.
19. Altman v. New Haven Union Co., *supra* note 7.
20. Pushman v. New York Graphic Soc'y, 287 N.Y. 302, 39 N.E.2d 249 (1942). See also Yardley v. Houghton Mifflin Co., 108 F.2d 28 (2d Cir. 1939), *cert. denied,* 309 U.S. 686 (1940); Grandma Moses Properties, Inc. v. This Week Magazine, 117 F. Supp. 348 (S.D.N.Y. 1953); Wright v. Eisle, 83 N.Y.S. 887 (App. Div. 1903).
21. Grant v. Kellogg Co., *supra* note 9.
22. Letter from Copyright Office to author, May 24, 1967. See also discussion of bulk-filing plan of Professional Photographers of America, Inc., in CHERNOFF & SARBIN, PHOTOGRAPHY AND THE LAW 73–76 (1958).

23. Note, *Copyright—Study of the Term "Writings" in the Copyright Clause of the Constitution,* 31 N.Y.U.L.R. 1263 (1956).

24. RINGER & GITLIN, COPYRIGHTS 38–40 and cases cited, note 68 (rev. ed. 1965).

25. Kitchens of Sara Lee v. Nifty Foods Corp. *et al.,* 116 U.S.P.Q. 292, 31 C.O. Bull. 452 (W.D.N.Y. 1957), *mod'd and remanded,* 266 F.2d 541, 121 U.S.P.Q. 359, 32 C.O. Bull. 242 (2d Cir. 1959).

26. Copyright Pub. No. 46, Sept., 1958.

27. BENTLEY, EDITING THE COMPANY PUBLICATION 159–62 (2d ed. 1953); FERGUSON, EDITING THE SMALL MAGAZINE 97–106 (3d ed. 1963). These discussions deal with sources for house organ photographs but the suggestions are widely applicable to other public relations efforts.

28. Burton, *Business Practices in the Copyright Field,* in SEVEN COPYRIGHT PROBLEMS ANALYZED 99 (1952).

29. Unofficially reported in N.Y.L.J., Nov. 8, 1951, at 1172.

30. DOVER, EFFECTIVE COMMUNICATIONS IN COMPANY PUBLICATIONS 296 (1961).

31. Vargas v. Esquire, Inc., 166 F.2d 651 (7th Cir. 1948).

32. 119 Ind. App. 643, 86 N.E.2d 306, 14 A.L.R.2d 743 (1949).

33. See discussion of such situations in SIMON, THE LAW FOR ADVERTISING AND MARKETING 248 (1956).

34. These legends appear in promotional material of H. Armstrong Roberts and Ewing Galloway respectively.

35. Harlow v. Buno Co., 36 D.&C. 101 (Pa. Com. Pl. 1939).

36. Hull v. Curtis Publishing Co., 182 Pa. Super. 86, 125 A.2d 644 (1956). See also Jenkins v. Dell Publishing Co., 251 F. 2d 447 (3d Cir. 1956) *cert. denied,* 357 U.S. 921 (1957) (purchase of photographs from World Wide Photos, Inc.).

37. Reed v. Continental Optical Co., *supra* note 32.

38. These forms are taken from the files of the author and of several large national companies and film producers.

39. Burton v. Crowell Publishing Co., *infra* note 43.

40. Peck v. Tribune, 214 U.S. 185 (1909).

41. Zbysko v. New York American, Inc., 228 App. Div. 277, 239 N.Y.S. 411 (1930).

42. Jackson v. Consumers Publications, Inc., 256 App. Div. 708 (N.Y. App. Div. 1939); Heyman v. Dodd, Mead & Co., 260 App. Div. 573 (N.Y. App. Div. 1940).

43. 82 F.2d 154 (2d Cir. 1936). See also Tolley v. Fry & Sons, Ltd., [1930] A.C. 333, 16 B.R.C. 1031.

44. Bentley, *supra* note 27, at 166–67.

45. See, *e.g.,* Sydney v. MacFadden Publishing Co., 242 N.Y. 208 (1926). This citation does not appear in the original quotation in the text.

46. For an interesting example of the delivery and use of a "wrong" photograph, see Emanuel v. Free Lance Photographer's Guild, 28 Misc. 2d 503, 219 N.Y.S.2d 626 (App. Term. 1961) and comments thereon in HOFSTADTER & HOROWITZ, THE RIGHT OF PRIVACY 262 (3d ed. 1964).

47. Mazzara's Case, 2 City Hall Rec. (N.Y. 1858); Snively v. Record Publishing Co., 185 Cal. 565, 198 Pac. 1 (1921).
48. Wamsley v. Atlas Steamship Co., 50 App. Div. 199 (N.Y. App. Div. 1900).
49. Lake v. Railway Express Agency, 98 N.Y.S.2d 202 (1950). The court filed no opinion but the facts and evidence are discussed at some length in Chernoff & Sarbin, *supra* note 22, at 54–55.
50. Goor v. Navilio, 177 Misc. 970 (N.Y. 1941).
51. Willard Van Dyke Prod., Inc. v. Eastman Kodak Co., 12 N.Y.2d 301, 189 N.E.2d 693 (1962).
52. Nathan v. Fotoshop, 5th Dis. Mun. Ct., Manhattan (N.Y., 1951). No opinion was written in this case but it is discussed at length in Chernoff & Sarbin, *supra* note 22, at 53.

Chapter 10

Trademarks

A. BASIC CONSIDERATIONS

B. PUBLIC RELATIONS, ADVERTISING AND TRADEMARKS

C. DEFINITIONS OF MARKS AND OTHER TERMS

D. REGISTRABILITY OF MARKS

E. CHOICE OF A TRADEMARK

In the public relations and promotional context the various steps between the original choice of a trademark and its eventual use on the product are many and sometimes frustrating.

Du Pont has humorously portrayed these problems in the accompanying "Name Game" which first appeared in a DuPont house organ and is here reproduced by permission.

What follows in this chapter is a documentation of most of the "stops" on this road to commercial success.

THE NAME GAME

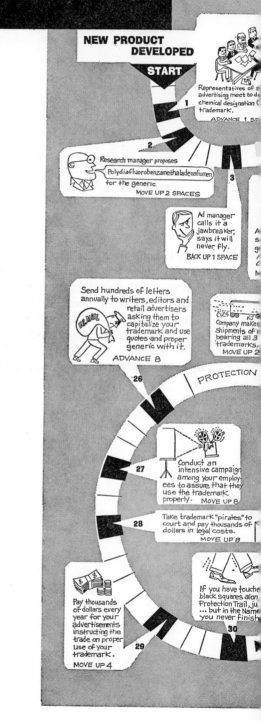

Chapter 10

Trademarks

A. BASIC CONSIDERATIONS.

1. Function of a Trademark.

It is initially important to keep in mind that the term "trademark" may sometimes be a misnomer. All too frequently, other types of marks, names or styles are lumped as "trademarks." Included here are such *sui generis* references as service marks, certification marks, collective marks, grade marks, process marks, style marks, corporate names, trade names and assumed or fictitious names. These have special characteristics and legal sequelae.

A trademark is generally taken to be a word, phrase, symbol or other device which identifies the *source* of goods and distinguishes such goods from those originating elsewhere. It is not a description of the goods.

However, in the modern commercial context, a trademark does more than this. It acts as a guarantee of quality. It is an advertising and promotional tool. It aids in reaching the "buying decision." It may be the deciding element to a customer faced with competitive brands having essentially the same characteristics and qualities. It is part of the overall corporate image and acceptance of the producer or manufacturer. It contributes to the introduction and distribution of new products. It transfers acceptance from one item in a "company line" to another.

Practically all of these functions are under the umbrella of this comment of the Supreme Court: [1]

> If it is true that we live by symbols, it is no less true that we purchase goods by them. A trademark is a merchandising shortcut which induces a purchaser to select what he wants, or what he has been led to believe he wants. The owner of the mark exploits this human propensity by making every effort to impregnate the atmosphere of the market with the drawing power of a congenial symbol. Whatever the means employed, the aim is the same—to convey through the mark, in the minds of potential customers, the

desirability of the commodity upon which it appears. Once this is attained, the trademark owner has something of value.

In certain ways the other types of marks and names mentioned above have some of these same functions even though they are significantly different.

2. How Trademarks Are Acquired.

Trademarks are acquired by *use* thereof, usually in interstate commerce. A mark may not be registered in the United States unless it has first been so used. It is the "date of first use" which is an important factor in contested claims over the same or similar marks.

Actual registration does not give the basic right to a mark. That comes from the use. Registration is merely a supplemental procedure to record and define rights. Some excellent marks are not even registered, the owners relying on common law rights acquired by long-term use, promotion and public acceptance of the mark.

Provided proper records are maintained, it should not be too difficult to prove date of first use. See Section 44 below as to record-keeping. Sometimes, however, such first use is merely a token (one-time) use— made only for trademark registration purposes and not the beginning of consistent and continuous use thereof on the goods. This may involve some dangers if not subject to proper explanation. It may open the door to possible attack in subsequent litigation.

In *Fort Howard Paper Co. v. Kimberley-Clark Corp.*,[2] for example, such a single shipment had been made and was not followed up for some 18 months with regular shipments, marketing tests being made during this interim. The opinion goes on to say:

> There is no question on the record presented but that first ship-
> ment of "HI-DRI" was made by the applicant at the request of its
> legal department to establish a basis for the registration which it
> now seeks, and that the shipment involved only a dollar and
> ninety-one cents worth of paper products. The recipient of the
> shipment, however, was a drug chain which apparently had no
> connection with applicant; the goods were shipped under a com-
> mercial type label, invoiced, and paid for in the usual manner for
> small shipments; and there is nothing to suggest that these goods
> were not offered for resale or that the shipment was anything but a
> bona fide sale. The fact that a sale in commerce was made ex-
> pressly for registration purposes is not damaging, *per se,* where
> circumstances indicate an intention to continue such use.

Despite this holding, it is probably safer to continue to make shipments —albeit small shipments—of the goods in interstate commerce under the label of the new mark. Establishment of the date of the first use is eased.

After the date of first use has been established, the application for registration should be filed promptly. The sooner it is filed, the sooner the registration will be processed and, presumably, the registration issued, thus permitting use of federal registration indicia.

3. Kinds of Marks.

Trademark law and literature recognize a wide variety of kinds of marks and have come to classify them on different bases. A threshold understanding of these distinctions and nomenclature is important. Some of the more important classifications are:

(a) *As to Registrability.*

This is a legal dichotomy and is limited to the registrable and the nonregistrable.

(b) *As to Purpose.*

The principal breakdown is:
Trademarks
Service marks
Certification marks
Collective marks
Membership marks
Radio/television marks
Publication marks
Slogans
Grade, style, process marks
Corporate names and styles
Fictitious or assumed names
Trade or commercial names

Some of these categories are not "marks" in even the broadest application of the term. Others may fall into several categories, one of which qualifies it as a registrable trademark, aside from its being, for example, a slogan or a grade mark. These terms and categories are defined and discussed in Part C and Sections 8 to 16 below.

(c) *As to Strength or Protectibility.*

Acknowledging that a term is a trademark or service mark, there is a further breakdown:
Coined or fanciful
Arbitrary
Suggestive
Descriptive

The coined or fanciful mark is considered the "strongest" from the point of view of protectibility although the arbitrary mark is sometimes considered essentially as strong provided it has not been diluted by use on other types of products. The descriptive is the weakest without question and may not even be registered except as discussed in Section 12 below.

4. Trademark Statutes and Registers.

There has been a widely spaced succession of federal trademark statutes. These are the Trademark Acts of 1881, 1905, 1920 and 1946. The 1946 Act is popularly known as the Lanham Act.[3] The Lanham Act superseded the Trademark Acts of 1905 and 1920.

The Lanham Act established two "Registers": the Principal Register and the Supplemental Register, the former essentially succeeding the Act of 1905 and the latter the Act of 1920.

Registration under the 1905 Act or on the Principal Register under the Lanham Act is constructive notice of the registrant's claim of ownership and *prima facie* evidence of the validity of the registration, registrant's ownership of the mark and its exclusive right to use the mark in interstate commerce on the goods named in the certificate. It also gives the right to sue in the United States courts and to prevent importation of goods bearing an infringing mark. Additional rights are given when an affidavit or declaration of incontestability is later filed as discussed in Section 46 below.

Registration under the Act of 1920 or on the Supplemental Register under the Lanham Act gives none of the above rights except the right to sue in the United States courts. Thus, if possible, registration should be sought on the Principal Register. See Sections 8 to 16 below.

B. PUBLIC RELATIONS, ADVERTISING AND TRADEMARKS.

5. Choosing the Trademark.

PR and advertising practitioners are important in the choice of a trademark. Usually this process is a corporate team effort and both of these functions can contribute much to the final choice. The varied members of the team and their lines of communications are shown generally in the chart on pages 336–337.

The extent of the PR/advertising contribution will depend upon the basic relationship of staff or counselor to the company. The inside department is usually more involved although there does appear to be a growing inclination to bring in the outside PR consultant. Much also depends upon the degree or depth of the liaison between the PR and legal departments as discussed in Chapter 1.

Since the trademark may be a significant contributor to the overall corporate image, the PR people should be in the picture from the beginning. Their contribution goes far beyond mere conceptualization. They apply their continuing understanding of public attitudes. They may handle initial research. They analyze the results of test-marketing. They may save much time and money in screening out psychologically unacceptable marks. They have even been known to assist in convincing legal counsel that the latter's inherent aversion to the descriptive or suggestive mark should be forgone. They sometimes tip the scales in the choice between use of the "house mark" and a new or different mark.

6. Promotion of the Trademark.

Once the mark has been adopted, the PR function continues its usefulness. As a company communicator in constant touch with the press and the public, the PR man is an important link in the promotional process. This is true both as an originator and as a recipient of playback. So effective is this function that some PR counsel offer a specialized service to clients for this sole purpose. The PR departments of advertising agencies seem more likely to recognize their importance in this context than other PR practitioners. This may be due to their association with the "straight" advertising efforts of their agency, the latter being quite obviously concerned in the promotion and advertising of the trademark.

Practically every PR tool or technique can be useful in the promotion of a trademark, whether it be a new or old mark. Specifically trademark-oriented campaigns or promotions need no stress here. However, even the routine PR effort—developed and used for other purposes—can help in trademark promotion, if only through proper use of the trademark notice in news releases, etc. Negatively, a failure to recognize this requirement may do considerable harm to the company's trademark promotion and protection effort. See Chapter 18, Section 15.

It has been suggested that trademark promotion is an area in which cooperation between legal and PR counsel is particularly important since the contribution of each is significantly affirmative whereas, in other PR contexts, legal counsel may have only a screening function.[4] There is no question that the liaison is here very important. At the same time, the "rules of the game" to be followed by the PR practitioner are relatively simple. See Section 22 below.

7. Policing the Trademark.

Here, also, the PR department or counselor is usually of considerable significance. It is usually its function, among other things, to use a clipping service and to maintain company scrapbooks. Thus the PR man may be the first to spot infringements or misuse of company marks. He should then channel these to company legal counsel for appropriate action. The PR man's constant contacts with the press are invaluable in promoting and preventing improper trademark references. He may, for example, place stories about the trademark in the press, both public and trade.

Once the misuse has been detected, it may fall to either the legal or the PR counsel to write the "sorry-to-bother-you-but" letter to the offending newspaper or magazine. From the point of view of future company relations with that particular publication, the PR man is undoubtedly in a better position to make the contact. He probably also is more likely to write a letter which will be less offensive. One very experienced PR director has said of such policing letters:

> The necessity for protecting trademarks can be an exceedingly annoying item for a public relations man. We have had cases when FORTUNE or the SATURDAY EVENING POST or LIFE or TIME has run an extremely valuable piece about ————— but has, in the course of the article, misused a trademark. It always seems hard to have to call the author to task for what we know seems to him a highly trivial flyspeck on the frame of a most valued work. We do it because we know how important it is, but it hurts horrid.

As to the form of such a letter see Section 39 below.

By virtue of the PR man's significant knowledge of the public and corporate minds, he is frequently consulted in the preparation of the paid "trademark advertising," frequently used to protect a mark as discussed in Section 35 below. PR departments have not infrequently— either on their own initiative or at the request of counsel—prepared booklets and other policing informative materials used in patrolling company trademarks. Some companies even assign a PR man permanently to their legal departments for this purpose or, vice versa, a lawyer to their advertising or PR departments.

C. DEFINITIONS OF MARKS AND OTHER TERMS.

In both the legal and practical contexts, it is important to distinguish among the various types of marks and other terms which are not recognized as "marks" at all—quite apart from the question of registrability. Even as among the four basic types of marks specifically recognized by the Lanham Act (see Subsections (a) to (d) below) it may be definitive of a party's rights to distinguish carefully. Thus, in the *National Trailways Bus System* case,[5] the court said:

> It is my opinion that plaintiff's marks should have been registered as Collective Marks rather than Service Marks . . . The defendant should have the opportunity to prove, at a trial, the invalidity on that account of the plaintiff's marks.

(a) Trademark.

The term "trademark" includes any word, name, symbol, or device or any combination thereof adopted and used by a manufacturer or merchant to identify his goods and distinguish them from those manufactured or sold by others.[6]

(b) Service Mark.

The term "service mark" means a mark used in the sale or advertising of services to identify the services of one person and distinguish them from the services of others. Titles, character names and other distinctive features of radio or television programs may be registered as service marks notwithstanding that they, or the programs, may advertise the goods of the sponsor.

(c) Certification Mark.

The term "certification mark" means a mark used upon or in connection with the products or services of one or more persons other than the owner of the mark to certify regional or other origin, material, mode of manufacture, quality, accuracy or other characteristics of such goods or services or that the work or labor on the goods or services was performed by members of a union or other organization.

(d) Collective Mark.

The term "collective mark" means a trademark or service mark used by the members of a cooperative, an association or other collective group or organization and includes marks used to indicate membership in a union, an association or other organization.

(e) Coined or Fanciful Marks.

These are marks which did not exist in the language before being "made up" for use as a mark. KODAK is the traditional example. They are "brand new" combinations of letters or syllables which, aside from their trademark use, have no meaning.

(f) Arbitrary Mark.

This type of mark is a word or phrase which is already in the language but is applied to a product—perhaps even illogically or irrationally. CAMEL and LUCKY STRIKE are examples when applied to cigarettes.

(g) Suggestive Mark.

This is a mark which does not describe the product or immediately convey to a person the nature or character of the product but is a more or less subtle, indirect, ingenious, fanciful, imaginative, poetic or allegorical reference to the product, its nature, use, purpose or attribute.

(h) Descriptive Mark.

This is a mark which is not the generic name of the product or a substitute name therefor but which describes its nature, purpose or characteristics so clearly that a person would easily and quickly think of the *type* of product in question.

(i) Technical Mark.

This is not so much a type of mark as it is a category containing coined, fanciful, arbitrary and suggestive marks, whether they be trademarks, service marks, collective or certification marks.

(j) Radio and Television Marks.

These marks are specifically referred to in the second sentence of the definition of service marks in Subsection (b) above. Amdur defines such marks as

> an expression of language (such as the name of a program), a sound (such as a station chimes), the name, tag-line, mannerism and other characteristics of a radio or television entertainer, etc. which is used for: (a) purposes of identification, or (b) purposes of entertainment.[7]

(k) Membership Marks.

This category includes the emblems and names of fraternal organizations, Greek-letter fraternities, etc., veterans groups, labor unions, trade associations and similar collective groups.

(l) Grade, Style, Process and Ingredient Marks.

These marks are those which identify a particular grade or style of goods within a company's line, a process used to fabricate or manufacture the goods, or an ingredient of the finished product. See Section 16 below.

(m)   Trade Name and Commercial Name.

The terms "trade name" and "commercial name" include individual names and surnames, firm names and trade names used by manufacturers, industrialists, merchants, agriculturists, and others to identify their businesses, vocations, or occupations; the names or titles lawfully adopted and used by persons, firms, associations, corporations, companies, unions and any manufacturing, industrial, commercial, agricultural, or other organizations engaged in trade or commerce and capable of suing and being sued in a court of law.

(n)   Corporate and Assumed Names.

These names are included in the definitions of trade names and commercial names in Subsection (m) above. The corporate name is the style of a business duly incorporated under the laws of a state. The assumed or fictitious name is a style (not corporate) used by an individual, partnership and (in some states) by a corporation which is different from the parties' or corporation's "real" name. Such names are creatures of state law.

Generally, these names as such are not registrable as trademarks although a registrable trademark may be a part of the corporate or assumed name. For example, "Du Pont" and "Kodak" are both part of corporate names and both are trademarks. Such names—corporate or noncorporate—are treated the same as trademarks in infringement cases.[8]

D. REGISTRABILITY OF MARKS.

8. Generally.

The question of registrability of marks breaks down into three parts:

(a)   Marks not subject to registration on either Register because of certain basic disabilities.

(b)   Marks acceptable on the Principal Register.

(c)   Marks acceptable only on the Supplemental Register.

This "negative first" approach is used herein because it may be useful in the preliminary screening of prospective marks in avoiding considerable lost motion, time and even perhaps expense.

9. Disabilities on Both Registers.

Under §2 of the Lanham Act, the following four disabilities will prevent registration on either the Principal or the Supplemental Register:

(a)   immoral, deceptive, or scandalous matter or matter which may disparage or falsely suggest a connection with persons, living or dead, institutions, beliefs or national symbols or bring them into contempt or disrepute; or

(b) use of the flag, coat of arms or other insignia of the United States or of any state, municipality, or any foreign nation; or

(c) use of the name, portrait or signature of a particular living individual except with his written consent or the similar attributes of a deceased President of the United States without the consent of his widow, during her lifetime; or

(d) resemblance to a previously registered mark, or a mark or trade name previously used and not abandoned in the United States, so as to be likely to cause confusion or mistake or to deceive purchasers, subject to certain provisions for concurrent registrations.

See Sections 25 to 29 below.

10. Acceptability on the Principal Register.

A trademark, service mark, certification mark or collective mark will be accepted on the Principal Register provided, according to Section 2 of the Lanham Act, it consists of a mark "by which the goods of the applicant may be distinguished from the goods of others" *unless* it is subject to the disabilities enumerated in Section 9 above and, *additionally,* consists of a mark which

(a) when applied to the goods of the applicant is merely descriptive of them, or

(b) when applied to the goods of the applicant is primarily geographically descriptive or deceptively misdescriptive of them, except as indications of regional origin, or

(c) is primarily a surname.

11. Eligibility for the Supplemental Register.

All marks capable of distinguishing the applicant's goods will be accepted on the Supplemental Register provided:

(a) They are not registrable on the Principal Register.

(b) They have been in lawful use in commerce for the year preceding the filing of the application. Use for the one-year period means exclusive use. If another has been using the mark for a period of time, registration will be refused.[9]

(c) They are not subject to any of the four disabilities set out in Section 9 above.

Under Section 23 of the Lanham Act, the mark may consist of any trademark, symbol, label, package, configuration of goods, name, word, slogan, phrase, surname, geographical name, numeral or device or any combination of the foregoing.

12. Secondary Meaning.

If marks which originally were ineligible for the Principal Register because they fell under the inhibiting provisions of Section 10 (a), (b) or (c) above have later "become distinctive of the applicant's goods," Section 2 (f) of the Lanham Act permits their registration thereon. Proof of "substantially exclusive and continuous use thereof as a mark by the applicant in commerce for the five years preceding the date of the filing of the application for its registration" will be considered *prima facie* evidence of such distinctive character.

This provision is essentially a recognition of the doctrine of "secondary meaning." A mark is considered to have acquired such secondary meaning when it has come to mean to the public that the product or service to which it is applied comes from a particular source or supplier.[10]

Despite the above five-year presumption provision, no particular duration of use is necessary or determinative. Also, the one-year use requirement for admission to the Supplemental Register discussed in Section 11 above should not be confused with this five-year presumption.

Inasmuch as the final test is probably the public consciousness of the meaning of the mark, the scope and intensity of advertising and promotion of a mark are very important in seeking to establish secondary meaning. The greater and the more continuous the distribution of the product and the promotion of the mark on the product, the more likely is the public to recognize the mark as indicative of origin. On the other hand, mere volume or extent of such promotion will not *per se* prove secondary meaning. As with the time element, each case must stand on its feet.

Secondary meaning is, in effect, the opposite of generic meaning, discussed in Section 31 below. Rights otherwise not available may be acquired by secondary meaning. Under the generic meaning concept, rights—even in a registered mark—may be subsequently lost.

While secondary meaning may "save" a mark originally non-registrable, it must be recognized that the doctrine has several weaknesses which should be kept in mind if a company intends to depend prospectively on secondary meaning for eventual registrability.

One such weakness is that the monopoly ordinarily accorded a mark is limited. For example, the registration will be limited to the specific goods in connection with which the secondary meaning has been attained.[11] It will not even be extended to other goods which may fall into the same Patent Office Class.[12] See Section 26 below.

Another weakness is that, even if secondary meaning has been attained, it must be demonstrated that it has not been lost thereafter, especially if a competitor used the same mark prior to the litigation testing the secondary meaning issue.[13]

Also, secondary meaning cannot improve a mark which is *generic*. Thus, in *In Re Automatic Radio Manufacturing Co., Inc.*,[14] the applicant had used AUTOMATIC for 46 years, had sold $150 million of goods bearing the mark and had spent approximately $5 million in advertising such goods in practically every advertising medium. Registration was refused because

> . . . no sign or form of words can be appropriated as a valid trademark which from the nature of the fact conveyed by its primary meaning others may employ with equal truth and with equal right for the same purpose.[15]

13. Slogan Registration.

Slogans are generally accepted for registration on the Principal Register.[16] Thus, "You Can Look Up to PREFORMED"[17] and "From Maine's Cool Breeze to Florida's Keys"[18] have been accepted as trademark and service mark respectively.

Not every slogan will be accepted. It must be capable of identifying the source of the product or service. If it is a mere statement of fact or description of a product, it cannot be registered. Thus, registration even on the Supplemental Register was refused for the slogan "Soil It—Wash It—Never Needs Pressing" in connection with neckties.[19]

One of the most interesting recent cases is the *Excedrin* case in which protection of the phrase "Extra Strength Pain Reliever" was sought in state court litigation.[20] The plaintiff introduced the results of surveys indicating that this slogan enjoyed the same "identification with Excedrin" as did the slogan "Put A Tiger In Your Tank" with Esso. The New York court said:

> The substantiality of the association ratio of "Excedrin" with its slogan, as shown by the survey, establishes that it has achieved a degree of distinction with plaintiff's product which amounts to a "secondary meaning," or, minimally, to the kind of popularity and commercial value which will be protected against competitive encroachment.

14. Registration of Publication Titles, etc.

Of very considerable specific interest to communications generally is the registrability of the names or titles of publications, columns, inserts, catalogues, etc. Generally, such names are registrable as trademarks provided they identify the source of the material (the "goods") and the printed matter has an identifiable existence of its own. See Chapter 18, Section 14 for a fuller discussion.

15. Registration of Marks on "Advertising."

Generally speaking, use of a mark only on a company's advertising will not permit registration.[21] It is being used on the advertising—not on the "goods"—and since the user is not in the business of selling "advertising," the advertising is not goods. The same is true of marks on letterheads and the business forms used by a company.[22] Such items are merely an adjunct to the company's business and not its "goods in trade."

In some instances a mark on "advertising" having some degree of physical substance, frequency and identification and the title of a house organ may be difficult to distinguish. In such cases the mark will usually be registrable if it satisfies the tests delineated in Chapter 18, Section 14.

On the other hand, a substantial catalogue, while admittedly having an advertising function, is generally regarded as "goods" itself and the mark used thereon will be registered. In the leading case of *Ex parte The Oskamp Nolting Co.*,[23] the following attributes of the catalogue were considered persuasive: its considerable size, profuse illustration including some color, the high cost per copy, issue of annually updated contents, distribution to an established and selected mailing list of customers and prospects. These generally add up to the catalogue's having an independent substance, identity and desirability—sometimes being considered as a reference book instead of a mere adjunct to the sale of the merchandise it offers.

Somewhat parallel to this situation is the question as to whether use of a mark in a company's advertising but not on the goods themselves is such a trademark use as to permit registrability as a mark for the goods. Generally speaking, this is not acceptable.[24] Under Section 45 of the Lanham Act, the mark must be placed on the goods, their containers or the displays associated therewith. If the mark appears on the displays but not on the goods, such use is now sufficient.[25]

16. Grade, Style and Ingredient Marks.

Grade or style marks are those which are used to distinguish a particular grade, style, model or unit within a company's line, the entire line of goods or merchandise usually bearing an overall mark or a "family" mark. They are registrable if they also indicate origin.[26] This is well illustrated in the automobile industry. Practically every automobile manufacturer has a series of different model or style marks, each thereof applicable only to a particular unit within the line offered to the public under the "family" name or mark.[27]

Frequently, an ingredient will be given a special name—perhaps originally as an advertising gimmick in an effort to affix the adjective "only" to it—and this may be registrable if it comes to designate an identifiable substance. LANOLIN-D was accepted for registration.[28] The Examiner had originally refused registration on the theory that LANOLIN-D was nothing more than a name for an ingredient. However, the Board reversed and held that the mark should be registered because it was more than a mere technical name for an ingredient.

17. Changes in Trademark Style.

It was long thought that a mark, once adopted and registered, should not be changed—especially if used in a handlettered form, in some distinctive typeface, or as a device or representation of some sort. This is not true. Thus, one of the early "Coca-Cola cases" held that the use of that trademark was not limited to the well-known script, hyphenated or unhyphenated, form but was protectible as a trademark in any form.[29]

Many marks have been changed—largely for purposes of modernization—and rights are not lost thereby.[30]

The test would seem to be whether the changes are so substantial as to lose the identification and unique nature which the trademark has enjoyed and through which it has come to be recognized by the public. These examples are usually given: the figures of Psyche in the White Rock trademark, Aunt Jemima and the picture or figure used in the Old Dutch Cleanser trademark. All of these have been modernized and no values lost in the process.

If changes are made, however, the original trademark registration should be amended so as to bring upon the record the new and current mark. On occasion, the Patent Office may not accept the new mark for amendment, in which case a new registration should be filed. This does not mean that rights have been lost or diluted in any way.

18. Duration and Renewal of Registration.

Registrations under the Lanham Act remain in force for 20 years from the date of registration—not from the date of first use—and may be renewed for periods of 20 years from the expiration dates unless previously cancelled or surrendered. As to cancellation, see Section 46 below.

To be eligible for renewal the mark must be in use in interstate commerce at the time the renewal application is filed unless the non-use is excused by special circumstances and is not due to any intention to abandon the mark. Renewal applications must be filed within the six-month period before the expiration of the registration or within three months thereafter upon payment of a small additional fee.

19. State Registration.

In addition to the federal trademark registration system, the states have their own somewhat parallel systems. In some, only trademarks and not the other categories of federally-recognized marks will be accepted. First use is here also the criterion as between competing marks. Thus Coca-Cola Company was able to prevail over a prior Illinois state registration because of its prior usage of COCA-COLA even though it was unregistered in Illinois.[31]

State trademark registrations should not be confused with state registrations of assumed or fictitious names, which are strictly the creatures of state statute and are essentially business names, not brand names. Furthermore, state registrations of such fictitious names—or even corporate names—will not prevent an adverse trademark registration of a similar name.[32]

State registrations have a definite value, especially during the early stages of the use of a new trademark. A federal registration may take a year or two to be completed and the certificate issued. A state registration may usually be obtained within a few days. This means that a notice of the state registration may be used from the outset. A state registration does not justify use of ® under Section 29 of the Lanham Act. A typical acceptable legend for such registration is "T.M. Reg." Such a trademark legend seems to have a considerable psychological deterrent effect.

State registrations, on the other hand, do not give too much legal protection, although they do assist in proving date of first use, if a conflict on that should later arise, and may also be worthwhile because they sometimes impose criminal sanctions for deliberate or knowing infringement of a mark registered in the state. Some states, such as New York,[33] also have a so-called "anti-dilution statute" under which additional rights are conferred.

E. CHOICE OF A TRADEMARK.

20. The Legal/Practical Problem.

The choice of a "good" trademark is an intimate mingling of legal and practical considerations. There may well be no other reasonably routine corporate effort which presents quite the same legal-practical relationship. The insistence of the lawyer frequently runs head-on into the needs and desires of the sales, marketing, PR and advertising people. In the last analysis, however, it is management which must make the decision and the decision may favor the practical and promotional demands as against the legal. For excellent discussions of all aspects of this multifaceted dialogue, see *Trademark Selection: The Management Team Method* and *Trademarks in the Marketplace* (1960 and 1964 respectively), published by the United States Trademark Association.

21. The Legal Considerations.

Among the characteristics of a potential mark which most appeal to the lawyers on the company team are the following:

(a) *Registrability on the Principal Register.*

A mark registered on the Principal Register has several elements of protection not accorded other marks. Such registration is "constructive notice" to the world of the registrant's claim of ownership. This makes it easier to protect—especially in situations in which another party may have later adopted the mark in another part of the country into which distribution of the registrant's goods may not yet have penetrated. Also, under Section 15 of the Lanham Act, such a registered mark becomes generally incontestable provided the procedures referred to in Section 47 below are followed.

(b) *Relative Strength of the Mark.*

Marks are loosely divided into strong and weak marks. A strong mark is usually coined, fanciful, arbitrary. Again, KODAK is the traditional example of a strong mark. Common marks such as UNIVERSAL, STAR, GOLD MEDAL or BLUE RIBBON are usually considered examples of weak marks. The strong mark will be given wider protection than the weak mark. Strong marks may even prevail over the same mark for quite different goods. KODAK for photographic equipment was able to knock out the same mark on bicycles.[34]

Weak marks, on the other hand, may not be able to prevail over the same or similar junior mark even as to products which seem close to those covered by the senior mark. BLUE RIBBON, a weak mark, could not be protected by Pabst against the same mark on malt syrup, close though the latter product may seem to be to beer.[35]

PARISIENNE was considered a strong mark and its use on stainless steel flatware was protected against a junior use on glass stemware [36] while PRESTIGE was considered a weak mark and no likelihood of confusion was found because of its use on both silver-plated flatware and glass tumblers.[37]

(c) *Avoidance of Descriptive Marks.*

Descriptive marks may not be registered on the Principal Register. Their hope is the Supplemental Register and possible Principal Register acceptance after they have acquired secondary meaning. Legally, they are not good marks. Furthermore, even if so registered, they are difficult to protect and thus do not appeal to the lawyer. See Sections 10 and 12 above.

The reasons for this lack of "legal appeal" have been well described by the Trademark Management Committee of the United States Trademark Association as being: [38]

> (1) the absence of an original right to exclude others from using the same word or words to describe their goods; (2) the limited aura of protection; (3) the uncertainty of being able to produce facts which prove validity of the word as a trademark; and (4) the expenditures of money, time and energy required to create a secondary meaning—and such expenditures may, in the final analysis, be for naught. It may be true that a market can be quickly developed by use of a descriptive term but it may be as quickly lost if a Court finds that there is no right to exclude others from using the same term.

One of the real difficulties in this area is that encountered by even the trademark specialist in trying to decide whether a contemplated mark is merely suggestive (therefore registrable) or is descriptive (therefore immediately unprotectible). Many, many cases have turned on this question. Trademark counsel are usually careful to warn of this gray area and the inherent dangers of the descriptive mark. If a company eventually uses one, it should do so only with its eyes open.

(d) Similarity of Mark and Goods.

Even when searches indicate that a mark is probably "available" for use, the lawyer will still be concerned if the "references" shown in the searches indicate the possible similarity between the prospective mark and one already in use. The question is: just how much difference in products will be necessary to permit registration of the new mark when the two marks are the same or quite similar although the products appear somewhat different? The parallel question is how much difference in the marks will be necessary when the products are the same or somewhat similar. These matters are dealt with in Sections 25 to 29 below.

22. Promotional and Public Relations Considerations.

In a very thoughtful and discriminating discussion of *Public Relations Thinking in Trademarks,* William G. Werner, then Director of the Procter & Gamble Division of Public Relations and former president of both the United States Trademark Association and Public Relations Society of America, said by way of introduction to his subject: [39]

Recognition of the significance of public attitudes and opinions toward trademarks is fully as important in assuring their proper use and protection, I believe, as is recognition of the law.

The importance of this will be most quickly apparent if we keep in mind that a good trademark is essentially a "bridge" between the owner of the mark and the public. This "bridge" function differs in its importance, of course, with varying conditions. Regardless, however, of these differences, it seems quite plain that the strength of any trademark—no matter how well chosen—depends, really, upon the attitudes and preferences at the other end of the bridge—at the public's end of it.

It is this interest in the public attitudes at "the other end of the bridge" which has produced the package of attributes and characteristics which business management, acting through its marketing, public relations, advertising, sales, merchandising and design staff and consultants, have come to believe a trademark should have. There does not appear to be any single roadmap guaranteed to guide the businessman to a successful trademark. At best, the most that can be done by those charged with selection of a trademark is to keep in mind factors which have in the past made, or contributed to the making of, a successful mark. Among these are:

(a) Brevity.

There seems to be a current trend toward the adoption and use of short (three to six letters) one-syllable marks. TAB, TIDE, PLEDGE, FINISH and DIAL are a few examples. Sometimes a shorter form of the mark is practically "forced" on the user by the public such as COKE for COCA-COLA, PEPSI for PEPSI-COLA and BUD in place of BUD-WEISER. These "nicknames" seem good evidence of the public's predilection against the longer marks, no matter how well-accepted and respected they may have become.

(b) Rememberability.

Obviously, a mark should be easy to remember. In fact, the various guidelines adopted over the years may only be factors contributing to this factor of memorability.

(c) Keying to Product and Potential Buyer.

A product intended for use by women presumably should not have a "masculine" mark. At the same time, family buying habits are such that some masculine-use products are bought by the wives.

(d) Readability and Verbal Use.

Marks which require any substantial degree of memory or intensive thought before they may be read, written, spoken or recognized are probably poor marks. Foreign terms are in this category. Pronunciation, spelling and even visual or auditory apprehension do not come too easily.

(e) Good Graphic Reproduction.

Due to the demands of various advertising and other graphic media, a mark—especially one which is handlettered or stylized—should not clog with ink or look cluttered and blurred if the reader or customer happens not to have 20-20 vision. The same is true of marks reduced in size.

(f) Adaptability to All Media and Circumstances.

This is different from the factor immediately above. A mark must be recognized by the public regardless of the source from which it comes—the printed page, the outdoor board, the radio speaker or the television tube. Not every mark is equally noticeable, forceful or memorable in all media. Consideration should also be given to adaptability for product label use, appearance on tightly packed store shelves, etc. In short, it must be "visible" under all possible anticipated circumstances.

(g) Acceptability of Color.

Some marks originally were used in a specific color such as Mobil's FLYING RED HORSE and BLUE SHIELD and BLUE CROSS of the hospitalization plan. Most, however, originate in black and white. With color being used more and more in newspapers, magazines and television, a mark should be adopted with an eye toward the possibility of increasing its impact in these media through the use of color—whether it be the same color at all times or variable colors as circumstances or surroundings may dictate.

(h) Pleasant Connotations.

This is merely part of the traditional mandate against "negative selling." A trademark should not have any unpleasant implications. It should surround the product with a pleasant or happy aura. The meanings and implications in foreign languages and cultures should be assessed also even if the mark is not necessarily to be used abroad.

(i) Storytelling Effect.

Here we get into the area of the descriptive/suggestive dichotomy. Descriptive marks undoubtedly tell a story better than merely suggestive marks but lawyers have a definite aversion to the descriptive mark. The effort here is to subtly and indirectly use the mark to create an aura for the product or suggest its attributes, rather than to describe the product. The suggestive mark may make the promotion of a product—especially a "new" product—much easier and such marks are generally considered among the most viable.

23. Trademark Searches.

Trademark searches are both a legal and practical prerequisite to trademark selection. Without reasonable assurance that a mark is "clear" and available, it is folly to invest anything in its promotion. The first question is at what point in the trademark adoption process should searches be made. Not infrequently hundreds of possible marks may be under initial consideration. Eventually, this is winnowed down to a dozen or less, any one of which might be feasible although, of course, among them will be priorities. It seems to be agreed by both lawyers and marketing people that the searches should be made at this point.

Initially searches are made in the United States Patent Office. They are usually made by trademark counsel or one of the trademark companies since the Patent Office itself cannot make them. The information included in such search reports will generally include back "references" which may appear to preclude use and registration of the new mark, comments about the acceptability for registration of the mark such as its descriptive nature, need for acquisition of secondary meaning and other pertinent suggestions or admonitions.

However, such searches produce information only as to federally registered marks. Other sources must therefore be covered. Among these are the state registration rolls. But even these include only registered marks. Further investigation is necessary as to unregistered marks. There are several private collections of marks, both registered and unregistered, which may be searched for nominal charge. Among them are the Trade-Mark Bureau of the United States Printing and Lithograph Company, Cincinnati, Ohio and the Trademark Service Corporation, New York City.

Valuable information may also be obtained from trade sources such as specific-industry-oriented Gold Books, Green Books, Red Books, etc. Some companies even alert their salesmen or rackjobbers to scan supermarket shelves for possibly unregistered but senior similar marks.

Despite all of these efforts, there is always the possibility that a prior, similar but undiscovered mark will cause difficulties. Probably the best example of this is the GENIE-JEENIE conflict.[40] Colgate-Palmolive adopted GENIE as a mark on a new household cleaner. After careful searches, the mark was registered. Three million dollars was invested in a West Coast sampling campaign. It then developed that JEENIE had been in use locally for 20 years as a mark on a product selling at the rate of about $25 per month. Although Colgate-Palmolive is reported to have eventually settled the matter for a nominal sum, a year had passed and

Colgate-Palmolive "was out of business . . . That was a multi-million dollar fiasco," as one executive associated with the situation has described it.[41]

24. The Eventual Solution.

After all of the legal requirements have been honored, all of the practical needs and purposes explored and satisfied, all of the research completed and the chosen mark satisfactorily searched and cleared, the distillate therefrom is probably going to be a compromise, perhaps not entirely acceptable to anyone. Yet this compromise is often the only solution. Trademark selection is becoming more and more difficult.

Even then, there is no guarantee that the chosen mark will be successful. The "Edsel Story" needs no repetition here. The unhappy ratio of failures to successes in new product introduction probably is, in part at least, attributable to the mark used on the product. This seems inescapable in view of the similarity between successful and unsuccessful products marketed under different marks by different companies which have essentially the same resources and expertise.

F. CONFUSION BETWEEN MARKS.

25. Avoidance of Similarity.

It has been said that "those who adopt trademarks should not enter a field where doubts can be reasonably entertained as to the likelihood of confusion, and if they do, it is at the risk of successful interference and restraint by the first user." [42]

This legal inhibition is, of course, always coupled with a very practical possibility: the dissipation and loss of perhaps millions of dollars of advertising and promotion if a conflicting mark is adopted and eventually lost.

The test, under the Lanham Act and the cases, is whether an allegedly conflicting mark is "likely to cause confusion or mistake or to deceive purchasers." Actual confusion need not be shown. Likely or potential confusion is sufficient.[43] Furthermore, registration will be refused under the Lanham Act, even if the senior mark has not been registered, as long as it has been "previously used in the United States by another and not abandoned."

Confusion or mistake may exist as a result of similarity of either the marks themselves or the goods upon which they are respectively used. Not infrequently the two are interrelated.

26. Patent Office Classifications.

The Patent Office has developed a classification system for trademarks, service marks, certification marks, collective marks and membership marks. Changes in marketing practices and the development of new products and product types dictate the addition of new classes from time to time. The classification follows:

CLASSIFICATION OF GOODS

Class   *Title*

1. Raw or partly prepared materials
2. Receptacles
3. Baggage, animal equipments, portfolios, and pocketbooks
4. Abrasives and polishing materials
5. Adhesives
6. Chemicals and chemical compositions
7. Cordage
8. Smokers' articles, not including tobacco products
9. Explosives, firearms, equipments, and projectiles
10. Fertilizers
11. Inks and inking materials
12. Construction materials
13. Hardware and plumbing and steamfitting supplies
14. Metals and metal castings and forgings
15. Oils and greases
16. Protective and decorative coatings
17. Tobacco products
18. Medicines and pharmaceutical preparations
19. Vehicles
20. Linoleum and oiled cloth
21. Electrical apparatus, machines, and supplies
22. Games, toys, and sporting goods
23. Cutlery, machinery, and tools and parts thereof
24. Laundry appliances and machines
25. Locks and safes
26. Measuring and scientific appliances
27. Horological instruments
28. Jewelry and precious-metal ware
29. Brooms, brushes and dusters
30. Crockery, earthenware, and porcelain
31. Filters and refrigerators

Class   *Title*

32. Furniture and upholstery
33. Glassware
34. Heating, lighting, and ventilating apparatus
35. Belting, hose, machinery packing, and nonmetallic tires
36. Musical instruments and supplies
37. Paper and stationery
38. Prints and publications
39. Clothing
40. Fancy goods, furnishings, and notions
41. Canes, parasols, and umbrellas
42. Knitted, netted, and textile fabrics and substitutes thereof
43. Thread and yarn
44. Dental, medical, and surgical appliances
45. Soft drinks and carbonated waters
46. Foods and ingredients of foods
47. Wines
48. Malt beverages and liquors
49. Distilled alcoholic liquors
50. Merchandise not otherwise classified
51. Cosmetics and toilet preparations
52. Detergents and soaps

CLASSIFICATION OF SERVICES

Class   *Title*

100. Miscellaneous
101. Advertising and business
102. Insurance and financial
103. Construction
104. Communications
105. Transportation and storage
106. Material treatment
107. Education and entertainment

CERTIFICATION MARKS

A. All goods on which a certification mark is used.
B. All services in connection with which a certification mark is used.

MEMBERSHIP MARKS

Class 200. Collective Membership. All marks which are used to indicate membership in an organization or group.

Collective marks other than those indicating membership are classified in the classes for goods and services depending upon the goods or services with which the mark is used.

Even this classification system has proved to be merely a starting point. The Trademark Office has developed a detailed breakdown of goods within each of the numbered classes. These are used as basic guides for processing trademark applications. They will be found in full in *Notes From the Patent Office*, Section 1, Part 4, Notes 1 and 2.

Many states use the same federal classification system. Inasmuch as many state trademark registration statutes permit registration of trademarks only, their classification system includes nothing beyond Class 52. See Section 19 above.

27. Similarity of Goods.

Prior to the Lanham Act, registration of a mark was refused if a similar mark had been used on merchandise having the "same descriptive properties" and the new mark, therefore, might result in confusion or mistake. The "same descriptive properties" test no longer obtains under the Lanham Act which will not permit registration of a mark which resembles one already registered or in use if it will be likely "to cause confusion or mistake or to deceive purchasers." This is a more difficult test. However, this change does not mean that "similar descriptive properties" will no longer be considered as a factor. They do have "considerable importance" even today.[44]

The basic question is whether there is likely to be a confusion of goods and of the sources from which the goods originate if the two marks are allowed to exist side by side. In deciding this issue, there are several factors which are considered.

(a) Classification of Goods.

This refers to the Patent Office Classes which are described and detailed in Section 26. Even though the goods may be different, they may still fall into the same numbered class. In one of the several ARROW cases, Cluett Peabody was able to stop the use of ARROW on belts because they fall into the same general class of men's apparel as did Cluett Peabody's collars and shirts.[45]

At the same time, the mere fact that competing goods are in the same class is not definitive. It was held, for example, that FOG CUTTER as a mark on men's and boys' jackets, raincoats, etc. was not likely to be confused with the marks FOGGERS and BRITISH FOGGERS used on ladies' and misses' dresses, coats, etc.[46] The court considered the fact that one mark applied to men's wear and the other to women's wear. Yet both fell into Class 39, "Clothing."

(b) Use of Goods Together.

Some goods may be quite different, fall into different classes, but still be of such a nature that they are commonly used together. Thus, in another of the ARROW cases, registration of a mark on collar buttons was refused because collar buttons are used together with shirts and collars for which Cluett Peabody already was using ARROW.[47] Also, SPRITE was refused registration for insulated containers such as chests because of senior mark SPRITE on soft drinks.[48]

(c) Sale in the Same Store.

Sometimes non-competing goods may be quite different, be used for different things, but generally offered to the public in the same kind of store. If this is the case, the junior mark may be held to be confusingly similar to the senior mark.[49]

(d) Purchase by the Same Type of Person.

This is somewhat akin to Subsection (c) above. If the same general segment of the community—judged by social, economic, or other standards—is likely to purchase the two types of goods, then the junior use will be rejected.[50] Thus, similar marks on mascara and eyelash curlers were considered likely to be confusing.[51] In the leading *Del Monte* case, registration was refused for canned coffee when the senior users of DEL MONTE objected because they used it on the well-known California fruit products.[52]

(e) Use for the Same Purpose.

Sometimes the same mark may be used on goods which are quite different but are used for the same purposes—not infrequently by the same type of purchaser. This occurs with some frequency in connection with food items. Such registration will generally be refused.[53]

(f) Impact of Dominant Word.

In certain competing marks, a particular word or syllable may be dominant—especially when consideration is given to the type of product on which the mark is used. In such cases, confusion is held to be likely. Thus, the owners of FIGURE FARE and FIGURE were able successfully to oppose the registration of FIGURE CONTROL in connection with dietary products.[54] The court felt that the word "figure" was dominant in both marks, especially when used in conjunction with diet foods, and that the latter mark would therefore cause confusion.

The following is a sampling of cases decided in a single year (1966) in which the same or essentially the same mark was used on products which were considered insufficiently different to avoid the likelihood of confusion. In each instance, registration was refused to the first-mentioned mark because of prior registration of the second.[55]

SPRITE (insulated containers shaped like jug)—SPRITE (soft drinks).

HOLIDAY RAMBLER (travel trailers)—RAMBLER (passenger automobiles).

THE HERITAGE COLLECTION (electric lighting fixtures)—HERITAGE (line of household furniture).

JOCKEY with drawing of jockey (shoe polish)—JOCKEY with similar representation (men's wear).

GOLD MINE SPARKLE (ice cream bars)—SPARKLE (fluid milk).

INTERARMCO (pistols, rifles, etc.)—ARMCO (steel and steel products).

FUSIONCOTE (plastic-lined metal drums)—FUSIONKOTE (abrasion- and chemical-resistant paint).

SIDEWINDER (radio receiver-transmitter)—SIDE WINDER and design (rotary farm implements including brush cutters).

EXECUTIVE (tennis rackets)—EXECUTIVE (golf clubs).

A gold band mark (bituminous fiber sewer pipe)—orange painted band (metal pipes and tubing).

OX-BOW (restaurant design mark)—OX-BOW cattle ranch also selling processed beef.

BJ (animal feed mixes and racks)—BJ (well tools, fertilizer mixing machines and equipment).

HOLLAND and HOLLAND INK (ink products)—HOLLAND COLORS (chemical colors).

COUNTY FAIR (fresh bread and baked goods)—COUNTY FAIR (frozen fruit and cream pies).

AMERICAN (microphones)—AMERICAN ELITE (electronic equipment).

SANISPEC (spectacle frame cleaner)—SPECS (eyeglass cleaner).

IOTHANE (wood surface plastic finish)—DIOTHANE (concrete surface synthetic resin coating).

FABIANO (men's trousers)—FABIANOS (women's dress and sport shoes).

CARPETSHIELD (carpet cleaning compound)—RUG-SHIELD (rug protective compound for stains).

ORANGE JOY (orange juice)—GRAPE JOY (grape juice).

BRIDGE MINTS (candy)—BRIDGE (chewing gum).

28. Similarity of Marks.

Obviously the same mark should not be used on the same or similar goods. The difficult question is how much resemblance between marks will be tolerated in the basic effort to avoid confusion. Each case must essentially stand on its own legs. The application of the "appearance, sound and meaning" test has been described in these words: [56]

> In determining likelihood of confusion between trade marks on identical goods it is proper to consider their appearance, sound and meaning, but a combination of all three factors need not necessarily exist, and an opposition to registration may be sustained if marks are identical or so similar in meaning that confusion as to origin is deemed likely.

It is extremely difficult to posit which of the three factors (appearance, sound or meaning) will be considered dominant in a given case or even how a case will be decided on the basis of any one of these factors. The two Uneeda Biscuit cases point this up. The National Biscuit Company using UNEEDA successfully opposed registration of IWANTA [57] but failed against HAVA.[58] The three-way test was applied in both cases but with different results, IWANTA being held likely to confuse because of the greater similarity in meaning and the somewhat similar appearance.

If products (such as "bottled pop") are usually bought by verbal order or as a result of "impulse buying," sound is usually considered the most important factor. Therefore BEEP was held to conflict with VEEP [59] and LEMON-UP with SEVEN-UP.[60] Yet SUN-UP was held not to conflict with SEVEN-UP.[61]

A leading case on the importance of meaning held CANNED LIGHT to be confusing with BARRELLED SUNLIGHT for use on paint even though appearance and sound vary greatly.[62]

Much depends on the type of product bearing the allegedly conflicting mark. No firm canons of interpretation are possible. As an example, TESTROID was refused registration against the opposition of TESTROLIX on ethical pharmaceutical preparations because of similarity in sound and appearance when written.[63] It was pointed out that prescriptions are often telephoned to the pharmacist (sound) and even when written, the prescriptions may not "always be unmistakably legible" (appearance). The possible danger from mixing up the two preparations undoubtedly was a strong factor in the decision, which might well have been different if a different type of product was involved.

29. "Free Ride" Doctrine.

In addition to these trademark tests, the courts appear to be applying the "free ride" doctrine with increasing frequency where exactly the same mark is being used. The courts consider the use of an identical mark as "evidence of intention to make something out of it—either to get the benefit of [the senior user's] reputation or of its advertisement . . ." [64]

This doctrine is being applied in trademark infringement cases, unfair competition cases, and copyright cases.[65]

G. PROTECTION OF TRADEMARKS.

Much of what has already been said about the choice and use of trademarks applies with equal force to their protection. Certain types of marks are easier to protect than others. Some are almost impossible to maintain, protect and develop. There are certain steps which every company should take to protect its marks—quite apart from the degree of depth or scope of such measures. It has been suggested that every trademark user "should assume the worst" and therefore take every possible precaution in connection with its mark or marks.

30. Trademark Notices or Legends.

The simplest protective step is the use of the proper trademark registration notice whenever the mark is used. Once a mark has been registered in either the Patent Office or a state, it should always carry the appropriate notice or legend. This should appear on the product itself, its container or packaging, shipping cartons, hangtags, and wherever else it may be "displayed with the mark" as required by the Lanham Act. Also, the appropriate notice should be used in all of the company's advertising, labeling, display material, catalogues, house organs, promotional material and wherever and whenever the mark is used.

If the mark has been registered in the Patent Office, the notice should be "Registered in U. S. Patent Office," "Reg. U. S. Pat. Off." or the more conventional ®. None of these notices should be used, however, unless the federal registration has actually been completed and the certificate issued and received. Premature use of such federal registration notice is improper and may be the basis for refusal of registration.

As discussed in Section 19, many companies obtain a state registration prior to the federal registration. None of the foregoing notices should be used in the event of a state registration, For such registration, "T. M. Reg." or something similar should be used. Later, when federal registration is completed, the state notice is removed and the federal notice replaces it.

The notice—even the innocuous ®—may sometimes offend the aesthetically-inclined art director or account executive. In such cases, an asterisk may be placed "on the shoulder" of the mark with an asterisked explanation elsewhere on the label or in the advertisement indicating the registration.

31. Danger of Generic Meaning.

The target of all protective measures is the prevention of the mark's deterioration into the generic or common name for the product with which the mark has been used or displayed. When this occurs, the mark no longer designates the source of the product but rather the kind of product. Just as a descriptive mark may not initially be registered, so too may rights in an otherwise valid registered mark be lost if it has been permitted to acquire a generic meaning.

Many once-valuable trademarks have fallen by the wayside for this reason. The two most commonly cited are "cellophane" [66] and "aspirin," [67] both of which were once valuable trademarks but are now merely descriptive. The recent loss of rights in "Thermos" for insulated bottles will also probably come to be cited as a prime example of this danger.[68]

Some of the court's language in the "aspirin case" is enlightening. The court said that Bayer had permitted the public to believe that "aspirin" meant only "a kind of drug to which for one reason or another they had become habituated." Therefore no one company would be permitted to prevent "the trade" from using "the only description which will be understood" by its customers.

32. "Anti-generic" Devices

One of the most effective protective devices is to couple the trademark and the generic word which describes the product. Thus, DuPont uses "Lucite® acrylic resin." When the trademark is used in handdrawn form or some special configuration, the generic name may be used immediately beneath or after the mark in any style of composition but is usually considerably smaller.

Another device is to use the trademark on a variety of different products. FRIGIDAIRE, for this reason, is used as a trademark on and with such diverse products as refrigerators, cooking ranges, air conditioners, dehumidifiers, food freezers, washing machines and dryers, etc. This avoids the possibility that "frigidaire" (in lower case) will come to mean *any* electric icebox. In England, such a home appliance is widely referred to as "the fridge."

Still another method is to add to the product label or advertising a line such as "PDQ is XYZ's registered trademark for its widgets" or "the PDQ brand of widgets," thus clearly demonstrating that PDQ is a trademark and widgets is the descriptive or generic term for the product. Both of these approaches are frequently observed on drug products.

33. Generic Use in Dictionaries.

As a trademark is promoted and used, it may appear to be so popular that lexicographers will include it in their dictionaries as a generic term. *Webster's Third New International Dictionary* includes many registered trademarks, although in its preface it points out that "it confines itself strictly to generic words." A random check of 65 registered trademarks in that dictionary showed 44 of them listed as generic words.[69] Trademark owners reacted promptly to this apparent invasion of their rights.

This "dictionary use" of a mark should be avoided or policed as much as any other "lower case use" in any mass media. However, it seems that such dictionary use will not be determinative of the owner's rights—nor should it be. One court has referred to this in these words: [70]

> Trade-names for popular products, as used by one manufacturer, may become so widely known as sometimes to be used as a synonym for the generic name itself. Striking examples of this are such names as "Kodak" and "Vaseline." Both these are defined in the dictionary and yet they are trade-marks, the use of which by anyone outside the firms which have originated them would constitute an infringement. The fact that a large part of the public may associate a trade-name with the generic name for a product is a tribute to the skill with which the firm has popularized the name. To put a penalty upon such skill and to say that the generalization of the trade-name by the public as a result of the originator's publicity must deprive him of his monopoly in the name would, in the absence of special circumstances, be the height of injustice.

34. Use of a Mark in Advertising.

Undoubtedly one of the best methods of developing a secure mark is to use it not only on the goods themselves but also in a continuing and extensive advertising effort. Whenever the mark is used in the advertising, it should be treated as a trademark. This can be done in many ways.

As discussed in Section 30, the trademark notice should be used with the mark. Additional typographic techniques may be used. The mark may be presented in its customary handlettered form. If printed characters are used, the mark must be at least capitalized—if not printed in solid caps. So-called "lower case use" should be avoided at all times. The mark should not be used as a possessive or as a verb. Its form and spelling should not be changed.

For the sake of appearance, especially if a mark is used frequently throughout the headlines or body copy of an advertisement, special typographic treatment need not be given except for the initial caps. However, this may be done only when the use of the term as a trademark is clearly indicated elsewhere in the advertisement.

35. Trademark Educational Advertising.

An effective method of preventing misuse of trademarks is the special, protection-oriented trademark educational advertisement or campaign. Usually this will appear in the general or trade (especially the communications) media although direct mail campaigns are also used. A wide variety of copy, art and layout techniques are used. Some are straightforward and serious; others are humorous, perhaps using cartoons. Some derive from the importance of using everyone's name correctly; others are practically courses in trademark law, stressing the "fragile" nature of trademarks. One of the commonest themes is the need for use of an initial cap on the trademark, no matter how the plea or argument is presented.[71]

One of the best and most famous pieces of trademark protection literature is the humorous booklet published by The Coca-Cola Company in 1953 under the highly appropriate title *The Case for the Upper Case.* So concerned was this company with its marks COCA-COLA and COKE that it also produced a film strip in color with recorded sound for which the booklet serves as a "libretto," the combination being intended "primarily for the information of the working press and students of journalism."

Using a cartoon technique and employing dialogue between the famous Don Marquis characters of Archy the cockroach and Mehitabel the office cat, booklet and film strip discuss the history of trademarks, their purposes, their value to owner and press alike and above all, the proper way to refer to a trademark in editorial matter. The theme as to such proper use, punched hard in several ways, is:

1. Spell it right.
2. Capitalize it.
3. Use it right.

36. Loss by Nonuser.

Just as rights in a trademark are initially acquired by use of the mark, so too may rights therein be lost by a failure to continue such use. This is one aspect of "abandonment" of the mark. Under Section 45 of the

Lanham Act, a mark is deemed abandoned when its use is discontinued with intent not to resume, intent being inferred "from circumstances." Nonuse for two consecutive years is "prima facie abandonment." Each case stands on its own facts and since abandonment is in the nature of a forfeiture, strict proof is required before it will be found to have occurred.[72]

Although nonuse for a protracted period may be satisfactorily explained,[73] it is important that records be maintained to prove the reasons for the nonuse and the intention to continue or resume use of the mark. Otherwise the registrant may lose its rights.

37. Innocent Misuse of Trademark.

Most misuse of a trademark involves no ulterior or sneaky motives; it is quite innocent. This may include misuse by a registrant's own wholesalers, jobbers or distributors, editors of the mass media, book authors and even competitors. However, the fact that the misuse is accidental is no rationale for the failure by the registrant to police the use of its mark.

Furthermore, the registrant should not relax supinely and take action only when it happens to learn of such misuse. The registrant should have a continuous and well-organized policing program. This would include use of a clipping service, continuing or periodical searches of subsequent filings or registrations and even such obvious—but sometimes overlooked —efforts as examination of telephone directories and the "Yellow Pages." Some companies retain legal counsel or trademark companies for this purpose.

38. Mass Media Misuse of Trademarks.

A prolific source of trademark misuse is the mass and trade media. Writers and editors will—usually innocently and inadvertently—use a trademark as a generic term. This frequently is referred to as "lower case use." A registrant probably has the right to expect nothing more from such media than the use of an "initial cap" on its trademark. However, "lower case use" should not be tolerated and every such instance should elicit from the registrant, its counsel or PR department, a letter warning against a repetition of the error. For the form of such letter, see Section 39 below.

Most of the trademark educational advertising discussed in Section 35 above is directed at editorial misuse. It solicits editorial use of initial caps and a generic term in conjunction with the mark.

Beverly W. Pattishall, former president of the International Trademark Association and chairman of the Patent, Trademark and Copyright Section of the American Bar Association, in addressing a meeting of press representatives, quoted from a March, 1963 *Pageant* article referring to what he described as "the most astonishing example of misuse of the famous COCA-COLA trademark that I have ever heard": [74]

> But if newspaper and magazine editors are occasionally stubborn, novelists are well-nigh impossible. In fact, by far the most offensive abuse of any company's trademark occurred in a novel. The trademark was "Coke." The novel was John Steinbeck's *The Wayward Bus*, published in 1947.
>
> To begin with, *The Wayward Bus* has some half-dozen references to Pepsi-Cola, all properly capitalized, and in not unpleasant contexts. Then, on page 128, comes:
>
> "Now, let's have a couple of cups of coffee," he said. And to the blonde, "You rather have a coke?"
>
> "No. Coffee. Cokes make me fat." And just 54 pages later:
>
> "Got any coke?" he asked.
>
> "No," said Breed. "Few bottles of Pepsi-Cola. Haven't had any coke for a month. It's the same stuff. You can't tell them apart."
>
> Naturally, an "I-hate-to-bother-you-but" letter was dispatched to Mr. Steinbeck. With admirable restraint, the Coca-Cola people protested only against his writing "Coke" as "coke."
>
> And Mr. Steinbeck blandly wrote back that "in English when a word is spelled with a small c and is still acceptable, it has become a great word. Only the small need to capitalize."

39. Suggested Policing Letter Form.

Whenever an editorial lapse in trademark use is found, a letter should be directed to the publisher or editor in order to prevent, if possible, a repetition of the misuse. The following form may be used—appropriately varied to suit the specific misuse or surrounding circumstances.

> Dear —————:
>
> We want to thank you for your friendly reference to ————— in your issue of —————. Your recognition is appreciated.
>
> However, should you have the occasion hereafter to refer to ————— or any of the other trademarks of our company, these trademarks should be treated somewhat differently. ————— is a registered trademark and it is our desire to protect it and our other trademarks.
>
> It would be appreciated if you would use either initial or solid caps when mentioning ————— and also add a generic or descriptive word immediately after each mention of the trademark. Of course, it would be even better from our point of view if you would add ® each time you refer to one of our trademarks. It is to both your interest and ours that trademarks be respected. We are sure that you will understand that misuse by a publication of a

valuable trademark might contribute to a dilution or even loss of rights. Obviously, we want to avoid this.

We are taking the liberty of enclosing a trademark manual which we have prepared and given wide distribution. This identifies our company's registered trademarks and also may assist you in connection with the proper use thereof in your publication.

May we thank you for your cooperation and courtesies in assisting us in our efforts.

40. Third-Party Advertising Misuse.

When a trademark is not used properly in the advertising of third parties, this will usually be at the retail level. The categories of errors most likely to be seen are:

(a) Lower case use of the mark.

(b) "Xyz-type" or "Pdq-style" mentions. These may also fail to use the initial cap, doubling the error and confusion. Not infrequently investigation proves that this hyphenated technique is deliberate with the user looking for a "free ride," at the same time recognizing that the advertised merchandise does not bear the trademark in question.

(c) Failure to use generic term with the mark.

In a review of textile advertising during 1966, the Better Business Bureau of Metropolitan New York found that 481 advertisements had failed to comply with its retail advertising guidelines and that 61 per cent of the errors involved use of trademarks without generic terms.[75] Of the violations 66 involved manufacturer's advertisements and the rest retail advertisements.

Whenever such errors are found, the registrant should put the advertiser on notice and correct it at once.

41. Prosecution of Infringers.

A failure by the trademark owner to take legal action against recalcitrant infringers may result in an "abandonment" of the mark. On the other hand, use or registration by others of the same mark for different goods which fall into the same general class does not, in and of itself, constitute an abandonment of the mark for the specific goods upon which a registrant has used the mark.[76] It may result in a weakening of the mark and a narrowing of a party's rights therein.[77] Even weak marks, on the other hand, are accorded the protection of the statute.[78]

A litigation program has an inherent danger if a registrant fails to take action against one or two infringers. Unless there is some valid reason for a failure to proceed in the isolated instances, the registrant may well be held to be estopped should it bring action later on. An interesting example of this is the *DuBois Brewery* case.[79] Anheuser-Busch had stopped 60 or 70 breweries from using its mark (by both litigation and notice) but had permitted DuBois to continue such use for 40 years. When suit was finally brought, DuBois prevailed.

42. Authorized Use by Third Parties.

Over the years more and more third parties have come to use a company's trademarks with the company's consent. Licensing of trademarks is increasing. With the growth of the franchise system has come an increase in such authorized use. In fact, some licensing and franchise programs would be impossible without use of the trademark. The trademark may well be the *deus ex machina* of the program.

If the third parties, regardless of their identity, use the registrant's marks properly and under appropriate agreements, the registrant runs little risk. The problem is that such programs must be continually policed.

Use by wholesalers, jobbers and other common types of customers usually can be covered with a trademark manual as discussed in Section 44 below. At the same time, they should be policed as with any other users.

43. Policing Franchises, etc.

Licensing and franchise programs present several problems of considerable scope and depth, especially if the mark is permitted to be used on products fabricated or compounded by the licensee or franchisee. It is necessary that the agreements contain provisions for product-quality control as well as trademark use control.[80]

Among the more common product-control provisions are those setting up quality standards, right of the franchisee to inspect and sample, to dictate changes, to advise on methods and buying sources, and to inspect records. Trademark use usually involves controls as to method of application or display of the mark on the product or place of business, use of the registration notice, mention of licensee's status, design of packaging, prior approvals by the franchisor, termination of trademark rights upon termination of franchise rights, destruction of non-conforming materials, labels, etc., duty of notification of infringements, keeping of records.

In addition to appropriate contract provisions the registrant should actually exercise both the quality controls and the trademark controls. The contract provisions should be enforced. Departures or malpractices by licensees should be stopped and, in extreme cases, rights should be terminated under the common contract clause making misuse of marks grounds for termination.[81]

H. MISCELLANEOUS.

44. Trademark Manuals.

More and more companies—especially if they use more than one trademark—are preparing and distributing so-called trademark manuals. These are booklets or brochures containing instructions for the use of company marks. Some are intended for use by company staff and personnel, others for external distribution to customers and the press. Most are of considerable length and substance, covering almost every aspect of trademark recognition and use. They carry various titles. Perhaps typical is *What You Should Know About DUPONT TRADE-MARKS.*

There is no question but that they are excellent tools for trademark protection, particularly because they *prevent* many possible future errors in such use—rather than merely calling attention to past errors.

45. Trademark Record-keeping.

It is not enough for a company to register and protect its trademark. It must also be able to *prove* at a later date what it has done. A careful system of trademark records must be maintained. It should cover all activity dealing with the mark from the very first use thereof. Even such first use may later come under attack.

The *Wilshire* case is an extreme but significant example of the need for adequate records. Two concerns started using the mark coincidentally in the East and West at the same time. Both expanded and finally met "head-on." The plaintiff had by far the larger sales volume under the mark but could not prove its shipments into the various states. The court realized the harshness of its ruling, but pointed out:[82]

> As between two well-nigh simultaneous users of a trade name this apportionment of territory would seem not a little harsh—45 states to 1. But the harshness, if any, is due to the fact that the plaintiff was unable to factually substantiate its extended territorial claims with any contemporaneous documentary, or even oral, proof. On the other hand, defendant's case was supported in detail by order blanks dated in 1935 and the following years, for substantial sized orders, from many states. It showed sales in 46 states for 1935 and 1936.

Among the records which should be maintained in connection with the adoption and first use of a mark are:

(a) Copies of invoices under which the goods bearing the new mark were shipped, showing specific mention of the mark thereon.

(b) Evidence of such shipment including signed freight bill of lading, express or post office receipt.

(c) Acknowledgment of receipt of the goods by the addressee or consignee, including, if necessary, a letter therefrom referring to the goods specifically under the trademark and the date received.

(d) Copies of the label or other applications of the mark to the goods, particularly if they were specially prepared for the initial shipment and are not the same as the printed labels or carton markings used thereafter on the goods.

(e) Any correspondence or other papers dealing with the shipment, including printing orders for labels, internal memoranda, instructions to salesmen, etc.

(f) Copies of news releases, trade publication articles, etc. dealing with use of the new mark.

Even after the mark is being used consistently, records should be preserved. The implications of the *Wilshire* case above are clear. These records should include:

(a) Evidence of volume of sales under the mark including states and markets to which shipped, number of customers therein, invoices carrying the reference to the mark (especially in multi-trademark companies), type of products shipped (in cases of "family mark" use), etc.

(b) Copies of advertising of the mark, including educational advertising, showing dates of publication or mailing (as to direct mail), dollar volume thereof, publications used and other evidence of the overall scope of advertising and promotion of the mark.

(c) All files dealing with policing of the mark including correspondence and litigated infringements.

(d) Evidence of use of clipping services and other affirmative steps taken in the policing such as instructions to salesmen and other field personnel.

Record-keeping of this kind and scope just does not "happen" even though some of the data might later be "dredged up" from routine company files. A special program is necessary. One department or individual should be charged with the responsibility. Furthermore, most companies today have a periodic file disposal program and these trademark records may thoughtlessly be disposed of, along with routine files no longer of any value. Yet case after case proves the need for records ten, twenty, even fifty years old. In the *Thermos* case,[83] evidence was introduced going back to the period before 1910.

46. Affidavit of Continued Use.

Section 8 of the Lanham Act provides:

(a) Each certificate of registration shall remain in force for twenty years: Provided, that the registration of any mark under the provisions of this chapter shall be canceled by the Commissioner at the end of six years following its date, unless within one year next preceding the expiration of such six years the registrant shall file in the Patent Office an affidavit showing that said mark is still in use or showing that its nonuse is due to special circumstances which excuse such nonuse and is not due to any intention to abandon the mark. Special notice of the requirement for such affidavit shall be attached to each certificate of registration.

47. Affidavit of Incontestability.

Section 15 of the Lanham Act provides for the filing of an Affidavit of Incontestability during the sixth year after registration if the mark is on the Principal Register. Such a filing enlarges the registrant's rights because thereafter a petition to cancel the registration will ordinarily not be allowed. However, a mark may still be canceled thereafter because

(a) the registration contains prohibited matter;

(b) the registration was obtained "fraudulently";

(c) of discontinuance of use;

(d) of misuse by an assignee of the mark so as to misrepresent the source of the goods or services;

(e) of loss of distinctiveness and significance as an indication of the source of the goods or services due to the registrant's improper use of the mark or failure to stop such use by others.

Certification marks may be canceled at any time for any of the above five reasons or for any of the following reasons:

(a) the registrant does not control the use of the certification mark;

(b) the registrant himself produces or sells the goods or services certified under the mark;

(c) permission is granted for use other than as a certification;

(d) discrimination among persons properly maintaining the standards subject to certification.

Notes

1. Mishawaka Rubber Co. v. S. S. Kresge Co., 316 U.S. 203 (1941).
2. 148 U.S.P.Q. 607 (P.O.T.T.A.B. 1966).
3. P.L. 489, 79th Cong., Ch. 540, 60 Stat. 427; 15 U.S.C., effective July 5, 1947.
4. For an interesting discussion of this interrelation, see the remarks of Charlotte Klein, Vice-President of Flanley and Woodward, Inc. in U.S. TRADEMARK ASS'N, TRADEMARKS IN THE MARKETPLACE 60–1 (1964).
5. National Trailways Bus System v. Trailway Van Lines, Inc., 222 F. Supp. 143, 139 U.S.P.Q. 54 (E.D.N.Y. 1963).
6. The definitions of trademarks, service marks, certification marks, collective marks, trade names and commercial names (p. 347) appear in Lanham Act, §45.
7. AMDUR, TRADEMARK LAW AND PRACTICE (1948).
8. Kimberley-Clark Corp. v. Marzell, 94 F. Supp. 254, 88 U.S.P.Q. 277 (D.C. 1950), aff'd, 196 F.2d 772, 93 U.S.P.Q. 191 (D.C. Cir. 1952); Drexel Enterprises, Inc. v. Hermitage Cabinet Shop, Inc., 266 F. Supp. 532, 152 U.S.P.Q. 484 (N.D. Ga. 1967); NIMS, UNFAIR COMPETITION AND TRADEMARKS 252 (4th ed. 1947).
9. Automatic Washer Co. v. Easy Washing Machine Corp., 98 F. Supp. 445 (N.D.N.Y. 1951).
10. Armstrong Paint Co. v. Nu-Enamel Corp., 305 U.S. 315 (1935); Condé Nast Publications, Inc., v. Vogue School of Fashions Modeling, 105 F. Supp. 325 (S.D.N.Y. 1952); in re Pilgrim Book Society, 149 U.S.P.Q. 658 (P.O.T.T.A.B. 1966); Capitol Tie Rack, Inc. v. Tie Rack Stores of Illinois, Inc., 150 U.S.P.Q. 357, N.D. Ill. 1966.
11. Curtis-Stepheson-Embry Co. v. Pro-Tek-Toe Skate Shop Co., 199 F.2d 407, 95 U.S.P.Q. 130 (8th Cir. 1952).
12. Sweetarts v. Sunline, Inc. et al., 150 U.S.P.Q. 361, 255 F. Supp. 771 (E.D. Mo. 1966).
13. Cinepix, Inc. v. Triple F Productions, 150 U.S.P.Q. 134 (N.Y. Sup. Ct. 1966); Goldman v. R.K.O. Radio Pictures, Inc., 149 Misc. 226 (1933).
14. 150 U.S.P.Q. 70 (P.O.T.T.A.B. 1966).
15. Quoted from Elgin Nat'l Watch Co. v. Illinois Watch Case Co., 179 U.S. 665 (1900).
16. In re Wisconsin Wine Works, 291 F.2d 958, 130 U.S.P.Q. 214 (C.C.P.A. 1961).
17. In re Preformed Line Products Co., 359 F.2d 907, 149 U.S.P.Q. 569 (C.C.P.A. 1966).
18. In re Lincoln Park Van Lines, 149 U.S.P.Q. 313 (P.O.T.T.A.B. 1966).
19. In re Superba Cravats, Inc., 149 U.S.P.Q. 852 (P.O.T.T.A.B. 1966).
20. Bristol-Myers Co. v. Approved Pharmaceutical Corp., 149 U.S.P.Q. 896 (N.Y. Sup. Ct. 1966).
21. Ex parte Wells Lamont Corp., 93 U.S.P.Q. 43 (Comr. 1952); Ex parte The

Catholic Digest, Inc., 111 U.S.P.Q. 444, 47 T.M.R. 378 (Comr. 1956); *Ex parte* Allied Chemical & Dye Corp., 47 T.M.R. 269, 111 U.S.P.Q. 344 (Comr. 1956).

22. *Ex parte* The Third National Bank of St. Louis, 1919 C.D. 26, 260 O.G. 562, 9 T.M.R. 326, 10 T.M.R. 52 (Comr. 1919); *Ex parte* Bank of America Nat'l Trust & Sav. Ass'n, 48 T.M.R. 1425, 118 U.S.P.Q. 165 (Comr. 1958).

23. 19 T.M.R. 261, 1 U.S.P.Q. 264 (Comr. 1929).

24. Western Stove Co. v. Roper Corp., 82 F. Supp. 206 (S.D. Cal. 1949). As to cases prior to the Lanham Act, see DeLong Hook & Eye Co. v. Hump Hairpin Mfg. Co., 297 Ill. 359, 130 N. E. 765 (1921); Gray v. Armand Co., 24 F.2d 878 (D.C. Cir. 1928).

25. Western Stove Co. v. Roper Corp., *supra* note 24.

26. Gilson Bros. Co. v. Wheel Horse Products, Inc., 150 U.S.P.Q. 204 (P.O.T.T.A.B. 1966); A. G. Spaulding & Bros., Inc. v. Bancroft Racquet Co., 149 U.S.P.Q. 391 (P.O.T.T.A.B. 1966).

27. Bell Co. v. Pack & Motor Car Co., 107 U.S.P.Q. 243 (Comr. 1955).

28. *In re* Purex Corp., Ltd., 149 U.S.P.Q. 308 (P.O.T.T.A.B. 1966).

29. Coca-Cola Co. v. Nashville Syrup Co., 220 Fed. 157 (D.C. Tenn. 1912), *aff'd,* 215 Fed. 527 (6th Cir. 1914).

30. Dwight S. Williams Co., Inc. v. Lykens Hosiery Mills, Inc., 109 U.S.P.Q. 328 (4th Cir. 1956), *cert. denied,* 352 U.S. 840 (1957); Vacuum-Electronics Corp. v. Electronic Engineering Co. of California, 150 U.S.P.Q. 215 (P.O.T.T.A.B. 1966).

31. Coca-Cola Co. v. Stevenson, 276 Fed. 1010 (S.D. Ill. 1920).

32. State trademark records are separate from corporate or fictitious name records. However, *some* states search *all* such records before accepting a new trademark registration and will refuse the latter if it conflicts with *any* prior registration.

33. N.Y. Gen. Bus. Law, McKinney's Consol. Laws, c. 20, §368-d (1961). See also Ideal Toy Corp. v. Fab-Lu, Ltd. (Inc.), 266 F. Supp. 755, 152 U.S.P.Q. 500 (S.D.N.Y. 1966), *aff'd,* 360 F.2d 1021 (1966).

34. Eastman v. Kodak Cycle Co., 15 R.P.C. 105 (1897).

35. Pabst Brewing Co. v. Decatur Brewing Co., 148 Fed. 110 (7th Cir. 1922).

36. Imperial Knife Associated Cos., Inc. v. National Silver Co., 150 U.S.P.Q. 209 (P.O.T.T.A.B. 1966).

37. Home Decorators, Inc. v. Federal Glass Co., 133 U.S.P.Q. 484 (P.O.T.T.A.B. 1962).

38. U.S. Trademark Ass'n, Trademark Management 34–5 (1955).

39. Address before the 76th annual meeting of the United States Trademark Ass'n, New York, June 23, 1954, reprinted in 44 T.M.R. 774 (1954).

40. Conley v. Colgate-Palmolive Co., 125 U.S.P.Q. 2 (N.D. Cal. 1959).

41. For a fuller and informal description of this case, see U.S. Trademark Ass'n, Trademarks in the Marketplace 10–11 (1964).

42. Plough, Inc. v. Intercity Oil Co., 26 F. Supp. 978 (E.D. Pa. 1939).

43. North Star Manufacturing Co. v. Wells Lamont Corp., 193 F.2d 204 (C.C.P.A. 1951).

44. Alligator Co. v. Larus & Bros., 196 F.2d 532 (C.C.P.A. 1952); Pep Boys v. Guth Co., 197 F.2d 527 (C.C.P.A. 1952).

45. Cluett, Peabody & Co., Inc. v. Wright, 46 F.2d 711 (C.C.P.A. 1952).

46. David Crystal, Inc. v. Budd & Votaw, 145 U.S.P.Q. 718, 346 F.2d 623 (C.C.P.A. 1965).

47. Cluett, Peabody & Co., Inc. v. Hartogensis, 41 F.2d 94 (C.C.P.A. 1930).

48. Coca-Cola Co. v. Hamilton-Skotch Corp., 146 U.S.P.Q. 502 (P.O.T.T.A.B. 1965).

49. J. R. Clark Co. v. Queen Mfg. Co., 150 U.S.P.Q. 73 (P.O.T.T.A.B. 1966).

50. Imperial Knife Associated Cos., Inc. v. National Silver Co., *supra* note 36.

51. Younghusband v. Kurlash Co., 94 F.2d 108 (C.C.P.A. 1938).

52. California Packing Corp. v. Tillman & Bendel, Inc., 40 F.2d 108 (C.C.P.A. 1930).

53. Heller & Co. v. Southern Cotton Oil Co., 4 F.2d 955 (D.C. Cir. 1925).

54. Duffy-Mott Co. v. General Mills, Inc., 148 U.S.P.Q. 225, 354 F.2d 394 (C.C.P.A. 1966).

55. These cases will all be found reported in 146–9 U.S.P.Q. (1966) and are indexed therein under the marks in question.

56. Hancock v. American Steel & Wire Co. of New Jersey, 203 F.2d 737 (C.C.P.A. 1953).

57. National Biscuit Co. v. Baker, 95 Fed. 135 (S.D.N.Y. 1899).

58. National Biscuit Co. v. Pennsylvania Baking Co., 285 Fed. 1018 (D.C. Cir. 1923).

59. The Coca-Cola Bottling Co. of New York, Inc. v. Krim-Ko Corporation, 148 U.S.P.Q. 396 (P.O.T.T.A.B. 1965).

60. Seven-Up Co. v. Balsh, 44 U.S.P.Q. 171 (Com'r Pats. 1940).

61. Seven-Up Co. v. Tropicana Products, Inc., 148 U.S.P.Q. 604 (C.C.P.A. 1966).

62. Boydell Bros. v. United States Gutta Percha Co., 22 F.2d 1006 (D.C. Cir. 1927).

63. Conal Pharmaceuticals, Inc. v. Starr Pharmacal Co., 148 U.S.P.Q. 753 (P.O.T.T.A.B. 1966).

64. Aunt Jemima Mills Co. v. Rigney, 247 Fed. 407 (2d Cir. 1917).

65. Great A. & P. Tea Co. v. A. & P. Radio Stores, Inc., 20 F. Supp. 703 (E.D. Pa. 1937) (trade name case); Ideal Toy Corp. v. Fab-Lu, Ltd. (Inc.), 152 U.S.P.Q. 500, 266 F. Supp. 755 (S.D.N.Y. 1966) (copyright case).

66. Du Pont Cellophane v. Waxed Products Co., 85 F.2d 75 (2d Cir. 1936).

67. Bayer Co. v. United Drug Co., 272 Fed. 505 (S.D.N.Y. 1921).

68. Amer. Thermos Prod. Co. v. Aladdin Industries, Inc., 207 F. Supp. 9 (D.C. Conn. 1962), *aff'd*, 321 F.2d 577 (2d Cir. 1963).

69. A.A., Jan. 15, 1962, at 12.

70. Metz Laboratories v. Blackman, 275 N.Y.S. 407, 153 Misc. 171 (1934).

71. For a discussion of a variety of trademark educational campaigns, see Diamond, *Advertising Can Preserve Trademark Rights*, A.A., Dec. 19, 1966, at 56.

72. Tisch Hotels, Inc. v. Atlanta Americana Motor Hotel Corp., 149 U.S.P.Q. 256 (N.D. Ga. 1966).

73. Fort Howard Paper Co. v. Kimberley-Clark Corp., *supra* note 2; Field Enterprises Educational Corp. v. Grosset & Dunlap, Inc., 150 U.S.P.Q. 517 (S.D.N.Y. 1966).

74. Address of Beverly W. Pattishall to the 1963 meeting of the Georgia Press Institute, reprinted in *Better Journalism For a Better Tomorrow,* School of Journalism, University of Georgia (1963).

75. BETTER BUSINESS BUREAU OF METROPOLITAN N.Y., HOW VIGILANCE HELPS AN INDUSTRY—A REPORT ON THE TEXTILE INDUSTRY 4 (1967).

76. A. G. Spaulding & Bros., Inc. v. Bancroft Racquet Co., *supra* note 26.

77. Condé Nast Publications, Inc. v. American Greeting Corp., 141 U.S.P.Q. 149 (C.C.P.A. 1964).

78. Contour Chair-Lounge Co., Inc. v. The Englander Co., Inc., 139 U.S.P.Q. 285 (C.C.P.A. 1964).

79. Anheuser-Busch, Inc. v. DuBois Brewing Co., 175 F.2d 370 (C.C.A. 3, 1959).

80. Elgin Nat'l Watch Co. v. Illinois Watch Case Co., 179 U.S. 665 (1900).

81. For an excellent discussion of trademark licensing, see U.S. TRADEMARK ASS'N, TRADEMARK LICENSING, DOMESTIC AND FOREIGN (1962).

82. Cohn-Goldwater Mfg. Co. v. Wilk Shirt Corp. 147 F.2d 767 (2d Cir. 1945).

83. *Supra* note 68.

Chapter 11

Deception and Unfair
Trade Practices

A. DECEPTION AND THE FEDERAL TRADE COMMISSION

B. OTHER FEDERAL ANTI-DECEPTION CONTROLS

C. STATE CONTROLS OF DECEPTION

Chapter 11

Deception and Unfair
Trade Practices

A. DECEPTION AND THE FEDERAL TRADE COMMISSION.

1. Deception and Government Controls.

Deception is the foundation upon which a considerable portion of governmental regulation of communications is premised. This is true not only of the Federal Trade Commission (FTC) but also of nearly every other government agency or department—without regard to other regulatory approaches which naturally vary from agency to agency.

Government controls of false and deceptive business practices extend beyond control over a company's paid advertising. The interdiction is against *deceptive and unfair acts and practices*. This may include practically everything which a company does in its external activities. The word "advertising" is not even mentioned—except in the limited context discussed in Section 17 below—in the FTC Act under which the Commission proceeds against deception.

Some of the earliest FTC actions involved deceptive publicity such as an announcement that a company had developed new products or methods,[1] the distribution publicly by one company of deceptive copies of FTC or court records involving a competitor,[2] the use of the "false front" technique.[3]

2. Public Relations Activities and Deception.

When misleading claims or other statements appear in paid advertising, there is generally no question that the FTC or other appropriate government agency has jurisdiction. However, a question may sometimes arise in the practitioner's mind as to the legal status of deceptive news releases, publicity and other PR communications.

Implicit in this duality is the scattered belief that, no matter how effective publicity and public relations may otherwise be, they do not "sell merchandise." This is erroneous. PR literature documents substantially the significant and direct contribution to product sales of publicity and PR—whether it be a news release and its resultant story or a feature article in a magazine. PR has been described as a "profit tool." [4] David Finn writes that public relations "merchandised to the customer" pays off in "sales results that can be measured." [5] A utility company acquires a new franchise and many new customers through its news releases and PR campaign.[6] Among the "well-defined goals and objectives" of publicity and PR is their use "as a sales tool" and in "direct mail advertising." [7] The publicity and other efforts of the ethical pharmaceutical manufacturers, discussed below, further validate these conclusions.

Very much to the point also is the fact that some publicity and similar promotion are intended to be "disguised advertising" as sometimes charged by editors. Publicity has been called "a new means of sales communication" and *Business Week* has pointed out that at times "smart public relations can be more useful and cheaper than advertising." The National Industrial Conference Board, in discussing new product introduction, has found that "these activities (publicity and public relations) are more important than the paid advertising." [8]

From all of this we can only conclude that such activities do "sell merchandise." Since this is true, deception therein should be and is actionable if material. See Section 5 below.

Even a casual examination of "new product news" in the press indicates that editors are careful to distinguish between it and "news" in its usual sense. The editor alters somewhat the language of the release. A typical item as printed may read, "This new model *is said to have* 75% greater capacity." The editor has inserted "is said to have" in place of the news release's "has." This editorial perspective is indicative of the true nature of the release and the disavowal of editorial responsibility for the accuracy of the "news" being printed.

It is interesting to note in this connection that in 1923 N. W. Ayer circulated to editors a statement of the principles upon which its publicity releases were based. One of them was to vouch for the truthfulness of the release.[9] Presumably every reputable company and PR man will assume this responsibility. This would apply, not only as to the product characteristics, but also as to the company's status, resources, personnel, etc. These publicity ploys, if deceptive, are as much subject to FTC action as misrepresentations about the product. See Section 7 below.

Legal editorial attitudes generally confirm this. One such comment points out: [10]

> "Deceptive acts or practices in commerce" are unlawful. The phrase "acts or practices" is so broad and inclusive that the question as to whether a particular business activity is subject to the law has rarely been at issue. *It appears that any business activity may be subject if it tends to make a deceptive impression on a customer or the public.* (Emphasis added.)

This broad language would apply, without question, to deceptive releases, publicity and other relevant company communications.

Except for the element of payment, there is very little practical difference between the news item based on a news release and the so-called "reader" advertisement. Under the Bourne Newspaper Publicity Law of 1912 such "readers" must be marked ADVERTISEMENT if paid for. A misleading claim in such an item would undoubtedly be legally deceptive.

In 1967 the FTC had occasion to comment critically about the confusion and deception which may arise from a failure to use ADVERTISEMENT over a reader and has pointed out "that in some instances the format of the advertisement may so exactly duplicate a news or feature story as to render the caption ADVERTISEMENT meaningless and incapable of curing the deception." [11] Although the FTC statement did not so indicate, it appears that it was based upon the mailing of many thousands of copies of an article-format advertisement which had originally carried ADVERTISEMENT but did not carry such legend when reproduced and mailed.

Even if the issuer of the release attempts to claim that it was the news medium—not the issuer—which actually brought the deception to the attention of the public, the issuer would be met by the well-accepted rule that one may not "insulate himself against responsibility for deception" if he "furnishes another with the means of consummating a fraud." [12]

The *Murray Space Shoe* case [13] is an interesting example of the judicial attitude toward culpability for deception arising from PR or publicity. In this case, the company apparently did not use paid advertising. Instead it circulated reprints of articles about it and its special shoes. These articles had previously appeared in various newspapers and magazines. From the articles themselves, as quoted by the court, it is clear that some of them were based on interviews with Mr. Murray, the inventor of the special shoes. Both the FTC and the court held that the deceptive and exaggerated claims which appeared in the articles and reprints were proper basis for an FTC order.

What has been said about news releases and publicity applies also to the house organ, discussed at length in Chapter 18. If an article in a house organ promotes a product with deceptive claims, this also would be actionable. See Chapter 18, Sections 5 and 6. Also, cases such as *Griffin v. Medical Society* [14] speak of articles even in publicly circulated magazines or society journals as "someone's advertisement in disguise."

The validity of such a judgment and view can be specifically documented—aside from the general sales effects of publicity and PR as discussed in Section 2 above. Dover speaks of "sales achievements" resulting from material contained in house organs. He points to "millions of dollars in sales for Allis-Chalmers from its *Reporter* including the sale of equipment for an entire brick plant, carload-lot sales to an entirely new customer for Monsanto's weed-killing chemical sprays through an article in *Monsanto Magazine,* increased electrical consumption because of a story in Hartford Electric Light Company's *Illuminator.*[15]

It follows that an article in a house organ containing a deceptive representation would be actionable if it dealt in a material aspect with a product or the company. This would include direct descriptions of products and their uses, case histories of product use and any other type of article or item which deceptively promoted the company or its products.

The use of promotional articles as vehicles of deception came under attack in the 1959–62 "Kefauver drug hearings." One editorial source, in commenting thereon, said: [16]

> The makers of so-called "ethical pharmaceuticals" . . . have been having some rough times at the Kefauver hearings. Their products are not advertised to the public, but like most other businesses, the pharmaceutical companies have an inescapable need to inform the public on various phases of their activities. . . .
> [T]hey rely on "public relations." But public relations is an uncertain tool. So, in some cases, various refinements are introduced to get maximum exposure for the client's sales story.
> The Kefauver committee testimony makes it clear that ethical standards of manufacturers of ethical drugs are not necessarily of the highest order when it comes to planting news stories beneficial to the promotion of their products, . . .

There is nothing magic about the fact that advertising is paid for. A deception charge can be premised on many different things. Thus, the words of a salesman are attributable to his employer and if such language —oral though it be—is deceptive, misleading or unfair, it can be, and has been, the basis for FTC action. The carefully prepared news release, officer's speech or interview, or other company communication is certainly as much a "company act" as the statement of a salesman in the field.

There is always the danger that an editor may delete or distort parts of a news release. As a result the news story as it finally runs may be deceptive even though it was quite proper and truthful when prepared and issued by the company. The editor is not the agent of the company. As an independent editor, his actions cannot be legally attributable to the honest company or PR man. As to other aspects of this problem, see Chapter 1, Section 10.

3. Incidence of Deception in PR Material.

It is, of course, impossible to assay the degree or frequency of deception in this context. Yet there is definite evidence that it exists—disagreeable though this conclusion may be.

Among the reasons periodically given by editors for refusing to run releases are inaccuracy and misleading content, as discussed more fully in Chapter 4, Section 20. From time to time the public relations trade press itself contains news of such "dishonest publicity practices." Thus, in 1967, *Public Relations News* reported the comments of an electronics trade publication which maintained that it "recently discovered four misstatements in a publicity release about a new line being introduced by a highly respected manufacturer." [17] *PRN* then pleads for "candor and scrupulous accuracy in all publicity work."

At about the same time the *Public Relations Journal* commented editorially upon a survey of media refusals of releases. One important element was "too many handouts contain misleading angles." The editorial then added that "these public relations practices (including 'misleading angles') appear much too often on similar 'universal' lists of complaints from the press." [18]

Scattered through the rulings of the SEC is evidence of misrepresentation in financial news releases, appearances before meetings of financial analysts, etc.—some thereof apparently "qualifying" for criminal prosecution. See Chapter 22 generally.

Inaccuracy and false claims or representations are not confined to news releases. They may appear, for example, in newsfilm and news clips. There is evidence that TV station news editors are wary of being subjected to "ridicule" and insist on "honest dealings" since they "have no time to check every detail of a film story." [19]

This continuing comment from such varied and responsible sources is significant. We can only conclude that this is a meaningful and continuing problem, whatever its quantitative impact may be.

4. Importance and Jurisdiction of the Federal Trade Commission.

The Federal Trade Commission is the principal "policeman" of business practices, including its promotional, PR, advertising, merchandising and marketing efforts, particularly as they may involve deceptive practices and techniques. Accordingly, its philosophy, attitudes, definitions and rulings—especially when confirmed by the courts—are particularly significant. As developed below, other government agencies look to the FTC in their own scrutiny and control of deception within their respective jurisdictions.

The jurisdiction of the FTC stems from the broad and ill-defined language of Section 5 of the FTC Act. Historically the first case before the FTC involved deception. However, the Commission's approach in its earlier days was the protection of competition—not of the public or the consumer. It was only the impact of deception upon a company's competitors which incited FTC action. It was not until 1938 that the FTC was legally competent to view deception as a direct danger to the customer and the consumer.[20]

The FTC now attacks deception by virtue of its jurisdiction over both "unfair methods of competition" and "unfair or deceptive acts and practices." This is a statutory concept well-rooted in federal regulatory law.[21] It is the outgrowth, in part, of the common law doctrine of "unfair competition." Unfair competition itself is an ever-changing and evolving concept. Similarly the perimeter of FTC controls is changing and expanding. This is particularly true as to:

(a) the Commission's attitude toward the need for more affirmative disclosure—as against the more passive negative attacks on active deception, and

(b) its defense and enforcement of national policy, such as civil rights,[22] and

(c) its more aggressive drive for "consumer protection," discussed more fully in Chapter 19, Sections 25 to 29.

5. Federal Trade Commission Deception Guidelines.

As defined by the FTC, a deceptive practice is one which has the capacity to deceive in a material aspect. This basic and simple definition is not always easy to apply to specific fact-situations.

Over the years the FTC and the courts have developed a series of general rules implementing this basic definition. Most of these rules deal with deception but some apply to acts and representations which are probably better defined as unfair. These rules have proved to be valuable guidelines, both as to past rulings of the FTC and for prophylactic screening by business.

(a) Representations must be considered in their entirety and as they would be read or heard by those to whom they are intended to appeal.[23]

(b) The law is not made for the protection of experts only but for the public which includes the ignorant, the unthinking and the credulous who do not stop to analyze but are governed by appearance and general impression.[24]

(c) Appeals addressed to a special audience (children, the elderly or "the worried") are held to stricter standards even though they might not deceive a typical reader or consumer.[25]

(d) Actual deception need not be shown and the capacity to deceive is sufficient to make a statement deceptive.[26]

(e) The literal truth of the representation is no defense if the net overall impression is misleading.[27]

(f) Only material untruths—those contributing to the buying decision—are legally deceptive and actionable but there is a tendency to consider all misrepresentations as material.[28]

(g) If the statement is ambiguous and one meaning is true and the other false, it will be considered as deceptive in order to protect the public and competition.[29]

(h) An intent to deceive is not a prerequisite to legal deception but existence of such intent may be definitive in a "close" case.[30]

(i) Even if the maker does not know that the representation is false, the capacity to deceive and the effect on competition are the same.[31]

(j) False and deceptive claims are construed differently and more strictly than is contract fraud or deceit.[32]

(k) Material misrepresentations as to extrinsic matters—those which do not deal with product quality—such as product source, price, etc.—are also deceptive.[33]

(l) The public is deceived if it does not get what it has been promised even though it may actually get something better, because of the discrepancy between representation and fact.[34]

(m) Subjective claims and representations such as those dealing with flavor or taste generally are not screened by the same standards as are objective claims, subject to demonstrable proof.[35]

(n) "Puffing" and the making of clearly exaggerated claims such as "amazing" are normally not considered deceptive.[36]

(o) Partisan and favorable presentation of truthful and fair claims is not deceptive.[37]

(p) A statement may be deceptive even though it is true if it does not prove the claim purportedly being validated.[38]

(q) Silence may be actively deceptive if the failure to make a limiting or explanatory statement is necessary because of the nature of the affirmative claims actually made.[39]

(r) Language and words will be construed and interpreted in their usual or primary meaning and a high degree of proof will be required to show that they were used in some special or secondary meaning.[40]

(s) Unfair or deceptive practices include deception in appeals or announcements which make the "first contact" with the prospect—such as "lead pullers" or new product news, even though they may not themselves affect the eventual buying decision.[41]

6. Other FTC-Administered Anti-Deception Laws.

The FTC Act is not the only Congressional mandate administered and policed by the FTC. Subsections (a) to (e) below deal with such other laws—at least as to their anti-deception aspects.

(a) Wool Products Labeling Act. (1939) [42]

Under this Act, wool products must be properly labeled and an affirmative disclosure of fabric content made. It is an unfair or deceptive practice to misbrand a wool product. Details as to required labeling are contained in printed materials readily obtainable from the FTC. If the wool product is misrepresented or deceptively promoted, this would also be actionable under the FTC Act. However, the Wool Products Labeling Act deals essentially with the deceptive labeling.

(b) Fur Products Labeling Act. (1951) [43]

This statute protects against misbranding and false labeling of fur products and the false and deceptive advertising of such products. Section 5 of the Act defines "falsely or deceptively advertised" as any "advertisement, representation, public announcement, or notice which is intended to aid, promote, or assist directly or indirectly in the sale or offering for sale" of any fur product. In other words, the deceptive practice may take place, not only in a paid advertisement in its commonly accepted sense, but in any "public announcement" or other communication intended to aid in making the sale.

Section 5 of the Act then goes on to explain six specific matters which will constitute deception. These explanations, together with much other useful information concerning the advertising, promotion and sale of furs and fur products, are contained in materials readily obtainable from the FTC.

(c) Flammable Fabrics Act. (1953) [44]

This law does not concern deception. Its thrust is against movement in interstate commerce of wearing apparel and fabrics which are so highly flammable as to be dangerous when worn about the body.

(d) Textile Fibre Products Identification Act. (1958) [45]

This act protects producers and consumers against both the misbranding and false advertising of the fibre content of textile fibre products. Section 3 of the Act interdicts the advertising of such products which are "misbranded or falsely or deceptively advertised within the meaning of this Act or the rules and regulations promulgated thereunder, . . ." Section 4 then defines advertising disclosure requirements:

> [A] textile fibre product shall be considered to be falsely or deceptively advertised if a disclosure or implication of fibre content is made in any written advertisement . . . unless the information as that required to be shown on the stamp, tag, label or other identification . . . is contained in the heading, body or other part of such written advertisement, except that the percentages of the fibre present . . . need not be stated.

This provision seems to limit the requirements to the more customary forms of advertising and probably does not include publicity releases.

(e) Fair Packaging and Labeling Act. (1966) [46]

This statute, which became effective July 1, 1967, deals with detailed requirements as to consumer-product labeling such as label location and type size of certain information. It is administered by both the FTC and FDA. As this is written, the FTC has not yet promulgated final regulations, necessary to implement the Act's provisions. This law does not actually involve deception or deceptive practices, unless deception can be postulated on the basis of lack of label information or the misdirection of customer attention by placement of label information.

7. Subject Matter of Deception.

The FTC, having jurisdiction over false and deceptive practices in all industries and as to all products—subject to certain limited exceptions—has developed a broadly-applicable "catalog of deception." Any material deceptive or unfair practices in connection with the following product characteristics, representations, promotional methods or competitive activity, may be considered as actionable.[47]

Business status, advantages or connections.
Comparative data or merits.
Competitors and their products.
Composition of goods.
Condition of goods.
Conditions of manufacture.
Connection of others with goods.

Content.
Dealer or seller assistance.
Demand, business or other opportunities.
Earnings and profits.
Fictitious affidavits.
Fictitious or misleading guarantees.
Financing.
Formal regulatory and statutory requirements.
Free goods or services.
Free test or trial.
Government approval, action, connection or standards.
History of product or offering.
Identity of product.
Individual attention.
Individual special selection or situation.
Indorsements, approvals and testimonials.
Jobs and employment service.
Legality or legitimacy.
Limited offers or supply.
Manufacture or preparation.
Nature of product or service.
Old, reclaimed or reused product as new.
Opportunities.
Patent or other rights.
Premiums and prizes.
Prices.
Prize contests.
Promotional sales plans.
Qualities or properties of product or service.
Quality of product or service.
Quantity.
Refunds, repairs and replacements.
Results.
Safety.
Sample, offer or order conformance.
Scientific or other relevant facts.
Scientific tests.
Seals, emblems and awards.
Securities.
Services.
Size or weight.
Source or origin.

Special or limited offers.
Specifications or standards conformance.
Success, use or standing.
Surveys.
Terms and conditions.
Tests and investigations.
Trademark registration or use.
Trade secrets.
Type or variety.
Undertakings, in general.
Unique nature or advantages.
Value.

8. Parties Responsible for Deception.

A wide variety of individuals and business entities may be responsible for deceptive promotion or advertising. The basic test applied by the FTC as to joinder of respondents is that it considers responsible all who create, place, contribute to, are responsible for, or have control over the misrepresentations.[48] Each case stands on its own feet—varying according to the actual responsibilities and factual situation.

(a) The Company.

The primary responsibility is that of the company which uses and benefits from the questionable practice. Ordinarily, this is the business, the name of which appears on or in the promotional material. However, some cases have included as respondents subsidiary or affiliated companies which are engaged in or actually a part of the deceptive program.[49]

(b) Corporate Owners, Officers and Employees.

In addition to the company, those of its owners, officers and employees who control or manage its sales and promotional practices are frequently joined in the FTC action.[50] The purpose is to prevent the culpable individuals from "folding up" an existing corporation after an Order is entered and thereafter reorganizing under a different name or as a new entity and resuming the offending promotion. PR or advertising directors or managers responsible for the original advertising or release sometimes fall into this category.

(c) Public Relations or Advertising Agency Firm.

These service entities have long been joined as respondents in appropriate cases.[51] Since the "payola" and quiz show scandals of 1959 and

1960, this policy has been consistent. These entities are now joined if they "prepared and placed" or "participated in" the deceptive representations or were the "active, if not the prime mover" in creating the advertising or if they were "significantly contributing" to it.[52] As the Commission's original decision in the *Colgate* case put it, the agency will be held liable if it can ". . . be shown to have had such connection with the wrong as would make [it] an accomplice were it a crime, or a joint tortfeasor, were the corporation an individual." [53]

While these cases have usually involved advertising agencies and TV commercials, the same inclusionary rules apply to PR firms under similar circumstances of control, creativity, origination or participation.

(d) Agency Officers and Employees.

In some cases advertising agency officers or employees have been held equally culpable.[54] Usually such respondents will be top officers of the company or the account executive handling the client in question. In some of these cases, the agency employee was originally joined as a respondent but later dropped from the case by preliminary Commission ruling or the action dismissed as to him for lack of sufficient evidence.[55]

(e) Third-Party Producers and Sources.

If the offending promotion or advertising is not prepared by the advertiser or its agency but by another third-party source—with no knowledge of any irregularities by advertiser or agency—such third-party originating source will be liable.[56] The company and the agency probably will not be held. In the 1964 *General Motors* case [57] which was terminated with a consent order, it was made clear that the agency would not be responsible if it did not participate in the erroneous tests (the representations in issue), "neither knew nor had reason to know" of the deception and acted "in good faith upon a written certification signed by the testing agency or the manufacturer with respect to the factors tested."

As to the testing agency or the other outside source, it would be culpable as participating in or contributing to the deception—as an accomplice or joint tortfeasor.

(f) Media.

The responsibility of media for carrying deceptive advertising or releases does not appear to have been definitely settled.[58] It does appear that media will be joined by the Commission under appropriate facts. In 1960 FTC Chairman Kintner said: [59]

> The Commission has rarely joined the publishing medium as a party respondent and then only when the medium was engaged in

the promotion of a product on a profit-sharing basis. However, there is no express exemption for media.[60] The question whether the Commission *should* join media in appropriate cases has been the subject of much public comment recently.

In my opinion the public and moral responsibility . . . must be shared by the media—the newspapers, magazines, periodicals and the broadcasting media. Whether this sharing of public and moral responsibility also should involve a sharing of legal responsibility to the extent that media are cited as parties respondent is another matter, involving serious policy considerations.

Chairman Kintner also warned, in discussing broadcasters' responsibilities: [61]

It may well be . . . that broadcasters have prepared and produced advertisements for radio and television. In such cases where it appears that the law may have been violated, . . . the broadcaster might well be in the same position as the advertising agency. On the broader question of including a broadcaster as a respondent where it is solely the conduit of the allegedly false and deceptive advertisement, a different and more novel legal theory is involved.

The reference to prior joinder of the medium by Mr. Kintner is probably premised on cases such as *Chamber of Commerce v. FTC* [62] in which a trade paper was ordered to cease "[p]ublishing . . . false and misleading statements concerning the financial standing, the business or the business methods of . . . Equity Co-operative Exchange . . ." The Minneapolis Chamber of Commerce apparently was seeking to end the competition from the Exchange in certain grain operations. Other elements in the case indicate that the Chamber and the medium were themselves deeply involved in the questioned representations and that the paper was not merely a vehicle for deceptive articles or advertising.

Comments similar to those of Chairman Kintner have since been made by Chairman Dixon.[63] However, no case has yet come to our attention in which the medium has been held responsible for deception in the usual frame of reference. As to the right or duty of the medium to refuse to carry advertising generally, see Chapter 4, Sections 19 to 25.

B. OTHER FEDERAL ANTI-DECEPTION CONTROLS.

The Federal Trade Commission is not the only federal agency or activity which deals with deception. Sections 9 to 17 do not necessarily include all of the federal policing agencies or corporations but these are among the most important and are typical and representative.

9. Food and Drug Administration.

Except for regulation of prescription drug advertising discussed below, the Food and Drug Administration is not concerned with deceptive advertising of food, drugs, cosmetics and devices—otherwise under its control as discussed in Chapter 19.[64] The Federal Trade Commission controls such product promotion and advertising. The FDA's interest in deception stems from control of label and labeling (misbranding) of such products. In 1954 the FDA and the FTC formalized these separate areas of responsibility and competence with a liaison statement.[65]

However, under the doctrine of "accompanying literature" as part of labeling, the FDA has extended its grasp—approved by the courts—over some materials which are essentially promotion or advertising.[66] Sales or explanatory literature will fall within this definition if supplementary to the label even though the buyer receives it apart from the product.[67]

The FDA considers a product misbranded if its "labeling is false and misleading in any particular." [68] This is one of the most important departures from the materiality requirement of the FTC referred to in Section 5(f) above. Otherwise, essentially the same rules about deception are applied by the FDA and the FTC. See Section 5 above. Thus, labels have been held misleading if they deceive the group to which they are intended to appeal; if they are ambiguous; if they are factual but "taken as a whole" are misleading; the construction is to be against the seller.[69]

The FDA is, however, more strict about affirmative disclosures than is the FTC. It requires reference to any respectable contrary authorities if probative authorities are mentioned or discussed even though the latter are more substantial. Problems can be avoided by obtaining from the FDA an advisory letter approving a label in advance.[70]

Another source of deception control is the power of the FDA to establish standards of identity of specific foods to "promote honesty and fair dealing in the interest of consumers." This includes dietary foods and "economic adulteration" of other foods with substitutes.[71]

Since 1964 the FDA has had control of prescription drug advertising.[72] The regulations thus far issued attempt to avoid deception by requiring substantial affirmative disclosure—particularly as to the drug's generic name [73]—as against its brand name—and of a summary of side effects, contraindications and effectiveness. Generally, the approach is to require a "fair balance" between the favorable and unfavorable in advertising the drug.[74]

10. Alcohol and Tobacco Tax Division, Internal Revenue Service.

Alcoholic beverages are probably the subject of more closely policed controls than any other type of product except, perhaps, drugs. Most of these deal with deceptive advertising and labeling and promotion.[75]

The Alcohol and Tobacco Tax Division administers and controls advertising content. Its Regulations 4, 5 and 7 refer respectively to the labeling and advertising of wine, distilled spirits and malt beverages. Each Regulation is separate, but they have much in common insofar as deceptive advertising of their respective subject matter is concerned.

The definition of deception follows rather closely that of the FTC, forbidding any statement "which is false or misleading in any material particular." While allowance for "puffing" is made, unrestrained use of superlatives is frowned upon.[76]

Also forbidden is "any statement, design, device or representation of or relating to analyses, standards or tests, *irrespective of falsity,* which [are found] to be likely to mislead the consumer." (Emphasis added.) [77] The ATTD also interdicts misleading guarantees, defining such deception as "any statement, design, device or representation of or relating to any guarantee, *irrespective of falsity,* which [is found] likely to mislead the consumer." (Emphasis added.) This goes beyond mere falsity in both references since even truthful guarantees and test results are banned provided they mislead the consumer.

11. Federal Home Loan Bank Board; Other Federal Financial Institution Control Agencies.

Various types of financial institutions are subject to deception controls by several federal agencies or corporations. Important and typical are the savings and loan associations, jurisdiction over which falls to the Federal Home Loan Bank Board and the Federal Savings and Loan Insurance Corporation. The FSLIC anti-deception provision—applicable to all federally-chartered associations and all insured state-chartered associations —is broad and blunt.[78]

> *Advertising must be accurate.* No association shall use advertising
> . . . *or make any representation* which is inaccurate in any partic-
> ular or which in any way misrepresents its services, contracts, in-
> vestments or financial condition. (Emphasis added.)

Two aspects of this regulation are worthy of specific note:

(a) "Representation" is mentioned as disjunctive from "advertising." This includes all forms of promotional or public relations statements dealing with the indicated subjects.

(b) The usual (FTC) requirement of materiality has been removed. See Section 5(f) above. The ban is broad and without exception. In theory at least, even the most minor or seemingly unimportant deviation from fact could render an association subject to inquiry and possible sanctions—even if it did not deceive. It appears that FHLBB polices such deceptive practices closely and "when practices have been subject to criticism, informal communications have been utilized, with desired results." [79] No formal proceedings have yet been instituted despite the scope of the regulation.

A specific and special provision of the Federal Deposit and Insurance Corporation (FDIC) seeks to prevent deception as to FDIC membership of the institution and the extent of insurance by prescribing in precise detail certain *mandatory* signs and advertising requirements, subject to certain defined options and exceptions. An exact "official advertising statement" is required.[80]

The provisions of the other agencies relative to national banks and banks with accounts insured by the FDIC, etc. may be taken as generally similar.

As evidence of this, several of the agencies and corporations on occasion cooperate when faced with interrelated or similar problems involving deceptive promotional practices by institutions under their respective controls. In December, 1966, for example, the Controller of the Currency, FDIC, FHLBB and the Federal Reserve Board simultaneously sent similar letters to controlled institutions outlawing certain "misleading claims" about the interest rates being paid. This action had apparently become necessary because of the "rate war" among the institutions arising from the then tight money market.[81]

The "principles," as they were called, are of continuing importance because of the highly competitive money needs and practices of the various types of institutions involved. They are:

> The interest rate paid depositors or shareholders must be stated in terms of the simple annual rate of interest. Neither total returns over a period of time, as a result of compounding interest, nor the annual rate achieved by compounding may be used unless the simple annual rate is given equal prominence.
> Advertisements showing that a depositor may—through combining accounts in various ways—receive insurance on accounts totalling more than $15,000 Federal insurance ceiling are forbidden.
> The word "profit" may not be used to describe the depositors' earnings of interest on deposits.
> Financial institutions will be required to state the fact if an advertised rate of interest is payable only on accounts beyond a specified size or accounts held for specific lengths of time.

12. Securities and Exchange Commission.

Restrictions on securities promotion are deeply rooted in the deception concept. However, such controls of the Securities and Exchange Commission, the New York Stock Exchange, the National Association of Securities Dealers, and other regulatory bodies are discussed in Chapter 22.

13. Department of Agriculture.

The Department of Agriculture, through the Agricultural Marketing Service, enforces the provisions of the Packers and Stockyards Act (1921).[82] Section 202 of the Act prohibits an "unfair and deceptive practice or device" by a concern under its jurisdiction. Action has been taken against deceptive advertising as well as against promotional practices probably more properly classified as unfair.

In one case a packer claimed that a pound of its frankfurters was "as nourishing as a pound of steak" and that "we use whole rounds, where your round steaks come from," contrary to the facts.[83] The packer accepted a consent order whereby it agreed to stop

> . . . representing in any advertisement, by *use of any statement,* or any photograph, illustration or sketch, alone or accompanied by a statement, directly or by implication, the nutritive value of its frankfurters or the class or grade of the meat used by [it] in the manufacture of its frankfurters. (Emphasis added.)

Proceedings have also been brought because of alleged bait advertising as an unfair and deceptive practice.[84]

In 1962 the Agricultural Marketing Service issued a statement of policy against promotional plans whereby prizes are given to retailers and their employees under the so-called "point system" to promote the retail sale of the packer's products.[85] Several proceedings were later brought for violation of this rule and consent orders were accepted in both cases.[86]

The rationale of the policy statement was the prevention of "a marketing practice under which sellers tend to compete in the sale of their products on the basis of . . . personal gifts, rather than on the basis of the merits and prices of the competing products." See Chapter 13, Section 1 for further discussion of this governmental attitude.

The Department also administers the Poultry Products Inspection Act and under this statute has, among other things, created "standards of identity" for various poultry products. Under a 1964 regulation implementing this function, the Department maintained that it was deceptive to label and promote as "chicken" soup a product which contained less than two percent poultry meat on a ready-to-serve basis.

This regulation was, in effect, upheld by the Supreme Court when it refused to review a circuit court ruling approving the regulation and the department's power to make it.[87]

14. Civil Aeronautics Board.

The Civil Aeronautics Board, under Section 411 of the Federal Aviation Act of 1958,[88] may order a carrier or ticket agent to end any "unfair or deceptive practices or unfair methods of competition in air transportation or the sale thereof." This provision was enforced by the CAB against an airline held responsible for falsely advertising and otherwise promoting "lowest fares in history." [89] Public relations releases are known to be scrutinized by the CAB in addition to the carriers' paid advertising; and, in appropriate cases, warning letters have been issued.

15. Federal Communications Commission.

The Federal Communications Commission has jurisdiction over "false and deceptive advertising over the air." [90] This control is indirect and delayed, although of a continuing nature. It is implemented, in substantial part, by a general notice issued to station licensees, advising them to adhere to the rulings and other pronouncements of the Federal Trade Commission, which releases and circulates such materials directly and regularly to all licensees.[91] The FTC and FCC have issued a liaison statement dealing with their consultation program.[92] The FCC notice to licensees is based on this statement.

At the same time, if the FCC is alerted to any specific deceptive broadcast advertisement, it seeks an explanation from the broadcaster about it. When a station license comes up for renewal, the station's file is carefully reviewed. If it contains such correspondence, etc. and other materials referring to the station's carrying deceptive advertising or itself using such advertising—including deceptive use of ratings as to share of market or viewers—such matters are considered in the renewal proceedings. Fines and forfeitures have been levied against stations or applicants for carrying bait advertising and other forms of deceptive advertising,[93] including their own promotion. See Chapter 13, Section 29.

16. Post Office Department.

The principal deception control of the Post Office Department is founded on the so-called postal fraud statutes, of which there are two, one criminal and the other administrative.[94] These laws both require use of the mails to obtain money or property by means of false or fraudulent pretenses with an intent to defraud.[95] Mail fraud cases—using that term broadly—carry heavier sanctions than do the deceptive advertising procedures of the FTC and the other federal and state agencies discussed throughout this chapter.

This requirement of intent in both types of cases makes conviction more difficult but by the same token the sanctions are more drastic: possible prison sentence under the criminal statute and the marking of addressee's mail "fraudulent"—plus other sanctions—under the administrative statute.

Another difficulty under the fraud statutes is that a difference of professional or other competent opinion about the allegedly false or fraudulent statements may result in dismissal. Although the drastic 1902 rule of the *American School of Magnetic Healing* case [96] has been interpreted and applied more narrowly, it would appear that allegedly deceptive claims can be justified as honest opinion only if there is a recognized conflict of opinion on the subject.[97] This, of course, is a less vigorous rule applied by the FTC, even though the penalty, if the government is successful, is more severe.

In a fraud prosecution—even if it is successful—the fraud order must be limited to the prior fraudulent material. It cannot be broad and general or be used as a basis for later enforcement proceedings arising from dissimilar deception as may a broad FTC order.[98]

17. Oleomargarine Amendment to the FTC Act.

The FTC Act contains a special provision, added by subsequent amendment, as to false and deceptive oleomargarine advertising. It is different from the usual, loosely-worded, broad "FTC approach." It stems from the nature of the product and the continuing "feud" between dairy interests and oleo producers and marketers. This definition is: [99]

> In the case of oleomargarine or margarine an advertisement shall be deemed misleading in a material respect if in such advertisement representations are made or suggested by statement, word, grade designation, design, device, symbol, sound, or any combination thereof, that such oleomargarine or margarine is a dairy product, except that nothing contained herein shall prevent a truthful, accurate, and full statement in any such advertisement of all the ingredients contained in such oleomargarine or margarine.

This is one of the relatively few statutes which define prohibited advertising with particularity. Broad and general statutes are of little basic help until they are explained, supplemented or applied by court decisions, agency rulings, rules, guides and other similar materials. When legislators see fit to particularize as to the nature of the deception in question, we have better initial and continuing guidelines.

C. STATE CONTROLS OF DECEPTION.

18. Importance.

Despite the powers of the Federal Trade Commission, state regulation of deception continues important—in fact, it may be considerably increasing in impact. The FTC's jurisdiction is limited to interstate commerce. The intrastate vacuum must be filled—and is filled—by state law. While actual enforcement—criminal or civil—may have been thus far sporadic and limited, there is a growing trend toward wider and deeper enforcement by both attorneys general and local district attorneys. Furthermore, the growing "consumer protection" movement—discussed in Chapter 19, Sections 25 to 29—is giving new impetus in many states to the attack on deceptive practices of all kinds including advertising and other forms of local promotion.[100]

19. Sources of Specific Information.

The deception control statutes of the various states and the ordinances of the larger cities are not well compiled. The two best such compilations are:

(a) "State Advertising Legislation," a study published in 1945 by *Printers' Ink* and prepared by Burt W. Roper of the Bureau of Foreign and Domestic Commerce of the Department of Commerce.

(b) The Statutory Appendix to a lengthy Note, "The Regulation of Advertising" in Volume 56 of the *Columbia Law Review,* beginning at page 1097 thereof and published in November, 1956.

Additional sources for information as to statutes subsequent to 1956 are the Better Business Bureaus of the larger cities, the Legislative Bureaus of the various state legislatures and the Attorney General's offices in several states.

In states which have Consumer Frauds Bureaus, Consumer Bureaus or Consumer Counsels—the names vary—these organizations have considerable information about such statutes, limited usually to the state in question, and their enforcement. See Chapter 19, Section 29.

20. Printers' Ink Statutes.

Beginning in 1911, so-called Printers' Ink Statutes—sponsored by that trade publication—have been adopted. Forty-seven of the fifty states now have them on their books. These are criminal statutes. Their actual form varies somewhat but the following is the text as originally suggested and adopted in many states:

> Any person, firm, corporation or association who, with intent to sell or in any way dispose of merchandise, securities, services, or anything offered by such person, firm, corporation or association, directly or indirectly, to the public for sale or distribution, or with intent to increase the consumption thereof, or to induce the public in any manner to enter into any obligation relating thereto, or to acquire title thereto, or an interest therein, makes, publishes, disseminates, circulates, or places before the public, or causes, directly or indirectly, to be made, published, disseminated, circulated, or placed before the public, in this State, in a newspaper or other publication, or in the form of a book, notice, handbill, poster, bill, circular, pamphlet or letter, or in any other way, an advertisement of any sort regarding merchandise, securities, service or anything so offered to the public, which advertisement contains any assertion, representation or statement of fact which is untrue, deceptive or misleading, shall be guilty of a misdemeanor.

Eight states require proof that the advertiser actually knew of the untrue or deceptive statement and this renders enforcement more difficult. Another eight require proof that the advertiser should have known thereof. Only in larger cities such as New York, Philadelphia and Detroit have any concerted efforts been made to enforce these statutes. Even here, the effort has been limited. It has been estimated that the New York County District Attorney's Office obtains only about ten convictions per year for false advertising—a minimal number inasmuch as most deceptive advertising is probably at the local level—as against interstate advertising subject to the jurisdiction of the FTC.[101]

21. Deceptive Advertising of Specific Commodities.

Many states have "specific-commodity statutes" which contain provisions against deceptive advertising, the product, purpose and language varying considerably. Specific examination of the particular state statute is necessary. A state's general statute against deceptive advertising is not ousted by the specific statute. If there is a relevant specific-product statute, the latter should then be consulted. There are certain types of products which have been covered very widely by specific state deception laws: alcoholic beverages, agricultural products, foods, drugs, dairy products, and securities.

Some specific laws have more value because their meaning fully pinpoints specific types of deceptive practices. These may be enforced and policed by various state licensure bodies. Noteworthy are those dealing with real estate dealers, funeral directors, optometrists, hearing-aid dealers, watchmakers, etc. Other statutes—especially those affecting product, as against service, promotion and advertising—still adhere to the general "false advertising" approach without any significant or meaningful enlargement of that term.

Notes

1. Walter Kidde & Co., 36 F.T.C. 431 (1943).
2. F.T.C. Stips., Nos. 1478, 2105, TRADE REG. REP. ¶7659.48.
3. Adolph Harper, 4 F.T.C. 488 (1922).
4. Skinner, *Public Relations Is a Profit Tool*, P.R.J., April, 1957, at 13.
5. Finn, *Public Relations in Marketing*, in HANDBOOK OF PUBLIC RELATIONS 61 (Stephenson ed. 1960).
6. *A PR Department Helps Win New Customers* (Case Study No. 1081), P.R.N., Oct. 31, 1966, at 3–4.
7. Harris, *Merchandising: The Publicity Pay-Off*, P.R.J., May, 1966, at 30–32.
8. These several quotations are from SELDIN, THE GOLDEN FLEECE 207, 211 (1963).
9. HOWER, HISTORY OF AN ADVERTISING AGENCY 447–48 (1st ed. 1939).
10. TRADE REG. REP., *supra* note 2, at ¶7524.
11. *Statement in Regard to Advertisements That Appear in Feature Article Format*, F.T.C. Release, Nov. 28, 1967.
12. F.T.C. v. Winsted Hosiery Co., 258 U.S. 483 (1922); Irwin v. F.T.C., 143 F.2d 316 (8th Cir. 1944).
13. 304 F.2d 270 (2d Cir. 1962).
14. Griffin v. Medical Society, 11 N.Y.S.2d 109 (1939).
15. DOVER, EFFECTIVE COMMUNICATION IN COMPANY PUBLICATIONS 51–52 (1959).
16. *How to Promote "Unadvertised" Drugs*, A.A., Feb. 19, 1962, at 16.
17. P.R.N., Nov. 6, 1967, at 1.
18. P.R.J., June, 1967, at 6.
19. Kalser, *Newsfilm for Industry*, P.R.J., June, 1958, at 7.
20. For a discussion of the broadened thrust of F.T.C.-administered policing of deceptive and unfair practices, see SIMON, THE LAW FOR ADVERTISING AND MARKETING 499–506 (1956).
21. For an excellent discussion of legislative "delegation" of authority and its limits under such broad mandates to an administrative agency, see JAFFE, JUDICIAL CONTROL OF ADMINISTRATIVE ACTION, ch. 2, at 28–86 (1965); FRIENDLY, THE FEDERAL ADMINISTRATIVE AGENCIES: THE NEED FOR BETTER DEFINITION OF STANDARDS, *passim* (Harvard Law School Holmes Lectures, 1962).
22. See F.T.C. Complaints in Dkt. Nos. 8750 and 8751 as described in F.T.C. Release, Dec. 8, 1967, including separate statement by Chairman Dixon questioning the issuance of the complaints and describing the actions as being "radical" changes in F.T.C. policy.
23. Charles of the Ritz Distributors Corp. v. F.T.C., 143 F.2d 676 (2d Cir. 1944).
24. Florence Manfacturing Co. v. J. C. Dowd and Co., 178 Fed. 73 (2d Cir. 1910); P. Lorillard Co. v. F.T.C., 186 F.2d 52 (2d Cir. 1950).
25. Doris Savitch v. F.T.C., 218 F.2d 817 (2d Cir. 1955), *aff'g, per curiam*, 50

F.T.C. 828 (1954); Stauffer Laboratories, Inc. v. F.T.C., 343 F.2d 75 (9th Cir. 1965).

26. Ford Motors Co. v. F.T.C., 120 F.2d 175 (6th Cir. 1941).

27. Koch v. F.T.C., 206 F.2d 584 (6th Cir. 1953).

28. Pep Boys—Manny, Moe & Jack, Inc. v. F.T.C., 122 F.2d 158 (3d Cir. 1941); F.T.C. v. Royal Milling Co., 288 U.S. 212 (1933).

29. United States v. Ninety-five Bottles of Vinegar, 265 U.S. 438 (1924); Murray Space Shoe Corp. v. F.T.C., 304 F.2d 270 (2d Cir. 1962).

30. F.T.C. v. Algoma Lumber Co., 291 U.S. 67 (1934); Riviera Trading Corp., F.T.C. Dkt. No. 8465, TRADE REG. REP. ¶16,489.

31. Gimbel Bros., Inc. v. F.T.C., 116 F.2d 578 (2d Cir. 1941).

32. F.T.C. v. National Health Aids, Inc. 108 F. Supp. 340 (D.C. Md. 1952).

33. See Note, *Extrinsic Representations in Advertising Under Section 5(a) of the Federal Trade Commission Act*, 114 U. OF PA. L.R. 725 (1966).

34. F.T.C. v. Royal Milling Co., *supra* note 28; Kerran v. F.T.C., 265 F.2d 246 (10th Cir. 1959), *cert. denied*, 361 U.S. 818 (1959).

35. Bristol-Myers Co., 46 F.T.C. 162 (1949), *aff'd*, 185 F.2d 58 (4th Cir. 1950).

36. Kidder Oil Co. v. F.T.C., 117 F.2d 892 (7th Cir. 1941); Carlay Co. v. F.T.C., 153 F.2d 493 (7th Cir. 1946).

37. F.T.C. v. Sterling Drug, Inc., 317 F.2d 669 (2d Cir. 1963).

38. Hutchinson Chemical Co., 55 F.T.C. 1942 (1959).

39. F.T.C. v. Alberty, 44 F.T.C. 475 (1948), *rev'd*, 182 F.2d 36 (D.C. Cir. 1950), *cert. denied*, 340 U.S. 818 (1950); Keele Hair & Scalp Specialists, Inc. v. F.T.C., 275 F.2d 18 (5th Cir. 1960).

40. C. Howard Hunt Pen Co. v. F.T.C., 197 F.2d 273 (3d Cir. 1952).

41. Better Living, Inc. v. F.T.C., 54 F.T.C. 648, *aff'd per curiam*, 259 F.2d 271 (3d Cir. 1958); Exposition Press, Inc. v. F.T.C., 295 F.2d 869 (2d Cir. 1961), *cert. denied*, 370 U.S. 917 (1962).

42. P.L. 850, 76th Cong., 15 U.S.C. §68 (1964).

43. P.L. 110, 82d Cong., 15 U.S.C. §69 (1964).

44. P.L. 88, 83d Cong., 15 U.S.C. §1191 (1964).

45. P.L. 897, 85th Cong., 15 U.S.C. §70 (1964).

46. P.L. 89-753, 35 L.W. 33 (1966).

47. This list is based on the F.T.C. 1953 Annual Report. The full list, without deletions, will be found in SIMON, THE ADVERTISING TRUTH BOOK (1960).

48. See TRADE REG. REP., *supra* note 2, at ¶9527.

49. Regina Corp. v. F.T.C., 322 F.2d 765 (3d Cir. 1963). See generally TRADE REG. REP., *supra* note 2, at ¶¶7524.01, 7524.21, 7527.

50. F.T.C. v. Standard Education Soc'y, 302 U.S. 112 (1937); Standard Distributors, Inc. v. F.T.C., 211 F.2d 7 (2d Cir. 1954).

51. Colgate-Palmolive Co. *et al.*, v. F.T.C., 326 F.2d 517 (1st Cir. 1963), *rev'd*, 380 U.S. 374 (1965); Carter Products, Inc. v. F.T.C., 186 F.2d 821 (7th Cir. 1951); Carter Products, Inc. v. F.T.C., 323 F.2d 523 (5th Cir. 1963); Revco D.S., Inc., *et al.*, F.T.C. Dkt. No. 8576, TRADE REG. REP. ¶17,287 (1965).

52. See cases cited, *supra* note 51.

53. Colgate-Palmolive Co. *et al.*, F.T.C. Dkt. No. 7736, 59 F.T.C. 1452 (1963).

54. Revco D.S., Inc., *supra* note 51; Patterson, F.T.C. Dkt. No. 7318, 56 F.T.C. 478 (1959); Eversharp, Inc., F.T.C. Dkt. No. 7811, 57 F.T.C. 841 (1960); Brown & Williamson Tobacco Co., F.T.C. Dkt. No. 7688, 56 F.T.C. 956 (1960); Standard Brands, F.T.C. Dkt. No. 7737, 56 F.T.C. 1491 (1960).

55. Patterson, *supra* note 54; Dollar Vitamin Plan, Inc., F.T.C. Dkt. Nos. 8636–37, Trade Reg. Rep. ¶17,602.

56. Peerless Products, Inc. v. F.T.C., 284 F.2d 285 (7th Cir. 1960).

57. F.T.C. Dkt. No. C-804, 3 Trade Reg. Rep. ¶25,737 (1964).

58. For a general discussion of media responsibility, see Baum, *Self-Regulation and Antitrust: Suppression of Deceptive Advertising by the Publishing Media,* 12 Syracuse L. Rev. 289 (1961).

59. Kintner, *Media Responsibility in the Improvement of Advertising,* address before the Northwest Newspaper Advertising Executives Association, F.T.C. Release, May 27, 1960, at 9.

60. F.T.C. Act, §14(b), 15 U.S.C. §54(b) (1964).

61. *Self-Discipline or Stricter Governmental Control—Which Will Advertising Choose?* address before the Advertising Federation of America, Washington, D.C., F.T.C. Release, Feb. 5, 1960, at 19.

62. 13 F.2d 673 (8th Cir. 1926).

63. Dixon, *A Look at the Ethics of the Press,* F.T.C. Release, Jan. 16, 1968.

64. The authority of F.D.A. stems from the Federal Food, Drug and Cosmetic Act of 1938, 21 U.S.C. §301 *et seq.*

65. Trade Reg. Rep., *supra* note 2, at ¶9850.

66. Kordel v. United States, 335 U.S. 345 (1948); United States v. Urbitlit, 335 U.S. 355 (1948); Alberty Food Products v. United States, 185 F.2d 321 (9th Cir. 1950).

67. United States v. Vitasafe, 345 F.2d 864 (3d Cir. 1965), *cert. denied,* 382 U.S. 918 (1965).

68. 21 U.S.C. §§343 (a), 352 (a) and 362 (a) (1964).

69. See discussion and cases cited, 80 Harv. L. Rev. 1005, 1106–1107.

70. Research Labs, Inc. v. United States, 167 F.2d 410 (9th Cir. 1948), *cert. denied,* 335 U.S. 843 (1948).

71. 21 U.S.C. §§341, 352 (d), (f) (1964).

72. *Id.* §352 (n) (1964).

73. See Abbott Laboratories v. Gardner, 228 F. Supp. 855 (D.C. Del. 1964), 352 F.2d 286 (3d Cir. 1965), *cert. granted,* 383 U.S. 924 (1966), *rev'd,* 35 L.W. 4433 (1967).

74. Goodrich, *The State of the Law and Compliance,* in Compendium of Medical Advertising 51–54 (1967).

75. For specific regulations and rulings referred to in this section as well as in many others, see CCH Liquor Control Law Reports; Nat'l Better Business Bureau, Do's and Don'ts of Advertising Copy §7.

76. FA-123, Oct. 15, 1937; FA-181, Jan. 6, 1940.

77. FA-181, Jan. 21, 1937; IRS Ruling 54-341, I.R.B. 1954-33, 20.

78. F.S.L.I.C., Rules and Regulations for Insurance of Accounts §563.27 (1966).

79. Letter to author, dated April 7, 1967.

80. FEDERAL DEPOSIT INSURANCE CORP., RULES AND REGULATIONS §§328.1-3 (1964).
81. N.Y. Times, Dec. 19, 1966, at 1, 22.
82. 7 U.S.C. §181 et seq. (1964).
83. Dep't of Agr., P. & S. Dkt. No. 3623 (1965).
84. Dep't of Agr., P. & S. Dkt. No. 3650 (1966).
85. Rule 203.3, 27 F.R. 11254, as corrected, 27 F.R. 11547 (1962).
86. Dep't of Agr., P. & S. Dkt. Nos. 3109 and 3500 (1965).
87. Borden Co. v. Freeman, 369 F.2d 404 (3d Cir. 1966), cert. denied, 35 L.W. 3355 (1967).
88. P.L. 85-726, 72 Stat. 731, 49 U.S.C. §1301, etc. (1965).
89. United States v. Eastern Airlines, Inc. 192 F. Supp. 187, AV. L. REP. ¶17,538 (D.C. Fla. 1961).
90. F.C.C. Inf. Bull. No. 3-G, Dec., 1966.
91. *Licensee Responsibility with Respect to the Broadcast of False, Misleading or Deceptive Advertising,* F.C.C. Release 61-1316, Nov. 7, 1961.
92. *Liaison Between F.C.C. and F.T.C.,* F.T.C. Statement, April 6, 1957, TRADE REG. REP. ¶9565.
93. Journal Co., 2 F.C.C. 609 (1936); WREC Broadcasting Serv., 10 P. & F. RADIO REG. 1323 (1955); MOSER & LAVINE, RADIO AND THE LAW 58 (1959).
94. 18 U.S.C. §1341 (criminal) and 39 U.S.C. §4005 (administrative).
95. Reilly v. Pinkus, 338 U.S. 269 (1949). See also Ague, *Intent to Defraud in Postal Fraud Orders Cases,* 38 TEMPLE L. Q. 61 (1964).
96. 187 U.S. 94 (1902).
97. Reilly v. Pinkus, *supra* note 95; Fanning v. Williams, 173 F.2d 95 (9th Cir. 1949).
98. Donaldson v. Reed Magazine, 333 U.S. 178 (1948); Summerfield v. Sunshine Book Co., 221 F.2d 42 (D.C. Cir. 1954), cert. denied, 349 U.S. 921 (1955).
99. F.T.C. Act, §15, 15 U.S.C. §55 (1964).
100. For useful discussions of state controls and consumer protection by the states see 80 HARV. L. REV. 1005 (1967); 56 COLUM. L. REV. 1018 (1956). The editors of both reviews have explored these poorly documented areas by correspondence with state and other officials and this correspondence is reflected in the Notes at considerable length.
101. A good source of information as to enforcement is the correspondence by editors of the *Harvard Law Review* in the course of their preparation of the Notes referred to, *supra* note 100, and discussed in some detail in notes 49-117 thereof.

Chapter 12

Testimonial Techniques

A. INTRODUCTION

1. Definitions
2. History of Testimonials
3. Public Relations Use of the Testimonial Technique
4. Procurement Methods

B. TESTIMONIALS AND ENDORSEMENTS

5. Paid Testimonials
6. Fictitious Testimonials
7. Deceptive Testimonials
8. Competency of Endorser
9. Testimonial Restrictions in Federal Trade Practice Rules
10. National Better Business Bureau Policy
11. Industry Code Provisions
12. Implied or Indirect Testimonials
13. Testimonial Letters
14. Editorial Endorsements
15. Competitive Endorsements
16. Professional Society Member Testimonials
17. Corporate Endorsements
18. Government Endorsements
19. Requirements for Military Testimonials
20. Use of Professional Models
21. Endorser's Approval of Testimonial
22. Liability of Endorser

C. TEST AND SURVEY RESULTS

23. Use of Test Results
24. Use of Survey Results

D. AWARDS, CERTIFICATIONS AND SEALS

Chapter 12

Testimonial Techniques

A. INTRODUCTION.

1. Definitions.

Traditionally, the terms "testimonial" and "endorsement"—they seem to be used interchangeably—were confined to third-party laudatory statements about a product.[1] Today, the testimonial tool is being varied, extended and expanded. No longer is the basic definition adequate. It is probably more accurate to speak of "testimonial techniques." This seems almost mandatory since many of the same practical and legal postulates and ramifications apply to the newer uses.

Even a "traditional" testimonial may frequently appear without any attribution to the celebrity whose photograph dominates the page. The mere conjunction is sufficient. The increased incidence and exploitation of awards of excellence, certifications, comparative or absolute test results and the various public relations and publicity efforts keyed to third-party sources or identities are all essentially testimonial in character and must be recognized as such.

When a product appears as a prop on the stage, in a motion picture or on television and is handled and used by some well-known and popular star or personality, this is more than mere "reminder" exposure. It is also an implied testimonial with a subtle but cogent effect. See Section 12 below.

We have therefore used "testimonial" and "endorsement" in this broad, modern sense in this chapter unless there is some indication otherwise.

2. History of Testimonials.

The use of the testimonial as a sales device is well rooted in the history of publicity and advertising. Beginning with the wiles of the press agent, the testimonial had a constant appeal and proved itself a potent sales producer. It is difficult to scan a history of advertising—especially if it is illustrated—without being impressed by the frequent incidence of cancer-cure letter testimonials.[2] Other products began to use the testimonial technique. J. Walter Thompson pioneered in the use and expansion of the testimonial but elevated his sights considerably. The testimonial was now based, not on emotionally glowing letters from "a satisfied customer" but rather on the cultured ecstasies of society women and, in at least one instance, of a reigning queen.[3]

The testimonial device is sometimes classified as a "hard sell" technique. It is no surprise that during the depression days of the 1930s the testimonial was used with greater frequency. At the same time, the impact of motion picture and radio stars was increasingly felt and "identification" with such celebrities was a source of popular "escape." Even today, the testimonial has lost nothing of its usefulness although its structure, substance and purpose have changed in certain ways.

The testimonial has been "cleaned up" over the years. The legal requirement that a company may not say in the form of a testimonial anything which it could not otherwise say in its news releases or advertising copy has had a lot to do with this. This has helped to make the testimonial become more believable. The claims it makes out of the mouth of the endorser must be open to substantiation.

The testimonial has had its ups and downs. The paid testimonial, when it first came into use, seemed to be a common reason for attack on the entire testimonial device. The story is told of a publisher who tried to convince an advertising agency "that the paid testimonial was in such bad repute that it had ceased to be an effective advertising weapon." The agency man is said to have insisted: "Well, here is the testimonial. Here is the release signed by the woman herself. What is dishonest about that? Suppose she doesn't use the product. She says she does. She's the liar, not we."[4] Hower tells us that N. W. Ayer in 1923 "refrained from using offensive types of appeal . . . [and] consistently refused to buy testimonials from anyone—film star, society matron or hero of the hour . . ."[5]

3. Public Relations Use of the Testimonial Technique.

The testimonial started life as an advertising device and, of course, continues so today. However, the technique and its allied methods have more and more become public relations tools although in somewhat different dress. The approach may be indirect but it is, nonetheless, the testimonial technique.

Institutional advertising may be the instrument. Perhaps it appears in a company internal house organ reporting appreciative letters from the public about help received from company employees. It may be used in a filmstrip at a P.T.A. meeting showing a happy-faced local housewife (identified by name) making a comment about the company's new anti-pollution filters. The national celebrity who appears in some company-staged event may be the vehicle. A news release may go out, relating suggestions for new product uses received from customers. It may be used in award exploitation. The company's annual report to stockholders may carry a story with pictures about "the youngest stockholder." The company president may be interviewed about a National Cancer Society report showing the company's cigarettes as having the lowest tar and nicotine content.[6]

The device is limited only by the imagination. Yet all of these are essentially testimonial in character. As such, they are subject to most of the same legal rules applicable to the customary product testimonial. See Section 12 below.

4. Procurement Methods.

Testimonials usually are obtained from one of several sources:

    (a) Spontaneous customer letters.

    (b) Professional testimonial bureaus.

    (c) Agents of athletes, actors and others in the limelight.

    (d) Publicity departments of theatrical or motion picture studios.

    (e) Research results including mail surveys and in-depth interviews.

Except for the spontaneous letter, these procurement channels are highly organized. Some athletes and other celebrities have special corporations through which testimonials are obtained. Some persons in public life—perhaps in more dignified callings—handle this aspect of their own public relations through their lecture bureaus or personal agents. The professional testimonial bureau may represent a wide variety and large number of individuals. They will handle all of the details of the procurement, even making sure that the endorser actually uses the product before signing an endorsement. In this context, it is not unusual for a company to supply a prospective endorser with the product in order to assure proper use of the product for a reasonable length of time as a prerequisite to the endorsement.

These highly organized channels are nothing new. They are the outgrowth of earlier disreputable testimonial bureaus which, it is reported, "procured a senator's endorsement for $75.00 and a Congressman's for $40.00."[7]

Organized channels of this sort may simplify testimonial procurement but they may also create a gap between the endorser and the advertiser or

sponsor. This presents no legal problems provided the endorser himself
signs the authorization for use of his name, photograph and testimonial,
personally certifying that he has used the product, the circumstances,
period and results of such use, his opinion of the product, etc. It is not
enough to obtain an authorization signed only by the intermediary. Such
approval may be necessary in a particular sense for other reasons but
should not be relied upon to foreclose privacy actions. This is especially
true in New York, which requires written approval of an individual for
any commercial or advertising use of his name or photograph. See Chapter 8, Section 8. Such a "record" is also necessary for protection against
future Federal Trade Commission investigations and litigation.

B. TESTIMONIALS AND ENDORSEMENTS.

5. Paid Testimonials.

The paid testimonial is today the rule rather than the exception. This
is a "fact of life" undoubtedly well-known and accepted by the public
whatever its substantive opinion of such endorsement may be. At one
time the Federal Trade Commission held that the advertiser's failure to
disclose that a testimonial had been paid for was deceptive. The rule was
changed in 1932 in the *Northam Warren* case [8] where the court held that
such disclosure was not required. The court said:

> Because a prominent person ventures an opinion without being
> requested to do so is no guarantee either of veracity or good judg-
> ment. If the testimonials involved here represent honest belief of
> the endorsers, there is no misrepresentation concerning the prod-
> uct, and no unfair competition is created. We have no right to
> assume that endorsers of commercial products falsify their state-
> ments because they have received compensation. There are no
> misrepresentations and the Commission was without jurisdiction.

Although paid testimonials may be used, nevertheless no claim may
directly or indirectly be made that such testimonials were unsolicited or
unbiased.[9]

The *Northam Warren* case dealt with testimonials in print advertising.
The same rule obtains as to paid broadcast testimonials. However, these
present an interesting aspect of this problem, particularly the "slice of
life" or candid interview type of commercial. The testimonial may be
recorded and filmed on the street—even without the endorser's knowledge. However, the endorser is paid when releases are obtained. Obviously, there should be nothing deceptive about such a commercial or
testimonial.

The Television Code follows this judicially approved rule, merely requiring that "Personal endorsements (testimonials) shall be genuine and reflect personal experience. They shall contain no statements that cannot be supported if presented in the advertiser's own words." [10]

6. Fictitious Testimonials.

A fictitious testimonial is one which was never given by the putative endorser. It may be said to have been created out of the whole cloth. This is not likely to occur with testimonials used by the average reputable company. Today the problem is with the partly fictitious testimonial. It may have been altered from its original form or it may have been used for a product other than the product actually endorsed.

Fictitious testimonials have long been the target of the Federal Trade Commission.[11] Such testimonials are considered to be both a deceptive and unfair trade practice, affecting both the public interest and the user's competitors.

A fictitious testimonial also involves serious exposure to right of privacy actions and even, in appropriate cases, suits for defamation. As to privacy, see Chapter 8, Section 20. As to defamation, the leading case of *Peck v. Tribune Co.*[12] held that the use of a fictitious and unauthorized testimonial of a nurse in favor of a certain brand of whiskey carried an actionable innuendo as to her personal habits. See Chapter 7, Section 7.

Another type of fictitious testimonial is that which uses indefinite and high-sounding claims of endorsement by intangible or ill-defined groups such as "druggists of America," "Hollywood stars," "French and Swiss chefs," "Chambers of Commerce," "independent experts," etc. Many F.T.C. rulings have interdicted such testimonials as unfounded and deceptive.[13]

A claim may be made—often innocently—in the general form of "over 1,000,000 satisfied customers." In the user's mind, this is premised upon sales of the product to over 1,000,000 different buyers. "Buyers" and satisfied customers" are not the same thing, even if but a handful of complaints have been received. Whenever representations of this nature are made, the F.T.C. almost invariably seeks justification—proof which normally is impossible to produce or obtain. Sometimes a survey may be made in order to develop a "ratio of satisfaction" upon which such claims may be premised. Even this is no justification for such claims unless the sample is adequate and the survey properly constructed according to acceptable standards to justify the extrapolation. See Section 24 below.

7. Deceptive Testimonials.

Generally speaking, no claim may be made in a testimonial which could not otherwise be made in the advertising.[14] As to tests of deception generally, see Chapter 11, Section 5.

As with copy claims generally, the misrepresentation, to be actionable, must deal with a material aspect of the claim. In the leading *R. J. Reynolds Tobacco Co.* case,[15] an order had been issued by the F.T.C. prohibiting claims that cigarettes aided digestion, relieved fatigue, etc. It prohibited the use of any testimonials "which were not factually true in *all* respects." On appeal, the court deleted this omnibus requirement and said:

> It seems to us that this all-inclusive language is too broad and goes beyond any concern of the Commission. A testimonial, for instance, might not be "factually true in all respects" but still immaterial to the subject of the instant proceeding in that it bore no relation to the public interest, and it would virtually make the petitioner [the advertiser] an insurer of the truthfulness of every statement contained in a testimonial, no matter how immaterial or beside the issue in controversy it might be.

8. Competency of Endorser.

Even if an endorsement is quite genuine, it still may be legally deceptive if the endorser is not competent to express an opinion on the product or service involved. This lack of competence arises in two ways. The most obvious is for the putative endorser never to have used the product. This occurred, as an example, when Mickey Mantle, in 1961, endorsed a brand of milk which he did not drink. This produced the following comment from the National Better Business Bureau: [16]

> When Mickey Mantle recently promised the Federal Trade Commission that he would quit endorsing a brand of milk he does not drink, he focused attention on a deceptive practice which lowers the standards of the advertising business to those of the charlatan.

The second type of situation in which this occurs deals with the endorser who may have used the product very extensively and be sincerely satisfied with it and yet lacks the training or knowledge to express an opinion about it.[17] This is most likely to occur with drug claims where the endorser has no medical expertise, or with claims for products which require engineering or other technical competence of an endorser.

Failure to use the product will outlaw endorsements as to both objective and subjective characteristics of the product. Lack of expertise or training, however, applies only to objective and not to subjective opinions and endorsements. Thus, opinions about taste or flavor may be given by almost anyone. Since these are purely individual reactions, no special knowledge or experience is required.

9. Testimonial Restrictions in Federal Trade Practice Rules.

If there is evidence that misuse of testimonials is rampant in an industry covered by a set of Federal Trade Practice Rules, there is likely to be a specific rule—rather finely detailed—on the subject. Distortion of critics' reviews and comments has long been recognized as a questionable and unfair promotion practice in book publishing. Therefore, the Rules for the Mail Order Book Publishing Industry, as promulgated by the F.T.C. after consultation and hearings with members of the industry, represent a good exposition of the Commission's views on testimonials, pinpointed to specific illegal industry practices: [18]

> *Deceptive testimonials*—It is an unfair trade practice for any member of the industry to use any testimonial or purported testimonial, or representation with respect thereto, which is false, misleading, or deceptive; or to cause any testimonial or part thereof to be used in such manner as to have the capacity and tendency or effect of misleading or deceiving purchasers or prospective purchasers into the belief:
>
> (a) That the testimonial was given without solicitation or payment therefor, when such is not the fact; or
>
> (b) That the testimonial was given by a school, library, or other institution, when in fact such testimonial was given by an individual connected therewith but acting in a personal capacity and not officially on behalf of such school, library, or other institution; or
>
> (c) That the testimonial is a bona fide and genuine testimonial given by a person whose name is used in connection therewith, when the testimonial was not given by such person, or when the testimonial was not given with respect to the particular book or books to which it purports to relate, or when the testimonial is otherwise inapplicable or misleading or deceptive.
>
> In order to avoid deception in the use of bona fide and genuine testimonials, the complete testimonial should be given wherever practicable, and words, phrases, sentences, or other parts of such testimonial shall not be separated from their context, or rearranged or otherwise used in such manner as to have the capacity and tendency or effect of misleading or deceiving purchasers or prospective purchasers in any respect.

10. National Better Business Bureau Policy.

The policy of the National Better Business Bureau in policing testimonials has been widely recognized and represents a good synthesis of the legal requirements. It has developed the following six criteria: [19]

(a) *The testimonial should be genuine.* This does not mean merely the possession of a statement from the endorser setting out the favorable comment. It means rather that the *facts* stated in the endorsement are correct.

(b) *The testimonial should represent the honest and sincere opinion of the endorser.* It is assumed "in the absence of a statement to the contrary" that a testimonial represents that the endorser is a current user of the product and really believes what he said about it.

(c) *The endorser should be competent.* See Section 8 above.

(d) *Testimonials should not contain any misstatement of fact.* See Section 7 above.

(e) *The testimonial should contain no misleading implications.* The testimonial may be literally and technically correct and yet be misleading because of its implications. This is a specific application of the general rule that representations must be considered as a whole and taken in the light in which they would be understood by the average reader or listener. See Chapter 11, Section 5 (a) and (b) .

(f) *The testimonial should reflect the current opinion of the endorser.* Generally speaking, "stale" endorsements should not be used. This is particularly true if there have been changes in the product.

(g) *The publicized portion of a testimonial should fairly reflect the spirit and content of the complete testimonial.* It is deceptive to isolate or excerpt the laudatory portion so as to give the impression that the entire testimonial was of the same general tenor when, as a matter of fact, negative or contrary portions have been deleted.

11. Industry Code Provisions.

Because of the generally different techniques of public relations, the PRSA Code of Professional Standards does not contain any provisions as to testimonials *per se* but, in its condemnation of "false fronts," provides:

> A member shall not make use of any individual or organization purporting to serve or represent some announced cause, or purporting to be independent or unbiased, but actually serving an undisclosed special or private interest of a member or his client or his employer.

This would seem to interdict false or misleading testimonial practices arising from such technique but it is understood that this section of the Code "was not designed to take care of the situations arising out of the improper use of testimonials."

As to the more common testimonial methods, they would be tested against the Code's general requirement of "adhering to generally accepted standards of accuracy, truth and good taste" and its prohibition of the "dissemination of false or misleading information." This would seem to follow by analogy to the "ground rules" of the FTC as to both testimonials and deception generally. See Chapter 20, Section 9.

Most industry codes contain specific provisions as to their use. The Advertising Code of American Business provides: "Advertising containing testimonials shall be limited to those of competent witnesses who are reflecting a real and honest choice." The Creative Code of the American Association of Advertising Agencies enjoins against "testimonials which do not reflect the real choice of a competent witness." [20]

12. Implied or Indirect Testimonials.

There are many testimonial techniques—especially in various public relations activities—which may not appear to be of a testimonial character. They are not what might be called "real" testimonials. They are indirect or implied.

A typical example is the actor in an industrial motion picture intended for public relations or promotional use. The actor is likely to be shown using, handling, or otherwise associated with the company's product. The script may even call for some favorable comment from the mouth of the actor. Releases specifically covering such incidental or indirect testimonials should be obtained—especially if the actor is a "name" whose other endorsement activities may be limited because of his association with this particular product in the film.

Another example is the celebrity who is paid to appear at some special public relations event. Photographs may be taken of the celebrity using or perhaps just standing next to the product. If there is any public news coverage of the event, the company could not properly be charged with violating his rights. However, such photographs are frequently used for subsequent exploitation purposes. This presents the problem of adequate releases. In this type of case, it is sometimes assumed that the "usual" release will be sufficient. This is not always the case. Such releases are customarily limited to the particular event or appearance for which the celebrity is being compensated. The release should be broad enough to cover such subsequent exploitation and even the initial use of the product in the film or in the special event.

13. Testimonial Letters.

Letters from "satisfied users"—frequently unsolicited—are a common source of endorsements used in company or product promotion. Unless a letter contains permission to use it publicly, as some do, it may not be so used without obtaining permission from the writer.

If such endorsements are solicited, that fact does not prevent their use. However, no affirmative or implied representation should be made that they are unsolicited.

14. Editorial Endorsements.

"Editorial endorsements" are the promotional use of "quotes" which originally appeared in magazine articles or books—not infrequently technical or learned in nature. Even assuming that the author was competent to make the judgment in question and that it is otherwise legally acceptable, such material should not be used for commercial purposes of any kind unless clearance and permission have been obtained from both the original copyright owner and the author.

A leading case on this subject is *Henry Holt & Co. v. Liggett & Myers Tobacco Co.*[21] which deals at length with various legal facets of the use of editorial material for publicity purposes.

The plaintiff had published and copyrighted a "scientific" book under the title *The Human Voice, Its Care and Development*. The author had written that tobacco had no adverse effects on "the auditory passages." The defendant published and widely circulated a publicity and promotional pamphlet *Some Facts About Cigarettes* and copied, "although not exactly," three sentences from the copyrighted book, giving credit to the source but without permission of either the publisher or the author.

The plaintiff sought and obtained an injunction against further infringement, destruction of the printing plates and an accounting for profits and damages. Several points were made by the court in so ruling: the copying of only three sentences was not controlling because they were "those portions of the author's work which are pertinent to the subject of the defendant's pamphlet"; alteration and some paraphrase is no defense; reference to the source does not excuse the infringement; the attribution may "cast reflections upon the author's ethics" and bring down upon him "the term 'commercialist' "; no proof of prior damages is needed to obtain an injunction.

Periodicals are sometimes cautious about permitting their contents to be used for such purposes. There are several reasons for this. Such use is a dilution of the publication values of the periodical. Since commercial use usually *follows* periodical publication and availability, the publication does not gain much from the added exposure. Also, the publication may become liable to members of the public who rely on the "tie up" between periodical and product advertising as discussed in Section 22 below.

The growing publication policy against use of editorial matter as a commercial testimonial is well illustrated by the stand taken by *Reader's Digest*. The *Digest* has told its readers:

. . . our readers are again cautioned to appraise with skepticism advertisements—in the press or on the air—of trade name products which imply *Reader's Digest* endorsement. To purchase such products on the basis of a semblance of *Digest* support for claims in the advertising is to lay oneself open to the possibility of deception.

The publication's overall position has been thus described:

No reference to, or use of, the *Reader's Digest* is permitted in any advertisement appearing in the *Digest*. . . . No quotation from a *Reader's Digest* article about a consumer product, nor reference to an article, nor reference to the *Digest* by name, or as a leading national magazine may be used in any form of advertising, in print or on the air.

15. Competitive Endorsements.

Since endorsements have a very real value to their users, an effort will usually be made to protect that value. The prime source of dilution is the testimonial for a competitive product by the same endorser. This problem is particularly acute with so-called "professional" endorsers whose income and personal advancement may depend upon high pressure and continued publicity through every possible channel including the commercial endorsement—perhaps over a limited period of years. The classic example may well be the actress, Constance Talmadge, who is reported to have signed 400 endorsements in one day, just before a new film opened.[22]

The contract with the endorser should therefore specifically provide against such competitive activity, preferably spelling out exclusive rights quite clearly. Questions may arise as to just what products or types of products are "competitive." Under such a contract a company may sue the endorser for breach of his obligation if he endorses a non-acceptable product. Also, under the relatively new doctrine of "right of publicity," an injunction may be obtained against continued use of the conflicting endorsement.[23] See Chapter 8, Sections 39 to 44 as to the right of publicity generally.

16. Professional Society Member Testimonials.

Many professional societies or associations have specific prohibitions against their members signing endorsements. This is true, either directly or indirectly, of bar associations, medical societies, engineering and other scientific and professional groups. These restrictions usually apply whether or not the endorser is identified as a society member. Although the responsibility for complying with the professional society's code is the member's, publications of professional societies will usually refuse advertising or ignore news releases containing such endorsements. The Association of Industrial Advertisers felt it necessary in 1965 to circulate a a special notice to its members about the enforcement of such a policy by professional journals.

At least one court has refused to accept such professional association canons as legally declarative of enforceable public policy. In *Spock v. Pocket Books, Inc.*[24] the plaintiff had agreed to the inclusion of advertising in a paperback edition of his famous book on child care. Later he sought to prevent such inclusion since it might imply that Dr. Spock had endorsed the advertised products, a relationship forbidden by the AMA. Since Dr. Spock could not show that his agreement contravened any statute or case law, the court refused the relief he sought.

The court pointedly referred to the permission given by the American Dental Association to exploit its findings as an endorsement of a popular brand of toothpaste.

In a sense, this restriction is, as to the medical and dental professions at least, akin to the Television Code provision that "physicians, dentists or nurses, or actors representing physicians, dentists or nurses shall not be employed directly or by implication" in commercials involving "services or over-the-counter products involving health considerations." [25]

17. Corporate Endorsements.

During recent years, a relatively new type of testimonial has come into use. This might be called the "corporate endorsement." This may take several forms. The frequently-used case history technique is, in effect, a testimonial by the user of the product. It is therefore subject to the same rules as any other endorsement or testimonial.

The "product tie-in" is frequently used, such as tying a detergent to a washing machine. The exploitation then implies that the appliance manufacturer thinks so highly of the detergent that it supplies it with its washing machines. The F.T.C. has held that this claim may not be made unless it is also disclosed that the detergent has been supplied by its manufacturer without charge. Also, the Commission requires that the samples of the soap packed with the machine must be similarly labeled.[26]

18. Government Endorsements.

Under the general requirement that the contents of an endorsement must not be false or deceptive, it has been held by the F.T.C. that a claim that the product has been approved or is used by the United States government or any of its agencies, if not true, is an unfair and deceptive practice.[27]

On the other hand, an aspirin promotion which referred to the findings of a "government-supported" medical team would not seem to convey a misleading impression that the government had endorsed or approved the findings, but only that the team, as was truly the case, had been paid by the government.[28]

Caution must also be exercised in referring to various agencies of the government such as the Bureau of Standards or the Federal Trade Commission. On occasion, these agencies may, in particular cases, have had certain contact with the product and may even have issued opinions about the product and its usefulness. However, such comments are usually not endorsements and no claim of such endorsement should be made under these circumstances. Furthermore, the F.T.C. has shown itself quite alert if even a slight advertising, promotional or PR lapse or error occurs in connection with comments about regulatory agency or court rulings. See Chapter 1, Section 16.

19. Requirements for Military Testimonials.

All branches of the service have specific and quite detailed controls covering testimonial use of personnel photographs, service insignia and references to the service. The basic military posture as this is written appears in a Department of Defense Directive issued on March 22, 1966. It provides:

> A. All civilian personnel and military personnel on active duty, are prohibited from using their civilian and military titles or positions in connection with any commercial enterprises or in endorsing any commercial product. . . .
> B. All retired military personnel and all members of reserve components, not on active duty, are permitted to use their military titles in connection with commercial enterprises. Such use of military titles shall in no way cast discredit on the military services or the DoD. Such use is prohibited in connection with commercial enterprises when such use, with or without the intent to mislead, gives rise to any appearance of sponsorship, sanction, endorsement, or approval by the military services of the DoD.

The following summary is representative and is based upon U.S. Navy Public Affairs Regulations.[29]

The Navy encourages cooperation with advertisers (except for tobacco and alcoholic advertising), reserving the right to approve layouts for security purposes. Approved materials may be released for commercial use in the same manner as to other civilian media.

Official information materials are to be incidental to commercial promotion and must not directly or indirectly benefit any private or commercial venture. Use of military titles is prohibited if use thereof "gives rise to the appearance of sponsorship, sanction, endorsement or approval by the military service of the Department of Defense."

Promotion, exploitation or advertising must not indicate that a product has undergone service tests, disclose data from such tests, indicate that a product is used by the Navy to the exclusion of similar products by other manufacturers or imply Navy responsibility for the accuracy of the claims or for compliance with laws protecting the rights of privacy of military personnel.

Reproductions of Naval insignia and uniforms may be used in advertising and publicity "providing the dignity of the insignia [or uniform] is not compromised."

Testimonials from Naval personnel are not banned *per se,* but the person giving the testimonial must not be specifically identified by name, grade or rank, nor may he receive monetary compensation, even for modeling fees. It is permissible, however, to use such expressions as "says a Navy captain." Testimonials from Naval personnel must be so presented as to make it clear that the views expressed are those of the individual and not of the Navy Department.

Names and pictures of Naval personnel may not be used for advertising without first obtaining permission from the personnel in question and submission of completed layout and scripts to the Officer of Information of the District, Fleet or Force Commander for review and clearance.

All branches of the services, through their Information Officers, are active and cooperative in supplying photographs for use in company publications but this will usually be limited to use with stories which do not have commercial slants.

20. Use of Professional Models.

Not infrequently, professional models will be used in endorsement activities. This presents two different problems.

A professional model whose picture is to be used will routinely sign a written release. See Chapter 8, Section 30 et seq. This release does not normally give the right to use her name or to attribute to her any testimonial. In some instances, a testimonial from a professional model may be very useful as in cosmetic or fashion promotion. If this is to be used, additional appropriate releases should be obtained and all of the other cautions exercised.

The second problem is quite different. A professional model's photograph may be used but the copy implies that it is some one else—perhaps a doctor, a housewife, or any other person whose "expertise" might be favorable to the product. This is particularly true in connection with health claims where the attractive face and body shown may be completely at variance with the actual appearance of the endorser.

If the professional model is used, there should be "appropriate disclosure" using a legend such as "Photographs were posed by professional models." It is for this reason that, not infrequently, such a legend flashes across a television screen during a commercial embodying such talent. In certain ways, this requirement ties in with the "men in white" position of the Television Code. See Section 16 above.

21. Endorser's Approval of Testimonial.

Many testimonial layouts use the photograph and name of the endorser as well as the language of the testimonial. This may be the principal feature of the advertisement. Even assuming releases and clearances, further approval should be obtained from the endorser covering the layout and all of its various elements. Some even go so far as to have proofs specifically approved by the endorser so as to obviate any future claim arising from errors in the advertisement as it finally appears. See Chapter 8, Section 35 also.

22. Liability of Endorser.

This question does not appear to have been authoritatively decided as yet. However, such responsibility is not difficult to envisage in an appropriate case. Several cases—some going back many years—have laid the groundwork. In the early days of the century, an English bicycle dealer sold a bicycle under the name of "Times Cycle," apparently trying to suggest that the august London *Times* was somehow connected with it. The *Times* obtained an injunction against the use of "Times Cycle." The order was premised essentially on the *Times*' risk of responsibility if someone were to be injured in using the bicycle.[30] An early American case involving Thomas Edison resulted in an injunction sought by the inventor against the unauthorized use of his name, photograph and so-called "certificate"—really a fictitious testimonial. The court reasoned— once again—that Edison ran the risk of being held liable should a purchaser of the product be injured.[31]

This entire question is part of the larger problem of product liability about which, at the present, judicial concepts are changing. The courts are becoming much more liberal in denying the need for privity or a directed commercial relationship between manufacturer and claimant and, in other ways also, are reducing the burden on the plaintiff. This is particularly true as to claims for personal injury as against those for financial loss.

At the same time, there is a tendency to continue the distinction between a factual representation and mere opinion. Thus the endorser who expresses his opinion about a product faces less of a potential liability than the person whose endorsement spells out factual claims about the product. The same is true of the test laboratory whose results are used in product promotion. Here the ground for responsibility most likely to be used in the future is negligent representation. By analogy to the liability of accountants, engineers, etc., the laboratory's responsibility for its mistakes is becoming greater.[32]

One argument which will undoubtedly motivate courts in the future in this trend toward expanding endorser and laboratory liability is the fact that both the endorser and the test laboratory know that their representations are specifically intended for commercial exploitation and not merely for internal use of the product manufacturer.

C. TEST AND SURVEY RESULTS.

23. Use of Test Results.

Exploitation of product test results must satisfy the same overall legal tests as any other form or vehicle of publicity and promotion. However, they present several specialized problems. The increased trend toward use of test results—especially comparative tests—appears to have focused F.T.C. attention thereon. Commission action against deceptive activities in this area is relatively simple, since it depends merely upon comparison of the actual test results and the publicity, advertisements or other promotion constructed around the figures or results. It is not necessary—except in limited situations—to go behind the results themselves. The deception usually is obvious when a side-by-side comparison is made.

Most of the cases of unfair or deceptive practices involving tests and their commercial use and exploitation fall into three categories:

(a) Improper claims that tests have in fact been conducted when such is not the case.

(b) Use of tests which are improper, unfair, rigged, invalid or otherwise misleading because of their inherent character or techniques.

(c) Deceptive use or exploitation of the test results even though the tests themselves and their results are proper.

Some of the specific kinds or areas of deception, falling into one or more of the above categories, are: [33]

Garbled, distorted or exaggerated claims, usually resulting in ambiguity or affirmative misrepresentation.

Overall performance claims which do not indicate relative performance of the various factors tested, in some of which the advertised product suffers by comparison.

False references to the organization making the tests.

Failure to indicate that the advertiser itself made the tests and implying outside and independent laboratory testing.

Use of non-standard products in tests.

Deletion of adverse portions of test results and use only of favorable portion thereof.

Comparison of advertiser's best line with competitors' cheaper or poorer quality lines.

Tests in which a substitute and not commercially available formulation was used in place of a competitive brand.

Use of tests which would be ruinous to the competitive product if actually used.

Reliance on tests which were really only laboratory experiments.

Reference to tests based on so-called "standards" when industry test standards had not been established.

The F.T.C. is requiring more and more affirmative disclosure of the details and the surrounding circumstances of the test being exploited. This is particularly true of cases which end in consent orders. Thus the advertiser was required to disclose that the testing methods used were not independently and finally determined by the testing agency, in connection with representations concerning appliance tests, if such was the case.[34]

24. Use of Survey Results.

Surveys and tests have much in common although tests usually deal with product features, characteristics or performance whereas surveys are usually concerned with the use or acceptance of the product or public attitudes concerning the product or the company. Unless surveys are represented as dealing with subjective matters, they will be assumed to be based on objective criteria—as product tests are.

Promotion based on surveys is subject essentially to the same legal requirements as is similar use of test results. See Section 23 above. The F.T.C. has prohibited use of survey statistics which are not justified by survey results.[35] In the leading *Ipana* case a claim was made that "twice as many dentists personally use Ipana Tooth Paste as any other dentifrice preparation.[36] This was based on the choice of 621 of the 66,000 dentists in the United States, 10,000 of whom had received questionnaires. The next choices received 258, 189, 144 and 128 votes respectively. It was held that such survey results did not justify the claim. The court said:

This is not to express the opinion that all advertisements based upon surveys must be barred, but merely that the information in the possession of the manufacturer in this case was insufficient to support its advertisements . . .

D. AWARDS, CERTIFICATIONS AND SEALS.

25. Exploitation by Award Winners.

Awards of various kinds are becoming an increasingly useful and frequent tool of business. They are now a well-recognized public relations technique, valuable to both the maker and the winner.[37] The legitimate award—most of them are both legal and properly administered—is more than merely a promotional or public relations device. It is a significant and fundamental "guarantee" of quality or merit and makes a meaningful contribution to the buying decision. However, some such awards are mere "gimmicks" on the part of either the maker or the winner. Some are the result of "a deal between a gullible manufacturer or his advertising hucksters and some self-seeking, completely unqualified promoter." [38] Such awards are subject to criticism on moral or ethical grounds as well as for legal reasons—usually as a deceptive or unfair trade practice within the jurisdiction of the F.T.C.

The Commission has proceeded in many cases in which false claims were made of awards for either product or company.[39] These cases have involved unjustified claims of specific named awards from well-known institutes, organizations and other legitimate sources and also of such general claims as "Blue Ribbon Winner" or "First Prize."

Some claims of awards are made indirectly as in the case of a watch manufacturer which used "Oscar" in its promotion. The company was required to show in its advertising that it was using such reference by license agreement only—rather than having won an award in competition with other watches.[40]

An important requirement in the winner's promotion of any award or certification is that it must conform carefully thereto and should not make excessive claims, either as to its nature, extent, meaning or substance.

26. Propriety of Award Contests.

Awards are usually granted to products or companies on the basis of some kind of contest or competition. The deception and irregularity may exist in the techniques or the machinery by which the awards are made. The F.T.C. has moved in many such cases.[41]

The granting of awards will usually be prohibited unless they are based on contests which satisfy certain basic requirements such as: the contests must actually be conducted; the judging must be impartial and be by competent persons; an adequate and representative number of different products and competitive products must be involved; the tests or standards used must be adequate and proper for the purpose; there can be no rigging of the contest; the competing companies must have no control over the competition nor make any financial contribution to it or its sponsors. See Chapter 13, Section 38.

27. Use of Certifications.

Claims that an article, its characteristics or performance is "certified" may not be made except under certain conditions. The most basic is that there be no misrepresentation, direct or implied, as to the *fact* of certification when no such certification has ever been issued.[42] The identity of the organization issuing the certification must be disclosed and, if it has any connection with the advertiser, this fact must be affirmatively disclosed also. Claims have been prohibited unless the certifying institution or source is qualified and competent to judge the matters being certified.

In one case an advertising agency executive had set up a testing and certification organization. Its name and certification were used in the advertising of a company represented by the agency. This was held by the F.T.C. to be an unfair and deceptive practice because the relationship among the parties was not disclosed.[43]

28. "Seals of Approval."

Seals of approval or commendation are issued by some magazines or by their testing laboratories, not infrequently as a prerequisite to the periodical's acceptance of advertising for the product. Some independent testing laboratories also issue such seals after appropriate tests, and permit their use in product marketing. Such seals may be misused in several ways—by either the manufacturer or the periodical.

The manufacturer may misuse it by including it in its promotion without authorization or permission. The periodical or laboratory may never have tested the product, no less issued a seal. This is obviously misleading—similar to a fictitious testimonial. The misuse may be more subtle. Permission may have been granted for use of the seal but the accompanying advertising copy may make claims for either the product or the implications of the seal which go beyond those covered by the seal.[44] The advertiser may use the seal in conjunction with a product for which it was not issued although issued for another product in the manufacturer's line.

29. Irregularities in Issuance of a Seal.

The F.T.C. has taken action in several instances against seal-issuing organizations because seals purportedly evidencing testing were issued for products which had not, in fact, been tested.[45] In one such case, terminated by a consent order, the complaint alleged that, contrary to representations of prior testing, the seal was issued for some services and products solely on the recommendations of the magazine's staff who were not qualified technicians or medical experts, or on the basis of tests or reports submitted by the applicant for the seal, or on the basis of an editorial staff decision based on the reputation of the applicant.[46]

Inasmuch as a seal is a "certification mark," similar to those issued by trade associations to industry members who satisfy certain requirements or standards, the above Commission decisions are also relevant thereto. The Commission requires that the trade association issue its certification mark or seal of approval to all industry members on a non-discriminatory basis. If the association were to issue its mark or seal to some companies or products without requiring strict adherence to the announced standards or test, as in the above cases, this would appear to be discrimination in favor of such company or product. See Chapter 19, Section 22 for a fuller discussion of the F.T.C. position and rulings on this issue.

30. Contract Breach in Use of Seals.

Before a manufacturer is allowed to use a seal of this sort—even assuming that its product satisfies the necessary tests—it must usually sign an agreement spelling out the extent of the permission granted and other terms and conditions governing use of the seal. The agreement may cover such matters as duration of the permission, the product covered thereby, certain production requirements such as size of the seal in print media, loss of the seal rights if quality deteriorates, requirements as to advertising in the publication issuing the seal, etc.

It is important that these various requirements and conditions be met by the advertiser. There have been instances in which expensive plates have had to be destroyed or redone because of lack of conformity to the terms of the agreement. Particular attention should be paid to the agreement if anything is used in the advertising beyond the seal itself—such as additional copy claims based upon the tests preceding the issuance of the seal.

31. Check List.

The following is a check list of questions which should be considered and appropriately resolved before a testimonial, endorsement, award, certification, test or survey result is used in company promotion, public relations or advertising. The answers to these several questions will be found in appropriate sections of this chapter.

Is the exploitation testimonial in character?

What is the probable and foreseeable extent of the use to be made of the endorsement?

Have full and otherwise appropriate releases been obtained?

Are specific approvals of the final form of the promotion necessary?

If no releases are available, what is the "calculated risk/promotional value" ratio?

Has any consideration been paid to the endorser?

Are any "unsolicited" claims being made with paid testimonials?

Is the testimonial "fictitious" or can its existence be validated?

Does the testimonial libel anyone?

Does it violate anyone's right of privacy or publicity?

Is the testimonial deceptive in any way?

Is the endorser competent and qualified?

Does the endorser use the product?

Is the testimonial the sincere and current belief of the endorser?

Does the exploitation or publicity fairly reflect the contents of endorser's entire statement?

Will there be any public confusion between the endorser as an individual and any organization or activity with which he is associated?

Has permission been obtained for use of a testimonial letter?

Has use of an "editorial endorsement" been permitted by the copyright owner and/or author?

Do competitive endorsements present any danger of dilution?

Are there any "professional society" problems with either the endorser or the society?

Have any and all necessary government clearances been obtained?

Do military testimonials conform to requirements of the Department of Defense and the service involved?

Are the product-test results valid?

Does the promotion of a test conform to the test?

If the company made the tests, will this be disclosed?

Does the exploited survey conform to proper research standards?

Has the award itself been made properly?

Is the exploitation of an award deceptive or non-conforming?

Is use of a "seal" properly limited?

Does use of a "seal" conform to its basic contract requirements?

Is "certified" being improperly exploited?

Are there any special or relevant statutory requirements or limitations?

Notes

1. For an excellent and entertaining discussion of the various facets of the use of testimonials, with many examples and suggestions, see FREEMAN, THE BIG NAME (1957).
2. For the history of testimonials generally, see TURNER. THE SHOCKING HISTORY OF ADVERTISING 16–17, 135–6 (1953); ROWSOME, THEY LAUGHED WHEN I SAT DOWN 44–59 (1959); PRESBREY, HISTORY OF ADVERTISING 533–5 (1929); HOWER, HISTORY OF AN ADVERTISING AGENCY, *passim* (1939).
3. THE WORLD OF ADVERTISING 268 (Advertising Publications, Inc. 1963).
4. ADVERTISING: YESTERDAY/TODAY/TOMORROW 448 (Printers' Ink Books, 1962).
5. Hower, *supra* note 2, at 157.
6. Philadelphia Inquirer, March 19, 1967, p. 10.
7. Presbrey, *supra* note 2, at 426.
8. Northam Warren Co. v. F.T.C., 59 F.2d 196 (2d Cir. 1932).
9. F.T.C. v. Inecto, Inc., 70 F.2d 370 (2d Cir. 1935).
10. NAT'L ASS'N OF BROADCASTERS, THE TELEVISION CODE 15, IV, 15 (11th ed.).
11. See cases collected, 2 TRADE REG. REP. ¶7671.
12. 214 U.S. 185 (1909).
13. See cases collected, 2 TRADE REG. REP. ¶7671.39.
14. See cases collected, 2 TRADE REG. REP. ¶7675.
15. R. J. Reynolds Tobacco Co. v. F.T.C., 192 F.2d 535 (7th Cir. 1951).
16. Nat'l Better Business Bureau, Serv. Bull., Periodical No. 1951, Sept. 20, 1961. See also *What Brand Did Ruth Smoke?* Printers' Ink, Sept. 29, 1961, and *Testimonials: Sense and Nonsense,* A.A., Sept. 26, 1961.
17. See cases collected, 2 TRADE REG. REP. ¶7848.
18. 2 TRADE REG. REP. *supra* note 13, at ¶41,150.
19. NAT'L BETTER BUSINESS BUREAU, DO'S AND DON'TS OF ADVERTISING COPY §2.20–26.
20. ADVERTISING ADVISORY COMM. TO THE SECRETARY OF COMMERCE, SELF-REGULATION IN ADVERTISING 73 (1965).
21. 23 F. Supp. 302 (E.D. Pa. 1938).
22. Freeman, *supra* note 1, at 18.
23. Haelen Laboratories, Inc. v. Topps Chewing Gum, Inc., 202 F.2d 866 (2d Cir. 1953).
24. 266 N.Y.S.2d 77 (1965).
25. Nat'l Ass'n of Broadcasters, *supra* note 10, at §XI (5) (a).
26. F.T.C. Dkt. No. 7542, 2 TRADE REG. REP. ¶3060.18.
27. TRADE REG. REP., *supra* note 13, at ¶7673.96.
28. F.T.C. v. Sterling Drug Co., Inc., 215 F. Supp. 327, *aff'd* 317 F.2d 669 (2d Cir. 1963).
29. NAVSO P-10.5 (Rev. 12-65) Part D, Chapter 1, §8 D-1801-2.
30. Walter v. Ashton, [1902] 2 Ch. 282.
31. Edison v. Edison Polyform Mfg. Co., 73 N.J. Eq. 136, 67 Atl. 392 (1907).

See also *Liability of Advertising Endorsers,* 2 STAN. L. REV. 496 (1950) for a general discussion of the grounds of endorser's liability.

32. For an extended discussion of this potential liability of testing laboratories, see Comment, *Potential Liability of Non-Manufacturer Certifiers of Quality,* 10 VILL. L. REV. 708 (1965).

33. See cases collected, 2 TRADE REG. REP. ¶7865.78-98.

34. F.T.C. Dkt. No. C-795, 2 TRADE REG. REP. ¶16.999.

35. See cases collected, 2 TRADE REG. REP. ¶7865.661.

36. F.T.C. v. Colgate-Palmolive Co., 58 F.T.C. 442 (1961).

37. For discussions of awards and their use in public relations, see: CANFIELD, PUBLIC RELATIONS 225, 245, 266 (3d ed. 1960); HANDBOOK OF PUBLIC RELATIONS 518-9, 576-7, 605 (Stephenson ed. 1960); Stewart, *An Award Can Be a Public Relations Plus,* P.R.J., April, 1960.

38. Remarks of Earl Lifshy, Managing Editor of *Retailing Daily,* reported in A.A., June 25, 1951, at 1.

39. See cases collected, 2 TRADE REG. REP. ¶7865.06; Better Living, Inc. v. F.T.C., 259 F.2d (3d Cir. 1958).

40. F.T.C. Stip. No. 8385, 2 TRADE REG. REP. ¶25,486.

41. See cases collected, 2 TRADE REG. REP. ¶7865.18.

42. See cases collected, 2 TRADE REG. REP. ¶7865.54.

43. Revco D. S., Inc. *et al.,* F.T.C. Dkt. No. 8576, 2 TRADE REG. REP. ¶17,287.

44. In addition to F.T.C. action, the issuing organization is likely to take action against such misuse for reasons discussed in Section 30 of the text.

45. F.T.C. Dkt. No. 3872, 32 F.T.C. 1440 (1941).

46. F.T.C. Dkt. No. C-1133, 2 TRADE REG. REP. ¶17,751 (1966).

Chapter 13

Contests and Lotteries

A. INTRODUCTION

B. CHANCE

C. CONSIDERATION

D. POLICING OF CONTESTS

E. MISCELLANEOUS

Chapter 13

Contests and Lotteries

A. INTRODUCTION.

1. The Contest as a Promotional Device.

Modern business regards the contest as one of its most valuable and adaptable tools. It is used for almost every possible business purpose and in an ever-increasing variety of dress and structure. It may be a simple point-of-purchase product sale stimulator, a public relations-oriented high school student essay contest, a device to build a sales organization, a trade association promotion to build public interest in an industry, part of a fund-raising drive, a means toward developing a publication's image among advertisers or a method of improving stockholder interest in their company. The purposes are almost limitless.

Just as its purposes are so varied, so too are its cognate techniques. These two variables are often interrelated. This heterogeneity has caused many legal complications and considerable confusion. It has even led to differing judicial interpretation, varying from state to state or as between federal and state enforcement policies. Precedents, even in a given jurisdiction, may not be relied upon blindly. The Supreme Court has recognized this legal maze and has said:

> Enforcing such legislation has long been a difficult task. Law enforcement officers, federal and state, have been plagued with as many types of lotteries as the seemingly inexhaustible ingenuity of their promoters could devise in their efforts to circumvent the law. When their schemes reached the courts, the decisions, of necessity, usually turned on whether the scheme, on its own peculiar facts, constituted a lottery. So varied have been the techniques used by promoters . . . and so clever have they been in applying these techniques to feigned as well as legitimate business activities, that it has often been difficult to apply the decision of one case to the facts of another.[1]

437

The contest is often only one part of an overall campaign addressed to the public. Yet it is a part which, by its very nature, creates as much public or consumer involvement as any other form of promotion or marketing, even down to the ultimate buying decision in contests which require "proof of purchase." This is one of the factors behind the deep and continuing interest of so many branches of government in the legality of a contest and their concern that it may actually be an illegal lottery.

The proliferation of contests has, in some government circles, come to be regarded as part of an increasing non-price and non-quality competition with which certain consumer-oriented industries seem involved. The question being asked is whether the customer is more concerned with the prize than with the price or quality of the product.[2] Thus, in 1967, the Federal Trade Commission conducted an investigation of sweepstakes along with other devices such as trading stamps.

Another result of the growth of the contest, especially the sweepstakes, has been the parallel growth of the contest companies. These concerns handle all of the many contest details, including planning, preparation of the rules, purchase of prizes, direct mail materials, processing of entries, judging where necessary, awarding of prizes, disputes over awards, even obtaining Post Office Department approval of the plan.

2. Judicial Approval of Contests.

The "lottery concept" is technical and limited. Some, however, view any device as somehow immoral and even illegal if it means "something for nothing." This was also the attitude of the Federal Trade Commission until 1953 in connection with the use of FREE in any appeal. Furthermore, there is no taint in a scheme merely because it has a commercial function and is used to sell merchandise or to develop public interest in a product or a company.

The courts have agreed that the contest is a legal business device when it does not violate the lottery strictures. For example, in the *Garden City Chamber of Commerce* case,[3] discussed more fully in Section 21 below, the court said, "Manifestly this is a joint effort to promote window shopping, which hitherto has not been deemed even faintly illegal or immoral."

3. Definition of a Lottery.

The Supreme Court has defined a lottery as "the distribution of prizes according to chance for a consideration." [4] While other courts or statutes have defined a lottery in somewhat different terms, all agree that there must be three basic elements in a lottery: prize, chance and consideration. This definition, in whatever form it may be used, is relatively simple. However, the application of the definition may be quite difficult in certain situations.

One thing is clear. If any one element in this triumvirate does not exist in a given promotion, it is not a lottery, whatever else it may be.

4. Screening a Contest.

While the presence of all of these elements is necessary in order to constitute a lottery, the National Association of Broadcasters has suggested that the analysis of a contest/lottery plan is simplified if the following successive determinations are made: [5]

(1) Is there a prize? (If the answer is "yes," then go to question #2.)
(2) How will it be decided as to whom the prize will be awarded? Will the award be made on the basis of skill or is there "chance" involved? (If there is an element of "chance," then go to question #3.)
(3) What must one do to participate? Do the requirements for participation constitute consideration?

5. Prize as a Lottery Element.

A contest, by the connotation of the term, implies the award of one or more prizes. A prize may be defined as "some advantage or inequality in amount or value" or "anything of value." [6] It may be money, merchandise, travel accommodations, a percentage discount on purchases, a free pinball game, a service to be rendered or anything else, tangible or intangible.

B. CHANCE.

6. Definition of Chance.

Chance is the concept most popularly associated with lotteries. Some hold that there is a lottery merely because chance exists. Little thought is given to the equal necessity of consideration. Some state statutes take this approach.[7] This was the attitude of the Supreme Court in 1878 when the chance element and lotteries were described as having "a demoralizing influence upon the people." [8] Even though public and judicial attitudes may have changed with the years,[9] it is still true that chance must exist in order to have a lottery. Without chance, there is no lottery.

Generally speaking, chance exists if one cannot foresee with reasonable accuracy the event upon which the prize depends; if the outcome "is beyond a person's will or influence"; or if "after the exercise of research, investigation, skill and judgment [a contestant is unable] to foresee the occurrence or non-occurrence of an event." [10]

Chance is not confined to the method of selecting the winners. Its four most important aspects are:

(a) the naming of the winner.

(b) the sequence of several winners of the same prize.

(c) the amount, if any, of the consideration required of participants.

(d) the size or nature of the prize.

7. Degrees of Chance.

In certain contexts the *degree* of chance is important. The federal lottery statute holds a lottery to exist if the plan depends "in whole or in part" on chance. The federal enforcement agencies follow the same mandate. Thus a plan is banned under federal law if it depends to any degree on chance. Several examples are given by the Post Office Department: [11]

(a) Guessing the number of beans in a jar might be approximately possible for a trained mathematician but still, even using such professional skill, some chance exists.

(b) First solving a problem requiring considerable skill, with the winner being picked by lot from those who have correctly solved it.

(c) The sponsor's failure to adhere to the rules in a contest admittedly requiring skill by actually deciding winners on the basis of chance.

(d) "Placing" all of the teams in a baseball league in the order in which the contestant believes they will finish the season involves chance even though success depends to some degree upon baseball expertise.

These examples all assume that prize and consideration are also present in addition to the element of partial chance.

It is therefore necessary to avoid any plan which involves prize and consideration plus even a degree of chance if contest advertisements or materials are to be carried by the mails or announcements are to be made over radio or TV.

The states vary in their attitudes on this matter. Some hold a lottery to exist *only* if the outcome depends upon "pure chance" with no element of skill involved. Others outlaw a contest which involves some skill as long as an element of chance is also present.

The "pure chance" approach is exemplified in *Hoff v. Daily Graphic*,[12] a New York case which involved movie title choices based on cartoons published in the newspaper. The court said:

> The test of the character of the game is not whether it contains an element of chance or an element of skill, but which is the domi-

nating element that determines the result of the game. The allegations in the complaint clearly indicate the exercise of judgment
and taste in the selection of titles, both by the contestant and by
the judges, and while taste is to a certain extent individual, and
perhaps at times fanciful, nevertheless the exercise of it is far
removed from blind guesswork or chance.

This dichotomy is of considerable importance to the purely intrastate or
local contest and is discussed in Section 31 below. However, national or
even regional contests must respect the federal doctrine—not merely
because of the mails or radio and TV—because this approach protects
against problems in states which do not adhere to the pure chance
doctrine.

8. Chance in Selection of Winners.

In the modern commercial contest—as in the traditional gambling
lottery—the principal incidence of chance is in the selection of the winners. In a sweepstakes, for example, we have selection by lot. This is true
even though the choice may be made by computer instead of a drawing
from the old-fashioned "wheel."

However, winners may be selected by chance through less obvious
methods. Thus a plan which awards equal prizes to the first 50 women to
enter a store is based on chance as is dependency on the relative dates of
the postmarks on the entries.

9. Chance as to Sequence of Winners.

Chance may be present solely in dictating the order in which prizes are
awarded. Thus all participants may win the same prize but receive them
over an extended period of time. If the other elements are present, this
would be a lottery. Such an arrangement may seem more like a distribution of premiums but the *seriatim* distribution, decided by chance, will
be decisive.

This situation is not to be confused with cases in which the consideration paid by the individual participants depends on chance as discussed
in Section 11.

10. Chance in Connection With Size of Prize.

Ordinarily the number and size or value of the prizes are predetermined
at the opening of a contest. However, the prizes may vary with certain
circumstances which develop throughout the course of the contest. If such
changes are the result of chance, the plan is a lottery, assuming that
consideration is also present.[13]

For example, the Post Office Department, in an unpublished letter ruling, has described the following situation as a lottery. A regional bowling alley trade association promoted a tournament in which the winning man and woman contestant would each receive a $100 prize. The number and size of the additional prizes were to depend upon the number of persons who participated, each thereof paying one dollar for the privilege. Obviously, the number of participants could not be ascertained in advance nor could the breakdown between men and women be known at the outset. Chance therefore dictated the number and size of the prizes.

This is an example of what is sometimes referred to as a "pool case" in which the size or value of the various prizes—perhaps also the number of winners—depends on the size of the money pool created by the contestants themselves. In the 1930s many of the so-called "bank night" plans were of this character and were considered lotteries under the applicable state laws. The same is true even though the pool is created by the sponsor but its size is keyed to the number of contestants or some other chance event provided, once again, that the contestants, though not contributing directly to the pool, have paid some form of consideration in order to enter.

The same legal logic is basic to the very common provision in contest rules that duplicate prizes will be awarded in the event of ties. Obviously, if the tie is to be broken by a toss of a coin or some other form of pure chance, legal chance is present. If the total amount of the first and second prizes is divided between the two winners, the element of chance is also present. This would also be true should the order of the prizes be determined by the relative priorities of the postmark dates on the entries of the tied participants since such dates clearly depend on sheer happenstance.[14]

A company's representative may call at various homes, selected at random, and offer the housewife a full case of the product if she has three packages of the product in the house but only one package if she does not. This is a lottery. Consideration is present, as discussed below in Section 18, and the size of the prize depends on chance as does the initial selection of the houses to be visited. The National Association of Broadcasters has indicated that the Rules of the Federal Communications Commission forbid carrying announcements of such programs which usually urge the housewife to stock up with the product.[15]

11. Amount of Consideration Dependent Upon Chance.

Every participant may receive exactly the same prize but pay a different amount of consideration to participate. Such an arrangement makes the plan a lottery if the amount of consideration depends on chance.

The so-called "suit club" is the traditional example of this arrangement. Fifty suits are to be awarded to fifty men. Each pays in one dollar a week. At the end of the first week one gets his suit, his identity depending on pure chance. The second week another person gets his suit, having paid two dollars. This arrangement is a lottery even though the suits may be worth fifty dollars and no deception is otherwise involved.[16]

Variations of this may suffer from the same fault. For example, certain of a store's charge account customers may receive a prize each month but the nature and value of the prize depend on the amount of purchases made during that month by the individual customer. The customers are "bracketed" according to volume of purchases and some of those in each bracket receive a certain gift, varying by brackets. Here the choice of winners is random and chance is present even though a customer may select the bracket by making purchases. Consideration is also present and we have a lottery.

12. "Best" and "Most" Contests.

The "best" answer contest is very common. It usually involves the submission of an essay, slogan or some other effort. These are then judged on certain specific objective standards and prizes are awarded accordingly. The familiar "Complete this sentence in 25 words or less" contest is typical. These are usually considered legal even though prize and consideration are present. The necessity of skill and judgment in the writing of the answers avoids the element of chance.[17]

However, such contests must be judged on certain specific and announced standards. No matter how unobjectionable the contest may be at the outset, if it appears that chance did in fact control the selection of the winners, the contest has degenerated into a lottery. This the Post Office Department has illustrated with the example of a best-slogan contest in which 8000 entries were received in the last two hours of the contest but the winner was announced just one hour later.

In the *Brooklyn Eagle* case,[18] a "best" essay contest was involved. The court said that "best," without more, could mean "the best written, the best expressed, most persuasive, longest, shortest or the best from any other viewpoint." This was condemned. If a contest is to be based on skill, rather than chance, the specific criteria should be both defined at the outset and adhered to consistently by competent judges. As to this obligation of the judges, see Section 38 below.

"Most" contests take many forms. Usually they depend upon skill and competence. Therefore, they are not lotteries even though prize and consideration be present.[19] Such contests may end in ties with greater frequency than "best" contests. Duplicate prizes should be given in such instances or tie-breakers provided for in the rules at the beginning.

The "popularity contest" is a version of the "most" contest. Usually, coupons or votes are distributed with purchases and the winner is the holder of the most coupons, amassed either through individual purchases or through pooling with others. Chance is generally held to be absent although there is some state authority to the contrary.[20]

13. "Take and Break" Promotions.

"Take and break" schemes are almost always packaging promotions. Some form of coupon or prize of varying value is enclosed in the box and the purchaser has no way of knowing its nature until after the purchase is made. This is essentially a "gift enterprise" as discussed in Section 18 below. The Federal Trade Commission and the courts have uniformly condemned such schemes.[21]

The *Mother's Oats* case [22] is typical of one type of such scheme. Each package contained one of the letters M-O-T-H-E-R-S. A winner had to collect all seven letters but the contestants could not tell in advance which letter was in a particular package. Only one out of each 500 boxes contained the letter "O." This was held to be a lottery, the consideration being the purchase of the product.

Modern versions of this arrangement have been used but without the necessity of making a purchase. This is probably legal since consideration (in the generally accepted sense) is not present. So appealing has this arrangement been that the classified advertising columns of many newspapers carry pleas for certain "letters" needed by the advertiser to complete the required name or sequence.

14. Puzzle Contests.

Puzzle contests are usually considered legal because chance is absent.[23] If the puzzle is so simple that the barest amount of "skill" is needed to solve it, chance may be present unless some other "skill" element is added. This may be an additional essay to be judged as discussed in Section 12 above. Tie-breakers may also be used.

Under the doctrine of the *Reed* case,[24] it may be postal fraud if the full nature of a puzzle contest is not revealed at the outset. Thus participation may be initially described as "free" and later, in conjunction with the tie-breakers, consideration (usually a cash payment) may be required.

On occasion the easy initial puzzles are used only as "bait." The tie-breakers, although announced in the rules and requiring no consideration, are of extreme difficulty, susceptible of solution only by skill of "exceptional caliber." Though probably legal, this type of "come-on" contest has been severely criticized by the National Better Business Bureau as "a scheme to deceive and exploit the public" and should be avoided.[25] It is not at all unlikely that the Federal Trade Commission would, in a proper case, consider such tactics as an unfair, if not a deceptive, practice.

C. CONSIDERATION.

15. Definition of Consideration.

Consideration has long since been defined as "a thing of value." [26] The meaning of this simple phrase has undergone more change than any other concept of contest/lottery law. There is no help in the federal lottery statute, which does not even mention consideration. State statutes are equally deficient. Many of the judicial definitions are loose and perhaps meaningless except in the obvious cases in which participants must pay money or make a purchase of some sort.

The confusion and change have occurred in connection with the important question of whether the participant's personal physical activity will supply consideration and, if so, the degree of such effort which will push an otherwise legal contest over the line into the lottery area.

The Post Office Department, the earliest and still today the most important government policeman of lotteries, has said that "there was a time" when it applied "a strict rule" under which *any* personal activity was consideration; then it moved on to the "time-and-effort" rule and now considers only "substantial time and effort" to be consideration. The Post Office Department concedes that the "law is now largely confined to schemes where money, merchandise, or other things of value are given by the contestants." [27]

16. Traditional Contract Consideration.

One of the complexities of contest consideration is the persistence in certain jurisdictions of the so-called contract concept of consideration. At one time, all "lottery cases" followed this traditional concept. They held that consideration was present if there were any detriment to one party or any benefit to the other party. They held that a person who did something, no matter how trivial, for the benefit of the other, gave consideration. Thus, the Federal Communications Commission at one time said, "A commercial benefit to the promoter satisfies the consideration requirement."

In connection with contests, this trivial personal effort, not legally required of a contestant, may involve answering the telephone, visiting a store to register, listening to the radio or watching TV, clipping a coupon and mailing it to the advertiser, etc.

The application of the contract concept persisted throughout the earlier days of the lottery when it was a gambling device. The "retreat" therefrom seems chronologically keyed to the growth of the contest as a business promotion technique. Without this change, the flood of sweepstakes and other business-oriented contests would not have been possible.

17. Payment of Money.

If the payment of money is required for participation, consideration is obviously present. In the customary form, this involves such things as purchase of raffle tickets, contribution to a charity, purchase of merchandise as discussed in Section 18, etc. Sometimes participation appears to be "free" but payment is required later—in connection with tie-breakers, perhaps.

Merely sending in an entry by mail involves the payment of postage, an expenditure of money. So, too, is the carfare spent to visit the sponsor's store. Ordinarily this is considered as merely incidental and not such payment as to constitute consideration. It is not "a contribution in kind to the fund or property to be distributed." [28]

18. The "Gift Enterprise" or "Proof of Purchase."

A gift enterprise has long been recognized by the law as any arrangement whereby the purchase of a product is necessary as a prerequisite to eligibility for a prize awarded by chance or lot. The federal lottery law specifically prohibits gift enterprises as do many state laws.[29]

While the term "gift enterprise" has fallen into relative disuse, the concept has not. Today it is more likely to be called "proof of purchase." This may take the form of a boxtop, a label, a sales slip, or some other physical evidence that the participant has purchased certain merchandise. The same is true if a "free" ticket or chance is issued to the customer at the time of purchase. The prohibited element is the requirement that a purchase be made.

Thus, if the elements of prize and chance are present, the purchase supplies the necessary consideration to make the plan a lottery. This is true even though the entrant pays the usual price for the article and receives fair value. In fact, he may even pay less, this sometimes being used as an additional promotional device. Consideration is still present.

19. Calling at a Place of Business.

Many promotion schemes require contestants in a lucky number drawing to call at the sponsor's place of business to register or otherwise qualify for a contest. No purchase is necessary. At one time this was considered a lottery, the consideration being furnished through the otherwise unnecessary effort of coming to the store.[30] This was based on the traditional contract concept of consideration. However, this is not now generally deemed to be consideration.

In 1947 the Post Office Department ruled that "if it is merely required that one's name be registered at a store to be eligible for the prize, consideration is not deemed to be present." [31] At the state level, the cases have gone both ways, some holding that lottery consideration exists and others taking the contrary view as discussed in Section 32 below.

In the *Caples* case,[32] the Circuit Court for the District of Columbia ruled against the existence of consideration in this situation. Probably any personal activity is allowable provided it is not extreme. Where the line will be drawn is still not clear.

The *Garden City Chamber of Commerce* case [33] raises some interesting questions. Here each participant in a "treasure hunt" received, without charge, a numbered card. He was required to "window shop" all of the sponsoring stores. Each store had a numbered item in its window. If the number corresponded to the number on the card, the holder received the merchandise. A large number of store windows were involved and it undoubtedly took the participants a substantial amount of time and effort to check all windows. Yet the court held that consideration was not present, saying, in part, "the consideration requisite to a lottery is a contribution in kind to the fund or property to be distributed" and also that

> . . . the Solicitor [of the Post Office Department] has ruled that to be consideration, which by no common-sense process of reasoning can be so designated; no authority has been cited, nor discovered by independent effort, which vindicates [this] position . . .

This is what may be considered as the federal view on this question. By and large, it is also the state position, although there is here a minority of states which adhere to the older position, as discussed in Sections 31 and 32 below.

The Post Office Department has generally accepted the doctrine of the *Caples* case but has nevertheless circumscribed its application in several ways. It maintains, for example, that if registration cards are also given out when a customer makes a purchase, this will create a lottery even though other cards are given out without a purchase. Its ruling states: [34]

> The fact that there is "free" participation would make the scheme nonetheless a lottery if, in addition, chances to participate for some are coupled or given with purchases or other consideration. Such schemes are lotteries as long as some pay, even though others

play free. Thus, the mere fact that there is provision for a "free chance" to participate does not remove the element of consideration from a scheme which otherwise constitutes a lottery.

Furthermore, the Post Office Department apparently will not clear a lucky number drawing—in supermarkets, for example—unless it is satisfied that the entry cards are available only outside the checkout booths near the front entrance. The Department wants to be sure that a person can walk in off the street and get a card. She is not to be subjected to the practical psychological pressures of "impulse buying" by entering the sales areas of the supermarket in order to obtain the card. This physical in-store arrangement was involved in the *"Split the Dollar"* case discussed in Section 32 below.

Notwithstanding the relaxation of the federal rule, some states still hold that contestants' coming to the sponsor's place of business or being present at a given time or event is consideration. In the most recent such case—as this is written—the Ohio Attorney General rules: [35]

> A promotional game which requires a participant to go onto the premises of a commercial enterprise to obtain a token necessary for participation, although no purchase is required to obtain the token, is a scheme of chance.

The same ruling held a promotion to be a lottery if "a participant had to pass through a check-out line" to participate. The basic premise of the ruling appears to have been that consideration was found in getting "people to come into the store" and "being exposed to goods being offered for sale in order to compete. . . ."

This opinion was issued at the peak of the gas station and supermarket use of "games" of various kinds in 1967 and the gasoline companies operating in Ohio cancelled such promotions. There was also some concern by these companies that the Attorney General might proceed against their charters if they used such "games," considered to be illegal lotteries.[36]

Other states have reached the same conclusion on this issue.[37] There is also authority going the other way [38] and multi-state promotions should be alert for these variations.

20. Use of Facsimiles.

Many "proof of purchase" promotions try to remove the consideration element by permitting the use of "reasonable facsimiles" instead of actual boxtops, labels, etc. Until relatively recently, the Post Office Department accepted this technique and held that no consideration was present provided the facsimiles "were easily made from the advertisement announcing the contest." Each case was decided on an individual basis.[39]

Now, however, Post Office Department policy is to accept such schemes only if the alternative type of entry is limited to writing in one's own handwriting "in plain block letters" the product name or other specified term.

21. Expenditure of "Considerable Time and Effort."

Although the question of calling at the sponsor's place of business has been settled, certain other types of personal activity are frequently required of a participant. Are they consideration?

In the "giveaway case" the Supreme Court said that "personal activity" is "not the kind of 'price' or 'thing of value' paid by a participant in a lottery which the law contemplates as an essential element of a lottery." [40] This would seem to make it reasonably clear that personal activity such as the required presence at the drawing or award of the prizes is not consideration. The Post Office Department so holds. Of course, it would be consideration if admission were charged as with a drawing between the halves of a regular football game.

The court in the *Garden City Chamber of Commerce* case imposed rather stringent requirements on such activities by saying they would not be consideration unless "factual data are employed to support a finding that the average participant would be required to put forth a 'substantial' effort, whatever that means." [41]

From past cases and rulings the following are not consideration: calling at a sponsor's store, visiting a number of stores to look for the posting of one's name, visiting the same store a number of times, answering the telephone, going to the house door, listening to the radio or watching the TV, reading a newspaper or magazine and cutting out a coupon, spending a few cents for postage on coupons or entry blanks, writing down a simple phrase or name and keeping it on hand, window shopping, mailing in a license number or social security number, obtaining a free bingo card at a store, opening a charge account, telephoning a certain number, witnessing a product demonstration at a store or taking a free ride in an automobile.

Exactly how far the courts and governmental agencies will go in allowing extended personal activity is not clear. An extrapolation of past changes and trends seems to indicate that most activity which is reasonably consonant with the normal activities of the participant will not be regarded as consideration.

22. Use of Entry Blank in Newspaper or Magazine.

Traditionally a favorite contest method has been the newspaper coupon, to be mailed to the sponsor with the name and address of the contestant. Today, with advances in printing and binding methods, many magazines have bound into them perforated mailing cards which are entry blanks.

Prior to June, 1965, such arrangement was legal under Post Office Department rulings *only* as to cards bound into *subscription* copies. Publishers controlled their press runs so that the cards did not appear in newsstand copies. Since then the Post Office Department has permitted the entry cards in newsstand copies as well, provided that the following conditions are met:

(a) The publication is not a co-sponsor or intended beneficiary of the prize promotion.

(b) There is no prior announcement to the public by the advertiser or the publisher that an issue will carry the prize offer, and there is no more than one-time publication of the contest.

(c) The advertisement contains no suggestion or invitation that other copies of the magazine be obtained to secure additional entry forms, numbers, etc.

(d) There is no promotional advertising over radio, television or otherwise, advising that entry materials for the contest are to be published in any magazine.[42]

23. "Sweepstakes."

During recent years, the "sweepstakes" has become the most common type of promotional contest. Early in 1967 it was estimated that approximately 55% of all national contests were sweepstakes, with the so-called "statement" form running second at about 20%.[43]

In its usual form, a sweepstakes is based on pure chance. It survives the lottery laws because consideration is not present. The entry card may be bound into a magazine; it may be picked up by the public at a supermarket or other retail outlet without the necessity of making a purchase; it may be received through the mail. All of these have been construed not to provide consideration in the lottery context.

It is usually not too difficult to obtain clearance from the Post Office Department on a sweepstakes promotion. However, the state laws vary and in a limited number of states the sweepstakes is illegal. A continuing campaign has been waged in various state legislatures for laws which would permit sweepstakes in the states in question. To a degree, these efforts have been successful but not across the board. Also, some progress has been made through judicial interpretations. In some states, new statutes have been adopted but the sweepstakes or other forms of contests are permitted only under certain limited conditions. The state laws are discussed in Sections 31 and 32.

24. Broadcast Contests.

Contests promoted over radio and TV must conform generally to the same legal requirements as any other. However, due to the nature of the medium, additional rules may apply. The basic federal laws covering such offers and advertising are set out in Section 29 below.

The Supreme Court pronouncement in the broadcast "give-away case" [44] is today a basic precedent as to the "personal activity" aspects of consideration. The Federal Communications Commission had proscribed certain programs as "illegal devices appealing to cupidity and the gambling spirit" if they selected participants by lot, telephoned them, and required them to have the sponsor's merchandise on hand, or if they had to be listening to the program and to answer questions based thereon or to do certain other things. On appeal, the Supreme Court overruled the Commission and said, ". . . as far as we are aware [no case] has ever held that a contestant's listening at home to a radio or television program satisfies the consideration requirement [of a lottery]." However, possession of the sponsor's product is still consideration under the traditional "gift enterprise" rule discussed in Section 18.

Due to time limitations, it is not always possible to explain the contest rules in full detail on the broadcast program. The National Better Business Bureau early insisted that if an answer or entry was to be sent in "direct response to a broadcast announcement," all rules and complete details should be broadcast.[45] If the participant is to obtain from a store or other source (such as a newspaper) an entry blank containing all such information, the broadcast announcement need not be complete.

D. POLICING OF CONTESTS.

25. Policing of Contests in General.

One of the problems facing the contest sponsor is the multiplicity of governmental policing agencies. Also, there are instances in which different enforcement authorities take different positions.

Generally speaking, however, a plan approved by the Post Office Department for admission to the mails will probably be acceptable to other federal authorities and to most state authorities. Even this cannot be said with complete assurance because of certain state statutes or local social or religious attitudes as discussed in Sections 32 and 33 below. However, an approval by the Post Office Department upon the sponsor's inquiry would be strong evidence that there was no intentional or knowing violation of a state statute which might be more restrictive than the federal law.

26. Post Office Department.

The most active lottery-control activity of the federal government is the Post Office Department, which enforces the following language of Section 1302 of the Criminal Code of 1948:

> Whoever knowingly deposits in the mail, or sends or delivers by mail;
> Any letter, package, postal card, or circular containing any lottery, gift enterprise, or similar scheme offering prizes dependent in whole or in part upon lot or chance . . .
> Any newspaper, circular, pamphlet, or publication of any kind containing any advertisement of any lottery, gift enterprise, or scheme of any kind offering prizes of any kind dependent in whole or in part upon lot or chance, or containing any list of the prizes drawn or awarded by means of any such lottery, gift enterprise, or scheme, whether said list contains any part or all of such prizes—
> Shall be fined not more than $1,000 or imprisoned not more than two years, or both; and for any subsequent offense shall be imprisoned not more than five years.

This Congressional mandate is repeated in Section 124.51 of the Postal Manual. Also, mail "destined for a scheme of this kind" is stamped LOTTERY MAIL and returned to the sender under Title 39, Section 4005 of the U.S. Code. The rulings of the Post Office Department are discussed throughout this chapter at appropriate sections.

The Post Office Department will give an advance "mailability ruling" to newspapers and other members of the public. The "question, with a full statement of the facts," may be submitted directly, or through the local postmaster, to the Office of the General Counsel, Mailability Division, Post Office Department, Washington, D.C. 20260.

The Department advises that such rulings "will be furnished as promptly as circumstances permit." It has been our experience that "same-day" service is sometimes possible if one first discusses the matter with the Department counsel and then submits in person the request for the ruling. The General Counsel's Office is most cooperative.

27. Federal Trade Commission.

The Federal Trade Commission is an active arm of the government anti-lottery enforcement. Its approach is that a lottery is an "unfair method of competition" under Section 5 of the Federal Trade Commission Act, discussed at length in Chapter 11, Section 4.

Its jurisdiction over lotteries was validated by the Supreme Court in the *Keppel* case,[46] decided in 1934. The Court said that the "common law and criminal statutes have long deemed [lotteries] contrary to public policy" and therefore they are unfair even though they are not deceptive.

Of course, the jurisdiction of the Federal Trade Commission is also premised on the use of lottery technique "in commerce," meaning interstate commerce. Purely intrastate lotteries or lottery devices are beyond the Commission pale. Intrastate use of such methods is not the end of the matter, however. It has also been held that if lottery devices or materials are shipped across state lines although later used in purely intrastate sales, the Commission can take action.[47]

The "lottery test" used by the Federal Trade Commission is generally the same as that applied under the criminal statutes enforced by the Post Office Department and the Federal Communications Commission and requires the same triumvirate of prize, chance and consideration.

Many of the Commission cases have involved sales at retail and have been concentrated to some degree in the areas of "pushboard" cases and sales of candy. However the rulings and jurisdiction of the Commission apply with equal force to any form of lottery or lottery device. The same is true regardless of the product or industry involved.[48]

There is another important aspect of the Federal Trade Commission cases. In many such cases, the users of the devices have not been the respondents. The actions have been instituted against the manufacturers of the devices. Such manufacturers do not themselves engage in a lottery and therefore claim they are not within Section 5 of the Federal Trade Commission Act. Nevertheless, the Commission and the courts have consistently held a cease and desist order to be proper on the ground that the manufacturer has put devices into the hands of others for the purpose of conducting a lottery.[49]

This may become quite important to large national manufacturers who distribute "promotion kits" or "sales kits" to their customers if such materials involve some form of lottery method. It is likely that the Commission will move against the manufacturer rather than the individual retail outlets since, by doing so, the practice can be inhibited at its source and, furthermore, many of the retailers involved are probably operating only in intrastate commerce.

28. Federal Trade Practice Rules.

One of the business-cooperation programs of the Federal Trade Commission is the Federal Trade Practice Rule, discussed at length in Chapter 19, Section 17. In industries in which questionable "contests" are a problem, rules have been adopted to control such unfair trade practices. A typical "lottery rule" reads as follows:

> It is an unfair trade practice to sell, distribute, or promote the sale or distribution of any industry product or other merchandise by means of a game of chance, gift enterprise or lottery scheme.

In other industries the contest problem may not involve lottery questions but, rather, other unfair and improper practices such as some form of misrepresentation. Thus, in the Portrait Photographic Industry Rule 7, we have the following mandate:

> It is an unfair trade practice to make, or cause to be made, directly or by implication, through advertising of any kind, or otherwise, any false, misleading, or deceptive statement as to "contests" of any type or description.
>
> (a) Among the practices inhibited by this section are:
>
> (1) Representing or implying that a specified sum of money or monetary amounts in awards will be made to winners in a contest unless the specified sum or amounts in awards is made in cash.
>
> (2) Failing to disclose in the advertising of any contest the conditions and requirements which govern the selection of contest winners, including the extent to which such selection is governed or influenced by the purchase of advertiser's merchandise.
>
> (3) Representing, directly or by implication, that awards in a specified number or value will be made in any contest unless such awards are actually conferred.

29. Federal Communications Commission.

Section 1304 of the Criminal Code of 1948 (the lottery broadcasting section) provides:

> Whoever broadcasts by means of any radio station for which a license is required by law of the United States, or whoever, operating any such station, knowingly permits the broadcasting of any advertisement of or information concerning any lottery, gift enterprise, or similar scheme, offering prizes dependent in whole or in part upon lot or chance, or any list of the prizes drawn or awarded by means of any such lottery, gift enterprise, or scheme, whether said list contains any part or all such prizes, shall be fined not more than $1,000 or imprisoned not more than one year, or both.

This provision applies even to the broadcasting of lottery information in states—New York and New Hampshire—in which lotteries have been legalized. The legality of the lottery under state law does not preempt or protect broadcasting concerning such activities.

However, there appears to be some latitude as to lottery information broadcast only incidentally and having news value in its own right. This follows from the position of the Post Office Department as to similar lottery information in the news columns of newspapers. Thus mention of the name of the first prize winner and the amount of his prize is probably acceptable but serious questions arise about mentioning the second, third, etc. winners.[50]

This is an important restriction in such states. New York lottery officials have said that their promotional efforts are severely restricted because of such mail and broadcast bans.[51]

The Supreme Court has specifically upheld the Federal Communications Commission's control of lotteries in the "give-away cases" and the Commission has supplemented the statute as interpretative thereof: [52]

> (b) The determination whether a particular program comes within the provision of paragraph (a) of this section depends on the facts of each case. However, the Commission will in any event consider that a program comes within the provisions of this paragraph (a) of this section if in connection with such a program a prize consisting of money is awarded to any person whose selection is dependent in whole or in part upon lot or chance, if as a condition of winning or competing for such prize, such winner or winners are required to furnish any money or thing of value or are required to have in their possession any product sold, manufactured, furnished or distributed by a sponsor of a program broadcast on the station in question.

The FCC has consistently taken action against violators of the lottery statute, including fines or forfeitures of from $500 to $10,000, renewal of license for only one year instead of the customary three years revocation of license, admonishment of the licensee. These penalties have resulted from violations such as the broadcast of lottery information, the rigging of contests, a failure to pay prizes as announced, deceptive advertising of contests, etc.[53]

30. TV Code Contest Provisions.

The National Association of Broadcasters, through its TV Code, has promulgated provisions relative to contests. These generally reflect the federal law and its judicial interpretations but go beyond them, especially as to fairness and completeness of information. The TV Code language is: [54]

> (a) Contests shall be conducted with fairness to all entrants, and shall comply with all pertinent laws and regulations. Care should be taken to avoid the concurrent use of the three elements which together constitute a lottery—prize, chance and consideration.
>
> (b) All contest details, including rules, eligibility requirements, opening and termination dates should be clearly and completely announced and/or shown, or easily accessible to the viewing public, and the winners' names should be released and prizes awarded as soon as possible after the close of the contest.
>
> (c) When advertising is accepted which requests contestants to submit items of product identification or other evidence of purchase of products, reasonable facsimiles thereof should be made acceptable unless the award is based upon skill and not upon chance.
>
> (d) All copy pertaining to any contest (except that which is required by law) associated with the exploitation or sale of the sponsor's product or service, and all references to prizes or gifts offered in such connection should be considered a part of and included in the total time allowances as herein provided.

Radio Code provisions are generally the same and stem from the same source.

31. State Laws and Nullification Clauses.

It is usually relatively easy to ascertain the legality of a promotion under federal laws—if only by obtaining a Post Office Department letter ruling. The rigors of state laws present additional problems not always susceptible of solution. It has been said: [55]

> How do you know if your mailing is legal? Have your lawyers check out state laws, as well as recent court decisions, then make the best guess possible. Usually, it's not a good idea to bring [the] promotion to state or local officials *before* mailing; nine times out of ten they turn it down.

While the "nine times out of ten" reference is extreme from the author's experience, the overall comment is basically sound. Gray areas do exist. See Section 19 above. For this reason a "nullification clause" should be used to protect the sponsor in jurisdictions in which these problems may arise. Such a clause may read: "This offer is void where taxed, prohibited, illegal or in any way restricted or regulated."

The more geographically widespread the promotion, the more necessary is a nullification clause since it is usually impossible to prevent advertising or other promotional materials from crossing state lines into so-called "difficult" jurisdictions. At the same time, it should be remembered that the administration of the contest should be consonant with the policy behind the nullification clause. For example, prizes should not be distributed to apparent winners in states which ban the promotion.

32. Recent Changes in State Laws.

During the 1960s several states modified their positions on the consideration question, especially the requirement that contestants visit a store or perform some other kind of personal activity. These changes have come through various combinations of constitutional amendment, legislative enactment and judicial interpretation. Undoubtedly they arose from an appreciation of the changes in the "lottery" from a purely gambling technique into a business or sales method. The following are representative.

In Florida the lottery statute was amended in 1965. Now a retailer may distribute prizes by chance provided the contestants do not have to "pay any tangible consideration . . . in the form of money or other property or thing of value" nor make a purchase.[56] The winners must be notified at their last known address and the mass media are permitted to carry advertising about such contests.

It should be noted that this amendment grants only *retailers* an exemption from the general lottery law under certain indicated conditions. The law, even now, does not permit *national* advertisers to operate a sweepstakes, for example, even though such sponsor otherwise conforms to the terms of the amendment. Thus a national gasoline marketer sent numbered tickets to its credit-cardholders throughout the country, including Florida. Prizes were distributed by lot. The cardholder was required to have his ticket validated at a local Florida gasoline station. The visit to the gas station was deemed to be consideration and not within the 1965 exemption.

Illinois amended its statute in 1961 and described a lottery as a scheme in which prizes are distributed by chance among persons who "paid or promised to pay consideration" to enter.[57] In 1963 it was still held that the traditional, common law theory consideration continued in that state.[58] Finally, in 1964, the Illinois Supreme Court held the "Split the Dollar" game to be legal since consideration could not be found in indirect benefits accruing to the store owner from having the participants visit his stores or in their physical efforts to do so and thus obtain the necessary lucky number combinations.[59]

Nebraska required a constitutional amendment in 1962, supplemented by a legislative change the following year, to define lottery consideration as the payment of money for the purchase of property, etc. or "the expenditure of substantial time and effort." Now, as set out in the accompanying legislative Committee Report, drawings are permissible if participants merely have "to go to a store to register" or qualify by "mailing in an entry blank which could be obtained without charge."

33. Local Variations in Lottery Law Enforcement.

State lottery statutes are usually criminal in nature and, as such, are enforced by the district attorneys in the several counties within a state. There have been instances in which a plan is legal under state law but has been, nevertheless, the source of police action in a few counties. Usually this is based on socio-religious or seasonal grounds.

The socio-religious aspect stems from a local religious consensus which is "anti-giveaway" even though the promotion in question may not be illegal. The district attorney, whose personal feelings may also be involved, is not unnaturally responsive to such local feeling.

The following is an example of the seasonal variation. A manufacturer of outboard motor boats ran a dealer-incentive sales contest, planned for the summer season. It was legal in the state. Yet the Attorney General's office warned the sponsor not to use the plan in certain counties which had a large summer-resident and tourist influx. The reason was his knowledge that these counties, regardless of the legality of the plan, took a very "hard-nosed" attitude about promotions which were premised on such traffic. The manufacturer wisely—however unhappily—withdrew the contest in these counties.

Contest sponsors should ascertain such conditions from local sources.

34. Private Enforcement of Lottery Laws.

Aside from being criminal offenses, business-building lotteries can have a serious adverse effect on competitors who, as one court has said, "should not be forced to meet unlawful competition by becoming a violator of the law." [60] Accordingly, private actions for injunctive relief against a competitor's lottery have been sustained. These have generally been brought in connection with a local, traffic-building scheme which has caused a diversion of customers to the lottery operator.[61]

On the other hand, there does not appear to be any right to recover monetary damages in such situations.

E. MISCELLANEOUS.

35. Mass Media and Lotteries.

There are essentially two aspects of the lottery problem which concern the mass media, whether print or broadcast.

 (a) Contests by which a medium promotes its own circulation or growth.

 (b) The indirect effects upon the medium of carrying paid advertising of others which is itself suspect under the lottery laws.

As to the medium's own promotions, the medium is in the same position as any other business concern. The same rules apply, but print media are subject to an additional limitation. Ordinarily, coupons clipped from paid advertisements in a newspaper or magazine will not raise a consideration problem. A contestant is not required to buy the advertiser's product to participate. On the other hand, the contestant must buy the "product" (in this case, the newspaper) in order to obtain the coupon if the newspaper is itself the sponsor of the contest. This brings the arrangement within the definition of a "gift enterprise," discussed in Section 18 above.

In a contest sponsored by an advertiser, both print and broadcast media are involved, although for different reasons. The newspaper distributes a portion of its circulation through the mails. Newspapers have long enjoyed a special postal status, frequently referred to as the "mailing privilege." If the newspaper carries advertising for a lottery, the publisher may face questions about admission to the mails and the continuance of the mailing privilege. For this reason, publishers are alert to prevent the acceptance of any lottery advertising. As discussed in Section 26, if a publisher "knowingly" mails issues carrying such advertising, he is subject to the penalties of Section 1302 of the U.S. Criminal Code of 1948 and the parallel provisions of the Postal Laws and Regulations.

It is this media concern about lottery advertising which is a prime reason why the advertiser or sponsor should obtain an approval from the Post Office Department. Newspapers, when offered such advertising, frequently insist upon such Post Office Department approval. This is particularly true when dealing with types of plans which may use "a new twist" and with which the media may not be familiar. There have been instances in which media schedules have been upset because the advertiser was not able to satisfy promptly this demand by the newspaper.

The broadcast media have essentially the same problem under criminal law even though policed by the Federal Communications Commission, which has ruled in several cases that station promotions which offended the lottery were prohibited.[62] See Section 29 above. The "give-away cases," discussed in Section 24, limit this power of the Commission. The Federal Communications Commission Rules and Regulations, discussed in Section 29, apply to self-serving promotions of the stations as much as they do to commercially sponsored programming or announcements.

36. Charitable Sponsorship of Lotteries.

Business is frequently called upon to assist with or participate in fund-raising for some worthy cause such as a local charity or service organization. The public relations function frequently looks in this direction. Such fund-raising efforts not infrequently use giveaways, lucky number draws or bingo games.

The mere fact that the promotion is for a hospital or other worthy institution does not protect it from attack as a lottery if, in fact and in law, it is a lottery. The worthy motive is immaterial. Certain states, such as New York and Nebraska, have adopted special legislation permitting bingo games, etc. on behalf of such institutions if certain conditions are met. These are exceptions to the general rule.

The Post Office Department has ruled that advertising of bingo games, etc. is a postal violation even though the reference is only circumlocutional such as "Game Tonight" or "Money" if in fact the reference is to a game of chance such as bingo. The same is true of broadcast promotions of such activities. At the state level, local enforcement officers often "wink" at such games but this enforcement attitude does not affect the basic legal character of the game or plan.

37. Check List of Contest Rules.

Basic to any properly operated contest, regardless of its nature, is a well-constructed set of contest rules. These should be carefully designed and written so as to cover all prerequisites and eventualities which intelligent forehandedness can foresee. The rules should be checked with legal counsel as a matter of course.

Whenever prior approval is to be sought from a governmental agency such as the Post Office Department, a simple plan is to submit the rules themselves, thus complying with what the Department describes as a "full statement of the facts" as explained more fully in Section 26 above.

The following list is not intended to be a "canned" set of rules for any specific type of contest. It is a check list of subject matter which should be included in the rules if appropriate to the particular contest. Obviously, not every item will be included for every contest. Some are mutually exclusive. For example, item (g) indicating that no purchase is required is incompatible with item (m) which describes the required proof of purchase. Inclusion or exclusion will be dictated by the nature of the contest. In some instances comments have been added below. These are not by any means exhaustive of the particular subject. The check list items should be read in conjunction with other relevant portions of this chapter.

(a) Requirements as to name, address and, possibly, demographic information about the contestant, if necessary.

(b) How entries are to be handled by contestants; whether they are to be mailed, dropped into a box at the dealer's place of business, etc.

(c) Termination date of contest including latest acceptable post-marked date, for example.

(d) Persons eligible to enter. This usually includes everyone who otherwise qualifies except for personnel (and their families) of the sponsor, its advertising agency, the company managing the contest for the sponsor, etc. Perhaps only those twenty-one and over are eligible.

(e) Multiple entries, if permissible. Information about limitations thereon (weekly, for example) if appropriate.

(f) Required choices on entry such as YES/NO as to order for merchandise of sponsor.

(g) Specific mention that no purchase is required if that be the case.

(h) Duplicate prizes to be awarded in case of ties.

(i) Clear description of essay, slogan or other submission which may be required.

(j) Basis upon which entries will be judged, being specific and clear.

(k) Decision of judges is final, together with naming of judges or references to their qualifications or positions.

(l) Validation of entry provisions, if required, such as being stamped at dealer's store.

(m) Nature of proof of purchase, if appropriate.

(n) Acceptability of facsimiles or writing name of product in block letters on plain sheet of paper, etc.

(o) All entries become the property of the sponsor.

(p) Participants (perhaps prize winners only) agree that sponsor may use their names and photographs in announcing prizes, subsequent company promotions, news releases, advertising, etc.

(q) Description of tie-breaker provisions if contemplated, possible or likely.

(r) Description of prizes with kind, value, etc. detailed. No exaggeration or misrepresentation thereof.

(s) Information as to substitute or alternative prizes at discretion of winner, if involved.

(t) Method of notifying winners: by mail, posted at dealer's store, announced in newspapers, etc.

(u) Allowance of time for delivery of prizes by sponsor; instructions where to pick up prizes; etc.

(v) Information as to payment of sales taxes, etc. on prizes by winners, if necessary.

(w) Contest void and not available wherever taxed, illegal, regulated, etc.

The impact of the rules upon the sponsor's relations with contestants and winners is discussed in Section 38 below.

38. Relations With Contestants.

The rules of a contest are the basis of the relationship between the contest sponsor and the contestants. They constitute an offer to all prospective contestants and this offer becomes a contract when a contestant meets the conditions set forth in the rules.[63]

If a contestant has satisfied those conditions and is the winner but the sponsor refuses to deliver the prize, the contestant may sue and recover for the prize. Thus, in a so-called "showcase contest," the sponsor displayed on TV a variety of merchandise. The viewers were to estimate by mail as closely as possible the prices of the various items. The plaintiff did so. The court held that the plaintiff could recover the prize from the contest sponsor because she had complied with the conditions, giving the most accurate estimate on a particular item.[64]

Once a contract has come into existence by virtue of the publication or announcement of the rules and by the compliance of the contestant with those rules, the sponsor may not change them at any time thereafter.[65]

Most contests, whether dependent upon skill or chance, provide that the decision of the judges is final. Such a rule is enforceable against a contestant if the judges are not guilty of a lack of good faith, gross or intentional mistake, fraud or the making of a decision contrary to the express rules of the contest.[66]

Another frequent rule provides that the contest is not open to the employees (or members of their immediate families) of the sponsor, its advertising agency or of the contest company. This has produced varied legal results. It may be expected that the phrase "immediate family" would be construed as not to disenfranchise anyone except the employee himself and those close—perhaps blood—relatives who live under the same roof with him. Thus, the father of an employee was permitted to recover his prize under such a rule because it was shown that the son-employee was over twenty-one, married and living separate from the father.[67]

39. Special Contest Service Marks.

A company may operate the same or similar contest periodically, perhaps giving it some distinctive name or even using a distinctive design or configuration in connection with it. Such name or design is not a trademark but a service mark, the general characteristics of which are discussed in Chapter 10, Part C, Subsection (b). Of course, the company's regular trademark is likely to be used also.

As to the service mark (name, design or combination thereof) this should be treated as would any other mark owned by the company. It should be registered under both federal and state laws. Even if the company may not initially regard such service mark as important nor worthy of registration—perhaps not even considering the possibility of repeated use in later contests—it should bear the designation that it is a service mark although, of course, there should be no indication of registration at that time.

Notes

1. A.B.C. *et al.*, v. United States, 110 F. Supp. 374 (S.D.N.Y. 1953), *rev'd*, 347 U.S. 284 (1954).
2. This is also the basis of the F.T.C. investigation started in late 1966. See also Comment, 10 VILL. L. REV. 597, at 600 (1954).
3. Garden City Chamber of Commerce v. Wagner, 100 F. Supp. 769 (1951), *stay denied*, 192 F.2d 240 (2d Cir. 1951).
4. A.B.C. *et al.*, v. United States, *supra* note 1, at 598.
5. NAT'L ASS'N OF BROADCASTERS, BROADCASTING AND THE LOTTERY LAWS 4–5 4th ed. 1962).
6. Baedaro v. Caldwell, 156 Neb. 489, 56 N.W.2d 706 (1953); Carl Co. v. Lennon, 86 Misc. 255, 148 N.Y.S. 375 (1914).
7. See, *e.g.*, Conn. Gen. Stat. §8667 (1949).
8. *Ex parte* Jackson, 96 U.S. 727 (1878).
9. In Dandy Products, Inc. v. F.T.C., 332 F.2d 985, 1964 Trade Cas. ¶71,139 (6th Cir. 1964), the court rejected the defense that "the moral climate of the community had changed" so as to exculpate the respondent, charged with a lottery practice.
10. People v. Lavin, 179 N.Y. 164, 71 N.E. 753, 66 L.R.A. 601 (1904).
11. U.S. POST OFFICE DEP'T, THE LAW VS. LOTTERIES 8–9 (1963). See also cases cited in United States v. Rich, 90 F. Supp. 624 (1950).
12. 132 Misc. 597, 230 N.Y.S. 360 (1928). See also Westerhaus Co. v. Cincinnati, 165 Ohio 327 (1956).
13. Public Clearing House v. Coyne, 194 U.S. 497 (1904).
14. U.S. Post Office Dep't, *supra* note 11, at 9.
15. Nat'l Ass'n of Broadcasters, *supra* note 5, at 6–7.
16. Savoy Mfg. Co. v. F.T.C., 152 F.2d 65 (2d Cir. 1945).
17. Pickett, *Contests and Lottery Laws*, 45 HARV. L. REV. 1196, at 1212 (1932).
18. Brooklyn Daily Eagle v. Voorhies, 181 Fed. 579 (E.D.N.Y. 1910).
19. Pickett, *supra* note 17.
20. Amlie Strand Hardware Co. v. Morse, 176 Minn. 598, 224 N.W. 158 (1929); Com. v. Jenkins, 159 Ky. 80, 166 S.W. 794 (1914).
21. See cases collected, 2 TRADE REG. REP. ¶¶7123.10, .70.
22. United States v. Jefferson, 134 Fed. 299 (C.C.W.D. Ky. 1905).
23. Pickett, *supra* note 17, at 1214–15.
24. Donaldson v. Read Magazine, 333 U.S. 178 (1947).
25. NAT'L BETTER BUSINESS BUREAU, DO'S AND DON'TS IN ADVERTISING COPY §2-265.
26. Pickett, *supra* note 17, at 1206.
27. U.S. Post Office Dep't, *supra* note 11, at 6.
28. Garden City Chamber of Commerce v. Wagner, *supra* note 3.
29. Horner v. United States, 147 U.S. 449 (1893).
30. Affiliated Enterprises v. Waller, 40 Del. 28, 5 A.2d 257 (1939); Maughs v. Porter, 157 Va. 415, 161 S.E. 242 (1931).

31. U.S. Post Office Dep't, Postal Bull., Feb. 13, 1947, at 2.

32. Caples Company v. United States, 243 F.2d 232 (D.C. Cir. 1957).

33. Garden City Chamber of Commerce v. Wagner, *supra* note 3.

34. U.S. Post Office Dep't, *supra* note 11, at 6–7. See also Idea Research and Development Corp. v. Hultman, 1 R.R.2d 2104 (Dist. Ct. Iowa 1964); *In re* KTOK Radio, Inc., 7 R.R.2d 694 (F.C.C. 1966).

35. Ohio Att'y Gen. Op. No. 67-064, July 15, 1967.

36. *Ohio Official Rules Giveaways Violate State's Law*, A.A., July 24, 1967, at 38.

37. Herald Publishing Co. v. Bill, 142 Conn. 53, 111 A.2d 4 (1955); Boyd v. Piggly Southern, Inc., 115 Ga. App. 628, 155 S.E.2d 630 (1967); Glover v. Malloska, 238 Mich. 216, 213 N.W. 107 (1927); United-Detroit Theaters Corp. v. Colonial Theater Enterprises, Inc., 280 Mich. 425, 273 N.W. 756 (1937); Maughs v. Porter, *supra* note 30. See particularly Lucky Calendar Co. v. Cohen, 19 N.J. 399, 117 A.2d 487 (1955), and State v. Grant, 162 Neb. 210, 75 N.W.2d 611 (1956) (later reversed by statute) for good discussions of cases of other jurisdictions going both ways on this issue.

38. See, *e.g.*, Minn. Att'y Gen. Op., 1948–49 Trade Cas. ¶62,371 (holding requirement to visit store not violative of Minn. Unfair Trade Practice Act); State v. Stern, 201 Minn. 139, 275 N.W. 626 (1937); see comment on State v. Grant, *supra* note 37.

39. U.S. Post Office Dep't, *supra* note 11, at 6–7.

40. *Supra,* note 1.

41. Garden City Chamber of Commerce v. Wagner, *supra* note 3.

42. U.S. Post Office Dep't News Release, June 4, 1965.

43. Blair Contest News Bull., Jan.–Feb., 1967.

44. A.B.C. *et al.,* v. United States, *supra* note 1.

45. Nat'l Better Business Bureau, *supra* note 25, at §§3–7.

46. F.T.C. v. R. F. Keppel & Bros., Inc., F.T.C. Dkt. No. 1816, *rev'd*, 63 F.2d 81 (3d Cir. 1933), *rev'd and F.T.C. order reinstated and aff'd*, 291 U.S. 304 (1934).

47. Zitserman v. F.T.C., 200 F.2d 519 (8th Cir. 1952).

48. See cases collected, 2 TRADE REG. REP. ¶7123.

49. *Id.* ¶7123.90. See also Peerless Products v. F.T.C., 284 F.2d 285 (7th Cir. 1960).

50. Nat'l Ass'n of Broadcasters, *Anello Clarifies Intent of Lottery Law*, TV Code News, June, 1967, at 1, 3.

51. *Ad Curbs Limit N.Y. Lottery Sales, State Official Says*, A.A., July 17, 1967, at 12.

52. This restriction, essentially the same for AM, FM and TV stations, is found in §§3.122, 3.292 and 3.656, respectively, of the F.C.C. Rules and Regulations.

53. See, *inter alia*, cases cited *infra* note 62.

54. NAT'L ASS'N OF BROADCASTERS, TELEVISION CODE, §XII, at 18 (1966).

55. *The Reporter of Direct Mail Advertising*, Dec. 1964, at E2.

56. Fla. Stat. §849.092 (1965).

57. Ill. Rev. Stat., ch. 38, §28-2 (b) (1961).

58. Midwest TV, Inc. v. Waller, 44 Ill. App.2d 401, 194 N.E.2d 653 (1963).

59. People v. Eagle Food Centers, Inc., 46 Ill. App.2d 24, 196 N.E.2d 366 (1964), *rev'd,* 31 Ill.2d 535, 202 N.E.2d 473 (1964).
60. Featherstone v. Independent Serv. Station Ass'n, 10 S.W.2d 124 (Tex. Civ. App. 1928).
61. Glover v. Malloska, *supra* note 37; California Gasoline Retailers v. Regal Petroleum Corp., 50 Cal.2d 844, 330 P.2d 778 (1958). See also Greater Akron Gasoline Dealers Ass'n v. Standard Oil Co. of Ohio (C.P. Ct. Summit City, Ohio), A.A., May 22, 1967, at 18 (not officially reported).
62. *In re* WRBL, 2 F.C.C. 687 (1936); *In re* KXL, 4 F.C.C. 186 (1937); *In re* WMBQ, 5 F.C.C. 501 (1938).
63. Las Vegas Hacienda, Inc. v. Gibson, 77 Nev. 25, 359 P.2d 85, 87 A.L.R.2d 645 (1961).
64. Moreno v. Marbil Productions, Inc., 296 F.2d 543 (2d Cir. 1961).
65. Holt v. Wilson, 55 S.W.2d 580 (Tex. Civ. App. 1932).
66. Furgille v. Disabled Amer. Veterans Serv. Foundation, 116 F. Supp. 375 (S.D.N.Y. 1952); Endres v. Buffalo Auto. Dealers Ass'n, 29 Misc.2d 756, 217 N.Y.S.2d 460 (1961).
67. Bryant v. Deseret News Publishing Co., 120 Utah 241, 233 P.2d 355 (1951).

Chapter 14

The Company and the Community

467

E. MISCELLANEOUS

Chapter 14

The Company and the Community

A. INTRODUCTION.

1. Chapter Purposes.

The thrust of this chapter is the legal exposure of a company engaged in a broad-based community relations program.[1] "Community" is here used in a geographical or social sense as meaning the immediate local area in which the company or its plant is located and throughout which the influence of the company is felt.

In a sense, we are here dealing with details—not long-range policy or ultimate aims and results. It is assumed that a community relations program has been adopted and its overall concepts approved.

At the same time, some of the purely local projects invite legal problems which are equally applicable to similar corporate programs on a national scale. The legal involvements in "bicycling" an art exhibit around four adjacent county-seat high schools differ essentially only in degree from those of a traveling art show hung in museums in 20 cities from coast to coast over a period of two years.

Some of the subjects may seem trivial and, in fact, are—if viewed on an individual basis. Cumulatively, however, they may mount into a massive and costly load. Again, the only difference is one of degree between the school girl who snags her dress on a rough concrete block wall during a class plant tour and the local housewife who breaks her leg when she trips on an unlighted company parking lot after an amateur musical revue in the plant auditorium. Both are in-plant accidents and the company is subject to the same legal duties.

Although the use of company or personal foundations may be important in community activities, they are not here considered. Such long-range programs involve legal and tax approaches which are generally beyond the scope of this work.[2] So too is the corporate gift of a substantial community facility such as a park, hospital, community center or other permanent community structure or adjunct. Such projects depend on extended negotiations and relatively unique legal considerations, too ramified to discuss herein.

2. Community Relations and Corporate Powers.

Since 1935, the Internal Revenue Code has permitted business corporations to make "contributions" or donations up to five percent of taxable income without proof of any direct corporate benefit. If contributions exceed that amount, the excess must be justified as a business expense.

However, the right to make such contributions also involves the power of a corporation under the corporation laws of the state wherein the company has been organized.

At common law—unchanged by statute—a corporation could not make a donation of its property and any donation was considered *ultra vires* or beyond its proper powers. Gradually, there developed a concept of direct corporate benefit which would justify a corporate donation. In the leading *Steinway* case,[3] decided in 1896, the New York court said:

> It is a question, therefore, in each case, of the logical relation of the act to the corporate purposes expressed in the charter. If that act is one which is lawful in itself, and not otherwise prohibited, is done for the purpose of serving corporate ends, and is reasonably tributary to the promotion of those ends, in a substantial, and not in a remote and fanciful sense, it may fairly be considered within charter powers. The field of corporate action in respect to the exercise of incidental powers is thus, I think, an expanding one. As industrial conditions change with them, an act becomes permissible which at an earlier period would not have been considered to be within corporate power.

The *Steinway* case dealt with the donation of a hospital for employees. The court believed that this was a promotion of corporate ends in a substantial and not in "a remote and fanciful sense." The gift was therefore considered within the corporate charter powers.[4] The last cases which seem to have been decided in this legal area are *A. P. Smith Mfg. Co. v. Barlow et al.*[5] and *Union Pacific Railroad Co. v. Trustees, Inc. et al.*[6] These two cases held that donations to Princeton University and to a charitable foundation respectively were proper even though the charters of the two corporations involved did not expressly grant the power to make charitable contributions. The courts said that such power existed "even though there might not be express statutory privilege granted under the laws of the state."

At the present time, it appears that only Arizona, Idaho, and Montana do not have corporation laws which recognize the power of a business corporation to make donations for charitable, scientific, religious or educational purposes.

Notwithstanding the fact that the states have now generally granted corporations the right to make donations to what is broadly described as "charities," legal writers have recommended that discretion be exercised in connection therewith, one pointing out: [7]

> [T]he board of directors should use good judgment in the exercise of the power. Donations should be reasonable in amount in the light of the corporation's financial condition, bear some reasonable relation to the corporation's interest, and not be so "remote and fanciful" as to excite the opposition of shareholders whose property is being used. Direct corporate benefit is no longer necessary, but corporate interest remains as a point.

Even though state statutes are today reasonably permissive, justification of certain community-relations expenditures as business expenses may be necessary under federal tax laws as discussed above.

In *United States v. Jefferson Mills*,[8] a company was faced with a need for better-educated employees. It contracted with the local school board to upgrade the local educational program and paid the school board for such additional training. The court held that this was a "valid decision" by the company's officers and that the cost was properly deductible as an "ordinary and necessary business expense." It was held not to be a contribution or a gift, limited to five percent of taxable corporate income.

These matters have direct implications for public relations practitioners who may be involved in such corporate matters:

(a) Decisions as to such contributions should be made at a high level of management. In some companies this is handled through a special committee which reports either to the Executive Committee or directly to the Board of Directors.

(b) The PR director of a corporation should not take it upon himself to commit the company to a charitable or community gift or commitment without first receiving approval from the requisite echelon of management. This approval may be indicated by a declaration of policy by the Board delegating specifically the right to make such contributions to certain types of activity and subject to certain limitations.

(c) All public announcements relative to such donations—matters which are routinely within the province of the PR department or PR counsel—should, if possible, describe in some detail the purpose thereof, indicating its relationship to the corporation's interests. In the case of a contribution to a local hospital, Community Chest, Boy Scout activity, etc., the corporate interest in the community is obvious.

Even the earlier cases, decided before the statutory amendments permitting contributions of this sort generally, seem to have been much more lenient in connection with corporate contributions made to institutions or activities in and around the community or area where the corporation operated. On the other hand, such donations were not approved by the courts when made to institutions in areas in which the corporation had no interest and did no business.

(d) Stockholders have a definite interest in the nature and amount of corporate donations. Questions are asked at annual meetings —not always by a so-called "professional stockholder"—relative to these matters. The PR director should therefore brief the chairman of the meeting about these matters so that his answer to stockholders' questions may be both accurate and politic.

(e) Many such contributions originate with the corporate PR director, who believes that they will serve a worthwhile and specific corporate PR purpose. In making such recommendations to management, he must be mindful of the problems discussed above. In so doing, he is both serving management and fulfilling his PR function.

3. Community Relations and Trade/Plant Secrets.

Any program which commits the company to a continuing liaison between the company—and company personnel—and the community may raise questions of plant security or trade secret protection. There are well-documented—although not publicized—instances of an almost paranoiac fear by management that in-plant visitation and public contacts with the community will, somehow or other, compromise such secrets.

As with any management function, a proper perspective must be maintained. While company secrets may be very important, there is no reason why their existence should emasculate the community relations program. Both functions can exist side by side if both are appropriately managed.

For a further discussion of this important possible contretemps, see Chapter 17, Section 14.

B. COMMUNITY USE OF COMPANY PREMISES.

4. In General.

Company public relations and community relations involve many relationships with the public—or selected sectors of the public—which require the use of company premises by the public. In most such situations, the public is specifically invited to visit the company premises. Sometimes this invitation is a general and continuing one; at other times it will be for a specific event or purpose and at a specifically limited or designated time.

Assuming, therefore, that members of the public are upon company premises either by permission or invitation—not as trespassers—the company has certain legal obligations and duties to such persons. These are discussed in Sections 6 to 11 below.

5. The Public Relations Obligation.

Inasmuch as the company PR man or department will usually be responsible for setting up and operating programs of this kind, it is mandatory that he appreciate their inherent problems. For this purpose, he should consult with company counsel *before* these programs are organized or announced.

They must be properly structured—if only because the company will need proper insurance coverage to protect against possible claims from injured members of the public. More than this, however, mishandling matters of this sort may lead to adverse—perhaps disastrous—community impact.

6. Bases of Company Liability.

When members of the public are upon company premises, a basic question is the nature and extent of the company's responsibility for any injuries which they may suffer. This liability depends upon the status of the person involved. There are two basic categories: licensee and invitee.[9]

Generally speaking, a licensee is a person who enters upon a company's premises with its consent and nothing more—not by invitation, express or implied. Ordinarily such a person enters for his own purposes, not those of the company. The classic example is the person allowed to take a short cut over company property for his own convenience. In the public relations context, tourists who gratuitously ask permission to visit a plant are considered licensees since they enter by consent but have not been invited.[10] As to such groups *invited* to inspect a plant, see below.

If the visitor is merely a licensee, the company generally owes him no duty except to refrain from willfully or wantonly injuring him.[11] On the other hand, if he is an invitee, the company—as the owner and occupier of the premises—owes him a duty of reasonable and due care.[12]

One line of cases, followed in certain states, considers the visitor an invitee only if the purpose of his presence on the company's premises constitutes an "economic benefit" to the company. The obvious example is the customer who visits a store to make a purchase.

The second line of cases is based on the "public invitation" theory and disregards the necessity of the existence of an economic benefit. These cases base the public invitation [13]

upon the fact that the occupier, by his arrangement of the premises or other conduct, has led the entrant to believe that the
premises were intended to be used by visitors, as members of the
public, for the purpose which the entrant was pursuing and that
reasonable care was taken to make the place safe for those who
enter for that purpose.

Under the economic benefit test, the courts have strained to find—in
less obvious situations—"some even more tenuous economic advantage,
in the form of *advertising or good will, . . .*" [14] In their effort to reach
what they apparently consider to be a just decision, the courts have been
free in finding the economic benefit in such things as tourists visiting a
factory at the invitation of the owner.[15] Of course, the result would be
the same if such courts admittedly adhered to the public invitation theory. See Section 7 below. Also, the modern trend appears to be to make of
the visitor an invitee if possible in order to protect the visitor under the
duty of due care to which he is then entitled.

7. Company Invitations to the Public.

The invitation by the company to enter upon its premises may be
implied or express. When the storekeeper opens his front door for business, this is an implied invitation and the customers who enter are invitees. However, in the public relations context, the invitation is almost
always quite specific. Therefore, the dual theories discussed in Section 6
above do not have too much impact. Yet the distinction between the two
theories continues important in view of the lack of uniformity among all
jurisdictions.

The specific invitation, in a sense, vitiates the plaintiff's need to show
"economic benefit" to the company. Realistically, however, the entry by
the public for a plant tour, the holding of a women's club meeting in the
company lounge, the use of a diamond on company premises by a Little
League team—all are for the benefit of the company.

Most states now apply the invitation theory. Yet it is only recently that
it has been applied to a purely public relations use of the premises. We
find such a holding in *McKinnon v. Washington S. & L. Ass'n,*[16] decided
in 1966 by the Washington Supreme Court.

In this case the defendant concern held "open house" for a period of
three days when it opened its place of business in 1962. A large sign was
displayed inviting the use by "local clubs and organized groups for meetings and conferences, either during regular office hours or in the eve-
nings," referring to a large room and a kitchen located at the rear of the
business premises. Many local organizations did, in fact, use the room for
its meetings.

There was a special outside entrance and walk to this meeting room for use by the public. In the grass and near the edge of this concrete walk was a sprinkler head. The plaintiff, an adult leader of a Girl Scout group, while on the concrete walk, struck the sprinkler head with her foot, fell and was injured. Washington had not theretofore applied the public invitation theory but did so in this case. The court said:

> The undisputed facts indicate that a segment of the public was invited by defendant association to use its building for group meetings. Under these circumstances, it was incumbent upon defendant to exercise reasonable care in making the premises safe for the purpose for which they had been held open. On these facts we hold as a matter of law that plaintiff was an invitee at the time of her fall.

In *McKinnon* the invitation was extended by a sign and group reservations were made by specific contact with the concern. However, the invitation may be extended in many other ways. The company may write to local groups or school principals. The company may announce a schedule of plant tours in the local newspapers. Employees may be advised by announcements on in-plant bulletin boards that facilities are available for meetings, etc.

Whatever the method of invitation, in most states members of the public who come upon the premises in response thereto are invitees. Accordingly, the company generally owes such invitees a duty of due care and will be held responsible for injuries if it has been negligent. As to limitations on this general rule, see Section 8 below.

While PR invitations to the public are usually specific and overt, they may also be implied. It has been held, for example, that a child who enters a gas station to get a free comic book is an invitee.[17] So too are persons who attend free lectures or demonstrations open to the public.[18] The economic benefit to the company may be slight or non-existent in these cases but the plaintiffs would recover on the invitation theory.

8. Limitations on Company Responsibility.

While persons on the company premises in the course of PR-oriented activities have the right to anticipate that the company will use due care in the maintenance of the premises for their use by the public, there are certain limitations to the company's obligations.

One of the important prerequisites to invitee status is that the invitee use only the portion of the premises allotted to his use. Thus, a member of a plant-tour group who wanders away from the conducted tour and explores on his own some other part of the plant, becomes only a licensee

as soon as he leaves the group, even though he was an invitee originally.[19]

The same is true of an invitee who "wants a closer look" at an operating machine and leaves a group, and is injured when he leaves the permissible area.

If the company maintains toilet facilities for use by invitees, that status
continues during use thereof.[20] However, if the facilities are only for
company-employee use and not for the public generally, use by a member
of the public makes the user only a licensee—again, even though the user
was an invitee when he entered the premises by specific invitation.[21]
This is merely a specific example of the invitee's leaving designated areas
for his own purposes. This situation may also be affected by local Board
of Health regulations.

9. Open Houses and Plant Tours.

Open houses and plant tours are frequent community relations tools.
The exposure of the company in such cases is the same as in *McKinnon*
discussed in Section 7 above. In that case, however, the area to which the
public was admitted was a special, separate room or area. In the open
house or plant tour, the public is conducted through the company plant
—perhaps when the plant and its equipment are in operation.[22]

Injuries to persons on such guided plant tours do occur—no matter
how carefully the company may plan and supervise the event. Participants are invitees to whom a duty of due care is due. See Sections 6 and 7
above.

In one such case, the defendants operated a bakery and creamery,
doing a wholesale business over several counties. Proud of their up-to-
date machinery and their sanitary operations, they widely "advertised"
that their products "were not touched by human hands." They invited
the public to inspect their equipment and methods. Four or five classes
from the local high school went through the defendant's plant each year
and were shown the machinery and methods. The court said: [23]

> It is a reasonable inference from the evidence that this was one of
> the defendants' methods of advertising their products; that it was
> done through arrangements with the school authorities to bring
> classes there. . . . These classes came by appointment. . . .

When the appointment was made, the defendants instructed their employees about the demonstration the class was coming to see; "to specially
clean up the place and have things in readiness, to have as little machinery running as possible and to give demonstrations of their work." A
department supervisor was instructed to work with them "like any teach-
er with a class of students in school."

A member of one class, so invited to defendants' plant, was seriously injured when her hand was caught in an unprotected ice crusher. The company was held liable.

There is now no question that a company is liable for lack of due care if a member of the public is injured while going through the plant "on a conducted tour" where the company supplies the guide, points out the nature of the operation, perhaps gives samples of the product.

It is interesting to note that the court in the above case quoted and adopted the following language: [24]

> A recognized, practical method of advertising, and one of the best means for increasing business is to get the general public to visit a mercantile or manufacturing plant for the purpose of acquainting them with the modern hygienic system of conducting same, as well as familiarizing the visitor with each department and the operation thereof; that such visits on the part of the public result in benefit to the company whose plant is thus inspected is generally admitted, *though the benefit that may accrue to the company after the visit of any particular individual may be long delayed.* (Emphasis added.)

This is an unusually perceptive judicial description and appreciation of the long-range character and efficacy of public relations. This is particularly true since it appears in a *1920* case, at a time when public relations had not yet acquired definite substance and purpose. Although the courts may appreciate the same values as the PR practitioner, nevertheless such value judgment is the foundation upon which company liability is premised when it opens its "house" to the invited visitor.

In another case a plant was opened to a trade association, the members of which made an inspection tour by invitation of the plant foreman, a member of the association. Another member of the group was killed during the tour and the company was held liable.[25]

10. Athletic Activities.

A frequent community-oriented program—especially for companies in smaller towns—is the maintenance of athletic facilities, use of which by the public is permitted and even encouraged. If the public—or teams from local schools or leagues—are invited to use the facilities, those doing so are clearly invitees and have a right to expect the company will use due care in maintaining the grounds, etc. See Section 7 above.

If the company merely permits—in a sense, "winks at"—pickup baseball games on its premises by local schoolboys, such players would be licensees only.[26] On the other hand, if the company grades and lays out a diamond and then permits the boys to play there, they have now become invitees and the company has a duty of due care.[27] There is now an implied invitation to the community that the field has been "fixed up" for use by the boys. If, however, the boys climbed over a high fence to play on a field reserved for company use they would be trespassers—not even licensees—since they lack the company's consent to use it at all.

If members of the public are invited as spectators and enter company grounds, they are also invitees. As to this, see Chapter 21, Section 15. It is immaterial that they do not pay an admission.

Liability may arise, not only from negligent maintenance of the company's premises but also from negligence in supervising or controlling the athletic events themselves.[28] This is true whether the events take place on or off the company's premises. Thus, if the company sponsors and controls an event off its own premises, the company must treat those attending as invitees.

Inasmuch as the element of "control" is so important in situations such as this, the company would not be responsible if an employees' "athletic association" operated the grounds or managed the events at which members of the public might be injured. As to this, see Chapter 21, Section 16.

11. Company Safety Precautions.

PR men and companies recognize the importance of safety during plant tours and open houses. Special precautions are frequently taken—in addition to the normal care taken to protect the working employees.

Some companies prepare and distribute to the plant manager or superintendent—also to the safety director if there is one—special manuals dealing with such public visits. One company with scattered plants provides a 20-page brochure under the title "Playing Host." In addition to instructions as to organizing and handling such events from the public relations point of view, it has this to say about safety:

ACCIDENTS REALLY HURT

Accidents to employees, of course, are to be avoided *at all times*. But we should be *doubly* careful to guard the safety of visitors. They are not familiar with the plant and the possible dangers.

Few things make a worse impression than accidents. If one person in a group visiting an XYZ plant should be injured, the accident would be the one thing that would stand out in the minds of our visitors. Little else would be mentioned in telling of the visit to XYZ.

Accidents hurt us all in many ways. We all have a great deal to gain by guarding our safety, the safety of our fellow workers and the safety of guests who come to see us.

*   *   *   *

MORE ABOUT SAFETY

You'll have some special safety problems during Open House. Ordinarily, parking space is ample for a group visiting your plant. But crowds usually are so large for Open House that you'll have to make parking arrangements at nearby lots.

You'll need signs directing your guests to these lots. . . . You'll need two or more policemen to direct traffic. . . .

Mere announcement of a "safety first" policy is not enough. There must be a constant follow-up. The courts, in "invitee" cases, analyze the nature of the precautions taken by the company to foreclose injury to the invitee. They also query in detail the precise efforts made by company employees to protect the visitors, almost step by step. Lack of care and caution (both before and during the visit) is evidence of culpable negligence.

C. COMMUNITY RELATIONS AND COMPANY MAIL.

12. In General.

Most companies and their PR directors are acutely aware of the importance of direct mail as a community relations tool. Some, however, may not be equally aware of the need for proper handling of incoming mail, much of it from members of the community.

The basic difficulty stems from the variety and scope of that mail. The incoming "lawyer's letter" is easy enough to recognize. Even the letter addressed to "Mr. President" is likely to get proper routing and treatment. The unnoticed legal pitfalls lie in letters addressed generally to "XYZ Company."

Much of this consumer or public mail will prove innocuous. On the other hand, mishandling of even one or two pieces may prove legally expensive. The careful mail-handling blueprint described in Section 15 below evidences this. From such seemingly routine matters as "complaints" may stem serious legal involvements. They may lead to product liability suits, civil rights charges, to defamation actions, etc. See Section 13 below.

Considerable preliminary planning may be necessary. The first consideration is the screening and routing to the proper department for handling and reply. Some companies consider this so important that the screening is not left to a mail-room clerk but is assigned to a knowledgeable middle-echelon officer—perhaps attached to the PR department. Some companies are known to maintain "logs" in which is entered every piece of general mail.

The specific routing of each letter to the proper department—public relations, sales, legal, etc.—will depend upon its nature, the relative ability of each department to dispose of it properly and expeditiously and, above all, the potential legal exposure which it may posit. As to a specific routing program, see Section 15 below.

13. Complaints.

The handling of complaints is a constant strain upon community relations and usually falls to the PR department or a branch thereof. In the multi-plant company, they may be handled at each plant. In the multi-product company, product complaints are likely to be handled by the product division. This decentralization of responsibility requires "home office" direction. All staff involved therein should operate uniformly. To insure this, some companies distribute specific instructions—sometimes amounting to a separate manual—to appropriate personnel.

A basic premise in handling complaints—whether considered from the PR or legal point of view—is that the reply should not prejudge the accuracy or validity of the complaint. Usually, unless the complaint is a frequent one—the PR man or other staff may not have the necessary information to evaluate it. Furthermore, an open admission of a defect in the product may later turn up in court as an "admission against interest," binding upon the company.[29]

It is important to check all facts before framing a reply. This is a legal necessity. If adverse facts develop, it usually will be advisable—even necessary—to pass the complaint along to the legal department. As to establishing PR/legal liaison in preparation for such procedures for situations of this sort, see Chapter 1.

14. Idea Submissions.

Almost every company will receive unsolicited submissions of allegedly new ideas and suggestions for use by the company in developing new products or improving old ones, sales and promotional methods, administrative procedures, and practically every aspect of company operations. These submissions definitely warrant special treatment. This is also true when they are received by outside PR counsel, advertising agencies, management consultants, etc. For several methods of handling these submissions, see Chapter 6, Sections 5 to 11.

15. Distribution of Responsibilities.

In recognition of the many different kinds of questions which may be involved in incoming mail—as well as the varying degrees of legal exposure which each may implicate—one large national company distributes its incoming "public mail" on the following basis:

(a) *To the product division involved:*
Correspondence dealing with premiums.
Inquiries about product availability.
Material requiring sales follow-up.
Product quality complaints.
Requests for advertised offers.

(b) *To Consumer Service, Public Relations Department:*
Questions involving two or more products or overall company activities.
Inquiries about use of products in the home.
Complaints about products in home use.
Technical inquiries about chemical composition, additives, etc.— unless coming from a government source.
Correspondence with medical, dental, teaching, engineering or other professions.
Requests for materials available in the department.

(c) *To the Public Relations Department:*
Inquiries from writers, editors and publications, as well as stock-holders.

(d) *To the Legal Department:*
Correspondence involving possible "product liability" claims and mentioning injury or loss from purchase or use of any company product.
Submission of ideas for new products, advertising, promotion, etc.
Correspondence from federal, state or municipal governments or agencies, regardless of its nature.
Complaints about pricing practices, price discrimination, trade practices, civil rights matters.
Correspondence relating to existing litigation.
Correspondence concerning matters previously handled by legal department.

Some companies require that other departments rout to the Legal Department any correspondence if there is the least question about their own ability to handle it properly, even though that department may have originally received the letter under the standing directions of the company.

In smaller companies this degree of diffusion may not be necessary or even possible. The PR Department and the Legal Department (or outside counsel) will be the two usually involved in such companies.

D. CULTURAL PROGRAMS.

16. Growth and Scope.

More and more corporate interest is being directed toward the support, in various ways, of community-oriented cultural programs. These have a broad sweep and include such diverse activities as traveling art shows, sponsorship of TV classical drama, underwriting of local orchestral concerts, literary contests of all kinds, in-plant employee choruses and instrumental groups, print media advertising—largely institutional—using fine art, support for seminars, contributions of works of art to museums, etc.[30]

The varied scope of these corporate excursions into the arts creates a medley of legal relationships and exposures. Some of these are alien to those with which most companies are routinely concerned. The more important thereof are discussed in Sections 17 to 23 below. If the cultural event is held on company premises, Sections 4 to 11 above are relevant.

Some question has arisen as to whether such programs are to be justified on a corporate economic benefit basis or merely as an esoteric contribution to the public's esthetics.[31] From the evidence to date it would appear that a considerable corporate benefit may be demonstrated—whatever the peripheral values may add to the cultural scene.[32] This may become important tax-wise or for other legal reasons. See Section 2 above.

17. Fine Arts Programs.

Corporate support of the fine arts as part of a community relations program is constantly increasing.[33] The use of the fine arts program has increased to such an extent that some PR firms maintain a separate "Fine Arts Department" to service the art programs of their clients.[34]

To a considerable degree the legal questions are the same whether the program is the hanging of a permanent collection in the company's lobby or the sponsorship of an annual, juried competition and traveling art show, hung in museums and colleges throughout the country. There are, generally, two legal areas involved in such fine art support:

    (a) Relationships with the artists.

    (b) Relationships with the "exhibitor"—the museum or gallery in which the exhibit is hung and presented to the public.

18. Relationships With Artists.

Whether the exhibit is based on the purchase of existing—even "old"
—paintings or the sponsorship of a competition for new works, the basic
question is the extent of the rights acquired by the company.

These rights will, of course, depend upon the extent and result of
negotiations with the artist or his agent. If a competition is the vehicle,
they will depend upon the terms of the "invitation" extended to the
artists and of the documents used in making the "purchase awards."
Usually the company will buy outright some of the winning entries. It
may require only limited rights in the other entries—perhaps only the
right to reproduce them. As to acquisition of such rights generally, see
Chapter 9, Sections 5 to 11. If "purchase awards" are being made, this
would imply acquisition of all rights through purchase but this should be
made clear.[35]

If only limited rights are to be acquired, their nature should be indicated clearly in the "invitation." The right to reproduce may be limited
to use in the show's catalog, for general promotion and publicity for the
show or it may call for unlimited distribution, even unconnected with the
show. Specific concepts and needs will dictate their amplitude.[36]

The company should also be certain that it acquires the right to use
the artist's name and artistic biography in the promotional materials as
well as for supplemental purposes if deemed necessary. There have been
instances when the artist has objected to such use—especially when he
has no right to prior approval of the text or purpose thereof.

The sponsoring company will usually reserve to itself the first option to
purchase all submitted or accepted works. Beyond this, the terms of the
competition may provide that all accepted works are to be considered
available for sale to the public. However, in fairness to the artist, the
company should only "accept bids" for the works with the final decision
left to the artist. The sponsor charges no commission and the purchase/
sale transaction should be consummated between artist (or his agent)
and the buyer.

The company should not be a "middleman" in the matter. If it so acts,
it may find itself subject to a morass of sales tax payments and reports in
every state in which a sale is made even though the company does not
otherwise "do business" in those states.[37]

19. Sponsor/Exhibitor Arrangements.

There does not appear to be any hard and fast pattern as to the
relative responsibilities and contributions of the sponsor and the exhibitor. In general, however, the sponsor pays for the development of the

concept, assembly of the collection, its documentation and the overall coordination. The exhibitor seems to be responsible for the installation and hanging of the show and security during the exhibition. Transportation costs may be paid by either or may be shared.[38]

Whatever the arrangements are, they should be clearly spelled out between the parties although no specific form need be used. A letter defining the relative obligations is sufficient.

Whatever the arrangement may be, it should be uniform as to all exhibitors so that later developments will not run afoul of some forgotten, special provision. However, some company experience shows that certain exhibitors do not have the resources—either financial or physical—to assume the usual duties. The sponsor may well decide to assume the added responsibility.

With traveling shows—going from one museum to another—it should be crystal clear at what point in time or physical act the duties of one exhibitor end and those of the next begin. This applies also to liability for inter-exhibitor transportation costs.

20. Responsibility for Physical Safety of Works.

It appears that the sponsor will usually be responsible for the safety of the exhibited works from the time they are received in good condition until they are delivered to the carrier for return to the artist after the close of the show. If "fine arts" insurance will be obtained by the sponsor, this should be indicated with an understanding when the coverage begins and terminates. For example, the Mead Corporation's "invitation" to its annual competition and traveling exhibit provides:

> The Mead Corporation will insure all works of art which have been accepted for exhibition during the period of the exhibition and while in transit. Mead will bear no responsibility for other works which have been submitted. Artists may insure works at their own option.

21. Handling of Publicity.

The sponsor will normally prepare and supervise all national promotion and publicity. It will also usually supply all such material to the local exhibitors. On occasion it will actively handle and supervise the local efforts. The sponsor, however, but rarely releases any local publicity without the knowledge and approval of the local exhibitor.

The reverse should also be true. The local exhibitor should be required to clear any locally-developed publicity materials or promotional events with the sponsor. This is necessary since the sponsor is the party responsible to the artist. Local efforts must be consonant with the sponsor/artist arrangements. If there should be any violation of these arrangements, the sponsor would be liable to the artist.[39]

22. Company Musical and Theatrical Activities.

Aside from contracts with sponsored talent, the principal concern in musical and theatrical activities is the royalty obligations. These depend upon the type of performance involved.

It should be assumed that royalties are due for performance of all musical or dramatic works.[40] There are certain exceptions, discussed below.

As to musical works, the copyright covers only works performed "for profit." This has been construed to include performances which do not carry a separate admission fee or charge but which are incidental to profit-making business purposes or activities, such as the operation of a restaurant, this being considered as "given in furtherance of a commercial enterprise." [41]

On the other hand, public performances by charitable, educational or similar organizations are not considered "for profit" even though an admission fee is charged or the performance occurs at a fund-raising event.[42] This may be a consideration to the company sponsor in setting up its basic arrangements with community charitable events or drives.

As to dramatic works or musical works classed as "dramatico-musical compositions," the "for profit" requirement is absent. The copyright owner's rights cover all public performances, whether or not for profit under any interpretation of that term.[43]

Some union questions may arise when company employees perform in public. These should be explored with local union officials if there is any question about such conflict.

23. Employee Participation.

Some cultural activities are built around company employees. This may be an employee orchestra, a rank-and-file art show or an in-plant theatrical group.

In some instances it has been found advisable to obtain from such participants—particularly if the activity is a continuing one—a release to protect the company from "after hours claims," especially for off-premises accidents. This is even more desirable if the company uses its own vehicles and drivers to transport the company "talent."

It has been held, for example, that the company is liable for injuries to one employee in a vehicle driven by another employee when the vehicle was being used for the promotion of "legitimate and important interests of [the] employer's business, namely, harmony, co-operation and good will among the employees." [44] A public performance by a company group or cast would certainly seem to fall into this category.[45]

In any event, the PR director or other company official supervising such ventures should take appropriate steps to protect both the company and the employee-members of the entertainment group with appropriate insurance coverage.

Workmen's compensation laws may cover injuries to employees under these circumstances although this is open to question and should be preliminarily explored under the laws of the state or states in question.

If such employee cultural activities are "run" by a truly independent employee association, as some are, the company has no responsibility. This applies to personal injuries, royalty payments and any other obligations or exposures arising by reason of such events or activities. See Chapter 21, Section 16 for a further discussion of such associations.

E. MISCELLANEOUS.

24. Activities on Public Property.

When the company sponsors an event in a public place, on a public street or any location freely open to the public, the company may be liable—under a standard of due care—if a member of the public is injured.

When the company sponsors such an event to which the public is "invited" by advertising and publicity or merely "attracted" by the event itself, the members of the public are "invitees as a matter of law" and have the right to assume that the company "would take reasonable precaution for their safety." [46] This is true even when the event is held on a public street, closed off by arrangement with the municipality and with the local police on hand.[47]

If, however, the company does not have control over the premises (such as a public hall) where the event is being held, the company would not be liable. Control is the key to liability. On the other hand, if the company "takes over" the premises, puts its own people in charge of all activities and of the premises generally, the company would be required to use due care to protect the public. This follows under the general rules discussed above.

25. Effect of Presence of Police.

Well-attended community relations events—either on or off the company premises—will ordinarily be patrolled by a police detail. See Section 11 above. Assuming that the company is required to use due care to protect the public guests as "invitees"—see Sections 6 to 10 and 24 above

—the presence of police does not automatically satisfy the obligation to use due care.

In most cases the courts have held that it is still up to the jury to decide the factual question of due care even if police are admittedly present when the injury was suffered. In company-sponsored soap box derby cases, for example, the company was not exculpated when a member of the public was struck by one of the home-made cars despite the presence of "police lines" and other police coverage.[48] At least one New Jersey case, however, has gone the other way and protected the company under such circumstances.[49]

26. Use of Independent Contractors.

A community event may be "sponsored" in the sense that a company pays for it but the management and control of the entire event are in the hands of an independent contractor. The most obvious example is the appearance of a theatrical or dance group at the local high school and the only connection the company has with it is to pay for the appearance of the company through reimbursing the local school authorities. In other cases the company may itself make the arrangements but turn over the program to an independent contractor. Normally, in both of these situations, the company is not liable if anyone is injured because of the operation of the event.[50]

A prime example of this would be a public fireworks display. Under most state laws such displays are legal only if run by a duly qualified and licensed company or individual. When it is so handled, the sponsors are not liable for injuries.[51] The company is here insulated from liability just as it is in instances in which an employee association operates and controls an athletic or other event. See Chapter 21, Section 16.

27. Permits, Licenses, etc.

Some of the most routine company community relations events—even those on company premises—will require compliance with local ordinances and other regulations. The use of police, temporary no-parking signs, the closing of streets, use of municipal premises, fire marshal approvals, various forms of permits or licenses—these are all typical of the seemingly endless parade of municipal contacts required for a continuing community relations program.

Local ordinances affecting these and many other needs vary. It is impossible to deal specifically with them in this work. However—as a result of state constitutional or statutory provisions—a municipality is generally authorized to permit and facilitate most of the companies' needs in this context and to cooperate with business in its efforts to serve the public interest in this manner. This includes the use of municipal property for such company programs.[52]

A company committed to such a program will find it productive and convenient to develop a close and forehanded rapport with all of the municipal officials charged with jurisdiction over such matters. This is probably simpler than to rely on company counsel to make such contacts. At the same time company counsel should be aware of all such events and the relationships involved.

28. Public Relations and the "Good Samaritan."

A company will undoubtedly go out of its way to "help out" some local public or civic endeavor whenever possible. Notwithstanding the company's good intentions, serious legal questions arise as to the company's liability for such endeavors.

As an example, the airconditioning equipment of a cancer research activity broke down, endangering the lives of 80,000 mice and rats, specially bred for research. Two airlines promptly sent to the laboratory large portable blowers used to aircondition planes while on the ground. A front-page story announced that the "airlines are helping out as a public service, free of charge." [53]

If a "Good Samaritan" undertakes to help another out of his predicament, he will generally be liable if any further injury or damage results from the Good Samaritan's negligence.[54] This is as true of a company which tries to help as it is of the doctor who volunteers to aid a stricken person on the street or in a theater at the call of "Is there a doctor in the house?" [55] There may not be any obligation to help in the first place but if such aid is rendered, it must be carried through without any fault or negligence.[56] So serious is this, as applied to doctors, that they have sought—in some states successfully—statutory relief therefrom. However, such statutes are of no help to the corporate "Good Samaritan."

To be avoided is the impulsive *promise* by a PR man—perhaps in response to an unexpected telephone call—to help without being sure that proper aid can and will be furnished. The traditional rule is that such a gratuitous promise—not leading to action—will not be a premise for liability.[57] Some states, however, are retreating from this position [58] or construing the most trivial of acts as the beginning of actual assistance. Even telling the caller to telephone back later may be so construed.[59]

This discussion of possible legal exposure should not prevent a company from helping its community when it can. It is merely a warning to handle such assistance properly. Some companies are known to approach such calls for aid with forehanded planning with the local authorities, setting up various flexible plans in anticipation of the more likely calls for local assistance.

For example, large plants in small towns may have their own fire equipment or ambulance and cooperative arrangements with the local fire department carefully blueprinted. Plant security guards have no authority off the premises but, if properly deputized by the municipality, may assist local police. Company dispensaries, staffed by competent personnel, may be very helpful to the public. Company employees having special skills—ascertained by advance screening—may be made available to municipal authority or the local Red Cross for *aid under their direction*.

The more advance planning and training the company does, the more efficient will be the assistance and, furthermore, the less likely that a charge of negligence can be leveled against the company.

29. Community Contests.

Company-sponsored community contests are common. They vary widely in substance, form, methodology, rules and purpose.[60] Normally such contests will not suffer from any legal infirmities as a "lottery" inasmuch as they are almost invariably based on skill—perhaps requiring an essay. Parenthetically, it must be remembered that reputable or charitable sponsorship will not save a "contest" from being illegal if, in fact, it is truly a lottery. See Chapter 13 generally as to contests and lotteries.

Most complaints about such company-sponsored events come, not from the Post Office Department or some other government agency, but from disgruntled contestants disputing the award of the prizes. There are two basic rules to be followed:

(a) The announced rules of the contest are binding on the company. They should not be changed in any way during the contest and all thereof, especially the provisions as to judging, should be scrupulously followed. The rules are the "offer" and the contestant's compliance therewith is the "acceptance" from which a contract arises.[61]

(b) If the rules provide, as they usually do, that the decision of the judges is final, their awards will be upheld provided the judges are not guilty of bad faith, gross or intentional mistake, fraud or a decision contrary to the announced rules.[62]

Although a contest may be announced as based solely on skill and the rules so provide, the awards may actually be made haphazardly and without regard to skill. This introduces the element of chance and will convert a contest into a lottery if consideration is also present.[63] Ordinarily, of course, a company-sponsored contest will not require consideration in the PR context. However, a contest might require some small cash contribution to a local community or civic activity. This could create the necessary consideration in such a case.

30. Merchandise Contributions.

Community-minded companies and their PR departments are often approached for contributions of merchandise for various community or civic affairs—to be used as prizes or to be resold for charitable purposes. The great majority of these contributions go to legitimate community activities and such donations serve a proper community and PR purpose.

However, some of the largest national companies have been mulcted of substantial amounts of merchandise by phony promoters using "charity" as bait. Usually surplus merchandise is sought. Its disposal in this manner —with resultant tax savings because of the purpose of the donation—may seem attractive both fiscally and PR-wise. However, mail fraud cases successfully prosecuted by the Post Office Department prove that these tempting large-scale "tax deduction situations" must be carefully investigated.[64] Local Better Business Bureaus will usually have a dossier on such schemes or can obtain useful information from other Bureaus throughout the country.

Notes

1. For discussions of community relations policy and techniques, see CUTLIP & CENTER, EFFECTIVE PUBLIC RELATIONS 251–67 (3d ed. 1964); McCarty, *The Image in Your Community*, in DEVELOPING THE CORPORATE IMAGE 49–69 (Bristol ed. 1960); Ducas, *Corporate Citizenship*, in HANDBOOK OF PUBLIC RELATIONS 383–406 (Stephenson ed. 1960); Newsome, *How to Identify Your Company with the Community Goals*, P.R.J., July, 1962, at 18; Schmidt & Carousso, *What to Do About Cementing a Public's Friendship*, id. at 31.

2. For a relatively brief but very instructive legal program for establishing a foundation, see Eaton, Sugerman, Mansfield, Cutler, *How to Draft the Charter or Indenture of a Charity so as to Qualify for Federal Tax Exemption*, 8 PRAC. LAW. No. 6, at 13; No. 7, at 87 (1962).

3. Steinway v. Steinway and Sons, 40 N.Y.S. 718 (1896).

4. See Dodge v. Ford Motor Co., 204 Mich. 457, 171 N.W. 557 (1919).

5. 13 N.J. 145, 98 A.2d 581 (1953).

6. 8 Utah 2d 101, 329 P.2d 398, 39 A.L.R.2d 1179 (1958).

7. Garrett, *Corporate Donations*, 22 BUS. LAW. 297, 301 (1967). For an excellent discussion of "corporate giving," see Hacker, *When Big Business Makes Gifts (Tax-Deductible)*, N.Y. Times Magazine, Nov. 12, 1967, at 34.

8. 259 F. Supp. 305 (N.D. Ga. 1965), aff'd, 367 F.2d 392, 35 L.W. 2219 (5th Cir. 1966).

9. For an overall discussion of the relative obligations to licensees and invitees, see PROSSER, TORTS 385–408 (3d ed. 1964).

10. Benson v. Baltimore Traction Co., 77 Md. 535, 26 Atl. 973 (1893); Roe v. St. Louis Independent Packing Co., 203 Mo. App. 11, 217 S.W. 335 (1920).

11. See James, *Tort Liability of Occupiers of Land: Duties Owed to Licensees and Invitees*, 63 YALE L.J. 605 (1954).

12. Indermaur v. Dames, (1866) L.R. 1 C.P. 274, 35 L.J.C.P. 184, aff'd, L.R. 2 C.P. 311, 36 L.J.C.P. 181. See Prosser, *Business Visitors and Invitees*, 26 MINN. L. REV. 573 (1942); James, *supra* note 11.

13. 2 HARPER & JAMES, TORTS §27.12, at 1478 (1956).

14. Prosser, *supra* note 9, at 396.

15. Gilliland v. Bondurant, 51 S.W.2d 559 (Mo. App. 1932), aff'd, 332 Mo. 881, 59 S.W.2d 679 (1933); Deach v. Woolner Distilling Co., 187 Ill. App. 524 (1914).

16. 414 P.2d 773 (Wash. 1966).

17. Edwards v. Gulf Oil Corp., 69 Ga. App. 140, 24 S.E.2d 843 (1943).

18. Bunnell v. Waterbury Hosp., 103 Conn. 520, 131 Atl. 501 (1925).

19. RESTATEMENT, TORTS §343, Comment *b* (1939).

20. Randolph v. Great A. & P. Tea Co., 2 F. Supp. 462 (E.D. Pa. 1932), aff'd, 64 F.2d 247 (3d Cir. 1933).

21. McNamara v. Maclean, 302 Mass. 428, 19 A.2d 544 (1939); Mullen v. M. & M. Hotel, 277 Iowa 1061, 29 N.W. 3 (1940).

22. See Cutlip & Center, *supra* note 1, at 199–200, 262–63.

23. Gilliland v. Bondurant, *supra* note 15.

24. Quoted and adapted from Roe v. St. Louis Independent Packing Co., *supra* note 10.

25. Corbin v. Haws Refractories Co., 277 Pa. 126, 120 Atl. 811 (1923).

26. Adams v. American Enka Corp., 202 N.C. 767, 163 S.E. 367 (1932); Indiana Harbor Belt Ry. v. Jones, 202 Ind. 139, 41 N.E.2d 361 (1942).

27. Millum v. Lehigh & Wilkes-Barre Coal Co., 225 Pa. 214, 73 Atl. 1106 (1909).

28. Gwynn Oak Park v. Becker, 177 Md. 528, 10 A.2d 652, 8 N.C.C.A. (n.s.) 1 (1940); Silverstein v. Camp David, Inc., 59 N.Y.S.2d 6 (Sup. Ct. 1945).

29. See generally V WIGMORE, EVIDENCE §§1455–69.

30. See Cutlip & Center, *supra* note 1, at 327; Ahlfeld, *Art Program Relates to Community-at-Large*, P.R.J., March, 1967, at 17; Stuart, *Bamberger's Crusades to Bring Culture to New Jersey*, P.R.J., Jan., 1963, at 18; P.R.N., April 22, 1963, Jan. 27, 1964, Sept. 19, 1966, Dec. 12, 1966, Feb. 6, 1967, March 13, 1967, April 17, 1967.

31. Letter of George Alan Smith, P.R.J., June, 1967, at 42.

32. See Ahlfeld, *supra* note 30.

33. See Normoyle, *Art Shows on the Road,* P.R.J., April, 1960, at 22.

34. The author is indebted to Nina Kaiden, Ruder & Finn Vice President and Director of its Fine Arts Department, for certain background information and material used in the preparation of Sections 18 to 21 of the text.

35. Pushman v. New York Graphic Soc'y, 287 N.Y. 302, 39 N.E.2d 249 (1942).

36. For a discussion of the general policy against permitting photographs of paintings hung in an exhibition or art show, see *No Photographs,* 8 BULL. COPYRIGHT SOC. 363 (1961).

37. See generally 1 CCH ALL-STATE SALES TAX REP. ¶¶1-021, 2-025, 050, 3-125.

38. See Normoyle, *supra* note 33, at 23.

39. This liability depends upon the interpretations of the agreement between artist and sponsor. The rights and obligations of the parties are similar to those involved in limited consents and waivers in right of privacy cases. See HOFSTADTER & HOROWITZ, THE RIGHT OF PRIVACY 73–87 (1964).

40. See WALLS, THE COPYRIGHT HANDBOOK FOR FINE AND APPLIED ARTS 105 *et seq.* (1963).

41. *Id.* at 108–09.

42. *Id.* See also 17 U.S.C. §1; Copyright Office Circular No. 58.

43. Copyright Office Circular No. 8.

44. Ackerman v. Jennings Co., 107 Conn. 393, 140 Atl. 760, 56 A.L.R. 1127 (1928).

45. Bamback, *Music as a Public Relations Tool,* P.R.J., March, 1959, at 25.

46. Watford v. Evening Star Publishing Co., 211 F.2d 31 (D.C. Cir. 1954); Macon Tel. Publishing Co. v. Graden, 76 Ga. App. 230, 53 S.E.2d 371 (1949).

47. Murphy v. Jarvis Chevrolet Co., 310 Ill. App. 534, 34 N.E.2d 872 (1941).

48. Watford v. Evening Star Publishing Co., *supra* note 46; Murphy v. Jarvis Chevrolet Co., *supra* note 47.

49. Bango v. Carteret Lions Club, 12 N.J. Super. 52, 79 A.2d 57, *cert. denied,* 7 N.J. 347, 81 A.2d 522 (1951).
50. See Prosser, *supra* note 9, at 480; James, *Vicarious Liability,* 28 TUL. L. REV. 161 (1954); Harper, *The Basis of the Immunity of an Employer of an Independent Contractor,* 10 IND. L.J. 494 (1935).
51. Crowley v. Rochester Fireworks Co., 183 N.Y. 353, 76 N.E. 470 (1906); Haddon v. Lotito, 399 Pa. 521, 161 A.2d 160 (1960).
52. 64 C.J.S., *Municipal Corporations,* §§1818–23, 1831–32.
53. Philadelphia Bull., June 16, 1967, at 1.
54. See cases and authorities cited, *infra* notes 55–59.
55. See Notes, 75 HARV. L. REV. 641 (1962); 51 CAL. L. REV. 816 (1963).
56. See Seavey, *I Am Not My Guest's Keeper,* 13 VAND. L. REV. 690 (1960); Seavey, *Reliance Upon Gratuitous Promises or Other Conduct,* 64 HARV. L. REV. 913 (1951); RESTATEMENT (SECOND), AGENCY §378 (1958).
57. Thorne v. Deas, 4 Johns. R. 84 (N.Y. 1809).
58. Dudley v. Victor Lynn Lines, 48 N.J. Super. 457, 138 A.2d 53 (1958), *rev'd on other grounds,* 32 N.J. 479, 161 A.2d 479 (1960).
59. O'Neill v. Montefiore Hosp., 11 App. Div. 2d 132, 202 N.Y.S.2d 436 (1960).
60. See extension of remarks of Senator Kenneth B. Keating (N.Y.) as to high school contest sponsored by *Newsday* in Congressional Record, Jan. 24, 1963, at A236; description of "Math Day" sponsored by National Life Insurance Co. in cooperation with the University of Vermont (Case Study No. 994), P.R.N., Jan. 25, 1965, at 3.
61. Moreno v. Marbil Productions, Inc., 296 F.2d 543 (2d Cir. 1961); Holt v. Wilson, 55 S.W.2d 580 (Tex. Civ. App. 1932).
62. Furgille v. Disabled Amer. Veterans Serv. Foundation, 116 F. Supp. 375 (S.D.N.Y. 1952); Endres v. Buffalo Auto. Dealers Ass'n, 29 Misc. 2d 756, 217 N.Y.S.2d 460 (1961).
63. U.S. POST OFFICE DEP'T, THE LAW VS. LOTTERIES 8 (1963). See also Carlini v. United States Rubber Co., 36 L.W. 2376 (Mich. Ct. App. 1967) and cases cited therein.
64. U.S. Post Office Dep't Gen. Release No. 180, Nov. 27, 1967.

Chapter 15

Research and Its Legal Application

A. INTRODUCTION

B. ADMISSIBILITY OF SURVEY EVIDENCE

C. PROBATIVE VALUE OF SURVEYS

D. RECOMMENDATIONS OF THE 1960 JUDICIAL CONFERENCE

Chapter 15

Research and Its Legal Application

A. INTRODUCTION.

1. Growing Use of Survey Evidence.

Surveys of various kinds—usually based on the sampling technique—are being used more and more as evidence in an increasingly broad variety of litigation and administrative agency procedures. Much of this evidence is public opinion research.[1]

The courts and administrative agencies have become increasingly amenable to the introduction into the record of the results of such studies. However, similar progress is not as evident when appraising the weight accorded such evidence, even assuming that the surveys are conducted in accordance with proper standards and methodology.

Such surveys and their use in litigation and administrative procedures should be considered with the following legal and practical areas in mind:

(a) Their basic reliability and validity.

(b) Judicial and agency attitudes as to the propriety and admissibility thereof.

(c) Proper presentation of, and testimonial support for, such evidence.

(d) Evidentiary weight accorded thereto in the decision process.

2. Involvement of Public Relations Personnel.

The public relations practitioner is, by the very nature of his function, becoming more and more involved with a wide variety of research. A considerable portion of this deals with studying public opinion. He uses it as a preliminary tool in planning a PR campaign or program; he uses it to investigate the results and effects of such corporate activities.[2]

The depth and nature of the PR involvement varies. Much of the actual research may be done by a separate research organization. The planning and the evaluation of the research frequently fall to the public relations man. It is he who often "figures out what the research means."

In a survey conducted by Champion Paper Company, about 20 percent of the replies to the question "What responsibilities might fall under the normal functioning of a PR department?" indicated "survey research" as one such responsibility.[3]

More and more, the PR practitioner or firm is a member of the "research team." This is even more likely when the research is prospectively intended for use in litigation—to support a legal position or merely for use in negotiations looking to avoid litigation.

Much of the research with which the PR man is concerned is naturally oriented toward public relations or allied corporate activities. It is not designed for legal use. Yet this research may later become quite relevant and useful in such matters. It has been suggested that studies undertaken before any legal issue has developed may be entitled to more weight than those undertaken in connection with either pending or prospective litigation.

An interesting example of the usefulness of what might be called routine public relations research arose in the *Household Finance* case.[4] In this 1952 case, it was shown that the plaintiff had, since 1948, made periodic surveys to determine public recognition of its trade symbol. The public recognition of the symbol was the issue in the 1952 case and the earlier surveys were admitted by the court. Surveys, intended originally merely to assist in the evaluation of the company's PR or promotion campaigns, thus were later significantly useful in assisting to protect its legal rights.

Because of the growing incidence of certain federal statutes—especially the antitrust laws or those concerned with other aspects of competition or promotion—business has become ever more aware of possible future legal complications whenever it plans activities such as mergers, acquisitions, invasion of a new market, the meeting of competition, advertising strategy, etc. In such business developments, advance research of various kinds has become a valuable tool.[5] It is merely common sense—in view of the possibility of litigation—to be certain that these studies will be legally acceptable if the company is called upon to defend its actions.

Quite apart from this, all research—even if apparently of a routine character—should be undertaken and managed with an eye toward possible legal use. This should normally entail little additional effort or expense. Research which is valid and in accordance with proper research standards and techniques is likely to be deemed valid and acceptable under legal standards as well—provided that it is material to the eventual legal issue.

3. Validity of Public Opinion Surveys.

Quite apart from the legal precepts being discussed by the court, the question usually uppermost in the judge's mind is whether or not the particular survey before him is reliable and valid. While, to the best of our knowledge, no reported opinion has ever openly asked the question, "Can we *really* depend on this evidence?" this seems to be the—perhaps unconscious—approach taken by the courts.

Some of the earlier cases made no effort to hide the judge's personal antipathy for such evidence. One court referred to the study as having been conducted "in a vacuum with Professor Quiz in charge." Others— perhaps merely more circumspect—described the evidence as "highly artificial"; [6] pointed out that the "questions and questionnaires are very biased"; [7] off-handedly admitted the survey "for whatever it may be worth." [8]

These earlier attitudes may well have been justified for a variety of reasons. A fair proportion of the studies presented to the courts were psychological tests of various kinds or surveys conducted in college classrooms [9]—all clearly divorced from both the atmosphere and behavior of the marketplace.[10] Beyond this, adequate techniques and standards had not yet been developed; interviewers were frequently untrained; samples were badly constructed; surveys were planned and managed by inexperienced personnel; generally, research had not yet come of age. Add to this the 1936 *Literary Digest* election poll which dropped upon such research a cloud from which it took years to emerge.

While opinion research may even now not be an exact "science" such as chemistry and physics, most courts and agencies now recognize that a properly-conducted study based on sampling does, within its admitted margin of error, give an accurate picture of the opinion of the universe or population in question.

The catch-as-catch-can period has passed. Methodology has been greatly improved and standardized. Accuracy within close and tolerable limits has been demonstrated. Personnel training has been amplified and intensified. Research literature has proliferated and become increasingly professional. Even the legal literature on the subject has become more frequent and perceptive. Both business and government have come to rely extensively on sampling techniques and studies as a foundation for policy and administration.[11]

Equally important from the judge's side of the rail is the fact that opinion surveys have become much more frequent and commonplace. The courts have now had considerable experience with them. Familiarity in this instance has not bred contempt but rather an affirmative and open-minded receptivity for a properly conducted study.

So apparent is this change in judicial attitude that some judges have affirmatively made their own surveys, informal though they may have been, and have commented upon them constructively in their opinions.[12]

Apart from technical legal rules of admissibility (see Sections 6–11 below), and the gradual disappearance of an elementary skepticism, courts have come to learn that such surveys can do much to shorten the trial of a case. See Section 19 below.

4. Types of Surveys.

Legally, all "surveys" are not treated alike. So important is this that the 1960 Judicial Conference carefully explained its own, specifically-limited definition of "sample." It confined it to "the physical examination of parts to establish the character of the whole, . . . such as . . . a count of units or the results of test borings." The Conference then applied "poll" to the opinion survey, the type of investigation with which we are here principally concerned. The Conference recognized that research practitioners define "sample" differently. As to the recommendations of the Conference generally, see Section 19 below.

While sampling is usually basic to all of the following types of surveys, they differ significantly within themselves.

(a) Opinion Surveys.

The ascertainment and measurement of opinions, attitudes, feelings, beliefs, etc. about a particular matter. The subject matter is largely subjective.

(b) Behavior Studies.

The investigation, usually by observation, of human behavior and reaction as overtly manifested.[13]

(c) Studies as to Physical Facts.

The investigation, examination or observation of objectively observable facts such as compliance with specifications,[14] traffic counts, etc.[15]

(d) Surveys of Market Data.

The sampling of statistical information on market data such as share of market, types of contracts in use, costs throughout an industry or the extent of tax involvement.[16]

5. Legal Issues Compatible With Survey Evidence.

A wide variety of legal issues lend themselves to survey evidence. As indicated in Section 4 above, opinion research is not necessarily pertinent. Other forms of research may be needed. Under the pressures of "necessity" (see Section 9 below) this catalogue may well be expanded in the future. Parties facing any of the following areas of litigation should consider survey evidence as prospectively useful:

(a) Trademark and Tradename Infringement.

This was the initial area of use of opinion survey evidence. Such cases require proof of confusion or the possibility of confusion in the public mind resulting from the use of the same, similar or related trademarks or tradenames. See Chapter 10, Sections 25 to 29. Inasmuch as public confusion is a reflection of "state of mind," use of an opinion survey is clearly warranted.[17]

(b) Unfair Competition.

Cases charging unfair competition or the use of unfair or deceptive trade practices—whether in Federal Trade Commission cases or private litigation—are akin to those involving trademark infringement. Here also public deception and confusion are important elements of proof. An opinion survey can contribute much to the resolution of the issues.[18]

(c) Misleading Advertising.

A basic issue is the net impression which allegedly false or deceptive representations make upon the public to which they are addressed. Proving this—one way or the other—can sometimes be difficult. Cases not infrequently, therefore, turn on the personal impression or expertise of the hearing examiner or of the members of the FTC themselves. While so-called "consumer witnesses" may be called to testify as to the meaning of an advertisement, the FTC has adversely commented upon their use.[19] An opinion survey can present such public attitudes and impressions and has been used for such purposes.[20] Such evidence is more valuable than that produced by conflicting witnesses called in substantial numbers by opposing parties—obviously selected in accordance with the needs of the parties.

(d) Deceptive Packaging or Labeling.

Again, opinion surveys are useful to present the attitude and beliefs of the public as to whether packaging or labeling is deceptive and sufficiently informative.

This type of application will probably become more important in view of the passage of the Fair Packaging and Labeling Act of 1966,[21] discussed further in Chapter 11, Section 6 (e). The new law deals with standards in packaging and labeling including deception and sufficiency of information. Judging by the testimony at the Congressional hearings prior to adopting of the Act, there is a considerable difference of opinion as to the extent, if any, to which the public is being confused or misled by present packaging and labeling practices. As this is written, rulemaking under the Act has already been instituted by the FTC, the FDA and the Commerce Department. It will probably be extended and sometimes bitter. Opinion research may be introduced in connection therewith—probably by industry and perhaps even by the government under the investigatory powers of the various agencies.

(e) Market Data.

The presentation of a large mass of market data can be an involved and time-consuming procedure. A properly-prepared survey can bring such data before the court in relatively brief compass and perhaps with even greater effectiveness. The study concentrates in one place information drawn from a variety of sources.

To introduce such information piecemeal by live testimony or separate exhibits could mean possibly thousands of pages of stenographic transcript which must be later correlated and integrated. The survey makes analysis by the trier of the facts—judge or jury—much simpler and more effective, quite apart from the time saved.

Antitrust cases are prime examples of such survey use although it is not limited to such cases.[22]

(f) Fair Trade Cases.

In enforcement actions by a manufacturer of its fair trade program, the defense is frequently made that the manufacturer has not enforced its price structure against the defendant-retailer's competitors. Studies of the prevailing prices of the fair-traded merchandise may be used in such a defense. However, opinion research is not here the basis of the study. It is rather a factual investigation of the prices.[23]

(g) Transportation Utility Practices.

Such cases have already occasioned the use of surveys of different kinds. In the "captive-audience" case,[24] a survey of bus passengers' attitudes and opinions about in-bus radio broadcasts was used before the Public Utility Commission. Although criticized by the Court of Appeals, it was considered by the Supreme Court as "a proper matter for determination by the Commission."

In another bus case,[25] the operators were resisting a change in route. They produced a survey based on questionnaires filled out by passengers in order to show riding habits and volume of use within the affected area.

In some of the current planning for metropolitan transportation system integration and operation, opinion surveys have been used to investigate passenger opinions and intentions. They have dealt with frequency of use, potential and future riding habits if fares were to be adjusted, etc. These have frequently been handled by public relations personnel of the lines or Authorities involved.

(h) Utility Rate Cases.

Utility rates sometimes depend upon reproduction cost of physical plant, usually very extensive. Studies based on sampling of the physical condition of the plant have been offered and accepted in such cases.[26] The purpose is to avoid the onerous and expensive examination of every single unit of the plant by projecting condition and value from the sample to the entire installation. Some state commissions have refused or adversely criticized such survey methods in this context.[27] Sampling of output in order to ascertain compliance with specifications is a frequent technique.[28] The utility cases referred to in Subsection (g) above are other examples. The Conference Report alludes to such matters as the simple "count of units and the result of test borings." [29] These surveys are not based upon opinion research but on physical examination of the sample being used.

(i) Zoning.

Surveys of various kinds, including opinion surveys, have been used in zoning cases.[30] Aside from survey sampling based on physical condition or other characteristics of properties or neighborhood areas, opinions of residents have been studied. The studies may involve opinion and intention of residents as to their future plans for removal. Slum clearance projects may also involve such studies.

(j) Municipal "Suburban Captures."

A growing effort is being made by cities to "capture" some of the growing suburban and exurban areas which have acquired substantial taxables through new industry and real estate developments. Ascertainment of the desires of the citizens in such areas presents an important prospective use for opinion research. Public relations campaigns by the local plants are considered important in contributing to the outcome of these studies. Such surveys would be of significant value to state legislatures which are usually constitutionally or otherwise legally responsible for such realignment.

(k) Civil Rights.

Many aspects of the civil rights picture lend themselves to the use of surveys. This is evident in such matters as methods of educational integration, busing, etc. As in Subsection (j) above, attitudes and opinions on possible amalgamation of city/suburban school districts—suggested in several metropolitan areas—may be ascertained by such studies. Such studies may be quite significant as against the highly-charged emotional or political harangues which inhibit real progress in this program.

Such investigation must go beyond mere "head-counts" of Negro/white pupils and teachers. Attitudes must be ascertained. They may be persuasive to both government and the people themselves. This seems to be a subject which lends itself particularly to "public relations treatment" in one use of such survey results.

(l) Change of Venue.

If local prejudice seems to preclude a fair trial in a criminal case, a change of venue may be necessary. Proof of community opinion and of the opinion of the prospective jurors is important in such a case or situation. Opinion surveys are useful in proving such matters.[31] Because of the apparently increased use of criminal prosecutions under the anti-trust laws, attended by increased preliminary government publicity, this type of evidence may become of greater importance in the future.

B. ADMISSIBILITY OF SURVEY EVIDENCE.

6. In General.

Admissibility, in this instance, deals essentially with the "hearsay rule." At the risk of oversimplification, the resolution of these two questions is fundamental:

(a) Is opinion survey evidence hearsay?

(b) Assuming that it is hearsay, is it still admissible under any recognized exception to the hearsay rule?

Having disposed of these two questions, the court must then decide whether the evidence is material.

7. The Hearsay Objection.

One of the traditional objections to the introduction of survey evidence is the charge that it is "hearsay." [32] Even today, although this objection has been considerably discredited, it still is heard. In one of the early cases, Judge Woolsey called it "solidified hearsay." [33]

The charge that survey evidence is hearsay is founded largely on the fact that the respondents (interviewees) are not present in court, subject to cross-examination. The only witnesses usually in court for cross-examination are the interviewers—only a few may be present—together with those who designed and managed the survey. Also sometimes present may be an independent "expert" to validate the research methods used.

There is no question that such evidence would be hearsay if the survey were being offered to prove the truth of the facts concerning which the interviewees had been asked questions. This, of course, is not the case. What is being offered in evidence is merely the fact that respondents said certain things or reacted in certain ways.

Whether or not these things are factually correct is beside the point. In fact, such evidence is frequently offered to prove that the respondents were wrong, that they did not know what they were talking about, that they were misinformed, that they were confused. Confusion and ignorance are often of greater probative value than knowledge and veracity.[34]

Aside from the evidentiary aspect, it is the inaccuracy of much public thinking which makes opinion research so important in public relations planning. The research contributes significantly to the two-way dialogue with the public and, abrasive though it may be, enables the public relations function to perform more efficiently.

Just as such opinion research is far from hearsay to the public relations practitioner, so too, evidence thereof is now no longer considered hearsay in the legal sense.[35] On the other hand, if for any reason a court should deem such evidence to be hearsay, it still should be admissible under two well-recognized premises relative to exceptions to the hearsay rule: necessity and trustworthiness as discussed in Sections 9 and 10 below.

Furthermore, the hearsay objection is confined largely to surveys dealing with the opinion, belief or understanding of the interviewees. It does not appear to be relevant to proof of physical facts even though such proof is offered in the form of a report based on sampling.[36]

8. State of Mind Evidence.

Opinion research usually involves ascertaining the "state of mind" of the public by interrogating a sample of that public or the appropriate segment (universe) thereof. Such "state of mind" evidence has long been admitted—quite apart from the opinion survey context—apparently beyond the hearsay frame of reference even though "hearsay" has frequently been raised as an objection by the opponent.

In the early leading case of *Elmer v. Fessendon*,[37] Justice Holmes was dealing with proof as to why the plaintiff's employees had left his employ. The plaintiff's superintendent sought to testify as to statements and explanations made by the employees when they left. This evidence was refused but, on appeal, Justice Holmes said:

> If, as may be assumed, the excluded testimony would have shown that the workmen when they left gave as their reason to the superintendent that the defendant had told them that the Board of Health reported arsenic in the silk, the evidence was admissible to show their belief in the presence of poison as their reason . . . such declarations made with no apparent motive for misstatement may be better evidence of the maker's state of mind at the time than the subsequent testimony of the same persons.

Justice Holmes adhered to this concept when, as a Supreme Court Justice, he wrote the opinion in the *Danbury Hatters* case.[38] He held that evidence was admissible as to the reasons expressed by customers for refusing to buy Loewe hats. Whether these reasons were rational or proper was beside the point. The evidence was offered merely to prove that these customers had expressed and spoken of their reasons in a certain manner—in short, it proved their "state of mind."

In the more modern setting of the *Franklin National Bank* case,[39] the New York Supreme Court—affirmed by the New York Court of Appeals and the United States Supreme Court—admitted a survey dealing with the public understanding of terms describing savings accounts. The Court discussed the survey evidence at length and pointed out:

> A party endeavoring to establish the public state of mind on a subject, which state of mind cannot be proved except by calling as witnesses so many of the public as to render the task impracticable, should be allowed to offer evidence concerning a poll which the party maintains reveals that state of mind. Not only does this fit the pattern of the "state of mind" exception to the hearsay rule, but it is not hearsay at all, since it is the fact that such answers were given to which the witness swears, and not the truth or value of the facts contained in such answers.

This language refers to state of mind evidence as being both an "exception to the hearsay rule" and "not hearsay at all." This duality is, in practice, relatively unimportant. The significant factor is that such evidence is admissible.

9. The "Necessity" Requirement.

Even if this type of evidence should be considered as hearsay, it still is admissible as an exception thereto. This may also apply even if it is sought to prove through the survey the truth of what the interviewers said—not merely that they said it. To qualify as an exception to the rule, however, in a given case, there must be a showing that the evidence is both necessary and has a circumstantial guarantee of trustworthiness.

Nearly every case in which such evidence is offered—not merely opinion surveys—involves the exploration of large masses of information, attitudes of perhaps hundreds or thousands of people, examination of innumerable similar or related facts or situations and other circumstances of broad and encompassing scope, volume or number.

One of the earliest and most bitter condemnations of calling large numbers of the public to testify "live" was voiced by a member of the Federal Trade Commission in 1928 when he wrote: [40]

> I want to register my protest at the way in which this case was tried. About a thousand witnesses from all walks of life were permitted to testify as to whether the use of the word "Castile" when applied to a soap made exclusively of olive oil, had the tendency to deceive the public. . . . Even admitted that they could [qualify as experts on deception], this piling up of cumulative evidence is an inexcusable outrage on the public. . . . About 700 such witnesses were subpoenaed to testify at Spokane. What justification can there be for such performances? . . . This class of testimony has caused the Federal Trade Commission to waste hundreds of thousands of dollars.

The survey technique and its subsequent trial use cuts across the cumbersome and perhaps even impossible trial procedure. It makes it possible to present in reasonable compass the evidence in question.

Many courts and administrative agencies have recognized the necessity aspect of survey evidence and admitted it on that ground.[41]

10. The "Trustworthiness" Requirement.

In addition to showing a need for use of survey evidence as discussed in Section 9 above, it is also necessary to demonstrate that the results of the sampling are trustworthy. This involves basically a demonstration through witnesses of the methodology used and its conformity to accepted practice, with results varying only to a tolerable and ascertainable degree.

A statistical expert can testify as to the projection of the sampling to the universe under scrutiny. This satisfies one aspect of the trustworthiness requirement, covering such matters as design of sample, amount of the predictable error, allowance for this inherent error, etc.[42]

Trustworthiness of the interviewing, editing and tabulating aspects of the survey can be shown through the testimony of the persons who were responsible for these functions. This would include the interviewers, the supervisors and the project manager.

Their testimony, subject to cross-examination in open court, should demonstrate that each step of the survey was managed and performed in accordance with accredited methodology. It should cover such matters as training and experience of the interviewers, adherence to interviewing instructions, methods of editing, etc. As additional evidence of trust-worthiness, all the "raw" materials such as the interviews and other documents should be available in court and offered as evidence.

It should be made clear that survey methodology seeks "to avoid the same hazards as does the hearsay rule" so that the approved methodology is, in effect, itself a guarantee of trustworthiness.[43]

11. Materiality of Survey Evidence.

Assuming that the hearsay question has been resolved in favor of ad-missibility, a court may still refuse to admit survey evidence if it is not material or germane to the issues of the case. There is nothing unusual about this. All evidence is appraised in this light.

In one case, for example, the issue was the effect of a certain safety device upon employee efficiency. A study was admitted by the lower court, demonstrating that the employees did not "desire" to use the device. The question of the employee's "desire" was not the issue. There-fore the study and its results were immaterial. This the appellate court recognized and for this reason, in part at least, reversed the lower court.[44]

Some courts appear to treat materiality—at least as to materiality of the universe—as something to be considered in determining the weight to be accorded the survey after it has been admitted. These cases, how-ever, do not specifically refer to materiality in this context. In the *Cadillac* case,[45] the issue was the possibility of confusion among boat "pur-chasers" between a boatbuilder's use of "Cadillac" and General Motors' use thereof on its automobiles. The plaintiff's survey materials, when examined in detail by the court, led to the well-justified comment that "[t]he individuals among whom this poll was taken were not, in the vast majority of cases, 'purchasers' in any sense of the word. Indeed many . . . had no interest in boats at all." In effect, therefore, the sample was drawn from the incorrect universe.[46]

The question of materiality would therefore appear to be involved in two contexts: the issue and the universe.

It has been strongly suggested that counsel should not be involved in the construction or management of surveys intended for eventual court use. See Section 19 below. This restriction should be limited to the conduct of the survey itself. It is almost mandatory that counsel be consulted preliminarily in order to be certain that the issue and universe are material.

C. PROBATIVE VALUE OF SURVEYS.

12. Weight Accorded Survey Evidence.

Once a survey has been admitted, it falls into the evidentiary hopper with all of the other evidence, testimony and exhibits—the entire record. The trier of the facts—judge or jury—must now consider this evidence-mix, evaluate each part of it, attempt to reconcile inconsistencies, appraise the honesty and knowledgeability of witnesses and, generally, reach a conclusion on the basis of that record.

Courts and administrative agencies have shown a definite tendency toward admitting opinion surveys with greater frequency and alacrity. On the other hand, there does not appear to be a similar tendency to consider the surveys—once admitted—as determinative or even overly significant in regard to the issues.

In only a relatively few cases has there been a specific indication of the affirmative weight accorded the survey by the court and the court's reliance thereon.[47] This is true even in cases in which the court did not specifically criticize the survey.

One apparent reason for this may be the current rule that errors or defects in an opinion survey go only to the weight accorded it [48]—not to the question of admissibility. This may have created something of a "so what?" approach. The court or agency can always ignore or minimize the study by according it little or no probative value, once it has been admitted. This conclusion is fortified by the fact that admission is more likely in administrative agency hearings or before judges sitting without juries. In both instances, the weighing of the evidence is within the control of the individual who admitted it in the first place.

Comments of agencies and courts about probative value make it clear that the survey evidence merely reinforced other convincing evidence,[49] was disregarded completely in the opinion,[50] was expressly considered of doubtful or little value,[51] or the case was decided "the other way" whatever the comment about the survey.[52] This is true in the more recent cases as well as in the older cases, decided in a period when opinion surveys generally were either inadmissible or at least suspect if admitted. One commentator has put it this way: [53]

> The review of the cases also indicates that survey evidence has played a relatively insignificant role in most cases where it has been admitted.

13. The Decision To Use a Survey.

What has been said in Section 12 above—the relatively insignificant impact of a survey—has much to do with the preliminary decision as to the use of a survey. This results from the time needed to make a survey and the cost thereof.

Cost is an important factor. Inasmuch as every litigation tactic is, to some extent, a balancing of cost against contribution to the case, this inability to pinpoint the practical effectiveness of even the best survey may cause even affluent parties to hesitate—sometimes to use a study of limited size or scope.

Notwithstanding this, however, certain guidelines have emerged.

(a) The well-designed and properly conducted study will have some probative value. It is possible that it may contribute a sufficient "plus" to tip the scales in a close case.

(b) In confusion cases, the other potential evidence of confusion may be slight. A study may be the only way to get such evidence before the court.

(c) A study becomes almost mandatory if the opposing party is known to have undertaken a study of its own. Here the effect may be only negative—counterbalancing the possible affirmative influence of the opposing study.

(d) If both parties present surveys, the significance of the better of the two may be increased. As one court said,[54] "The survey of one side may be subject to such severe criticism as to make the opponents' 'look good' by contrast." See Section 14 below.

(e) In administrative agency cases, the agency itself may have premised its Complaint on a survey. The respondent in such cases is under heavy pressure to make and present a countervailing study. It may become almost a matter of self-defense.

(f) In trials of complex issues or involving very extensive documentation, a survey—not a public opinion survey—may become necessary and, on a relative basis, may actually be less expensive in the long run.

(g) A failure to present a study may elicit adverse criticism from the court.[55]

14. The "Thermos Bottle" Case.

The "Thermos Bottle" case [56] presents an interesting and valuable case history involving two different kinds of surveys being offered in the same case. The issue was whether "Thermos" had become a generic term.

Preliminarily, the court pointed out that there was sufficient evidence —apart from the opinion polls taken by each of the parties—to show that "Thermos" had become a generic word in the English language as used in the United States, saying, "[T]he polls tend to corroborate what the court has found to be demonstrated by the other evidence in the case."

The court—perhaps with tongue in cheek—at the beginning of its discussion of the two surveys also said:

> The method of polltaking adopted by each of the parties reflects their respective views of the law and *each method was designed to elicit the kind of evidence each wished to bring out.* (Emphasis added.)

The court then discussed the plaintiff's survey, intended to show that "Thermos" was well-recognized as a trademark by a substantial minority of consumers. Some 3,650 members of the public had been asked:

> Please name any trademark or brandnames with which you are familiar, for vacuum bottles, insulated bottles, or other containers which keep the contents hot or cold.

The court said that this obviously focused the minds of the interviewees on trademarks and the plaintiff had therefore assumed that all responses, whether written with a capital "T" or small "t," were clear cases of trademark recognition. About one-third of the interviewees answered "thermos" in one form or another.

While complimenting the plaintiff's interviewers for honest, conscientious work done with "commendable detachment," the court found that the weight to be given the results was adversely affected by (a) the poor design of the question; (b) most of the interviewees appeared to have a higher than average educational and economic status and, therefore, were not a representative cross-section of the consuming public; (c) those who testified in court had been interviewed by plaintiff's counsel; and (d) they had seemed "emotionally conditioned" in favor of the plaintiff.

The survey conducted for the defendant attempted to comply with the principles adopted by the 1960 Judicial Conference (see Part D below) and the court was "satisfied that this poll or survey was conducted in accordance with those standards."

The court did not—having made the above observation—deal at great length with the defendant's survey except to say that it was:

> . . . particularly impressed with the high degree of credibility of the interviewers who testified; their conscientiousness in carrying out their duties and their complete lack of bias. They did not know the purpose of the survey as it related to the trial; they did not know when they conducted the interviews for whom the sur-

vey was being made or that it was to be used in litigation; they
had never talked with the attorneys nor had they been interviewed
or given any instructions by them; and as each took the stand she
had no knowledge of what the trial was about.

15. Preferred Methodology and Presentation Techniques.

Despite the increasing number of "survey cases," the courts have been
slow to develop any firm guidelines for either counsel or researchers
which will, in effect, "guarantee" either admissibility or substantial
weight to the results of such studies. One federal court has said: [57]

> We know of no fixed formula which has been generally recognized
> as a standard for conducting surveys in an attempt to ascertain
> public opinion. There is no sufficient ground, however, to say that
> one system of polling in a particular field would be as effective as
> some other method in a different field. The system used by the
> plaintiff has been severely criticized . . . It may be entirely possi-
> ble that the system adopted by the plaintiff . . . would be as
> effective as any other method.

Probably the closest to a definitive blueprint has come from the recommendations of the 1960 Judicial Conference. See Section 19 below. While
involving a different [58]—although parallel—aspect of survey use, these
recommendations are clearly indicative of the possible future standards
which may be applied by courts in weighing survey results and assessing
their probative value. The five elements suggested as necessary standards
are:

(a) Surveys should be conducted by recognized experts.

(b) The data gathered should be accurately reported.

(c) The sample design, questionnaire construction and interviewing should follow generally accepted standards in the field of such
surveys.

(d) The sample should be designed and interviews conducted independently of attorneys.

(e) The interviewers should be trained and have no knowledge of
the litigation or the purpose for which the survey is being done.

These suggestions are, in the main, fairly general. The cases do, on the
other hand, give some indications of preferred specifics. For example, a
probability sample is apparently to be preferred.[59] The best method of
court presentation of survey results has crystallized to some extent. The
court in the *Franklin Bank* case [60] recommended the following:

> The evidence offered should include calling the planners, super-
> visors and workers (or some of them) as witnesses so that the Court

may see and hear them; they should be ready to give a complete exposition of the poll and even its results; the work sheets, reports, surveys and all documents used in or prepared during the poll taking and those showing its results should be offered in evidence, although the Court may desire to draw its own conclusions.

16. Effect of Acknowledged Errors.

It is acknowledged that opinion surveys based on sampling do contain certain well-recognized and inherent errors. This is true of even the best planned and conducted study.[61] However, these errors are part of accepted methodology and compensation can be and is made for them in accordance with accepted standards. They are not the vital mistakes which lead to polling debacles like the *Literary Digest* poll of 1936 or the various pre-Truman-Dewey election polls of 1948. Such errors, when of a customary, anticipated and explicable nature, do not militate appreciably against either the admission of the survey evidence or the weight to be given thereto.

In the *United Shoe Machinery* case [62] the court itself suggested the nature of the study and later commented upon the "distortions" inherent in the sample and the survey results but nevertheless based its opinion to a considerable degree on such results.

In the *Thermos* case,[63] the trial court discussed the surveys at considerable length, apparently finding the defendant's survey superior to that of the plaintiff. The court said it was "particularly impressed by the high degree of credibility of the [defendant's] interviewers who testified . . ." and then went on to comment:

Here and there in the testimony it was brought out that some human error had occurred in a particular interview, but an adequate allowance had been made for such error in computing the results of the poll.

On the other hand, basic errors or misconceptions in methodology such as insufficiency of the sample, choice of an incorrect universe or the other matters referred to in Section 17 below, may have a very considerable effect upon both the admissibility of the results and the weight to be accorded the evidence, if admitted. See also, in this context, Section 14 above.

17. Defects in Reported Cases.

A study of the cases cited throughout this chapter—without reference to whether or not the survey in question was admitted—produces the following list of specific defects upon which various courts have commented. Some surveys suffered from several of these shortcomings; others from only one; all, however, were criticized by the courts for at least one of these indicated reasons:

   (a) improper universe,
   (b) improper design of sample,
   (c) improper type of sample,
   (d) sample too small,
   (e) slanted questionnaires,
   (f) leading questions,
   (g) overcasual interviewing,
   (h) offering of prizes to interviewees,
   (i) flattery of interviewees,
   (j) mail questionnaires,
   (k) telephone interviews,
   (l) use of substitute interviewees,
  (m) oral leading and hints by interviewers,
   (n) survey made after institution of suit,
   (o) competing surveys in conflict,
   (p) inclusion of incomplete interviews,
   (q) influence of interviewing locale,
   (r) inaccurate and non-reflective tabulation,
   (s) variations from marketplace conditions,
   (t) lack of supportive expert testimony,
   (u) questionnaires not made available to other party,
   (v) survey results contrary to other evidence,
  (w) no specific or demonstrable margin of error,
   (x) unexplained and missing questionnaires,
   (y) oral as opposed to written reports,
   (z) emotional involvement of interviewees,
  (aa) contact between attorney and interviewees,
  (ab) obvious irregularity or laxity in procedure,
  (ac) partisan choice of interviewees,
  (ad) inexperienced personnel.

Some of these errors are found in the earlier cases and presumably would not be repeated in a survey designed and conducted according to currently approved methodology.

18. Protection of Anonymity of Respondents.

Several courts have commented favorably upon the use of interviewees (respondents) as live witnesses, subject to cross-examination. This raises certain questions under the Codes of Ethics of both the American Marketing Association (AMA) and the American Association for Public Opinion Research (AAPOR).

The AMA Code provides,

> if a respondent has been led to believe, . . . that his anonymity will be protected, his name shall not be made known to anyone outside the research organization or research department, or used for other than research purposes.

The AAPOR Code provides: "We shall protect the anonymity of every respondent. We shall hold as privileged and confidential all information which tends to identify the respondent."

These standards were originally adopted in order to protect respondents and their names or identities from being followed up in some manner or other such as by mailing list use or some other form of playback considered unethical. It is doubtful whether such protection was intended to apply in connection with testimony before a court. At the same time, if a respondent is advised in advance that he may be called to testify, this is likely to lead to a colloquy vitiating the validity of that particular interview and the data developed therein.

There have been instances in which the project managers have refused to identify in court the respondents interviewed in the study. This does not appear to have contributed to any adverse judicial attitude or finding. It certainly should not—at least when an expert witness or the project manager explains the reason for such anonymity.

D. RECOMMENDATIONS OF THE 1960 JUDICIAL CONFERENCE.

In 1960, the Federal Judicial Conference produced a lengthy Report on various evidentiary techniques useful in expediting the trial of protracted cases. Among the matters considered in detail was "the proper use of samples and polls." [64]

Although the basic interest of the Conference was the protracted case, its recommendations relative to surveys and their use apply with logic to any case in which such evidence may properly contribute. The discussion in the Conference Report is probably our most cohesive analysis of the problem and its solution. This portion of the Report has therefore been quoted verbatim in Section 19, altered only as to headings and subheadings. The footnotes have been omitted.

An important caveat is in order. The Report uses the term "sample" differently from the way in which research practitioners use it, the former confining it to physical matters although in normal procedures it refers to both human beings and inanimate objects. See Section 4 above.

19. Full Text of Sample/Poll Segment of the Report.

PROOF OF FACTS REQUIRING RESORT TO BULK UNDERLYING DOCUMENTS OR TO
NUMEROUS WITNESSES: SAMPLES AND POLLS

Recommendation: Scientifically designed samples and polls, meeting
the tests of necessity and trustworthiness, are useful adjuncts to conventional methods of proof and may, under certain circumstances, contribute
materially to shortening the trial of the protracted case.

Definition of "Sample" and "Poll" as Terms Are Used Herein.

Discussion. Both samples and polls are designed to obtain a result applicable to the entire universe by examining representative portions thereof and projecting the results. For clarity of discussion, we use "sample" to
mean the physical examination of parts to establish the character of the
whole, *i.e.*, personal examination by the sampler of objectively observable
facts such as, for example, a count of units or the results of test borings.
On the other hand, a "poll" (or opinion survey) as used herein refers to
the interrogation of part of the population to be examined and the projection of the data thus obtained to the whole.

Thus, for present purposes, a sample is confined to observable facts,
whereas a poll may involve the reporting by interviewees of (1) what they
have seen, think, do or believe, or (2) why they think, act or believe in a
certain way.

Principal Problem Is Admissibility.

Scientifically designed samples and polls have received increasing acceptance in recent years in government and in industry. The important
question to be considered in a given case is whether the contemplated or
proffered sample or poll is admissible under existing rules of evidence.

*Samples: Admissibility More Often Depends Upon Correct Methodology
Than Upon Application of Hearsay Rule.*

Samples. When a sample is offered through the testimony of the sampler, the report on the sample examined (*i.e.*, on the count of units or the
test borings, in the examples noted above) usually does not involve hearsay. In order to project this report, however, the burden of proof rests upon the offeror to show, by the testimony of a statistical expert, that the
sample was selected in accordance with accepted principles of sampling so
that it properly represents the universe. Once this is established, there
remain only questions of relevancy, materiality and weight.

The same reasoning applies to the type of survey portions of the universe to testify as to the particular facts in issue with which each is familiar. The crucial question is whether the selected witnesses collectively have been chosen by proper sampling methods so as to justify the inference that their testimony accurately reflects the testimony which would have been given by the universe as a whole.

Polls: Circumstances Where Hearsay Is Not Involved.

Polls. As noted above, polling, unlike sampling, involves the ascertainment of facts by interrogating others on their observations, actions, motivations, or beliefs. Sometimes, as a matter of substantive law, what is said by an interviewee may be relevant and admissible not for the truth of what he said but for the fact of the statement; for example, where state of mind is an issue and what is said is evidence of that state of mind. Thus polls have been held admissible to prove statements of interviewees as evidence of state of mind in unfair competition, and antitrust cases. This kind of "poll" is actually a "sampling," for the outward manifestation of the "physical fact" to be proved, state of mind, has been personally observed by the sampler-witness. A poll of this kind involves no hearsay.

Polls: Circumstances Where Hearsay Is Involved and Admissibility Depends Upon Applicability of a Recognized Exception to the Hearsay Rule.

On the other hand, polls may also be offered to prove the truth of the assertions made by the interviewees and thus are hearsay, admissible only if they fall within an exception to the hearsay rule. It is not recommended that there be created a general exception to this rule which would allow the admission of all polls into evidence. However, in a given case the factors of necessity and the circumstantial guarantee of trustworthiness may be such that a particular survey could properly be admitted to prove the truth of the facts reported within recognized principles of evidence.

Proof of necessity does not require a showing of total inaccessibility to proof of the facts desired to be shown, but the offeror must show the impracticability of making his proof by conventional methods.

In evaluating the trustworthiness of a particular survey attention should be centered on the nature of the fact or facts to be proved thereby, and the manner of conducting the survey. If a poll records the interviewees' observations or knowledge of objective facts such as color, number, size, etc., it may, if properly conducted, possess the elements of trustworthiness sufficient to be admitted. If, on the other hand, a poll records subjective data such as the beliefs, opinions or motivations of the interviewees, its trustworthiness may well be less; the showing of necessity in such case should be stronger, and the question of trustworthiness should be more closely scrutinized.

Polls: Admissibility Is Dependent on Correct Methodology.

The offeror has the burden of establishing that a proffered poll was conducted in accordance with accepted principles of survey research, *i.e.,* that the proper universe was examined, that a representative sample was drawn from that universe, and that the mode of questioning the interviewees was correct. He should be required to show that: the persons conducting the survey were recognized experts; the data gathered was accurately reported; the sample design, the questionnaire and the interviewing were in accordance with generally accepted standards of objective procedure and statistics in the field of such surveys; the sample design and the interviews were conducted independently of the attorneys; and the interviewers, trained in this field, had no knowledge of the litigation or the purposes for which the survey was to be used. Normally this showing will be made through the testimony of the persons responsible for the various parts of the survey.

Polls: Questions Going to Admissibility Should Be Raised and Resolved Prior to Offer.

While it is desirable that questions going to the admissibility of the poll be raised, and if possible decided, prior to the time it is offered, no procedure should be adopted which in effect would place the burden of disproving admissibility on the opposing party. Thus, merely making available to the opposing party the documents underlying the poll, and names and addresses of the samplers and interviewees, so that they can be interviewed, cross-examined or the trustworthiness of their answers otherwise checked, should not be held to place upon the opposing party the burden of proving the proffered poll untrustworthy.

Polls: Advance Planning.

In certain instances and with the consent of all parties, it may be desirable to consider at pre-trial a proposed poll so that the flaws in mechanics may be eliminated, to the extent possible, before the poll is taken. However, participation in such a procedure should not be made compulsory.

Notes

1. For extended consideration and discussion of the opinion polls and surveys as well as other forms of sampling research, see: BARKSDALE, THE USE OF SURVEY FINDINGS AS LEGAL EVIDENCE (1957); SIMON, THE LAW FOR ADVERTISING AND MARKETING, ch. 26, at 471–482 (1956); *Report of the 1960 Judicial Conference,* 25 F.R.D. 351, 425–30 (1960) (referred to hereafter as "Conference Report"); OPINION RESEARCH CORP., THE USE OF SURVEYS IN LEGAL ACTIONS (1964); Sorenson and Sorenson, *The Admissibility and Use of Opinion Research Evidence,* 28 N.Y.U.L.R. 1213 (1953).

2. CUTLIP & CENTER, EFFECTIVE PUBLIC RELATIONS, ch. 7, at 108–126 (3d ed. 1964); Robinson, *Research in Public Relations,* P.R.J., Jan., 1961, at 19.

3. Cutlip & Center, *supra* note 2, at 93. For an excellent study in depth of the PR involvement with research, see FOUSS, THE ROLE OF RESEARCH IN PUBLIC RELATIONS (1963), a thesis submitted in fulfillment of requirements for an M.S. in Public Relations, Boston University School of Public Relations and Communications. The author indicates that approximately 90 per cent of the PR practitioners questioned foresee either an increasing or a quantitatively similar role for PR research in the future.

4. Household Finance Corp. v. Federal Finance Corp. *et al.,* 105 F. Supp. 164 (D.C. Ariz. 1952).

5. OPINION RESEARCH CORP., THE USE OF SURVEYS IN LEGAL ACTIONS 2–3 (1964).

6. Procter & Gamble Co. v. Sweets Laboratories, Inc., 137 F.2d 365 (C.C.P.A. 1943).

7. S.C. Johnson & Son, Inc. v. Gold Seal Co., 90 U.S.P.Q. 379 (Comm'r Pat. 1951).

8. United States v. J.I. Case Co., 101 F. Supp. 856 (D.C. Minn. 1951).

9. See Barksdale, *supra* note 1, at 50–57.

10. See Burtt, *Measurement of Confusion Between Similar Trade Names,* 19 ILL. L. REV. 320–336 (1925).

11. For several examples and further references, see Conference Report, *supra* note 1, at 427, note 128.

12. See La Touraine Coffee Co. v. Lorraine Coffee Co., 157 F.2d 116 (2d Cir. 1946), *cert. denied,* 329 U.S. 771 (1946); Triangle Publications, Inc. v. Rohrlich *et al.,* 73 F. Supp. 74 (S.D.N.Y. 1947), *mod'd and aff'd,* 167 F.2d 969 (2d Cir. 1948).

13. Opinion Research Corp., *supra* note 5, at 4.

14. *Id.* at 15.

15. See, *e.g.,* Eighth Ave. Coach Corp. v. City of New York, 170 Misc. 243, 10 N.Y.S.2d 170 (Sup. Ct. 1939), *aff'd,* 259 Supp. Div. 870, 20 N.Y.S.2d 402 (1940), *aff'd,* 286 N.Y. 84, 35 N.E.2d 907 (1941).

16. See, *e.g.,* State Wholesale Grocers v. Great A. & P. Tea Co., *infra* note 23;

United States v. E. I. du Pont de Nemours & Co., 177 F. Supp. 1 (N.D. Ill. 1959).

17. United States v. Eighty-eight Cases, etc., 187 F.2d 967 (3d Cir. 1951), *cert. denied,* 342 U.S. 861 (1951).

18. See cases cited, 25 F.R.D. 427, note 131.

19. James S. Kirk & Co. v. F.T.C., *infra* note 40.

20. Rhodes Pharmacal Corp. v. F.T.C., 208 F.2d 382 (7th Cir. 1953), *rev'd,* 348 U.S. 940 (1955).

21. P.L. 89-755.

22. United States v. United Shoe Machinery Corp., 110 F. Supp. 295 (D.C. Mass. 1953), *aff'd,* 347 U.S. 521 (1954); United States v. J. I. Case Co., *supra* note 8.

23. See also, as to price surveys, State Wholesale Grocers v. Great A. & P. Tea Co., 258 F.2d 831 (7th Cir. 1958).

24. Public Util. Comm'n v. Pollak *et al.,* 191 F.2d 450 (D.C. Cir. 1951), *rev'd on other grounds,* 343 U.S. 451 (1952).

25. Eighth Avenue Coach Corp. v. City of New York, 170 Misc. 243, 10 N.Y.S.2d 170 (Sup. Ct. 1939), *aff'd,* 259 App. Div. 870, 20 N.Y.S.2d 402 (1st Dep't 1940), *aff'd,* 286 N.Y. 84, 34 N.E.2d 907 (1941).

26. Illinois Bell Tel. Co. v. Illinois Commerce Comm'n, 111 N.E.2d 337 (Ill. Sup. Ct. 1953); Illinois Bell Tel. Co., UTIL. LAW REP. §16, 714 (Ill. Commerce Comm'n 1955); see also Rose, *The Bell Telephone System Rate Cases,* 37 VA. L. REV. 699 (1951).

27. Southern Bell Tel. & Tel. Co., 4 P.U.R.3d 195 (Ala. Pub. Serv. Comm'n 1954).

28. Barksdale, *supra* note 1, at 122.

29. Conference Report, *supra* note 1, at 425.

30. 66 HARV. L. REV. 498, 513 (1953).

31. United States v. Hiss, 185 F.2d 822 (2d Cir. 1950), *cert. denied,* 340 U.S. 948 (1951); Note, *Local Prejudice in Criminal Cases,* 54 HARV. L. REV. 679 (1940).

32. Elgin Nat'l Watch Co. v. Elgin Clock Co., 26 F.2d 376 (D.C. Del. 1928). See also Barksdale, *supra* note 1, at 44-6 and cases cited note 42.

33. John B. Stetson Co. v. Stephen L. Stetson Co., 14 F. Supp. 74 (S.D.N.Y. 1936), *mod'd and aff'd,* 85 F.2d 586 (2d Cir. 1936), *cert. denied,* 299 U.S. 605 (1936).

34. Quaker Oats Co. v. General Mills, Inc., 134 F.2d 431 (7th Cir. 1943).

35. United States v. Eighty-eight Cases, *supra* note 17; Standard Oil Co. v. Standard Oil Co. *et al.,* 252 F.2d 65, 76 A.L.R.2d 600 (10th Cir. 1958); see also Barksdale, *supra* note 1, at 46 and authorities cited, note 43.

36. See Sprowls, *The Admissibility of Sample Data into a Court of Law,* 4 U.C.L.A. L. REV. 222 (1957) and authorities cited and discussed therein.

37. 151 Mass. 359, 24 N.E. 208 (1889).

38. Lawlor v. Loewe, 235 U.S. 522 (1915).

39. People v. Franklin Nat'l Bank, etc., 200 Misc. 557, 105 N.Y.S.2d 81 (Sup. Ct. 1951), *rev'd,* 281 App. Div. 757, 118 N.Y.S.2d 210 (1953), *aff'd,* 305 N.Y. 453, 113 N.E.2d 796 (1953), *rev'd,* 347 U.S. 373 (1954).

40. James S. Kirk & Co. v. F.T.C., 12 F.T.C. 272 (1928), *rev'd*, 59 F.2d 179 (7th Cir. 1932), *cert. denied*, 287 U.S. 663 (1932).

41. United States v. E. I. du Pont de Nemours & Co., *supra* note 16; People v. Franklin Nat'l Bank, etc., *supra* note 39; Eighth Avenue Coach Corp. v. City of New York, *supra* note 25.

42. Conference Report, *supra* note 1, at 429, note 134.

43. Barksdale, *supra* note 1, at 146–7, 153.

44. Baldisarre v. West Oregon Lumber Co., 193 Ore. 556, 239 P.2d 839 (1952).

45. General Motors Corp. v. Cadillac Marine & Boat Co., 226 F. Supp. 716 (W.D. Mich. 1964).

46. The same situation was apparently present in S.C. Johnson v. Johnson, 266 F.2d 129 (6th Cir. 1959), and was also treated there by the court as affecting the weight to be accorded the evidence.

47. International Milling Co. v. Robin Hood Pop Corn Co., 110 U.S.P.Q. 368 (Comm'r Pats. 1956); United States v. E. I. du Pont de Nemours & Co., *supra* note 16.

48. Rhodes Pharmacal Corp. v. F.T.C., *supra* note 20; General Motors v. Cadillac Marine & Boat Co., *supra* note 45.

49. General Motors Corp. v. Cadillac Marine & Boat Co., *supra* note 45.

50. Procter & Gamble Co., 96 U.S.P.Q. 272 (1953); Admiral Corp. v. Penco, Inc., 106 F. Supp. 1015 (W.D.N.Y. 1952), *aff'd*, 203 F.2d 517 (2d Cir. 1953).

51. General Dry Batteries, Inc. v. Ray-O-Vac Co., 45 T.M. Rep. 588 (Comm'r Pats. 1955).

52. Campbell Soup Co. v. Armour & Co., 81 F. Supp. 114 (E.D. Pa. 1948), *aff'd*, 175 F.2d 795 (3d Cir. 1949), *cert. denied*, 338 U.S. 847 (1949).

53. Barksdale, *supra* note 1, at 141.

54. Du Pont Cellophane Co. v. Waxed Products Co., 6 F. Supp. 859 (E.D.N.Y. 1934), *mod'd*, 85 F.2d 75 (2d Cir. 1936), *cert. denied*, 299 U.S. 601 (1936).

55. National Fruit Prod. Co. v. Dwinell-Wright Co., 47 F. Supp. 499 (E.D. Mass. 1942).

56. American Thermos Prods. Co. v. Aladdin Industries, Inc. 207 F. Supp. 9 (D.C. Conn. 1962), *aff'd*, 321 F.2d 557 (2d Cir. 1963).

57. Standard Oil Co. v. Standard Oil Co., 110 U.S.P.Q. 122 (D.C. Wyo. 1956).

58. These recommendations were made in connection with *admissibility* of surveys when the survey is offered to prove the *truth* of the assertions made by the interviewees and thus are hearsay. Conference Report, *supra* note 1, at 428–9.

59. People v. Franklin Nat'l Bank, etc., *supra* note 39.

60. *Id.*

61. Barksdale, *supra* note 1, at 31–33.

62. United States v. United Shoe Machinery Corp., *supra* note 22.

63. American Thermos Prods. Co. v. Aladdin Industries, Inc., *supra* note 56.

64. Conference Report, *supra* note 1, at 425–30.

Chapter 16

New Product Introduction

A. INTRODUCTION

B. DEFINITION AND APPLICATIONS OF "NEW"

C. SPECIFIC LEGAL CONSIDERATIONS

Chapter 16

New Product Introduction

A. INTRODUCTION.

1. Unique Legal Characteristics.

The introduction of a new product[1] exposes the PR practitioner and all others concerned with it to certain new legal concepts or special aspects of general legal rules which may not already be part of their legal panoply. Some are more restrictive than usual; others give greater flexibility to the marketer.

A prime example of the unique legal nature of the introduction of a new product appears in the proceedings brought against Armour & Company under the Packers and Stockyards Act, charging a violation arising from a coupon refund promotion resulting in sales below cost. An order was entered prohibiting such practices.[2] However, the order carved out this exception: *"Provided:* that this order shall not apply to the *introduction of a really new meat product."* (Emphasis added.)

2. Chapter Scope.

Other unusual legal applications, both statutory and judicial, arise in the legal areas discussed in this chapter, the purpose of which is to pinpoint, collect and discuss within a consolidated framework the various legal concerns with which new product introduction must work. Most of the subjects are dealt with at length in other chapters and cross-references thereto will be found at appropriate points below. An effort has been made to maintain a considerable degree of selectivity.

We are not here concerned with "new products" as meaning "unused" products.[3] Meanings such as this are incorporated into and defined in the Wool Products Labeling Act and the Textile Fiber Products Identification Act to which reference is directed. See Chapter 19, Section 17.

"New" is discussed herein in the context of "new product," "new invention," "new process," or "new principle."

3. Role of Public Relations.

The contribution and value of public relations in new product introduction are increasing. This is true regardless of company size or functional organization, or the nature of the new product.

The PR Director is a member of the new product marketing team in
many companies.[4] The National Industrial Conference Board concluded
that new product public relations and publicity "sometimes . . . are
more important than paid advertising." [5] Singer has attributed the "most
successful new product introduction in [its] history" to its PR program;
Scott Paper's "paper caper" helped introduce the new paper dresses and
received "a big play in the press and TV." Fleishman's new corn oil
margarine managed to get into the A & P stores because of public demand developed from a Clementine Paddleford column which originated
at a press luncheon.[6]

PR's role seems to start in some cases with playback from the public,
guiding the company in its initial new-product conceptualization—even
before development of the product begins.

Cutlip and Center equate "the image of the managerial executive
heading a drive to get out the voters and his public relations executive or
counsel in a marketing huddle concerning the introduction of a new
product." [7]

4. Need for Early Legal Consultation.

The new product team should give early and frequent consideration
to the possible legal complications it may face. Their incidence and
importance will naturally vary. If the new product is a pain killer, a
cigarette, a diet food, a new tire or some other product in which the
various governmental agencies—federal or state—are particularly interested, the legal involvement may be most intensive. Probably new industrial products pose the fewest problems but, even here, there are legal
ramifications.

Legal questions are often inextricably intertwined with the practical
problems of new product introduction, and may, on occasion, be so basic
as to control other phases of the project. One of the most obvious is the
impact of existing patents.

Legal counsel should routinely be a member of the new product team.
While he will usually act only in an advisory capacity with few, if any,
decision-making powers, his advice will often be both a prop and a curb
for the team or managerial decision. The extent of his successful contribution may depend upon the nature of the continuing liaison which has
been previously developed with counsel. It has been suggested that new

product development and introduction is probably the context which best tests the usefulness of company legal counsel. See Chapter 1.

5. Legal Clearance of Publicity and Promotion.

All new product announcements of any kind should be routinely cleared by legal counsel. This is necessary for company protection against many different legal claims or charges ranging from patent infringement suits by private individuals to broad, inhibitory action by the regulatory agencies. It may also be vitally necessary for considerations of corporate "trade secrets" security as discussed in Chapter 17.

The following procedures and requirements of Du Pont are a good example of such clearance and some of the likely problems in clearing publicity: [8]

> It is normal procedure for the legal counsel assigned to a department to approve every new product announcement. Where the responsibility falls may vary, depending on whether the Public Relations Department is in primary charge of the announcement or the operating department is the primary initiator.
>
> In the highly regulative product areas—agricultural chemicals, pharmaceuticals, etc.—legal approval is thorough, routine and automatic.
>
> In almost every case of the announcement of new products, there is a question or patent protection, liability, and in some cases various government regulations.
>
> To cite the procedure in our most active department, everything except the items that fall into continuing product publicity is checked with the Textile Fibers Department legal counsel. The Textile Fibers Department checks with him on everything it proposes to do in new product announcements, price changes, etc. That is its responsibility. Then we check what is going to be said about what Textile Fibers proposes to do. This is the Public Relations manager's responsibility.
>
> It can be said that everything in the public relations area is checked with Legal—the Legal Department representative of the announcing department, not our Public Relations legal counsel.
>
> The details of the procedure and the responsibility may vary, but the principle does not.

Du Pont, of course, is a large company with a company legal department staffed with attorneys having specialized experience in many legal fields. However, these procedures are pertinent to any company although it may consult outside counsel. The smaller the company and the more infrequent the introduction of a new product, the more care should be exercised.

Legal clearances may also be required—with some new products—from federal agencies. This is discussed in Section 18 below.

B. DEFINITIONS AND APPLICATIONS OF "NEW."

6. Definition of "New."

In the legal configuration it has not always been possible to know with any assurance when a company is promoting a "new" product. Only recently has the word come to have any reasonably specific meaning as a legal "word of art." The principal source of such definition in the past has been the decisions of the FTC.[9] These have not laid down any broad, generally applicable meaning. The cases have been decided on their specific facts.

Typical is *Prima Products, Inc. et al. v. F.T.C.*[10] in which a concrete-waterproofing paint was promoted with a claim that it involved a "new principle." The promotion had included the distribution of reprints of an article by a New York University professor which had appeared in *Forbes* with a later condensation in *Reader's Digest*. These reprints were held to be deceptive because the public might construe such language to mean that the product's "combination of materials" constituted the new principle when the constituents were not really new.

In another case [11] a thermographic printing method was represented as "a new process" when in fact it had been "used by the trade for years." The Commission entered an order against the company for misrepresenting the process as "new."

In 1967 the FTC issued its Advisory Opinion No. 120 defining the permissible use of "new" and the period during which it could properly be so used. It provides, in relevant part: [12]

> [T]he word "new" may be properly used *only* when the product so described is either *entirely new* or has been *changed in a functionally significant and substantial respect*. A product may not be called "new" when only the package has been altered or some other change made which is functionally insignificant or insubstantial. . . . However, the time period during which a particular product may be called "new" will depend upon the circumstances and is not subject to precise limitations; any selection of a fixed period of time or a rigid cut-off date would have to be arbitrary in nature. [I]t would be preferable, considering the absence of precedents, to establish a tentative outer limit for use of the claim, while leaving itself free to take into consideration unusual situations which may arise. Thus, the Commission's position was that until such time as later developments may show the need for a different rule, *it would be inclined to question use of any claim that a product is "new" for a period of time longer than six months*. This general rule would apply unless exceptional circumstances warranting a period either shorter or longer than six months were shown to exist. (Emphasis added.)

While Advisory Opinions are not necessarily binding except upon the applicant therefor, this statement may be relied upon—as far as it goes—as the position of the FTC on this subject. See Section 8 below.

7. Industry Concepts of "New Products."

It is important to appraise possible conflicts between the FTC definition of "new," discussed in Section 6 above, with the thinking of the marketer. In view of the continuing, almost emotional, seeking after and use of "new" in marketing appeals, this could be a serious problem.[13]

Unfortunately, the FTC has not been overly specific in its statement, using expressions such as "entirely new" and "changed in a functionally significant and substantial respect." Against these mandates, industry approaches to "new products" should be carefully scrutinized.

Richard D. Crisp, Director of Marketing of Carson/Roberts, has suggested 15 "concepts" as essential to a "useful, tested framework for an organized approach to creative new product development." [14]

These 15 concepts may be thus grouped and summarized:

(a) Changes in flavor, size, color, shape, quality and minority or sub-market appeal.

(b) Changes in packaging for purposes of physical convenience in use, time-saving, assembly of related-product needs, variety of sizes, flavors, etc.

(c) New uses or end-function of existing product.

(d) Combination of two products into one.

(e) A combination of any of the above.

Applying the FTC test, certain of these "concepts" would clearly not qualify a product as "new." Promotion of a new use or size for an unchanged product is an example. Apparently aware of this, Crisp, in discussing changes in size, says:

> Differentiation of a product by size is particularly meaningful if there is a *functional reason* for making a product in different sizes. . . . I suggest that you *approach it from a consumer-use viewpoint.* . . . If the consumer changes the size of your product before using it, there is often a real opportunity to demonstrate that you can do the size-changing better and cheaper. (Emphasis added.)

This analysis might qualify more of the above change-concepts under the FTC requirements if it can be demonstrated that the marketer's analysis of the "consumer-use viewpoint" is correct. However, a change in shape, for example, would not qualify unless shape is "functionally significant and substantial" to the buying decision as to the product in question.

Some well-qualified marketing people are questioning the realities of industry concepts about new products—especially when viewed from the consumer's position in the marketplace. Louis A. Collier, H. J. Heinz Marketing Vice-President, writing under the conclusory title "The Difference Must Be Real," says: [15]

> Why has "newness" become such a relative term to the home-maker, that it is almost meaningless? If you have a job in market-ing, are you inclined, like me, to refuse to answer on the grounds of self-incrimination?
>
> Take off your business hat and make like a consumer. How many products can you name that seemed absolutely new to you in the past ten years? What about *New from X Company, Restyled Widget X, New-Formula Brand X, Gismo X in New Decorator Colors, New Process Brand X, New Super Brand X, Improved Brand X, Electrified Brand X, New Quick Opening Brand X, New Easier-To-Serve Brand X.*

Collier then goes on to discuss misconceptions about the distinctions between "new products" and "marketing innovations" or differences be-tween "product differentiation" and "product innovation." He appears to agree with the FTC when he says:

> There should be the same reluctance to consider new packaging a product innovation. . . . Packaging will continue to be a major *merchandising* innovation but, with exceptions like the invention of aerosol dispensing, packaging *per se* will seldom represent basic product invention. (Emphasis added.)

8. Duration of "Newness."

Recognizing the dangers in a too rigid cut-off limit for permissible use of "new," the FTC has adopted a "tentative outer limit" of six months, indicating that it "would be inclined to question" any claim of newness after that period. See Section 6 above. The Commission's awareness in this respect has been fortified by industry queries on the subject, one trade paper editorializing somewhat archly: [16]

> The Commission may have stumbled into a real semantic bramble bush in its effort to arrive at a clear and precise definition. Some things stop being new long before six months, while others can be new much longer. A newspaper isn't new after a couple of hours, for instance. A new car becomes used as soon as it leaves the showroom. A new baby is a new baby for perhaps six weeks, and a new potato stops being new after only a couple of months.
>
> But a new house remains new for several years. A road can

retain that designation for a decade—or until a newer one is built. A television show that remains on the air as long as six months is certainly a veteran by that time. But a new idea can be new for 50 years or more.

* * * *

Six months after the issuance of the FTC's new ruling on "new," will it still be a new ruling? Or will it be referred to as the old "new" ruling?

This closing facetious query was borne out when the Commission— some six months later, in October 1967—revised its initial position in part. The revision dealt with test marketing of new products and said: [17]

> [T]he six months rule announced in its earlier opinion does not apply to the bona fide test marketing of a new product. So long as the test marketing program does not cover more than 15% of the population, so long as the test period does not exceed six months in duration and so long as it is being conducted in good faith for test purposes only, the Commission stated that it did not intend to apply the six months rule until the test period had ended and the product had been introduced to the general market.

While conceding that test marketing required a revision of its position, the Commission refused to concede that six months was too short a period in view of "the average life of packaging materials and advertising literature." It desired to minimize losses to an advertiser but pointed out that the advertiser, knowing it is limited as to the permissible period in which "new" may legally be used, could predict "with reasonable accuracy" the quantities of "new" promotional materials and thus hold its wastage to a minimum. It also repeated its willingness to consider applications for permissible periods longer than six months.

Any company seeking a longer period will probably have the burden of proving to the Commission that the market realities dictate a relaxation of the rule. The Commission has said that the "general rule would apply unless exceptional circumstances . . . were shown to exist." [18] On the other hand, the probabilities are that the Commission would itself take the initiative if it had reason to believe that a shorter period were in order under "exceptional circumstances."

Interesting questions may also arise from the efforts of creative copywriters seeking to avoid—not evade—the FTC rule. For example, a product may be admittedly on the market for more than six months but it still is the "latest" or the "newest" model. Is such a claim permissible after six months?

9. "Breakthroughs."

The word "breakthrough" has apparently been so overworked that it causes "some editors to laugh out loud when they read it" in publicity releases.[19] Improperly used, its legal implications may cause government agencies to show their teeth but not as a by-product of laughter. Donald Van Deusen of National Research Company suggests that "breakthrough" is "a fair and accurate description" if it represents a development "of major importance representing a capability that has been sought for many years." Warning against the "sensationalized account" in news releases, he recommends as a worthwhile preliminary test the ability "to tell them [the editors] why." [20]

The same approach should inhibit use in publicity and promotion of such expressions as "the greatest advance in so-and-so years," particularly if the product change may be appraised on an objective basis. As to the objective/subjective aspect of the situation, see Chapter 11, Section 5.

10. Regional Use of "New."

Under the FTC rule discussed in Section 6 above, the expanding marketer may face questions about calling his product "new" when he introduces it into a new market more than six months after it was elsewhere introduced. It is definitely "new" and available for the first time in that market. May he promote it as "new" in that market?

While there has been no decision on this, by analogy to the FTC position on price representations, it would appear that such a claim would be permissible in the new market under these circumstances.[21]

11. Franchises as New Products.

PR counsel are serving national and regional franchise chains more frequently and are also rendering a broader spectrum of services. It has been said: [22]

> [T]here is also a trend toward a new form of assistance, public relations. [It is] a form of business assistance that has proven itself with too much historic impact to elaborate on. It is more important to note that franchising companies are increasingly turning to professional public relations for a variety of purposes, . . .

From a promotional point of view and as far as the local public is concerned, a new franchisee in a new community is essentially a "new product." This is true although the franchise chain may have operated elsewhere for some time. By their very nature, franchises are local operations and this should be the frame of reference within which "new" should be judged. See Sections 6, 8 and 10.

When the PR firm assists in the development and opening of a local franchisee, it is exposed to many different local legal procedures. Since some PR firms assist even in the choice of the site, the involvement may start with local zoning laws. PR firms experienced in franchising have found that it is useful to retain local legal counsel to steer them through the maze of applicable state laws and local ordinances, which may vary tremendously as successive franchise units come under contract and into operation.

12. Effect of Mergers and Acquisitions.

The "urge to merge" is producing some interesting and sometimes difficult problems in the "new products field." When a company acquires another concern, it may consider the acquired products as "new" from its own point of view. Yet, from the public's perspective, such products are definitely not new and the acquiring company should not endeavor to promote them as new.

There is often a temptation to announce "a new product in the XYZ family of good foods" or in some similar fashion. This is incorrect because it implies that the product itself is new. "ABC is now a member of XYZ's family of good foods" would avoid this implication.

Furthermore, the acquiring company should investigate carefully through its own counsel before continuing the same appeals and representations as were previously used. They may be suspect. Some merger contracts contain warranties by the acquired company that all of its marketing methods, PR and promotional practices, advertising, etc. have been conducted legally. Such warranties are particularly useful if the acquired products are alien to the field in which the acquiring company operates—a typical example being the acquisition of a consumer-products concern by an industrially-oriented firm.

C. SPECIFIC LEGAL CONSIDERATIONS.

13. Trademarks.

Legal texts concerning trademarks are plentiful but their concern is almost exclusively with technicalities of registration and protection of the marks. The trademark "glamor cases" usually deal with infringements. Yet they are the last stop on the trademark road—a road which started with the original choice of the marks, in many cases as part of the introduction of the product which carries the mark.

Only relatively recently has there begun to develop a small body of literature dealing with the *choice* of a mark. Much of this is coming from non-legal sources. This is as might be expected. The Marketing Director, the PR Director, the Advertising Manager—they are the people who are going to be charged with making the mark *produce*. This is not the job of the lawyer. He can only advise as to legal perils which a particular mark may face; he cannot and should not judge the marketplace value of the mark.

Unless a company is content with its existing "family mark" on its new products, the company faces the problem of trademark choice almost every time it offers something new. This is a recurrent problem—one which is becoming more difficult as time goes on. Even the computer is now being used in the probing for new, acceptable, powerful marks for new products. As new products proliferate, availabilities narrow. In short, the search for new marks is becoming increasingly troublesome at the same time that it becomes more important. Public awareness of brand names is increasing and reliance upon public goodwill and acceptance dominates the marketplace.

In discussing the choice of a trademark, William Werner of Procter & Gamble and a past president of PRSA, has said: [23]

> The naming and marketing, the nurturing and protecting of a trademark affects an extremely valuable asset of the company. This asset each year becomes more and more valuable as you pour dollars' worth of advertising and promotion and selling into it . . .
>
> We are surrounded with good will problems, the good will of the American public and the protection of the company's good name. We are surrounded with public relations problems. All of this has to do with our relations with the public, the public's concept of us.

It has been estimated that American business invested over $6 billion in new product development in 1966. Of this, 70% was "wasted on ideas that did not develop or products that did not survive in the market-place." [24] There is good reason to believe that a fair share of this "waste" was properly attributable to mistakes in the initial choice of a trademark for the new product.

This importance of the mark is becoming better recognized. It may have been formerly confined to the marketer. The PR man has long appreciated its importance. It is gaining acceptance with management.

There appears to be a growing tendency in some companies to select several alternative new marks for a new product and to test these—sometimes over a considerable period—coupling trademark-testing with product-testing. This may lead to a considerable interval between choice of the mark and its eventual use in normal promotion and volume sales —perhaps a year or two.

The law is not unaware of this temporal hiatus between the choice and the eventual regular use of a mark. Thus, one company used a new mark initially on $1.91 worth of merchandise. Due to testing needs, it was 18 months later before the mark was used on regular volume shipments. The mark was upheld against later attack.[25] It is against this background that company communicators and marketers should give careful thought to the practical/legal problems discussed in Sections 20–24 of Chapter 10. See also Section 8 above.

14. Patents.

Ordinarily the PR man or other company communicator has little to do with the patentability of the new product or patents in general. This will be the chore of company counsel, the Research and Development Department or other technical personnel. However, "patent language" is often important in new product announcements, whether they deal with entirely new products or refinements of existing products.

The communicator will normally rely on the technical staff for specific language and instructions. Some companies *require* such reliance. Monsanto, for example, requires that all speeches, technical and professional papers, advertising, internal publications, printed communications and photography be cleared by the divisional Clearance and Review Committee which has the duty [26]

> . . . to review and approve for release all materials originating in that division. . . . Staff department directors are responsible for the review and clearance of material originating with their departments. Where technical information is involved, the committee or director shall secure the approval of the Patent Department.

On the other hand, the PR man may find the study of patents quite useful—especially some of the older and expired patents which are somehow relevant or antecedent to the new product. The author has been informed by several PR men that they have been "sparked" by language in such patents—obtaining ideas which have led to successful releases and even unique promotions, unusual displays and "stunts," resulting in extended publicity and traceable sales.

This is in line with the comments of the Director of the Office of Information Services, U.S. Patent Office, who has said that there are "seven occasions when a search or intensive study of patent literature is appropriate and highly important." Of these, several deal with new product development, one being "[f]or writer, magazine or press source materials in every conceivable field of applied technology." [27]

Louis J. Collier, marketing vice-president of H. J. Heinz, goes even further,[28] suggesting that the alert product innovator should

> search patent registrations for many years back to pick the brains of other . . . inventors . . . (and) check century-old registrations for unmarketed ideas that might have been ahead of their age. They may be right now.

15. Copyrights.

New product introduction, promotion and publicity pose only one unusual copyright problem. Yet this may be critical if not handled properly.

In the vernacular, "there is no second chance in copyright." This means that the proper copyright notice must be used the very first time that new material is "published." Since new product introduction necessarily involves much new and distinctive material, this rule becomes unusually pertinent.

Labels, explanatory leaflets, operating manuals, instruction booklets, guarantee cards, descriptive matter of all kinds, house organs or specific new-product articles therein should all carry the copyright notice. If it is desired to protect certain of these, the same language should not be used in initial news releases which obviously are not subject to copyright since it is intended that their contents will be reprinted.

As to copyright generally, see Chapter 5.

16. New Product Testing.

One of the most tangible legal aspects of new product introduction is product testing. Such testing is almost a prerequisite for successful new product publicity, public relations, promotion or paid advertising. Referring to such testing as "research," David Finn has said: [29]

> Research for individual products is particularly important when a new principle is involved or a new method of dealing with an old problem is introduced. The public is often skeptical about innovations and the only way to persuade it that there are real advantages to something new is to substantiate a claim with research information that it is convincing. *This is particularly important in regard to public relations for the product,* for here the experts are the targets of persuasion, and they are sure to have their critical guard up even more than the lay public.
> There have been instances in the marketing of certain types of products in which superficial research information was used for promotional purposes with transitory success. This has been true,

for instance, in the drug field where borderline products have been introduced with an impressive amount of scientific jargon but without valid testing. *It would be extremely difficult, if not impossible, to undertake a public relations project on behalf of such an unproven product,* for the experts who would have to be convinced first of the quality of the product would be aware of the inadequacy of the research. (Emphasis added.)

Garth Bentley, a knowledgeable house organ editor, observes that the company publication "is at its best" in dealing with new products because "any new product or service is news." [30] He then goes on to suggest that stories about new products should include detailed description and pictures; functions and intended uses, exclusive features, points of superiority, type and size of potential market, unusual ingredients, unusual facts leading to its discovery, invention or design, unusual or revolutionary steps in its manufacture and unusual uses.

With few exceptions, these suggested story lines are, to some degree, premised upon product tests or research. Pointing this up, Bentley stresses, as "good openings" for new product stories, "exclusive features or superiority *when endorsed by laboratory tests.*" (Emphasis added.)

Test results have become even more important in relation to the growing consumer protection movement of the 1960s.[31] One of the basic demands of government on behalf of consumers is for a greater flow of accurate product information from producer or manufacturer. In explaining the "[c]onsumer's increased self-awareness and self-assertiveness in the marketplace," Commissioner Mary Gardiner Jones of the FTC has said: [32]

> [I]t is reflective of the American consumer's desire to be treated as a mature and rational individual with a genuine desire *to participate intelligently in the marketplace, to make purposeful decisions* about the myriad of choices that marketplace offers and *to act on the basis of knowledge and self-interest* rather than simply to react on the basis of the emotional appeal of an advertising message. (Emphasis added.)

Much of President Johnson's 1967 Consumer Message to the Congress was premised upon what he called "the ever increasing complexities of products available in the market" and "the realities of modern life and a sophisticated marketplace." [33]

This cry for increased product information has been accompanied by an increased governmental interest in its accuracy—evidenced by accelerated Congressional, FTC, FDA and other agency activities—particularly through the statutory or adjudicative application of the doctrine of "affirmative disclosure." It has included even such suggestions as a mandatory "Info Tag" on consumer products.[34]

This interest is likely to be more intensive as to new products—quite apart from the necessary threshold clearances and advance approvals discussed in Section 18 below. For example, this is generally true of the FTC, particularly if unusual claims are made or if there is any public playback to the Commission.

Generally speaking, when research and test results are used in promotion, there must be a showing that it was the company's own laboratory which made the tests—if such was the fact.[35] The independent PR counselor or publicist will normally accept his client's own research results. If the counselor "neither knew nor had reason to know of the falsity of the representation," he would not be held responsible for any invalid tests.[36]

If the tests have been made by an independent source and without the participation of the counselor, he may protect himself by obtaining "a written test report from those making the tests" and if he "acts in good faith upon a written certification signed by the testing agency of the manufacturer or seller, with respect to the factors tested." [37] This also protects the counselor if the invalid tests were made by the client should the counselor obtain such a certification from the client.

However, if the announcement or publicity goes beyond the tenor and results of the tests, the PR man will not be protected—probably even if he obtained the above certification.[38]

Mass media feature stories detailing test results as evidence of product improvement or superiority are likely to produce from the publication a demand for validation. Some national media have learned the necessity for this through unhappy experience. See Section 20 below.

This is an editorial requirement akin to the demands of the advertising side of the publication. Thus, when American Motors made claims of certain technical superiority for its 1968 "Javelin" model as compared with the Ford "Mustang," *Life* insisted on substantiation.[39] As to such requirements of media generally, see Chapter 4, Section 20.

17. Representations in General.

Representations made in the announcement and introduction of new products are subject to the same general restrictions and requirements which affect similar promotional activities for "old" products. On the other hand, the occasion is one which may generate an excess of enthusiasm by the PR man and others engaged in such seminal operations.

This is particularly likely to occur if the innovation involves a truly new—perhaps currently unique—product, process or other invention. There may be a temptation to use some rather florid expressions, descriptions, comparisons and promises of performance in publicity, interviews or statements which are hopefully intended to develop into magazine or newspaper articles.

They may be warranted by the facts. However, if this cannot be demonstrated on an objective basis, such glowing expressions should be avoided. Thus, in Rule 9 of the FTC's Trade Practice Rules for the Hearing Aid Industry, adopted in 1965,[40] expressions such as "amazing new discovery," "revolutionary new discovery," "radically new and different," "sensational new laboratory development," "remarkable new electronic device," "brand-new invention," "new miracle scientific aid," are interdicted "when not *fully* justified by the facts." (Emphasis added.)

Expressions such as this are clearly improper if even the simple word "new" would not be appropriate under FTC and court decisions.

Beyond misrepresentations about novelty (see Sections 6 and 7 above) and preliminary product testing (see Section 16 above), the principal areas of error are performance or benefit claims. In a sense, these are related to the results of the testing, whether it has been in the laboratory, clinic or field.

Most lapses occur when the promotion goes beyond the actual test results and attempts to extrapolate—perhaps without foundation—into other areas.[41] Even the rewording—for purposes of facility of expression or understanding—of basic and unassailable product or service realities may make a release or other announcement deceptive or otherwise unfair. Probably the classic example of the effect of *changing a single word* is the phrase long used by an insurance company: "Retire in 15 years *with* $300 a month" as against "Retire in 15 years *on* $300 a month."

Lawyers familiar with screening of PR and publicity materials are always alert to this fault in new product announcements. This is one of the reasons why larger companies require departmental legal counsel— sometimes even technical staff—to screen these materials and do not confine such clearance to public relations department counsel. The former are more likely to adhere to the product limitations and to be keenly aware of additions or extensions thereto.

As to deceptive, misleading or unfair claims and representations generally, see Chapter 11.

18. Government Clearances.

Promotion of some new products requires advance government-agency approval and clearances; others *may* be so cleared if desired.

The advisory opinion procedure of the FTC permits advance approval if desired. New product introduction would seem to be an ideal situation for taking advantage of such procedure since a prerequisite to such approval is that the proposed course of action or claim is not yet in use. This would seem to apply to all new products. On the other hand, the Commission will not render an opinion "where the proposed course of action is such that an informed decision thereon could be made only after extensive investigation, clinical study, testing or collateral inquiry." [42]

This procedure also covers promotional and merchandising methods in addition to matters which may involve possible deceptive practices.

Drug promotion is *sui generis* and is likely to become ever more so in the future. New drugs must be approved before they may be marketed—even to physicians. Labels must be approved and all marketing or promotional materials should follow the labels. Except in "extraordinary circumstances," preclearance of advertising is not required. FDA regulations contain 34 specific practices which should be avoided so as not to be charged as "false, lacking in fair balance or otherwise misleading."

The FDA's *Compendium of Medical Advertising*, published in 1967, will prove very useful in this situation.

"Brochures, mailing pieces, bulletins, . . . catalogs, house organs, literature reprints and similar pieces of printed matter" are among the promotional matter which are subject to the "full disclosure" requirements of the Act and under FDA regulations.[43]

Alcoholic beverages are closely regulated and new labels are to be approved. Promotion should follow the labels, as approved by the Alcohol and Tobacco Tax Division of the Internal Revenue Service, Department of the Treasury.[44]

New securities require advance clearance of publicity, etc. in the sense that approval of the securities by the SEC is required and publicity and promotion must be confined to approved matters and figures. See Chapter 22 as to financial PR generally.

19. Promotional Aids and Allowances.

The introduction of a new product presents an unusual opportunity to escape the strictures of the Robinson-Patman Act.[45] The basic premise of the Act is that all competitors must be treated proportionately alike as to promotional services or payments. This requirement does not apply if a particular retailer carrying the new product has no competitors in the sale of that product. In the leading *Atalanta* case, a federal court said: [46]

> [T]he existence of another competing purchaser of a product of like grade and quality must also be shown and proof thereof is an essential part of the Commission's case.

Therefore, if the manufacturer confines his initial new-product thrust in a given market to a single retailer—a local chain, for example—the manufacturer can give all kinds of publicity, PR, promotional and other assistance to that single customer or "purchaser." This may include local press conferences, sidewalk sampling, demonstrators, paid advertising of all kinds, promotional contests, extended local publicity, etc.

However, once the new product is made available through other outlets in a given market, this freedom of action ceases and the manufacturer must then adhere to the general rules applicable to promotional aids under the Act and must accord or make them available to all competitors on the requisite proportionately equal basis.

To take advantage of this exclusion from the Act's application, the new product must be "new." In this context its novelty or distinctiveness is appraised on the basis of its not being of "like grade and quality." The question has produced considerable contention and commentators have referred to its "fluid state." Rowe summarizes the problem: [47]

> In brief, even minor *physical* variations in a seller's otherwise comparable products may dispel a conclusion of their "like grade and quality" while *brand* variations have ordinarily been ignored by the Federal Trade Commission—although some of the judicial declarations indicate that *all* commercial factors bearing on product competition and price should be taken into account.

Generally speaking, it may be assumed that "artificial distinctions in [the] product" will not change the grade or quality.[48] The 1955 Attorney General's Committee Report recognized as exempted from the Act products having "actual and genuine differentiations . . . adapted to the several buyers' uses, and not merely a decorative or fanciful feature." [49]

The "fluid state" of the "like grade and quality" concept continues and if the "new product" is not clearly and distinctively novel, counsel should be consulted before adopting promotional methods premised on the non-applicability of the Act.

20. New Products and the Securities Markets.

An important aspect of new product public relations and publicity is its probable effects upon company stock prices on the securities markets.

Probably the best recommendation as to any new product publicity in this context is that it should always be "conservative" and should not be premature or misleading. The New York Stock Exchange requires in such cases: [50]

> [Such corporate news] necessitates careful adherence to the facts, appropriate restraint and good judgment. . . . Premature announcements of new products whose commercial applications can-

not yet be determined realistically, overly optimistic forecasts, exaggerated claims, and unwarranted promises should be avoided. If subsequent developments indicate that performance will not match earlier projections, this should be reported and explained.

The same caution should be exercised in other public relations activities quite apart from a formal announcement—for example, articles appearing in major magazines dealing with apparent technical "breakthroughs" resulting in new products. Some of these have been clear overstatements as to the invention or new technique or the product's efficiency, novelty or importance to the company involved. Usually articles like this do not appear in such media without the cooperation of the company's public relations arm. Such stories have played havoc with the price of the company stock.

The Special Study of Securities Markets published by the SEC in 1963 documented situations involving such things as a low cost process for desalination of sea water and a currency-sensing machine capable of distinguishing a $1 bill from a $100 bill, neither of which eventually lived up to the claims made for it.[51] See Chapter 22, Section 6.

In September, 1963, an article appeared in a major national magazine about the development by a listed company of an allegedly new device which could be used for the detection of diseases, including cancer. The stock shot up from 21 to 31 in one day and within a few more days was priced at about 43. By this time the Amex market for the stock was chaotic and the Exchange suspended trading. Meanwhile, it appeared that the device was not new, having been described in a scientific journal some four years earlier, and that the claims made for it were over-optimistic.

In October, 1964, a somewhat similar situation arose when another listed company announced plans to manufacture and distribute a new kind of low-cost camera for color pictures. The stock reacted dramatically but again it turned out that the development was neither so new nor so effective as the company had pictured. The SEC suspended trading in the stock, the SEC release stating: [52]

> Information furnished by the company and its officials in public statements and releases, and information otherwise publicly disseminated with respect to recent developments in the business operations of the company were misleading or omitted to state material facts. . . . Under these circumstances the Commission is of the view that public investors are unable to make an informed judgment in evaluating [the] securities.

In order to avoid a dislocation of company security prices because of new product announcements, some financial PR counsel withhold such announcements until after the markets have closed on Fridays so that the weekend intervenes before trading is resumed. This permits the absorption of the news by the market and the public and may result in a more orderly reaction thereto.

There are three situations which pose difficult questions in this new product/financial PR context.

(a) SEC and securities exchange attitudes about publicity on new products may be complicated by the effects of other laws or the postures of other federal agencies. The former may require announcements of new developments or products but the latter may insist upon delay. Bert Goss has discussed one such possible anomaly: [53]

> The new Food and Drug Administration regulations apparently prohibit a company from public discussion of new drugs before they are approved for marketing. Yet, let us suppose that the medical journals report highly promising new miracle drugs. If the sponsoring drug company does not, or cannot, mention the factual development, is it guilty of the omission of information required by the SEC and the New York Stock Exchange? In other words, would the drug company, in trying to obey the spirit and letter of one law, be guilty of violating still another law?

(b) Announcements of new products—especially major product changes or technical breakthroughs—should be very carefully appraised before issuance if the company is about to "go public." Even if such an announcement may seem to be "normal" publicity and the projected announcement is scrupulously fair and non-deceptive, there is always the possibility that the SEC may nevertheless consider the announcement as a company effort to "precondition the market" for the prospective public offering. Corporate counsel are prone to advise against the announcement under such circumstances. See Chapter 22, Sections 33 and 34.

(c) PR counsel may be approached by newsmen or feature writers who have "heard" that the company has developed a startling new process or is about to introduce a commercially-exciting, new major product. The company may not be ready to announce it as yet. "No comment" may produce a distorted story. Giving full and accurate details may be out of order for any number of reasons including the posture of the SEC discussed above. The company may be forced to make a statement nevertheless if a story does appear. See Chapter 22, Sections 19 and 35.

21. Industrial Espionage.

New products—by their very nature—are a constantly attractive target for industrial espionage during their developmental stages. Assuming that there has been no "leak" about the new product during the research and development stage, there is still a danger within this focus during the marketing plans stage. Once market testing has begun, the "seal of secrecy" is, of course, broken.

There have been several well-publicized cases in which marketing and promotional plans—not technology—have been stolen by employees or others and have been offered to the competition. Both company people and outside personnel have been involved. See Chapter 17, Section 4. From public indications, the competition has been "honest" and has called in the police, the district attorney or the FBI. As to industrial espionage generally, see Chapter 17.

At the same time it must be recognized that all companies have a legitimate interest in the new product activities of their competition. Without engaging in illicit spying or other forms of industrial espionage, there is available to them a vast area of legitimate marketing intelligence, the exploration and use of which is not only legitimate but usually necessary to competitive balance and progress. See Chapter 17, Section 6.

Notes

1. For a discussion of the many facets of new product introduction, see New PRODUCTS MARKETING (Printers' Ink Books, 1964), to which this author contributed the chapter "Call Your Lawyer Before, Not After," at 247.
2. *In re* Armour and Co., U.S.D.A., P. & S. Dkt. No. 2815, H. Exam. Dec. and Order, May 19, 1967.
3. For cases involving "new" as meaning "unused," see 2 TRADE REG. REP. ¶7765.40.
4. John McLaughlin, Director of Sales, Kraft Foods Co., quoted in Skinner, *Public Relations Is a Profit Tool*, P.R.J., April, 1957, at 13.
5. N.I.C.B. Bulletin, *New Product Development*, quoted by SELDIN, THE GOLDEN FLEECE 211 (1963).
6. The three "PR success stories" are taken from an interview with Leroy Baxter, J. Walter Thompson vice president and director of PR-publicity, quoted in *PR Arm Helps JWT Service Ad Clients*, A.A., June 12, 1967, at 6.
7. CUTLIP & CENTER, EFFECTIVE PUBLIC RELATIONS 324 (3d ed. 1964).
8. E. I. du Pont de Nemours Co., Public Relations Dep't Internal Memorandum, June 16, 1967, quoted by permission.
9. See cases cited and explained, 2 TRADE REG. REP. ¶7765.30-.351, .45.
10. 209 F.2d 465, 1954 Trade Cas. ¶67,663 (2d Cir. 1954).
11. F.T.C. Dkt. No. 5762, Stip. 8653.
12. F.T.C. Ad. Op. Dig. No. 120, April 15, 1967, 2 TRADE REG. REP. ¶17,914.
13. See, *e.g.*, Roberts, *The Image and Product Publicity*, in DEVELOPING THE CORPORATE IMAGE 180–187 (Bristol ed. 1960); Collier, *infra* note 15.
14. Crisp, *Fifteen Ways to Go about Developing a New Product*, A.A., Oct. 31, 1966, at 115–124.
15. Collier, *The Difference Must Be Real*, in NEW PRODUCTS MARKETING, *supra* note 1, at 243.
16. *What's "New" at FTC*, A.A., May 1, 1967, at 16.
17. F.T.C. Ad. Op. Dig. No. 146, Oct. 24, 1967, 2 TRADE REG. REP. ¶18,088.
18. F.T.C. Ad. Op. Dig., *supra* note 12.
19. Van Deusen, *Technical Publicity Means "Special Handling,"* P.R.J., June, 1964, at 26.
20. *Id.* at 27.
21. See F.T.C. Pricing Guides, 2 TRADE REG. REP. ¶7897.
22. KURSH, THE FRANCHISE BOOM 30–31 (1963).
23. U.S. TRADEMARK ASS'N, TRADEMARK SELECTION 7–8 (1960).
24. CUMMINGS, NEW PRODUCTS DIGEST, quoted in *Wasted Ideas*, P.R.J., June, 1967, at 6.
25. Fort Howard Paper Co. v. Kimberley-Clark Corp., 148 U.S.P.Q. 607 (P.O.T.T.A.B. 1966).
26. *Monsanto Security Guide*, at 12. See WADE, INDUSTRIAL ESPIONAGE AND USE OF TRADE SECRETS 59–62 (1964).

27. Fleischmann, *The Treasure Trove Open to All,* in NEW PRODUCTS MARKET-ING, *supra* note 1, at 267.

28. Collier, *supra* note 15, at 244.

29. Finn, *Public Relations and Marketing,* in HANDBOOK OF PUBLIC RELATIONS (Stephenson ed. 1960).

30. BENTLEY, EDITING THE COMPANY PUBLICATION 101 (1953).

31. For a discussion of the consumer protection movement and the desire for more product information, see generally the text, Chapter 19, Sections 25–29.

32. Remarks of Mary Gardner Jones, *"Consumerism" and the Role of Marketing —A Comparative Analysis of the Consumer Abroad and at Home,* before Rochester Chapter, American Marketing Association, Sept. 27, 1967, F.T.C. Release, 3–4.

33. See text, Chapter 19, Sections 25–29.

34. See H.R. Rep. No. 2374, 90th Cong., 1st Sess. (1967).

35. See 2 TRADE REG. REP. ¶7865.

36. Revco D. S., Inc., *et al.,* F.T.C. Dkt. No. 8576, 2 TRADE REG. REP. ¶17,289 (1965).

37. General Motors *et al.,* F.T.C. Dkt. No. C-795, Consent Order entered July 27, 1964, 2 TRADE REG. REP. ¶25,737.

38. See Merck & Co. *et al.,* F.T.C. Dkt. No. 8635, 2 TRADE REG. REP. ¶17,246, 17,503; 17,629 (1966).

39. *American Motors Drive Compares Javelin, Mustang, A.A.,* Sept. 11, 1967, at 1, 8.

40. 2 TRADE REG. REP. ¶41,181.

41. See, *e.g.,* Merck & Co., *supra* note 38.

42. F.T.C., RULES OF PRACTICE §1.51 (1963).

43. 21 C.F.R. §1.105 (1), §1.106 (b) (c) and §1.104.

44. For regulations on labeling, advertising and promotion of wine, distilled spirits and malt beverages, see 27 C.F.R., ch. 1, parts 4, 5 and 7, reprinted as I.R.S. Publication No. 449 (Feb. 1961).

45. P.L. 692, 74th Cong., 49 Stat. 1526, 15 U.S.C. §13 (1938).

46. Atalanta Trading Corp. v. F.T.C., 258 F.2d 365, 370 (2d Cir. 1958).

47. ROWE, PRICE DISCRIMINATION UNDER THE ROBINSON-PATMAN ACT 63 (1962).

48. Atalanta Trading Corp. v. F.T.C., *supra* note 46, at 371.

49. REPORT OF THE ATTORNEY GENERAL'S COMMITTEE TO STUDY THE ANTITRUST LAWS 158 (1955).

50. N.Y. Stock Exchange, *Company Manual,* A-20 (1965).

51. H.R. Doc. No. 95, 88th Cong., 1st Sess., pt. 3, at 91–93 (1963).

52. *SEC Suspends Trading 10 Days in Fotochrome,* Wall St. Jour., Oct. 12, 1964, and *Trading in Fotochrome Set to Resume Today on American Exchange, id.,* Oct. 29, 1964.

53. Goss, *Common Sense of the PRSA Financial Code,* P.R.J., April, 1964, at 8. See also, Page, *Instant Reporting—Is It Necessary?,* Sat. Rev., Feb. 3, 1968, at 58.

Chapter 17

Industrial Espionage and Trade Secrets

Chapter 17

Industrial Espionage
and Trade Secrets

A. INTRODUCTION.

1. Frame of Reference.

Our concern here is with two related subjects: trade secrets and industrial espionage, the latter being, in effect, a violation of the former. With American industry and business spending many billions every year on basic and product research and more billions on competitive distribution of its products, both old and new, the importance of protecting its research, products and marketing plans from a competitive eye is becoming a major concern of business.

Companies may prefer to treat as a trade secret some new process, machine, product, system, etc., rather than obtain 17-year protection through patent disclosure and proceedings. Even if the innovation is patented when completed, it must be treated as a trade secret during its development. Under either circumstance it is a prime temptation to the industrial spy or the unethical competitor.

2. Definition.

Industrial espionage is not difficult to define. It is the "stealing" of another's trade secret through illegal or unethical means. Some have suggested that explicit definition is not necessary. The words themselves instantly conjure up an under-the-table, dark-of-the-moon, booze-and-blondes picture in a business context.

It is not merely *obtaining* the secrets of the competition. Seeking out and learning through open or legal means the innermost secrets of another company is quite legal. It is even considered ethical in most quarters. Furthermore, such information is sought constantly. It may be necessary to business growth and success—perhaps, in some cases, necessary for business survival.

The shades of impropriety are many. It may run from clear-cut criminality such as breaking into a laboratory at night to the ethically hazy area of "picking the brains" of a competitor's salesman at a trade show.[1] Even the legal definition of the same physical act—surreptitiously copying oil maps, for example—may vary, depending upon the particular interpretation of a statute. See Sections 11 and 12 below.

As to definitions of "trade secret," see Section 8 below.

3. Frequency and Incidence.

There is a considerable difference of opinion as to the incidence of industrial espionage. Some sources estimate that the loss to American industry through industrial espionage may mount as high as two to three billion dollars annually.[2] These estimates may, to some degree, be influenced by front-page reports of episodes which smack of the Mata Hari and James Bond influence.

This seems to be borne out by the more careful studies in this field. The most frequently cited is the 1959 *Harvard Business Review* project [3] which came to the conclusion that industrial espionage was less common than generally suspected—even among knowledgeable businessmen— that when rumors were discounted and hard facts sought, the evidence showed a relatively small number of documented industrial espionage cases.

In another study, some 25% of the 700 members of the American Society of Industrial Security reported in 1964 that they had been "victims of thefts involving process or product secrets." [4] However, the Society attributes such losses more to indifferent security and employee supervision than to overt industrial espionage.

However, the Harvard study did show that an ex-employee has little loyalty to his former employer and, while he might not engage in industrial espionage as that term is generally accepted, his scruples about revealing secrets of his former employer are not too strong.

More recent studies performed by Dr. Edward Brink [5] and his graduate students at the University of Pennsylvania Wharton School seem to confirm these results: that industrial espionage definitely exists but is not as prevalent as the popular press seems to believe.[6]

The true frequency and effect of industrial espionage are not likely to be accurately documented. Respondents in even carefully-managed surveys are likely to be "against sin" in reporting their own activities and overly suspicious in assessing the activities of competitors. This lack of specific and accurate information should have no effect on future attitudes since it *is* well-documented that such a theft, when it does occur, may involve the loss of millions.[7]

4. Functional Areas Involved.

It is generally assumed that industrial espionage is confined to the illicit acquisition of scientific or technical information. The most widely publicized cases have undoubtedly involved such data.[8]

However, the Harvard study referred to in Section 3 above showed that the business manager was most interested in information about the competition's immediate activities and not so much the long-range. This interest was found to concentrate on competitive pricing practices, promotional strategy, research and development, sales figures, manufacturing processes and costs, expansion plans, bid data, product styling, financing needs and plans, patents and executive compensation and, more to point, *in that order of priority*.[9] The highest priority, therefore, seems to be accorded to advance information about the immediate moving of goods into the consumer's hands rather than about future developments.

The legitimate techniques of marketing intelligence, discussed in Section 6 below, may be able to supply such distributional information with greater facility than information on new or presently incomplete product or process research. This may explain why the latter is more frequently the subject of unethical or illegal methods. Yet there are well-documented cases of industrial espionage dealing with these distributional practices at both the wholesale and retail levels.

In 1967 the Supreme Court dealt with the *Utah Pie Co.* case,[10] an antitrust action which turned, in part, on evidence of "predatory intent" of which in-plant spying was a part. Pet Milk Co. was engaged in a marketing battle in Salt Lake City with Utah Pie (the plaintiff), historically the area's principal frozen-pie supplier. One of the plaintiff's major customers was Safeway Stores. Pet went after that account and "candidly admitted" that "it had sent into Utah Pie Co.'s plant an industrial spy to seek information that would be of use to Pet in convincing Safeway that Utah Pie was not worthy of its custom." While Pet denied that it had ever used any of this information, the Court held that "the jury was not foreclosed from considering the predatory intent underlying Pet's mode of competition." The Court affirmed for the plaintiff.

Other cases have involved the theft of marketing information. In 1964 an employee of Procter & Gamble's advertising agency tried to sell the company's confidential marketing strategy to Colgate-Palmolive.[11] In 1965 a Procter & Gamble employee attempted to sell Colgate confidential plans for marketing "Crest" toothpaste.[12] Colgate turned both down.

These cases are particularly significant because of the apparent mobility of advertising and marketing personnel, especially those in the junior echelons. The siren lure to such men is supposed to be higher salaries and "better prospects." It is not unlikely that such "hiring away of employees" may sometimes be keyed to the competitive information which they bring with them.[13]

5. Public Relations Involvements.

The PR man may find himself much concerned with trade secrets and their possibly concomitant industrial espionage.

(a) The PR man's concern with employees, direct or indirect, means a constant interest in these matters. It includes the hiring process, the preparation of new-employee manuals, explanatory articles in company/internal house organs, employee-termination procedures and contacts, continued exposition of company policy to both rank and file and the highly-skilled, technical echelons.

(b) As the voice of his company or client the PR man is primarily responsible for press relations in what is almost always an important or intriguing story. His posture will depend upon the company's relation to the case. Engberg reports one instance of this arising from the *Hirsch* case.[14]

Dr. Hirsch had been employed by DuPont for a number of years in its development of the "chloride process" of making titanium dioxide. He left DuPont and went to work for American Potash. DuPont sought and obtained an injunction in May, 1964 against both Hirsch and American Potash—thereby preventing the chemist from working on this process for his new employer. Hirsch stayed with American Potash but in connection with other matters. In November, 1964, according to Engberg, the PR counsel for American Potash sent a memorandum about the case to the *Saturday Evening Post,* inferentially critical of the Court's decision. The *Post,* however, did not carry any story about the case. Engberg also discusses the PR counsel's relations with legal counsel for American Potash.[15]

(c) The PR man may have much to do with the corporate decisions as to whether action, criminal or civil, should be brought against the spy, employee or competitor involved. This usually presents a mixed PR/legal problem and may pose delicate questions about company policy —both internal and external. See Chapter 1.

(d) The PR man may himself be more or less responsible for the loss of the trade secret—quite innocently. What appear to be routine releases—sometimes required by the SEC or stock exchange rules—may be the vehicles. The author is familiar with several instances in which a series of related releases over a period of time either "gave the whole story away" or so alerted the competition that it began to "dig"—with considerable success.

(e) PR considerations are frequently important in the preparation of the company security manuals referred to in Section 16 below. These deal with external, as well as with internal, measures and may involve sectors of primary concern to the PR man. He should, therefore, contribute considerably to the preparation of such guides or manuals. He will also probably have a continuing responsibility for the proper implementation of certain security measures—especially as they concern such matters as public plant-tours, open houses, visits by the press, free-lance writers, etc.

6. Marketing Intelligence.

Marketing intelligence is a relatively new aspect of marketing. The Wharton School's Dr. Edward Brink, a leader in the development of the marketing intelligence concept, has thus defined it: [16]

> Marketing intelligence flows from marketing information, which is first gathered by utilizing such tools as marketing research, distribution cost analysis or even operations research, and then organized. Marketing intelligence is information which is selected, evaluated, interpreted and expressed in such a way that its application to a marketing problem, present or potential, is clear.

More and more companies are creating marketing intelligence departments or units although they may not denominate the activity by that name.[17] One of the barriers to more rapid adoption of marketing intelligence as a business-planning tool is the feeling—in some circles at least—that it is coupled with industrial espionage. The word "intelligence" does have a largely military connotation of secrecy, deception, even undercover spying. Yet some of our earliest newspapers bore the proud logo "Intelligencer." Some still do.

Marketing intelligence is premised upon the acquisition of information by legitimate means. Industrial espionage not merely connotes, but usually relies on, illicit techniques. The dichotomy is an important one and is legally recognized.[18]

People in marketing intelligence are greatly concerned with the ethics of their techniques. Several studies have indicated that ethical premises loom large with marketing executives—especially in information acquired through certain specific sources or methods.

The conclusions reached in one such study [19] indicate, among other things, that businessmen believe that ethical considerations are important in gathering information; company policy is the main force that assures ethical methods; state and federal laws are the second most important deterrent from illegal information-gathering; espionage—

pirating of personnel or information secured through a business intermediary such as a common customer—are the most objectionable practices in the gathering of information; marketing-information acquisition is not inherently unethical; most intelligence work is generally overt; information gathered surreptitiously is not an important part of the information flow; covert practices are costly and they are effective only in the short run.

B. TRADE SECRETS.

7. General Legal Background.

Industrial espionage and the protection of trade secrets involve essentially the following different legal areas:

(a) *Common Law Doctrine of Trade Secrets.*

Historically, aside from patent law, this is the primary basis upon which the inventor or developer of new methods, processes and products relied. It is still a powerful legal protection. See Section 8 below.

(b) *Contract Rights.*

Contract rights are premised upon trade secret rights. A contract may go further, spelling out the developer's further rights and additional obligations of others not to use or divulge the trade secrets. See Sections 17 and 22 to 25 below.

(c) *Criminal Statutes.*

These federal and state laws make certain aspects of industrial espionage a criminal offense. See Sections 11 and 12 below.

8. Definition.

Trade secrets have been the subject of many definitions as different courts confronted their existence and the necessity for protection. They have been described as:

> [A] plan or process, tool, mechanism, or compound known only to its owner and those of his employees to whom it is necessary to confide it.[20]

*   *   *   *

> . . . nothing more than a private matter.[21]

*   *   *   *

> [A]lmost any knowledge or information used in the conduct of one's business may be held by its possessor in secret.[22]

The most frequently cited definition is that of the *Restatement, Torts:* [23]

> Any formula, pattern, device or compilation of information which is used in one's business, and which gives him an opportunity to obtain an advantage over competitors who do not know or use it.

A trade secret is nonetheless a trade secret even if it suffers from any of the following alleged infirmities:

(a) It resulted from the specialized application of knowledge in the public domain.[24]

(b) It consists of several different components, any or all of which are in the public domain.[25]

(c) It is the same "secret" which others have independently discovered by their own efforts.[26]

(d) It could have been discovered by resorting to sources not used by its developer.[27]

(e) It might be duplicated or copied through "reverse engineering." [28]

(f) It did not require any great "genius" or special ability to develop the product or processes in question.[29]

(g) It does not rise to the degree of "inventiveness" required by patent standards.[30]

From the looseness of the term and the variety of situations to which it may be applied stem most of the practical problems faced by owners of trade secrets—especially the precautions needed to protect and maintain their integrity. See Sections 13 to 20 below.

9. Common Law Basis of Protection.

The law has long protected trade secrets, quite apart from their modern statutory armor discussed in Sections 11 and 12 below. In the 1865 case of *Peabody v. Norfolk,* the Massachusetts Supreme Court said: [31]

> If [a person] invents or discovers, and keeps secret, a process of manufacture, whether a proper subject for a patent or not, he has not indeed an exclusive right to it as against the public, or against those who in good faith acquire knowledge of it; but he has a property in it, which a court of chancery will protect against one who in violation of contract and breach of confidence undertakes to apply it to his own use, or to disclose it to third persons.

The *Restatement, Torts* has delineated the doctrine of the *Peabody* case and of many other subsequent decisions by this "general principle": [32]

One who discloses or uses another's trade secret, without a privilege to do so, is liable to the other if: (a) he discovered the secret by improper means; or (b) his disclosure or use constitutes a breach of confidence reposed in him by the other in disclosing the secret to him; or (c) he learned the secret from a third person with notice of the facts that it was a secret and that the third person discovered it by improper means or that the third person's disclosure of it was otherwise a breach of his duty to the other; or (d) he learned the secret with notice of the facts that it was a secret and that its disclosure was made to him by mistake.

The inclusion of items (c) and (d) in the above rule—dealing with the liability of third persons—is one of the reasons that many well-advised companies will put subsequent employers on written notice of the now-departed employee's status and obligations. It also accounts for the refusal of some companies to assign new employees to the same field or project in which they were working in their previous employment.

Inasmuch as so many of the leaks of trade secrets are due to the "mobile employee," the following statements from the *Restatement, Agency* as to an agent's responsibility, both during and after his employment, are relevant: [33]

Unless otherwise agreed, an agent is subject to a duty to the principal not to use or to communicate information confidentially given him by the principal or acquired by him during the course of or on account of his agency or in violation of his duties as agent, in competition with or to the injury of the principal, on his own account or on behalf of another, although such information does not relate to the transaction in which he is then employed, unless the information is a matter of general knowledge.

*   *   *   *

Unless otherwise agreed, after the termination of the agency, the agent: (a) has no duty not to compete with the principal; (b) has a duty to the principal not to use or to disclose to third persons, on his own account or on account of others, in competition with the principal or to his injury, trade secrets, written lists of names, or other similar confidential matters given to him only for the principal's use or acquired by the agent in violation of duty. The agent is entitled to use general information concerning the method of business of the principal and the names of the customers retained in his memory, if not acquired in violation of his duty as agent; (c) has a duty to account for profits made by the sale or use of trade secrets and other confidential information, whether or not in competition with the principal; and (d) has a duty to the principal not to take advantage of a still subsisting confidential relation created during the prior agency relation.

10. Judicial Attitudes.

Most trade secret or industrial espionage cases—aside from possible criminal actions—are injunction proceedings. They are addressed to the discretion of the court and are resolved on equitable principles. Accordingly, judicial attitudes—apart from legal requirements as to proof—are unusually important in these cases.

Ordinarily, three things must be proved by a trade-secret plaintiff:

    (a) The plaintiff must have a trade secret and actually treat it as such.[34]

    (b) The defendant must have learned of it under circumstances or through a relationship requiring him to keep it confidential.[35]

    (c) The defendant must have violated the confidence.[36]

Overshadowing these requirements, however, is proof of the defendant's bad faith. One legal writer has said: [37]

> [I]n a close case, the court is normally swayed by the element of bad faith, or reprehensible conduct on the part of the particular employee, or of the competitor if the employee has been used as a tool. Thus, while every court applies the well-known *Restatement* definition of a trade secret [see Section 8 above], what really counts is not how valuable the information may be, nor how secretly it has been maintained, but rather how badly the employee may have behaved. Conversely, where there is no proof of the employee's bad faith, the courts are much stricter in determining whether the employer has a trade secret.
>
>   *   *   *   *
>
> The information may be of little value, and secrecy may be only in keeping it from competitors, but if the defendant has behaved badly enough the court will grant relief. Likewise, if the information is of unquestionably great competitive value and has been carefully guarded, the court will grant relief even though the employee is free of blame.

The closing comment about the secret being "carefully guarded" validates the continuing need for internal security precautions with a company's trade secrets. Such methods are discussed in Sections 13 to 19 below.

11. National Stolen Property Act.

The National Stolen Property Act,[38] a federal statute, normally applies only to the theft of tangibles and their transportation across state lines.[39] It ordinarily does not subject intangibles such as trade secrets to its provisions.[40]

Two cases indicate some departure from this rule. In the *Lester* case [41] and in the *Seagraves* case [42] the statute's phrase "goods, wares or merchandise" appears to have been liberally construed and relaxed. In *Lester* it was applied apparently to the intangible information contained on maps—even as to such maps as were not physically stolen or removed from the owner's possession. The others had been photographed by the defendant. In *Seagraves,* the court expressed agreement with the comment, "It is the idea, not its material paper embodiment, which is valuable."

It has been suggested that the federal courts will "most probably" follow this expanded application of the Act.[43] In 1965 an amendment was introduced to the Act which would bring trade secrets within its scope.[44] This bill does not appear to have made much progress.

12. State Stolen Property Statutes.

General *theft* statutes, as well as the common law crime of larceny, apply only to theft of "personal property," an expression normally construed to apply only to tangible personal property and not to intangibles such as ideas or trade secrets.[45]

Some states, however, have expanded their statutes so as to cover technical and scientific information, making them the subject of larceny. The New York statute [46] covers under grand larceny in the second degree

> property of any value consisting of a sample, culture, micro-organism, specimen, record, recording, document, drawing, or any other article, material, device or substance which constitutes, represents, evidences, reflects or records a secret scientific or technical process, invention or formula or any phase or part thereof.

Similar statutes have been enacted in Illinois [47] and Georgia.[48] These statutes protect secret information but apply only when the information is physically taken, not copied by the thief.

The New Jersey,[49] Pennsylvania,[50] Wisconsin [51] and Nebraska [52] statutes prohibit copying of the material, thus removing the requirement that the tangible record of the secret material be physically taken from its owner. Georgia has amended its earlier statute by providing that copying of trade secrets is also a criminal act.[53]

Generally speaking, under such statutes "copy" is defined as any "facsimile, replica, photograph or other reproduction of an article in any note, drawing or sketch made of or from an article." [54]

The New Jersey Act defines "trade secret" as "the whole or any portion or phase of any scientific or technical information, design, process or procedure, formula or improvement which is secret and of value . . ." and makes culpable "any person who, with intent to deprive or withhold from the owner thereof the control of a trade secret, or with an intent to appropriate a trade secret to his own use or to the use of another, . . . steals the embodiment of the trade secret or makes a copy thereof."

This statute requires that an "embodiment" or "copy" be taken. This is said to have been included in order to protect an ex-employee who unconsciously remembers secrets which he rightfully learned while employed by the owner thereof.[55]

Most of these statutes apply only to the piracy of scientific and technical information. Except for the Wisconsin statute, they do not appear to cover business information not categorized as scientific and technical information or data. This exception may be quite important to the public relations practitioner and his client. The owner of a PR firm probably would not be protected if an employee pirated the trade secrets of his employer. These are not scientific or technical data unless research results, for example, qualify as technical information.

C. PROTECTIVE METHODS.

13. Corporate Policy.

Basic to any company program concerning protection of trade secrets is high-level management policy. Security measures cannot normally be imposed on a hit-and-miss basis. As a company grows, protection may be overlooked. Yet, even the smaller company should be aware of its security needs. This awareness should start with top management.

One of the first management decisions to be made is a more-or-less formal recognition that the company *has* trade secrets and will treat them as such. It is clear from the cases [56] that a company will face serious problems when it suddenly decides to bring a trade-secret suit after "the horse was stolen" even though the company never treated the matter as secret or took any steps to protect it.

Some companies are more "trade-secret-minded" than others. Some go so far as to permit an intensive security program to interfere with other corporate necessities such as their community relations. PR practitioners have found that some companies carry this to extremes. Edward Pendray, for example, has described some trade secrets as "no secrets at all, merely a form of company paranoia" and then goes on to write: [57]

Many industries, particularly the older ones, such as chemicals, glass, steel, metals, etc., are particularly "secret" conscious, and in several notable instances this fetish for secrecy has been carried to an extreme. I have been called in to deal with several situations where the habit of secrecy has prevented proper development of public relations and community relations.

Many plant managers, disliking the "nuisance" of community relations activities, such as plant visits, etc., use the need for alleged protection of trade and plant know-how secrets to avoid doing what they ought to do, often to the serious detriment of the company. In several cases I have had to combat and break down a lot of secrecy over mythical "trade" and "plant secrets" in order to cure serious community relations disturbances.

In one very large company there was, until a short time ago, a rule that no officer or employee of the company was to talk with people in the community, or other "outsider" on any topic whatsoever, on pain of being fired. For violating this rule, two or three top men had been fired and, as a result, all the others followed the rule to the letter. Community relations got so bad that the community held meetings to consider how to run the company out, even though it was a major employer. Zoning restrictions were passed against the company. Local people became reluctant to work for it.

Obviously management's decision should be a balanced one and go no further than the facts reasonably require and vis-à-vis the problems referred to above.

Having taken this first step, the company should lay out a continuing program to implement the original decision. Much of what follows in this chapter deals with such implementation. Furthermore, management should review its security program from time to time—even if the company has a full-time security officer. In some companies this review falls to the public relations director, reporting to management.

14. Physical Security.

Physical security of plant and office is a necessary prerequisite to the overall company program. Some studies showing a high percentage of companies within an industry as subject to industrial espionage or other forms of leaks, have also indicated that many of the losses resulted from "indifference" to this aspect of the program.[58]

Physical security is generally beyond the scope of this work. There is a considerable body of specific literature on the subject.

Good plant security will help prove that the company considered certain processes, machines, etc. as trade secrets. Putting sensitive areas "off limits" is one example. Company files should contain photographs of wall and door signs posted on or in such areas.

15. Communications Elements.

Company communicators play an important role in the prevention of trade secret compromise. Many of the prophylactic measures are part of a continuing communication program directed to company employees and other persons or companies. While this program leans to a large extent upon assistance from the legal department or company counsel, the communicator has the face-to-face, grass roots function which makes the program work. In his context the company's formal agreements are essentially communications tools.

The various elements and steps in a suggested trade secret security program—largely communications of various kinds—would include the following, many of which are cross-referenced to suggested forms: [59]

(a) Basic determination of the sensitive/non-sensitive according to function, project, and/or other basis.

(b) Standards for assessment of *specific* dangers of prospective violations of security.

(c) Overall company security manual. See Section 16 below.

(d) Trade secret agreement at time of hiring. See Section 22 below for forms.

(e) New-employee manual containing a statement of company policy and referring to new-employee agreements under (d) above.

(f) "Sign-out" procedures for terminated employees. See Section 25 below for forms.

(g) Notices to future employers of "obligated" personnel. See Section 26 below for forms.

(h) Bulletin board "reminder" materials (in sensitive areas, departments or plants) stating company policy.

(i) Occasional internal house organ articles.

(j) "Special event reminders" for such occasions as in-plant learned society meetings or even company staff meetings attended by "unobligated" personnel.

(k) Procedures for transferred, reassigned, reclassified or promoted employees. See Subsection (e) above.

(l) Agreements with consultants.

(m) Procedures and forms for invention disclosure to company by employees, consultants and others.

(n) Clearance program for external communications. See Chapter 16, Section 5.

(o) Document and blueprint legends, usually by rubber stamp or in the "title block." See Section 28 below for forms.

(p)   Legends on passes for the public, salesmen, repeated visitors, casual labor (company-hired or otherwise), plant-tour members, etc. See Section 27 below for forms.

(q)   Treatment of governmental inspectors, etc.

(r)   Treatment of outside personnel such as insurance underwriters, contractors and their work force, in-plant caterers, industrial cleaning and maintenance staffs, etc.

(s)   Agreements with government sources which may require disclosure, including government contracts.

(t)   Instructions to personnel relative to requirements by governmental, military, space, etc. agencies or of outside companies with which the company has a relationship for security relative to *their* confidential materials. See Section 20 below.

(u)   Internal "breach of security" reports. See Chapter 7, Section 5.

(v)   Procedures for reporting and other handling of trade secret thefts, especially to various police authorities. See Chapter 7, Sections 21 and 23.

16. Security Manuals.

Whatever the actual incidence of industrial espionage may be, more and more companies are coming to appreciate its importance and potential dangers. This has led to a reconsideration of security measures and the preparation and use of security manuals or guides.

These materials are usually intended as supplements to physical plant and office security measures. Locked doors and safes may protect against the "spy" in the James Bond sense, but the security manual seeks to protect—insofar as protection is possible—against the machinations of the employee or other person who has a right—even the need—to pass through the locked doors and open the locked safes.

The form and extent of detail of such publications varies considerably. However, their thrust and substance are consistent. Ordinarily a manual will include the materials outlined in Section 15 above, together with explanations and instructions as to the use thereof. In a sense, a security manual becomes a very useful "security bible," expressing company policy as to a wide variety of security matters.

17. Employee Agreements.

The keystone of a trade secret protection program may well be the employee restrictive convenant. Since the law impresses a duty of loyalty upon the employee, such an agreement may not be absolutely mandatory. However, a survey of trade secret litigation has shown: [60]

[T]here are comparatively few cases where, with no restrictive agreement, the employer has been successful against a former employee. Without such an agreement it is easier for the employee to establish that during his employment the employer did not claim certain information to be a trade secret and that the employee had no reason to consider it a trade secret. Such an agreement also helps to establish that the employer has taken positive steps to keep his trade secrets confidential, and that they are disclosed to employees only in strict confidence.

While there seems to be little doubt as to the efficacy of such agreements, there is a significant business sector which believes that they may cause employee resentment. The employee may feel that the company is trying "to lock them in" and prevent their professional or technical progress. One large company PR Director has observed that the highly-skilled, scientific staff man may easily become "temperamental" about such agreements. Some have even "walked out" on their term contracts because they did not like "the atmosphere" believed to be created by these restrictions.[61]

Such resentment is more likely to occur when an entire industry or an individual company *first* begins to use these agreements after operating without them. For example, the publishing industry traditionally did not require them. In 1967 two publishers, Macmillan and Harcourt, Brace & World, began to require them of their editors. Most editors are said to have signed the agreements but some publicly criticized them as "loyalty oaths." [62]

Normally there will be two agreements. The first will be signed when the employee is hired and the second—the "sign-out agreement"—when the employment ends. The latter is largely confirmatory of the original hiring agreement and has been described to the author as "a psychological kick in the pants."

For forms of these agreements, see Sections 22 to 25 below.

18. Distinction from Covenants Not To Compete.

Employee trade secret agreements and employee covenants not to compete are both restrictions upon the activities of the employee. Yet they are quite different in content and result. They have also received different legal treatment.[63] In the *Hirsch* case, for example, the court was careful to point out that Hirsch had not signed an agreement not to compete but had signed an agreement "not to use or disclose any of the plaintiff's trade secrets without its prior written consent." See Section 5 above.

The covenant not to compete with the former employer must be reasonable in extent as to duration, geographical area covered and the nature or scope of the forbidden business or service. The legally support-able convenant not to compete is almost invariably limited and "expires" by its terms. For a fuller discussion of restrictive covenants against competition by employees, see Chapter 3, Sections 10 to 31.

On the other hand, the trade secret agreement permits the employee to compete with the former employer almost without any restriction. The single exception is that he must respect his former employer's trade se-crets and may not use them in any way. Aside from this, the ex-employee is a free agent. The trade secret restriction may be perpetual in dura-tion.[64]

As further evidence of the difference between the two types of restric-tions, many companies use trade secret agreements with non-employees such as consultants, contractors and sub-contractors, free-lance designers, suppliers, outside service companies and personnel such as insurance companies and their employees. The covenant not to compete would be inapplicable in these relationships.

19. Methods of Disclosure.

Even if the company obtains "tight" trade secret agreements from em-ployees and third parties, it is still necessary to prove that the defendant had access to, and did learn, the *specific* trade secret involved. The ex-treme case would be a chemist working on product X in the company's plant at A and later being charged with stealing process Y from plant B some 500 miles away.

The problem is resolved if the company maintains a careful "log" or other continuous and detailed record of trade secret access. The log should be signed by every individual having any form of access—physical access to the building or off-limits area; access by permissive use of com-pany documents, drawings, etc.; presence at relevant company confer-ences, meetings or discussions; etc.

Some companies prefer to use highly specific agreements, pinpointing the specific process or working area to which access is given. This may be coupled with a prohibition against unauthorized intrusion into other areas or plants.

20. Protection of Secrets of Others.

A company of any size is likely to have responsibilities to protect trade secrets revealed to it by others. These third parties may be:

(a) Company customers who have divulged information necessary to company activities on the customers' behalf.

(b) Various elements of government, including the military, to whom security of personnel, plant and process is very important.

(c) Individuals with whom the company may be negotiating and who must reveal trade secrets on a confidential basis in order to permit intelligent negotiation. See Section 30 below.

(d) Other concerns with which the company may be discussing a merger or acquisition.

Company procedures and communications should provide for whatever security may be necessary to meet these demands. Staff personnel may have a different perspective in such situations and additional indoctrination will be required. Breach of such security may expose the company to claims, loss of business or, in certain government relations, criminal action.

D. FORMS.

21. In General.

The following forms are suggested for use in the several situations and relationships which may involve the exposure of company trade secrets. Inasmuch as a company's daily activities are such that it is almost impossible to avoid *some* disclosure, these forms will help satisfy such peremptory needs.

As with any "forms," these should be used with care and, presumably, after consultation with legal counsel. They may require changes so as to conform to specific needs and circumstances.

In some of the following sections more than one form is suggested. Such groupings are usually mutually exclusive and portions of each form within the section may overlap.

Other forms which may be useful in this context will be found in Chapter 3, Sections 32 to 36.

22. Trade Secret and Patent Agreement.

(a) The undersigned employee, in consideration of his employment or continued employment by Company, agrees:

1. All improvements, discoveries or inventions (whether or not deemed patentable) conceived, devised, made, developed or perfected by him during the period of his employment and related in any way to the business, including development and research, of Company, shall be promptly disclosed to and become the property of Company, and employee shall assist in obtaining the grant of patents, both domestic and foreign, with respect to such improvements, discoveries or inventions and for vesting title to such patents in Company. This agreement applies to improvements, discoveries and inventions conceived, devised, made, de-

veloped or perfected during off-duty hours and away from the employer's premises as well as to those conceived, devised, made, developed or perfected in the regular course of employment.

2. Any improvements, discoveries or inventions (whether or not deemed patentable) devised, made, developed or perfected after an employee leaves the employ of Company are within Paragraph 1 if conceived during such employment, and any such improvements, discoveries or inventions devised, made, developed or perfected within six months from cessation of employment shall be conclusively presumed to have been conceived during employment.

3. All information of a business or technical nature imparted to or learned by the employee in the course of his employment with respect to the business of Company or its affiliates, including the improvements, inventions and discoveries of Paragraph 1, shall be deemed to be confidential and shall not be disclosed by him to anyone outside the employ of Company or its affiliates without its express authorization, unless such information has been made generally available to the trade. If an employee leaves the employ of Company, such authorization to disclose information must be obtained in writing, and he shall not take with him any original or copies of any drawings, other documents, or development or pre-production models containing or disclosing confidential information. The business and technical information developed and acquired by Company is among the employer's most valuable assets, and its value may be unwittingly destroyed by casual dissemination. All employees are therefore expected to safeguard this information as carefully as other property of the employer.

(b) I hereby agree, in consideration of my employment or continued employment, not to use or divulge, without the company's consent, any confidential information acquired through my connection with the company.

23. Post-Employment Consultant Agreement.

(a) Upon termination of the active, full-time employment which is the subject of this employment agreement, Employer may at its option retain employee as a part-time consultant for any period up to an additional three years after termination of full-time employment, requiring not more than 8 hours of his time per month and paying him monthly 30 per cent of his average salary during the three years next preceding termination of active full-time employment; and during such period of retainer as a consultant, employee is forbidden to accept any employment competitive with any activity related to his activity with Employer.

24. Agreement Not To Compete.

See Chapter 3, Section 34 (a) to (f) for suggested forms of this character. See also Section 18 above.

25. "Sign-Out" Agreement.

(a) I acknowledge that I have received all salary and compensation due me during my employment by XYZ Company which terminated on this date. I certify that I have complied with all provisions of the "New Employee Agreement" which I signed upon my employment and that I have not done or in any way been a party to or knowingly permitted, any of the following:

(1) Disclosure of any confidential matters or trade secret of the XYZ Company.

(2) Retention of any confidential materials, documents or drawings issued to or used by me or others during my employment.

(3) Copying any of the above.

I acknowledge that I have again been carefully and fully advised by Mr. —————— of my continuing obligation to preserve as confidential, and not to reveal to anyone or use for myself or anyone else, any trade secrets, know-how or confidential matters learned by me during, or by reason of, my employment by XYZ Company, and I reaffirm such obligations as more fully set forth in the "New Employee Agreement."

I agree that XYZ Company may inform in writing my new employer, ——————, of my said obligations, provided only that I receive a copy of such letter or other communication.

(b) I again agree that I will not in any way or at any time hereafter disclose or reveal to my new employer or to any other party, or use in any way for my own purposes, any secret or confidential information, trade secrets, records or other materials learned by me or disclosed to me during my employment by XYZ Company, and I state that I have retained and now possess no written or graphic materials (or copies thereof) relative to any thereof.

26. Letter to New Employer.

(a) We understand that Mr. ——————, a former employee of ours, has accepted employment with your company as a —————— working in the field(s) of ——————.

Our best wishes for success go with Mr. —————— in his new endeavor. However, we think you should be aware that, at the time Mr.

———————— entered our employ, he executed an employment agreement, certain provisions of which remain in force after his separation from XYZ. A copy of his agreement is attached for your review.

We wish to call your attention to the provisions which refer to information and materials considered confidential by our company. During the course of Mr. ————————'s employment with us, he was given access to confidential information and documents which are XYZ's trade secrets.

While we do not intend or desire in any way to impair Mr. ————————'s employment opportunities or performance, we do expect and feel confident that he will honor his employment contract with XYZ by keeping confidential and not using any of our company's classified information or trade secrets during the course of his new employment.

(b) We understand that Mr. ———————— is now in your employ, having been formerly employed by us as a ————————.

This is to advise you that Mr. ———————— continues bound by a non-disclosure agreement, signed by him while in our employ, a copy of which is enclosed. While we do not anticipate in any way that Mr. ———————— will breach his agreement or that your company will seek to induce him to do so, we believe it advisable to bring this matter to your attention.

Mr. ———————— is, of course, receiving a copy of this letter.

May we wish Mr. ———————— continued success in his career.

27. Legend for Plant Pass.

(a) In consideration of XYZ Company granting me permission to enter its (insert plant or laboratory), I hereby covenant and agree that all knowledge, information or experience which I may acquire thereby, and particularly any knowledge, information or experience which I may acquire with reference to the manufacture of the said plant's products, shall and will be held by me in confidence, and that I will not disclose, divulge or reveal the same or any part thereof, directly or indirectly, to any person or persons, or make any use of the same for myself or others.

28. Document Legend.

(a) This document contains confidential trade-secret information and is the sole property of XYZ Company and must be returned to or "sighted" by the issuing office on or before ———————— 19——. No reproduction or disclosure of any of its contents is permitted at any time.

(b) This document is the property of the company and the recipient is responsible for its safekeeping and disposition. It contains confidential information of company which must not be reproduced, revealed to unauthorized persons or sent outside the company without proper authorization. The disposition of this document shall be:

( ) Return to originator ( ) Destroy after reading
( ) Retain in secure files ( ) ——————————

(c) This document, blueprint or drawing is the confidential property of XYZ Company and must be handled and returned in accordance with the provisions of the "Employee Non-Disclosure Agreement" of XYZ Company.

[This form also covers blueprints and drawings as well as company documents. See Section 29 below. It should be used only with employees and only if the employees have signed the non-disclosure agreement referred to therein.]

(d) CONFIDENTIAL. Property of XYZ Company.

29. Drawing/Blueprint Legend.

(a) This drawing is the property of XYZ Company and must be accounted for and returned to the company. Information hereon is confidential and must not be reproduced, revealed to unauthorized persons or sent outside the company without proper authorization.

(b) See Section 28 (c) above.

(c) This drawing and all information hereon are the confidential property of XYZ Company. This drawing is CONFIDENTIAL and its contents may not be disclosed. Return this drawing promptly to

——————————.

(d) This drawing is the property of XYZ Company and must be returned, without reproduction or duplication, at any time upon request, but in any event on completion of the work or job. While in the possession of the recipient, it must be properly safeguarded against revelation or disclosure to any one except those employees who require it for the work or job. The recipient must keep confidential and require his (its) employees to keep confidential the information contained hereon.

30. Third-Party Disclosure Agreement.

(a) In consideration of the mutual promises herein contained and an actual or potential business association between

(Company or Individual)

———————————————————————————————————————

and XYZ Company, XYZ agrees to keep confidential the following specific information disclosed to it subject, however, to any terms as to use or otherwise the parties herein or otherwise have agreed to:

(Specific listing of precise information to be kept confidential)

_____

_____

_____

It is further agreed that XYZ Company will not be bound by this agreement for longer than _____ years from its execution date nor will XYZ be bound by it if at the time of the execution hereof XYZ (a) already has said information in its possession; or (b) is in the process of developing it; or (c) if the information classified herein as confidential is already in or subsequently enters the public domain; or (d) if said information is furnished or made known to XYZ by any other person, firm or corporation as a matter of right.

(b) See forms in Chapter 6.

Notes

1. For a lively description of industrial espionage in most of its ramifications, see ENGBERG, THE SPY IN THE CORPORATE STRUCTURE (1967).
2. N. Y. Times, March 16, 1965, at 53; Time, March 26, 1965, at 76. See Fortune, May, 1956, at 118; Cosmopolitan, Feb., 1958, at 71.
3. Furash, *Problems in Review—Industrial Espionage,* 37 HARV. BUS. REV. 7 (1959).
4. *"Viewpoint,"* Chemical Week, Sept. 12, 1964, at 89.
5. Edward L. Brink, *The Current State of Marketing Intelligence,* paper presented before the American Marketing Association Winter Conference, Dec. 29, 1964.
6. See, *e.g.,* Barker, A Study of the Ethical Status of Marketing Intelligence in American Business, at 112–15. Thesis prepared in partial fulfillment for the requirements for the degree of M.B.A., Wharton School, University of Pennsylvania (1965).
7. See, *e.g.,* N.Y. Journal American, March 18, 1966, p. 2, reporting that secret synthetic rubber information of Montecatini and B. F. Goodrich, offered to Du Pont, was worth $2 million.
8. American Cyanamid Co. v. Fox, 140 U.S.P.Q. 199 (1964); United States v. Bottone, 365 F.2d 389 (2d Cir. 1966); American Cyanamid Co. v. Sharaff, 309 F.2d 790 (3d Cir. 1962).
9. Furash, *supra* note 3, at 10.
10. Utah Pie Co. v. Continental Baking Co. *et al.,* 386 U.S. 685, 35 L.W. 4373 (1967).
11. A.A., July 13, 1964, at 74.
12. A.A., Aug. 9, 1965, at 3. For extended discussion of this case, see Engberg, *supra* note 1, at 101–3.
13. Harvey Smith, *Sources of Single Competition Information,* address before N.I.C.B., Oct. 28, 1964, at 1–4; Barker, *supra* note 6, at 93–94.
14. E. I. du Pont de Nemours & Co. v. American Potash & Chemical Corp. & Donald E. Hirsch, 200 A.2d 428 (Del. Ch. 1964).
15. Engberg, *supra* note 1, at 116–17.
16. Edward L. Brink, *Marketing Intelligence and Long Range Planning,* paper presented at the 47th Annual Conference, American Marketing Association, June 17, 1964, at 1. Dr. Brink is the author of *Marketing Intelligence,* scheduled for 1968 publication.
17. Brink, *supra* note 5, at 1–4.
18. See, *e.g.,* Heyman v. Ar Winarick, Inc., 207 F. Supp. 78 (S.D.N.Y. 1962), *aff'd,* 325 F.2d 584 (2d Cir. 1963); Schaefer, Inc. v. Mohawk Cabinet Co., 165 F. Supp. 688 (N.D.N.Y. 1958).
19. Barker, *supra* note 6.
20. Victor Chem. Works v. Iliff, 299 Ill. 532 (1921).
21. Kaumagraph Co. v. Stampagraph Co., 235 N.Y. 1, 138 N.E. 485 (1923) (Pound, J.).

22. E. O. Smith v. Dravo Corp., 203 F.2d 369 (7th Cir. 1953).

23. RESTATEMENT, TORTS §757, Comment b (1939).

24. Winston Res. Corp. v. Minnesota Mining & Mfg. Co., 350 F.2d 134 (10th Cir. 1965).

25. Sperry Rand Corp. v. Rothlein, 241 F. Supp. 549 (D.C. Coun. 1964).

26. Minnesota Mining & Mfg. Co. v. Technical Tape Co., 23 Misc.2d 671, 192 N.Y.S.2d 102 (Sup. Ct. 1959).

27. *Id.*

28. Schulenberg v. Signatrol, Inc., 33 Ill2.d 379, 212 N.E.2d 865 (1965); Stone v. Goss & Grasseli Chem. Co., 65 N.J. Eq. 756 (1903).

29. A. O. Smith Corp. v. Petroleum Iron Works Co., 73 F.2d 531 (6th Cir. 1934).

30. Riess v. Sanford, 117 P.2d 694 (Cal. 1941); Fairchild Engine & Airplane Corp. v. Cox, 50 N.Y.S.2d 643 (Sup. Ct. 1944); Booth v. Stutz Motor Car Co., 24 F.2d 416, *aff'd,* 56 F.2d 962 (7th Cir. 1932); E. O. Smith v. Dravo Corp., *supra* note 22.

31. 98 Mass. 452 (1865).

32. RESTATEMENT, TORTS, *supra* note 23, at §757.

33. RESTATEMENT, AGENCY §§395, 396 (1958).

34. Allen-Qualey Co. v. Shellmar Products Co., 36 F.2d 623 (7th Cir. 1930); Victor Chem. Works v. Iliff, *supra* note 20.

35. Du Pont Powder Co. v. Masland, 244 U.S. 100 (1917).

36. RESTATEMENT, AGENCY, *supra* note 33 and cases cited in state annotations.

37. Harding, *Trade Secrets and the Mobile Employee,* 22 BUS. LAW, 395, 398 (1967) (footnotes omitted).

38. 18 U.S.C. §§2311–17 (1964).

39. Reynolds v. United States, 152 F.2d 586 (5th Cir. 1946) *cert. denied,* 327 U.S. 803 (1946); Gordon v. United States, 164 F.2d 855 (6th Cir. 1947), *cert. denied,* 333 U.S. 862 (1948).

40. American Cyanamid Co. v. Sharaff, *supra* note 8.

41. United States v. Lester, 282 F.2d 750 (3d Cir. 1960).

42. United States v. Seagraves, 265 F.2d 876 (3d Cir. 1959).

43. Comment, *Industrial Espionage: Piracy of Secret Scientific and Technical Information,* 14 U.C.L.A. L. REV. 911, 917–18 (1967).

44. H.R. Rep. No. 5578, 89th Cong., 1st Sess. (1965).

45. See, *e.g.,* State v. Cougscher, 227 Ore. 1, 360 P.2d 764 (1961); Palm Springs–La Quinta Development v. Kieberk Corp., 46 Cal. App. 2d 234, 115 P.2d 548 (1941) (intangible information on cards distinguished from the cards themselves).

46. N.Y. Penal Law, §1296 (1964).

47. 38 Ill. Rev. Stat. §15-1 (1965).

48. 26 Ga. Code Ann. §2643 (1966).

49. N.J. Stat. Ann. §2A 119-5.1 to 5.4 (1965).

50. Pa. Stat., Tit. 18, §4899.2 (1965).

51. Wis. Stat. §943.205 (1965).

52. Neb. Rev. Stat. §§28-548.01–.03 (Supp. 1965).

53. 26 Ga. Code Ann. §§2644–46 (1966).

54. N.J. Stat. Ann., *supra* note 49, at §5.1 (d) ; Neb. Rev. Stat., *supra* note 52, at §.01 (4).

55. James M. Fulton, *Protection of Intellectual Property Against Industrial Espionage and Theft,* address before American Management Association, March 17, 1965, at 11.

56. See Harding, *supra* note 37, at 398–401.

57. Letter to author, dated October 24, 1967.

58. Chemical Week, *supra* note 4.

59. This outline has been developed on the basis of the security practices of several companies, and reference has been made to the *Monsanto Security Guide* and *Procedure in Establishing Protective Program for Trade Secrets,* suggested by Evans Kahn of American Cyanamid Co., reprinted as Appendix "A" to Harding, *supra* note 37, at 407–11.

60. Harding, *supra* note 37, at 402.

61. Letter to author, quoted by permission but without attribution.

62. N.Y. Times, Sept. 18, 1967, p. 43.

63. For a discussion of both types of restrictions and their legal treatment, see Hudson Foam Latex Prods., Inc. v. Aiken, 82 N.J. 508, 198 A.2d 136 (1964).

64. Harrison v. Glucose Sugar Refining Co., 116 Fed. 304 (7th Cir. 1902). See Lezdig, *Protecting Trade Secrets When Employees Move,* 21 Bus. Law. 325, 333–34 (1966).

Chapter 18

House Organs and Company Books

A. INTRODUCTION

B. HOUSE ORGANS: COMMERCIAL/JOURNALISTIC

C. RIGHT OF PRIVACY

D. TRADEMARKS

E. COPYRIGHT OF HOUSE ORGAN

F. THE ROBINSON-PATMAN ACT

G. SYNDICATED HOUSE ORGANS

H. COMPANY BOOKS

Chapter 18

House Organs and Company Books

A. INTRODUCTION.

1. Chapter Scope.

This chapter collects and discusses certain practical matters having legal overtones or implications for the house organ editor or sponsor. Its purpose is to integrate legal subjects and specific segments of legal areas which may present problems in the planning, editing, management and distribution of such company or association publications. The treatment of such subjects is limited to the peculiarities of the house organ; it is not intended as a full discussion but, instead, is keyed to other chapters and sections for fuller information and detail generally.

The development of this chapter in this manner stems directly from the suggestions of the Southern Industrial Editors Association in connection with the author's appearance before its 1964 Institute.[1]

2. Nature, Purposes and Classification.

The house organ—by whatever name it may be known—is a well-recognized public relations tool and has long proved its value for a variety of company purposes. "House organ" is, in fact, an umbrella term which includes such more-specifically directed company publications as the employee publication, "customer book," stockholder magazine, industrial publication and other company publications. The specific "public" to which the house organ is directed and for whom, presumably, it is edited may vary but its basic purpose is to serve the interests of the company sponsor.

In format, content and appearance the publications go from pole to pole. Management interest and editorial competence are equally uneven. This contributes considerably to the confusion about, or even absence of appreciation for, the legal questions which revolve around their publication and distribution.

Public relations people and editors have gradually developed a tripartite classification of house organs:

    Internal,

    External,

    Internal-External combination.

This breakdown also has definite legal implications, some broad enough to include all three, and others relevant only to one category.

The sheer size of the house organ and its cumulative readership argue for an understanding of the legal exposure flowing from its publication. In 1963 Emerson Foote cited estimates of the number of house organs as from 7,000 to 50,000 and the total circulation as "anywhere from a conservative 200 million to 350 million," pointing out that he "knew of no other means of communication which can produce a comparable audience in this or any other country." [2] Other sources have suggested figures similar to these.

3. Increase in Legal Exposure.

The impact of the law on company publications has increased considerably over recent years. This was to be anticipated. There are several reasons for it:

    (a) An overall increase in the impingement of law and government on all business and all forms of communications.

    (b) An increased public awareness of its legal rights and remedies in connection with publishing, broadcasting and all forms of communications.

    (c) The tremendous burgeoning of the house organ as a company public relations tool, both internal and external, a part of the "communications explosion," as discussed in Section 2.

    (d) The change in orientation and substance of many house organs with many becoming more sophisticated and containing much which would qualify for inclusion in the public mass media.

    (e) The diversification of the purpose of house organs and the readership to which each is addressed. A single company may have separate publications intended for plant employees, salesmen, various echelons or segments of management or supervision, customers—even customers of a single division—or the public at large. Each may provide a company or editor with an entirely different group of legally-oriented questions.

    (f) The growing inclination to discuss controversial matters in house organs has introduced additional legal and even tax problems.[3]

B. HOUSE ORGANS: COMMERCIAL/JOURNALISTIC.

4. The Tripartite Orientation.

The house organ really has a three-way commitment or orientation:

(a) As a *journalistic* effort. In certain ways at least, it is part of "the press."

(b) As a *commercial* "captive publication," not to be confused with a "trade publication." Its primary function—perhaps its ultimate function—is to serve the business and commercial needs of its sponsor.

(c) As an *advertising* medium. It may be institutional advertising or product advertising or both as circumstances dictate.

From this tri-directional focus flow certain legal implications, not always easy to define or, for that matter, to discover. The interrelation of the journalistic, commercial and advertising introduces some problems perhaps unique in the communications legal field.

5. Commercial Nature of House Organs.

A basic question from which may stem several dichotomic legal conclusions is whether the house organ is a purely advertising, commercial or trade venture as a whole, as to portions only or, finally, not commercial at all.

Examination of a wide variety of such publications demonstrates that —aside from its overall public relations purpose of improving the sponsor's image or increasing its public acceptability—the house organ contains a substantial though varying amount of material dealing specifically with the sponsor, its policies, operations and even specific products and prices.

The mere fact that the house organ is published for company purposes and, indirectly, for its profit is not determinative any more than is the fact that mass media publications are admittedly published for the profit of the publisher.[4] However, the house organ would appear to be substantially different from the *public* press. Quite probably—this is not yet altogether clear—it does not share the protected position of the public press posited by the Supreme Court in the *Hill* case as discussed in Chapter 8, Section 22.

Probably a better approach is to consider separately each individual article, story, comment or item in the house organ in question rather than the house organ as an entirety. Thus, there should be no question that an article which promotes a specific product in the sponsor's line is a commercial, trade or advertising use. The same would seem to be true of an article or other writing which promotes the sponsor company or its products generally. This approach becomes more convincing if we were to consider the particular part of an article as having been physically separated from the issue in which it appears and then distributed separately. If as direct mail literature, for example, it would be an advertisement or for commercial purposes, then it should be so considered when included in the house organ.

By the same analysis, an article which is merely of general interest—not confined to product or company promotion—would seem to partake of the newsworthy character of stories appearing in the public press.

6. House Organs as Product Advertising.

Separate articles or features of the house organ fall into several different categories. One of the most important is product publicity or promotion. Many house organs consistently use such material—sometimes to the exclusion of other matter. The more general trend seems to be to limit such content but almost all contain some of it.

A survey by *Dun's Review and Modern Industry* of house organ content indicated that the "runner-up topics" were "new developments and policy changes and company products and services." [5] This is true of both the internal and the external house organ.

The trademark cases discussed in Section 14 below relative to registration of house organ names or titles refer quite specifically to the commercial nature of such publications involved, with descriptions such as:

(a) distributed freely and mainly for advertising purposes;

(b) house organ or advertising medium;

(c) The primary purpose of the publication was to advertise the applicant's business;

(d) devoted very largely to the advertising of applicant's merchandise.

This line of cases is a recognition of both the overall promotional and advertising character of the house organ as well as of the specific product advertising content thereof.

Some portions of house organs may not be out-and-out product advertising. They may be more subtle but, nonetheless, effective product promotion. In this category are research and development stories, case histories of product use by customers, new product announcements and promotion, price policy items, suggestions and instructions concerning sales approaches such as multi- or parallel-product use, etc. These would seem to fall into the general class of product publicity and advertising despite their more indirect nature, and even though they may sometimes be directed to the sponsor's own plant or sales personnel rather than to prospective customers or "the trade."

C. RIGHT OF PRIVACY.

7. The Specific Problem.

One of the most important continuing legal pitfalls faced by house organ editors is the application of the right of privacy, discussed at length in Chapter 8. We are here concerned with the special or unusual applications of that legal doctrine to the house organ. Some of these arise from the tripartite character of the house organ described in Section 4 above and from the varied character of house organ contents.

It has not as yet been clearly judicially determined whether a publication such as a house organ is the same as a newspaper—at least insofar as the right of privacy is concerned. However, there are cases which have pointed the way and which appear to indicate that the house organ generally will not be considered in the category of a newspaper but rather as advertising or as a commercial or trade effort of the sponsor.

In *Griffin v. Medical Society* [6] plaintiff's complaint was held sufficient when it alleged that plaintiff's "before and after" photographs were published in a journal as part of an article entitled "The Saddle Nose" and written by certain physicians whose names appeared thereon. The defendants argued that the photographs were not used for advertising purposes and therefore the plaintiff had no recourse under the New York privacy statute. The court rejected this argument saying, *inter alia,*

> An article even in a scientific publication may be nothing more than someone's advertisement in disguise. . . . That the article . . . with the accompanying photographs of plaintiff was published . . . to advertise the defendant physicians and their handiwork [is] a fair inference . . . (Emphasis added.)

If an article in a learned or scientific journal may be considered as "someone's advertisement in disguise," certainly a self-serving article in a company-published house organ should be so considered.

However, even *if* a house organ should be considered as such, there still would persist some of these special aspects. It is for this reason that the item-by-item approach suggested in Section 5 above appears more logical and certainly more conducive to safety. Briefly restated and applied directly to the privacy concept, each article or section of each issue of the house organ should be analyzed separately. The privacy strictures may apply to some but not to others.

8. Use of Employee Names, Pictures and Stories.

House organ use of the names or photographs of the sponsor's employees or stories about their activities is commonly found in internal house organs (as "personals" or otherwise) and sometimes even in external publications. It should not be assumed that a person's status as an employee waives his right of privacy. The various situations merit different attitudes.

If a factual item is used as a "personal" in an internal house organ, it may well be considered as newsworthy to the readership of such a publication. Presumably this would qualify under the well-recognized exemption accorded the public press. On the other hand, if used in an external or even a combination house organ, it is doubtful whether it would so qualify. Mention of an employee's company or plant activities would be more likely to avoid a privacy violation claim than would an item dealing solely with the employee's personal life. Probably a story about an employee as a member of the company bowling team would be considered to have a company orientation rather than a personal-life implication.

Sometimes employee pictures and names are used in conjunction with such things as employee safety campaigns or other news directed toward increased plant efficiency. There is some indication that such purpose removes the possible stigma of a privacy violation. Thus, in *Thomas v. General Electric Co.,*[7] an employee was photographed at his machine and the picture was used by the company without the employee's consent in order to improve the company's efficiency and promote employee safety "and for no other purpose." The company defeated the employee's privacy suit. Furthermore, some cases have held that employees who know that their pictures are being taken for company use will be considered as having impliedly waived their right to object. In *Johnson v. Boeing Airplane Co.,*[8] the plaintiff was an employee of Boeing, knew his picture was being taken and "guessed" that it would be used in company promotion. The court found this to constitute an *implied waiver* by the employee despite his later claim for compensation for the use of his picture.

Such assumption of implied waiver or consent should not be taken as a firm ground for using the name and picture in external house organs. This would seem to follow from cases such as *Brizinski v. Doall Corp. and Popular Science Publishing Company, Inc.*[9] which held that the publication was not liable for publishing the employee's photograph which had been sent to it by Doall, apparently in connection with a news release, but implied that the employer was liable.

This entire subject is an ambiguous segment of privacy law. It does seem clear that "claims based on use of a name or picture 'for advertising purposes' . . . have received much more liberal treatment than those grounded on use 'for purposes of trade.' " [10] However, this was said by a New York court in construing a statute which refers specifically to both such uses, a situation not present in other states. This would appear to give greater protection to the use of names and photographs in those portions of house organs which do not partake of the clearly advertising function.

9. Employee Consents.

There is no question but that house organ editors are better advised to obtain written releases from employees before using their pictures and names in house organs. This is generally accepted by editorial commentators in the field.[11] While, in specific instances, such releases *may* not be mandatory, safety dictates that they should be obtained.

There are two procedures which are most commonly used.

(a) When the plant or other photograph is taken, the release is signed and then keyed by number or other code to the photograph. The release specifically indicates the use to be made of the employee's name or picture. Many an editor or PR man is accompanied in such picture-taking by a clerk or secretary whose sole function is to get the releases signed, sometimes even handing the employee a dollar bill as consideration.

(b) When an employee is first hired, a general and forward-looking release is signed, covering all such prospective uses by the company of name, photograph and personal history or activities.

Some union contracts have provided that all union members covered by the contract give their permission in advance for such matters. Such a provision should not be relied upon since the permission should be signed by the employee himself. Otherwise the vagaries of implied consent or waiver would probably apply.

10. Effect of Employment Termination.

Even assuming that an employee's name and picture may be safely used during the period of his or her employment, no use should be made thereof after the employment has been terminated. For example, in *Colgate-Palmolive Co. v. Tullos*,[12] the employee had specifically given the employer the right to use her photograph but recovered $1200 for its use after the employment had been terminated. Similarly in *Wendell v. Conduit Machine Co.*,[13] the employee voluntarily posed for his picture for company use. Long after his employment ended, he sought an injunction against further use. Equitable relief (the injunction) was refused on grounds of "culpable negligence amounting to constructive fraud" due to the extended delay but the prior assent was not deemed evidence of a permanent grant to the employer.

11. Reprinting News Item in House Organ.

Not infrequently the house organ editor will pick up from a newspaper or magazine and reprint a news story or picture pertinent to the company's products or activities. Aside from questions of copyright infringement (see Section 20 below), privacy rights may be involved if someone's name or picture was used in the original news story and as reprinted. This becomes clearer if we think of the house organ piece as a separate item of direct mail, for example, as suggested in Section 5 above.

In *Flores v. Mosler Safe Co.*,[14] the newspapers had carried a news story of a fire which mentioned the name of the plaintiff several times as having been on the premises at the time of the fire. This use of plaintiff's name was privileged. The defendant reprinted the original news coverage, including photograph and story, in a "circular" which it distributed, with added copy suggesting the purchase of Mosler safes to protect business records in a fire. The company argued that the mention of Flores was merely incidental to the advertising copy. Holding that the circular was a solicitation for patronage, the court considered it advertising and held the complaint to be legally sufficient.

Some company publication editors appear to appreciate these dangers and black out the eyes in news photographs or delete names, addresses and other identifying indicia from news stories when used in this manner.

There seems to be an exception to this rule when the house organ— even the mass media advertising—of a *publisher* uses reprints of photographs or stories which had previously appeared in magazines or periodicals published by that very publishing company. In *Shirley Booth v. Curtis Publishing Co.*,[15] the defendant had used Shirley Booth's picture (with her knowledge) in a resort story in *Holiday*. Later the defendant republished the same picture as part of a promotional advertisement in *The New Yorker* and *Advertising Age* as a sample of the contents of *Holiday*. Following the apparent rule in New York,[16] this was held to be only "incidental" use of the photograph and not actionable. A distinction was drawn between such use and a "collateral" use to advertise a product directly. There was a vigorous dissent from this view on the basis of the *Flores* case and subsequent legal comment has criticized the holding, maintaining that the dissent is "more consonant with a liberal interpretation of the New York statute." [17]

12. Articles of General or Instructive Interest.

House organs frequently print articles of general interest, perhaps of an informative or instructional character. Here the editor is on firmer ground vis-à-vis the right of privacy. If the articles are about reasonably current newsworthy subjects and the person mentioned therein has a definite association with the subject, the likelihood is that the house organ would not be liable—essentially for the same reason that the public media would be protected in such cases. See Chapter 8, Section 22.

Furthermore, mere incidental mention of the individual in such material has been held not actionable, especially where the name used is not likely to promote particularly the sale of a product or the image of the company generally as discussed in Section 11 above.

Some such articles deal with developments of new equipment or company research and mention the names of the employees or even outside persons responsible for such design, improvements, etc. If the reference to the individual is merely a truthful association with the product, there would seem to be no liability. It has been held, for example, that paid advertising which truthfully credited to a contract designer the development of certain devices was not actionable.[18]

13. Fiction.

Should a house organ carry any "fiction," its exposure would be the same as that of any periodical or book publisher if identifiable persons are mentioned therein. See Chapter 8, Section 9. It would seem that the house organ sponsor should be under no greater liability unless a court should decide that the entire house organ was "tainted" by its commercial aspects. Yet exculpatory language should be used—as it is in most publisher-author agreements.

D. TRADEMARKS.

14. House Organ Title as a Trademark.

It is surprising to find that many house organ names or titles have not been treated as trademarks by their editors or company sponsors. In most cases such names are registrable as trademarks [19] although the names of some publications which are loosely referred to as house organs may not be.[20]

In the landmark case of *Ex parte The Curtis Publishing Co.*,[21] the Patent Office held that the name of a so-called magazine published by

Curtis was registrable as a trademark since it was "merchandise" even though it was "distributed freely and mainly for advertising purposes." It contained some literary matter as well as advertising. Prior to 1913 such titles were not considered registrable.

In *Maryland Assurance Corp. v. Van Sant*,[22] another leading case, the publication in question was described as a "house organ or advertising medium." It was a monthly periodical with the title "Protection" and was issued solely for the interests of the insurance company's agents. The publication was not sold, had no subscription price, was distributed to a regular mailing list, contained some general insurance and other articles but its prime content was information about the sponsor company. "Protection" was held to be registrable.

From the cases it appears that a title of a house organ will be registered if it satisfies the following tests:

     (a) The publication is issued periodically.

     (b) The contents of each issue is different, in part at least.

     (c) A portion (even as small as 20 per cent) is "literary matter" or "matter of general interest," with these terms being rather loosely used.

     (d) It is not "mere advertising" although the inclusion of advertising does not prevent registration *per se*.

     (e) It is mailed or otherwise distributed to a regular list.

     (f) The format and theme of successive issues are reasonably consistent.

     (g) The publication has become a "recognizable thing in its own right." [23]

Practically all current house organs, regardless of "mere size, binding or appearance," will satisfy these standards. It is therefore noteworthy that so many house organ sponsors have made no effort to protect their titles. The author has examined hundreds thereof and a very considerable portion do not carry any registration notice on the title, presumably because it has not been registered. This is an omission which should be remedied since the proliferation of house organs has been and continues to be such that "good names are running out." Many conflicts already exist and more are likely to occur in the future.

The "Concrete FACTS" case,[24] decided in 1966, is an example of conflicting claims to the same title for use in the same industry. The applicant had used the title since 1953 and the opposer since 1950. It was only when the applicant sought to register the title on the Principal Register that the matter came to issue. The opposer prevailed by reason of prior use of the title.

15. Use of Company Trademarks.

Among the details which the house organ editor should police is the proper use of the company's own trademarks. These trademarks are usually valuable company assets even though they do not appear on the corporate balance sheets. They should be treated accordingly. Many house organs do not respect them.

An examination of many house organs—also of successive issues of the same house organ—indicates certain common failings.

(a) "Lower Case Use."

Frequently—perhaps because of long familiarity—the trademark is written as a noun or adjective and even as a verb in different tenses. This must be avoided at all times. See Chapter 10, Section 38.

(b) Failure to Use Registration Notice.

The notice should be used at least once in each separate article, story, section, etc. of the house organ. Typographic needs may dictate that it not be used every time a trademark is mentioned. Some house organs list company trademarks on the masthead, title page or at the foot of the table of contents. See Chapter 10, Section 30.

Company trademarks must be used properly because of the possibility that misuse may contribute to the mark's becoming generic. One of the most damning pieces of evidence on this issue would be a company's failure to refer properly to its own marks in a publication under its own control. This problem is worsened if a mark has not been registered. This may occur with either old or new marks but seems particularly noticeable in house organs as to new marks. House organs frequently are media for announcing or promoting new products being marketed under new brand names or marks. See Chapter 16 as to new product introduction.

16. Use of Other Trademarks.

Not infrequently house organ articles or other pieces will use words which are really the trademarks of other companies. This is especially true if the house organ content deals with developments in a given industry or field. These marks must be respected with the same fidelity which the editor and the sponsor have a right to expect in connection with the use of the sponsor's own marks in the public press or other house organs. Frequently they are not.

The basic rule is simple: use the mark as a proper noun and capitalize it as you would any name. See Chapter 10, Section 38.

E. COPYRIGHT OF HOUSE ORGAN.

17. Company Attitudes.

The house organ, as a printed and publicly distributed periodical, presents no special problems insofar as copyright procedures are concerned. The principal question seems to be the apparent disinclination of editors and companies even to consider the possibility of copyright. Examination of representative house organs shows that they may contain material which should be so protected. Some are considered ephemeral by management—in some instances properly so—but they should be copyrighted in many cases in which such protection has been ignored.

It probably is something more than coincidence that companies which are jealous of their corporate image generally and careful of the various elements which contribute to it, are more likely to copyright their house organs and any other published company materials—even those issued periodically or episodically.

Decisions adverse to copyright are usually premised on the "hope" that other publications will act as "multipliers"—picking up and reprinting material from the house organ, thus giving broader exposure without additional cost. This undoubtedly makes sense. However, it can still be achieved even though the house organ is copyrighted.

The copyright notice should be accompanied by a legend indicating either that (a) reprinting is permitted provided full credit is given and the copyright notice appended to the reprinted material, or (b) that requests for permission to reprint should be addressed to XYZ and will be promptly answered. The permission is granted with the specific requirement that the copyright notice be appended.

18. When to Copyright.

The basic decision on this matter should be dictated by a consideration of the contents of the house organ. Inasmuch as the contents will probably have a reasonably consistent character or nature—though varying from issue to issue—an examination of a half-dozen issues or so should give a clear indication of the need for protection. Among the types of material, the use of which should point to protection, are:

(a) Original writing of apparent literary value, even though such material may deal with purely company matters and have been written by company personnel.

(b) Articles purchased from free-lance writers, especially those who may have some stature in their fields. Even though only first periodical rights may be purchased, protection of the author may dictate copyright of the house organ. Some contracts with authors or their agents require such a procedure. Also, the company's rights and interests in such literary property should be considered.

(c) Original artwork or photography which may have current or prospective value or which may have been reasonably expensive. Also, such graphics may be later used in other types of company promotion, advertising, etc. and their original appearance in the house organ is the appropriate point at which copyright should be obtained.

(d) Technical writing prepared by various departments of the company may be used. This may deal with new products and models or even the description, details or methods of use of existing products. Since an editorial—rather than an advertising—approach or concept is used in house organs, such materials may be more extensive and detailed than similar copy in the advertising of the company. Copyright at this point can be valuable and may later be the basis of important company protection against misuse by competitors. Even if the new product may be subject to present or prospective patent protection, this should not color the decision.

(e) Product-use case histories require protection in some instances. These may have been costly to develop and should be protected.[25] Furthermore, some customers will cooperate with a company with the understanding that the use made of the case history be limited in certain ways or that it be used only in "full text" as approved by the customer without any possible emasculation in other media or use by others, even trade journals. Copyright is a useful method to comply with such requirements.

19. Whole Issue Copyright Notice and Registration.

Since a house organ is a "periodical," the copyright notice should appear on the title page of the issue, on the first page of the text or under the title heading or masthead. If the cover contains art or other graphics considered valuable, an *additional* notice may be used thereon.

The copyright should be registered with Form B (Periodical manufactured in the United States). Each issue must be separately registered since there is no such thing as a "blanket" copyright which will protect the general idea or format of a house organ or other periodical or a series of issues as a whole. See Chapter 5.

20. "Inside" Copyright Notices.

In addition to the overall copyright of each issue of the house organ, it may be necessary, advisable or desirable to use other copyright notices in connection with specific parts of its contents.

(a) If an item is being reprinted from some other source—either company or external—and carried a copyright notice on its original publication, the same form of notice should be used on that item when reprinted. This may be different from the whole issue copyright notice. Such notice should appear on the first page of the article, picture or other item reprinted. On occasion such reprinted material will also have to carry, in addition to the appropriate copyright notice, a slug indicating that it is reprinted with the permission granted by the copyright owner.

(b) Some material may be picked up—with permission of course —from a newspaper or magazine which is subject to whole issue copyright but in which the individual news story or feature naturally does not carry its own copyright notice. It is all too easy to neglect to attach the appropriate copyright notice to that item in the house organ. Such omissions have been observed from time to time even in well-edited house organs.

(c) An article or photograph may appear for the first time in the house organ but the company may be required by the creator to add a separate copyright notice on it—probably in the creator's name—because the company has not purchased all rights in the material. The full issue copyright may not protect the author.

(d) It may be advisable to affix a separate notice to a particularly valuable photograph, technical drawing or even fine art. Such material is separately registrable in a different Class and the separate notice may facilitate this.

(e) House organs may use syndicated features, the terms of purchase of which require a specific and separate copyright notice, even though the material has never been theretofore published. If the syndicated material is really "boilerplate"—perhaps in mat form or ready for offset reproduction—the necessary notice will automatically be picked up when reproduced. However, the material may be reset for the house organ and the required copyright notice lost in the process. Furthermore, some house organ editors have a disinclination to use such notice in a desire to avoid possible implications of syndicated material use.

F. THE ROBINSON-PATMAN ACT.

21. Involvement of House Organs Generally.

It may seem to the house organ editor or even to the sponsoring company that the provisions of the Robinson-Patman Act would have little, if any, effect on such publications. Yet this may not be true unless the contents and distribution of the house organ are properly controlled and handled.

Basically, the Act was intended to prevent a manufacturer or advertiser from dealing unfairly or in a discriminatory manner with some of its customers, favoring the larger or more important. The house organ can be a tool of such favoritism and discrimination.

The Act requires that competing customers be dealt with on *proportionately equal terms*.[26] A failure to do so results in discrimination and a violation of the Act. There are basically two channels through which such discrimination—with resultant violation of the Act—can develop. The first is the mismanagement of the contents and of the distribution of the publication and the second is the acceptance of assistance from company suppliers or sources in its publication. Put another way, the first deals with Section 2(e) of the Act which, in this context, deals with the furnishing of services on an improper basis, and the second involves the acceptance, under Section 2(f) of the Act, of improper contributions or services from others.

Quite probably the house organ sponsor does not deliberately discriminate in the use or distribution of its house organ, although some instances of such deliberate misuse have occurred. Inadvertence is usually the premise. This lack of intent, however, is no defense.

22. Discrimination Among Sponsor's Customers.

Internal house organs are not likely to involve any Robinson-Patman Act problems since their distribution is limited to the employees of the sponsor and customers are but rarely concerned. However, the external or internal-external combination house organ may be misused and result in violations of the Act.

It is a common practice for an external house organ to be distributed very widely to the distributors, wholesalers, retailers and other customers of the sponsor. When one copy of the publication is sent to each customer, no problems arise. However, some companies supply multiple copies (sometimes by the hundred or even more) to customers for their own further use. The wholesaler or other recipient then redistributes these copies to its salesmen or even to its own customers. These publications can be of real help to the wholesaler in his sales program, dealing, as many of them do, with new product announcements, product characteristics and performance, and other matters useful in promoting sales of the sponsor's products.

Clearly a wholesaler or other customer who is given a disproportionately large supply of such publications—as against its competitor—is being helped significantly in his merchandising and selling chores. His competitor is at a disadvantage and discrimination has occurred. Such discrimination has been recognized by the Federal Trade Commission as a violation of the Act.[27]

Nor is this discrimination limited to the wholesale level. Some retailers receive substantial supplies of the house organ for display and free distribution to their own consumer customers. This is definitely an aid to the retailer and if a competitor does not receive similar, proportionate assistance, there could well be a violation of the Act.

This situation falls into sharper and more practical focus if the house organ is recognized for what it is—an important sales aid. Few would question the possible impropriety if we were dealing with only clearly descriptive sales materials—perhaps single sheets or small leaflets—which are so commonly given to customers as a sales aid.

23. Acceptance of Discriminatory Contributions.

Some—perhaps not too many—house organs accept paid advertising. This advertising comes principally and not unpredictably from company suppliers and sources. Section 2(f) of the Act contains sanctions against the customer who knowingly *accepts* disproportionate services or payments. This presents some difficult problems and decisions for the house organ sponsor—especially if such paid advertising is important to the house organ budget.

The question becomes particularly acute—with probable sponsor culpability—if the sponsor or the editor deliberately and affirmatively solicits such paid advertising with the knowledge or "reason to believe" that similar assistance is not being accorded to the sponsor's competitors. The mere fact that the sponsor's competitor is not receiving similar advertising—it may not even have a house organ—is not necessarily fatal provided the house organ advertiser provides such competitor with usable and acceptable alternative services, etc.

Undoubtedly the leading case is that involving the A & P's *Woman's Day,* a paid circulation house publication which accepts very substantial quantities of advertising.[28] The Act was held to be violated because of the mismanagement of the paid advertising of the A & P's suppliers. While this is certainly an "extreme" case, nevertheless its implications for house organs are clear.

24. Control of Distribution of Circulation.

A goodly share of the sponsor's exposure stems from the distribution patterns of the external house organ. The house organ editor may not control this distribution. The sales department, for example, may have a considerable voice in the matter. Perhaps the public relations director has the final say in the makeup of the mailing or other circulation lists and patterns. Once again, the solution lies in open communication between the various departments including legal counsel.

Another aspect of circulation control involves the company's having a variety of house organs. Some may present these Robinson-Patman Act questions. Others may not. A clear-cut policy should be adopted for each of them.

Discrimination in distribution of house organs may result from actions of the jobber or wholesaler. This is usually beyond the sponsor's control and it would not seem likely that the sponsor would be responsible under the Act. However, if the "jobber" were really a sponsor's branch instead of an independent business, then such discrimination would be chargeable to the sponsor.

G. SYNDICATED HOUSE ORGANS.

25. Nature and Use.

Most sponsors of house organs think of them as company publications prepared entirely by, or under the direction of, company staff. This may generally be true but there are many companies which use syndicated publications which are really house organs. Usually such syndicated publications will be used by the smaller manufacturer or retailer.

The size, content and format supplied by the syndicator varies widely. A common type is an eight-page publication, all of which is preprinted uniformly for all users and then imprinted on the cover with the name of the individual sponsor. Some allow a page or so for the sponsor's special material or advertising.

26. Exclusivity.

Ordinarily, a syndicator will protect the sponsor against a competitor's use of the same material. The scope of this protection will vary and the sponsor should be certain as to its extent if such exclusivity is important to it. This should be done by agreement before the sponsor contracts for any extended period.

Inasmuch as syndicated house organs are usually used only by retailers or other relatively local concerns, the protection is usually limited to use by a direct competitor in the same business or industry within a sponsor's marketing area. However, this may be insufficient for the purposes of the sponsor. Even though a sponsor may be only a regional or local concern, it may desire protection on a national basis—at least against use of the same material by other companies within the same industry or selling products which are directly or indirectly competitive with those of the sponsor.

27. Trademark Aspects.

It would be a most unusual relationship which would permit a single sponsor of a syndicated house organ to acquire any rights in the title or name used by the syndicator. The same is true even though the sponsor may have the right to prefix its own name to the title. This means that a sponsor using this syndicated house organ for a lengthy period of time will not acquire the same rights or exclusive reader acceptance which the sponsor's own, privately-prepared house organ may expect to achieve over the same period of time.

There have been some instances in which an individual sponsor has, by contract, acquired licensee rights in the name of the syndicated house organ. These have resulted from specific agreement and definitely are exceptions to the general rule.

28. Copyright Protection.

Frequently, syndicated house organs will carry a copyright in the name of the syndicating source. On occasion, the individual company using such a house organ will want to protect by copyright the company matter which it adds to the syndicated material. This presents no particular problems.

An additional copyright notice should be placed on the page or pages added by the sponsor. The notice should contain the name of the sponsor, not the syndicator.

29. Miscellaneous Legal Questions.

Even though an individual sponsor has no control over the contents of the syndicated material, it does nevertheless have the same responsibility and liability for legal irregularities therein as it would have if it prepared its own house organ. Among the possible types of exposure are libel, right of privacy violations, copyright infringement, etc.

A sponsor should therefore take the precaution of checking out the contents of each issue before its distribution. This may require special arrangements with the syndicator, especially if the copies bearing the sponsor's imprint and individual material are drop-mailed by the syndicator as part of its service to its customers. The least the sponsor should require is a written undertaking by the syndicator to protect the sponsor against such liability and to hold it harmless in the event of claim or suit.

H. COMPANY BOOKS.

30. Characteristics and Legal Results.

The publication of "company books" or "sponsored books" as a public relations tool is markedly increasing. As might be expected because of the variety of purposes motivating such publications, they appear in a wide variety of form, content, methods of distribution and even sponsorship and absorption of costs.[29] Some of these variables create a multiplicity of legal relationships and problems.

Some such volumes are frankly laudatory histories of the company or of the "founding father," exuding pride in company success. Others are industry histories, commemorative volumes, "guide books" about use of company products, handbooks of various kinds and for various purposes.[30] Most are published by commercial publishers. The cost may be split by sponsor and publisher, or paid entirely by the sponsor. Profits, if any, may be variously divided.

Various "types" of authors do the writing and we have here a multiplicity of legal results and needs. Some books are illustrated. Others contain financial data. All of these aspects create legal questions, discussed in Sections 31 to 34 below.

31. Authorship: Copyright and Contract Questions.

Company books may be authored by members of the company's PR staff, outside PR or advertising agency staff, a free-lance writer, or a "big name" author. Sometimes the final manuscript is a mixture of several of these sources. The book may be "a book without an author" as Du Pont frankly described its *Du PONT The Autobiography of an American Enterprise*. It may contain limited and designated material prepared by a "big name" as does National Gypsum Company's *Design for Growth* to which Bruce Barton contributed the introduction.

This variation in authorship and contribution provides some interesting copyright questions. Not infrequently company books bear the copyright of the sponsor. This is legally acceptable, especially when the book is written by the PR staff or other employee "in the case of works made for hire."

Some such books do not carry the name of any author. In a sense, we have an anonymous volume despite the known identity of the corporate sponsor. Since the copyright statute is somewhat inconsistent about the need for an author's "name," the safest method is to use the name of the sponsor or publisher.[31] If it is intended that the real author is to retain any rights in the book, this should be spelled out in an agreement and the named sponsor or publisher should serve as a trustee for the author.

32. Publication Contracts.

Company books usually are printed and published by trade publishers although some are printed by commercial printers and then published and distributed by the sponsor. If published by a regular publisher, several changes will be necessary in the usual author-publisher contract, using the term "author" in reference to the sponsor, as is usually the case in company books.[32] Among these changes are the provisions for:

(a) Contributions by the sponsor to the cost of the volume including possible sharing thereof with the publisher.

(b) Commitment by the sponsor to purchase a specified number of copies from the publisher and the price at which such copies will be bought.

(c) Responsibility for advertising or other promotion of the volume.

(d) Sharing of the profits, if any, resulting from the sale of the book.

(e) Obligation of the publisher to keep the volume in print, also disposition of overstock, if any.

(f) Relative rights to copyright.

(g) Ownership of company materials reproduced in the work.

Not every one of the above provisions will be pertinent in a particular case nor will every situation be treated alike. However, special consideration should be given to their application.

33. Miscellaneous Problems.

As with any substantial literary effort, a company book involves a miscellany of legal questions. Furthermore, some of these are somewhat complicated by the nature and purpose of the book in contradistinction to the customary historical or similar work. Among them are:

(a) *Right of Privacy.*

Ordinarily an historical, educational or technical volume may be treated as "newsworthy" and therefore not too much concern is needed about the right of privacy. However, a company book, no matter how educational or factual it is, may be considered as an advertising or promotional venture of the sponsor. Caution would ordinarily dictate that releases be obtained from living persons named in the book. However, the recent Supreme Court decision in the *Warren Spahn* case probably accords some protection. See Chapter 8, Sections 9 and 12.

(b) Defamation.

A company book is subject to the same legal strictures as any other book insofar as libel is concerned. Additional caution should be exercised because of the nature of the book since it is possible that malice may be inferred therefrom should derogatory mention be made of competitors or other persons having special relationships to the sponsor. See Chapter 7 generally.

(c) Unfair Competition.

Many company books, especially if they presume to tell the story of the sponsor's entire industry, may contain references which may be grounds for an unfair competition action by a competitor. There is even the possibility that a competing *industry* may have such grounds.[33]

(d) Financial Material.

Inasmuch as many company books may stress the company's strength, industry leadership, growth, size, etc., some contain a multiplicity of references to financial and statistical matters throughout their text.[34] Some even include balance sheets and operating statements. These inclusions must be accurate and satisfy the strictures of the SEC and other control agencies, governmental or otherwise. This is especially true since a favorite method of distribution thereof is to company stockholders, financial analysts and others of influence in the financial field.

(e) Deceptive and Unfair Practices.

While it is unlikely that a company book will deliberately include deceptive material, the danger is a very real one since the purpose of the book may be "puffery." This may cross into positive deception, susceptible to policing by the Federal Trade Commission or other governmental agency charged with supervision of the sponsor's industry. Even "restrained" company volumes have been known to skirt very close to deceptive or unfair trade practices.

34. Screening by Legal Counsel.

The manuscript of every company book should be carefully screened by legal counsel. The legal aspects and implications discussed above dictate this. Furthermore, publishing contracts frequently permit the publisher's attorneys to do this and also contain somewhat onerous provisions should any legal liabilities arise by virtue of the content of the work.

While this screening is necessary, counsel must realize that the volume is intended as a literary work and not a "law book." The lawyer should screen and advise. He should not try to write the book himself. What was stressed in Chapter 1 as to the limitations on the lawyer's contribution to PR activities generally, applies with particular relevance to the company book.

Notes

1. Reprinted under the title *You, the Law and Your Company,* in HIGHER GROUND FOR JOURNALISM, School of Journalism, University of Georgia, 1965. See also Weslager, *The Legal Responsibilities of an Employee Publication,* Printers' Ink, Nov. 21, 1947, at 40.
2. Emerson Foote, *New Opportunities in America's Fastest Growing Mass Media,* address before the 17th Annual Southern Industrial Editors Institute, reprinted in COMMUNICATIONS CARTOGRAPHY, School of Journalism, University of Georgia, 1964.
3. For a discussion of such matters, see Avery, *Company Publications and Politics,* P.R.J., Nov., 1959, at 28; Kimball, *Politics for Corporate Employees,* P.R.J., Aug., 1959, at 6.
4. Sidis v. F-R Publishing Corp., 113 F.2d 806 (2d Cir. 1940), *cert. denied,* 61 Sup. Ct. 393 (1940); Lahiri v. Daily Mirror, Inc., 162 Misc. 776 (1937).
5. As quoted and discussed in CUTLIP & CENTER, EFFECTIVE PUBLIC RELATIONS 183 (3d ed. 1964).
6. 11 N.Y.S.2d 109 (1939).
7. 207 F. Supp. 792 (W.D. Ky. 1962).
8. 175 Kans. 275, 262 P.2d 808 (1953), discussed in 67 HARV. L. REV. 1433 (1954).
9. 31 Ill. App.2d 191, 175 N.E.2d 577 (1961).
10. Gautier v. Pro Football, Inc., 304 N.Y. 354, 107 N.E.2d 48 (1952).
11. For a discussion of this problem by an experienced house organ editor, see BENTLEY, EDITING THE COMPANY PUBLICATION 225–6 (1953).
12. 219 F.2d 617 (5th Cir. 1955).
13. 74 Misc. 201 (N.Y. 1911).
14. 20 N.Y.2d 276, 164 N.E.2d 853, 196 N.Y.S.2d 975 (1959).
15. 15 App. Div.2d 343, 223 N.Y.S.2d 727 (1962); *aff'd,* 11 N.Y.2d 907, 182 N.E.2d 812 (1962).
16. Shubert v. Columbia Pictures Corp., 189 Misc. 734 (N.Y. 1947); Merle v. Sociological Film Corp., 166 App. Div. 376 (1915); Moglen v. Varsity Pajamas, 13 App. Div.2d 114, 213 N.Y.S.2d 999 (1961).
17. See *e.g.,* HOFSTADTER & HOROWITZ, THE RIGHT OF PRIVACY 217 (1964).
18. Brociner v. Radio Wire Tel., Inc., 15 Misc.2d 843, 133 N.Y.S.2d 743 (1959).
19. Giannini Controls Corp. v. Litton Precision Prods., Inc., 150 U.S.P.Q. 387 (P.O.T.T.A.B. 1966); *Ex parte* The Scholl Mfg. Co., Inc., 40 U.S.P.Q. 254, 29 T.M.R. 175 (Comr. 1939); *Ex parte* The Griffith Laboratories, Inc., 31 T.M.R. 424, 50 U.S.P.Q. 512 (Comr. 1941).
20. *Ex parte* The Catholic Digest, Inc., 47 T.M.R. 378, 11 U.S.P.Q. 444 (Comr. 1956); *In re* Commonwealth Engineering Co. of Ohio, 50 T.M.R. 209, 120 U.S.P.Q. 415 (P.O.T.T.A.B. 1959).
21. 1913 C.D. 268, 197 O.G. Pat. Off. 1000, 4 T.M.R. 79 (Comr. 1913).
22. 1924 D.C. 39, 326 O.G. Pat. Off. 469, 14 T.M.R. 114 (Comr. 1924).

23. For an excellent discussion of these requirements, see *Notes from the Patent Office*, §1, Part 5, Note 8.

24. Martin-Marietta Corp. v. Expanded Shale, Clay & Slate Institute, 150 U.S.P.Q. 385 (1966).

25. On this type of feature generally, see Borno, *How to Organize and Staff a Business Features Program*, P.R.J., Feb., 1967, at 21.

26. For a discussion of this requirement and of the Act generally, see ROWE, PRICE DISCRIMINATION UNDER THE ROBINSON-PATMAN ACT (1962).

27. See, *e.g.*, F.T.C. v. Simplicity Pattern Co., Inc., 360 U.S. 55 (1959).

28. State Wholesale Grocers v. Great A. & P. Tea Co., 258 F.2d 831 (7th Cir. 1958).

29. For a general discussion of the company book, see Cutlip & Center, *supra* note 5, at 184–6.

30. For an excellent explanation of the handling of a sponsored book, see *Using the Sponsored Book as a PR Tool*, P.R.N., April 3, 1967 (Case Study No. 1101) concerning THE REMINGTON HISTORICAL TREASURY OF AMERICAN GUNS.

31. See generally, on this somewhat confusing situation, Bates, *Copyright by Anon.*, 52 A.B.A.J. 1140 (1966).

32. For a form of author-publisher agreement intended for the customary relationship, see RINGER & GITLIN, COPYRIGHTS 171–180 (rev. ed. 1965).

33. See the discussion of the "trucker-railroad" case in Chapter 23, Section 4 of text.

34. See Nelson, *The Company Sponsored Book,* P.R.J., March, 1959, at 22 for a description of company book content including financial references.

Chapter 19

Government Relations and Regulation

Chapter 19

Government Relations
and Regulation

A. INTRODUCTION.

1. The Public Relations Function and Government.

In one sense, all PR activity may be "involved" in one way or another with government, using the term in the broadest sense to include the executive, legislative and judicial branches. Put another way, every chapter in this work deals with some phase of the PR man's possible concern with government. This follows if the PR man and his company or client equate "government relations" with "law."

However, our concern in this chapter is with the more practical government-oriented PR functions and the PR man's responsibilities and activities—apart from the more general, broadly applicable *legal* obligations which apply to the business communicator.

The growing intervention of government in the operation of business and the lives of the individual citizen—without any characterization as a "welfare state"—naturally posits more and more PR involvement with and by government. In this framework, PR does not differ from any other function of business.

At the same time, the "communications explosion" and the PR concept of the "two-way street" demand—and have produced—a seemingly disproportionate increase in government-oriented PR. This government thrust has led to such comments as: "No corporation or association of any consequence can afford to ignore Washington. Regardless, Washington will not ignore them." [1]

In 1963, John Hill made a "random sampling" of the problems put to his firm "week in and week out for which we are asked to find or to help to find the answers." Of the eighteen specific problems which he outlines, eleven specifically deal with some form of governmental regulation, activity or relationship. Another three appear to present prospects of developing similarly. Only four of his eighteen examples seem clearly devoid of any governmental tinge.[2]

Here is the "track record" of an experienced PR counselor and firm—indicating clearly the impact of government on the PR function.

Before delineating these varied contexts of PR interest or activity, it is immediately suggestive and fundamentally necessary to understand that government and the citizen (individual or corporate) must "communicate" if government is to perform its proper limited functions and the citizen is not to be overwhelmed by government. Otherwise, there may be an end to our political and governmental system as we know it. In a very special way, communication acts as a curb on unrestrained governmental power and as the first line of defense of the citizen. After all, the voice of the ballot box is merely another means of communication.

Such communications must lead to understanding between government and the private sector. While lack of communications usually leads to lack of understanding, communications proliferation does not inevitably result in understanding. It is all too easy to speak without being either heard or understood. Philip Elman of the FTC, a highly perceptive administrative agency member and winner of the 1967 Rockefeller Public Service Award—basing his words on long experience in the Justice Department and the FTC—has said: [3]

> An obvious answer to the problem of inadequate communications between business and government is more communication.
> . . . [but] more communication between business and regulatory agencies is not enough; there must also be a greater effort at mutual understanding.
> . . . [T]he problem of friction, hostility and misunderstanding will doubtless persist until there is a fundamental change in attitude—on both sides.

2. Categories of Interest and Activities.

The interests and activities of the PR practitioner fall into, or are affected by, the following general categories:

(a) Employment by a government agency or unit as a "PR man" or a "publicity man" although these classifications are legally taboo. See Section 9 below.

(b) Private sector public relations and publicity directed to the government as a sub- or separate public. See Section 19 below.

(c) Routine company regulation by government agency. See Sections 19 to 24 below.

(d) Government investigations involving a company or an industry. See Sections 6 and 7 below.

(e) Company litigation by or against the government. See Section 13 below.

(f) Adverse government publicity involving company or client. See Sections 5 to 11 below.

(g) The government and its various agencies as a source of information. See Sections 15 to 18 below.

(h) Non-adversary liaison with government. See Section 3 below.

(i) Acting as independent public relations or advertising counsel for governmental agencies. See Section 35 below.

(j) Government media and materials. See Section 17 below.

(k) Engagement in lobbying. See Chapter 23.

(l) Activity as "foreign agent." See Chapter 24.

(m) Political public relations, generally beyond the scope of this book.

3. Non-adversary Liaison with Government.

Some of the most important and productive PR activity in the government arena is entirely non-adversary and intended to have essentially the same results as similar efforts in the private sector: to make friends and influence people. It has many purposes, some of which are interrelated but still functionally distinctive.[4] Company PR programs should ordinarily have at least the following purposes:

(a) Prophylactic.

This is sometimes considered "image-building." Its purpose is to create a generally good relationship with government and the overall belief that the company is a good citizen, trustworthy, reliable and a law-abiding member of the business community. It is a long-range program and is normally directed toward a broad spectrum of government officers and personnel.

(b) Fact Finding.

This can be everything from a "mechanical" pick-up of news releases and reports from the administrative agencies to research in depth on a specific problem. It usually will involve government records rather than government personnel. Prosaic though it may appear, it is highly important and may be the foundation for important management judgments. It is also sometimes ignored by a company which either is unaware of its importance or relies on Washington-originated newsletters or "services," valuable though they may be.

(c) Exploratory.

This goes beyond mere fact-finding and seeks to ascertain on an ethical plane, in advance of general availability, the "thinking" of an administrative agency or a Congressional committee. It must be distinguished from advocacy of the company's position and is generally preliminary in character. Action or comment by one branch of government may spark exploration with another branch. It is essentially a "listening" function —born of intelligent inquiry.

Personal contacts of this sort may be improper if they become *ex parte* communications within the scope of the agency's rules. The rules of each agency should be consulted.

(d) Interpretive.

Much of the information developed in the fact-finding and exploratory processes requires interpretation. Government pronouncements are frequently ambiguous or, in the case of the agencies, represent a multiplicity of views.

For example, late in 1967, the FTC issued a proposed "revised version" of new rules to prevent misbranded wool imports from entering domestic channels of commerce under the Wool Products Labeling Act of 1939. This revision came after at least 14 months of consideration of the matter by the Commission. Yet, after all this time and effort and after public hearings, it required *four* separate "versions, dissents and statements" to present the views of the *five* Commissioners.[5] This kind of "split-thinking" is not uncommon.

This necessary interpretation will be done by company counsel insofar as the legal implications thereof are involved. On the other hand, the PR man, in constant touch with the source, may be better able to interpret and explain the background and contributing factors leading to "gray area" announcements. Familiarity here breeds understanding.

(e) Fact Supplying.

One of the most useful and constant activities is supplying information *to* the government people. They need honest, direct information and welcome sources which can supply it. This is not lobbying. Companies which have created an essential rapport with an agency will frequently be called upon for information concerning the entire industry of which they are a part. The same is true of the industry trade association.

(f) Advocative.

In addition to supplying information to a government agency, it may become necessary at times to "take a stand" and to advocate a position on behalf of the company or the industry. Such informal advocacy may sometimes prevent formal proceedings and considerable adverse publicity.

It takes many forms: individual confrontation by the PR man, legal counsel or a company officer; group meetings between government personnel and trade association officers or committees; the submission of written views; etc. However, whatever its form, the PR man is normally instrumental in seeking such opportunities and setting up the confrontation or submission.

(g) Cooperative.

This includes a multitude of continuing "services" to government personnel—all quite open and above-board—which "make life a little easier" for them. Usually such opportunities will not develop until after both sides have come to understand and trust each other. It may consist of such trivia as acting as a catalyst to set up a meeting with a third party; a few days' delay in issuing a company statement; assistance to an agency in co-sponsorship of a "briefing conference"; etc.

(h) Advisory.

Government—both federal and state—is making greater use of "advisory committees" drawn from business. Intended as a cross-section of interest and knowledge within an industry, the membership is usually made up of top officers from several companies and/or trade associations. Invitations are likely to be extended to officers of companies whose prior contacts with government have been satisfactory and workable—not necessarily humble or complaisant—again the result of constant contact and development of a quietly understanding relationship.

Such committees may bring to their members (and their several companies) added stature in the public mind, itself no mean result for good public relations.

(i) Responsive.

Government personnel—at all levels—are "people." They appreciate the amenities of personal intercourse and react favorably to them. They like, for example, to be congratulated on a speech or statement. Such events present an opportunity for constructive comment and assistance. To our knowledge, more than one delicate situation has been "saved" by just such a reaction. Such activities need not be "personal." Even a formal letter is useful and welcome.

B. GOVERNMENT PUBLICITY AND PUBLIC RELATIONS.

4. Purposes.

Government-originated publicity—in its many forms—has many purposes. Statements, news releases and speeches may be used to explain to the public the functions and purposes of an agency or an activity. They may seek public cooperation in some government program. They may implement a court's decision such as the 1954 Supreme Court school-integration ruling. They may seek support for pending legislation desired by the executive. They may announce appropriations. They may report routinely on the day-to-day official activities of an agency or the passage of some bill. They may be mere copies of, or notices about, public records. They may be reactions to rumors or "leaks." They may promote government personalities. They may criticize individuals or companies.

Probably there is little concern about, or objection to, many of these—despite the admittedly political or personal orientation of some of them. However, the concern does exist when such government publicity is used for other purposes—ends which are grossly self-serving, unduly prejudicial to private interests or of no service to any public or governmental purpose. Without any reference whatsoever to particular philosophies of government, the intelligent citizen resents and resists government-spawned publicity which is unfair and one-sided, perhaps subtly developed to create antagonism toward the private sector or to develop a prejudicial atmosphere for certain prospective proceedings, programs or projects.

In theory, at least, the prime function of government publicity is truthful information. Yet even conservative government officials sometimes admit that its purpose may actually be more self-serving. Thus Frederick Mueller, when Secretary of Commerce, addressed himself to "Government's True Role in Public Relations." While proudly pointing to his department's "open-door policy on information" and its activities as "the world's biggest collector of economic data," he nevertheless wrote: [6]

> The *creation of public confidence* is Federal public relations in its finest aspect. . . . [K]eeping the public aware that *the motivating spirit of government is good* also is a potent force in growth. . . . Giving such assurance to the people is a role of government in public relations. (Emphasis added.)

Despite its obvious restraint and its keying to the democratic process, such rationalization is self-serving and contributory to the prestige and maintenance of a desirable governmental image.

5. Publicity as a Regulatory Tool.

There can be no doubt that publicity is often used by government as a regulatory tool at the executive, legislative and/or administrative levels. A well-publicized presidential speech can have such results. Congressional committee hearings may also make an industry "behave itself" through the threat of new and adverse legislation. See Section 6 below.

At the agency level publicity or the threat thereof can be an ambivalent weapon. As indicated in Section 7 below, the SEC uses publicity to "inhibit unlawful activities." The FTC considers as "a major objective" of its economic reports the achievement of "significant remedial results by publicity on important economic problems." [7]

Wide publicity is sought by the same agency for its Guides, Trade Regulation Rules, etc. in the belief that such publicity will permit the honest business man to know what the law is and to conform to its mandates, a laudatory purpose but nonetheless regulatory.

Conversely, the agencies believe that the *absence* of publicity will contribute toward the acceptance by prospective respondents of consent orders. The threat of public adjudicative proceedings is frequently mentioned as a reason for a suggested lack of resistance to agency proceedings. For example, one Commissioner, in discussing the new Rules which permitted "consent negotiations in the investigational stages of a proceeding," said: [8]

> The procedure is of advantage to respondents, since it may eliminate at least some of the unfavorable publicity inherent in many investigations when a party's suppliers, customers or competitors must be interviewed in order to secure the information necessary to determine whether a complaint should issue.

In other words, the *threat* of increased publicity is used as a tool to induce a prospective respondent to "go along" and agree to a consent order though the government agency may not have enough facts or information to decide preliminarily whether there has been a violation. For further discussion of this technique and result—especially as it affects smaller businesses—see Section 11 below.

A prime example of "regulation by publicity" was the FTC investigation of a so-called "child appeal" advertising and public relations campaign by television manufacturers in 1950. The first advertisement in the campaign—apparently a test and used in only a few markets—appeared on November 13, 1950. Complaints about the campaign's orientation and theme immediately came into the FTC and the Commission announced at once that it was instituting an investigation. *Three days* later the campaign was withdrawn and the advertising agency handling it, in effect, apologized for it.

The Supreme Court has recognized the impact of adverse publicity resulting from governmental action. In *Gardner v. Toilet Goods Association* [9] the Court was dealing with the right of the Association to "pre-enforcement relief" against certain new FDA regulations requiring advance approval of color additives in cosmetics. The Court upheld such preliminary right. After pointing out that use of a color additive which does not satisfy FDA premarketing clearance procedures may lead to injunctive action, criminal prosecution and seizure, the Court went on to say:

> The price of noncompliance is not limited to these formal penalties. Respondents [members of the Association] note the importance of public good will to their industry, and *not without reason* fear the disastrous impact of an announcement that their cosmetics have been seized as "adulterated." (Emphasis added.)

See Section II below.

6. Congressional Investigations and Publicity.

The customary purpose of Congressional investigations is to develop information which will serve as the basis for new or modified legislation. Much such legislation has, in fact, stemmed from such investigations. Unfortunately some investigations—whatever their original and stated purposes may have been—have degenerated into "side shows" designed to satisfy the personal ambitions or individual beliefs of some committee chairman.[10] Francis Rourke points out: [11]

> No aspect of congressional activity other than investigations is as capable of attracting the attention of the public and of the communications facilities that both direct and reflect public interest. Investigations are a form of entertainment, even if they stir in the minds of some observers recollections of the Roman amphitheater or of the public trials and executions of revolutionary regimes. . . . [T]hey can compete with other forms of entertainment with which politics and political events are in competition for the voter's attention.
>
> *   *   *   *
>
> [T]he publicity attached to investigations may also serve a wide variety of self-interested purposes for congressmen or congressional blocs. The fact that prominence in a well-publicized investigation has enormous self-promotional possibilities for the individual legislator needs no documentation here. As the examples of Kefauver and Nixon in recent history reveal, the power of publicity can easily short-circuit the traditional dependence of the individual legislator upon length of service for power and prestige.

Not only are such investigations vehicles for personal power but they may frequently be disasters for the personal reputations of witnesses. In theory, such witnesses are merely contributors to evidence for new laws. In reality they are treated in both Congressional and readers' minds as being themselves on trial. Witnesses have committed suicide. Others have lost employment and been harassed for years thereafter; the perfectly legal "taking the Fifth Amendment" has created doubts and even vilification in public sentiment.

Self-seeking publicity and personal discreditation may be the normal results of these investigations. Such results are, however, often compounded by the deliberate tactics of the investigators. Probably the best remembered are those of Senator Joseph McCarthy. Among his tools was a continuing stream of statements about individuals under investigation, mostly based upon secret executive sessions, with much of it later to be discredited in the public hearings.

Similar techniques are sometimes used today. These include early-in-the-day news releases dealing with that day's testimony (not yet actually taken or in the public record), timed to meet early deadlines for the newspapers and wire services. Even though some of the testimony may later (the same day) refute the earlier releases, the damage has been done. The refutation rarely catches up with the accusation. Persons, companies or industries under investigation have learned to counter such tactics with their own "early" releases or news conferences so that the answer appears in the same story as the charge.

Edward Bernays, in writing of his activities during the 1938 investigation of A. P. Giannini and The Bank of America, comments ruefully about "government by headlines" and says: [12]

> The real case was being fought in the arena of the entire United States through the newspapers. The hearing room was only a platform for the participants to talk to the larger audience outside. . . . I could not wonder, as I watched Government attorneys presenting their case, whether professional zeal dominated their actions or whether they were functioning to gain good will with a sympathetic public or possibly to show how forceful they were and thus get themselves more secure and better-paid jobs outside of government.
>
> * * * *
>
> It was surprising to me that the U.S. Government should be using publicity as a weapon instead of relying on the law alone to win this case. For that is what was done. When headlines favorable to us appeared in the late-afternoon Washington editions of the newspapers, the SEC attorneys rushed statements about the case to the morning newspapers to kill any favorable impression. This happened more than once . . .
>
> * * * *
>
> Usually statements of the counter-offensive (Giannini's statements) did not make the same newspaper editions that carried the original Government accusation, which I think the SEC was fully

aware of and which was part of the strategy. In this case, fore-
warned by a ticker service, the morning papers carried our side of
the story too. Still I felt this was an injustice and suggested to A. P.
(Giannini) that he take the offensive against publicity tactics of
the Government. (Parenthetical matter added.)

While these comments were made in connection with SEC charges, they
describe well some of the tactics of certain publicity-eager Washington
personalities in all kinds of investigations. More than that, however, they
fortify the conviction that even in the Thirties, the importance of public
opinion in what presumably was a "legal matter" was deeply appreciated and that techniques—some not so subtle—had already been developed to create the desired public reaction and atmosphere.

7. Investigations and Publicity by Administrative Agencies.

Most administrative agencies have investigative powers, varying from
agency to agency and subject generally to the provisions of the Administrative Procedure Act.[13] Normally, these investigations—especially if
they involve an individual company only—will be undertaken and pursued without much public fanfare.[14]

They may be live field investigations or merely by correspondence—a
more or less polite inquiry asking for information and unaccompanied by
any threat of legal pressures.

They may, on the other hand, be in the form of a hearing—not
adjudicatory—but again they will usually be non-public, not even being
listed on the calendar of the agency.

On occasion, however, they will be open, public investigatory hearings.
This is more likely to be the case when the practices of an entire industry
or of a substantial segment of an industry are under inquiry. Sometimes a
public hearing is necessary under the requirements, for example, as to an
agency's rule-making powers.[15]

Some agencies are specifically given the authority to announce the
results of investigations. Among them is the FDA which, as discussed
more fully in Section 11 below, may publicly report concerning health
hazards after making an investigation. This right has been upheld
judicially.[16] The same right was upheld as to the SEC in a ruling that the
Commission did not abuse its discretion by announcing that an investigation was going to be made.[17]

Perhaps two of the most "notorious" agency announcements concerning preliminary governmental investigations were that made by FDA
through the Secretary of Health, Education and Welfare in 1959 concerning cranberry contamination by a chemical weedkiller and that of
the Public Health Service in 1955 concerning alleged dangers in the polio

vaccine from Cutter Laboratory, later acknowledged by PHS to be due to failure of certain of its own tests.[18]

The Sierra Club/Internal Revenue Service dispute of 1966 presents a more recent and rather "novel" example of investigation publicity and its effects on the party involved. On June 9, 1966 the Sierra Club, a tax-exempt organization under §170 (c) of the Internal Revenue Code, placed full page advertisements in New York and Washington newspapers, opposing the construction of Grand Canyon dams. *Four days* later IRS announced that it planned to investigate and reevaluate the Club's tax-free status because of its alleged efforts to influence state and federal legislation.[19] In December, 1966 such status was revoked.

If an organization is named in the IRS *Cumulative List,* donors to the organization may rely on deductibility of their contributions unless, among other reasons, they were aware that revocation of the tax-exempt status was imminent. What effect the early publicity release may have had on contributions to the Club is not clear. It is not difficult to posit very severe adverse results since tax-exempt status is so important to such contributions.[20]

In some cases in which the FTC has sought to hold a public hearing, its right has been questioned. In at least a few cases, the FTC did not proceed rather than meet charges that such a hearing violated the constitutional rights of the investigated party.[21] The parties under investigation had claimed that they had the same rights to counsel as in private hearings.

It has also been held that the procedural safeguards of the Administrative Procedure Act [22] applied to investigative hearings as well as adjudicative proceedings.[23] However, these rights are subject to certain limitations.[24]

The rights of a party under investigation should also be considered—especially insofar as detrimental publicity is concerned—in the context of the discussion of pre-adjudicative hearing publicity in Section 11 below. Logically, there are certain similarities. Jaffe and Nathanson have suggested that "perhaps the line between informal, investigatory hearings, and formal, adjudicatory or adversary hearings, is not crystal clear." [25]

8. Speeches by Administrative Agency Members.

"Speechmaking" is a well-known and highly-regarded PR technique in both private and government sectors. On the government side, Senators, Congressmen and administrative agency members constantly appear before trade associations and public groups of all kinds. In many of these appearances, the speaker espouses or explains the functions or purposes of his agency or discusses its future plans. Much of this oratory is salutary. It clarifies for the audience—through press pick-up, for the public generally —the nature, purpose and direction of the agency. It is a valuable communications tool.

Many sectors of business follow these speeches closely. They indicate much of the general "thinking" of the agency by which a company may be licensed, controlled or policed. Not infrequently such public comments are the first indication of prospective agency trends or policy changes.

Probably the most famous and most frequently cited such occasion was the "vast wasteland" speech of Newton Minow, then Chairman of the FCC, at a convention of the NAB.[26] It was in such a speech that Everette MacIntyre of the FTC first adverted substantially to the then prospective FTC program of Trade Regulation Rules—now probably one of the most important and controversial FTC methods of industry regulation.[27]

However, such speeches may raise serious legal issues. A principal issue is "prejudgment" of individual cases before the agency of which the speaker is a member. In the *Texaco* case,[28] for example, Chairman Dixon of the FTC had made a speech in Denver in 1961 before the National Congress of Petroleum Retailers. The substance of Mr. Dixon's speech—in his own later description of the occurrence—was: [29]

> [T]here was good reason to believe some unlawful price discrimination and price fixing was going on and the Federal Trade Commission proposed to do something about it. I also read off, from the various pending and completed cases, the names of the major oil firms then being proceeded against by the Commission.

Later Texaco took exception to Mr. Dixon's sitting in judgment on it in such a case and, on appeal to the circuit court, it was held that the Chairman had "prejudged" the pending cases before the Commission (including the *Texaco* case) and was thus "disqualified" from hearing them.

The effect of such "outside" utterances is not altogether clear. Other cases have not disqualified agency members or other government officials for prior speeches, letters or reports to Congress which had indicated a position on practices or cases which later came before them for adjudication. In the *Marquette Cement Manufacturing* case,[30] for example, FTC members were not disqualified because of their "reports" to Congress that the cement industry's basing point pricing practices were illegal. The court said:

> [T]he fact that the Commission had entertained such views as the result of prior *ex parte* investigations did not necessarily mean that the minds of its members were irrevocably closed on the subject of the respondents' basing point practices.

In the *National Lawyers Guild* case,[31] Attorney General Brownell was not disqualified to adjudicate whether the Guild should be designated a subversive organization because of a speech declaring "the evidence shows that the National Lawyers Guild is at present a Communist dominated and controlled organization fully committed to the Communist Party line . . ."

The attitude of the circuit court in *Texaco* was premised on its earlier position in the well-known *Amos Treat* case.[32] SEC Commissioner Cohen had been disqualified from hearing an SEC fraud case because he had earlier been on the SEC staff and had had some contact with the case in such capacity. The court there said:

> [A]n administrative hearing of such importance and vast potential consequences must be attended, not only with every element of fairness but with the very appearance of complete fairness. Only thus can the tribunal conducting a quasi-adjudicatory proceeding meet the basic requirement of due process.

In the *Permian Basin* case [33] Commissioner Black of the Federal Power Commission refused to disqualify himself—nor did the Commission itself find any disqualifying bias—because Mr. Black had previously, in a speech, appealed to a group of natural gas *retailers* to fight any legislation which would take from the FPC its jurisdiction over prices charged by natural gas *producers*. The producers charged that the Black speech indicated his "bias against independent producers as a class."

Agency members have long sought to remove any imprimatur of "official" from their public remarks and many of them—their staff people, also—warn preliminarily in their speeches that their opinions are their own and not those of the Commission. However, this does not appear to satisfy the "prejudgment" charge.

Since the *Texaco* decision agency members are going further—their obvious purpose being to forestall, if possible, any future accusation of this sort. For example, Commissioner Reilly of the FTC addressed The Trade Relations Association in September, 1967. His subject was reciprocal trade relations between two companies—what may be called "one hand washing the other." The opening paragraph of his remarks, according to the FTC release, read as follows: [34]

> Before proceeding I want to emphasize that my remarks today were prepared without reference to any matter, formal or informal, currently before the Federal Trade Commission, and while my attitude toward reciprocity as an abstract question will certainly emerge in the course of my remarks, I have formed no opinion as to specific fact situations involving specific firms which may come before the Commission in the future.

When FTC Chairman Dixon was testifying before a Senate subcommittee, he prefaced his statement by saying: [35]

> You understand, of course, that I labor under some disability in discussing matters now receiving attention by the Commission and its staff. I have carefully avoided any discussion or even significant understanding of the facts, in order that I may remain impartial in my consideration, anticipating that adjudicative proceedings may be presented for determination. I believe, however, that I can offer some general comments with propriety.

9. General Criticism of Government "Public Relations."

It is a generally accepted fact that essentially every branch of government employs public relations and publicity people. Yet—in the federal structure at least—nowhere will there be found a job classification or responsibility using the words "public relations" or "publicity." Furthermore such terminology is *legally* unacceptable. The PR practitioner in government service is usually a "public information officer," a "director of public information" or a "press aide."

"Public Relations" is still a "dirty word" in government circles.[36] This stems from a traditional hostility to the function on the part of Congress notwithstanding the legislators' own reliance on, and use of, the function. This antipathy goes back, as a matter of affirmative statute, to 1913 when Congress directed that: [37]

> No money appropriated by any Act shall be spent for the compensation of any publicity expert, unless specifically appropriated for that purpose.

This mandate was prompted by an advertisement of the United States Civil Service Commission seeking a "publicity expert whose . . . affiliations with newspaper publishers and writers is extensive enough to secure publication of items prepared by him." This 1913 statute continues on the federal lawbooks.[38]

Indicative of the still-lingering Congressional antagonism to publicity and public relations as elements in federal activities, paid for with Congressionally-appropriated funds, are the repeated annual budgetary inquisitions by the House Appropriations Committee. Thus, in 1965, the United States Travel Service was closely questioned as to why about one-half of its budget was spent with advertising and public relations firms both here and abroad.[39]

When President Kennedy was concerned about the fate of his foreign trade policy in 1962, he added to the White House staff Carl Levin, Washington vice-president of Schenley Industries, to head up a public relations program. A knowledgeable Washington correspondent said this about the appointment: [40]

> In the government lexicography, "public relations" is a "hate word"—several degrees lower than "Madison Avenue." So the rose must be called by another name. And at this advanced stage of his career, Mr. Levin finds himself engaged in "education."

The *apparent* purpose of the thousands of public relations men, publicity people, writers, etc. on the federal payroll is therefore "education" or conveyance of information. This is true notwithstanding their acknowledged penchant for publicity and promotion for the agencies and departments they serve.

The press, also, has been vocal over the years in criticizing both the purely informational and the publicity activities of government. On the one hand they have decried lack of access to government information; on the other they have assailed, as self-serving and pseudo-political, efforts to provide them with seemingly "normal" news. Some of the latter criticism has been capsulized as "management of the news," "propaganda," "lobbying," "waste of the taxpayer's money," "free publicity for hungry politicians," "exploitation of the public," "glamorizing," "publicity for a bigger agency budget," etc.

The "lack of access" aspects may have been remedied by the passage of the Freedom of Information Act, discussed in Section 18 below. It is unlikely that the alleged perversion of the PR or publicity function will ever be resolved. It is too laden with emotional and political overtones to be subdued by statute or rational reappraisal although efforts are being made in those directions. See Section 12 below.

The criticism of federal PR or publicity activities carries over to state or municipal levels. The same charges are made and the same problems exist. They may even be intensified because state and local governments are "closer to the people" than the federal government. The misuse of local government publicity strikes closer to home with a resultant local reaction by both press and public which is deeper and more direct.

Within all three perimeters, however, the solution seems to lie in the same direction: a self-restrained and intelligent search by government for *balance* as to both the purposes of the PR and publicity and the tools used in achieving a desirable and legitimate end. See Section 12 below.

10. Irrelevant and Distorted Publicity.

Much of the constant flow of government publicity is salutary, illuminating and proper. A good portion of it is even mandated by such federal laws as the Freedom of Information Act. Some of it, however, is irrele-

vant, unnecessary, or designed to "accentuate the positive" and "minimize the negative"—sometimes to such an extent as to damage seriously
the private individual or company concerned.[41]

In the *Silver King Mines* case,[42] for example, the SEC had "automatically" issued news releases which were not relevant to the action and the
court said:

> In the issuance of such releases, the Commission did not give
> consideration to any questions of public justification, as contrasted
> to potential private harm. There was, in fact, no sufficient public
> justification, when compared to the potential harm to the individ-
> ual, to warrant the instigation of such publicity as mentioned
> above.

In the same case the court referred to an SEC explanation of a 1964
amendment of its Rules, the purpose of the change being to avoid criticism based on the charge that the SEC "tries its cases in the newspapers
before the respondent has an opportunity to defend itself." [43]

As another example, in hearings before the Senate Subcommittee on
Antitrust and Monopoly investigating possible anticompetitive effects of
TV rates, an allegedly deceptive chart showing corporate TV expenditures in the coffee industry was at issue. Committee counsel suggested
that the explanatory breakdown of the chart, demanded by Senator
Hruska, a minority member, be "put into an appendix" to the record.
Senator Hruska retorted, "Ah, that famous appendix. Put the thing in
the headlines and then on page 32 put a little correction of the headline." [44] Examples such as this could be multiplied and are well-known
to PR practitioners.

Even when distorted or unfair releases are issued and exception thereto
is taken by the parties affected, the agency is likely to give the parties
short shrift. The FTC for example has said, in such a situation, that a
news release is not part of the case record and therefore need not be
suppressed or explained properly by a supplemental release.[45]

However, some relief is possible by appeal to the courts as discussed in
Section 11 below.

11. Publicity Before Judgment.

In 1967 two cases brought into sharp focus the propriety of the issuance
of press releases and other publicity by government agencies *before* the
hearings on the government complaints. These were the *Cinderella
Schools* [46] and the *Diapulse* [47] cases.

Both cases turned on "pretrial publicity" and the right to a fair and
unprejudiced trial of the issues.

In *Cinderella* the FTC was enjoined from issuing any further news releases until final adjudication of a false advertising case since, as the court said, such releases give "the appearance of constituting a prejudgment of the issues." In *Diapulse,* the company sought an injunction against FDA releases during seizure proceedings, claiming that its rights had been prejudiced by an FDA "tirade of publicity by newspaper and radio." The court held that it had the power to issue the injunction but that the company had not, in fact, proved prejudicial publicity. The court said:

> A United States court has the inherent power—indeed, it is under a plain duty—to take whatever action may be necessary and appropriate to assure a fair trial, regardless of how the proceedings are labeled: criminal, civil, admiralty or otherwise. *The assurance of a fair trial includes safeguarding against prejudicial pretrial publicity, regardless of the type of action.* (Emphasis added.)

The court in *Cinderella* recognized the impact of the FTC's news release concerning the issuance of its complaint, pointing out:

> [The release] in general created and spread throughout the public and business community the impression that the respondents were guilty of unlawful and deceptive practices and were not honorable or ethical persons with whom to be doing business. . . . [Such an impression] is the inevitable consequence of the issuance and distribution of news releases by the Commission prior to the final adjudication of a quasi-judicial proceeding.

Coincident with this case, the FTC began to insert in its initial-complaint news releases "disclaimer" language in the form of the following NOTE: [48]

> (NOTE—A complaint is issued whenever the Commission has found "reason to believe" that the law has been violated and that a proceeding is in the public interest. It is emphasized that the issuance of a complaint simply marks the initiation of a formal proceeding in which the charges in the complaint will be ruled upon after a hearing and on the record. The issuance of a complaint does not indicate or reflect any adjudication of the matters charged.)

As this is written there has been no judicial determination as to the legal efficacy and acceptability of such language.

These holdings are specific applications of the language of the Supreme Court in the leading case of *Joint Anti-Fascist Refugee Committee v. McGrath.*[49] The court there said that federal publication of statements (in that case the government's list of "communist" organizations) will "cripple the functioning and damage the reputation of those organizations in their respective communities and in the nation" even without the opportunity to be heard. Justice Frankfurter, in his concurring opinion, explained further that such publicity can itself cause grievous harm, stating:

> This Court is not alone in recognizing that the right to be heard before being condemned to suffer grievous loss of any kind, even though it may not involve the stigma and hardships of a criminal conviction, is a principle basic to our society. Regard for this principle has guided Congress and the Executive. Congress has often entrusted, as it may, protection of interests which it has created to administrative agencies rather than to the courts. But rarely has it authorized such agencies to act without those essential safeguards for fair judgment which in the course of centuries have come to be associated with due process. . . . And when Congress has given an administrative agency discretion to determine its own procedure, the agency has rarely chosen to dispose of the rights of individuals without a hearing, however informal.

As suggested in this quotation, some administrative agencies do have Congressional authority to issue statements, reports and releases—however they may be described. Thus the FDA may: [50]

> . . . cause to be disseminated information regarding food, drugs, devices, or cosmetics in situations involving, in the opinion of the Secretary, imminent danger to health or gross deception of the consumer. Nothing in this section shall be construed to prohibit the Secretary from collecting, reporting, and illustrating the results of the investigations of the Department.

The SEC has also been authorized to issue statements and publish information concerning "any violations" of the 1934 Act.[51] A section of the Commission's *Manual of Administrative Regulations* is titled "Purpose of Publicity" [52] and states that publicity is an "important element in overall law enforcement activities of the Commission" since it, among other things, "tends to inhibit unlawful activities in the purchase and sale of securities by those who may not wish to risk the threat of exposure or possible imposition of statutory sanctions."

In 1958 and 1964 these Regulations were amended so as to restrict releases concerning the institution of public administrative proceedings and litigation to what is referred to as "bare bones releases." These are limited essentially to "an identification of the respondents, a brief reference to the general nature of the underlying charges, and an identification of the securities involved." [53]

On the other hand, it does not appear that the FTC has any Congressional mandate or authority under the FTC Act to issue such releases at the institution of an action.[54]

Even though an agency has the authority to publicize its actions, such publicity must be prepared and distributed with considerable circumspection. It may not be "prejudicial"[55] to the respondent and furthermore, as pointed out in the *Silver King Mines* case:[56]

> [A] unilateral or absolute discretion has not been granted to the [Commission] with reference to publicity; and *publicity which is arbitrary, capricious and unreasonable or for the purpose of bringing pressure to bear upon those involved in administrative or judicial proceedings . . . is beyond any grant of discretion or power to the Commission.* (Emphasis added.)

Throughout these admonitory cases run two grounds for restriction: prejudgment by the agency and premature publicity, prejudicial to the integrity of the respondents. The judicial attitude as to prejudgment in this context is similar to that shown in the *Texaco* case dealing with public speeches by administrative agency commissioners, discussed in Section 8 above.

As this is written, late in 1967, there was filed by Bristol-Myers Co. in the District Court for the District of Columbia an action seeking an injunction to bar the FTC from releasing any further publicity on the proposed FTC Trade Regulation Rule that would prohibit unproved advertising claims that one analgesic is speedier, stronger or longer lasting than another.[57] This is the first attack on the entire Trade Regulation Rule program of the FTC. See Chapter 20. The complaint recited a wide variety of factual, legal and constitutional reasons for the invalidity of the Rules and, as to this particular Rule, charged that the Commission's public statements on the proposed rule "have made Bristol-Myers look like a false advertiser and scofflaw" and further, that its "lawful advertising claims have been so severely prejudiced that, even if shown to be true, they may have to be dropped."[58]

This action is, therefore, undisposed of at this time and may well go far to test the validity and force of the entire Trade Regulation Rule approach by the Commission. It may also contribute to settling important questions about publicity used in connection with an agency's rule-making power. See Section 7 above.

However, even before the filing of the action, it seemed clear that the public statements made by the Commission in connection with this Rule —affecting, as it does, the advertising of a small group of companies and dealing with a single product—were likely to have an adverse public effect on the stature of the companies and the products in the eyes of the public.

12. Prospective Restrictions on Government Publicity.

Some sectors of government are coming to realize the need for caution and circumspection in the preparation of their press releases and other publicity. Addressing himself to the need for "corrective action," Philip Elman of the FTC has said: [59]

> For example, the Federal Trade Commission's policy of publicizing formal charges of violation of law, . . . has created particular sensitivity in its relations with the business community. . . . The Commission can and should make every effort to ensure that its press releases are fair, factual, and objective, and do not leave an erroneous impression as to the status of the proceedings.

As indicated in Section 11 above, the SEC now puts out "bare bones releases" as to public administrative proceedings and litigation, noting only the identity of the parties, the general nature of the charges and of the securities involved.

In June, 1967 the FHLBB—apparently as a result of the *Cinderella* decision—issued new rules which prohibit publicity on pending investigations of savings and loan associations subject to its jurisdiction. Unless specifically ordered by the Board, the entire investigatory and hearing record is not to be made public.[60]

Thus slow and irregular progress towards an end of prejudicial government agency publicity is being made. This is coming only through the gradual development of an "administrative conscience" under the impact of scattered court decisions. Something more is needed to accelerate the change. Action by Congress may be the answer.

A Congressional attempt has been made to curb—or at least circumscribe—administrative agency publicity. In 1966 an amendment to the Administrative Procedures Act passed the Senate but not the House.[61] This would have outlawed such preliminary publicity unless the respondent was accorded an equal opportunity to publicize his own comments at the same time and in the same document in which the agency publicity was issued.

In 1967, a similar Bill (S.924) was again introduced under the co-sponsorship of Senators Long and Dirksen. This provides, *inter alia,* as follows: [62]

> (c) PUBLICITY.—If a reviewing court finds that publicity which was issued by the agency or any officer, employee, or member thereof, did discredit or disparage a person under investigation or a party to an agency proceeding, that court may hold this to be prejudicial error and may set aside any action taken by the agency

against such person or party or enter such other order as it deems appropriate. It shall not be deemed prejudicial error, however, if such person or party has been given an equal opportunity to publicize his comments at the same time and in the same document in which the agency publicity was issued.

In the course of introducing the legislation, Senator Long castigated particularly the FTC, FDA and the SEC as being the source of "perhaps the most flagrant illustrations of this practice," referring to the agency press releases as "issued primarily for the purpose of trying the case in the newspapers. As a result, innocent individuals and businesses are often damaged; and the guilty are prematurely injured." [63]

The basic policy behind legislation of this kind was expressed by Senator Long in the following language:

> When dealing with this area of freedom of information, there are, of course, many problems involved. It must be clearly understood that this bill does not restrict and should not be used to restrict any information in any way. When an agency issues a complaint, that complaint is a public record. Our bill is aimed at preventing the disparaging press release which an agency often issues pursuant to the complaint for the sole purpose of degrading the subject of the complaint. Let no Federal agency think this bill would in any way give them the right to violate the freedom of information law. Let no agency think that it can withhold information the public has a right to know. What our bill demands of each agency is honesty and fairness in dealing with extremely vital and sensitive matters of public interest. It is our belief that if the principles of this bill are enacted, we would not only insure freedom of information but equality and fairness of information.

13. The "Public Relations" Decision.

In negotiations with a federal agency as to possible settlement of a prospective formal complaint, one of the basic premises to be considered is the susceptibility of the company to adverse publicity. Unless the company is clearly at fault and has no defense, a value judgment must be made as to whether to accept a consent decree or some other form of preliminary settlement which involves less exposure to public criticism.

Obviously the advice of legal counsel is fundamental on such matters as the adequacy of any available company defense, the legal posture of the company in any future triple-damage suits resulting from the settlement, etc. These matters are not within the scope of this work nor of the PR advisor to the company. If, however, legal counsel believes that a consent settlement *may* be in order, the final decision may well rest on public relations considerations. Here the advice of the PR counselor is likely to be vital and determinative. See Chapter 1, Sections 13 to 16.

Not every company is concerned to the same extent about such adverse publicity. *Ad hoc* decisions are therefore in order. In some instances they are not likely to be easy—especially if calculated risks are involved as to either legal or PR consequences.

The PR value judgment is likely to rest on the following—or some of the following—factors:

(a) Whether the company is in a monopoly position;

(b) The relative economic level of the company if it is in a competitive industry;

(c) The prestige of the administrative agency threatening the publicity sanctions;

(d) Whether the company competes on a price or a quality basis;

(e) The overall public relations awareness of the company.

The last factor may contribute much to the decision. While recognizing that the evidence may be "fragmentary," Rourke writes: [64]

> Insofar, at least, as the institutionalization of the public relations function occurs only in firms of relatively large size, there may also be said to be a positive correlation between size of firm and sensitivity to governmental control by the publicity sanction. This assumes that with the employment of a public relations specialist, a firm undertakes a decisive commitment to give public relations considerations important standing in its decision-making process. A corollary assumption is, of course, that the introduction of a specific spokesman for public relations considerations into the executive hierarchy results in a significant increment being added to the influence of the public relations factor in policy decisions.
>
> The quest for favorable publicity signalled by the employment by business firms and other institutions of public relations counselors is in part an attempt to avoid the obvious economic penalties that may follow in the wake of adverse public attention, such as a reduction in sales. In part, also, it is a product of the desire to establish and maintain more subtle assets such as the respectability and prestige in the eyes of the community. The manner in which these psychological and economic incentives are woven together is difficult to determine, but it is at least likely that they reinforce as well as relate to each other.

This 1961 appraisal may seem to conflict somewhat with the results of a 1966 *Yale Law Journal* survey.[65] It was found that "small firms appear to suffer more from adverse publicity." In discussing publicity resulting from public investigations, the survey revealed:

> [S]mall businesses are subjected to public investigation more often than large ones, and small firms appear to suffer more from the adverse publicity that sometimes follows the hearing. For example, small firms reported more injury than did large firms resulting

from public accusations against officers. This result seems natural since large firms often have institutional images unrelated to any particular officer. Moreover, small firms could not repair their images as easily by firing the officer since he was more probably a substantial owner. In highly fragmented industries many small firms complained that their competitors used public accusations to seek business. Large firms did not make similar complaints, apparently because their markets are more stable and because their customers would have considered such tactics bad form. The public hearing also exposes information which is normally guarded closely by small firms. The disclosure of this information could change a small firm's profit to a loss.

This is validated by Philip Zeidman, General Counsel of the Small Business Administration, who has said: [66]

I am convinced that the effects of a public regulatory action, or even a public investigation by a Federal regulatory agency, weigh more heavily on small business than on large business. . . . [F]or a small business, the effect of such an action may not as easily be overcome.

These comments emphasize the difficulty sometimes inherent in making a decision concerning corporate effects of government-originated publicity.

14. Counter-publicity.

If a company decides to "fight" a government action—or is forced to do so—the result may be a "publicity battle." Even routine government releases may be expected at each step in the litigation and the company must be prepared to counter them. The 1953 case of the FCC against Edward O. Lamb, seeking renewal of his Erie, Pennsylvania TV station license, is a prime example of such a "battle of releases." Later to be exonerated by the Hearing Examiner, Lamb was charged by the FCC with being linked to communist activities. Lamb fought the FCC publicity with newspaper advertisements and legal counteractions for libel, "matching broadside for broadside." This continued from the beginning to the end of the case and led to the comment: [67]

If this case represents a trend, the press release is as important a weapon in adversary proceedings before regulatory agencies as the legal brief, and newspaper publicity will come to occupy more of an attorney's attention than trial strategy.

There are certain legal dangers in the counter-publicity. Some of it takes the form of paid advertising, endeavoring to explain the company's position and to rebut the government's charges. In the *Imdrim* case [68] such a company advertisement was itself held to be deceptive and subject to district court action.

The susceptibility of purely PR counter-efforts to charges of deception was highlighted in the 1967 hearings of the Senate Monopoly Subcommittee on competition in the pharmaceutical industry. The Chairman, Senator Gaylord Nelson, complained about a four-page institutional advertisement in *Reader's Digest,* placed by the Pharmaceutical Manufacturers Association in its resistance to the "generic-name campaign" and to attacks on the allegedly high price of brand-name drugs. About 1 million reprints were sent to members of Congress, legislators, doctors and others but the caption "Special Advertising Section" was removed from the reprints which were in "article form." The FDA was said to believe that some parts of the campaign were misleading. The Justice Department and the FTC were described as "investigating" although they indicated that they could not prejudge the validity of the advertisements.[69]

The usual PR and publicity techniques are always open to the respondents or defendants in these cases. The "maneuverings" of the parties in the Bank of America litigation, described in Section 6 above, are instructive as to some of the available counter-measures. Legal counsel can be very useful in the public relations or publicity campaign and close liaison between the legal and PR arms should be maintained at all times when it becomes apparent that publicity values are likely to be involved in either an investigation or litigation. See Chapter 1, Sections 13 to 16.

C. ACCESS TO GOVERNMENT INFORMATION.

15. Purpose and Need.

The Senate Report on the 1967 Freedom of Information Act quotes the still significant comment of James Madison, who as Chairman of the committee which drafted the First Amendment, said: [70]

> Knowledge will forever govern ignorance, and a people who mean to be their own governors, must arm themselves with the power knowledge gives. A popular government without popular information or the means of acquiring it, is but a prologue to a farce or a tragedy or perhaps both.

Madison was but echoing the earlier words of Patrick Henry:

> To cover with the veil of secrecy the common routine of business is an abomination in the eyes of every intelligent man.

It is this need for informed public opinion, based on accurate and continuing knowledge of the activities—overt and otherwise—of government, which has led to the continuing struggle between press and public on the one hand, and the government, federal and state, on the other. It is not enough to permit government to "hand-feed" the public with such news or information as it may think sufficient. Harold Cross has said: [71]

> Citizens of a self-governing society *must* have the *legal right* to examine and investigate the conduct of its affairs, subject only to those limitations imposed by the most urgent public necessity. (Emphasis added.)

This right, recognized by the Founding Fathers, has become even more important as government has proliferated and has injected itself more and more into our society and the functioning of private and business intercourse.

The government's "right to know" about the activities of the private sector has been abundantly reenforced by statute and court over the years. We need only mention the annual income tax return and the innumerable "forms" which business must file. The public's correlative right has been but slowly implemented by a slow, steady, constant stream of litigation and sporadic statute. This has been true at both the state and federal levels.

16. The Governmental Tendency Toward Secrecy.

From the constitutionally-protected foundations, the historically documented struggles and the political or social argumentation, it is clear that the people of the United States—probably more than in any other country—have a deeply ingrained national aversion to secrecy in government. The counter-belief in open publicity for government is, in fact, the basis of our fundamental "checks and balances" system. Without open knowledge by one branch of the works and workings of the others, the system must fail.

Yet a great deal of secrecy exists in our government at all levels and in most sectors.[72] This tendency towards secrecy—now happily somewhat reversed as discussed in Section 18 below—represses the citizen, the press and even the several branches of government in their dealings with each other. In the latter relationship we might go so far as to pose the question of the marketplace: "Does Macy's tell Gimbels?"

Exemplifying the internal governmental refusals of information is the continuing effort made by a group of Congressmen during 1967 to obtain records and information as to the operation of the Office of Economic Opportunity. Because of reputed "scandals" OEO refused persistently to supply to the Congressmen the requested information despite the fact that, "except for the Department of Defense, the publicity staff of the Office of Economic Opportunity is the largest and most aggressive in the Government," according to Robert Allen and Paul Scott, who go on to describe it—as of mid-1967—in these specific terms: [73]

> Headed by Herbert Kramer, one time vice president in charge of public relations and advertising for a large insurance company, the press staff numbers around 50 and has a budget of more than $2.4 million.
> Around one-half million of that is for salaries alone. For these publicity agents, some with salaries exceeding $20,000, the anti-poverty program is juicy pickings.
> Kramer and his army of assistants have a high-speed duplicating machine that can pour out 2400 handouts an hour, 10 telephone lines, and Kramer or one of his lieutenants is available to newsmen around the clock.
> They send out a steady stream of OEO propaganda ranging from business-like newsletters to slick and elaborate magazines. Lately, OEO publicity has concentrated on glamorizing the scandal-racked Job Corps centers—which admittedly are in serious difficulty in Congress.

This is also an excellent example of the difference between the purely informational function and the "glamorizing" function of government PR and publicity.

Many reasons have been suggested for this inclination toward close-mouthed protection of official "secrets." Among them are:

    (a) National security.[74]

    (b) Monolithic isolation of government.

    (c) "Competition" between the several branches of government.[75]

    (d) Instinct and the personal insecurity of government personnel.

    (e) Traditional "mystique" of the "state."

    (f) Channeling of information through information officers oriented only toward favorable publicity.

    (g) Legislative philosophy of "limited disclosure" rather than "limited withholding."

    (h) Repeated specific Congressional mandates against disclosure and privileges to agencies to make non-disclosure rules.

    (i) Loose language of the "housekeeping act" of 1789 and Administrative Procedures Act of 1946.[76]

    (j) Executive prerogatives of non-disclosure.

    (k) Judicial approval of many forms of secrecy by the executive and legislative.[77]

Many of these factors which have accreted over almost two centuries of our national history have little sound basis; some are merely psychological shibboleths unworthy of honest men; others have been swept away by the Freedom of Information Act discussed in Section 18 below; still others are likely to stand far into the future because of their basic soundness or important judicial affirmation and support.

17. Nature of Government Informational Materials.

Generally speaking, there are two categories of government information with which the business world may be concerned:

(a) Information concerning government activities of all kinds. Such information is usually disseminated through a wide variety of day-to-day news releases, monthly cumulative reports, annual reports, copies of official documents, instruction materials, special reports, hearing testimony, correspondence in reply to specific inquiry, news conferences, etc.

(b) Materials distributed by the Government Printing Office, some of which may have no connection with government activities or which may result from research by government departments or agencies.[78] Usually such materials are priced quite reasonably—even nominally—compared to commercially printed matter. Much of it is of a character that would be unlikely to appear under a commercial colophon.

However, in recent years and particularly since 1967, several branches of the federal government have been considering their own publication of a great mass of information, largely in the scientific fields. This would be in direct competition with the business and industrial press. At least two such publications have already appeared: *National Standard Reference Data System* and *FDA Papers,* the latter published by the FDA at an annual subscription rate of $5.50. This is a "slick," four-color magazine competitive in every way with similar "books" available in the commercial publishing trade. Its contents, however, are completely oriented to FDA activities and some have characterized it as "an expensive reader-supported puffsheet for the FDA."

The future of this, apparently new, category of government-disseminated information is not clear. It has created considerable opposition in commercial printing and publication circles.[79] Furthermore, a governmental effort is being made to impose certain limitations on the tax-exempt status of "learned societies" and other groups which publish "journals" carrying advertising which produces a profit for the organization.[80]

These two programs, if carried to logical fruition, could lead to the government's increasing dominance of the "information explosion" and curtail substantially the private sector's participation therein.

18. Freedom of Information Act.

On July 4, 1967 the Freedom of Information Act became effective.[81] The importance of this new statute has already been equated—by both date and significance—with the Declaration of Independence.[82] Technically it is an amendment to Section 3 of the Administrative Procedure Act of 1946.[83]

The Act is the culmination of a long, continuous effort—beginning in 1941—when the Attorney General's Committee on Administrative Procedure unanimously agreed that the field of administrative law suffered from "an important and far-reaching defect": lack of adequate public information concerning the substance and procedure of administrative law. This the new law seeks to remedy and does remedy to a significant degree. It recognizes a basic public "right to know."

The new statute has been described as a "disclosure statute" rather than a "withholding statute" as had been the previous laws on the subject of access to government information. According to the Senate Report on the bill [84] the new law makes the following major changes:

> (1) It sets up workable standards for what records should or should not be open to public inspection. In particular, it avoids the use of such vague phrases as "for good cause found" and replaces them with specific and limited types of information that may be withheld.
> (2) It eliminates the test of who shall have the right to different information. For the great majority of different records, the public as a whole has a right to know what its Government is doing. There is, of course, a need for confidentiality in some aspects of Government operations and these are protected specifically; but outside these limited areas, all citizens have a right to know.
> (3) The revised section (3) gives to any aggrieved person a remedy in court.

The new Act represents an "about-face" both in theory and substance. Previously, government agencies could withhold essentially what they wished, even as to final opinions and public records which could be "held confidential for good cause shown." And, also, these were to be disclosed only "to persons properly and directly concerned" therewith.[85] Therefore, if something is *now* to be withheld, *the burden is on the government* to prove a right to withhold, rather than on the person seeking the information, as was usually the case in the past.

It had been charged that, under the old law, the withholding privilege was used as a subterfuge to "cover up embarrassing mistakes or irregularities" [86] or as a basis for the government official to "equate national security with job security." [87] Under the new statute, withholding will be justified only if the record falls within nine specific exemptions. Judicial review is now available. The official involved in the withholding will no longer be the one to make the final withholding decision.

The "any person" provision in the new law removes the requirement that the inquirer be "properly and directly concerned" with the requested data. The Attorney General had previously interpreted this to mean "individuals who have a legitimate and valid reason for seeking access to an agency's records." [88] Under this interpretation each agency had been "the primary judge" as to an applicant's interest in seeking information.

The Act specifically exempts nine types of records or information from the disclosure requirements. These exemptions deal with certain aspects of national defense and foreign policy, matters solely relating to internal agency procedures, information specifically protected by other statutes, trade secrets and information given the agency in confidence, internal agency or inter-agency communications, unwarranted invasion of the privacy of personnel, agency investigation materials, data concerning financial institutions and information concerning "wells."

Unless a record comes within these limited exemptions, it may not be withheld from the public. Further, these exemptions may not be used by an agency as authority to withhold information from Congress.

These exemptions—as is the Act generally—are explored at considerable length in the *Attorney General's Memorandum on the Public Information Section of the Administrative Procedure Act,* issued by the Department of Justice in June, 1967. This Memorandum is probably the best available source of authoritative explanation of the Act. It is "required reading" for all affected in any way by the Act and is obtainable from the Government Printing Office, Washington, D.C. at a cost of 25 cents. The Memorandum is also "intended to assist every agency to fulfill" its obligation under the Act "and to develop common and constructive methods of implementation."

The Act requires that each agency shall adopt "published rules" applicable to disclosure of its records in accordance with the Congressional mandate. These have been published in the Federal Register.[89] They are also available in the compiled Rules of the agencies. Quite naturally the availabilities differ from agency to agency by virtue of the varying jurisdiction and activities of the several agencies. Reference should be made to the Rules of the agency with which a person may be concerned.

The specific application of the Act and particular agency Rules will await future judicial determinations of specific instances. Several such cases are now pending as this is written.[90]

D. GOVERNMENT REGULATION.

19. Public Relations and Government Regulation.

From the point of view of public relations and the business communicator "government regulation" means essentially two things:

(a) Industry Regulation.

This includes all of the specific statutes, regulations and interpretations applicable to operations within a given industry such as banking, railroading, food processing, etc. Generally speaking, such particularities are beyond the thrust of this work.[91]

(b) Communications Regulation.

These are the "horizontal" regulatory measures which affect all communications activities of industry—quite apart from the specific nature of any industry. The control applies to the communication function rather than to the industry.

20. Basis of Communications Regulation.

The basis of communications regulation is "truth" and the thrust of government policing is against "deception." However, both "truth" and "deception" have come to be words of art as used in this legal area. As "public interest" and "the consumer" have come to be more and more the subject of expanded government interest and protection, the definition of both "truth" and "deception" has changed. Today, it is almost impossible to define with any certitude the limits of the terms.

Furthermore, "unfair" is often conjoined with "deceptive" in the interdictions. This opens the door to the exercise of a regulatory discretion which probably is limited only by the capricious and the arbitrary.

A further basis for some regulation is the protection or attainment of social or economic ends. Whether this is a proper control basis is not within our province here. However, it does appear as increasingly fundamental to current control philosophy. The FCC requirement of free air time for opponents of cigarets, discussed in Section 22 below, is an example. Much of this type of regulation is premised on "fairness" also. Thus this FCC anti-cigaret requirement is postulated under the Commission's so-called "Fairness Doctrine."

Chapter 11 deals at length with deception and fairness as the basis for government regulation and discusses these requirements as enforced by many of the government agencies.

21. Power of the Administrative Agency.

In the regulatory scheme, the federal administrative agency looms very large. Congress rarely undertakes the direct enforcement of sanctions or regulations. It leaves this to the particular administrative agency charged by Congress with that specific responsibility. The acquired "expertise" of the agency is said to be important.

The rulings of an agency, based on that expertise, ordinarily will not be upset by a court. Thus Justice Cardozo held in the *Algoma Lumber Company* case [92] that a court could not substitute "its own appraisal of the testimony" for that of the agency and that "the findings of the [agency], if supported by evidence, shall be conclusive." He went on to explain this by saying:

> [The Commission] was created with the avowed purpose of lodging the administrative functions committed to it in a "body specially competent to deal with them by reason of information, experience, and careful study of the business and economic conditions of the industry affected," and it was organized in such a manner, with respect to the length and expiration of the terms of office of its members, as would "give to them an opportunity to acquire the expertness in dealing with these special questions concerning industry that comes from experience."

Thus the administrative agency is much more than a mere "finder of fact." It has the power, except for arbitrary or capricious actions, to decide whether a particular act or practice is unfair or deceptive and therefore illegal and enjoinable.

22. Dangers of Regulation.

Since the end of the last century, government regulation of industry and business has become an accepted part of the fabric of American government. With its origins in the Interstate Commerce Commission and the Sherman Act, a philosophy has evolved which has lead both the government and the governed to walk a tightrope of compromise whenever new areas of regulation are suggested or become necessary.

Many volumes have been devoted to explanation of this philosophy and this process.[93] It was probably well summed up by Bert Goss in 1967 when, in discussing consumer protection by the government, he said: [94]

> Effective consumer . . . protection should include that which will work out for his benefit and convenience without undue cost or serious injury to the economy.

This is a statement of the effective and workable compromise so basic to progress and acceptable government regulation.

Unfortunately the power of regulation sometimes feeds on itself. Well-intentioned and even necessary controls can sometimes be pushed to extreme, illogical and burdensome limits.

The anti-cigaret campaign of the 1960's is sometimes cited as a prime example of this by even disinterested observers. It is not necessary to take sides on the basic cigaret/cancer-emphysema issue to see how "from a dubious premise [the government] has proceeded grandly to an absurd conclusion." [95] In 1964 the Surgeon General's report *Smoking and Health* appeared. Despite some questioned research, the FTC used the report as "proof" and sought to force cigaret packages and advertising to carry warnings which Congress believed too extreme. As a result—to limit the efforts of the FTC—the Cigaret Labeling and Advertising Law was passed.[96] However, Senator Magnusson and others continued to seek heavier sanctions against cigarets and their advertising. Senator Robert Kennedy sought a special tax based on relative tar and nicotine content as measured by the FTC.

Finally, in June 1967, the FCC, applying the "Fairness Doctrine" for the first time to commercial advertising, ordered all radio and TV stations to give cigaret foes a "significant amount of time" if the station carries cigaret commercials.[97] As this is written, this FCC ruling is under legal attack in the courts. Even FCC Commissioner Loevinger, though voting in favor of the order, said:

> No matter what the Commission now says about the distinction between cigaret advertising and other types, *it is establishing the principle that the Fairness Doctrine applies to commercial advertising,* as distinguished from paid political advertising. The Commission will be hard pressed to find a rational basis for holding that cigarets differ from all other hazards to life and health. . . . I am reluctant [to approve the order] because of concern that *this action may represent subjugation of judgment to sentiment.* (Emphasis added.)

When viewed against the background of the "consumer protection movement" generally, it is easy to understand Commissioner Loevinger's uneasiness about the supremacy of sentiment over judgment. It must also be remembered that these snowballing Congressional and administrative developments occurred in the face of a continuing and massive public relations and "educational" campaign by the tobacco industry.

Similar documentation of "emotional" regulation may be found in some aspects of the federal campaigns against brand-name prescription drugs and in favor of generic-name drug merchandising; the automobile safety requirements under the Automobile Safety Act;[98] and the court action against "the high cost of dying" instituted by the Justice Department late in 1967.[99]

The complaint about these government activities is not that they are "illegal" or not needed. It is with the emotional and even sometimes fanatic premises used and atmosphere created. A reader of newspaper releases from senatorial or federal agency information offices cannot help but believe that "the world will come to an end" if this or that legislation isn't adopted or this or that case won.

Business is all too often branded as some sort of Machiavellian ogre licking its chops at its successful bilking of the public, its glee changing to consternation and fear when the government seeks to save the public by ending the ogre's domination and machinations. Every semantic trick is used. Purple prose is ground out. The "hypoed" words come from so many government sources and functionaries that charges of "management" seem inescapable.

When the "packaging law" was finally adopted in 1966, it bore the legislative title "Fair Packaging and Labeling Act."[100] However, it was widely referred to by its sponsors and supporters as the "*Truth* in Packaging Bill." As time went on and the contents and target of the bill became clear, even government people had to admit that "truth" had little to do with the bill and that a businessman could still be in gross violation of the law no matter how truthful his packaging or labeling might be. Finally the absurdity of the nomenclature became apparent even to the bill's sponsors and the word "truth" gave way to "fair."

Another inherent danger in regulation is the conflicting jurisdiction between two or more agencies relative to the same product or activity. Examples are the FTC/Department of Agriculture conflicts as to food chains in their meat packing function[101] and the Comptroller of the Currency/Justice Department conflict in the bank merger cases.[102]

One court, in holding that a commodity broker was subject to both SEC and Department of Agriculture controls, has pointed out:[103] "There are numerous examples of businesses which are regulated by two or more regulatory agencies."

The dangers and ambiguities are compounded when the two agencies may have conflicting regulations or views. This occurs frequently in the above bank merger cases. It also exists in the presently pending FDA litigation and seizure because of labeling of Rheingold's Gablinger beer. The ATTR had cleared the label but FDA charged that its words "no available carbohydrates" implied that the beer was a weight-reducing product and therefore the label should contain calory content.

23. Roster of Federal Regulatory Agencies, Etc.

Federal regulation of the communications function is spread over many agencies, departments, bureaus, etc. The following alphabetical list is a roster thereof, together with an indication of the specific industries or areas with which each is concerned.[104] The scope of each unit's authority varies. All affect communications in some way but the specific thrust may vary over such particulars as publicity, promotion, advertising, labeling, speeches, mailings and other acts or practices.

Agriculture Department. Meat packers products; seeds; insecticides, fungicides and rodenticides; animal vaccines and drugs.

Alcohol and Tobacco Tax Division of the Internal Revenue Service. Distilled spirits, wines and malt beverages.

Civil Aeronautics Board. Airlines and ticket agencies, including fares, charges, contest promotions, etc.

Coast Guard. Representations concerning safety of American and foreign passenger vessels.

Commerce Department. References to Commercial Standards set by Bureau of Standards.

Customs Bureau. Claims made for certain imported products.

Defense Department. Advertising and promotion by defense contractors; use of all military and civilian personnel in PR, promotion, publicity and advertising.

Fair Employment Practices Commission. Employment practices.

Farm Credit Administration. Promotion of federal farm loans, etc.

Federal Aviation Administration. Public relations, publicity of contractors and bidders dealing with it.

Federal Communications Commission. All broadcasting activities.

Federal Deposit Insurance Corporation. Banks and institutions insured by it.

Federal Home Loan Bank Board. Federally-chartered savings and loan associations and state chartered associations insured by Federal Savings and Loan Insurance Corporation.

Federal Power Commission. Utilities subject to its jurisdiction, such as electric, gas, pipeline companies, etc.

Federal Reserve Board. Banks and institutions subject to its jurisdiction.

Federal Savings and Loan Insurance Corporation. See Federal Home Loan Bank.

Federal Trade Commission. Broad powers over unfair and deceptive practices in practically all industries and product categories.

Food and Drug Administration. Comprehensive controls of foods, drugs, cosmetics and devices.

General Accounting Office. Registration of and reports of lobbyists. (Prospectively, assuming passage of legislation referred to in Chapter 23, Section 21.)

Interior Department. Advertising on lands subject to its jurisdiction.

Internal Revenue Service. Tax status of publicity, promotion, public relations, advertising and similar expenses; tax status of political, legislative, institutional, publicity and advertising expenses; etc.

Interstate Commerce Commission. Representations concerning carrier rates and securities of common carriers subject to its jurisdiction.

Justice Department. Registration and reports by foreign agents.

Labor Department. Promotional practices of labor unions and by employers where labor practices are involved.

Library of Congress. Registration of copyrights, etc.

Narcotics Bureau. Narcotics and products containing narcotics.

National Labor Relations Board. Management/employee relations, communications and practices.

Patent Office. Patent agents.

Post Office Department. Mail fraud; contests and lotteries; pornography and obscenity; mailing privileges; direct mail controls.

Securities and Exchange Commission. Sale and promotion of securities.

Senate Clerk. Registration and reports of lobbyists. See General Accounting Office.

Treasury Department. Non-profit trade association tax status; marking of sterling silver; use of illustrations of United States and foreign coins, paper money, postage and stamps, bonds, securities obligations, etc.

All government agencies and departments. Use and reproductions of their official seals and insignia, grading stamps, badges, identification materials, etc.

24. State Regulation.

State controls, as with federal controls, are premised largely on "deception." Much of what is said in Chapter 11 is applicable here. However, state regulation in this area has not been effective nor very well enforced. Enforcement has been so sporadic that the public has come to ignore it and to look to the federal government in such matters.

The statute books of the several states are replete with a broad spectrum of both general anti-deception laws and specific product statutes.[105] These differ very considerably as to substance, form and procedure and are generally beyond the scope of this work.

The current consumer-protection program has led to many new state laws. These new statutes are usually of sweeping scope and applicable to many deceptive or unfair business practices, being patterned, in many cases, after the F.T.C. Act. Furthermore, their adoption has been accompanied, in some states, by new programs of consumer education and liaison. It may be expected that future state action against illegal communications or other practices will be taken under these new laws. See Sections 28 and 29 below.

E. CONSUMER PROTECTION.

25. History and Philosophy.

Any discussion of government regulation of business and communications must encounter and acknowledge "consumerism" and consumer protection as a vital fact of regulatory life. In theory at least, all government regulation of business has been intended as a direct protection of the public interest, which, again in theory at least, means protection of the community and the consumer. This certainly has been true since 1938 when the Wheeler-Lea amendments to the F.T.C. Act opened the door to action against business practices which were "unfair or deceptive" to the public, quite apart from their possible impact upon competition.[106]

Furthermore, exponents of consumer protection including Betty Furness—as this is written, the White House aide for consumer affairs—take the position that "consumer-type" activities by the government started in 1872 when Congress made it a crime to use the mails to defraud. Miss Furness then points to the Interstate Commerce Commission Act (1886), weights and measures protection (1901) and the Pure Food and Drug Act (1907) as other early milestones in consumer protection.

Despite this history, the "consumer" now has been set aside as a new "bloc" whose specialized protection is deemed necessary and to whom direct and forceful appeals for support are being made by government officials and politicians alike. Since the Kennedy campaign speeches of 1960, consumer protection has been a lively and apparently productive political issue during two presidential administrations.

This presidential context is appropriate because President Kennedy and President Johnson repeatedly put the prestige of their office behind the movement. Both frequently discussed, publicly and in messages to Congress, specific features of the snowballing drive for new laws, new regulations and new interpretations of existing laws.

As pointed out, there is really nothing new about "consumer-type" laws. The difference between the past and the present is largely semantic and atmospheric. As to semantics, the earlier laws were intended to protect the *public*. Frequent justification for them was found in the "*public* interest." Today, the word *public* has largely given way to the word *consumer.* The policy may be the same but the literary and oratorical garb is different—new, except for sporadic similarities in the 1930s.

The "atmosphere," as this is written early in 1968, is the big difference. The "consumer" is being split off from the rest of the country. This can only mean, split off from business and the sector which produces the things which the "consumer consumes." A wedge is being driven between two national elements which have historically been one. There were bilateral confrontations such as North/South, labor/management, farm/city. These were, at the time, divisions which were seemingly logical. The consumer/business split is not. Even the supporters of the consumer protection drive admit that "we are all consumers." [107] Yet the word is being given a symbolism which seeks to create a super-class, seemingly set apart from the culture and economy of which it is the very matrix.

Sharp, unilateral appeals are being made to this new bloc. Consumer meetings are being held all over the country. Supermarket picket lines have been encouraged. Sweeping promises of seemingly unending protection are being made. Local Consumer Councils are being formed. We have a Consumer Assembly, a Consumer Federation. The ghetto-dweller is being incited as a victimized and despoiled citizen. Labor's participation and support are being sought. Practically every PR technique is being used. Even in the Department of Agriculture—historically the voice of the farmer—a deputy director becomes the Deputy Administrator for Consumer Affairs and the department issues its annual yearbook under the title "Consumers All."

The political overtones are clear. Not the least is the fact that the average American is being turned into a complainer. He or she is being urged to "form committees, write letters . . . speak up and fight for your rights." President Johnson has said, "This is a consumer's administration. . . . Your Congressman should hear from you, too—loud and often." [108]

26. Effect on Public Relations.

It requires no crystal ball to predict that the PR function is going to be called upon with greater frequency and intensity to meet corporate problems—old and new—stemming from this quickening of the consumer protection movement. This is true whether the "consumer" is eventually considered as a new "public" or is equated with the traditional classifications of the community, the public or the various subpublics such as women, youth, the elderly, etc.

Both management and the PR man appear likely to find themselves wrestling with these new or intensified areas of concern:

(a) Basic company programs addressed to the consumer and consumer groups.

(b) Programs directed to government, concentrating on this consumer concept, including direct and personal liaison.

(c) Counseling as to legislative activity and trends for several years ahead.

(d) A greater emphasis upon relations with local government and the growing proliferation of local government units and personnel concerned with the consumer, as discussed in Section 29 below.

(e) Emphasis on company product-information campaigns emphasizing utility, serviceability and safety—perhaps even with a veering away from price.[109]

As a participant in the Public Relations News 1966 Forecast Forum, Bert Goss addressed himself to the PR and communications aspects of the consumer program and said: [110]

> Business faces a major problem in government relations. Our government is only beginning to put the legislation of the Great Society into effect. The success or failure of much of it will depend upon closer relations between government and business, or, more specifically, where the government seeks help and advice from business and whether business provides such support. Moreover, business must learn from the example of government itself and engage in total communication—personal contacts, lobbying, and PR—or its advice and suggestions may be overlooked and discarded because of attention accorded more insistent pleas from other elements of our society. It's a big task . . . to be done and needs to be done continuously, day in and day out, and at all levels. I hope business learns that.

This 1966 prognosis has proved to be accurate—at least into 1968—and its inter-related problems are becoming intensified and broadened.

27. Federal Consumer-Protection Activity.

President Kennedy campaigned for that office as "a lobbyist for the consumer" and in March, 1962 his presidential message to Congress announced four basic consumer rights: the rights to safety, to be informed, to choose and to be heard.

These four "rights" have already been implemented to a very considerable degree and, as this is written, many other bills are in the federal legislative hopper, with several Congressional committees actively holding hearings on them and other protective legislation.

At the White House level, a Consumer Advisory Council was appointed, which, in 1964, became the President's Committee on Consumer

Interests. Associated with it is the President's Assistant on Consumer Affairs. Esther Peterson was the first appointee, to be succeeded by Betty Furness.

By early 1968 Congress had passed the Fair Packaging and Labeling Act,[111] the Federal Child Protection Act,[112] the Automobile Safety Act,[113] the Highway Safety Act,[114] the Federal Cigaret Labeling and Advertising Act,[115] the Comprehensive Health Planning and Public Health Service Act,[116] among others. The Truth-in-Lending Act [117] was passed in 1968.

Congress is now holding hearings on such matters as drug prices and the effect of brand names, overall interests of the elderly, hazardous household products, controls over guarantees, automobile insurance charges and provisions and credit card misuse, some of which are already the subjects of pending bills.[118]

Administrative agencies are looking into such things as games of chance in supermarkets, effect of trading stamps on the cost of food, "cents off" promotions, loudness of TV commercials, educational or "public" television, cost of electricity to churches, cosmetic additives, children's aspirin, land sale methods, vending machine franchising methods, etc.

Bills or resolutions have been introduced for the creation of a new executive Department of Consumer Affairs,[119] a National Consumers Service Foundation [120] having supervision of a quality certification plan, dramatically called the Info-Tag,[121] and a National Commission on Product Safety.[122]

For the first time, the Senate has a permanent Sub-committee for Consumer Protection, now chaired by Senator Magnuson.

These are some of the trend-pointing federal laws, bills, investigations, rulings, etc. which may be expected, as this is written, to proliferate considerably with, as one Washington editor has said, "a barrelful of new legislation on the way affecting every aspect of production and sales" [123] and affecting, as Eric Severeid has said, "everything we eat, wear, use and hire." [124]

28. Federal/State Regulatory Cooperation.

One important limitation on regulatory action by any branch of the federal government has been, and is, the requirement that the offense, act or practice in question must be "in commerce" as that act is legally defined. This means essentially "in interstate commerce." Thus many practices, no matter how deleterious or offensive they may seem to be, are beyond the reach of the federal arm if they are performed within the borders of a single state—in "intrastate commerce."

It has long been recognized that this has been a real chink in the regulatory armor. State policing of such illegal practices has, for many reasons, been lackadaisical and indifferent. Many states do not have relevant laws under which State Attorneys General or District Attorneys could move even if they were so minded. There have been criminal fraud laws, a "Printers' Ink Model Statute" proscribing deceptive advertising, food and drug laws, regulatory product laws, etc. on the books of the states [125] but they were either not enforced or were so loosely written that they were not susceptible to enforcement. See Chapter 11, Section 20.

Within the last few years a new and active federal-state liaison has developed, leading to new state activity and statutes. The principal federal-state liaison—as might be expected—originated with the FTC which, in October 1965, began its cooperative program, appointing an Assistant General Counsel for Federal-State Cooperation. Close relations were established with all of the State Attorneys General and with many other state agencies, which report to the FTC on improper practices in their states. The FTC refers an increasing number of matters to them for action under state law, and the states, in turn, refer "interstate" practices to the FTC for action. In the last nine months of 1966, 327 cases were so referred, about 7 percent of all complaints received by the Commission in that period.

The FTC, in some cases, refers private complainants to the states even though the Commission could move, believing that grass roots enforcement is superior, if it is legally possible. The Commission believes that state action will increase considerably as more states become more interested in correcting "merely false and deceptive practices" in addition to the traditional crimes of fraud, larceny or obtaining money under false pretenses.

Probably the most important aid to the states is assistance in getting new laws on the states' books. These are of two types: (a) general laws interdicting false and deceptive practices, and (b) specific product laws such as those dealing with licensing of hearing aid dealers and regulation of correspondence and vocational schools. See Section 29 below.

Late in 1967 additional cooperative efforts were instituted by the FTC to implement the then new Fair Packaging and Labeling Act.[126]

Other federal agencies are cooperating with state agencies. In November, 1967, FDA "loaned" one of its top men to Illinois for six months to "assist Illinois agencies in setting up the enforcement machinery for the state's [new] Food, Drug, and Cosmetic Act." [127] This arrangement was made under the 1967 Federal Comprehensive Health Planning and Public Health Service Act.

29. State Consumer Laws.

As part of the current consumer-protection drive, many of the states have adopted, or are now adopting, new laws looking to action against a variety of unfair and deceptive practices and to consumer education. These have stemmed both from federal cooperation and action by the Council of State Governments. There are essentially three forms of such laws: [128]

(a) A law which would enable a designated State official to investigate and to enjoin "unfair methods of competition and unfair or deceptive acts or practices," similar to the authority contained in the F.T.C. Act. This form of legislation has been adopted in the States of Washington, Hawaii and Vermont. The law is administered in those States by the Attorney General. Vermont added a section to provide that the State Department of Agriculture, through its Extension Service, should carry on a related program of consumer education.

(b) The Council of State Governments suggested a draft of a law ("Unfair Trade Practices and Consumer Protection Law") which would enable the State official to deal with eleven specific kinds of deceptive practice and any others which "similarly" mislead the public. This has been adopted in Connecticut, New Mexico and Texas. The law is administered in New Mexico by the Attorney General, in Connecticut by the Commissioner of Consumer Protection, and in Texas by the Commissioner of Consumer Credit.

(c) Another form of law which seems to have considerable appeal is that adopted by Illinois is 1961 [129] giving the Attorney General power to investigate and to obtain a court injunction against

> The . . . use . . . by any person of any deception, . . . false promise, misrepresentation, or the concealment, suppression, or omission of any material fact with intent that others rely upon such concealment, suppression, or omission, in connection with the sale or advertisement of any merchandise (including real estate or services), whether or not any person has in fact been misled, deceived or damaged thereby . . .

This type of law permits the court to order restitution to any person actually damaged by the deceptive practice and to appoint a receiver in case of substantial and willful violation. Such laws have been enacted in Arizona, Delaware, Iowa, Maryland, Missouri, New Jersey, and North Dakota.

California has a law enabling the Attorney General not only to obtain an injunction but to collect civil penalties of up to $2,500 for each deceptive practice violation. Under that law penalties of $95,000 were collected from a concern selling encyclopedias in California. The Minnesota Attorney General obtained an injunction to stop the use of deceptive claims in advertising of automobile transmission repair services. The New York Attorney General has since 1959 carried on a very active program of consumer protection,[130] resulting in his obtaining return to the public of over $1,000,000 in 1966. Other states having somewhat similar laws and programs include Alaska, Kansas, Kentucky, Massachusetts, Michigan, Ohio, Pennsylvania, Rhode Island, and Wisconsin, about 26 in all.

F. BROADCASTING AND THE PUBLIC.

30. The "Public Interest."

While every business is involved with the public interest in some degree, probably none is an intimately concerned with it as broadcasting—both radio and television.

The very existence of the commercial broadcasting industry is based on good public relations. The individual radio stations and TV channels are *required* to serve the "public interest, convenience and necessity." [131] These few words could almost serve as a definition for public relations generally. John M. Couric, Vice President for Public Relations National Association of Broadcasters, has said: [132]

> You can find many good definitions of what public relations is. But I have one which I think fits the broadcaster.
> IT INVOLVES THREE BASIC ELEMENTS.
> First, public relations means finding what your public—your audience—wishes . . . what it needs . . . what it expects from you.
> Second, public relations means guiding your policies to fulfill these needs and desires.
> Now do these two points sound familiar to you? Of course, they do. I'm paraphrasing the Communications Act. Of course, most broadcasters are guided by these two points in their operations in the public interest, convenience and necessity.
> But, the third point . . . this is the point which is too often ignored and this is the capstone of public relations.
> The third point is:
> Public relations means communicating and interpreting your policies and your actions so your public will know that you are acting in their interests.
> In other words, public relations is the free flow of communications between you and your community. *FROM* you *TO* your

public. It means *guiding* public opinion, but it also means *being* guided by public opinion. (Emphasis in original.)

What Couric said could well be accepted by all PR practitioners. But in broadcasting, such an attitude and activity is a matter of legal necessity for survival.

Nor is this "two-way street" theory of public relations merely a voluntary effort by the broadcaster. In 1960 the FCC issued its Report and Statement of Policy in connection with its programming inquiry. It said, in part: [133]

> In this fulfillment of his obligation the broadcaster should consider the tastes, needs and desires of the public he is licensed to serve in developing his programming and should exercise conscientious efforts not only to ascertain them but also to carry them out as well as he reasonably can. He should reasonably attempt to meet all such needs and interests on an equitable basis. . . . [T]he Commission does expect its broadcast licensees to take the necessary steps to inform themselves of the real needs and interests of the areas they serve and to provide programming which in fact constitutes a diligent effort, in good faith, to provide for those needs and interests.

31. Licensee Renewal Procedures.

Every three years a radio or TV station must have its license renewed by the FCC. The licensees, in effect, submit their past performance to official scrutiny—especially as to how well they have served the public interest, convenience and necessity and as to their contemplated service in the future.

In 1965 and 1966 the Commission set up new requirements and forms for the renewal procedures as to radio and TV licensees respectively.[134] The major changes involve the efforts taken by a licensee to ascertain the needs and interests of the community being served. This information is contained in Part I of Section IV-B of FCC Forms 301, 303, 314, 315. Required exhibits are to delineate and report on the following:

> (a) The methods used by the applicant to ascertain the needs and interests of the public served by the station. Such information shall include (1) the major communities or areas which applicant principally undertakes to serve, and (2) identification of representative groups.
> (b) The significant needs and interests of the public which the applicant believes his station will serve during the coming license period, including those with respect to national and international matters.
> (c) Typical and illustrative programs or program series (ex-

cluding entertainment and news) that applicant plans to broadcast during the coming license period to meet those needs and
interests.

(d) The procedures applicant has or proposes to have for the
consideration and disposition of complaints or suggestions coming
from the public.

As the result of confusion among licensees, the FCC sent letters, under
date of June 22, 1966, to several licensees which had filed inadequate
responses, stating that the "purpose of the above question is to ascertain
full information with respect to": [135]

(a) The steps that have been taken to inform yourselves of the
real needs and interests of the area served by your station and to
provide programming which, in fact, constitutes a diligent effort,
in good faith, to provide for those needs and interests;

(b) such suggestions as may have been made as to how your
station could help meet the real needs and interests of the community from the viewpoints of those consulted;

(c) your evaluation of the relative importance of all such suggestions and the consideration given them in formulating the
overall program structure for your station; and

(d) the programming that you propose, either generally or specifically, to meet the needs and interests of the community as you
have evaluated them.

These requirements seem to accord closely with the approach a PR
practitioner might take on behalf of any company in designing a PR
program. It includes playback and research as to public needs and attitudes, both generally and as to the station (the company); an evaluation
thereof; specific plans and proposals based on such playback and evaluation.

The FCC recognizes that "there is wide disagreement over the details
that should be required" of each applicant in ascertaining such community needs and interests. It makes no recommendation as to specific methods of ascertaining this information, leaving that to the individual licensee. However, broadcast trade sources have particularized as to
practical steps to be taken. The following, from a broadcasting trade
paper, is illustrative: [136]

(1) Have members of your staff, especially those who belong to
various civic groups (e.g., service clubs, philanthropic organizations, PTA, citizens' associations, religious groups, and the like),
conduct oral surveys and submit periodic memoranda to you as to
the results and/or have brief questionnaires completed and tabulated for your use. Actually, the distribution and tabulation of
questionnaires on 3 x 5 cards would be less time-consuming than
posing the questions orally and preparing a memo on the results.

(2) Keep a record of community (program) contacts by your staff.

(3) Send out form letters, seeking opinions on programming.

(4) You might retain an independent survey firm.

(5) Periodically, broadcast a request for such information from your audience. You might offer a small prize for the best recommendations.

Regardless of the methods you employ to obtain documented indications of the interests of your audience, you should:

(1) Immediately set up procedures, policies, and plans to obtain such evidence;

(2) Examine the survey results carefully;

(3) Prepare a brief résumé of each survey to be included in your renewal application;

(4) Make some effort to adopt the meritorious suggestions received.

Once again much of this detail is essentially similar in structure and function to techniques which the PR man might well recommend to any company seeking public reaction to the company or information upon which to construct a long-range PR program.

Instructive as to the attitude of the FCC concerning station efforts to survey and ascertain local needs is its holding in the WBEL case.[137] One of the applicants for a new station license (Prudential) sought to have the Commission inquire as to "their respective efforts to ascertain the needs and interests of the community to be served." This was the St. Louis area. The Commission agreed to enlarge the issues in the case to include this question.[138]

In the course of its opinion the Commission described as "extensive and thorough" Prudential's efforts to ascertain such needs and interests, basing this comment on the following Prudential inquiries:

(a) 1554 questionnaires sent to persons in the community to be served.

(b) A telephone survey of 934 calls of which 391 were completed.

(c) Over 500 personal and telephone interviews with community leaders.

(d) The presentment of the results of all of the above to a "Permanent Program Advisory Committee" consisting of 21 community leaders who had been invited to continue to serve on the committee until Prudential's application was granted.

This ruling is also suggestive to PR and research people as to federal agency attitudes in other postures such as the nature, scope and purpose of similar surveys in deceptive advertising cases before the FTC. As developed in Chapter 15, Section 5, such evidence is admissible and valuable to show public attitudes as to the meaning of product claims and whether particular claims are likely to be deceptive or to confuse.

32. The United Church of Christ Case.

Further evidence of the growing importance of public opinion in the broadcasting field and its legal perimeters was the 1966 *United Church of Christ* decision of the District of Columbia Circuit Court, according a Jackson, Mississippi church the right to intervene in the FCC renewal proceedings of a TV station in that community.[139] Prior to this case, intervention in such proceedings had been limited to parties alleging some electrical interference or economic injury. It was assumed that the FCC itself could protect the public interest.

The court pointed out that it would be "an enormously complex and prohibitively expensive task" for the Commission to survey the performance of every station in the country and went on to say:

> [C]onsumers are generally among the best vindicators of the public interest. In order to safeguard the public interest in broadcasting, therefore, we hold that some "audience participation" must be allowed in license renewal proceedings. We recognize that this will create problems for the Commission but it does not necessarily follow that "hosts" of protestors must be granted standing . . . The Commission can avoid such results by developing appropriate regulations by statutory rulemaking . . .
>
> The responsible and representative groups eligible to intervene cannot here be enumerated or categorized specifically; such community organizations as civic organizations, professional societies, unions, churches and educational institutions or associations might well be helpful to the Commission. These groups can be found in every community; they usually concern themselves with a wide range of community problems and tend to be representatives of broad as distinguished from narrow interests, public as distinguished from narrow interests, public as distinguished from private or commercial interests.

From the point of view of the PR practitioner it is interesting to note how closely this judicial "community lineup" parallels public relations concepts about "community thought leaders" or the various publics with which communicators are concerned.

33. Broadcast of Industrial Films.

Companies and trade associations are using films to tell their stories with increasing frequency. Other industrial films are more public-service-oriented and limit carefully the mentions of the "sponsor." Probably the two most frequent media for such films—aside from the company's own employees or customers and the association's members or chapters—are public group showings and TV use on local channels.[140]

Other company-originated films or filmclips are news-oriented and are intended for use in station news programs.

Experience has shown that over-commercialism in such films will seriously retard their use by local stations and company mentions are therefore kept to a minimum. However, the Communications Act of 1934 requires identification of the sponsor on all commercial broadcasts. Accordingly, mention of the company is necessary in some clear form or other. It may be in the opening title frames or a closing slug.

Thus a company supplying such films may quite properly insert some company reference as a matter of legal necessity. It has been pointed out: [141]

> [N]ews directors are, when interviewed, alert to legal requirements of identification of "sponsor" of all materials aired—many look on a brief and logical company identification as not only reasonable but also a compliance with requirements.

The identification of the company should appear on even those films which are clearly public service instruments—such as a 28 minute film dealing with air pollution and without any stress whatsoever on the company's contribution to remedial measures. This is required for TV station logging purposes also.[142]

G. MISCELLANEOUS.

34. Government as a "Public."

It is well recognized in PR that government and government personnel and decision-makers constitute a separate and very important "public." Normally a company will plan its PR program so as to include that public, including therein the federal, state and local arms of government.[143]

More and more, PR directed to government is becoming a specialized field, similar in this respect to financial PR. The reasons are easy to understand: both its importance and intricacies are increasing. However, beyond this is the growing conviction that episodic approaches to government are not enough. Usually these approaches were confined to periods of legislative attack, Congressional or legislative hearings and the pendency of new laws.

Today government has made it clear that something more than even continuing direct appeals is necessary. Business has come to learn that "Congressmen read their mail." It knows that the community-at-large—through complaints to its elected representatives or to government administrators—is really the original source of most new anti-business legislation and regulatory policy. See Section 25 above.

Accordingly, a policy of "good corporate citizenship" is coming to the fore. This means convincing the grass roots communities—those who communicate with the lawmakers, either by letter or the editorial mouthpiece of the local newspaper—that a company is a good neighbor and should not be subjected to unfair or unnecessary restraints and controls. This has been put into focus by men such as John D. Harper, Alcoa president, who has said: [144]

> The intelligent exercise of public responsibility involves, first of all, a recognition that a business is a citizen in a very real sense, and must behave like a citizen in return for being allowed to operate within the community. Just as an individual citizen can't throw rocks through his neighbor's picture window without landing in jail, so the corporate citizen cannot wantonly abuse the public interest without public retaliation. A business, for instance, cannot disregard the fire and health laws, or deliberately make false claims in advertising. At least in the minimum sense, therefore, public responsibility is not an optional chore for business.
>
> Quite frankly, and unfortunately for all of us, there are some businessmen who still believe that public responsibility means living up to the letter of the law and not one inch beyond. . . . Their disregard for the public interest inevitably leads to public legislation, which may cause problems for all of us.
>
> Businessmen are perhaps the most vocal members of society in complaining about regulation. We must remember that we can prevent further regulation best by anticipating needs and meeting them voluntarily.

Thus, the basic approach is not necessarily to government but indirectly through the people who, in the long run, direct the thinking of government. This, in turn, requires prophylactic action and planning by the company or, as has been said, "from inside out." [145]

At the same time, the direct contact with government continues. Canfield lists 19 important elements in such a program.[146] See also Section 3 above.

Yet, despite good "grass roots" and community-leader acceptance, detrimental legislation or administrative rulings do loom frequently. Specific programs must be tailored to meet these thrusts. But even here, it has been said: [147]

> No law or regulation just happens. There is some reason for it, and it usually reflects the majority opinion of those who have been concerned with it. This is important; only rarely does a legislative proposal represent the opinion of *most* of the people; it represents the opinion of most of those who have *expressed* themselves about

it; that number might be very small, and most of them can be identified.

There is some belief that "lobbying" is the sum-total of the appeal by business to government. Lobbying may be important but it has a limited function. As against clearly partisan lobbying or other appeals, the most effective program is "education." This means a steady flow of honest, informational materials to the legislator or the government administrator. See Section 3 above.

35. Representation of Government.

Public relations firms or counselors are retained by government to perform PR, publicity and other duties on behalf of some government agency or program. This may be at the state, federal, or municipal level. It may involve military recruitment, promotion of state-produced fruit, tourist travel (federal or state), industrial development or any other of a wide variety of government-supported functions. The retainer may be for the customary PR services, institutional advertising, publicity, trade show promotion, general media advertising, direct mail promotion or, as in the private sector, any related services calculated to produce the necessary result.

Because of these similarities it is sometimes believed that there are but few differences between such government services and private service. Unfortunately this is not true. Some of the differences likely to be encountered are:

(a) Political relations may be important, more probably in state-financed promotions and publicity.

(b) The retainer is not likely to be for more than one year and without any automatic renewals because of legal budgetary requirements.

(c) Some contracts may not be firm as to total to be spent, especially as to purchase of paid space or time, and even approved budgets may be cut back during the program.

(d) In large programs, the retainers may be fragmented with several firms handling different segments of the promotion, resulting in liaison problems and excessive time.

(e) Excessive time may be needed for preparation and execution of agreements and not infrequently the service will be well under way before "final papers" are signed.

(f) Channels of reporting may be rather involved and require considerably more time or frequency.

(g) There is likely to be a demand for greater and more rapid evidence of "results."

(h) In some government quarters skepticism as to the value of the services will be indicated—especially with budget or appropriations committees—and embarrassment may result.

(i) Government accounting procedures may require different billing procedures with resultant travail, especially if computerized methods are in use.

(j) Payment of the PR firm's invoices may be delayed because of government auditing methods or just old-fashioned "red tape."

(k) Fees and reimbursable expense items may, in some cases, be subject to renegotiation.

(l) Scrupulous care must be taken that the services do not—accidentally or otherwise—include even the smallest amount of "personal PR" on behalf of government administrators whether or not this would serve the overall purposes effectively or is quite "incidental" to the program.

(m) The services may, for a long time after their apparently satisfactory completion, be subject to government investigation—even long after any legal statute of limitations may have expired.

(n) Record-keeping may be more cumbersome.

Most of these are not merely practical factors but also legal problems since they derive from statutory or judge-made requirements with which the PR firm must conform or to which it is subject.

36. Services for State-Affiliated Groups.

Many PR firms throughout the country, from time to time, come to serve various state-affiliated or state-controlled groups of minority interests. Principal among these are the special agricultural organizations probably operating under some kind of "marketing order." These have, as their principal purpose, the promotion of some specific and important state-produced product such as citrus fruits or apples.

Dissidents may question the propriety of such specialized groups and especially their fiscal and financial arrangements. A New York court ruled on this issue in 1966.[148] A successful referendum had been held as to the establishment of an "apple marketing order." The order provided for an assessment on all apple-producers in the state to create a fund to be used for promoting the sale of New York-grown apples. The Commissioner of Agriculture and Markets sought a declaratory judgment as to the referendum and marketing order. Both were upheld by the Appellate Division.

The court pointed out that the assessment was not a tax but fund-raising for a specific and proper purpose. The program was held valid as a proper exercise of the state's power to regulate for the public welfare, health, morals and the like.

However, the decision has been questioned by legal comment, which points out that under this ruling,[149]

> [T]here is no reason why, for example, the legislature could not pass a law to force bowling ball manufacturers to advertise, upon a recital that the sport is healthful, and it is in the public interest to stimulate industry by state-controlled advertising. This example is not much more extreme than the situation presented in the instant case, especially in view of the fact that the majority of the Appellate Division admitted that the apple industry constitutes a relatively small percent of the total agricultural output of the state.

37. Public Relations and Foreign Nations.

PR practitioners are becoming increasingly concerned about relationships with foreign laws and foreign governments—even when serving domestic companies.

Representation in the United States of foreign governments or companies raises threshold and continuing questions of compliance with the Foreign Agents Registration Act, discussed at length in Chapter 24. This normally accounts for most of the PR function's obligations under American law when serving such clients.

When serving American companies with overseas interests, the legal needs in foreign countries must be closely regarded and satisfied. Even the operation of a PR firm's branch office in a foreign country may necessitate incorporation in that foreign country, the employment of a certain percentage of foreign nationals and other "local" legal prerequisites.

Beyond this, the international PR operation which is managed from and in the United States runs into a plethora of foreign legal intricacies. Their multi-faceted nature prevents their discussion at length in a work such as this. The interpolation here of the problems is intended as an alerting to the existence and the frequently unusual nature of these multi-country or inter-country PR operations or even individual projects, programs or campaigns. Their sometimes "alien" or esoteric nature will be understood from the following sampling:

(a) An American company held stockholders meetings simultaneously in the United States, England and France with proceedings on closed circuit TV from all three countries via Telstar, requiring legal clearances and arrangements in all three countries.

(b) A war-time ally of the United States retained an American PR firm to promote a "Caravan" for American veterans who had fought in that country, with passports and visas needed for several countries and special plane clearances in both the United States and the foreign nations.

(c) An American company entered the Common Market and developed a "low-pressure" PR and publicity campaign directed to the potential customers in the Common Market as well as directly to the governments concerned. France objected for a time.

(d) Participation in a German trade fair was to be supplemented by certain "commercial entertainment" which used music and other materials copyrighted in Germany and other continental countries.

(e) The house organ of a French subsidiary of an American company carried a story about a member of the French government who demanded a legally-mandated "right of reply" in the house organ.

(f) An official of an American company spoke at an international trade association convention in Italy and found his remarks censored by the local government.

(g) A PR man traveling with a high-level representative of an American company in Sweden issued a press release indicating the company's interest in setting up a plant in that country, only to have the local newspapers delete all references to prices from the news release.

(h) The PR director of an American company visited a South American country where the company had a plant. At a local press conference he read a company statement—with the local PR man at his side—only to be reminded he had no standing because he was not licensed as a PR practitioner in that country.

(i) An American vitamin producer built a plant in a continental country (complying with all local laws) and then found that any prepared-in-America statements had to be cleared by several agencies of the foreign government.

(j) An American PR firm represented—together with client's attorneys—the company in negotiations for more favorable terms on a "concession" from a middle eastern nation.

(k) In one of the Scandinavian countries, the "Ombudsman"—as required and permitted by law—investigated an American company's communications to its employees in a local plant because the wife of one employee complained that her husband was being coerced by the company.

(l) An American PR firm was asked to "straighten out" a company with a branch factory in one of the emerging African countries which had allegedly paid its taxes to the "wrong" government because of a dispute between the groups claiming sovereignty.

Each one of these "episodes" implicated the organic law of the foreign country or direct relations with the government of that country. Some of the legal exposures were quite obvious before the activity was undertaken and were satisfactorily resolved during the planning stage. Others came as a "surprise." In a few cases the lack of forehandedness resulted in substantial difficulties for the American company. In all of these instances in which prophylactic inquiries had not been made, the minimum result was embarrassment and, it has been suggested, "another contribution to the legend of the Ugly American."

38. The "Newsman's Privilege."

The "newsman's privilege" is generally taken to mean the right of the press to withhold information as to the origin of news of which he may have learned. The reporter is traditionally zealous in "protecting his sources" and some have gone to prison for a refusal to testify as to the origin of their information.[150] This, then, is the "newsman's privilege" —the right to protect a reporter's sources. In either the state or federal forums this right has not been broadly established or recognized although in individual cases the reporter may escape prosecution for refusing to divulge his source.[151]

In the absence of statutory reform, it is generally held that a "newspaper correspondent must answer pertinent questions and disclose the sources of his information . . . if the questions be relevant to the proceedings." [152] The reporter is "under the same duty to testify, when properly called upon, as other persons." [153] The journalistic canon of ethics against disclosure must give way to the legal obligation to testify.[154]

Several fairly intensive campaigns have been waged to create this right by state statute—in the 1930s and in 1949–50. As a result some 12 states now recognize the right in various forms: Alabama, Arizona, Arkansas, California, Indiana, Kentucky, Maryland, Michigan, Montana, New Jersey, Ohio and Pennsylvania.[155]

The statutes vary somewhat but generally protect any employee of a newspaper, news service, newspaper syndicate, periodical, or radio or TV station or network who is a writer, reporter, correspondent or commentator or in any other capacity is involved directly in the gathering or presentation of news. Whether this would protect an editor or reporter of a company house organ is open to serious question although a good argument could probably be made in favor of such protection in certain cases.[156]

In the federal area, there has, as yet, been no protection legislation. Twenty-three bills have been introduced in the Senate and House from 1930 through the end of 1966. None of the bills received positive consideration.

Notes

1. Rosenbloom, *Effective Public Relations with Washington, D.C.,* 12 P.R.Q. No. 2, at 7 (1967).
2. Hill, *The Making of a PR Counselor,* P.R.J. June, 1964, at 22, reprinted from THE MAKING OF A PUBLIC RELATIONS MAN (1963).
3. Philip Elman, *Better Relations with Business,* address before American University's Fifth Annual Conference on Business-Government Relations in Marketing, F.T.C. Release, March 19, 1965, at 2, 4. For a discussion in depth of government-private sector communications, see *Business-Government Communication: A Symposium,* including Galpin, *Increasing Effective Communication with Government,* Morton, *Business and Government Are Not Adversaries,* and Powers, *Cooperation For Common Advantage,* P.R.J., Oct., 1966, at 73–76.
4. See Rosenbloom, *supra* note 1, *passim.*
5. *Notice of Proposed Rule Making, Rule 300.36,* F.T.C. Release, Nov. 1, 1967.
6. Mueller, *Government's True Role in Public Relations,* P.R.J., Nov., 1960, at 9.
7. Everette MacIntyre, *Government Regulation of Business—The Role of the Federal Trade Commission,* address before University of Rhode Island Conference on Social Studies, F.T.C. Release, July 19, 1967, at 9.
8. Everette MacIntyre, *FTC Promotes Fair Competitive Acts and Practices,* remarks before the Harvard Business School Club of Philadelphia, F.T.C. Release, Nov. 21, 1963, at 13.
9. 360 F.2d 667 (2d Cir. 1966), *aff'd,* 35 L.W. 4439 (1967). See also Abbott Laboratories v. Gardner, 35 L.W. 4433 (1967).
10. For discussions of the investigatory process generally, see McGEARY, THE DEVELOPMENTS OF CONGRESSIONAL INVESTIGATIVE POWER (1940); TAYLOR, GRAND INQUEST, THE STORY OF CONGRESSIONAL INVESTIGATION (1955); ROURKE, SECRECY AND PUBLICITY 113–130 (1961).
11. Rourke, *supra* note 10, at 118.
12. BERNAYS, BIOGRAPHY OF AN IDEA 614–17 (1965).
13. 5 U.S.C. §1005, 60 Stat. 240 (1946). See generally, as to investigatory powers and procedures, DAVIS, ADMINISTRATIVE LAW TREATISE, ch. 3.
14. As to the non-publicity policy of the S.E.C. in such cases, see LOSS, SECURITIES REGULATION 1153 (1951).
15. As to administrative rulemaking powers generally, see Davis, *supra* note 13, at ch. 6.
16. Hoxsey Cancer Clinic v. Folsom, 155 F. Supp. 376 (D.D.C. 1957).
17. Schmidt v. United States, 198 F.2d 32 (7th Cir. 1952), *cert. denied,* 344 U.S. 896 (1952).
18. See Rourke, *supra* note 10, at 126–28.

19. I.R.S. News Release No. 829, 7 CCH 1966 STAND. FED. TAX REP. ¶6607 (June 13, 1966).

20. For a detailed discussion of this case, see 80 HARV. L. REV. 1793 (1967), particularly at 1797–98, as to the effect of the early publicity.

21. Archer v. Lemke, 1962 Trade Cas. ¶70, 417 (N.D. Ill. 1962); Hall v. Lemke, 1962 Trade Cas. ¶70, 338 (N.D. Ill. 1962). See Note, 75 YALE L.J. 487 (1966).

22. *Supra,* n. 13.

23. Wanderer v. Kaplan, 1962 Trade Cas. ¶70,535 (D.D.C. 1962).

24. See F.C.C. v. Schreiber, 201 F. Supp. 421 (S.D. Cal. 1962); Larche v. Hannah, 177 F. Supp. 816 (W.D. La. 1959), *rev.,* 363 U.S. 420 (1960). See Note, 72 YALE L.J. 1227 (1963).

25. JAFFE & NATHANSON, ADMINISTRATIVE LAW CASES AND MATERIALS 525 (2d ed. 1961).

26. These remarks will be found in MINOW, EQUAL TIME: THE PRIVATE BROADCASTER AND THE PUBLIC INTEREST 49–55 (Laurent ed. 1964).

27. Everette MacIntyre, *Measures For Preserving Competition,* address before National Congress of Petroleum Retailers, Aug. 22, 1962, at 7–11.

28. Texaco, Inc. v. F.T.C., 336 F.2d 754 (D.C. Cir. 1964).

29. Dixon, *"Disqualification" of Agency Members: The New Challenge to the Administrative Process,* remarks before the Antitrust Law Section of the N.Y. State Bar Association, Jan. 27, 1965, at 8.

30. Marquette Cement Mfg. Co. v. F.T.C., 147 F.2d 589, 592 (7th Cir. 1945), aff'd 333 U.S. 683, 701 (1947).

31. National Lawyers Guild v. Brownell, 225 F.2d 552 (D.C. Cir. 1955), *cert. denied,* 351 U.S. 927 (1956). See also Lumber Mut. Cas. Ins. Co. v. Locke, 60 F.2d 35 (2d Cir. 1932); O'Malley v. United States, 128 F.2d 676 (8th Cir. 1942), *rev'd on other grounds,* 317 U.S. 412 (1943).

32. Amos Treat & Co. v. S.E.C., 306 F.2d 260 (D.C. Cir. 1962). See also R. A. Holman & Co. v. S.E.C., 366 F.2d 446, 35 L.W. 2174 (D.C. Cir. 1966), *rev. denied,* 36 L.W. 3224 (1967) (distinguished).

33. Area Rate Proceeding (Permian Basin Area), F.P.C. Dkt. No. AR61-1 et al. (Memorandum Opinion and Statement of Com. Black), Jan. 12, 1965.

34. Reilly, *Reciprocity—The End of Innocence,* remarks before the Trade Relations Association, F.T.C. Release, Sept. 18, 1967, at 1.

35. Statement before Subcommittee on Consumer Interests of the Elderly, Senate Special Committee on Aging, F.T.C. Release, Jan. 18, 1967, at 4.

36. Archibald, *Public Relations, Politics and Government,* P.R.J., June, 1967, at 40.

37. 5 U.S.C. §54 (1964), 38 Stat. 212 (1913).

38. For a discussion of this statute and the status of PR and publicity men in government generally, see W. W. Cohen, *Public Information in a Democratic Society,* P.R.J., Dec., 1967, reprinted from COHEN, THE VOICE OF GOVERNMENT (1968).

39. *Congressmen Eye PR Fees for U.S. Travel Service,* A.A., May 31, 1965, at 12, col. 3.

40. S. Cohen, *White House Uses Massive Effort to Educate U.S. on Foreign Trade,* A.A., Feb. 19, 1962, at 88.

41. Useful discussions of government activities in this area will be found in ROURKE, SECRECY AND PUBLICITY, *passim,* especially at 183 *et seq.* (1961); PIMLOTT, PUBLIC RELATIONS AND AMERICAN DEMOCRACY pt. II (1951); CUTLIP & CENTER, EFFECTIVE PUBLIC RELATIONS 378–387 (3d ed. 1964); Note, 80 HARV. L. REV. 1005, 1015 *et seq.* (1967).

42. Silver King Mines v. Cohen, *infra* note 56, at 673.

43. *Id.* at 671.

44. *Hearings on S. Res. 191 before the Subcomm. on Antitrust and Monopoly of the Senate Comm. on the Judiciary,* 89th Cong., 2d Sess., pt. 1, at 206 (1966).

45. *In re* Rodale, F.T.C. Dkt. No. 8619 (refusal to enlarge record), TRADE REG. REP. ¶17,243 (May 11, 1965). ("Accuracy of the release . . . is irrelevant to any issue before [the Commission].")

46. Cinderella Career and Finishing Schools, Inc. v. F.T.C. 1967 Trade Cas. ¶7202 (D.D.C.).

47. United States v. Diapulse Mfg. Corp. of America, 362 F. Supp. 728, 53 A.B.A.J. 472 (D.C. Conn. 1967).

48. Quoted from news release as to issuance of complaint in F.T.C. Dkt. No. 8748, Nov. 29, 1967.

49. 341 U.S. 123 (1952).

50. §705(b) of the Federal Food, Drug and Cosmetic Act, 21 U.S.C. §375(b) (1964).

51. 15 U.S.C. §78(u) (1964).

52. S.E.C., *Manual of Administrative Regulations* §161.03.

53. Id. §§161.05, 06.

54. Cinderella Schools, Inc. v. F.T.C., *supra* note 46.

55. United States v. Diapulse Mfg. Corp. of America, *supra* note 47.

56. Silver King Mines, Inc., *et al.,* v. Cohen *et al.,* 261 F. Supp. 666, 674 (D.C. Utah 1966). See also B. C. Morton Int'l Corp. v. F.D.I.C., 305 F.2d 692 (1st Cir. 1962).

57. Bureau of Nat'l Affairs, *Antitrust & Trade Regulation Report,* No. 332, A-20, Nov. 21, 1967.

58. *Id.* at A-22.

59. Elman, *supra* note 3, at 4.

60. *Washington Focus,* P.R.J., June, 1967, at 8.

61. §9(b) of S.1336, 89th Cong., 2d Sess. (1966).

62. S. 924, 90th Cong., 1st Sess. (1967).

63. 113 CONG. REC. S.1749-50, Feb. 8, 1967.

64. Rourke, *supra* note 10, at 146.

65. Note, *Small Business before the Federal Trade Commission,* 75 YALE L.J. 487 (1966).

66. Philip F. Zeidman, *Advertising and the Smaller Firm,* address before the Federal Bar Association Briefing Conference on Federal Controls of Advertising, June 3, 1966, S.B.A. Release, June 3, 1966, at 14.

67. Rourke, *supra* note 10, at 136.

68. F.T.C. v. Rhodes Pharmacal Co., 191 F.2d 744 (7th Cir. 1951), 208 F.2d 382 (7th Cir. 1953), *mod'd*, 348 U.S. 940 (1954).

69. B.N.A., *supra* note 57, at A-16.

70. *Infra* note 84, at 2.

71. CROSS, THE PEOPLE'S RIGHT TO KNOW xiii (1953). This work, together with its Second Supplement in 1959, constitutes the best available source of information as to access to state and municipal records. It is the standard reference work on the subject, detailing the statutes and case law on the subject.

72. One of the better discussions of the existence and development of governmental secrecy, written essentially for the layman, is Rourke, *supra* note 10, at 21–110.

73. Allen & Scott, *OEO Data Behind "Curtain of Secrecy," The Washington Report,* syndicated May 6, 1967.

74. See, *e.g.,* Atomic Energy Act of 1964, as amended.

75. F.T.C. v. Dilger, 276 F.2d 739 (7th Cir. 1960), *cert. denied,* 364 U.S. 882 (1960).

76. 5 U.S.C. §22; 5 U.S.C. §1002 (1964).

77. Among the leading cases dealing with judicial approval of various types of secrecy, see Totten v. United States, 92 U.S. 106 (1876); United States v. Coplon, 185 F.2d 629 (2d Cir. 1950); Boske v. Comingore, 177 U.S. 459 (1900); United States v. Reynolds, 10 F.R.D. 468 (E.D. Pa. 1950), *aff'd,* 192 F.2d 987 (3d Cir. 1951), *rev'd,* 345 U.S. 1 (1953).

78. See legislation adopted in 1919 giving Government Printing Office dominance in duplicating or printing government materials. 44 U.S.C. §111 (1964), 40 Stat. 1270 (1919).

79. *ABP Unit Warns Business Papers of Direct Government Competition,* A.A., May 29, 1967, at 1, 40.

80. T.D. 6939, 26 C.F.R. Ch. 1, Subch. A, Pt. 1, 1.513-2, 32 F.R. 17657 (Dec. 12, 1967).

81. P.L. 89-487, 89th Cong. S.1160 (July 4, 1966), 5 U.S.C. §1002 (1964).

82. Kass, *The New Freedom of Information Act,* 53 A.B.A.J. 667 (1967).

83. 5 U.S.C. §1002 (1964).

84. S. Rep. No. 813, 89th Cong., 1st Sess. 5 (1965).

85. Administrative Procedure Act, §3 (1946). See Administrative Procedure Act, S. Doc. No. 248, 79th Cong., 2d Sess. (July 26, 1946).

86. S. Rep., *supra* note 84, at 3.

87. Archibald, *supra* note 36.

88. Attorney General's Manual on the Administrative Procedure Act, August 27, 1947, at 25.

89. The various pages of the 1967 Federal Register at which these Regulations will be found are:

Agency for International Development, 9652, 9845.

Aging, Administration on, 12068.

Agriculture Department, 8822, 9605, 10118, 11895.

Agricultural Research Service, 9606, 10915.

Agricultural Stabilization and Conservation Service, 9608.

90. See, *e.g.,* The Tobacco Institute v. F.T.C., (D.D.C.) (complaint filed November 29, 1967).
91. Davis, *supra* note 15. See also the individual statutes, voluminous texts and reports of decisions relative to each agency's or industry's regulation.
92. Algoma Lumber Co. v. F.T.C., 291 U.S. 67 (1934).
93. See Davis, *supra* note 15, at ch. 1.

94. Bert C. Goss, untitled remarks before the 9th Annual Conference on Advertising/Government Relations of the American Advertising Federation, Feb. 6, 1967, reprinted in AMERICAN ADVERTISING FEDERATION, LET'S TRY COMMUNICATIONS 60 (1967).

95. *Dangerous Lengths—The Federal Crusade Against Smoking Has Gone Too Far,* Barron's, Oct. 2, 1967, at 1.

96. P.L. 89-92, §559, July 27, 1965, *eff.* Jan. 1, 1966, 34 L.W. 68 (1965).

97. F.C.C. 67-641, June 2, 1967.

98. P.L. 89-563, S.3005, Sept. 9, 1966, 35 L.W. 9 (1966).

99. United States v. National Funeral Directors Ass'n (E.D. Wis.). Complaint filed Nov. 24, 1967.

100. P.L. 89-755, S.985, 35 L.W. 33 (1966).

101. See discussion and cases cited, 1 TRADE REG. REP. ¶1388; 2 *ibid.* ¶7527.

102. See United States v. Philadelphia Nat'l Bank, 374 U.S. 321 (1964); United States v. First Nat'l Bank & Trust Co., 376 U.S. 665 (1965); United States v. Provident Nat'l Bank, 35 L.W. 4303 (1967); Bank Merger Act of 1966, 12 U.S.C. §1828 (c), 80 Stat. 7 (1967).

103. W.J. Abbott, Inc. v. S.E.C., 36 L.W. 2346 (W.D. Pa. 1967).

104. This alignment is based on a roster originally prepared by the author and appearing in the author's ADVERTISING TRUTH BOOK (1960). Acknowledgement is made to the staff of the Federal Trade Commission for assistance in connection with the original list.

105. See SIMON, THE LAW FOR ADVERTISING AND MARKETING, ch. 33, at 576–83 (1956).

106. The Wheeler-Lea Act, P.L. 447, 75th Cong., 15 U.S.C. §45 (1964).

107. Gale P. Gotschall, F.T.C. Assistant General Counsel for Federal-State Cooperation, *Role of the FTC in Consumer Protection,* F.T.C. Release, Dec. 1, 1967, at 1.

108. For an excellent and unbiased résumé and explanation of new consumer attitudes and appeals, see Arnold B. Barach (Senior Editor of *Changing Times*), *Consumerism—A Growing Force in Government,* remarks before the 20th National Conference of the Public Relations Society of America, Nov. 13, 1967.

109. See *The Consumer in the Marketplace—A Survey of the Law of Informed Buying,* 38 NOTRE DAME LAW. 555 (1963).

110. P.R.N., Jan. 17, 1966, at 3. See also remarks of J. Carroll Bateman, reported in P.R.N., Oct. 2, 1967, at 1.

111. *Supra* note 100.

112. P.L. 89-642, 80 Stat. 88 (1966), 42 U.S.C. §§1171–85 (1964).

113. P.L. 89-563, S.3005, 35 L.W. 9 (1966).

114. P.L. 89-564, S.3052, 35 L.W. 13 (1966).

115. P.L. 89-356, S.559, 34 L.W. 69 (1965).

116. P.L. 90-248, 36 L.W. 39 (1968).

117. 1968 Consumer Credit Protection Act of May 29, 1968. P.L. 90-321. For a full explanation of this important new law, see CCH TRUTH-IN-LENDING, LAW AND EXPLANATION (1968).

118. See, *e.g.,* S. 2727, 90th Cong., 1st Sess. (1967) (automobile warranties) ; S. 2728, *id.* (household appliance warranties) .

119. *E.g.,* H.R. 7114, 90th Cong., 1st Sess. (1967) .

120. This is part of a broad campaign to compel business to make available to the consumer more information about the products in the marketplace.

121. H.R. 2374, 90th Cong., 1st Sess. (1967) .

122. S.J. Res. 33, 90th Cong., 1st Sess. (1967) .

123. Barach, *supra* note 108, at 23.

124. *Id.* at 22.

125. A listing of state controls will be found in ROPER, STATE ADVERTISING LEGISLATION (1945) and in 56 COLUM. L. REV. 1097 (1956) .

126. *Letter to State Officials,* F.T.C. Release, Dec. 5, 1967.

127. F.D.A. Release 67-132, Nov. 6, 1967.

128. This discussion is indebted to Gotschall, *supra* note 107.

129. Ill. Stats. ch. 121 1/2 §261 *et seq.*

130. See Dole, *Merchant and Consumer Protection: The Uniform Deceptive Trade Practices Act,* 76 YALE L. J. 485 (1967) .

131. Communications Act of 1934, 48 Stat. 1064, 15 U.S.C. §21 (1964) .

132. John M. Couric, *Your Part in P.R.,* Presentation at National Association of Broadcasters 1959 Fall Conference, at 3.

133. Report and Statement of Policy re Commission EN BANC Programming Inquiry, F.C.C. 60-970, 25 F.R. 7291, 20 R.R. 1902, July 29, 1960.

134. F.C.C. Dkt. No. 13961, Report and Order F.C.C. 65-686, Aug. 13, 1965 (as to radio) ; F.C.C. 66-903, Oct. 10, 1966 (as to TV) .

135. Nat'l Ass'n of Broadcasters, *Lay Talks on Legal Problems Facing Broadcast Management,* Bull. 22, July, 1966, at 2.

136. *Revised Program Forms for TV Stations,* BM/E, Dec., 1966, at 15.

137. Salter Broadcasting Co. (WBEL) *et al.,* F.C.C. Dkt. No. 17209, F.C.C. 67R-242, 32 Fed. Reg. 8989 (1967) .

138. See also Chapman Radio and Television Co., F.C.C. 67-234, 7 F.C.C.2d 213 (1967) .

139. Office of Communication of United Church of Christ v. F.C.C., 359 F.2d 994, 34 L.W. 2533 D.C. Cir. (1966) . See 31 ALBANY L. REV. 133 (1967) .

140. See generally Westerman, *American Airlines: Films with a Point of View,* P.R.J., Dec., 1963, at 8; de Rochemont, *Brevity Key to Larger Audience Penetration, id.,* at 13; Barnum, *Inexpensive Way to Tell a Filmed Story, id.,* at 16; Andrews, *To Make Television Filmstrips Tell Company News— "Know the Territory," id.,* at 28.

141. Andrews, *supra* note 140, at 30. See also *Use of Motion Picture Films to Attain PR Objectives* (Case Study No. 1129) , P.R.N., Oct. 16, 1967, at 3; Romney Wheeler, *Public Relations Films for Television,* address before P.R.S.A. Trading Post Session, Nov. 14, 1967.

142. F.C.C. Rule §73.670 (a) (2) (i) (c) , (iii) .

143. For a discussion of relations with government, see CANFIELD, PUBLIC RELATIONS, ch. 11, at 290–312 (3d ed. 1960) .

144. John D. Harper, *Private Enterprise's Public Responsibility,* remarks before National Association of Manufacturers, Dec. 8, 1966.

145. Golden, *From Inside Out,* Sat. Rev., Nov. 11, 1967, at 95.

146. CANFIELD, PUBLIC RELATIONS, PRINCIPLES, CASES AND PROBLEMS 297–8 (3d ed. 1960).

147. Bowe, *What to Do About Unfavorable Legislation,* P.R.J., Sept., 1964, at 21.

148. Wickham v. Trapani, 26 App. Div. 2d 216, 272 N.Y.S.2d 6 (1966).

149. 31 ALBANY L. REV. 163, at 167 (1967).

150. See, *e.g.,* Garland v. Torre, 259 F.2d 545 (1958), *cert. denied,* 358 U.S. 910 (1958).

151. See STEIGLEMAN, THE NEWSPAPER AND THE LAW 196–97 (1950).

152. Rosenberg v. Carroll, *in re* Lyons, 99 F. Supp. 629 (1951). See also People *ex. rel.* Mooney v. Sheriff of New York City, 269 N.Y. 291, 199 N.E. 415, 102 A.L.R. 769 (1936); Garland v. Torre, *supra* note 150; Brewster v. Boston Herald-Traveler Corp., 20 F.R.D. 416 (D. Mass. 1957); Plunkett v. Hamilton, 136 Ga. 72, 70 S.E. 781, 35 L.R.A.N.S. 583 (1911).

153. Clein v. State, 52 So.2d 117 (Fla. 1951).

154. *In re* Wayne, 4 Haw. D.C. 475 (1914).

155. For specific citations to these statutes and a discussion of their terms and interpretation, see Library of Congress Legislative Reference Serv., *The Newsman's Privilege,* Senate Comm. on the Judiciary, 89th Cong., 2d Sess. at 12–14 (Comm. Print, 1966). Much of the background for this section of the text is drawn from this source.

156. The outcome may depend on the language of the specific statute, if any, involved. See, *e.g.,* Deltec, Inc. v. Dun & Bradstreet, Inc., 187 F. Supp. 788 (N.D. Ohio 1960).

Chapter 20

Self-Regulation and Codes of Ethics

A. FUNDAMENTALS OF SELF-REGULATION

B. CODES AND STANDARDS

C. SELF-REGULATION AND GOVERNMENT

D. POLICING OF SELF-REGULATION

667

Chapter 20

Self-Regulation and Codes of Ethics

A. FUNDAMENTALS OF SELF-REGULATION.

1. Introduction.

Self-regulation quite literally covers "a multitude of sins." Even in the limited communications and public relations contexts, it deals with ethics, compliance with legal mandates, observance of good taste, recognition of public needs, competitive dealings and relations with media. It ranges from clear-cut situations into nebulous "gray areas" about which even the most honest businessmen may differ. It encompasses nearly every day-to-day internal and external business activity.

It is sometimes not easy to understand or to evaluate. Its motives are mixed. Its objectives are often intangible. Its philosophy may even be negative. Yet business, particularly in its communications functions, has learned to accept it and to appreciate it as necessary—even fundamental.

This is particularly true of public relations. Public relations lives in a glass house and that house must always be in order. The best housekeeping policy is consistent and sincere self-regulation.

2. Definitions.

"Self-regulation," in its purest sense, is individual or corporate *self-discipline*. It develops when the individual or the company sets up its own operational standards and restraints. This was the original meaning of the term as detailed in Section 3 below. However, with the passage of time, changes in business relationships and the growth of trade associations, self-regulation has gone beyond this.

It now includes not only individual self-restraints but also group standards and restraints. It means the regulation of a concern under standards adopted by the company's peers—its competitors—on a basis presumably agreeable to the concern. When used in this chapter, self-regulation is used in this broad concept—individual and mass restraint.

3. History.

Self-regulation in public relations and publicity has relatively old roots.[1] As early as 1827 and 1842 ministers were speaking of the need of publicity to be "correct" and to "avoid the employment of falsehood, appeals to prejudice or passions and the proscription of those who do not fall in with particular opinions and practices." In 1882 a *lawyer* was using the term "public relations," meaning thereby "relations for the general good" in advising members of the Yale Law School graduating class.

The turn of the century brought widespread investigation and exposure of nefarious business and political practices by men such as S. S. McClure and Lincoln Steffens. This slowly lead to a realization by "big business" of the need for *disclosure,* if only as a defense against continued *exposure.* The stage was set for Ivy Lee, whose 1906 "Declaration of Principles" was essentially a statement of self-regulation and personal self-restraint: [2]

> This is not a secret press bureau. All our work is done in the open. We aim to supply news . . . Our matter is accurate . . . I send out only matter every detail of which I am willing to assist any editor in verifying for himself.

Without hiding the fact that he was working "on behalf of the business concerns and public institutions" he represented, he set for himself a standard of verity. Above all, he was under no compulsion to do this. In that period he could well have continued the arrantly promotional and unreliable "gimmicks" of the press agent. Instead, he aligned himself with truth and open-handed dealing with the press.

Practically contemporaneously with this came the statement of Theodore N. Vail, then but recently recalled to the American Telephone & Telegraph Company as its president. In replacing secrecy with publicity as a firm company policy, Vail said: [3]

> The only policy to govern the publicity is that whatever is said or told should be absolutely correct, and that no material fact, even if unfavorable but bearing upon the subject, should be held back. . . . Attempted concealment of material facts cannot but be harmful in the end.

Thus began overtly the intelligent self-restraint and adherence to truth which are the only approaches consistent with effective public relations. History later proved this.

This self-imposed policy was fostered as public relations and publicity services grew. It led to statements such as that circulated to editors by N. W. Ayer & Son in 1923 announcing the principles upon which its publicity releases were based—truthfulness which it vouched for and newsworthiness which it left to the individual editor.[4]

The PR practitioner early sought to eliminate what Appel called "the suspicion inherent in other forms of publicity, such as mere press agentry, ballyhoo, quackery, and propaganda."[5]

An interesting public-relations-oriented policy by media was developing at the same time.[6] Mindful of the need for the confidence of their readers, the agricultural papers early began to protect them against the "humbug and fraud" of patent medicine advertising, as the *American Agriculturist* put it in 1849. In 1880 *Farm Journal* began to guarantee its readers against advertising fraud. In 1892 Curtis began to refuse all patent medicine advertising and in 1910 issued the Curtis Advertising Code, probably the first detailed expression of "advertising acceptability."

At the turn of the century several series of articles in *Ladies' Home Journal* and *Collier's* exposed medical quackery and led to the adoption of the first pure food and drug law in 1906. Shortly thereafter (1911) the infant "truth in advertising movement," initiated by the media and nurtured by significant national and local advertisers, was formalized by the Associated Advertising Clubs of the World, later to become the Advertising Federation of America and, in 1967, the American Advertising Federation.

The seeds of this advertising truth campaign thus had their genesis in the public relations concepts and activities of media at a time when the testimonial of a Congressman could be bought for $40 and that of a Senator for $75. Finding the pages of important media closed to them unless they cleaned up their advertising, the advertisers soon found it good business to do so. In other words, business was finding it to be good "public relations" to produce more acceptable advertising.

The impact of the self-restraints of the PR man became felt upon the businesses which he counseled and served. By reason of the "two-way street" nature of successful public relations, business was coming to learn what the public thought and, above all, what the public wanted.

Business began to guide itself accordingly and to give its PR representatives "a better product to sell." This led to considerable self-regulation by business in areas which seemed little associated with public relations.

The early public relations trade associations were all interested in self-regulation. From its inception in 1948, PRSA established and maintained a committee on standards and professional practice. This led to the Society's first Code of Professional Standards in 1954, to be replaced in 1959 by a stronger Code and Declaration of Principles which has been further amended since then. As to the details of the Code and Declaration, see Section 9 below.

4. Purposes.

There are probably several motives or purposes behind any effort at self-regulation. Among them are:
  (a) To improve the public relations of a company or industry;
  (b) To avert increased government controls;
  (c) To improve internal conditions within an industry;
  (d) To serve the public interest more effectively;
  (e) To increase individual or industry-wide self-respect.

It is in no way deprecatory to say that these aims are essentially self-oriented—just as most of American business or, for that matter, just as most human beings are. While there undoubtedly are many altruistically motivated businessmen, behind most self-regulatory campaigns or standards is, in the last analysis, either the profit motive or self-defense.

Industry spokesmen have made no effort to hide this, pointing out, for example, on many occasions that if public relations, advertising and communications in general do not themselves take up the cudgels, government will. In 1962, several speakers at the annual meeting of the Association of Better Business Bureaus urged business to "intensify their self-regulation or risk increased regulation by the Federal Government." [7]

The National Association of Broadcasters in 1966 pointed out that its self-regulatory Radio Code and Television Code had two aims: to reflect broadcaster service to the public and to "maintain and preserve the freedom of self-determination," [8] a euphemism for the avoidance of stultifying governmental strictures.

Alluding to another aspect of this dichotomous motivation in a public relations frame of reference, J. Carroll Bateman, former PRSA President, has said: [9]

> This responsibility to his audience is an inescapable one. It is an altruistic responsibility, in one sense, but in the meeting of it enlightened selfishness is also served. For the public relations communicator, above all, needs the confidence of his audience if he is to communicate effectively.

5. Ethics and Self-Regulation.

We find in every discussion of self-regulation some reference to ethics and ethical concepts or purposes—even when the self-regulation may admittedly be self-centered. It is unimportant whether this is mere lip service. It exists. It must exist. Without the foundation of faith as in religion, or of long-standing tradition as in law or medicine, business self-regulation must rest upon some other foundation. That basis is the ethical concept of its times.

Ethics is frequently equated with moral principles. Percy Winfield, Professor of Law at Cambridge University, writing of ethics and law, has said: [10]

> Morality, then, rests on a consciousness of difference between good and evil. This consciousness influences the springs of action in a man's own nature; it works from within outwards and it is this internal character which distinguishes it from the law of the land and the conventions of society.

In his *A Preface to Morals,* Walter Lippmann wrote of this inward characteristic: [11]

> A man cannot cheat about faith. Either he has it in his bones, or . . . there is no conviction there to support him . . . Ethical codes cannot lay claim to unhesitating obedience when they are based upon the opinions of a majority, or on the notions of wise men, or on the estimates of what is socially useful, or on an appeal to patriotism. For they depend then on the force which happens to range itself behind them at a particular time; or on their convenience for a moment. They are felt to be the outcome of human, and therefore quite fallible, decisions. They are no necessary part of the government of the universe.

To be effective, then, true ethical restraints and self-regulation must come from the individual—not from government or industry-mandated rules or compulsion even though the individual may generally agree with them. This applies to companies as well as to individuals. The restraints, the desire to "do the right thing," the profession of ethical attitudes must come from the individual company. It "must be an essential ingredient in the day-to-day operations of the company . . . a positive and dynamic part of the behavior of the company and not considered to be a restrictive influence." [12]

It has been suggested that codes of ethics are really "nothing more than an expression of the universal human desire to have the rules of the game set down in writing."[13] While this may be a practical—albeit somewhat cynical—rationalization, codes adopted for this self-serving purpose are not likely to be effective in the long run. They lack the true inwardness of individual or corporate conviction. The individual, whether man or corporation, must truly be convinced and believe in the rightness of his activity—not merely in an acceptance of "the rules of the game."

The application of ethical principles often means a conflict between such tenets and the self-interest of business. This conflict is sometimes defined as the distinction between self-interest and service to the public. The mass communicator must "choose between being a less than fully effective technician and a less than scrupulous human being." [14] J. Carroll Bateman, in applying this dilemma to public relations, has said: [15]

> We need to affirm certain principles which will take precedence over the purposes of those who employ our talents, however noble those purposes may sound or even may be.

It is this necessity for personal ethical conviction and the subordination of individual interest which explains, in large part, the less-than-total success of various codes of ethics and much of the criticism in public and government circles of such self-regulatory measures.[16] This is coming to be more and more recognized by American industry and its communicators. They are developing and publishing statements and "company rules" firmly rooted in ethical conviction, quite apart from any attitude that such precepts are "good business." Some of them go far toward fitting the test of "current, well-considered statements of the ethical principles that should guide our officers and employees in specific situations that arise in our business activities, both domestic and foreign" as postulated in 1962 in "Call for Action," a report of the Business Ethics Advisory Council of the Department of Commerce.

This duality of achievements has been summed up well by Dr. Eric Goldman, an historian addressing himself to the needs of the PR practitioner: [17]

> The call is for doctors who, in addition to making a good living, will remember the Hippocratic oath; for teachers who are ready to lay aside their research long enough to teach the student—and it is for public relations men who do not forget that in representing a client, whether business, labor, or the Society for the Prevention of Cruelty to Animals, there is such a thing as the community and the national interest and that *it is the duty of a public relations man not only to persuade but to bring closer identity between what his client does and the larger needs.* (Emphasis added.)

6. Public Relations and Ethics.

The ethics of the PR man bear a heavy burden. Ordinarily, a person's ethics are his own concern. Only occasionally, when they intrude upon a neighbor, do they become of third party concern. This is not the case with the PR man.

If he is capable and, above all, respected, his ethics become those of his employer or client. Despite the many factors upon which a company's success may depend, all are subordinate or contributory to the company's acceptance and approval by the public. This eventually comes to depend upon a sound and ethical public relations policy, scrupulously honored. David Finn has thus described this capillary absorption: [18]

> Clarification of the company's ethical threshold in public relations is one of the major responsibilities of top management. . . . If this is left unspecified, management is failing to come to grips with the basic question of the company's role in society.
> [I]n a frequently disguised form, public relations performs the role of keeping management itself in line. When functioning well, it acts as the anvil against which management's moral problems can be hammered.
> This actually means that when businessmen apply themselves to establishing a public relations policy for their company, they are really concerned with significant ethical questions—without quite realizing it.

These more current analyses are simply a continuance of the much earlier realization by media that they must recognize and serve the needs of their readers and the public as discussed in Section 3 above. Once again, public relation's own ethics give polarity to the ethics of the businesses which it serves.

It is this magnification or extrapolation of PR ethics which makes so important the industry's and the individual's efforts in the drive toward ethical precept and conduct.

7. Value of Group Self-Regulation.

The principal value of group self-regulation lies in its ability to persuade and educate. If the education and persuasion are successful, the individual businessman or company may then become so "involved" and stimulated as to engage in true self-discipline. In a real sense, therefore, the impact of self-regulation is psychological. It has been said: [19]

> New codes, new regulations, new enforcement machinery will, in themselves, be meaningless and inconsequential unless and until the essential motivation for self-regulation has been reached and touched.

This is nothing more than the inwardness which ethics demands in order to be effective.

Education and persuasion have been clearly recognized by government and the law as being essentially the only techniques within the legally acceptable perimeter of self-regulation. As discussed in Section 21 below, any regulatory methods going much beyond this may run afoul of the antitrust laws.

This evaluation of self-regulation, both individual and group, appears again and again in the literature of self-regulation, which is voluminous and ever-increasing.[20] No company, seeking a self-regulatory policy, should grope in a vacuum. Reference to these back materials is mandatory.

B. CODES AND STANDARDS.

8. Preliminary Code Analysis.

Self-regulatory codes and standards—especially in communications—may be categorized or analyzed in several different ways:

(a) *Contents/Operations.*

Some proscriptions deal only with communications content such as permissible representations and claims. Others deal with the operational activities of industry members. This usually covers their relationships with competition, government, employees, the public, etc. These distinctions may be important, especially vis-à-vis the legality of the code or program. See Sections 19 to 22 below.

(b) *Legal/Non-Legal Matters.*

Codes may include provisions which are essentially only restatements of legal requirements. Others involve non-legal elements such as good taste or ethical precept. Some combine both. Some, seeming to adhere to legal mandate only, actually go beyond what government or court would require—even in seemingly legal areas.

(c) *Recommendation/Enforcement.*

Most codes are in reality merely considered group recommendations or suggestions for individual company conduct. Others either contain, or are otherwise subject to, sanctions and enforcement provisions. Here again, there may be legal considerations as discussed in Sections 19 to 22 below.

It is important that the individual company analyze its industry code or standards from these three aspects. The code's impact upon company economic well-being may depend upon a satisfactory resolution of questions posited by such analysis. The preliminary question of company adherence to a code may be involved. It may also implicate prospective company exposure to government prosecution.

9. Declaration of Principles and the Code of Professional Standards for the Practice of Public Relations.

In 1959 the Public Relations Society of America (PRSA) adopted a Declaration of Principles and Code of Professional Standards for the Practice of Public Relations. This replaced and strengthened a similar Code adopted in 1954.[21] It has since been amended in 1963 and 1966.

In addition, PRSA implements the Code with a procedure set forth in its Bylaws and has organized the PRSA National Judicial Council, operating through a series of panels and Grievance Boards. Their purpose is to hear complaints against PRSA members and when necessary, after due process, to discipline the members. In order to assure due process, carefully defined rules of procedure were adopted in 1965 for use by the panels.[22]

The Code states certain broad ethical concepts and also deals with relationships among its members, prohibited activities of members and certain affirmative duties of members.

The full text of the Declaration and Code follows:

DECLARATION OF PRINCIPLES

Members of the Public Relations Society of America acknowledge and publicly declare that the public relations profession in serving the legitimate interests of clients or employers is dedicated fundamentally to the goals of better mutual understanding and cooperation among the diverse individuals, groups, institutions and elements of our modern society.

In the performance of this mission, we pledge ourselves:

1. To conduct ourselves both privately and professionally in accord with the public welfare.

2. To be guided in all our activities by the generally accepted standards of truth, accuracy, fair dealing and good taste.

3. To support efforts designed to increase the proficiency of the profession by encouraging the continuous development of sound training and resourceful education in the practice of public relations.

4. To adhere faithfully to provisions of the duly adopted Code of Professional Standards for the Practice of Public Relations, a copy of which is in the possession of every member.

CODE OF PROFESSIONAL STANDARDS FOR THE PRACTICE OF PUBLIC RELATIONS

This Code of Professional Standards for the Practice of Public Relations is adopted by the Public Relations Society of America to promote and maintain high standards of public service and conduct among its members in order that membership in the Society may be deemed a badge of ethical conduct; that Public Relations justly may be regarded as a profession; that the public may have increasing confidence in its integrity; and that the practice of Public Relations may best serve the public interest.

1. A member has a general duty of fair dealing towards his clients or employers, past and present, his fellow members and the general public.

2. A member shall conduct his professional life in accord with the public welfare.

3. A member has the affirmative duty of adhering to generally accepted standards of accuracy, truth and good taste.

4. A member shall not represent conflicting or competing interests without the express consent of those concerned, given after a full disclosure of the facts; nor shall he place himself in a position where his interest is or may be in conflict with his duty to his client, employer, another member or the public, without a full disclosure of such interests to all concerned.

5. A member shall safeguard the confidences of both present and former clients or employers and shall not accept retainers or employment which may involve the disclosure or use of these confidences to the disadvantage or prejudice of such clients or employers.

6. A member shall not engage in any practice which tends to corrupt the integrity of channels of public communication.

7. A member shall not intentionally disseminate false or misleading information and is obligated to use ordinary care to avoid dissemination of false or misleading information.

8. A member shall be prepared to identify to the public the source of any communication for which he is responsible, including the name of the client or employer on whose behalf the communication is made.

9. A member shall not make use of any individual or organization purporting to serve or represent some announced cause, or purporting to be independent or unbiased, but actually serving an undisclosed special or private interest of a member or his client or his employer.

10. A member shall not intentionally injure the professional reputation or practice of another member. However, if a member has evidence that another member has been guilty of unethical, illegal or unfair practices, including practices in violation of this Code, he should present the information to the proper authorities of the Society for action in accordance with the procedure set forth in Article XIII of the Bylaws.

11. A member shall not employ methods tending to be derogatory of another member's client or employer or of the products, business or services of such client or employer.

12. In performing services for a client or employer a member shall not accept fees, commissions or any other valuable consideration in connection with those services from anyone other than his client or employer without the express consent of his client or employer, given after a full disclosure of the facts.

13. A member shall not propose to a prospective client or employer that his fee or other compensation be contingent on the achievement of certain results; nor shall he enter into any fee agreement to the same effect.

14. A member shall not encroach upon the professional employment of another member. Where there are two engagements, both must be assured that there is no conflict between them.

15. A member shall, as soon as possible, sever his relations with any organization when he knows or should know that his continued employment would require him to conduct himself contrary to the principles of this Code.

16. A member called as a witness in a proceeding for the enforcement of this Code shall be bound to appear unless, for sufficient reason, he shall be excused by the panel hearing the same.

17. A member shall co-operate with fellow members in upholding and enforcing this Code.

In addition to its basic Code and Declaration, PRSA in 1963 also adopted an official interpretation of the Code as it applies to financial public relations. This is set out in full in Chapter 22, Section 8. From time to time interpretations thereof are issued.

The PRSA self-regulatory procedure has been invoked as to many different types of infractions by members, hearings held, and discipline imposed or the charges dismissed as warranted by the evidence adduced at the hearing.[23] Some of the criminal cases referred to in Chapter 2, Section 15 resulted in action by PRSA or resignations by the members involved before such action was ripe.

Similar action has been taken by the British Institute of Public Relations under its Code of Professional Conduct. For example, in 1966, two members were suspended from membership for a period of one year (with a public announcement of the suspensions) for violation of the provisions against "false fronts." [24]

10. Code of Conduct of International Public Relations Association.

The International Public Relations Association (IPRA) was organized in 1955. One of its early accomplishments was the adoption at Venice in 1961 of a Code of Conduct which covers its approximately 300 members who are nationals of 35 countries, and who, under the IPRA Constitution, agree to abide by its Code of Conduct and to accept the rulings of its Professional Practices Committee as duly endorsed by its Council.

The basic precepts and argumentation of its Code are the same as those of the PRSA Declaration and Code. So, too, are many of its specific provisions. The influence of PRSA, one of IPRA's "founder bodies," is clear.

In October, 1967 the IV World Public Relations Congress—attended by approximately 1000 practitioners—convened at Rio de Janeiro. A substantial portion of the agenda was, directly or indirectly, addressed to various aspects of self-regulation, including a paper of the author, *The PR Man and His New Status.*[25]

11. Other Communications Industry Codes.

Nearly every organized branch of the communications industry has adopted a Code of Conduct, Declaration of Principles, Standards of Practice or a similar codification for its members. These vary in scope and content. Such variation may be due to the nature of the industry, basic thinking as to industry needs, relative level of ethical precept, usefulness of the general as against the specific pronouncement, extent of self-regulatory enforcement and considerations of the legally permissible limits of such codification.

In addition to the PRSA Code discussed in Section 9 above, the following communications associations have either adopted codes or standards or, without a specific code for its members, have a clear-cut policy as to self-regulatory activities:

> Advertising Federation of America, now the American Advertising Federation
> Advertising Association of the West, now a part of the American Advertising Federation
> Advertising Specialty National Association
> Agricultural Publishers Association
> American Association of Advertising Agencies
> American Newspaper Publishers Association
> Associated Business Publications
> Association of Better Business Bureaus
> Association of Industrial Advertisers
> Association of National Advertisers
> Direct Mail Advertising Association
> Magazine Publishers Association
> National Association of Broadcasters
> National Association of Transit Advertising
> National Business Publications
> National Editorial Association
> Outdoor Advertising Association

12. Advertising Code of American Business.

In 1965 the Advertising Federation of America in conjunction with the Advertising Association of the West (both now united as the American Advertising Federation) and the Association of Better Business Bureaus promulgated a "horizontal" code for all American business. Its nine elements are:

1. Truth . . . Advertising shall tell the truth, and shall reveal significant facts, the concealment of which would mislead the public.

2. Responsibility . . . Advertising agencies and advertisers shall be willing to provide substantiation of claims made.

3. Taste and Decency . . . Advertising shall be free of statements, illustrations or implications which are offensive to good taste or public decency.

4. Disparagement . . . Advertising shall offer merchandise or service on its merits, and refrain from attacking competitors unfairly or disparaging their products, services or methods of doing business.

5. Bait Advertising . . . Advertising shall offer only merchandise or services which are readily available for purchase at the advertised price.

6. Guaranties and Warranties . . . Advertising of guaranties and warranties shall be explicit. Advertising of any guarantee or warranty shall clearly and conspicuously disclose its nature and extent, the manner in which the guarantor or warrantor will perform and the identity of the guarantor or warrantor.

7. Price Claims . . . Advertising shall avoid price or savings claims which are false or misleading, or which do not offer provable bargains or savings.

8. Unprovable Claims . . . Advertising shall avoid the use of exaggerated or unprovable claims.

9. Testimonials . . . Advertising containing testimonials shall be limited to those of competent witnesses who are reflecting a real and honest choice.

These nine points are typical of most advertising or communications codes. Starting with a basic dedication to truth, they contain certain basic precepts which are usually broad *legal* rules pronounced by the Federal Trade Commission and the courts. Probably the only exceptions to this legal orientation are the provisions as to taste and decency, matters beyond the legal perimeter.

While the above Code is oriented towards the content of paid advertising, its relevance to public relations practice is clear—not only when the PR man uses paid advertising but also in his product publicity and other PR activities. See Chapter 11 generally.

13. Self-Regulation by Media.

The mass media have long been in the forefront of so-called "self-regulation." They continue so today. But this is not self-regulation at all.[26] It is a form of "private censorship," however altruistically oriented and resulting in considerable financial loss to the media through their refusal of advertising not considered acceptable. See Chapter 4, Section 19. More than this, however, many media are scrupulously careful about printing company news releases and may check them through independent sources before using them in their news columns or newscasts.

A form of such "self-regulation" not usually so considered is the now almost-universal media policy to refuse to print as "news" a release from a company which, directly or indirectly, implies that its continued use as an advertising medium is dependent on "editorial support" or "news" use of the company's releases. The strength of this editorial/advertising independence varies but has increased in recent years in both the mass media and the trade media.[27]

So interrelated are the elements within the industry that standards erected by one segment may have a serious impact on another. Probably the best example is the refusal of a newspaper or broadcasting station to accept an advertisement because the medium is conforming to either its own or an association standard. A company, violating no law, may find itself subject to "regulation" by the media. Presumably such regulation is not arbitrary or whimsical but rather founded on some acceptable rationale—usually protection of the public. At the same time, it must be recognized that the door has been opened to regulation which is not necessarily rational, logical or even well-intentioned. As to the media's legal position in this relationship, see Chapter 4, Section 23.

14. Communications Regulation in Industry Codes.

Many industries using, but not part of, communications have created their own industry-wide codes or standards. These cover many practices, some of them dealing with public relations, advertising, promotion and various other consumer- or public-related activities. These codes vary little from similar "horizontal" provisions in the self-regulatory guidelines discussed in Sections 9 to 12 above. Many of these provisions are merely restatements of basic legal rules, perhaps once again with greater specificity.

Some, however, require levels of performance or restraint above the applicable legal rule. In certain industries which have been under both popular and governmental scrutiny over the years—the distillers and the cigarette manufacturers are good examples—the codes contain restraints obviously keyed to these pressures. A portion of this falls into the good taste category but other parts deal with restraints which fall into no specific category but are rather detailed efforts to forestall further criticism and possible government action.

C. SELF-REGULATION AND GOVERNMENT.

15. Relation to Government Regulation.

Industry self-regulation and government-imposed controls have two basic differences: self-regulation is essentially voluntary and is generally adopted without compulsion or threat of penalty; further, it may operate in areas not dealt with by government controls. As to the latter, it has been pointed out: [28]

> [S]elf-regulation operates alongside a huge and complex system of government legislation. But it performs very different and specialized functions. Unlike government regulation, which is mainly concerned with questions of fact, and with punishing untruthful, fraudulent, deceptive and misleading claims and statements, self-regulation promotes higher standards of behavior and deals with larger questions of business ethics. It cannot be expected to assume the role of government . . . (Certain types of self-regulation are strictly forbidden for anti-trust reasons.)

Government does not seek to control questions of taste. Self-regulation usually does. Government seeks compliance only within the limits of the law. Self-regulation goes beyond this and seeks higher ethical standards. Government operates through "the big stick" of legal enforcement, even if it be only a threat in particular cases. Self-regulation offers the more palatable line of persuasion and education on a voluntary basis.

16. Government Attitudes Toward Self-Regulation.

From almost every level and segment of government has come resounding approval of communications' self-regulatory program and progress toward cleaning their own house. Presidents, administrative agency chairmen and cabinet members have reechoed this praise. Nearly every Federal Trade Commission Chairman and Commissioner has, over the years —especially since 1960—complimented all of the many self-regulatory codes and measures. The reason is simple, and has been repeatedly cited. Without self-regulation, the government would be unable to police business or its communications functions—even if it were to have "a policeman on every corner." [29]

At the same time—sometimes in the same speech—the government official tempers his compliments with very definite skepticism. Thus Federal Trade Commission Chairman Dixon has said: [30]

> I can say with assurance that my fellow Commissioners and I place little stock in evangelism as a substitute for law enforcement. . . . Tough policing is the backbone of voluntary compliance with the law.

On the other hand, Chairman Dixon, in commenting on the National Association of Broadcasters' TV Code, has said: [31]

> That this Code is subscribed to by so great a number of broadcasters is a spectacular demonstration of the self-restraint American business men freely impose upon themselves in the public interest [and the codes are evidence of] that vital force of freedom channelled by self-discipline and morality.

Such ambivalence undoubtedly has a basis in fact because self-regulation, based on education and persuasion as it is, rarely moves the hard-core offender to mend his ways.

The government must still move. The fault, however, is not all on the side of business. For example, late in 1957, the then FTC Chairman announced the creation of a liaison with various advertising groups, pointing out that "cooperation between business and government is still the cornerstone of FTC." Yet, four years before, in 1953, the FTC had attempted similar meetings, alternating between New York and Washington. The results of that project at cooperation were less than productive. *Printers' Ink* reported in 1957:

> . . . the FTC was presumably enthusiastic about the [1953] plan. A check by Printers' Ink at the time found that this feeling was shared by the advertising business. After much fanfare, however, the much-discussed union of a government agency and advertising never amounted to anything. Talk about it lingered for a while and then died away.

Despite its apparent desire for cooperation with industry, government seems to be passive in its general reaction. It meets with business committees when business committees take the initiative; it attends industry conventions and plays the part of a courteous guest. Rarely does it take the affirmative and ask business for its help or attend meetings for specific purposes—except, of course, as legally required in connection with its rule-making powers. Business advisory committees are frequently *ad hoc* creatures; their meetings, when they do take place, produce little specific result.

This is not to say that government does not have its doors open to communicators. It does. Much of this, however, is the result either of statute or mandatory rule. But this is not cooperation. It is policing, regulation and restriction.

The FTC has set up its Industry Guidance Program and even established a *separate* Bureau of Industry Guidance. Here again, the role seems passive, with the initiative remaining largely with business. On occasion the FTC does take the first step with, perhaps, the announcement of hearings looking toward a new Trade Regulation Rule. The incentive and purpose, however, are not simply a desire for amicable and informal cooperation, but rather as a preface to a new and specific regulatory rule—which in this case has the force of "law."

17. Federal Trade Commission "Codes."

Certain of the policing arms of the Federal government have promulgated what might be called "codes," compliance with which gives reasonable assurance of legal acceptability. In effect, they are a checklist for the guidance of business. Some even go beyond the purely "legal" and cover matters more accurately described as "ethical." Some of the provisions refer to public relations, advertising and promotional aspects of the covered industry. Many PR practitioners maintain complete files of these materials or, at least, of those which cover industries which concern them.

Among these "codes," those of the Federal Trade Commission naturally have the broadest impact. They fall into three general groups, each having somewhat different legal results.

(a) *Trade Regulation Rules* are a relatively new type of FTC "code." They are defined by §1.63 of the Commission's Rules of Practice in the following language:

> (a) *Nature and authority.*—For the purpose of carrying out the provisions of the statutes administered by it, the Commission is empowered to promulgate rules and regulations applicable to unlawful trade practices. Such rules and regulations (hereinafter called "trade regulation rules") express the experience and judgment of the Commission based on facts of which it has knowledge derived from studies, reports, investigations, hearings, and other proceedings or within official notice, concerning the substantive requirements of the statutes which it administers.
>
> (b) *Scope.*—Trade Regulation rules may cover all applications of a particular statutory provision and may be nationwide in effect, or they may be limited to particular areas or industries or to particular product or geographic markets as may be appropriate.
>
> (c) *Use of Rules in adjudicative proceedings.*—Where a trade regulation rule is relevant to any issue involved in an adjudicative proceeding thereafter instituted, the Commission may rely upon

the rule to resolve such issue, provided that the respondent shall have been given a fair hearing on the legality and propriety of applying the rule to the particular case.

The most important aspect is Section (c) thereof which, in effect, places upon business the burden of avoiding the application of the pertinent Trade Regulation Rule. The Commission has also said, ". . . it also simplifies the FTC's burden of proof in prosecuting cases." [32] In other words, this type of rule "has teeth in it." However, as this is written, the legal validity of the Trade Regulation Rules has not been judicially tested. There is a very significant segment of legal opinion which believes that they are unconstitutional, eventually to be overthrown by the courts.[33]

(b) *F.T.C. Guides* are the second "code" activity of the FTC. They are described in §§1.55–6 of the Commission's Rules of Practice in this manner:

> *Purpose.*—Guides are administrative interpretations of laws administered by the Commission for the use of the Commission's staff and guidance of business-men in evaluating certain types of practices. An unlawful practice common to many industries may be the subject of guides or they may relate to specific practices of a particular industry.
>
> *How Promulgated.*—Guides are promulgated by the Commission on its own initiative or upon application therefor by any interested person, when it appears to the Commission that guidance as to legal requirements applicable to particular practices would be beneficial in the public interest and would serve to bring about more widespread and equitable observance of laws administered by it.

The key word is "guidance." Guides are not *per se* enforceable as "law" although action is likely to be brought if a company does not follow their provisions. Also, the Commission staff uses them as firm guidelines in all negotiations for preliminary disposition of alleged improprieties through administrative and informal proceedings without the issuance of a formal complaint.

Guides have been issued thus far in connection with: Adhesives, Advertising Allowances, Audience Rating Claims, Bait Advertising, Cigarets, Debt Collection Methods, Fallout Shelters, Guarantees, Lipstick, Mail-order Insurance, Use of "Mill," Radiation Monitoring Instruments, Shell Homes, Shoes, Tile and Tires.[34]

(c) *Fair Trade Practice Rules.* Prior to 1967 the Commission promulgated a series of Fair Trade Practice Rules as its first effort at advance guidelines based upon consultation with the affected industries. When adopted, they did not have the force of "law" as do the current

Trade Regulation Rules. Over the years sets of such Rules for some 175 industries, national or local, have been adopted. Compliance therewith by the individual company was voluntary but non-compliance was likely to produce FTC action.[35] Apparently no new sets of Rules will hereafter be promulgated.

18. Other Government "Codes."

The Federal Trade Commission is not the only government agency which has promulgated guidelines or codes for communications or advertising behavior or those segments thereof over which the individual agency has jurisdiction. These take various forms. Some are Public Notices, Special Statements or Directives issued by the agency. Others appear in the Rules of the agency.

They vary widely in content and approach, depending largely on the nature of the industry concerned, the practices involved, the public interest to be served, etc. One thing is common to all of them: the deep-seated desire for enforcement of the federal law and insistence upon protection of the "public interest." These have proliferated as part of the "consumer protection program" and the new statutes adopted by Congress in connection therewith.

Certain of these—the more broadly applicable and important—are discussed elsewhere in this volume, particularly in Chapter 19 relative to Government Relations. Once again, wisdom dictates a familiarity with these blueprints of regulatory position for all communicators concerned with the industries, practices or patterns covered thereby.

D. POLICING OF SELF-REGULATION.

19. Self-Regulatory Dangers.

Self-regulation, even in its broad meaning, is generally a salutary process. Yet it may involve potential dangers of significant dimension. "Pure" self-regulation, as discussed in Section 2 above, avoids this danger since it involves only individual self-restraints, adopted by the individual and presumably "self-policed" by the individual himself. However, *group* self-regulation does present serious potential problems.

There can be no question that a company surrenders a portion of its independence when it becomes part of an industry-wide, group-self-regulatory program. This is true even if the program does not involve sanctions of any kind. The company submits itself to the mandate of its competitors although, presumably, on a basis acceptable to it.

Even without the possibilities of sanctions, a company is likely to comply with the industry rules if only to avoid the stigma, implied or expressed, of being a "renegade." The self-interest of other industry members may be diverse from that of a particular company. The others may, therefore, acting through industry associations or councils, bring pressures to bear on the company which are essentially self-serving, no matter how they may be dignified with the halo of self-regulation.

When sanctions are part of the self-regulatory process, the possible evil is multiplied. As Gilbert Weil has pointed out, "Once the processes of compulsion must be invoked, however, one has left the realm of true self-regulation and has entered that of government, albeit non-official." [36] This danger is quite real. It may be so sweeping as to posit the possibility of very substantial injury to a company.

Government regulation is surrounded by the safeguards of "due process." Trade association regulation may provide for hearings, representation by counsel, confrontation by one's accusers, the right of defense, and other procedures parallel to those of the regulatory agencies and the courts. Yet they lack the right of appeal through the courts, subject to constitutional and other protections. Therefore they lack due process as that term has come to be understood in our jurisprudential system.

20. Non-Sanction Policing.

Most group self-regulatory systems do not involve sanctions. This is presumably because of possible antitrust involvements as discussed in Sections 19 above and 21 and 22 below. Without sanctions, the results of the self-regulatory process depend upon the effectiveness of the program's campaign of persuasion and education. Such a campaign can be resultful. There is no doubt of that. Group pressures can be effective, quite apart from any group-induced personal convictions of the individual company. In fact, such pressures may be very substantial in order to prove that the industry is "really trying" and not "just going through the motions" of self-regulation.

Since one of the purposes of self-regulation is to avoid governmental controls, there is the likelihood that the industry will seek results at least as substantial as government would obtain through new legislation or implementation of existing controls. Not only may this lead to the adoption of supra-legal standards in the first instance but also to policing at least as vigorous as might be expected from a government agency.

21. Effect of Antitrust Law.

Even if no industry-administered sanctions are involved, there may be questions of antitrust involvement. Just where the line is drawn is not easy to define. Unofficial pressures may be of such substance as to invite antitrust litigation. For example, even though there is no agreement to refuse to deal with recalcitrants whose names appear on a published list, it has been pointed out that "the circulation of such information . . . had and was intended to have the natural effect of causing [others not to deal] with the concern listed." [37]

This nebulous legal area has thus been summarized by Lamb and Kittelle: [38]

> Because of the unlawful legal inferences that may be drawn from them, codes should not deal with trade practices on which agreements might be unlawful. Nor should they be used to bring uniformity of action in areas where it would be illegal to do so by agreement. Actually codes are safest if they are kept general in scope and wording. Perhaps they should do no more than to encourage association members to follow high moral principles in conducting their businesses.

When the self-regulatory program involves the imposition of sanctions against a recalcitrant industry member, the antitrust aspects become clearer—especially if the plan involves the reprimand, discipline or economic chastisement of the "wrongdoer," direct or indirect. In the leading case of *Fashion Guild of America, Inc. v. F.T.C.*, [39] industry members banded together to protect against style piracy in the women's wear industry. A program of checking instances of such piracy was set up as was a system of "courts" to enforce compliance. The Supreme Court struck down such an arrangement and pointed out:

> In addition to all this, the combination is in reality an extragovernmental agency, which prescribes rules for the regulation and restraint of interstate commerce, and provides extra-judicial tribunals for determination and punishment of violations and thus "trenches upon the power of the national legislature and violates the statute.

Even if the proscribed practices are patently illegal, this is insufficient provocation for an industry to arrogate to itself "legislative and judicial functions." On this issue the Court said:

> Even if copying were an acknowledged tort under the law of every state, that situation would not justify [the trade association] in combining together to regulate and restrain interstate commerce in violation of federal law.

The position of the FTC has generally followed this direction. FTC Chairman Dixon said in 1966: [40]

The question then arises as to whether an industry is privileged to crack the whip on the illegal few within it. What kind of discipline is acceptable? Who is to be the judge and jury? What assurance is there that the assessment of the facts will be impartial? And will the accused have a fair chance to defend himself? These are serious questions. We are no longer living in the days of the Old West when punishment was dealt out with more speed than accuracy. We are living instead, thank Heaven, under a government of law for which many generations of free men have fought. Although legal process sometimes may be frustratingly slow, it is the safeguard of our liberty. Thus, should any industry interpret self policing as conveying the privilege to mete out justice to offenders without due process of law, far more would be lost than gained. That is why I say that self policing must be reinforced by governmental authority. . . . [S]elf restraint serves to focus attention on those few who are out of step. They may even become so uncomfortably conspicuous that they will mend their ways. But if they don't, and persuasion fails, it is not your privilege to discipline them. Such is the sole responsibility of governmental authority—local, state or national.

Consonant with this, FTC Commissioner Elman has written: [41]

It is fundamental that the regulatory powers of government are too awesome to be turned over to private policemen, prosecutors, and judges—no matter how well-intentioned. Regulation of business—at least when it involves the imposition of fines and penalties for violations of prescribed standards of conduct—is the job of government agencies and officials bound by the limitations of due process and the rule of law. It runs against the basic grain of American society to permit private judges to hold "kangaroo courts" where punishments are imposed. The fundamental safeguards and retraints which protect the public against arbitrary or lawless official action are absent when the powers of government are sought to be exercised by private individuals or groups.

The approach of the Justice Department, which has parallel jurisdiction with the FTC, is clear from the words of Donald F. Turner, Deputy Attorney General for Antitrust: [42]

For good reasons, the law has always been suspicious of the potential abuse in private government of economic activity enforced by sanctions. Therefore, the use of sanctions within and without the group raises quite separate questions * * *. In short, the imposition of sanctions is indeed an assumption of legislative power by a private group which is likely to be intolerable under all but the most extreme circumstances.

The specific application of these general precepts is discussed in Section 22 below.

22. Federal Trade Commission Advisory Opinions.

In a series of advisory opinions, the FTC has dealt at length with a variety of types of trade association self-regulation efforts, some of them quite pertinent to the communications industry.

In *Advisory Opinion No. 4*,[43] a trade association published a booklet establishing "standards representing the ideal of a top quality industry product . . . as a goal for which the industry should be striving." The FTC advised that there could be no objection to such publication "provided it removes any procedure, practice or requirement that seals of approval be given to industry members who meet the standards."

Advisory Opinion No. 59[44] involved the right of "a proposed private group advertising review board to control advertising practices in a particular locality." The board's function was to "consider complaints of violations of advertising standards established by the organization." The board would hold hearings and render decisions on the complaints. If the advertiser refused to comply within a specified time, "a letter was to be sent to local media requesting them to require the advertiser to comply with the decisions of the panel." The FTC refused to approve this plan, saying,

> . . . [A]bsolute regulation of all advertising practices down to and including the determination of individual rights and the imposition of a penalty in the form of interference with the individual's right to advertise . . . is the ultimate authority which can only be exercised pursuant to legislative grant and subject to proper judicial review.

In *Advisory Opinion No. 64*[45] a trade association required of applicants for membership a pledge that they were following the FTC Trade Practice Rules for the industry involved. No enforcement program beyond the pledge requirement and referral of appropriate cases to the FTC was involved. The Commission advised that the inclusion of the pledge requirement would not, *per se,* violate the law, assuming that "the pledge would be required of all applicants alike."

In *Advisory Opinion No. 96*[46] the FTC approved a certification program by an association based on member-company availability of trained production personnel, certain test and quality control equipment and use of recognized production techniques. The approval was conditioned on the availability of the program and certification mark to all producers, present and future, whether or not they are association members; no greater cost for non-members; uniform mark to all who qualify; program supervision by a board truly representative of all companies with responsibility for insuring non-discriminatory access to the program; implementation of the program in a way which does not contravene Commission-administered laws.

In *Advisory Opinion No. 97*, [47] the Commission refused to approve a trade association program dealing with uniform delivery terms to all customers, local price schedules, payment terms and so-called "full requirements" agreements.

In *Advisory Opinion No. 128* [48] the Commission seems to have shifted —at least on a tentative basis—its overall position about self-policing, especially where sanctions are involved.

The Commission approved a Code of "a group of producers of products sold by door-to-door salesmen employed by independent sales agencies"—identified in the trade press as the magazine industry. Under the Code an "Administrator" is empowered to "impose fines" on sales agencies which violate the Code's provisions and to maintain records of the findings of willful violations. This was in lieu of the Code's earlier provision to permit the Administrator to recommend non-employment of salesman-violators. There are provisions for "appeals" from the Administrator's decisions. The Commission also indicated that all "coercion" was to be eliminated as to the joinder or resignation by the individual sales agencies.

The approval was granted for a three-year period; the Administrator is to submit reports to the Commission as to every complaint and its disposition; the Commission staff was instructed "to initiate periodic inquiries . . . to determine . . . as to how it is actually working."

Commissioner Elman vigorously dissented from the approval, his position generally being as quoted in Section 21 above. It seems clear that the majority of the FTC recognized that it may be attempting to break new ground in this legal area; hence its tentative and even speculative approval since there was "little recorded experience upon which to predicate" its opinion. Based on prior FTC rulings and court decisions, it would appear that Commissioner Elman's dissent represents the better view.

From these rulings certain guidelines emerge as to permissible limits of self-regulatory policing by trade associations:

(a) Programs, even if otherwise legal, must be available on the same terms and conditions to non-members as well as to members of the association.

(b) No coercion or restraints are to be applied to any company not participating in the program.

(c) Certification marks or seals may be awarded or their use permitted but on a non-discriminatory basis.

(d) Industry self-regulatory policing through pseudo-judicial machinery should be avoided.

(e) Methods which may foreclose a company from "the market" or render its activities more difficult should not be used.

(f) Permissive—as against mandatory—standards are more likely to be legally acceptable.

Notes

1. Dr. Eric F. Goldman, *Public Relations and the Progressive Surge,* address at the Annual Conference of P.R.S.A., New York, Nov. 19, 1965, published by Foundation for Public Relations Research and Education (1966), to which portions of this historical discussion are indebted.
2. As quoted in HIEBERT, COURTIER TO THE CROWD 48 (1966).
3. Quoted in Griswold, *How A.T. & T. Public Relations Policies Developed,* 12 P.R.Q., Fall, 1967, at 8.
4. Hower, *infra* note 6, at 447.
5. Appel, "Some Truths about Advertising," Introduction to Kenner, *infra* note 20, at xiv.
6. Acknowledgement is made for portions of this section to PRESBREY, THE HISTORY AND DEVELOPMENT OF ADVERTISING (1929); HOWER, THE HISTORY OF AN ADVERTISING AGENCY (1939); Kenner, *infra* note 20.
7. Bart, N. Y. Times, May 23, 1962, p. 71.
8. NAT'L ASS'N OF BROADCASTERS, THE CHALLENGE OF SELF-REGULATION 31 (undated).
9. Bateman, *A New Moral Dimension For Communications,* P.R.J., August, 1958, at 16–17.
10. Winfield, *Ethics on English Case Law,* 45 HARV. L. REV. 112, at 113 (1931).
11. LIPPMANN, A PREFACE TO MORALS 49 (1st ed. 1929).
12. Biehl, *Management Consultants and Ethics,* P.R.J., Feb., 1957, at 9.
13. LAMB & KITTELLE, TRADE ASSOCIATION LAW AND PRACTICE 147 (1956).
14. MERTON, MASS PERSUASION 185, reprinted under the title *The Moral Dimension* in THE ROLE OF ADVERTISING 479 (Sandage & Fryburger eds. 1960).
15. *In Search of Morality,* P.R.Q., July, 1963, at 26–27.
16. *How Ethical Are Codes of Ethics?* A.A., July 16, 1951, at 12.
17. Goldman, *supra* note 1, at 16.
18. FINN, STRUGGLE FOR ETHICS IN PUBLIC RELATIONS 9 (undated).
19. U.S. DEP'T OF COMMERCE, SELF-REGULATION IN ADVERTISING iii (1964).
20. Important sources in self-regulatory literature are the following: P.R.S.A., CODE OF PROFESSIONAL STANDARDS (1954, 1959, 1963, 1966); ROWELL, FORTY YEARS AN ADVERTISING AGENT (1906); ATKINSON, HOW CONFIDENCE BEGAN (1916); KENNER, THE FIGHT FOR TRUTH IN ADVERTISING (1936); BURNETT, SELF-REGULATION OF ADVERTISING (1950); NAT'L ASS'N OF BROADCASTERS, RADIO CODE AND TELEVISION CODE (var. eds. including 1967); ASS'N OF NAT'L ADVERTISERS AND A.A.A.A., THE INTERCHANGE PROGRAM (biennial eds.); SIMON, THE ADVERTISING TRUTH BOOK (1960); U.S. DEP'T OF COMMERCE, SELF-REGULATION IN ADVERTISING (1964); various articles (particularly those in the *Public Relations Journal*) cited in other footnotes to this chapter.
21. *Public Relations Execs Revise Ethics Code,* Printer's Ink, Dec. 3, 1954, at 33.
22. For an explanation of the PRSA Code machinery, see Decker, *The Path Towards Professionalism: PRSA's Code and How It Operates,* P.R.J., April,

1963, at 7, and *PRSA's Code: How the Practitioner and Public Are Protected,* P.R.J., March, 1967, at 26.

23. See Decker, P.R.J., March, 1966, *supra* note 22.

24. *British Society Suspends Two in Scandal,* P.R.J., June, 1966, at 5.

25. An excellent report on the IV World Public Relations Congress appears in P.R.N., Oct. 30, 1967 (Special World Congress Issue). As this is written, the author has been advised that the Proceedings of the Congress will become available in printed form during 1968.

26. See U.S. Dep't of Commerce, *supra* note 19, at 57–97 for a detailed discussion of the efforts of various media trade groups and individual media; SIMON, THE LAW FOR ADVERTISING AND MARKETING 335–351 (1956).

27. Hower, *supra* note 6, at 446–48. See also I.M.C. Letter, Council for Management of Change, Apr. 7, 1967, criticizing "rumor" of product publicity-paid advertising linkage.

28. U.S. Dep't of Commerce, *supra* note 19, at 48–50.

29. Kintner, *The Current State of Advertising at the Grass Roots,* Kansas City, Mo., F.T.C. Release, Nov. 21, 1960, at 6.

30. F.T.C. Release, May 30, 1961, at 1–2.

31. Nat'l Ass'n of Broadcasters, *supra* note 8, at 17.

32. F.T.C., *1953 Annual Report,* at 37.

33. At least one action has been filed at this time. This is an effort by Bristol-Myers, Inc., to prevent the F.T.C. from proceeding by such a rule in the analgesic cases.

34. See 2 TRADE REG. REP. ¶¶7893–7912 (1968).

35. These "guidelines" are now known as "Industry Guides" as a result of the apparent merger of the older Conference Rule program into the surviving Industry Guides program, as explained in Willard F. Mueller's *The FTC and Current Marketing Interfaces,* paper read before American Marketing Association, Washington, Dec. 28, 1967, F.T.C. Release (undated), at 13.

36. Gilbert H. Weil, Esq., *Industry Self-Regulation and Advertising Codes,* address at Federal Bar Association Briefing Conference on Federal Controls of Advertising and Promotion, Washington, D.C., June 2, 1966, distributed by Association of National Advertisers.

37. Eastern States Retail Lumber Dealers' Ass'n v. United States, 234 U.S. 600, at 609 (1914).

38. Lamb & Kittelle, *supra* note 13, at 149.

39. 312 U.S. 457 (1941). See also Radiant Burners, Inc. v. Peoples Gas Light & Coke Co., 364 U.S. 656 (1959); C-O-Two Fire Extinguisher Co. v. United States, 197 F.2d 489 (9th Cir. 1952); Standard Sanitary Mfg. v. United States, 226 U.S. 20 (1912); Eastern States Lumber Ass'n v. United States, 234 U.S. 600 (1914).

40. Paul Rand Dixon, *The Precious Ounce of Prevention,* address before Advertising Association of the West, Spokane, June 28, 1966, F.T.C. Release, at 11–12.

41. Dissenting Statement of Commissioner Elman, F.T.C. Ad. Op. Dig. No. 128, at 1–2 (1967). This Opinion is discussed in Section 22 of the text.

42. Turner, *Cooperation Among Competitors,* 35 Nw. U.L. Rev. 865, 870–71 (1967).

43. F.T.C. Ad. Op. Dig. No. 4, released Oct. 14, 1965, 3 TRADE REG. REP. ¶17,345.
44. F.T.C. Ad. Op. Dig. No. 59, released June 16, 1966, 3 TRADE REG. REP. ¶17,573.
45. F.T.C. Ad. Op. Dig. No. 64, released June 22, 1966, 3 TRADE REG. REP. ¶17,580.
46. F.T.C. Ad. Op. Dig. No. 96, released Oct. 19, 1966, 3 TRADE REG. REP. ¶17,723.
47. F.T.C. Ad. Op. Dig. No. 97, released Oct. 26, 1966, 3 TRADE REG. REP. ¶17,727.
48. F.T.C. Ad. Op. Dig. No. 128, released May 23, 1967, 3 TRADE REG. REP. ¶17,802.

Chapter 21

Corporate Employee Relations

Chapter 21

Corporate Employee Relations

A. INTRODUCTION.

1. Scope of "Employee Relations."

"Employee relations" is here—and in other chapters—used as an umbrella term. It goes beyond the normally-included programs such as employee communications (house organs, bulletin boards, etc.) or industrial and labor relations. It also includes physical and recreational activities which are employee-oriented, personnel relations such as hiring and termination, labor relations, community activities involving employees, counseling on employees' personal interests, employee suggestion plans, etc.

This inclusive definition is broader than that usually found in public relations text books [1] but—in the author's opinion, at least—is empirically suitable for all but the largest companies. This is particularly true in the PR frame of reference.

They all have one thing in common: the development of employee allegiance and understanding and the improvement of relations between company and employee.

2. Public Relations Contributions.

Since employee relations has so many facets and may be organizationally fragmented, it is difficult to generalize about public relations contributions. The PR director and staff may have no direct responsibility. Cutlip and Center point out that they have "a large stake in productive, pleasant internal relationships [and] can contribute much," and describe the PR role in employee relations as including: [2]

> (1) an overall concern for the success of the enterprise; (2) the attitudes employees reflect in their role as ambassadors of good or ill will for the firm in their relationships with customers, community, and other publics; (3) the responsibility for creating an en-

vironment favorable to the personnel, industrial relations function; (4) responsibility for encouraging and implementing two-way communication between managers and men.

Though the PR man may seem divorced from a particular function—such as employee hiring—the relevant informational process is often his obligation. Perhaps the PR man's most effective contribution is his two-way concept of "company-employee conversation." Other staff personnel engaged in some phase of employee relations may be trained only "in getting the job done." They may not look to the effects of their procedures except as they directly affect the company. By ascertaining employee reactions and desires, the PR man can advise and help modify these procedures or operations and thus cement employee loyalties and satisfaction.

Since the PR contribution and concern are indirect in some instances, conflicts with the personnel, industrial or labor relations function or department may arise—in what has been called "organizational politics." [3] This must be avoided by intelligent mutual understanding and clear managerial definition of function and jurisdiction. It is as important here as in the relationship between the members of the PR-legal team discussed in Chapter 1, Sections 7 to 10.

3. Variety of Legal Exposures.

Because of the "horizontal" PR integration with all aspects of employee relations, the PR man or department faces legal exposures of unusual character and dimension. The catalogue is long but a few examples illustrate its range.

It includes knowledge of the Wagner Act, the Taft-Hartley Act and other federal labor laws (especially as to unfair labor practices), the Equal Employment Opportunity Act and the Equal Pay Act, state Workmen's Compensation Acts, house organ problems, tort liabilities for employee injuries, requirements for company assistance in employee personal problems, postal laws concerning contests and lotteries, certain requirements of stock exchanges and the SEC, industrial espionage legal problems, etc.

These and others have their own specific potential and the exposure is increasing. New laws or new company programs produce new problems. So prolific of legal entanglement is employee relations that the PR staff may find itself devoting more time to legal counsel than to any other single responsibility.

This becomes clear when we recognize that employees are one of the several publics with which PR deals. All of the legal concerns which surround PR generally therefore apply to the employee public—plus the many legal specialties deriving from the unique company-employee relationship.

4. Communications Control.

Control of PR programs and their operational elements is always important. It would seem that employee communications—essentially internal communications—would present fewer control problems than external PR or publicity. The latter is always subject to the legitimate judgment of editor or publisher and sometimes to their whim or prejudice. The members of the external publics are essentially less homogeneous and their interests more varied. Playbacks from such publics may be more difficult to obtain or analyze.

These are practical concerns. Legally, however, the external communication is usually under the control of the company. It generally can and does—through its PR arm—control carefully what it says, when it says it, how it says it, and about whom it says it.

This is not always possible with internal communications. Employee communicating is considered more fruitful through personal contact. It has been forcefully said that "the basis and framework of any (good employee) communications program is the line organization." [4] The more diffuse or remote the ultimate corporate voice becomes, the greater the likelihood of legal mishap. The larger the company, the more likely is this to occur.

While the printed internal communication or factory public address system can be carefully controlled, this is not equally true of shop foremen and supervisors. The built-in dangers in the activities of these "line executives" are many. As Canfield says: [5]

> Oral communication also has decided limitations and cannot be relied upon to transmit information to employees. The communications of management are sometimes misunderstood and misinterpreted by line executives. Much of the original meaning of a message may be lost in the process of oral transmission. Many executives are poor oral communicators and cannot express clearly to workers messages from management. Some supervisors do not appreciate the importance of giving employees information about the business. . . . [L]ine executives may put their own interpretation on company information, color it with their own sentiments, or deliberately withhold information from employees.

This contretemps may be further amplified if the corporate voice is an "employee counselor." Likened in part to the military chaplain or the social service caseworker, such counselors may have a humanistic and personally sympathetic approach to the employee and his questions. As a company representative he may not hew to the legal line. While his motivation is worthy, from the company's legal position it may be unfortunate.[6]

These handicaps are coming to be better recognized by management and PR practitioners. Highly trained employee-communication specialists and consultants are being introduced. Companies are training their foremen, supervisors and counselors for this important informational function. Individual plant managers are being properly indoctrinated. Training in labor law and human relations (including their legal overtones) is being given.

Most companies are fully aware of the need for carefully prepared manuals, handbooks and other permanent materials directed to the employees themselves. There should be an equal awareness of a similar or even overriding need of similar tools for what may be called the "junior communicators," especially those who have the final, personal contact with the rank and file.

Notwithstanding these efforts, the PR man and company legal counsel must be ever alert to the *operations* of oral communications personnel, no matter how carefully they may have originally been structured and instructed.

B. EMPLOYEES' PERSONAL INTERESTS.

5. Introduction.

Most companies encourage their employees to consult the Personnel Director or other staff people about their personal interests.[7] These may be company-connected matters such as pension rights. They may be purely personal and private matters such as an automobile accident, choice of a daughter's college or a troubled domestic situation. Some may be resolved by a staff member. Others may be referred to company counsel or to an outside agency such as a local university's marriage counseling service.

There is nothing new about these programs or services. Some go back to the early days of the century, probably having their origins in corporate paternalism. The late Professor James MacLachlan of Harvard Law School, in discussing his early legal career shortly after his law school graduation in 1916, said: [8]

> We were . . . attorneys for what was then the Chicago Telephone Company, now . . . Illinois Bell. . . . There was a good deal of assistance given by the telephone company to its employees. . . ,

> To that extent we were running a kind of legal aid bureau and the younger men used to get a disproportionate share of these no-pay cases. . . . From that aspect, the practice was quite variegated.

The question naturally arises as to the posture of the company if it gives the employee "bad advice" and the employee or his family subsequently suffers some loss as a result thereof. This is no idle query in view of the many different situations about which the employee may seek guidance. Among them may be: [9]

(a) Personal wills.

(b) Handling of business relationships of the employee, such as department store charge accounts or the purchase of an automobile with subsequent collection efforts against the employee.

(c) Employee stock option or profit-sharing plans, social security and retirement rights.

(d) Title in which securities or other property (real or personal) should be held by the employee and his wife.

(e) Income tax returns, often described as "simple" when the questions are posed.

(f) Personal life or accident insurance of the employee.

(g) Divorce and separation.

(h) Automobile accidents and other casualty claims or defenses.

(i) Purchase of real estate.

6. Company Benefits.

One of the most important legally-oriented company-employee communications programs is that dealing with company benefits. It is estimated that by 1970 more than 30% of payroll will be going into fringe benefits. Apart from quantitative importance, the psychological value of a solid communications program is this field is tremendous. It deals with the employee's pocketbook and, above all, with his and his family's present and future security.

The employee's rights and interests must be calculated—then explained—on the basis of such factors as age, salary or wage scale, length of service, family structure, the various options available to the employee, contributions by the company, the employee, the government and possibly a union. Then, too, such a program must explain the mechanics and eligibility requirements for each segment of the benefits. As time passes, many of these factors inexorably change. This leads to continuing calculations and explanations.

All in all, the company is faced with a ponderous and increasingly onerous internal technical problem resulting in a complicated communicatory challenge. For example, Willard A. Weiss, an actuary and lawyer with long experience in this field, has estimated that some "750,000 calculations per employee" are required in the computerized analysis of an employee's rights and benefits. Weiss thus sums up the company's difficult communications problem: [10]

> Even high level employees have great difficulty in applying the formulae to their individual cases and estimating their present and future status. Efforts to indoctrinate supervisory employees in the system have been somewhat futile and result in great expenditures of time in attempting to counsel the rank and file.

Even in companies which administratively split off employee relations from public relations, the proper fulfillment of this explanatory program is important in a strictly public relations sense. Studies have shown that community understanding and appreciation of a company depend in part on its understanding of the company's benefits, their value and relative strength. Since this information is usually obtained by the community from the employees themselves, the importance of informing the employees properly and faithfully cannot be overemphasized.[11]

Such a program—together with its underlying administration—implicates two sources of legal liability:

(a) The *accuracy and validity* of the "arithmetic" or other data involved in developing the employee's rights and benefits.

This means compliance with criteria or formulae of federal/state statutes and their judicial interpretation, the rules, regulations, or approval of the relevant administrative agency; company-union contracts; individual employment agreements; contracts with insurance companies funding or underwriting benefits or company policy relative thereto.

The PR man usually must accept the "figures" prepared by specialized company staff or consultants. His concern is with the effect of errors, their ramifications and their legal and PR impact upon the overall employee program.

(b) The *method of communicating* the information to the employees and the degree of comprehension achieved.

Here the communicator must be sure that he is transmitting effective, understandable and unambiguous information. It is not enough to be accurate. Such accuracy must be embodied in language which is likely to be understood, taking into consideration the level of intelligence and comprehension of the employee and "the frailties of human understanding." If done ineffectively, the company may be liable for the employee's loss. See Section 7 below.

7. Basis of Company Liability.

If a company answers an employee's inquiry as to his rights, it is bound to "answer clearly" and use the care and competence which the employee "is justified in expecting." A failure to do so is likely to be considered negligence on the part of the company with resulting liability.

A leading case on this subject is *Gediman v. Anheuser Busch, Inc.,* [12] wherein the plaintiff was the executor of a former employee who had been a well-educated, high level executive of the defendant company. The employee had asked the company for an explanation of his rights under the company pension plan. The company's independent pension consultants prepared a memorandum for him, listing three alternative options, one of them a delayed distribution. The memorandum warned: "If your death occurs prior to your receipt of such distribution, the death benefit *would not be as much as* the death benefit described in (2) . . ." (Emphasis added.)

The employee chose this option but was killed before the indicated distribution date. The pension fund paid $32,780 to the estate; $79,000 would have been paid had the employee selected either of the other options.

The executor recovered the difference between the two amounts on the ground, as the court said, that the pension consultants "did not exercise that care and competence in obtaining and *communicating* the information which its recipient is justified in expecting." (Emphasis added.)

It should be noted that the employee had been accurately warned that one option would not pay as much as the other, but the court felt that the *language* used in putting the employee on notice of this fact was insufficient in view of the very large difference between approximately $32,000 and $79,000. The court said:

> When Barsi sought advice and defendant gave this, it was bound to take account of the frailties of human understanding . . . Barsi placed himself in defendant's hands. Defendant was not required to accept it: he could have suggested he consult his own advisors. Having undertaken to advise, the defendant was bound to advise clearly. . .

The basis of liability was negligence in failing "to advise clearly." It was not deceit or misrepresentation. In short, it resulted from honest but poor communications between employer and employee.

This is an application of the general warning of Justice Cardozo, who said that "one who assumes to act, even though gratuitously, may thereby become subject to the duty of acting carefully, if he acts at all." [13]

8. Employee Manuals.

Most companies, as part of their employee or personnel-relations programs, distribute one or more manuals which seek to explain various aspects of the employment relationship. In *Gediman,* such a manual had been distributed about the pension plan. The court, however, said:

> Neither the plan nor the employees' booklet, so beautifully clear to the experienced draftsman, used the kind of language that is fully understandable by even an intelligent layman; *perhaps it is just not possible to do so.* (Emphasis added.)

Decisions as to manuals will rest largely on overall company policy as to the alternatives discussed in Section 9 below. Assuming commitment to a cooperative policy, one or more manuals may help to avoid or skirt some of the company's possible liabilities.

(a) A manual reduces the explanations to positive and definite form. It avoids the vagaries of individual reaction and reply. Insofar as broad, general answers or explanations are sufficient and accurate, a manual is preferable.

(b) If the manual deals with matters which must be particularized for individual employees, generalities must be carefully policed and appropriate caveats used. There must be no lulling of the employee into reliance—perhaps to his detriment—on the manual.

(c) Manuals are unusually useful to companies with scattered plants or with decentralized or departmental responsibility for employee relations or counseling. A plant manager or supervisor may become almost a *pater familias* to his employees, enjoying a close personal relationship. This is conducive to much off-the-cuff "friendly advice," some of which is likely to be erroneous. Mandatory use of a manual can avoid some of these pitfalls.

(d) Manuals cannot "cover everything" and, in marginal situations, discretion would seem to dictate forbearance from "explanation by manual."

Canfield notes the subject matter of 12 separate "printed booklets or leaflets" used by some companies in "a complete employee orientation packet for new employees." [14] It may be suggestive that only one of them—described as an "Employee Benefit Handbook"—appears to deal with financial matters of interest to the employee.

9. Alternative Company Policies.

The employee in *Gediman* was a well-educated, high-level executive. Yet the company did not communicate with him with judicially acceptable effectiveness. It is, therefore, easy to understand the dangers implicit in endeavoring to explain some matters to the rank and file—presumably less well-educated or perceptive.

This poses the need for a clearly-defined top-management policy. This policy will probably result from a mixture of legal and PR thinking. This is one area in which close liaison and understanding by the PR-legal team are mandatory. Whatever the eventual policy may be, the following choices should be considered:

(a) The company may refuse to answer any questions by its employees or give them any information or advice. This probably is the only really safe course for a company to pursue. It should refer its employees to their own lawyers or other outside advisors.

(b) The company may give advice but accompany this with a clear and distinct "disclaimer," putting the employee on notice that it will not be responsible in any way, and, furthermore, that the employee should see his own personal advisor.

Neither (a) nor (b) is particularly attractive from the point of view of employee relations.

(c) The company can make very sure that its advice is both accurate and couched in language which the employee—regardless of level of education or intelligence—will clearly understand. This presents some very definite long-range problems in employee relations. More than that, the company may not be able to reduce some such advice to truly simple language on complicated matters—such as was the core of *Gediman*. Even a booklet dealing with Medicare involves some very difficult questions. See Section 8 above. This amounts to accepting a calculated risk as the price of improved employee relations.

10. Employees as Stockholders.

When employees become stockholders, the company not infrequently considers them as a "special kind" of stockholder although, technically, their position is no different from that of any "public" stockholder.

Employee-stockholders may receive special editions of the company's annual or interim reports. These may emphasize matters known to be of particular interest to employees. If they do receive special reports, they should also receive the regular reports distributed to all stockholders. Non-stockholding employees usually will also receive such special reports if they are used at all. This is part of the overall employees communications program. Special in-plant meetings are sometimes held—parallel to regular stockholder meetings.

These special reports sometimes add information not given in the regular reports—employment figures, for example. This would not appear to add any problems.

However, in revamping reports, care must be taken not to give any misleading data. There have been instances of this—springing usually from the desire to "simplify" the employee reports. See Chapter 22, Section 24.

11. Investment Information.

A growing type of company-employee communications is the explanation of investment principles to the employees. With the growing interest of the American public in corporate investments, this type of communication is becoming more common.

Such information—whether it be of a general character or beamed toward the company's own stock—should be highly factual and conservative. See Chapter 22, Section 3. The Department of Public Information of the New York Stock Exchange acts as a "clearing house" for a wide variety of information and source material very useful in the preparation of such employee communications.

The Exchange has "a variety of background articles and stock photos" which are available for such use. Arrangements can also be made for special photographs to be taken on the Exchange floor. Its Investors Information Department also "sets up special educational programs on how to invest—for company employees and other groups. Exchange-produced films on investment themes are also available." [15]

As long as this instruction and explanation are of a general character and confined to materials obtained from such sources, the company is not likely to become legally involved if employees misunderstand and suffer some alleged loss as a result. However, if information as to specific securities and issues is given—either to groups or in reply to individual inquiry—this may not be the case.

12. Special Liability Insurance.

In view of the general recognition of increased legal exposure in this area by corporations, their officers and directors, they have shown increased interest within recent years in liability insurance covering their activities and statements.[16]

This insurance also covers risks other than those involved in *Gediman.* This may involve, for example, protection of "insiders" breaching their duty to the corporation and other actions based on allegations of purely economic injury brought by stockholders or third parties. See Chapter 22, Sections 20 to 22. Traditionally, such losses are excluded from so-called "umbrella casualty policies" which protect a company and its agents from suits for product liability, libel and slander, etc.

This coverage is relatively new, first being written by Lloyds of London some 25 years ago. Any discussion of such policies and their effects is necessarily subject to a caveat that comments "are subject to rapid obsolescence." [17]

There are essentially two forms of policies although they are usually sold in one indivisible package. The first, using Lloyds' nomenclature, is "reimbursement for directors and officers liability insurance." This protects the corporation for lawful indemnification of its executives. The second is "directors and officers liability insurance." This protects the executives themselves against unindemnified losses.

All policies have a deductible amount of at least $20,000 and a co-insurance clause requiring the insured executive or corporation to contribute five per cent of any losses above the deductible amount. This is to protect the insurance company against a multiplicity of small claims.

The Lloyds policy insures against "any breach of duty, neglect, error, misstatement, misleading statement, omission or other act done or wrongfully attempted. . . ." Ordinarily coverage would be limited to losses flowing from innocent or negligent acts. Deliberate misconduct is probably not within the terms of the policy although this is not "wholly free from doubt." The Lloyds policy does not cover "acts of active and deliberate dishonesty committed . . . with actual dishonest purpose and intent. . . ."

It has been suggested that serious questions may arise as to coverage when a judgment is entered against the officer without any specification of fault, citing as an example the liability under §11 of the Securities Act of 1933, giving injured investors a cause of action against a broad class of persons connected with the issuance of a misleading registration statement. Here the aggrieved party need not prove that the defendant knew or had reason to know of the misstatement. The defendants can escape liability only if they can demonstrate the exercise of reasonable care.[18]

C. EMPLOYEE ATHLETIC ACTIVITIES.

13. Introduction.

Many companies have extensive employee athletic programs. These may include company-sponsored participation in community bowling, softball, basketball or golf leagues, employee athletic associations, athletic facilities on company property open to employees, their families and others for organized or casual sports or other activities such as picnics, support of Little League teams, even daily ten-minute calisthenics sessions on company time.

Company support may be given to employee theatricals or other "physical activities" which may not ordinarily be considered "athletic." To a considerable degree, however, company responsibility is essentially the same.

Company responsibility in these areas should be appraised as to the employees, their families and non-company-associated persons participating therein, either actively or as spectators.

The liability of the company may be premised on common law grounds, state workmen's compensation laws or other statutes. Unless otherwise indicated, this discussion is confined to situations and liability arising from common law because of the relationship of the parties.

Sections 14 to 16 below dealing with the liability of a company for injuries to its employees or members of the public in the course of employee athletic activities are not intended as inclusive discussions of the applicable tort law. They deal only with those special aspects of it created by the company's public relations or promotional interest in such events.

14. Injuries to Employees.

If an employee is injured in the course of a group-employee athletic event, his right to recover against the company is essentially the same as it would be against any other party.

Generally, a voluntary participant in a lawful game or sport contest assumes the dangers inherent in that game or contest and is precluded from recovery for injury or death resulting therefrom. On the other hand, that participant does not assume the risk of negligence—he may be precluded by his own contributory negligence—nor extraordinary risks involved therein unless he knew of them.[19]

The same rules apply to public participants injured in company-sponsored games. The status of the injured plaintiff makes little difference except from the point of view of proving assumption of the risks involved. Thus an employee who has frequently played baseball on a company diamond would be more likely to know of any unusual conditions than an outside participant playing thereon for the first time. This, however, becomes a question of fact.[20]

Also, it does not appear to be significant whether the game is played on the company premises or elsewhere except as to the question of whether the company should have known of the condition to which participants would be exposed with a resultant duty to rectify such conditions or clearly warn the participants.[21]

If the company is negligent in maintaining the site or running the game or contest, the company is generally liable unless contributory negligence of the employee can be shown.[22] The respective rights and liabilities of the company and the employee in this situation are essentially similar to those of any "invitee" as discussed in Chapter 14, Sections 6 to 11.

Most of the relevant cases have involved agricultural societies, county fairs, trotting race associations, etc. However, some cases have dealt with the question of the "liability of promoter or operator" which did involve PR activities.

One such case is *Hotels El Rancho v. Pray*.[23] The operators of a hotel, as part of their promotional activities "to increase the attractiveness of the hotel to tourists," ran a cross-country horse race with prizes to be given to the three winners. The race was not run on the hotel grounds but on other property which had been used for somewhat similar purposes previously.

As part of the promotional or "press-agentry" activities of the hotel (as the court put it), it arranged with the United States Navy to give bombing demonstrations. This resulted in the dropping of bombs on the area in which the race was later run and several large holes were made in the course. The plaintiff's horse hit such a hole and the plaintiff was killed.

In the court's opinion—written, coincidentally enough, by Justice Horsey—it was held that the hotel violated a duty "to furnish a reasonably safe place for the race" and "at least to warn the participants of the danger."

The plaintiff was held not to be contributorially negligent because of the extraordinary nature of the holes and there was no assumption of risk by reason of riding the same course previously in "treasure hunts" (also operated by the hotel for publicity purposes) before the holes were made. Even though the plaintiff rider may have assumed the risk of ordinary conditions, he did not assume the risk of an extraordinary situation of which he had no knowledge and which he could not be looking for, intent as he was on winning the race.

15. Injuries to Third Parties.

The liability of a company for injuries to third persons (other employees or members of the public) arising out of the recreational activities of employees appears to depend upon whether "such activities bear some genuine or substantial relation to the business of the employer."[24]

Not infrequently, the relation of the employer's business arises from the promotion of interests which fall definitely within almost any definition of employee relations. For example, a company has been held liable for injury to an employee riding in a company car taking employees to a dinner given by the manager "in order to promote legitimate and important interests of his employer's business, namely, harmony, cooperation, and good will among the employees."[25] On the other hand, the mere use of a company vehicle is not sufficient *per se* to indicate company liability.[26]

For such liability to exist, the employee must usually be acting within the scope of his employment or under the control or direction of the employer. Thus, in one case, no liability was found even though the company permitted employees to play baseball during their lunch hour on company premises.[27]

The mere fact that the company organizes the sports activity is not, of itself, a foundation for liability. It has been held, for example, that the company was not liable even though it entered a team in a city-wide "industrial golf league" and through its "athletic supervisor" recruited players from among its employees, provided them with uniforms and equipment and paid other expenses. One employee playing golf under this arrangement after working hours and "under no control or direction of his employer," hooked his ball and struck the plaintiff. The court pointed to the lack of control by the employer during the golf match when the injury occurred.[28]

The result would probably be different if, for example, the injury had occurred on company premises during a league baseball game on a diamond provided by the company and negligently maintained by it. The liability here would be premised on negligence and not on any doctrine of *respondeat superior* resulting from activities of the employees in the course of their employment.[29]

16. Employee Athletic Associations.

Many companies have organized employee athletic associations as the vehicle for athletic and other employee-participant programs. These groups are more or less "sponsored" by the company. The support may come from direct payments to the association by the company, allocations of profits from the vending machines on company premises, use of company premises for association purposes (indoor or outdoor), company underwriting of annual deficits, etc. Other support comes from employee dues or admission charges to the events or functions.

Most such associations are separately incorporated, with the actual leadership supplied by the employees after the initial company impetus.[30] As a matter of good employee relations, such leadership is to be encouraged—avoiding possible charges of company paternalism. Such management and control also serve to insulate the company from certain legal liabilities as discussed below.

The association may also run social or other types of events for the employees. In large companies the social function may be the responsibility of a separate employee association. Company liability is unaffected by such variance in organization.

Mere financial or other support of such associations does not appear to involve company liability for injuries occurring during their activities. On the other hand, if the association is merely a conduit or vehicle for company control and management of such events, the company would be responsible for such injuries. The use of the athletic association as a "device" or "fiction" will not protect the company. This becomes a question of fact, to be resolved on a case-by-case basis.

Klinsky v. Hanson Van Winkle Munning Co.[31] is a good example of the various problems arising from company assistance to an employees' athletic association. As usual, the athletic association had been separately incorporated. It ran an employee picnic at an outside picnic ground, not on company property. The company gave the association $1000 for the outing "seeking to promote good will among the employees." The association paid all of the outing costs out of this $1000 plus the proceeds realized from the sale of tickets. Later, the association returned the $1000 (which was not needed) to the company. In effect, therefore, the company underwrote—rather than paid—the expenses of the outing.

A woman guest was hit by a broken bat during an employees' baseball game. She sued "everybody": the company, the athletic association, the operator of the picnic grounds, the batter and others including the owner of the land upon which the picnic ground was operated. The court's opinion dealt in detail with the position of each of the various defendants.

As to the athletic association, the court held:

> [T]here was a fair inference that the association arranged for and ran the outing and that it had a duty to take measures to protect persons from injury from the ball game. No measures of this sort were undertaken by it or by anyone. We think that it was up to the jury to determine whether the association had control of the situation to such a degree that it could have averted the danger (citing cases).

The evidence showed that the officers of the association had ordered the printing of the tickets, collected at the gate and paid the bills for the outing. Its treasurer gave a meal guarantee to the picnic ground operator. It bought softballs and bats and paid for them even though the bill was made out to the company. A so-called Game Committee was appointed by the association which also bought playing cards, jump ropes, paddleballs, balloons, etc. for the children.

As to the company, the plaintiffs had claimed that the association and other persons "were acting on the company's behalf as instruments to maintain good labor relations." As to this, the court said:

> Their theory must be that the association and these persons were sufficiently subject to the company's control with respect to the details of the operation of the outing, as to be the agents of the company and to render the company liable for their negligent conduct (citing cases). There is no sufficient proof of this.

In other words, even though the company had assisted the athletic association by supplying funds in the first instance, it did not have such control over the athletic association as to make the association and its members agents of the company. Therefore, the company was not liable.

However, the rule and result might have been different if the picnic or outing had been held on company grounds. See Section 15 above and Chapter 14, Sections 6 and 10.

D. LABOR RELATIONS.

17. Scope of Discussion.

Labor relations is a very broad and ever-present subject in the modern industrial world, having many ramifications and involutions.[32] The discussion in Sections 18 to 27 below is confined to the communications aspects thereof. It deals largely with that element of the subject from the management side of the table.

No effort has been made to cover other facets of the program or relationship such as face-to-face collective bargaining or company lockouts. At the same time, these matters do have communicatory aspects which fall within the purview of the company public relations or industrial relations staff or counselor.

What follows is premised upon the provisions of the 1935 National Labor Relations Act (Wagner Act) [33] and the 1947 Labor Management Relations Act (Taft-Hartley Act),[34] together with the decisions of the National Labor Relations Board (NLRB) and the courts enforcing, interpreting or implementing these statutes.[35]

The Labor-Management Reporting and Disclosure Act of 1959 (LMRDA) [36] is also relevant but it is not herein considered. Under §203 (f) thereof, the employer, employer-association and labor-relations-consultant reporting requirements of the Act do not affect or amend the free-speech rights discussed in Sections 20 to 27 below.

It may be assumed for our purposes that the management-labor relation and its legal control have been preempted entirely by federal legislation. No effort has been made to discuss state labor relations laws (Little Wagner Acts) nor questions of federal jurisdiction.

18. Relevance of Public Relations.

One of the difficulties of generalizing about the status of the PR man in labor relations is his varied responsibility for, and relationship to, labor relations in different companies. In the smaller concern, he may be the sole person available. In the large, multi-plant operation he may be in either a peripheral or subordinate position, subject to the direction of the company, plant manager or the company legal counsel. His responsibility may vary from one of sole authority to that of "detail man," charged only with arranging press conferences.

Because of this broad spectrum of duties, it is almost mandatory that there be a clear definition of company policy, delineating the relative areas of staff responsibility.

This also applies to the PR counsel or consultant. Some such organizations handle client labor relations with the same personnel as serve other client needs. Some have separate departments whose work is confined to labor relations. Some handle only the external communications involved. Some are responsible for all phases thereof. Again it is difficult to generalize.

Whatever his capabilities may be, the PR man must always realize that he is legally the "voice of management" when he enters the labor arena. What he does—right or wrong—binds the company or client.

When a strike hits a company, the drama of the picket line, the police protection of company property, the front-page newspaper stories and pictures, and all of the other trappings of the moment tend to overemphasize the strike as an isolated episode. But strikes—even periodic collective bargaining—do not exist in a vacuum. They are only links in a chain—parts of a very important long-range program of the company. Seemingly routine PR activities and campaigns—apparently with no relationship to labor relations—can be exceedingly relevant.

Most managements have come to realize that overall or what might be called "pure" public relations is an important and integral part of their labor relations—something which should be undertaken and cultivated on a long-range basis.

There are essentially three areas in which continuing public relations can be most effective. These are (a) the development of an agreeable community climate, (b) the field of national labor legislation and (c) overall employee attitudes.

In discussing 20 years of his own experience with General Electric, Virgil Day wrote in 1966: [37]

> Where effective measures were undertaken to repair the public's misunderstanding concerning employee policies, hostility has

turned to open-mindedness and then to open support of a company's legitimate pursuit of business objectives—with all that means for job stability, improved wages, benefits and working conditions, and the prosperity of plant communities. Provided truthful and colorful communication of the employer's side of the story, communities appear far less willing to tolerate or support unthinking strike action than they did in those paralyzing waves of 1946 work stoppages.

Day then goes on to demonstrate how in 1947, 1959 and 1966, public opinion reacted favorably and with great force during congressional discussions of new labor legislation.

As to overall employee attitudes, nearly all employee-oriented long-range programs will contribute to employee understanding of the company image so that "when the chips are down," the company is not a "corporate ogre."

The *General Electric* case—discussed in Section 27 below—produced an insistent spate of comment from diverse sources, all pointing to the need for concentrated and continuous publicity and other PR efforts about the rights of management to communicate with its employees. For example, Theodore Iserman, an experienced attorney in the labor relations field, has said:

> This strange stretch of the labor law and constitutional guarantees should be called to the urgent attention of Congress because it concerns not only people in the employee and public relations field but all others interested in free speech, a free press and a free exchange of ideas.

John D. Baxter, senior editor of *Iron Age* and a knowledgeable observer of labor-management problems, has pointed out:

> Interviews with many corporate and trade associations counsels clearly point to the need for public relations men to aid in halting this whittling away of management rights. Their role can be a major one.

*   *   *   *

> Allied in the fight against this rights loss are top managers, corporate counsel and industrial relations executives. They can use expert public relations help to tell their story to the public and to its representatives in Washington, . . .

Thus, what might be called "routine" PR activities must be supplemented by specifically directed campaigns, generated by specific legal developments in this field. More and more is management recognizing the need for PR programs keyed to this problem.

The employee is also a member of the community. Campaigns directed to the community inevitably condition the thinking of the employees. These effects are both direct and indirect, the latter resulting from expressions of approval by non-employee members of the community. In some cases—perhaps in small towns in which the plant is particularly important—the relationship between community and employer may be so satisfactory that the local officials will help the employer against the union. It has been held that a company is responsible for the acts (unfair practices) of the local elected officials, such as the mayor, in the course of an organizing drive.[38]

19. Communication Tools Used.

In a hard-fought or protracted management-labor dispute—whether involving representation or collective bargaining—it is likely that every possible communications tool will be used by management to get its position before the employees and the community. Some of these are routine channels—such as internal house organs or employee manuals. Others are special materials used only during the stress periods.

The decisions of the NLRB and the courts have dealt with this varied panoply which has included:

Speeches by company officers, attorneys or other representatives.

Bulletin board materials and displays.

Internal or employee-directed house organs.

Personal conversations with individual employees or small groups of employees, both "in the shop" and "in the office."

Personal letters from management to the individual employee or his wife.

Employee manuals.

Plant public address system use.

Press conferences.

Mass meetings with employees—either on or off company time and property.

Paid newspaper or broadcast media advertising.

Free meals in company cafeteria.

Lucky number drawings for television sets and other prizes.

New-employee hiring indoctrination—whether printed or oral.

Community meetings.

Generally speaking, the same rules apply to all of these communications channels or media. Some, however, are subject to special criteria—such as the mass meetings of employees on company time and property as discussed in Section 24 below.

20. "Free Speech" Doctrine.

The rights and position of the employer to engage freely in a dialogue with its employees and the public during times of labor stress have evolved from a resolution of the conflicts between the basic free-speech rights of the First Amendment and the restrictive language of the federal labor laws.[39]

This has been done—as in other sectors of the free-speech conflict—by adhering to the basic right but subjecting it to certain restraints, the thrust of which is to prevent coercion of the employees in the exercise of their rights.[40] For the general principles underlying this philosophy, see Chapter 4, Sections 1 to 3.

The presently controlling legislation is found in §8(c) of the Taft-Hartley Act—frequently referred to as the "free speech section"—which provides:

> The expressing of any view, argument, or opinion, or the dissemination thereof, whether in written, printed, graphic or visual form, shall not constitute or be evidence of an unfair labor practice under any of the provisions of this Act, if such expression contains no threat of reprisal or force or promise of benefit.

An unending parade of "unfair labor practice cases" has passed before the Board and the courts in an effort to interpret and apply not so much the basic protective language of §8(c), but the exceptions "threat of reprisal or force" and "promise of benefit," involvement of which denudes the employer of its privilege of free speech.[41]

This provision concerning threat or promise is a more precise definition and classification of the limitations on employer free speech than the prior judicial generalities which had relied on constitutional grounds.[42] These expressions have caused much confusion and have resulted in what has been called "some enchanting problems in semantics." [43]

A frequent example of such semantics is found in the employer which does not threaten its employees with pay cuts or dismissals but describes what it believes to be the inevitable consequences of either initial unionization or demands for increased wages or other benefits. The employer may point out that it will probably be impossible for it to continue in business or that it will lose certain accounts under these circumstances. These are not threats. They are considered merely opinion or "prophecy." Such statements have been held permissible in many cases.[44]

There are four principal situations in which the issue of employer free speech is likely to develop in unfair labor practice cases. These have been summarized as: [45]

(a) An employer is alleged to have commited an unfair labor practice by making coercive statements (either oral or written) to his employees—that is, statements which contain threats of reprisal or force, or promise of benefit.

(b) An employer's statements are alleged to be unfair labor practices when they are considered in the context in which they were made, despite the fact that, standing alone, they contain no threat or promise of benefit.

(c) An employer's statements, although non-coercive, are alleged to be evidence of some other unfair practice on the part of the employer.

(d) An employer who has delivered a non-coercive speech to his employees on company time and property ("captive audience") is alleged to have committed an unfair labor practice by refusing a union's request for an opportunity to reply to the employer's speech on company time and property.

The same institutional author summarizes the "general rules" applied by the Board in meeting each of these issues:

(a) Employer statements or speeches to employees which contain threats of reprisal or force, or promises of benefit, are unfair labor practices and are not protected under the free speech provisions of the Act.

(b) Employer statements or speeches to employees which, on their face, do not contain any threat or promise of benefit may nevertheless constitute unfair labor practices when considered in the context in which they were made.

(c) Employer statements or speeches to employees which do not contain any threats or promises of benefit cannot be used as evidence of some other unfair labor practice on the part of the employer.

(d) An employer is privileged to make non-coercive speeches to his employees on company time and property, and does not commit an unfair labor practice by refusing a union's request for an opportunity to reply to the employer's speech under similar conditions, provided that the employer does not have in effect an unlawful broad no-solicitation rule.

These are dealt with in greater detail in Sections 21 to 26 below.

21. "Totality of Conduct" Concept.

Company communications, otherwise permissible under the basic "free speech" rule, may become illegal under the so-called "totality of conduct" doctrine. This is an amorphous, sometimes overriding concept whereby the company communication is not considered as an isolated incident, to be judged apart from other company statements or activities. As the Supreme Court said in the leading *Virginia Electric* case, [46]

Conduct, though evidenced in part by speech, may amount in connection with other circumstances to coercion within the meaning of the Act. If the total activities of an employer restrain or coerce his employees in their free choice, then those employees are entitled to the protection of the Act.

This doctrine *appeared* to be abandoned by the Board after the passage of the "free speech" amendment in the 1947 Taft-Hartley Act.[47] However, the Board still applies the reasoning behind the rule. It appraises the company statement in the *context* in which it is made.[48] Courts have applied the rule with different explanations, referring variously to "all the circumstances surrounding the utterance," [49] "the setting, the conditions, the methods, the incidents, the purpose, or other probative context," [50] "the substance and context of the statements and the position of the speaker in relation to the audience," [51] and taking the questions and statements "not merely by themselves but in the connection in which they are made." [52]

An interesting and clear-cut example of this rule arose in connection with a series of two letters from the employer. It was found that neither letter—considered separately—contained a threat or promise. Yet, when "considered jointly," they were not privileged and the Board set aside a representation election.[53]

One commentator has summed up the concept by pointing out: [54]

It is the configuration of factors—the interweaving of the words themselves, the form in which communicated, the quality of the union-management relationship, the character of the community —which determines whether there is promise of reward and threat of reprisal or not.

Unfortunately, questions under this doctrine are matters of fact— resolved by the Board or the courts on a case-by-case basis. The company communicator has no way of definitively knowing in advance whether a particular company statement, otherwise acceptable, will be considered coercive, threatening or promissory should its effect be subsequently litigated.

The cases give some guidelines but each situation may contain its own imponderables. With experience, however, the practitioner may acquire a "feel" for the circumstantial impact of a statement against the surrounding background of which it is a part.

22. Non-Privileged Statements.

Company statements which hold out promises of benefits to the employees or contain threats against them are generally held coercive and are likely to be considered non-privileged under §8(c) of the Taft-Hartley Act.[55] The following is a sampling of such company statements:

Attempts to discredit the representative of a certified union.

Circulation of anti-union petitions.

Letters to employees denying union's authority as bargaining representatives.

Questioning of employees about their union activities under circumstances reasonably indicating coercion threats—a very "touchy subject." The cases have gone both ways.[56] It is included in this section as a warning of its inherent problems.

Clear statement that employer will not bargain with the union even if it wins the election.

Statement that plant would be closed before employer would bargain with a union.

Direct or implied threats against employees.

Firm statement that working hours will be reduced (resulting in lesser weekly pay) if plant is unionized.

Implication that continued employment was dependent upon rejection of the union.

Statement that power at plant will remain turned off if union is not renounced.

Reminder that employees active in prior organization attempts were no longer with the company.

Letters to employees threatening to use delaying legal methods to prevent bargaining and implying thereby economic loss to the employees.

23. Privileged Statements.

From the cases—decided both before and since the "free speech" amendment of 1947—there have emerged certain guidelines and examples as to what an employer may say under the shield of free speech. In considering the following sampling, however, it must be recognized that, while a given statement may seem to be privileged, it *may* lose that posture if conjoined with other matters—even themselves privileged—under the "totality" concept discussed in Section 21 above.

Generally speaking, the employer may issue public statements, make speeches or circulate printed materials about the following matters or those which serve the following purposes: [57]

Extol or justify the company's wage policies, fringe benefits or other practices.

Answer union arguments or charges against the company and point out their fallacies.

Express its views regarding, and opposition to, labor unions generally.

Make comments about the background and character of the labor movement or the union in question.

Comment upon the checkoff system and the effect of the payment of union dues.

Bring to the attention of employees the activities of the union at other plants with adverse results.

Point out that union membership is not a requirement for continued employment.

Discuss union tactics—both generally and specifically.

Give facts to justify company action against specific employees in the union.

Explain to employees or to the public generally the effect of a strike on the community or the military or space effort.

Explain the price structure of the employer and its inability to make a higher wage offer.

Explain that company may lose orders or customers if it becomes unionized.

Write letters to employees explaining representation election procedures.

Give employees directly the state and terms of the current bargaining negotiations.

Explain the need for the company's remaining competitive in view of potential increased labor costs.

Request employees of a new plant to hold up for a year their decisions about joining a union.

Indicate company preference for one union as against another.

Indicate that current offer will be the last offer the company will or can make.

Predict the results of unionization.

Discuss possibility of company being required to close the plant or reduce working hours to avoid overtime.

Point out that there is no need for a union or that the union will not produce added benefits.

Remind employees about *prior* announcements of new or increased company benefits although they are not yet in operation.

Point out that wage increases are not tied to unionization.

Explain that payment of union dues is a waste of employees' money.

Circulate legitimate letters from other companies or customers as to their reaction to company's possible increased costs.

Expression of fear that union may demand changes in seniority structure and eligibility on multiple-plant basis.

Explanation that employees voting against the union would also be represented by the union.

Giving employees a free meal in company cafeteria after company hours and making a non-coercive speech thereat when attendance was voluntary.

Reminding employees about subsequent lucky number drawing for television set and other prizes, as previously announced.

24. Speeches on Company Time and Property.

Speeches by officers or other representatives of the employer are frequent labor relations tools. Generally speaking, such speeches are subject to the same free speech doctrine—as are any other company communication or statement. Consequently, they have been used in many instances as the foundation for charges of an unfair labor practice or to set aside an election.

Since a speech is, by its very nature, ephemeral, the speaker should speak from a prepared text. Admittedly, such a speech may not be as effective as would be the same remarks delivered more informally. However, caution clearly dictates that the remarks be prepared in writing before being delivered.[58] Furthermore, the speaker should not depart from his text.

As a general rule, any company speech to employees which contains threats of reprisal or promise of benefits is unlawful regardless of when or where it is delivered by the company officer or representative. See Section 20 above. However, employers are free to give non-coercive talks to their employees on company property and on company time and, in such event, to deny a union's request for the opportunity to reply thereto on company property and company time.[59]

There are two exceptions or limitations to this general rule. These exceptions are:

(a) The "24-hour" ban discussed in Section 25 below.

(b) The "captive audience" doctrine discussed in Section 26 below.

25. The "24-Hour" Ban.

Neither the employer nor the union may make a speech on company time within 24 hours immediately prior to a representation election conducted by the NLRB. Under this doctrine, announced in the *Peerless Plywood* case,[60] an election will be set aside if such a speech is made. On the other hand, such a violation is not considered an unfair labor practice.[61]

The 24-hour rule does not operate to prevent either the employer or the union from making speeches—on or off company premises—during this 24-hour period provided that the employees' attendance is voluntary and on their own time.[62]

Speeches may be made by the employer on company time prior to the 24-hour period.[63] Also, the 24-hour rule prevents neither the employer nor the union from circulating campaign literature to the employee on or off company property or from using any other campaign materials or campaigning methods even during the 24-hour period.[64]

26. "Captive Audience" Rule.

Speeches made by company representatives on company property are subject to the so-called "captive audience" rule. This is quite apart from the "24-hour rule" discussed in Section 25 above.

A speech on behalf of the employer—given on company time and property at any time—may be unlawful if the employer has a rule which forbids union solicitation on company property during *both* working and non-working time. Such a company rule is known as a "broad no-solicitation rule."

Under this doctrine of the *Livingston Shirt* case,[65] if the employer has no company rule against union solicitation or if solicitation is forbidden only during working hours, the employer may make speeches to the employees on company property and time—even without giving the union the opportunity to reply.

If the union is permitted to solicit and propagandize on company property after working hours, this opens the door to company speeches because there would, in such instance, be no "broad no-solicitation rule."

In certain limited instances, a broad no-solicitation rule does not operate to prevent on-property speeches by the employer. Department stores are typical of this because of the nature of that business whereby such a rule is necessary for its efficient operation.[66]

27. "Boulwarism."

"Boulwarism"—as it has come to be known in the vernacular—is a form of collective bargaining initiated by L. R. Boulware when he took over the labor relations of General Electric in 1947. It has been used by that and other companies since then. It is premised on a mixture of continuing company research and employee communications.[67] Our concern here is with the latter factor.

The company employs an intensive stream of communications directly to its employees and the public—some of the material originating at the company's home office but most of it stemming from the company's individual plants. This flow from company to employee continues year in and year out. It is not confined to the period during which collective bargaining is under way although it may peak at such times.

The posture of the company is that the company has the interests of the employee at heart and therefore its firm offer to the unions is "right," being based on intensive research and considerations important to the employees.

The importance of direct communications to the employees is evident in this summary: [68]

> (1) Management has a tendency to bypass the union and communicate directly with its employees on day-to-day problems. (2) Management attempts to win its employees' allegiance in competition with the union by convincing them that it is sincerely interested in their welfare and is doing its best to promote it. (3) Management follows a policy of firmness in negotiating with the union. (4) Management communicates its offers directly to its workers and the public, independently of the union.

The legal status of Boulwarism has not yet been definitively determined although it has been involved in several cases before the NLRB and the courts. In the well-known *General Electric* case [69] growing out of the company's 1960 contract negotiations, much stress was laid on "the great mass of employee communications to which G.E. employees were subjected." One employee received 100 items. Yet it was found that, of the great welter of company material, only in one instance was any of it coercive or improper.

Even though the NLRB decided against General Electric, it does not appear to have condemned Boulwarism as a method of bargaining. Other rulings have been premised upon the specific facts in other cases involving Boulwarism. Thus, in the *Philip Carey* case,[70] the NLRB was also faced with the same overall method of bargaining and said:

> [W]e are deciding the case only on its facts, and not passing upon any purportedly general technique of bargaining.

While the Examiner in the *General Electric* case did mention Boulwarism by name, the term will not be found anywhere in the NLRB's opinion. Until the courts finally decide otherwise, it may be accepted that Boulwarism as a concept or technique is not *per se* improper but that each case involving it will be decided on the facts. This is true of any form of bargaining including the original and commonly used "auction sale" give-and-take negotiation and compromise to reach a mutually acceptable result.

Boulwarism is significant because of its emphasis upon direct communications with the employees.

One of the possible dangers implicit in this may be, as was said in the *General Electric* case, that the company "elaborated its arguments far more fully to employees than it had at the bargaining table . . . [It] presented arguments to employees that it had not presented at all to the union negotiators."

The employer is generally not prevented from speaking directly to its employees. The important restriction on direct employee communication is that the company may not urge or solicit the employees to abandon or bypass their union in favor of dealing directly with the employer.

Thus, the employer may make every possible legitimate (non-coercive) effort to convince the individual employee directly that the company's position and offer are reasonable and that the union is being arbitrary. This is permissible as long as the company makes it clear that it will deal with the union and urge the employees to continue to deal through the union.

Notes

1. For general discussions of management-employee relations and communications, see Lerbinger, *Employee Communications,* and Schorr, *Small Industry* in HANDBOOK OF PUBLIC RELATIONS (Stephenson ed. 1960) at 439–75, 533–40, 553–55; DOVER, EFFECTIVE COMMUNICATIONS IN COMPANY PUBLICATIONS (1959); CUTLIP & CENTER, EFFECTIVE PUBLIC RELATIONS 223–39 ("The Employee Public") (3d ed. 1964); CANFIELD, PUBLIC RELATIONS 87–114 ("Employee Relations") (3d ed. 1960).

2. Cutlip & Center, *supra* note 1, at 232.

3. Cutlip & Center, *supra* note 1, at 212.

4. See Brennan, *The Image Among Your Employees,* in DEVELOPING THE CORPORATE IMAGE 41–48 (Bristol ed. 1960).

5. Canfield, *supra* note 1, at 95.

6. See generally NIELANDER & MILLER, PUBLIC RELATIONS 67–69 (1956).

7. For a general discussion of the problem and practical situations involved, see Davis, *Liability to Employees for Gratuitous Advice or Service,* 18 BUS. LAW. 1063 (1963).

8. J.M.M., *James Angell MacLachlan,* 18 Harv. L.S. Bull. May, 1967, at 2.

9. Many of these situations are discussed in detail in Davis, *supra* note 7, *passim.*

10. Weiss, *The Hardest Story Ever Told: Employee Benefits,* P.R.J., July, 1966, at 11–12.

11. Williams, *How Employees Influence a Company's Reputation,* P.R.J., May, 1959, at 11.

12. 299 F.2d 537 (2d Cir. 1962).

13. Glanzer v. Shepard, 233 N.Y. 236, 135 N.E. 275 (1922).

14. Canfield, *supra* note 1, at 102.

15. Rudick C. Lawrence, *Financial Public Relations and the NYSE,* remarks before the Public Relations Group of the Management Council of Southwestern Connecticut, Nov. 17, 1966.

16. See generally Note, *Liability Insurance for Corporate Executives,* 80 HARV. L. REV. 648 (1967).

17. *Id.* at 650.

18. Other discussions of this subject will be found in Bishop, *Indemnification for Corporate Insiders: Problems and Methods—Including Insurance,* in PROCEEDINGS OF 4TH ANNUAL CORPORATE COUNCIL INSTITUTE 328 (1965); Bishop, *New Cure for an Old Ailment: Insurance Against Director's and Officers' Liability,* 22 BUS. LAW. 92 (1966); Dyson, *The Director's Liability for Negligence,* 40 IND. L.J. 341 (1965); see also materials cited in Note, *supra* note 16, at note 12.

19. Annot., *Liability for Injury or Death of Participant in Game or Contest,* 7 A.L.R.2d 704, 706 (1949) and cases discussed therein.

20. Frieze v. Rosenthal, 148 Misc. 273, 264 N.Y.S. 378, *rev'd without op.,* 241

App. Div. 719, 269 N.Y.S. 1010 (1933). *Cf.* Hotels El Rancho v. Pray, *infra* note 23.

21. Hotels El Rancho v. Pray, *infra* note 23.

22. See Annots. and cases cited and discussed therein at 22 A.L.R. 610, 29 A.L.R. 29, 38 A.L.R. 357, 44 A.L.R. 203, 53 A.L.R. 855, 61 A.L.R. 1289, 98 A.L.R. 557, 138 A.L.R. 541, 141 A.L.R. 1315, 168 A.L.R. 896.

23. 64 Nev. 591, 187 P.2d 568 (1947).

24. Annot., *Liability of Employer for Injury Resulting From Games or Other Recreational or Social Activities,* 18 A.L.R.2d 1372 (1951). See also Annot., 56 A.L.R. 1127 (1928).

25. Ackerman v. Jennings Co., 107 Conn. 393, 140 Atl. 760, 56 A.L.R. 1127 (1928).

26. Stenzler v. Standard Gas Light Co., 179 App. Div. 774, 167 N.Y.S. 282, *aff'd without op.,* 226 N.Y. 681, 123 N.E. 891 (1917).

27. Harrington v. Border City Mfg. Co., 240 Mass. 170, 132 N.E. 721, 18 A.L.R. 610, 21 N.C.C.A. 668 (1921).

28. Rogers v. Allis Chalmers Mfg. Co., 153 Ohio St. 513, 92 N.E.2d 677, 18 A.L.R.2d 1363 (1950).

29. See, *e.g.,* Easler v. Downie Amusement Co., 125 Me. 334, 133 Atl. 905, 53 A.L.R. 847 (1926).

30. Schorr, *supra* note 1, at 539.

31. 38 N.J. Super. 439, 119 A.2d 166 (1955).

32. Probably the most accessible and current sources of labor relations law are the multivolume *Labor Law Reports,* published by Commerce Clearing House, and *Labor Relations Reporter,* published by the Bureau of National Affairs. Also useful is *United States Law Week* issued by the same publisher.

33. 49 Stat. 449, 29 U.S.C. §§151–58 (1935), as amended.

34. 61 Stat. 136, 29 U.S.C. §§141–44, etc. (1947), as amended.

35. The decisions are reprinted in the Reports of the N.L.R.B. and also in the various volumes of CCH Labor Cases.

36. 73 Stat. 519, 29 U.S.C. §153, etc. (1959).

37. Day, *Communication in Labor Relations,* 11 P.R.Q. 15 (1966). Sources for the quotations from Iserman and Baxter are: Iserman, *The Strange Stretch of the Labor Law,* P.R.J., May, 1965, at 10; Baxter, *Who Has the Right to Communicate with Employees?* P.R.J., May, 1965, at 8.

38. Clothing Workers v. N.L.R.B., 347 F.2d 128 (8th Cir. 1966); Colsen Corp. v. N.L.R.B., 347 F.2d 128, 35 L.W. 2346 (D.C. Cir. 1966).

39. For a general discussion and history of "Free Speech Under NLRA," see 3 CCH Lab. L. Rep. ¶5005, at 10, 211–15.

40. N.L.R.B. v. Virginia Elec. & Power Co., 314 U.S. 469 (1941).

41. See cases cited and discussed in 3 CCH Lab. L. Rep. ¶3880 ("Promises").

42. See, *e.g.,* N.L.R.B. v. Virginia Elec. & Power Co., *supra* note 40; N.L.R.B. v. Ford Motor Co., 114 F.2d 905 (6th Cir. 1940); Budd Motor Co. v. N.L.R.B., 142 F.2d 922 (3d Cir. 1944); N.L.R.B. v. Montgomery Ward & Co., 157 F.2d 486 (8th Cir. 1946).

43. See Dover, *supra* note 1, at 184.

44. See, *e.g.,* N.L.R.B. v. McCatron, 216 F.2d 212 (9th Cir. 1954); N.L.R.B. v.

Superex Drugs, 341 F.2d 747 (6th Cir. 1965); Sylvania Elec. Prod., 106 N.L.R.B. 1210 (1953); Safeway Stores, 122 N.L.R.B. 1369 (1959).

45. 4 CCH Lab. L. Rep. ¶5010, at 10,235.
46. N.L.R.B. v. Virginia Elec. & Power Co., *supra* note 40.
47. See, *e.g.*, Babcock & Wilcox Co., 77 N.L.R.B. 577 (1948); Minnesota Mining & Mfg. Co., 81 N.L.R.B. 557 (1949); John Deere Plow Co., 82 N.L.R.B. 69 (1949).
48. N.L.R.B. v. Kropp Forge Co., 178 F.2d 822 (7th Cir. 1949).
49. N.L.R.B. v. O'Keefe & Merritt Mfg. Co., 178 F.2d 445 (9th Cir. 1949).
50. N.L.R.B. v. Protein Blenders, 215 F.2d 749 (8th Cir. 1954).
51. Cary Lumber Co., 102 N.L.R.B. 406 (1953).
52. N.L.R.B. v. Fulton Bag and Cotton Mills, 175 F.2d 675 (6th Cir. 1949).
53. Boston Mut. Life Ins. Co., 110 N.L.R.B. 272 (1954).
54. Barbash, *Employer "Free Speech" and Employee Right,* 14 Lab. L.J. 317–18 (1963).
55. See cases cited and summarized at 4 CCH Lab. L. Rep. ¶5020.25–.4391.
56. S. H. Kress & Co. v. N.L.R.B., 317 F.2d 225 (9th Cir. 1963) (privileged); Blue Flash Express, 109 N.L.R.B. 591 (1954) (privileged), *overruling* Standard-Coosa-Thatcher, 85 N.L.R.B. 1385 (1949) (interrogation of employees held *per se* illegal); N.L.R.B. v. Minnesota Mining & Mfg. Co., 179 F.2d 823 (8th Cir. 1950) (non-privileged); Daniel Construction Co. v. N.L.R.B., 341 F.2d 805 (4th Cir. 1965), *cert. denied,* 382 U.S. 831 (1965) (non-privileged); Graber Mfg. Co., 111 N.L.R.B. 167 (1955) (non-privileged).
57. See cases cited and summarized at 4 CCH Lab. L. Rep. ¶¶5020.50–.992, 5025.20–.59.
58. See texts of employer's speeches reprinted in 4 CCH Lab. L. Rep. ¶5045.
59. N.L.R.B. v. Clark Bros. Corp., 163 F.2d 373 (2d Cir. 1947).
60. 107 N.L.R.B. 427 (1953).
61. Sparklette Drinking Water Co., 107 N.L.R.B. 1462 (1954).
62. Peerless Plywood Co., *supra* note 60.
63. *Id.*
64. *Id.*
65. Livingston Shirt Corp., 107 N.L.R.B. 400 (1953).
66. See discussion, 4 CCH Lab. L. Rep. ¶5015 as to effect of *Livingston Shirt* rule on cases such as *Bonwit Teller* and *Woolworth* in this context.
67. For discussion of "Boulwarism," see Northrup, Boulwarism (1964); Cooper, *Boulwarism and the Duty to Bargain in Good Faith,* 20 Rutgers L. Rev. 653 (1966).
68. McMurry, *War and Peace in Labor Relations,* 33 Harv. Bus. Rev. 48 (1955).
69. General Electric Co., 150 N.L.R.B. 192 (1964), on appeal to the Seventh Circuit.
70. Philip Carey Mfg. Co., 140 N.L.R.B. 1103 (1963).

Chapter 22

Financial Public Relations and Publicity

A. INTRODUCTION

B. DISCLOSURE

C. PROXY SOLICITATION PUBLICITY

D. PUBLICITY AND NEW ISSUES

E. MISCELLANEOUS FINANCIAL CONTROLS

Chapter 22

Financial Public Relations
and Publicity

A. INTRODUCTION.

1. Definition and Purposes.

The Public Relations Society of America (PRSA) in 1963 defined financial public relations as being [1]

> [T]hat area of public relations which relates to the dissemination of information that affects the understanding of stockholders and investors generally concerning the financial position and prospects of a company, and includes among its objectives the improvement of relations between corporations and their stockholders.

Harold Gartley, one of the earliest leaders in financial PR, said in 1957: [2]

> Financial Public Relations is, in essence, the telling and retelling of a company's story not only to its own shareholders but even more importantly, to the 30,000 men and women in the securities business.

Gartley supplements this definition by referring to four "practical purposes" of such activity. These help to explain the general definitions. They are:

(a) To achieve and maintain a FAIR evaluation of the company's securities in the marketplace.
(b) To provide well-priced "share money."
(c) To meet competition in the nationwide financial community.
(d) To prevent misunderstandings, and maintain loyalty of both shareholders and financial opinion leaders.

733

For similar definitions and some criticism as to purposes from government-control-oriented sources, see Section 6 below.

These definitions may be somewhat too limited when applied to "financial PR in action." They seem to confine the function to the dissemination of information about a *company*. However, the concept probably is a fair one—especially when financial PR conforms, as so much of it does, to the "Be Conservative" mandate of the SEC and the stock exchanges. See Sections 3 and 14 below.

In one sense, at least, these definitions include certain tools or techniques not always included in the PR kit. These include a considerable amount of paid advertising, "sales literature," radio and TV scripts and commercials, etc.—all of which are subject to the same rules and requirements as are what might be called "pure" publicity and public relations.

2. The Basic Disclosure Philosophy.

> Sunlight is said to be the best of disinfectants; electric light the most efficient policeman.

Thus, in 1914, in his provocative *Other People's Money*, Louis D. Brandeis urged publicity as the remedy for "social and industrial disease." [3] This was to become the basis of governmental regulation of securities. It was adopted in 1933 by President Roosevelt, in his message to Congress: [4]

> There is, however, an obligation upon us to insist that every issue of new securities to be sold in interstate commerce shall be accompanied by full publicity and information and that no essentially important element attending the issue shall be concealed from the buying public.
> The proposal adds to the ancient rule of caveat emptor, the further doctrine "let the seller beware." *It puts the burden of telling the whole truth on the seller.* It should give impetus to honest dealing in securities and thereby bring back public confidence. (Emphasis added.)

The Securities Exchange Commission (SEC) has frequently restated this philosophy in language of which the following is indicative: [5]

> A basic purpose of the Securities Act of 1933, the Securities Exchange Act of 1934 and the Investment Company Act of 1940 is to require the dissemination of *adequate and accurate information* concerning issuers and their securities in connection with the offer and sale of securities to the public, and the publication periodically of *material business and financial facts, knowledge which is essential to an informed trading market in such securities.*

There has been an increasing tendency . . . to give publicity through many media concerning corporate affairs which goes beyond the statutory requirements. This practice reflects a commendable and growing recognition on the part of industry and the investment community of the importance of informing security holders and the public generally with respect to *important business and financial developments*. (Emphasis added.)

The New York Stock Exchange reinforces this policy by pinpointing, as the first objective of its Listing Agreement: [6]

Timely disclosure to the public and the Exchange, of *information which may affect security values or influence investment decisions,* and to which stockholders, the public and the Exchange have a warrantable interest; . . . (Emphasis added.)

The specific application and requirements of the disclosure philosophy are discussed in Sections 9 to 26 below.

3. Unique Character of Financial Public Relations.

Financial public relations is probably unique, differing for many reasons from any other public relations area. For this reason—perhaps for more than any other—financial PR has, more and more, become the province of the specialist. At the same time, many a PR practitioner—whether staff or independent counselor—may find himself occasionally involved in what is really financial PR although this may not be immediately apparent. One example would be the house organ editor who includes, in a particular issue, an article about investment principles, perhaps dealing with the company's program for employee stock purchases.

A non-financial PR program may be premised on any one of several purposes or desired results. Applying this multiple-alternative approach to financial PR, Rudick Lawrence, vice-president of the New York Stock Exchange, has said: [7]

There are two divergent views of financial public relations. One school sees it as an effort to achieve, through PR techniques, a higher price for a company's stock. The other school regards it as an effort to tell investors and other audiences the full story about the company, its management, its finances, and its products.

Now, it may seem that the first view is cynical, the latter naive—with the best practical definition lying somewhere between the two. But at the New York Stock Exchange we think the second view is so naive as to be highly sophisticated. From our observations, this is the approach practiced by the most reputable, most hard-nosed—and most successful—corporations in the country.

It is this "full story" or disclosure requirement or purpose which makes financial PR the unique activity which it is. Subsections (a) to (q) below are merely examples of this dominating premise of disclosure. All contribute to the unique demand of this PR area and, in turn, result from it.

(a) *Insufficiency of Normal Ethical Standards.*

Even the most ethical or best-motivated PR practitioner or firm may fall short of adequately handling financial PR.

(b) *Specific Governmental and Exchange Requirements.*

Financial PR and publicity are the subject of many and different specific requirements or prohibitions originating with the Securities Exchange Commission, the National Association of Securities Dealers, the New York Stock Exchange and state commissions. These controls are the starting points for a proper understanding and administration of financial PR.

(c) *Continuous Policing.*

Financial PR is subject to continuous policing by these bodies. Not only do the "rules of the game" exist but their implementation is closely investigated and the rules enforced, on both a prophylactic and *post hoc* basis.

(d) *Unexplored Areas and Problems.*

Despite the cooperative attitude of the policing bodies and the growing mass of literature—both official and unofficial—on the subject, there are still "gray areas," within which PR practitioners must "come up with their own answers . . . [and] examine their own positions and make their own decisions." [8]

(e) *High Degree of Public Interest.*

There were said to be 20 million stockholders in the United States in 1965. The total will, according to some estimates, reach 30 million in 1975.[9] Public interest in financial PR and publicity is therefore significant and continuing—probably greater than is likely to exist in other areas of PR or publicity.

(f) *Sophistication of Public and Press.*

Nowhere else in public relations does a news release face such intelligent and sophisticated scrutiny from "publics" such as security analysts, exchange officials, bankers, brokers, "board watchers" and stockholders.

(g) Importance of Timing.

The enforced need for proper timing of publicity may be critical. Reference need only be made to the "timely disclosure" requirement. Company needs or benefits are relatively unimportant and may sometimes have to be overridden.

(h) Need for Accuracy.

Accurate reporting is mandatory in financial PR. This goes beyond mere reporting of facts. It includes reporting of opinion and judgment.

(i) Conservative Orientation.

Allied to accuracy is the need for conservative semantics. Whatever may be the power of the creative in other PR activities, it makes a limited contribution in financial PR. Understatement—not overstatement—is a built-in requirement in doubtful or ambiguous circumstances.

(j) Completeness Requirement.

Honesty in financial PR requires the telling of "the whole truth," not merely sketchy or conclusory comments, unexplained or unmitigated.

(k) Unfavorable Disclosure.

Perhaps relatively alien to public relations generally but often necessary in financial PR is the prompt disclosure of unfavorable news as well as the favorable. In a sense, this is part of the completeness requirement. Failure to disclose may here be even more important than actual disclosure.

(l) The "Open Door" Policy.

Normally, disclosure of company information is a unilateral matter within the control and discretion of the company and its PR people. This is not always true in financial PR. Quite apart from required reporting and disclosure, information is frequently sought by analysts, stockholders and other persons with legitimate interests—inquiries which cannot and should not go unanswered. Disclosures to such persons may require an immediate affirmative general disclosure.

(m) Internal Security.

Adequate internal security—sometimes almost of "cloak and dagger" character or proportions—is necessary to prevent "leaks" and rumors and to maintain positive control and appropriate handling of required disclosures.

(n) *Liaison Between Management and PR Arm.*

Intimate and continuing liaison between company management and its PR people—internal department or outside PR counsel—is necessary. So important is this that formal logistical planning is often necessary. So, too, may be the attendance of the PR man at Board meetings.

(o) *Increased Contact with Legal Counsel.*

Despite the seemingly routine character of many required financial PR activities, probably more contact with legal counsel is necessary than is customary in public relations activities generally.

(p) *High Level Corporate Responsibility.*

Financial PR is here more than a "function of management"; it is a direct *responsibility* of management. The Board of Directors and corporate officers may even be *personally*—as well as officially—involved if improprieties occur. It is unlikely that PR personnel will anywhere have as intimate a contact with top management as in financial PR.

(q) *Continuing Change.*

As recently as 1966, the New York Stock Exchange was able to say: "Financial communications are going through a continuing revolution." [10] These changes from time to time do not merely fill in some of the heretofore unanswered questions but may also stiffen requirements thought to be firm and well understood. The financial PR man or counsel must be on a perpetual alert for new developments. For an example, see Section 23 below.

4. Public Relations Involvement With Securities Regulation.

The basic philosophy of securities regulation is public disclosure as discussed in Section 2 above. The concern of all who engage in any form of financial publicity or public relations is therefore clear. This applies to the corporate PR practitioner, outside PR counsel and even a corporate officer or employee primarily charged with other functions and to whom such disclosure or publicity may be merely an additional assignment.

While much of the required and more formal forms of disclosure—a prospectus for a new issue or the filing of reports with the SEC, NASD or a stock exchange, for example—are the responsibilities of others than the PR practitioner, the latter still has serious obligations in supplemental or other "informal" promotional or publicity activities.

The PR practitioner is usually only a link—no matter how important a link—between the company (primarily responsible for the disclosure) and the "public" involved, be it the public-at-large, company stockholders, financial analysts, the financial press, etc. He may be the person who actually prepares the release, article or speech in question. He may, in fact, be the genesis or instigator of the disclosure—quite independently of his employer. But whatever his place in the "chain of command," he is essentially an intermediary, an agent. What he does binds his employer or client. See Chapter 2.

This requires the PR counsel to maintain close and continuing contact with management as well as legal counsel in order to use "reasonable care to ascertain the facts correctly and to disseminate only information which he believes to be accurate and adequate." His obligations may go even further as spelled out in the PRSA Interpretation discussed in Section 8 below.

Beyond this obligation to client or employer, financial PR counsel may be *personally* involved by reason of his activities. He may be considered an "insider" or subject to charges of conflicting interests, as discussed in Section 22 below. He or his firm may become personally liable to third parties in civil actions or under the criminal laws. See Sections 9 and 10 below and Chapter 2, Sections 15 and 16.

A PR practitioner may sometimes be a director of a company he serves. As a director, he has a statutory status as an "insider." See Section 22 below. The same rules against disclosure and trading apply to him as would apply to a member of a NYSE firm who is also a company director, as to whom the Exchange has said: [11]

> Every director has a fiduciary obligation not to reveal any privileged information to anyone not authorized to receive it. Not until there is full public disclosure of such data, particularly when the information might have a bearing on the market price of the securities, is a director released from the necessity of keeping information of this character to himself . . . [and] must meticulously avoid any disclosure of inside information to his partners, employees of the firm, his customers. . . .

All of these legal ramifications and sequelae lead to one solid conclusion: financial PR is not a field for the uninitiated or the inexperienced. Years of general PR expertise are no substitute for intensive study of the unique and definitive requirements of financial PR practice.

5. Internal and External Sectors Involved.

Financial PR seems to be an external activity. On the other hand, as far as the PR practitioner is concerned, it involves both external and internal sectors or elements, using those terms as distinct from "publics."

The practitioner is concerned—more or less intimately and continuously—with the following sectors. Furthermore, the legal obligations of the practitioner may vary as among these sectors, thus meriting some threshold attention. These sectors are:

    (a) Management.
    (b) Stockholders.
    (c) Company employees.
    (d) Financial community.
    (e) Financial press.
    (f) General public.
    (g) Government control agencies.
    (h) Quasi-governmental or private control agencies and groups.

Some of these sectors overlap. The most obvious overlap is that of government, which is involved with all of the others. Also, management and ownership may overlap, thus generating the "insider" problems discussed in Section 22 below. Interests of the stockholders parallel those of the stock exchange.

The needs of some sectors may seem, on occasion, to be disparate. Thus, the effort of management vis-à-vis corporate competition may seem to run head-on into the interests and "right to know" of stockholders. The "insider" rules may oppose management to the stockholders. There is, therefore, in financial PR, the need for balancing the various interests involved—for serving all fairly without impairment of the interests of any.

At the same time, a failure to appreciate the multiplicity of targets and purposes has, in some cases, led to unintegrated financial PR activities which—aside from being less than effective—are illegal. This is particularly true of smaller companies which may retain a financial PR counselor for limited purposes only—perhaps an appearance before a group of analysts. By divorcing the other elements of the program, the company fragments its efforts and, more important, exposes itself to criticism.

6. The Securities Exchange Commission "Special Study."

An understanding of financial PR is incomplete without some familiarity with the *Special Study of Securities Markets*, published in 1963 by the SEC.[12] This was a study in depth of the operation of all phases of the securities markets—the most intensive study thereof since the early 1930s when stock exchange and securities regulation became a prime interest of the federal government. It is referred to as the "Special Study" throughout the text of this chapter.

Part 3 thereof deals largely with "corporate publicity and public relations." [13] The investigation of financial PR and publicity is undoubtedly the most thorough ever made. It deals with nearly every phase of the subject and should be "required reading" for anyone engaged in financial PR.

At the outset, the Special Study makes it clear that it recognizes the importance of corporate publicity, saying:

> Informal corporate publicity is an important supplement to the disclosures required by the securities acts. In order to keep shareholders, the investment community, and the general public continuously informed of corporate developments, it is desirable for issuers to disseminate publicity through the channels of news distribution as well as by other means. This fact has been recognized by the Commission, which has encouraged publicly held corporations to employ publicity and public relations for these purposes.

Tracing the history of financial PR as "a specialized industry"—especially since the 1930s—the Special Study accepts the customary definitions, describing the "financial public relations consultant" as the person generally "responsible for communications for publicly held companies to their stockholders and the financial community" and footnoting the definition "financial public relations is public relations designed to influence the attitudes of the financial community." See Section 1 above.

The Special Study goes into detail as to the structure of the financial PR industry, its compensation arrangements, its functions, the governmental and other policing thereof, and even the promotional claims made by financial PR practitioners in obtaining new accounts. Against this background, it then deals at length with a wide variety of public relations situations which "have been used for purposes contrary to the letter and spirit of the securities acts." It documents examples of "misleading publicity [which] has directly affected the market price of securities."

It goes beyond a consideration of the results of financial PR. It delves into and delineates specific PR techniques and, in some portions thereof, blueprints entire financial PR campaigns. It almost reads like a do-it-yourself text.

It is made clear that much of financial PR is properly conducted and is not used for ulterior purposes or speculatory and improper reasons. However, the critical documentation of the following activities should be sufficient warning of the posture of the SEC:

(a) Optimistic sales and earnings reports and projections "which seem to be based primarily on wishful thinking."

(b) Glowing descriptions of new products still in the experimental stages.

(c)   Announcements of mergers and acquisitions which are only "vague possibilities."

(d)   Improper placement of articles in the public press.

(e)   Preparation by the PR man of a broker's or analyst's market letters.

(f)   Extensive junkets apparently unconnected with proper corporate purposes.

(g)   Undue stress in publicity on favorable news and developments.

(h)   Omission or understatement of adverse or unfavorable corporate developments.

(i)   Allocation to financial writers of shares of new "hot issues."

(j)   Constant importuning of analysts and financial writers by telephone and in person.

(k)   "Leaking" and creation of rumors "on the street" of impending stock splits, mergers, etc.

(l)   Favoring certain analysts with otherwise undisclosed but material news without making such developments public generally.

(m)   Acceptance of compensation in client stock, warrants or options.

(n)   Profitable sales of client securities after placing stories causing a price rise in the securities.

(o)   Direct contacts with and "tipping" of registered representatives to create interest in a client's securities.

(p)   Improper pre-filing press conferences and releases.

The Special Study also deals at some length with the effect of financial PR upon product sales and their possible interrelationship. It points out that "[t]he distinction between financial and product public relations is not always an easy one to draw," citing examples of product advertising and PR tied specifically to rises in stock prices. The converse was also found to be true: financial PR can be and has been used to sell a company's *products* and for other business purposes.

Quite apart from the financial PR context, these findings are otherwise significant. As discussed in Chapter 4, Sections 18 to 26, corporate public relations is a "trade" purpose even though it may appear to be directed only toward institutional or image-building functions. This finding by the Special Study fortifies the comments in that chapter.

7. The Control Agencies.

The financial PR practitioner should be familiar with the control structure within the shadow of which he and his clients or employer operate. This structure is an amalgam of federal and state legislation, governmental administrative agencies, quasi-governmental supervision, stock exchange rules and contract provisions, civil and criminal court enforcement and trade association inquiry.

The concern of financial PR with these controls is limited largely to those elements which deal with disclosure and publicity. Therefore, no effort has been made herein to explore other applications of such laws and the diverse interests or requirements of the policing authorities.[14]

The following subsections are intended only to direct the attention of PR practitioners toward the more important sources of regulation and the laws or programs which they administer. It is an "outline map"—not a "tour guide." The degree of interest of the PR practitioner in each will naturally vary—dependent largely upon the character of the concern or institution being served.

(a) *Securities and Exchange Commission. (SEC.)*

This is the principal federal control agency. It administers the following six federal statutes:

Securities Act of 1933,[15] dealing largely with the initial issuance of securities including many disclosure and filing requirements and restrictions.

Securities Exchange Act of 1934,[16] concerned essentially with "post-distribution trading" (including disclosure provisions) in listed and certain over-the-counter securities, the registration of exchanges and of broker-dealers.

Public Utilities Holding Company Act of 1935,[17] relative to electric and gas utility company financing and control structures.

Trust Indenture Act of 1939,[18] relevant to registration of corporate bond issues and the qualifications of the trustees thereof.

Investment Company Act of 1940,[19] concerned with activities and disclosure needs of investment companies (mutual funds) and the securities issued by them.

Investment Advisers Act of 1940,[20] regulating those in the business of advising others about securities transactions, again including certain disclosure provisions.

In 1966 the SEC published *The Work of the Securities and Exchange Commission*. This is a relatively brief but highly informative pamphlet which deals in broad strokes with the Commission's functions as pinpointed so briefly above. It should serve as an excellent "first primer" for those interested in the overall activities of the Commission. It also contains a listing of available SEC publications, a great many of which should prove very useful—even perhaps necessary—to the financial PR practitioner.

(b) National Association of Securities Dealers, Inc. (NASD.)

NASD is a voluntary, self-regulatory association of over-the-counter broker-dealers, the creation of which was provided for in a Securities Exchange Act amendment of 1938—often referred to as the Maloney Act. Among its functions—very important to financial PR and promotion—is the Association's enforcement of the SEC *Statement of Policy* concerning investment company advertising and supplemental literature and "communications."

Its "Rules of Fair Practice" are the basis of much other supervisory and enforcement activity as well as the continuing advisory service for its members.

Non-NASD members have been brought under similar regulation by the SEC pursuant to the 1964 amendments to the Securities Exchange Act.

Among NASD publications of considerable assistance to PR and publicity people are the *Reprint of the Manual* (1967) and *What You Should Know . . .* (1964). Both contain extended discussions and reprints of important materials referred to at various points in this chapter.

(c) Miscellaneous Federal Agencies.

Other federal agencies exercise regulatory controls—relevant to financial PR—over the promotional, publicity and advertising activities under their jurisdiction. Among them are the Federal Deposit Insurance Corporation (FDIC) in connection with banks with insured deposits. Other analogous federal controls over banks are exercised by the Comptroller of the Currency and the Board of Governors of the Federal Reserve System.

The Federal Home Loan Bank Board (FHLBB) and the Federal Savings and Loan Insurance Corporation (FSLIC) share responsibilities in connection with savings and loan associations—both federally- and state-chartered—which are so insured or otherwise within the jurisdiction of FHLBB.

Various other federal agencies—more concerned with organizational, operational or rate controls of industries or activities under their jurisdiction—also have some policing powers as to matters which fall within financial PR.

(d) State Regulatory Agencies.

Every state except Nevada has a Public Securities Commission—however it may be named—which has effective control over certain aspects of securities issue, promotion and disclosure. The SEC legislation specifically "saves" such state controls and contains several intrastate exemptions. Also, some special or general state statutes deal with civil or penal liability for securities fraud, misrepresentation, etc.[21]

For an example of such state regulation of securities communications, see the discussion of the *Allis Chalmers* case, in Chapter 4, Section 14(a).

Other state commissions, not specifically securities-oriented, have certain supervisory obligations over financial PR or promotion of the industries or businesses within their jurisdiction.

(e) New York Stock Exchange. (NYSE.)

The importance of the control programs of the NYSE over financial PR and publicity relative to listed securities and by its members cannot be overemphasized. Through its Listing Agreement, listed companies are required to meet very substantial and varied requirements as to proper and timely disclosure and filings. The promotional, among other, activities of its members are rigidly policed.

Basic materials and guidelines issued by the NYSE in these areas are the *Company Manual,* particularly Sections A-2 and A-3, relative to listed company disclosures and, as to NYSE members, *Communications With the Public,* a reprint of the Rules dealing with their advertising, market letters, research reports, sales literature, radio, television and writing and speaking activities.

(f) American Stock Exchange (AMEX) and Other Securities Exchanges.

AMEX and other securities exchanges follow generally the disclosure and related rules of the NYSE under their own listing agreements and membership requirements. Some such regulations are less stringent as is indicated in the tabulation on pages 753–756.

(g) Public Relations Society of America, Inc. (PRSA.)

PRSA is a voluntary trade association in the public relations field. It includes among its activities a self-regulatory program, within the structure of which financial PR looms large. This program is discussed in detail in Section 8 below. The PRSA also maintains a continuing liaison program with the SEC relative to the Commission's controls as they may affect PR practitioners.

8. PRSA Financial Public Relations Standards.

The Public Relations Society of America, Inc. (PRSA) adopted a Code of Professional Standards for the Practice of Public Relations in 1959 and amended it in 1963. These Standards replaced and strengthened a similar Code previously enacted in 1954.

In 1963 the PRSA Board of Directors approved the following "Interpretation" of this Code as it applies to financial PR practice:

1. It is the responsibility of the member practicing financial public relations to know and understand the rules and regulations of the SEC and the laws which it administers and the other laws, rules and regulations affecting financial public relations and to act in accordance with their letter and spirit. (See paragraph 2 of the Code.)

2. It shall be the objective of such member to follow the policy of full disclosure of corporate information, except in such instances where such information is of a confidential nature. The purpose of this objective is to enable an accurate evaluation of the company by the investing public and not to influence the price of securities. Such information should be accurate, clear and understandable. (See paragraphs 1 and 2 of the Code.)

3. Such member shall observe the confidential nature of certain of the information he has access to because of his employment and shall take every precaution to make sure this information is not used in a manner detrimental to his client's or employer's best interests. (See paragraph 5 of the Code.)

4. Such member shall disclose or release information promptly so as to avoid the possibility of any use of the information by an insider for personal gain. In general, such member should make every effort to comply with the spirit and intent of the "Timely Disclosure" provisions of the New York Stock Exchange Company Manual. Information deemed not confidential but which is not subject to a formal release shall be available to all on an equal basis. (See paragraphs 1 and 2 of the Code.)

5. Such member shall exercise reasonable care to ascertain the facts correctly and to disseminate only information which he believes to be accurate and adequate. Such members shall use reasonable care to avoid the issuance or release of predictions or projections of financial or other matters lacking adequate basis in fact. (See paragraph 7 of the Code.)

6. Such member shall act promptly to correct false or misleading information or rumors concerning his client's or employer's securities or business whenever he has reason to believe such information or rumors exist. (See paragraphs 1, 2 and 7 of the Code.)

7. Such member shall clearly identify to the investing public the sources of any communication for which he is responsible, including the name of the client or employer on whose behalf the communication is made. (See paragraph 8 of the Code.)

8. Such member shall not exploit the information he has gained as an insider for personal gain. However, this is not intended to prohibit a member from making bona fide investments in his company's or client's securities in accordance with normal investment practices. (See paragraphs 1 and 4 of the Code.)

9. Such member shall not accept compensation which would place him in a position of conflict with his duty to his client, employer or the investing public. Specifically, such member shall not accept a contingent fee or a stock option from his client or employer unless part of an over-all plan in favor of corporate executives, nor shall he accept securities as compensation at a value substantially below market price. (See paragraph 4 of the Code.)

10. Such member shall so act as to maintain the integrity of channels of public communication and to observe generally accepted standards of good taste. He shall as a minimum observe the publicly announced standards published by organizations representing the media of communications. (See paragraph 6 of the Code.)

As used throughout this booklet, the term "Member" includes both Active Member and Associate Member of the Society.

This interpretation, which was prepared for the PRSA Board by the Society's legal counsel, an Advisory Committee working with the SEC and the PRSA Committee on Standards of Professional Practice, is rooted directly in the Code and has the full force of the Code behind it. A violation of any one of its ten points would be subject to the same procedures and penalties as a violation of the Code.

Since this interpretation is so closely keyed to the basic PRSA Code, reference thereto should be made at all times and to all interpretations and amendments of the Code as may be made from time to time. See Chapter 20, Section 9. Copies of the Code, the financial PR Interpretation thereof and other interpretations and amendments may be obtained from the headquarters of PRSA, 845 Third Avenue, New York, New York 10022.[22]

B. DISCLOSURE.

As discussed in Section 2 above, the basis of federal securities control is the doctrine of disclosure. However, recognition of this is only the beginning unless, of course, a policy of "disclose everything" is to be followed. Such a policy is not only empirically unlikely but also operationally unsound.

The degree of disclosure, its subject matter, timing, logistics or mechanics, results thereof, etc. all present problems which involve judgment and experience as supplements to the requirements of government agencies and securities exchange policy. Sections 9 to 26 below deal with these various facets.

9. Federal Anti-Fraud Laws.

Disclosure and its legal impact are based, to a considerable degree, upon the anti-fraud provisions of the securities acts. We are not here concerned with fraud, deception and lack of disclosure in connection with issuance of securities—matters which arise largely in respect to formal documents (such as a prospectus) or steps taken in registering such securities. As to certain aspects of this, see Sections 31 to 35 below.

The basic federal anti-fraud provisions appear in §10(b) of the Exchange Act, providing: [23]

It shall be unlawful for any person, directly or indirectly, by the use of any means or instrumentality of interstate commerce or of the mails, or of any facility of any national securities exchange—

*   *   *   *

(b) To use or employ, in connection with the purchase or sale of any security registered on a national securities exchange or any security not so registered, any manipulative or deceptive device or contrivance in contravention of such rules and regulations as the Commission may prescribe as necessary or appropriate in the public interest or for the protection of investors.

The corresponding SEC Rule 10b-5 provides: [24]

It shall be unlawful for any person, directly or indirectly, by the use of any means or instrumentality of interstate commerce, or of the mails, or of any facility of any national securities exchange,
(1) to employ any device, scheme, or artifice to defraud,
(2) to make any untrue statement of a material fact or to omit to state a material fact necessary in order to make the statements made, in the light of the circumstances under which they were made, not misleading, or
(3) to engage in any act, practice, or course of business which operates or would operate as a fraud or deceit upon any person,
in connection with the purchase or sale of any security.

Rule 10b-5 has heen held to be valid and not so vague or ambiguous as to be unconstitutional.[25]

The key question is whether a "device or contrivance" is "deceptive" within the context of the Act and the Rule. The Rule pinpoints this more closely—insofar as financial PR practitioners are concerned—by a basic reference to "any untrue statement of a material fact," among other requirements for liability.

Any untrue statement or a technically true but misleading statement falls within the Rule.[26] Complete non-disclosure—the absence of any representations whatsoever—may violate the Rule if there is a duty to disclose. Such a duty is owed to the stockholders of a corporation by its directors, officers and controlling stockholders with reference to confidential information about the affairs of the corporation obtained by reason of their corporate position.[27]

Conduct which violates Rule 10b-5 may also involve a breach of a common law fiduciary duty. The fact that deception occurred *within* the corporate structure does not by itself avoid liability under the Rule.[28]

Whether non-disclosure or any other form of deception violates Subsections 1, 2 or 3 of the Rule is relatively unimportant.[29] The Supreme Court has said that the scope of Subsection 3 is so broad as to render Subsection 2 mere "surplusage."[30]

The anti-fraud provisions of §10b of the Act and Rule 10b-5 are separate and distinct from the "insider" provisions contained in §16 of the Act and further discussed in Section 22 below. §16 relates only to the liability of directors, officers and principal stockholders as therein defined. The anti-fraud provisions, on the other hand, are much broader and include "any person." §16 limits the liabilities of these insiders to certain indicated sanctions. A person involved under the anti-fraud sections may be subjected to liability beyond the limited sanctions provided in §16.[31]

The Rule is not limited in its application to officers, directors, and controlling shareholders. By its very terms, it applies to "any person." Whether a particular individual such as a public relations practitioner is liable for non-disclosure depends upon whether he is under a legal duty to disclose. Such an obligation, which is created by the Rule itself, notwithstanding the absence of any duty at common law, rests upon two principal elements announced in the leading *Cady, Roberts & Co.* case: [32]

(1) the existence of a relationship giving access, directly or indirectly, to information intended to be available only for a corporate purpose and not for the benefit of anyone, and
(2) the inherent unfairness involved where a party takes advantage of such information knowing it is unavailable to those with whom he is dealing.

In the application of this principle, no distinction can be made between directors, officers and controlling shareholders (as a separate group) and the employees of a corporation, at least those in responsible positions who acquire confidential information about the affairs of the corporation through their employment relationship.

Thus, an accountant,[33] a broker,[34] and a lawyer acting as "manager of . . . public . . . relations"[35] have been held subject to "a Section 10b action."

10. State Anti-Fraud Laws.

The anti-fraud laws of some states prohibit dissemination of false or misleading corporate publicity.[36] Of particular importance is the Martin Act, adopted in New York in 1955.[37] The provisions of the Martin Act are described as broader than those of the federal securities acts.[38] Section 352-c provides that it shall be illegal for any person "or any agent or employee thereof" to employ

> (a) Any fraud, deception, concealment, suppression, false pretense, or fictitious or pretended purchase or sale;
> (b) Any promise or representation as to the future which is beyond reasonable expectation or unwarranted by existing circumstances;
> (c) Any representation or statement which is false, where the person who made such representation or statement:
> (i) knew the truth; or (ii) with reasonable effort could have known the truth; or (iii) made no reasonable effort to ascertain the truth; or (iv) did not have knowledge concerning the representation or statement made; where engaged in to induce or promote the issuance, distribution, exchange, sale, negotiation or purchase within or from this State of any securities . . . ; regardless of whether issuance, distribution, exchange, sale, negotiation or purchase resulted.

The New York criminal law also makes unlawful the circulation of false statements for the purpose of affecting the market price of securities.[39] However, this act has been given a strict interpretation. Corporate statements in advertising, etc., apparently are regarded as mere "puffing." [40] The provision does not appear to have been intensively applied.

11. Relationship of SEC/Exchange Requirements.

The provisions of the securities acts mandate certain formal filings. Initially, these deal with registration of the securities and thereafter with the filings (among others) of Form 8-K, described by the SEC as "for current reports." As to matters to be reported on Form 8-K, reference should be made to the form itself in accordance with SEC Rule 13a-11. The tabulation on pages 753–756 will also serve as a guide.

This latter procedure is described as "a continuous disclosure system." However, Form 8-K need be filed only within ten days after the close of the month in which the specified event has occurred. Much important corporate news—even though later to be disclosed in Form 8-K—must be given proper publicity and airing at the time it occurs, prior to the time of the formal filing.

The timely requirements of the exchanges seek to fill this hiatus. Such timely "informal publicity" is not a substitute for the SEC filings but rather an additional precursor thereof. In recognition of the contemporaneous timeliness and the "gap-filling" effect of this informal disclosure, Ralph Saul, president of the American Stock Exchange, has said: [41]

> *First,* timely disclosure works in the world of "real" time—corporate developments are disclosed at the time of or shortly after they happen, rather than periodically. *Secondly,* timely disclosure requires prompt dissemination of information through news media so that all investors are placed on an equal footing. (Filed information under the 1934 Act, on the other hand, must be sought out, analyzed and then disseminated if it is to be useful.) *Finally,* timely disclosure calls for reporting many corporate developments not required by the technical reporting requirements of the 1934 Act.

12. Subject Matter of Timely Disclosure.

General definitions of the subject matter requiring immediate releases have proliferated. Among those from significant government, exchange and judicial sources are:

(a) "Material business and financial facts, knowledge of which is essential to an informed trading market in such securities." [42]

(b) "Information with respect to important business and financial developments." [43]

(c) "Information which may affect security values or influence investment decisions, and in which the stockholders, the public and the Exchange have a warrantable interest." [44]

(d) "Any material development in [a corporation's] affairs and operations, whether favorable or unfavorable, which might significantly affect the market for its securities or influence investment decisions." [45]

(e) "Facts which in reasonable and objective contemplation might affect the value of the corporation's stock or securities." [46]

(f) "[Facts to which] a reasonable man would attach importance in determining his choice of action in the transaction in question." [47]

13. Specific News To Be Released Immediately.

The general definitions in Section 12 above acquire practical significance when related to specific types of "corporate news" which have in the past been found by exchanges, courts, etc. to require timely disclosure or immediate release.

A minimum itemization of such developments would include the following:

Dividends or their omission or change.

Annual and quarterly earnings.

Preliminary but audited interim earnings.

Annual reports. See Section 24 below.

Stock splits.

Rights to subscribe.

Mergers and acquisitions.

Key management changes.

Major product developments and discoveries.

Contracts and awards.

Expansion plans.

Change of business purpose.

Defaults on senior securities.

Disposition of significant assets.

Security redemption.

Proxy materials involving non-routine matters.

Purchase of own securities in open market.

These and other matters which may require similar treatment are dealt with in the accompanying tabulation of "Reporting Requirements" originally appearing in the *Timely Disclosure Manual*, published and copyrighted by Edward Howard & Co. This material, in then currently updated form, also appeared in the April, 1966, 1967 and 1968 issues of the *Public Relations Journal* in articles by Robert W. Taft and Craig S. Thompson of the firm.[48] The April, 1968 tabulation is reproduced by permission of the copyright owner, Edward Howard & Co., and of the *Public Relations Journal*.

In commenting on the utility and value of the *Manual* in its original form, Rudick Lawrence of the NYSE has said: [49]

> There certainly is a need for a compendium of the various requirements of various agencies and organizations, and I believe this manual is a good, succinct approach to this need.

The tabulation contains the reporting and disclosure requirements of the SEC, NYSE, AMEX and the Midwest and Pacific Stock Exchange, together with "generally recommended publicity practice for all companies."

Particular attention should be paid to items marked "TD" which should be the subject of timely disclosure.

14. Required Informational Standard.

The basic standard for all corporate information filed with the SEC or announced to the public is "truth," but this overall concept needs definition—perhaps more in financial publicity than in any other "product" area.

Adopting SEC Rule 10b-5, it may be said that such materials—regardless of their form or the medium through which they are communicated—should not "make an untrue statement of a material fact or . . . omit to state a material fact necessary in order to make the statements made, in the light of the circumstances under which they were made, not misleading. . . ."

REPORTING REQUIREMENTS

REPORTING REQUIRED FOR:	SECURITIES AND EXCHANGE COMMISSION	NEW YORK STOCK EXCHANGE	AMERICAN STOCK EXCHANGE	MIDWEST AND PACIFIC STOCK EXCHANGE	GENERALLY RECOMMENDED PUBLICITY PRACTICE— ALL COMPANIES
ACCOUNTING— CHANGE IN METHODS OR CHANGE IN FISCAL YEAR:	8-K* may be required if change in method results in or is related to a material revaluation of assets or restatement of capital share account.	Notice to Exchange if change in method is substantial. 8-K if filed. Must disclose effect of any change in next succeeding interim and annual report.	8-K if filed. Same as NYSE.	8-K if filed. Notice of any material change.	Ordinarily no publicity at time of change. Recommend effort in subsequent financial reports to relate old and new financial methods/old and new reporting periods.
ACQUISITION OR MERGER:	8-K if company or majority-owned subsidiary acquires a significant (15 per cent increase in total assets or revenues) amount of assets or business other than in course of business or if registrant issues more than 5 per cent of additional securities. Proxy soliciting material or Registration Statement may also be required.	8-K if filed. No other formal notice required.	8-K if filed. Same as NYSE.	8-K if filed. Timely disclosure provisions apply.	TD: **Recommend publicity immediately following directors' action. Earlier comment may be required by unusual market action or by rumors circulating about event.
AMENDMENT OF CHARTER OR BYLAWS:	8-K if matter subject to stockholders' approval or if change materially modifies rights of holders of any class of registered securities.	Four copies of material sent to stockholders in respect to proposed changes. Certified copies of changes when effective. 8-K required for amendments to charter or by-laws.	8-K. Same as NYSE.	8-K. Certified copy and opinion of counsel, three copies of mailings to stockholders.	Recommend publicity if change alters rights or interests of shareholders.
ANNUAL REPORT TO SHAREHOLDERS:	Required by Section 13 of Securities Exchange Act of 1934 on Form 10-K to be filed no later than 120 days after close of fiscal year. Submit four copies of printed annual report with 10-K. Annual report must be delivered to shareholders with, or prior to, delivery of proxy material.	Published and submitted to shareholders at least 15 days before annual meeting but no later than three months after close of fiscal year. (See individual company listing agreement.) PROMPTEST POSSIBLE ISSUANCE URGED. Three copies to Exchange. Recommend release of audited figures as soon as available.	10 days before meeting but no later than four months after close of fiscal year. PROMPTEST POSSIBLE ISSUANCE URGED. Three copies to Exchange. Recommend release of audited figures as soon as available.	MIDWEST: Mail with or prior to notice of annual meeting a report containing balance sheet, income statement, analysis of surplus account covering period since last report. Consolidated, certified copy to Exchange. PACIFIC: Copies to Exchange and shareholders 15 days before meeting, not more than 120 days after close of year.	TD: Publicity required. Recommend release of annual financial information as soon as available; second release at time printed report is issued.

ally speaking, Form 8-K must be filed within 10 days after the close of each month during which an event occurs which must be reported on this form. There eptions, which should be discussed with counsel.

s which, in our opinion, are clearly timely disclosure matters have been marked TD. The NYSE "timely disclosure provisions" require issuance of a press re- "immediate release" basis to "one or more of the newspapers of general circulation in New York City which regularly publish financial news and simultaneously Jones & Company, Inc. and one or more of the other major national news services"—AP, UPI, Reuters. The Exchange manual also states, "When news of a d event which may affect the value of a company's securities or influence investment decisions is released shortly before the opening or during market hours s recommended that the Department of Stock List of the Exchange be notified by telephone no later than simultaneously with the announcement of the event to vs media." The manual then warns that the Exchange may temporarily halt trading until, normally, "15 minutes after appearance of the news on the Dow-Jones cker."

REPORTING REQUIRED FOR:	SEC	NYSE	AMEX	MSE and PSE	RECOMMENDED PUBLICITY PRAC
AUDITORS CHANGED:		Prompt notice of change in accounting firm which regularly audits company books.	Same as NYSE.		Normally no publi —consider mention annual report.
BUSINESS PURPOSES CHANGED:	8-K if registrant deems change of material of importance to security holders (consult counsel).	Prompt notice of any material change in general character or nature of business.	8-K if filed. Same as NYSE.	8-K if filed. PROMPT notice of any change in general character or nature of business.	TD: Recommend licity where cha may affect marke stock.
CAPITAL SURPLUS CHARGES:	8-K required for material restatement of capital share accounts.	Prior notice of any proposed substantial charge by company or by directly or indirectly controlled subsidiary.	Same as NYSE.	8-K if filed.	Depends on circu stances.
COLLATERAL REMOVED OR CHANGED:	8-K unless made pursuant to terms of an indenture qualified under Trust Indenture Act of 1939.	8-K. IMMEDIATE notice.	8-K. Same as NYSE.	8-K.	Depends on inden
CONVERSION RATES—CHANGES IN:	8-K if material change.	Prompt publicity on any change in convertible security, or termination of conversion privilege when conversions have been occurring or appear imminent. Notice by mail to holders of record. Immediate notice to Exchange.	8-K if filed. Same as NYSE.	8-K if filed.	TD: Publicity sh be timed to the e causing the chang termination of the version privilege. mediate notice to tistical services.
DECREASE IN FLOATING SUPPLY OF STOCK:	8-K if decreased more than 5 per cent of previously outstanding amount by payment of indebtedness or decreased more than 1 per cent by open market purchases.	Prompt notice when occasioned by actual or proposed deposit under voting trust agreements, etc., and brought to official attention of officers or directors.	Same as NYSE.	Same as NYSE.	Usually no publ except that TD sions may apply to purchase of stock on open ma
DEFAULT UPON SENIOR SECURITIES:	8-K if actual material default in principal, interest, sinking or purchase fund installment, etc., not cured within 30 days — and if indebtedness exceeds five per cent of total consolidated assets. 8-K if material arrearage in dividends not cured in 30 days for preferred registered or ranking securities.	8-K if filed. IMMEDIATE publicity and notification when and as soon as known.	8-K if filed. Same as NYSE.	8-K if filed. Publish promptly to holders. Notice to Exchange a reasonable time in advance.	TD
DIRECTORS OR OFFICERS— CHANGE IN OR CHANGE OF CONTROL	8-K if change in control of corporation. New directors, officers or other insiders must personally file Form 3.	PROMPT notice of any change. 8-K if filed.	8-K if filed. Same as NYSE.	8-K if filed. Same as NYSE.	TD: Immediat nouncement of change in dire officers or in co

REPORTING REQUIRED FOR:	SEC	NYSE	AMEX	MSE and PSE	RECOMMENDED PUBLICITY PRACTICE
DISPOSITION OF ASSETS:	8-K if company or majority owned subsidiary disposes of a significant amount of assets or business other than in normal course of business.	8-K if filed. In addition, prompt notice if disposition materially affects financial position of company or extent of its operations.	8-K if filed. Same as NYSE.	8-K if filed. Same as NYSE.	TD: Immediate publicity, especially when assets consist of an entire product line, division, operating unit or a substantial part of the business.
DIVIDENDS:		Prompt notice to Exchange and IMMEDIATE publicity. Exchange requires telephone alert when the action is unusual (increase, decrease, omitting, etc.). Immediate means even while meeting is still in progress.	Same as NYSE.	Publish promptly to shareholders any action. Notify Exchange.	TD: Publicity should be prepared in advance and released immediately on word of declaration. Publicity especially important when dividend rate changes.
FORM OR NATURE OF LISTED SECURITIES CHANGED:	8-K if constituent instruments defining rights have been materially modified or if rights are otherwise limited.	8-K if filed. At least 20 days prior notice of change in form or nature of securities or certificates.	8-K. Same as NYSE.	8-K. 10 day-prior notice.	TD
INTERIM EARNINGS STATEMENT:	Form 9-K for first half of fiscal year only. Send to exchanges involved and to SEC within 45 days of close of period.	Quarterly. Publicity required — shareholder mailing recommended but not required. No set time limit but four to five weeks after close of period considered usual.	Quarterly. Should be published within 45 days after end of fiscal quarter.	MIDWEST: Three copies to Exchange. PACIFIC: Semi-annual. Publish and submit four copies to Exchange.	TD
LISTED SECURITIES— CHANGE IN RIGHTS OR PRIVILEGES	8-K in event material modification or limitation — including restrictions on working capital or dividend payments.	8-K if filed. At least 20 day-advance notice of proposed changes. May require change in listing agreement.	8-K if filed. Same as NYSE.	8-K if filed. 10 day-prior notice. May require substitute listing application.	TD
LISTING ON ANOTHER EXCHANGE OR LISTING ON AN EXCHANGE:	Involved and extensive legal work is required.	(See Col. 1.)	(See Col. 1.)	(See Col. 1.)	Handled by exchange. Discuss with attornies and public relations counsel well in advance.
MATERIAL LEGAL PROCEEDINGS:	8-K at start and termination of material proceedings (see exceptions in 8-K item 3); any bankruptcy, receiverships, etc. or proceedings in which certain parties have interests adverse to company.	8-K sufficient unless proceeding bears on ownership, dividends, interest, or principal of listed securities or to institution of receivership, bankruptcy, reorganization proceedings, etc.	8-K if filed. Same as NYSE.	8-K if filed.	Usually not, unless suit generates substantial negative or misleading publicity about company.
MEETINGS OF STOCKHOLDERS:	8-K required when security holders' vote required except as to procedural matters, selection of auditors or uncontested election of management nominees as listed in proxy statement.	8-K if filed. Prompt notice and publicity on significant occurrences. Also at least 10 days advance notice of record date or closing transfer books —plus four copies of proxy material.	8-K if filed. Same as NYSE.	8-K if filed. MIDWEST: Three copies of proxy and notice to exchange. PACIFIC: Four copies of proxy material to Exchange.	Recommend inviting interested financial writers and advance preparation of news release.

REPORTING REQUIRED FOR:	SEC	NYSE	AMEX	MSE and PSE	RECOMMENDED PUBLICITY PRACTI
PROXY MATERIAL:	Three preliminary copies at least 10 days prior to shareholder mailing. Eight finals not later than date sent to holders, plus three to each exchange where listed. If company does not regularly solicit proxies, see Reg. 14C. Subsequent proxy material: file preliminary copies at least 2 days before stockholder mailing. Definitive copies filed before mailing.	Immediate newspaper publicity on controversial issues, especially when there is a contest. Prompt notice to be received not later than 10 days before record date. Four copies definitive proxy material. Ask for advance review in major matters. (See Exchange rules.)	Same as NYSE.	MIDWEST: Three copies definitive proxy material. PACIFIC: Four copies definitive proxy material.	TD: When a contest non-routine matters i volved. Normally pu licity not needed routine matters.
REDEMPTION OF LISTED SECURITIES:	8-K.	8-K. Immediate press publicity. Prompt notice to Exchange not less than 15 days before redemption date.	8-K. Same as NYSE.	8-K. Prompt publicity to holders and to Exchange a reasonable time in advance of redemption date.	TD: Usually advertis ment is required. W ten notice to securi holders.
REGISTRATION STATEMENT:	Involved legal proceedings and publicity practices. Consult legal counsel.	(See Col. 1.)	(See Col. 1.)	(See Col. 1.)	Publicity severely stricted. See appl able SEC releases.
REVALUATION OF ASSETS OR RESTATEMENT OF CAPITAL SHARE ACCOUNT:	8-K if material (company or significant subsidiaries).	8-K if filed. Prior supplement to listing agreement required for change in par value.	8-K if filed. Prior notice of change of par value of stock split, file listing application.	8-K if filed. Same as NYSE.	Depending on circu stances.
RIGHTS TO SUBSCRIBE:	Registration under the Securities Act of 1933. Prefiling notice limited by SEC Rule 135.	See regulations. Preliminary discussion necessary — immediate publicity. Important to work out time schedule with Exchange before any action taken. Notice to shareholders not less than 10 days in advance of the proposed record date.	Same as NYSE.	MIDWEST: Notify in time to afford holders an interim — satisfactory to Exchange — within which to record their interests to exercise their rights. Publish promptly to holders. PACIFIC: Immediate publicity. Ten days notice prior to record date.	TD
STOCK SPLIT OR OTHER CHANGE IN CAPITALIZATION:	8-K required for increase or decrease if exceeds five per cent of amount of securities of the class previously outstanding. IMPORTANT: Check with legal counsel.	For increase — copy of 8-K sufficient, except notice if through reissuance of previously reacquired listed securities. Issuance of additional amount requires prior listing approval. For decrease— see Redemption of Listed Securities and Treasury Stock Changes.	Same as NYSE.	MIDWEST: Notify of any proposed increase sufficiently prior to permit action on application for listing. Also if issue securities on parity with or senior to listed securities. PACIFIC: Issuance of additional amount requires prior listing authorization.	TD: As soon as de sion to put matter vote of shareholde is made.
TREASURY STOCK —INCREASE OR DECREASE:	Check Form 8-K, Items 7 and 8, for possible application.	8-K if filed. Notice within 10 days after close of fiscal quarter in which it takes place.	8-K if filed. Same as NYSE.	MIDWEST: 8-K if filed. Same as NYSE. PACIFIC: 8-K if filed. Notice within 15 days after close of fiscal quarter.	Normally no publici

Just what is truthful or not misleading has produced many adjectival and otherwise descriptive recommendations from knowledgeable sources. Perhaps the best is that of the NYSE: [50]

> A primary objective is that corporate news be handled in *proper perspective*. This necessitates *careful adherence to the facts, appropriate restraint and good judgment.* Any projections of financial data . . . should be very *soundly based, thoroughly qualified, and conservative.* [Other significant] news should be treated with the same *caution. Premature announcements . . . , overly optimistic forecasts, exaggerated claims, and unwarranted promises should be avoided.* If subsequent developments indicate that performance will not match earlier projections, this should be reported and explained . . . *Unfavorable news should be disclosed* just as promptly and as fully as favorable news. (Emphasis added.)

Notwithstanding the "best intentions in the world" of experienced financial PR practitioners, much of this still boils down to "good judgment." Some requirements are still vague. The situation has been likened to "a morality play in which the reassuring blacks and whites of wrong and right are both discouragingly grey." [51] In 1966, SEC Chairman Cohen quite frankly wrote: [52]

> A certain amount of uncertainty, of lack of rules, means that people have to continually examine their own decisions about whether what they want to do is legal.

One way to solve this dilemma—especially when there may be a question as to whether information given to one person or group such as a meeting of analysts, is publicly available—is "when in doubt, prepare the release." [53]

15. NYSE Recommended "Immediate Release" Procedures.

The NYSE has spelled out quite specifically the procedures it considers necessary for the purpose of "insuring immediate publicity of news releases." As of May 15, 1967, its *Company Manual* required: [54]

Procedure Insuring Immediate Publicity of News Releases

Release to Newspapers and News-wire Services: News which ought to be the subject of immediate publicity must be released by the fastest available means. The "fastest available means" may vary in individual cases and according to the time of day. Ordinarily, this requires a release to the public press by telephone, telegraph, or hand delivery, or some combination thereof. Transmittal of such a release to the press solely by mail is not considered satisfactory. Similarly, release of such news exclusively to the local press outside of New York City would not be sufficient for adequate and prompt disclosure to the investing public.

To insure adequate coverage, releases requiring immediate publicity should be given to one or more of the newspapers of general circulation in New York City which regularly publish financial news and simultaneously to Dow Jones & Company, Inc. and one or more of the other major national news-wire services noted below. When releases are made of news or information which presumably would materially affect security values or influence investment decisions, such releases should be given to the financial press and wire services for "immediate release" as promptly and simultaneously as circumstances permit. The foregoing distribution of releases should be regarded as a minimum. Many companies may wish to give additional distribution to their releases. Two copies of any press release should be sent promptly to the Exchange.

The New York City addresses and telephone numbers of these national news-wire services are:

Associated Press, 50 Rockefeller Plaza, PLaza 7-1111, Ext. 201; after 6:30 p.m. Ext. 231.

Dow Jones & Company, Inc., 30 Broad Street, HAnover 2-3115, Exts. 324, 325, 326; after 5:00 p.m., Exts. 451, 452.

Reuters Economic Services, 1212 Avenue of the Americas, 581-4250; after 5:30 p.m., 582-4035.

United Press International, 220 East 42nd Street, MUrray Hill 2-0400; Ext. 371; after 6:00 p.m., Ext. 325.

It is suggested that every news release include the name and telephone number of a company official who will be available if a newspaper or news-wire service desires to confirm or clarify the release with the company.

Telephone Alert to the Department of Stock List of the Exchange: When news of a material event which may affect the value of a company's securities or influence investment decisions is released shortly before the opening or during market hours (10 a.m. to 3:30 p.m., New York time), it is recommended that the Department of Stock List of the Exchange be notified by telephone no later than simultaneously with the announcement of the event to the news media. If the Exchange receives such notification in time, it will be in a position to consider whether, in the opinion of the Exchange, trading in the security should be halted temporarily. A delay in trading, which normally would last about 15 minutes after appearance of the news on the Dow-Jones news ticker, provides a period for the public evaluation of the announcement. A longer delay in trading may be necessary if there is an unusual influx of orders.

The telephone number of the Department of Stock List of the Exchange is 212–HA 2-4200. A telephone alert should be confirmed promptly in writing to the Department of Stock List.

As to "immediate release of dividend news," the NYSE, also as of May 15, 1967, requires: [55]

Recommended Procedure for Release: It has been found, in a number of instances, that avoidable delay in release of dividend news to the public press was due, primarily, to the fact that no one officer of the company had been specifically assigned the regular duty of releasing the dividend news as a routine part of the meeting procedure. In other cases, delay in the release was due to the prolongment of the meeting into the evening hours and deferment of the release until the following morning, either because of the inconvenience of making the release at a late hour, or because of an erroneous idea that, because of the lateness of the hour, immediate transmittal of a release would be of no avail. In still other cases, the delay was attributable to the fact that the Board meeting was held at a point distant from the company's offices and the release was deferred until the officers present at the meeting had returned to their offices.

These, and other obstacles to timely release of dividend news, can be avoided by the following procedure which has been adopted by many companies to expedite the release and publication of such news. A designated officer of the company is charged, specifically, with the responsibility for regularly making the dividend news release as a routine step in the procedure of the meeting, with alternates specifically designated to act in event of his absence. The officer so designated is usually one who, invariably, is either present at Board meetings, or represented at such meetings by someone who assumes his duties. The dividend action is placed well forward on the agenda for the meeting, ahead of routine matters. As soon as the action is taken, the designated officer, or his alternate, leaves the meeting and releases the news, by telephone or telegraph, to the newspapers and to the national news-wire services in the city where the meeting is held, or, in the event there is no financial news coverage at the point where the meeting is held, to the nearest center where such coverage is available. In addition, and at the same time, a telegram is sent to the Dow Jones news-ticker service, so that, regardless of how late in the day the release may be made, it will appear, at least, on the news ticker before the opening of the market on the following day.

Related Paragraph of Listing Agreement: The paragraph of the listing agreement requiring immediate publicity in respect of dividend action (or the postponed or omission of such action) is Paragraph 4 of Section III of the current form of listing agreement. Said Paragraph 4 of Section III is stated below in full (see *Paragraphs of Listing Agreement Relative to Dividend Actions*).

Notice to Exchange

The company's listing agreement also requires that the Exchange be given prompt notice of any dividend action in respect of listed stock, and further requires that the Exchange receive prompt notice, with a mimimum of ten days' advance notice, of the record date for any dividend declared on listed stock. The requirement as to advance notice of a record date is separately discussed below under *Date for Record of Holders or Closing of Transfer Books—Advance Notice.*

Notice of dividend action shall be given by direct communication to the Department of Stock List of the Exchange. News items or advertisements in the public press in respect of dividend action cannot be accepted by the Exchange as sufficiently authoritative for its purposes.

Such notice shall be given promptly, and may be given by letter, or by telephone or telegraphic communication, promptly confirmed in writing. Except under unusual, unforeseeable circumstances, it would seem feasible to send written notice on the day of the meeting, or to give telephone or telegraphic notice on the day of the meeting and send written confirmation thereof not later than the morning of the following day.

When it would reasonably appear that dividend action, or its omission, may substantially affect security values or influence investment decisions and when news of such an event is released shortly before the opening or during market hours (10 a.m. to 3:30 p.m., New York time), it is recommended that the Department of Stock List of the Exchange be notified by telephone no later than simultaneously with the announcement of the event to the news media. If the Exchange receives such notification in time, it will be in a position to consider whether, in the opinion of the Exchange, trading in the security should be halted temporarily. A delay in trading which normally would last about 15 minutes after appearance of the news on the Dow-Jones news ticker, provides a period for the public evaluation of the announcement. A longer delay in trading may be necessary if there is an unusual influx of orders. (See generally Section A2 of this Manual, *Agreements with Exchange—Procedure for Insuring Immediate Publicity of News Releases,* above.)

The telephone number of the Department of Stock List of the Exchange is 212–HA 2-4200. A telephone alert should be confirmed promptly in writing to the Department of Stock List.

Telephone or telegraphic notice should be given if the record date for the dividend is so imminent as to make it questionable that written notice will be received by the Exchange before the close of business on the tenth day prior to the record date (see *Date for Record of Holders or Closing of Transfer Books— Advance Notice* below).

When written notice is sent from a point normally more than one day distant from New York City by regular mail delivery, it is desirable that such notice be sent by air mail.

In July, 1968, during the pendency of the *Texas Gulf Sulphur* appeal, the NYSE issued its *Expanded Policy on Timely Disclosure.* The opening mandate is that a listed company "is expected to release quickly to the public any news or information which might reasonably be expected to materially affect the market for securities."

The NYSE goes on to direct that the decision-making group within a company should be kept as small as possible and if important information (judged by the above critical standard) gets beyond that small group, the information must be disclosed publicly at once. This raises questions as to the effect of the dictation of important memoranda or reports to even a confidential secretary of one of the decision-makers.

16. AMEX Required Procedure.

The AMEX procedures for timely disclosure and handling of such news provide: [56]

> As to procedure, information of this type should be issued as quickly as circumstances permit, to as broad an audience as possible, and on an "immediate release" or "not held" basis. It should be distributed to one or more New York City newspapers which regularly publish financial news, to the news-ticker service operated by Dow Jones & Company, Inc. and to the national wire services of the Associated Press and United Press International. Companies may also find it advisable to broaden their distribution to other news media of their choosing.
>
> When, in spite of proper precautions, inaccurate information or rumors, true or false, are circulated, companies are expected to clarify the situation promptly through a public announcement.

17. Logistics of Immediate Release.

Immediate release procedures require considerable advance planning or logistics. This should not be left to chance but should be planned on a firm pattern, especially if Board of Directors action is a preliminary to the release of the news. The planning involves management, inside PR staff and the company's financial PR counselor, if any.

The importance of planned timing was documented in the *Texas Gulf Sulphur* case wherein the court dealt at length with the exact timing (to the minute) of the various steps in the disclosure and the fact that a press conference was held *after* the Board of Directors meeting was completed.

The procedure breaks down into several phases:

    (a) Timing and scheduling of the meeting itself.

    (b) Agenda planning, with "timely release" matters well up toward the head thereof. See Section 15 above.

    (c) Advance warning to the Exchange of coming release, if necessary. See Section 15 above.

    (d) Identity of the specific individual charged with obligation to effect the release.

(e) Definition of the precise moment when news is to be released, preferably while the meeting is still in session.

(f) Mechanics of release handling and distribution, including availability of all detailed information necessary to get the news out as rapidly as possible including names, addresses, telephone numbers, etc. of wire services, newspapers, broadcast networks, etc. This has sometimes been the "horseshoe nail, for want of which the war was lost."

(g) Substance of the release as well as of any follow-up confirmation upon the initial disclosure.

(h) Possible advance preparation of anticipated release omitting precise or critical figures or data. See Section 19 below.

(i) Preparation for answering anticipated inquiries generated by initial release.

(j) Development of liaison and communications channels with or without outside PR counselor.

18. Interrelation of Company/PR Firm.

The procedures of timely disclosure will vary according to several factors. Most of these factors are tied to the basic question of whether the communications contact with the news services, etc. is made by the company or by its outside PR counsel.

PR firms charged with this responsibility may reduce their procedures to writing. Reproduced below by permission is the major portion of such a procedural memorandum under which Carl Byoir & Associates handles and *controls* timely disclosure:

> MEMORANDUM TO THE ENTIRE STAFF—ALL OFFICES
> FROM: GEORGE HAMMOND
>
> The subject of this memorandum is of the utmost importance, so I ask that you read it as many times as is necessary so that you will know exactly what is being asked of you. Further, I suggest that you make it a practice to read it again from time to time to be sure that you are handling your part of the operation perfectly.
>
> As you know, we have responsibilities for making public certain actions taken by the client, usually the board of directors, which have great importance to the financial markets. Our most usual assignment is relaying to the financial services and to the press, dividend action taken by the client's board of directors.
>
> We all understand that there is no uniform formula which we follow in doing this. In some cases a man present at the board meeting advises the public relations director of the company, who advises us to put out the announcement. In other cases, a member of the client organization calls the Dow Jones ticker, and perhaps

some other outlets, and we supplement this action by distributing a news release.

Everyone involved in this matter—client personnel or CB&A personnel—must observe this requirement: As soon as the board has taken action on a dividend (or on any other matter which may have a significant impact upon the appraisal of the company by the financial community), this action is to be made public *promptly*. This means, primarily, a statement to the Dow Jones ticker, made either by the client or by us. I cannot emphasize too strongly that this action should be taken *immediately*. It is not enough to wait until the board meeting is over, or when it is convenient to type out an announcement or a press release, or to do anything else that would delay the information.

The second requirement is one that we at CB&A *insist upon, as a matter of policy*. While circumstances may indicate that the action of the board can be forecast, *we do not want any releases prepared which include figures on the amount of the dividend*. A form of release can be prepared, but the amount per share is to be left blank. Theoretically, time is saved by running off a dividend release in advance and then holding it for a phone call saying that the board has taken action.

But all of you can clearly see that this is a most dangerous practice and is prohibited. It is quite possible for some new secretary to encounter such a release and assume that it had been cleared and released, which, if she acted on it, could get the client and ourselves into great troubles.

*   *   *   *

The Financial Department has been instructed that when a call comes in from a CB&A man giving information on board action which is to be put out immediately, this fact is to be typed and time-stamped and put in a special book which the Financial Department is keeping for this purpose. In this way we will know who called in the information, when it was called in, when we called the services, and when the release was made by us. All of these steps will be time-stamped and a permanent record kept.

This to account executives: I will require from you immediately a memorandum which I want you to write and have initialled for approval by the appropriate client official. This memorandum should tell me and the Financial Department *exactly* what procedure your particular client follows in making public such actions as are referred to in this memorandum.

1) Who is the person at the board meeting who is delegated to release information to us for prompt distribution.

2) What portion of the job is done by the client (name the man responsible); for what portion of the job are we responsible.

3) *From now on we will hold responsible the account executive to personally monitor the operation associated with board meetings*. Though I have great confidence in our staffers and secretaries, I do not want our responsibilities in these matters delegated beyond the account executive level. It is not asking too much to

expect that the account executive will know when the board is meeting (he must make it his business to find out). He should inquire what action may be taken by the board that will require instantaneous information distribution, and he should make certain that the information is properly and promptly given to our Financial Department, observing the rules I am stating.

Important: This does not mean that the account executive need interpose himself between the client and the Financial Department, if the routine established for your account specifically states that word from the client man specified will go direct to CB&A's Financial Department. This is a proper procedure but the account executive, even in such cases, should be in touch with our Financial Department so that he knows that the operation has gone off properly.

4) It will be the responsibility of the account executive to see the book in the Financial Department, as soon as the operation has been completed, so that he can make a note of the times at which the various steps of the job were done, and can report this to the proper client official. I recommend that a photostat of the page in the Financial Department book be given to the client for the client's records.

* * * *

But the fundamental itself is abundantly clear. So it behooves our executive staff and our account executives not only to operate wisely, as the client must, but it is also important that we counsel the client on whether or not certain situations fall into this area of importance and should be handled so precisely that the client cannot be criticized.

I want the matter of this memorandum discussed thoroughly with each client, and as I mentioned earlier, I want the reply memorandum from each account executive concerned to be in my hands not later than Friday of this week. This means that you will have to have the memo written and initialled, as requested earlier, and it will be kept on file here as our guideline to the handling of financial information affecting each client. I believe I can add that the client is just as much interested in this situation as we are, perhaps even more, and I believe he will be happy to cooperate in clarifying and making a written record of our procedures in this important area.

. . . GH . . .

This memorandum has been reproduced here at such great length because it "pounds" incessantly at the need for speed and adherence to formal pattern. The importance of this cannot be overemphasized.

This procedure involves the closest cooperation between PR firm and client. This is fundamental. A breakdown in either link vitiates the desired result. While this procedure originates with the PR firm, the client is expected to conform to it.

Fixed procedures of this sort protect all concerned. Also, in the event of a lapse in connection with a particular release, it fixes individual responsibility. It also provides to firm and client a permanent time record of the disclosure, even to the *minute*. See Section 17 above.

19. "Hold for Release" Disclosure.

The NYSE makes it clear that "Hold for Release" announcements are not to be used. Distributing information in this manner invites leaks and breach of the "hold" instructions. It places advance information in the hands of third parties, not normally entitled to it.

However, there are some situations in which the PR staff may *prepare* —but not distribute—a release in advance.

(a) The timing of dividend action can normally be foretold and there appears to be nothing improper in the forehanded preparation of a dividend announcement, leaving the amount of the dividend blank—to be filled in immediately upon action by the Board. This is merely a practical device to expedite the logistics of timely disclosure. See Section 18 above.

(b) In other cases, such as prospective mergers or acquisitions under negotiation, it may be appropriate to *prepare* a release and hold it in strict confidence within the company. It then is available if it becomes necessary to act very rapidly because of unexpected leaks or other developments. The company would be prepared if a call from an Exchange advises of floor rumors or unexplained excessive trading activity. The company then is in a position to issue a proper release promptly and avert either embarrassment or possible censure.[57]

Obviously, such a release must be kept currently updated as negotiations progress, eventually reaching a final form when the parties have agreed in principle at which time it should be distributed.

This is also true concerning research and development which have an apparent potential of important new products or product changes. Some companies are known to keep in their security files currently-updated draft releases covering all of their developmental projects. Once again, if it becomes necessary to dispel rumors or to stop leaks, the appropriate release is ready for immediate distribution.

(c) On occasion, the formal annual report may be issued on a "hold for release" basis if the company has previously issued a preliminary audited earnings report so that the annual report itself does "not contain any news which is likely to affect stock values or market activity." This should be avoided, however, if the annual report "discloses for the first time, any innovation or development that may affect total sales or earnings or the company's competitive position." [58]

20. When Is Corporate News "Disclosed"?

One phase of disclosure upon which there seems to be continuing dispute is: "what does 'disclosure' mean insofar as the time element is concerned?" In other words, when is news "public"? [59]

The NYSE takes the position that news is public when it "appears in the press." [60] Most public relations practitioners appear to feel that news is public when it is delivered to the Dow Jones news service, other press services or news services as are mentioned in the NYSE *Company Manual,* quoted in Section 15 above.[61]

The SEC believes that news is not public until a "reasonable time" has passed during which the public may digest and evaluate the information. This may require as much as "several days." [62] In the *Texas Gulf Sulphur* case, the SEC position was rejected by the district court, which ruled that disclosure was effective when it was announced to the press. The court further said that it was not for the court to fix a waiting period during which insiders having confidential information would be barred from trading in the corporate stock on the basis of that special knowledge. The court did, however, indicate that the SEC might issue regulations in this matter if it believed them necessary. However, the SEC believes that such regulations "would be undesirable." [63]

On appeal, however, the district court's position was reversed and the SEC attitude was, in effect, upheld. The Circuit Court said: [64]

> Before insiders may act upon material information, such information must have been *effectively disclosed in a manner sufficient to insure its availability to the investing public.* . . . [A]ll insider activity must await dissemination of the . . . official announcement.
>
> *   *   *   *
>
> The reading of a news release . . . is merely the first step in the process of dissemination required for compliance with the regulatory objective of providing all investors with an equal opportunity to make informed investment judgments. Assuming that the contents of the official release could be instantaneously acted upon, *at the minimum [he] should have waited until the news could reasonably have been expected to appear over the media of widest circulation, the Dow-Jones broad-tape,* . . . (Emphasis added.)

The court then went on to footnote a suggestion, as had the district court, that

> . . . the permissible timing of insider transactions after disclosures of various sorts is one of the many areas of expertise for appropriate exercise of the SEC's rule-making power, which we hope will be

utilized in the future to provide some predictability of certainty for the business community.

Presumably a further appeal will be taken by the company officers to the Supreme Court.

The impact of this decision upon the corporate and financial PR communities was impressive. Knowledgeable financial PR executives said variously: "Public relations in the business world will now have to live by a much stricter set of standards"; "[E]very sensible company will have to consider its financial public relations in a new light"; "[T]he decisions will increase the demand for more competent public-relations counsel"; "The rulings will upgrade the whole investment process." [65]

A firm and accepted solution to this question is very important to the position of "insiders." There seems to be a feeling that such persons deserve no special consideration in this context. Thus SEC Chairman Cohen has said: [66]

> If, in the insider area, this means that the business men decide *not* to buy in borderline cases, I have to think that's all to the good.

For a discussion of insider position generally, see Section 22 below.

21. Disclosure Assistance from Exchanges/SEC.

The literature dealing with timely disclosure is replete with "admissions" that there are many unsolved problems and "grey areas" in this area of financial publicity. This is recognized by the regulatory agencies and organizations, all of which appear not only desirous but eager to assist the company and its PR personnel in solving such situations.

Rudick Lawrence has said that "the Exchange acts more as a counselor than as a policeman." [67] Either the Exchange or the company may initiate the contact.[68] In addition, the Exchange periodically issues its Educational Circulars to cover situations coming to its attention from time to time.

Both the SEC and NASD have "an open door" and will discuss with an interested party its contemplated publicity or releases. They will do their best to make suggestions and to assist insofar as they are able. In connection with many such informal approaches, a letter may, on request, be written, confirming the SEC position. However, one SEC staff member of long experience has said that he could not recall the writing of such a letter in connection with public relations or publicity—despite the fact that frequently he and others do sit down to discuss these matters with the PR counsel for public companies.[69]

The apparent reason is that it is difficult to give precise answers when dealing with public relations and publicity in areas subject to Commission control. Furthermore, there seems to be an "historical sensitivity to censorship" at the SEC. Publicity naturally is closer to censorial areas than would be other corporate activities about which opinions might be sought. It is understandable that the SEC should be cautious about any activity which may open it to a charge of censorship, even indirect. See Chapter 4, particularly Section 14.

Staff personnel of the SEC and NASD are surprised and concerned by the apparent lack of knowledge in cases coming to their attention. As one told the author: "You would think that by the time people got ready to make a public offering, they would know enough about how to do it right. This includes the company people, their lawyers and public relations people." Another frequent comment is that "the PR man thinks he has a news item which the public is just hungering to read. He talks about the public's 'right to know.' When he is told that such publicity or news releases are subject to the rules, he says, 'But you just don't understand. This is news, not selling.' " See Section 34 below.

Government and quasi-government authorities look on releases to newspapers and other publicity or public relations activities as subject to the same standards as are paid advertising.

Both SEC and NASD staff appear to feel that the most common problems with which they are presented deal with *ambiguities* in the description of the past performance of a security and with its prospects. Not too often is an instance of clearly deceptive promotion involved.

22. PR Personnel as "Insiders."

One of the principal reasons for insistence upon timely disclosure is to prevent certain "insiders" from profiting through dealings in corporate securities upon the basis of information available to them but not available generally to the investing public.[70] See Section 9 above.

Under Section 16a of the Exchange Act, an insider is considered to be an officer, director or the beneficial owner of more than ten per cent of any listed class of equity security. Various statutory controls apply to their buying and selling activities.[71] We are not here concerned except insofar as the legal definition of "insider" may otherwise be extended to include other persons and be subject to other sanctions.

In 1966 Burson-Marsteller Associates made available the results of a "detailed survey to determine precisely what current policies and practices prevail in corporate disclosure" including the respondents' attitudes and practices as to "insiders." [72] Its follow-up survey, limited to the definition of "insiders," amplified one of the major and rather unexpected results of the initial study.

Some 80 per cent of the respondents in the second phase of the study saw the need to include as "unofficial insiders" their lawyers, accountants, PR men or others who were privy normally to confidential information. The same percentage, on the other hand, "say they have neither a written nor unwritten policy dealing with the situation." They are believed to feel that lawyers, CPAs or PR personnel "have enough sense of their own code of conduct not to take advantage of inside data."

Of course, the really important question is not whether a company considers its PR people as insiders but whether the law may so consider them. The recommendations in the Special Study relative to publicity and PR counselors did not include any reference to such possible insider status. On the other hand, it recommended that consideration be given to enactment of "criminal sanctions and civil liability for intentional or reckless dissemination by *issuers or their agents* of false or misleading statements" (emphasis added) affecting investment decisions. See Section 6 above.

In the *Texas Gulf Sulphur* case, one of the defendants was described by the trial court as "a lawyer who . . . was appointed secretary of the Company and manager of its public and Government relations." He was said by the court to have utilized "material undisclosed information to his advantage and violated Section 10 (b) [of the Exchange Act] and [Exchange Act] Rule 10b-5." See Section 9 above.

The PRSA Interpretation, discussed in Section 8 above, provides that "such member shall not exploit the information he has gained as an insider for personal gain" although this does not restrict him from "bona fide investments (according to) normal investment practices."

After the reversal in the *Texas Gulf Sulphur* case, financial PR executives made it clear that they consider themselves to be insiders. Among such comments were: "If a PR is not an insider with a client, then he should be" and "Assisting in major decisions is what we are paid for." [73]

The importance of this was fortified by the beginning of the so-called "second round" in the SEC attack on alleged insider activities. Late in August, 1968 the SEC brought an administrative proceeding against Merrill Lynch, Pierce, Fenner & Smith, Inc. and many of its officers, alleging that the brokerage firm had obtained inside information about the finances of Douglas Aircraft Company and passed this along to certain large institutional investors who then sold their Douglas holdings. Building on the *Texas Gulf Sulphur* foundation, the SEC now apparently is seeking to extend the insider restrictions to brokers and "outsiders"—companies and individuals who have no direct, internal relationship to a company. [74]

From the anticipated Supreme Court appeal in Texas Gulf Sulphur and the outcome of this latter extension of the insider doctrine should come many necessary answers.

There is no question that a PR practitioner may often be privy to important and undisclosed corporate information. If he should trade in the company stock at that time, both equity and the anti-fraud sections of the securities laws dictate that he would be considered an insider.

From another point of view, the affirmative duty of the PR man may not be so clear. The Byoir memorandum in Section 18 above points out "it is also important that we counsel the client on whether or not certain situations fall into this area of importance and should be handled so precisely that the client cannot be criticized."

There probably is no duty to do so at common law but certainly it would seem to be dictated by the depth-of-service concept which many PR firms have adopted. In a practical sense, the client is later likely to consider the PR firm derelict for failing to have brought the matter to its attention—should there be legal or other repercussions.

23. SEC 1968 Disclosure Study.

Late in 1967 the SEC announced "the formation of a Study Group within the Commission to examine the operation of the disclosure provisions" of the securities laws.[75] This had been foreshadowed by comments of SEC personnel throughout 1967, pointing to a variety of questions which have evolved from the disclosure philosophy over the years. The Study—probably similar in depth and scope to the 1962 Study discussed in Section 6 above—will be "comprehensive" and will delve into

> the effectiveness of present disclosure requirements in the light of changing trends in corporate finance and in the pattern of public stock ownership and trading activity, as well as the technological advances in the means of dissemination of information to the public.

As this is written the Study Group is at work. From its report may come answers to some of the questionable problems raised throughout this chapter including possible clarification of the question as to when corporate news is disclosed, resolving ambiguities raised by the *Texas Gulf Sulphur* case, discussed in Section 20 above.

PR people should, in any event, be alert to this prospective report which, quite probably, will either alter or increase financial PR and publicity burdens.

24. Annual Reports.

The annual stockholder's report has come a long way since the Borden Company issued the first one in 1858. More and more it is being given "professional-level concern with clear, expository, factual, briskly-moving, un-stuffy writing." It has even been referred to as a "unique art form." [76]

At the same time, this effort to "humanize" the annual report and to divorce it as to both form and content from the dry, technical and accounting-oriented publication of the past, has produced much concern. In 1967 Samuel Krasny was able to write: [77]

> What goes into the corporate annual report today has thrown the accounting profession into a turmoil and upended traditional concepts. It has aroused the protective instincts of the SEC and other government agencies. Auditors approach it with trepidation. Attorneys scan its contents with suspicion.
>
> [T]he spread of the investing public has created a concomitant increasing pattern of government, court, Exchange, and quasi-judicial interpretation regarding exactly what should go into annual reports and the way in which the facts are presented.
>
> * * * *
>
> [P]ublic relations counsel sometimes move through its maze of words and their possible legal pitfalls with an air of casual unconcern.

The challenge facing the public relations practitioner preparing an annual report is twofold: presenting financial information as clearly and attractively as possible and also, in other portions of the report (such as the president's introductory letter), avoiding statements "not completely consistent with the financial statements portion."

It has been charged that the non-financial statement portions of the reports may be inconsistent, overly optimistic or too selective of the facts and data mentioned. The same author points out:

> In the present atmosphere of search for change and improvement in corporate reporting, great gains have already been achieved though much more can be accomplished. Ferment is taking place in the accounting profession with the Accounting Principles Board issuing seven Opinions in four years (three major ones within the last several months) that are of great importance to the president's letter and the commentary. All are binding on both auditors and corporate financial people. Yet, the public relations profession, though participating, may not have been doing as much in projecting the full financial picture of a corporation to its shareholders and interested individuals as it might.

Even if a corporate financial PR man confers closely with accounting and legal counsel on a report for a given year, thus acquiring what may appear to be considerable expertise, this feeling of certainty should not carry over to the following year. This is a changing field and an Account-

ing Principles Board Opinion valid in a given year may not be applicable
in the years to follow. There is, therefore, a necessity for close and continuous liaison which cannot be escaped through the development of an
"annual format" or "copy theme."

25. Stockholder/Customer Contacts.

Many companies encourage their sales or promotion people to approach company stockholders—usually for product promotion and sales.
However, especially in smaller communities where a company plant may
be located—perhaps as an important local economic factor—the customer-
stockholder contacts may go beyond mere product or plant promotion.
Such contacts not infrequently are the responsibility of personnel not
having any particular expertise in stockholder or financial PR.

Such contacts should not reveal any confidential company information.
In an effort to build up a close relationship with the local public, some
company employees may unconsciously exceed the proprieties of the situation. In order to prevent this, one large, multi-plant company instructs its
people that "the stockholder . . . likes to be kept informed on company
activities, to have his views welcomed and, in general, to be regarded as
an active and keenly interested member of our business family." However, the company's instructions are quite specific:

> NOTE: If his questions are about aspects of the over-all Company
> with which you are not familiar, offer to obtain the information—
> but don't guess at the answers. NOTE. *Don't disclose confidential
> or unpublished information that you would not be willing to have
> made generally available.* (Emphasis added.)

26. Financial Press Relations.

Peripheral to disclosure is the possible distortion of the relationship
between a company or its PR people and the press. This generally involves direct or indirect payment of some kind by the PR man to the
writer. Rare though it may be, it has nevertheless occurred as was made
clear in the Special Study. See Section 6 above.

The PRSA Interpretation requires that its members "shall maintain
the integrity of the channels of communication." See Section 8 above.
This is essentially a mandate against making any payment or giving any
other consideration to the press. But it may go further—especially in the
disclosure context.

Apart from the question of immediate disclosure, other disclosures may
be made to a favored financial writer—either with or without expectation of some reciprocal favor for the client. This should be avoided.

Under the Regulations of the NYSE, for example, something disclosed to one member of the financial community must be disclosed to all.[78]

Furthermore, it may involve the anti-touting section (§17[b]) of the Securities Act providing:

> It shall be unlawful for any person to publish, give publicity to, or circulate any notice, circular, advertisement, newspaper article, letter, investment service, or communication which, though not purporting to offer a security for sale, describes such security for a consideration received or to be received, directly or indirectly, from an issuer, underwriter, or dealer, without fully disclosing the receipt, whether past or prospective, of such consideration and the amount thereof.

This anti-touting or anti-tipster provision is intended to prevent payment for purportedly unbiased published materials which "in reality are bought and paid for." [79]

C. PROXY SOLICITATION PUBLICITY.

27. Proxy Solicitation Generally.

The solicitation of proxies in listed companies is carefully and specifically controlled by §14 of the Exchange Act and SEC Rules adopted pursuant thereto. Such solicitation involves carefully blueprinted step-by-step activities with which financial PR people should be familiar.

As in any financial matter subject to governmental control, the principal—the "formal"—activities in proxy solicitation are the responsibility of the company and its counsel or, in the case of solicitation by non-management parties, of such party and his counsel. Yet the communications problems of proxy contests are so considerable and important that the PR man is a key cog in the machine.

Edward Bernays, writing under the chapter title "Power Struggles for Proxies," has said of a pre-SEC proxy war: [80]

> Theodore Dreiser and Frank Norris, in their most imaginative depictions of power struggles, did not match the realities of the struggle that occurred when two strong financial groups . . . went to war with each other in a short and decisive struggle for millions.

While the modern proxy battle—under the securities acts and the SEC rules—have become more stylized on the legal front, they have lost none of their vigor insofar as publicity in-fighting is concerned.

28. Nature of Public Relations Involvement.

The Special Study, while not exploring in any detail "the use of publicity in proxy contexts," made it crystal clear that "[t]he financial public relations industry is deeply involved in these contests in ways which are frequently a matter of concern to the Commission." [81]

The frequently-quoted remarks of a former SEC Commissioner are here quite pertinent: [82]

> A large number of the more difficult problems in any proxy contest result from the fact that a considerable portion of the corporation's outstanding shares are often held in street names and their ownership is constantly changing. No longer can participants in a proxy contest rely on being able to communicate with the beneficial owners indirectly through the solicitation of stockholders of record. As a result, the use of paid advertisements, prepared press releases, press conferences, and radio and television broadcasts, has become common in attempting to reach stockholders and to sway the opinion of the public and persons who may advise or influence stockholders with respect to giving, revoking or withholding proxies.

Such SEC recognition is well-fortified in the history of proxy battles and has led observers such as Beveridge to say: [83]

> From year to year, it becomes increasingly likely that financial public relations people will eventually be involved in a proxy contest. All financial public relations specialists, therefore, should possess a good theoretical knowledge of proxy fights. If they are exposed, they can rest assured they'll get a fast working knowledge, of course. But it is well to be prepared in advance for a lesson "under fire" can prove costly.

Among the specific contributions which the PR specialist can make are strategic and tactical planning before the fight begins, including a sound choice of "issues"; planning initial and subsequent appeals to stockholders, brokers (street names), institutional interests, other specifically-identified large-block holders; handling "news" and "breaks" from day to day; paid proxy solicitation advertising; analyzing, framing and publicizing answers to the charges of the opposition; consulting constantly with counsel and management; assisting in corporate "customer contacts" during the fight; handling or advising on employee relations including, in some instances, fairly high echelon officers and staff; planning the meeting culminating the fight, etc.

Many, if not all, of these PR and related activities have legal overtones. Everything should therefore be cleared with legal counsel. If liaison has been properly established and a two-way understanding created, a "legal-PR" conflict can be avoided. See Chapter 1, Section 8.

29. SEC Requirements for Proxy Publicity.

The Exchange Act makes it unlawful, with respect to listed securities, to solicit proxies in contravention of SEC Rules such as the prohibition of false or misleading written solicitations.[84] Material used in such solicitations must be filed preliminarily with the Commission for comment.

This requirement does not apply to "soliciting materials in the form of speeches, press releases, and radio or television scripts." However, eight "definitive copies" thereof must be filed with or mailed for filing to the Commission "not later than the date such material is used or published" and three such copies are to be similarly supplied at the same time to each national exchange upon which the issuer's securities are listed.[85]

The mere fact that "speeches, press releases and radio and television scripts" are not subject to "pre-publication" submission does not mean that they may be used without reference to the basic proxy solicitation statement which must be submitted.

All such auxiliary or supplemental releases, etc. should follow closely the data set out in the formally submitted written materials. Assuming that the formally submitted materials are acceptable as not false or misleading, it would seem to follow that any deviations therefrom might well be considered false or misleading and, therefore, improper.

Furthermore, "any reprints or reproductions of all or any part of such materials" are subjects to Rules 14a-6(a) and (b) which require their submission at least 10 days prior to the date "they are first sent or given to security holders." This presupposes that such reprints or reproductions are among "other soliciting material to be furnished to security holders concurrently [with the proxy statement]." Two days' prior submission is required if such reprints or reproductions are used as "additional soliciting material" furnished to security holders. Both time requirements may be shortened if authorized by the Commission for good cause shown.

These provisions apparently apply to copies of speeches, articles, releases, etc. which may originate from sources other than the parties soliciting the proxies. This assumes, of course, that such "third party" materials are furnished to the security holders in connection with the proxy solicitation and are therefore properly soliciting material or "additional soliciting material."

30. PR and Avoidance of Proxy Contests.

The knowledgeable financial PR practitioner can do much to avoid a proxy contest. In fact, good financial PR generally—without even thinking ahead to such possibilities—is one of the best prophylactics.

Beveridge, in discussing "How To Avoid Proxy Fights" and quoting at length from the comments of corporation attorney Bernard Chapman, "a veteran of several key struggles for corporate control," maintains that "the key is the market price of your stock." He continues:

> And how can you be assured of a properly valued stock?
> "By improving stockholder relations," says Chapman, "because the stockholders are the people who fix the price of your stock."
> He offers 12 suggestions for improving stockholder relations.
> 1. Maintain good relations with the press. "They can help you and will."
> 2. See that your story is told to investment bankers, brokers, security analysts and security salesmen. "They are the men who are in touch with your stockholders and your potential stockholders."
> 3. Get your story across to the public generally. "This is the pool of investors from which you and your raider must draw."
> 4. Not only should better stockholder relations be the concern of a qualified executive but also the company should consider hiring a good public relations firm to give him a hand.
> 5. Do some financial advertising.
> 6. Publish interesting, understandable and attractive annual reports.
> 7. Send interim reports to your stockholders. "You wrote your wife more than once a year when you were wooing her."
> 8. Conduct meaningful annual meetings. Avoid what's cut and dried.
> 9. Pay a fair and adequate dividend. "It goes without saying that you must operate at a profit."
> 10. Explain your future plans to your stockholders and the need for retained earnings for use in the business.
> 11. Encourage selection of top-flight businessmen for your board of directors, not a group of yes-men beholden to management.
> 12. Advise management to back its judgment with its pocketbook. "A substantial ownership of stock by management will not only cement the executives' interest with those of the stockholders but will also reduce the floating supply of stock and make it harder for insurgents to take over."
> "In short," says Chapman, "you must run a successful operation and you must tell the public about it."

The need for these tactics and the need to "tell the public about it" is—of itself—sufficient reason for a continuing corporate financial PR program.

D. PUBLICITY AND NEW ISSUES.

31. Securities Act Background.

The Securities Act restricts sharply the use of PR or publicity either before or in conjunction with a new security offering. Basically, the use and extent thereof are keyed to the filing and effective date of the registration statement. It breaks down into three parts: [86]

(a) Prior to Filing of Registration Statement.

§5 of the Act prohibits any activity by issuers, underwriters or dealers designed to further the public offer or sale of securities required to be registered or to stimulate offers to buy from brokers, dealers and investors prior to the filing of the registration statement.

(b) After Filing But Prior to Effective Date.

Once the registration statement is filed but before its effective date, oral offers for sale may be made, but a written offer may be made only by a statutory prospectus which includes the preliminary prospectus filed by the issuer as well as a summary prospectus provided for in the SEC Rules. So-called "tombstone advertisements" permitted by the Act and SEC Rule 134 may also be used. No sale may be consummated legally during the period prior to the effective date of the statement.

(c) After Effective Date.

Once the registration statement is effective, written statements may be made otherwise than by the statutory prospectus but only if such other offers are accompanied by or preceded by the final prospectus.

The term "offer for sale" is carefully defined in the Act to include "every attempt to offer to dispose of, or solicitation of an offer to buy, a security for value." The broad scope of this definition clearly demonstrates that "offer" is not to be narrowly limited to communications which include such words as "offer" or which refer specifically to the security.

This was designed to put an end to any selling effort or sales literature and publicity by issuers, underwriters and dealers intended for this purpose and used prior to the filing of a registration statement. It was recognized that a very effective sales campaign can be carried on without making express use of words such as "offer."

It is against this background that preregistration publicity must be viewed. The language is clear. Its overall purpose and implication are equally clear. Yet specific applications have caused dispute and grief.

32. The *Arvida* Case.

The landmark case as to "gun jumping" or prefiling publicity is *S.E.C. v. Arvida*.[87] Arvida was formed in 1958 as a private corporation and its principal promoter transferred to it large tracts of land in Florida. This was described in a news release on July 8, 1958. Later, on September 18, 1958, certain large brokerage firms agreed to underwrite an Arvida common stock issue. Another press release was issued and a press conference held. Wide publicity as to the company's plans and projects resulted and over $500,000 in "expressions of interest" came to non-underwriter brokers. An SEC Commissioner said: [88]

> The release read like a letter distributor might send to a prospective customer in an effort to persuade him to invest in the enterprize . . . (Furthermore) the information contained in this release and its manner of presentation were not recognizably consistent in many respects with the contents of the registration statement and prospectus subsequently filed with the Commission. (Parenthetical matter added.)

The SEC instituted an administrative proceedings against the two broker-dealers and also sought an injunction against them, the company and various individual defendants. The district court refused the injunction, holding the likelihood of "irreparable injury" had not been shown. Later, pending the appeal and after the effective date of the registration statement, a permanent injunction was entered by consent. The court found that although the underwriters appeared to be acting in good faith with no intent to violate the Act, they had violated §5(c).

Shortly after the *Arvida* case, the SEC suspended another firm from the NASD for 20 days for distributing, both before the filing and during the waiting period, several brochures, form letters, reprints of newspaper stories and advertisements, announcements of corporate activities, all stressing that a former governor of Maine was among the experienced management and that the company would invest in life insurance stocks which were an attractive investment.[89]

33. Permissible Publicity.

Under the Act as discussed in Section 31 above, the basic question is whether or not publicity issued during the indicated periods is part of the sales effort of the issuer, underwriter or dealer. SEC Commissioner Woodside in 1965 described the "very practical problem" created by this question. He said: [90]

It is at this point, however, that a very practical problem arises, calling for a very practical distinction to be made. The prohibition against prefiling offers, thus broadly defined, has never been considered by the SEC or the courts to make unlawful the bona fide dissemination of normal corporate information to the public, if the information is not part of a selling effort; in other words, if the circumstances do not suggest evasion and sharp practice. Whether a particular item of corporate publicity or institutional advertising constitutes an offer to sell made unlawful by the Securities Act can of course be a difficult question.

The distinction is a vital one, and is not a matter of mere form. Like so many other sophisticated legal distinctions, it can be made only by consideration of all the facts and circumstances of a particular case. Factors such as intent, knowledge and time are important considerations in determining whether an item of publicity will in a particular situation be regarded as an attempt to dispose of a security within the meaning of the Act. Accordingly, the Commission has never believed it appropriate to try to formulate a rule-of-thumb definition in this area; the approach has instead been on a case-by-case basis. But as the body of case history has evolved, I think that certain principles or guides have become apparent.

Generally speaking, the flow of normal corporate news unrelated to the selling effort may be continued. In fact, the Exchanges require that such news continue to be disclosed and make no exceptions for its nondisclosure during the "difficult" period. The SEC itself has taken this position. In the leading *Loeb, Rhoades* case [91] the SEC said:

> In the normal conduct of its business a corporation may continue to advertise its products and services without interruption, it may send out its customary quarterly, annual, and other periodical reports to security holders, and it may publish its proxy statements, send out its dividend notices and make routine announcements to the press. This flow of normal corporate news, unrelated to a selling effort for an issue of securities, is natural, desirable, and entirely consistent with the objective of disclosure to the public which underlies the Federal securities laws.
>
> Difficult and close questions of fact may arise as to whether a particular item of publicity by an issuer is part of a selling effort or whether it is an item of legitimate disclosure to investors unrelated to such an effort.

This ambivalent situation has produced considerable criticism of the SEC attitude. For example, Eliot Sharp, writing under the title, "What Are News and What Are Puffs Related to Corporate Security Offerings?" [92] says of Commissioner Woodside's remarks:

> SEC's interpretations of "important business and financial developments" often aren't in consonance with those of businessmen

and business writers and reporters. Indeed, even some of Mr. Woodside's colleagues in private practice disagree with his contention.

Sharp then goes on to point out that the prohibitory line could better be drawn between legitimate corporate news and corporate puffs since "what is 'publicity' to one is news to another." The situation is further confused, according to this writer, by the fact that a lawyer's definition of news is frequently different from that of the public or of the journalist.

Probably the only reasonably safe position to take under these circumstances is to "play the publicity straight," stick to the facts, not increase the number or frequency of releases, and generally use "last year's scrapbook" as a blueprint for issuance of publicity releases, appearances before analysts, etc.

The SEC's concern seems to be directed principally toward efforts to "pre-condition the market" or to "indirectly sell or offer the securities." Low pressure, factual and "historically normal" publicity efforts should, therefore, not meet censure or criticism.[93]

34. "News" Justification Argument.

The principal argument usually advanced as to the permissibility of publicity during the "gestation period" is that, in the eyes of both the public and the financial world, the financing, the company or the individuals involved are newsworthy. This was raised in the *Arvida* case, discussed in Section 32 above. The SEC rejected this argument. Its words are of particular value to both financial PR practitioners and the financial press itself. The SEC said: [94]

> The principal justification advanced for the September 19 release and publicity was the claim that the activities of Mr. Davis, and specifically his interests in Florida real estate, are "news" and that accordingly Section 5(c) should not be construed to restrict the freedom of the managing underwriters to release such publicity. We reject this contention. *Section 5(c) is equally applicable whether or not the issuer or the surrounding circumstances have, or by astute public relations activities may be made to appear to have, news value.*
>
> It should be clear that our interpretation of *Section 5(c) in no way restricts the freedom of news media to seek out and publish financial news.* Reporters presumably have no securities to sell and, absent collusion with sellers, Section 5(c) has no application to them. *Underwriters such as registrants are in a different position; they are in the business of distributing securities, not news.* Failure to appreciate this distinction between reporters and securities distributors has given rise to a further misconception. Instances have arisen in which a proposed financing is of sufficient public

interest that journalists on their own initiative have sought out and published information concerning it. Since such journalistic enterprise does not violate Section 5, our failure to question resulting publicity should not have been taken as any indication that Section 5 is inapplicable to publicity by underwriters about newsworthy offerings. Similar considerations apply to publicity by issuers. (Emphasis added.)

Woodside, in discussing the so-called "flow of normal corporate news," waves the red flag about "purported news items" when he says: [95]

This does not mean, however, that purported news items which tout the companies' securities or which dwell upon those financial aspects of the business ordinarily associated with the sale of securities would be viewed in the same light. *Even so-called institutional or product advertisement might sometimes be viewed with concern if timing and content indicate that its real purpose is to draw attention to the issuer's securities and thus condition the market* for an offering in progress or shortly forthcoming. The difficulty for an issuer generally arises from *the publication of special brochures, press releases and speeches dealing with the prospects of the issuer at or about the time a registration statement is to be filed or become effective.* When, shortly before the filing of a registration statement or during the pre-effective period, public communications of various sorts begin to emanate from issuers or underwriters which discuss in glowing and optimistic terms such aspects of a business as its finances, its earnings, or its growth prospects, stressing the favorable over the unfavorable, a question naturally arises whether in fact a campaign to sell securities has begun. Experience has shown that when particular difficulties in this area arise, they frequently occur because of the publication of valuation data or projections of future net income or dividends and other material which are normally considered to be objectionable in a registration statement. (Emphasis added.)

In its Release 3844 the SEC spelled out, as an adjunct to its general comments, 10 specific instances in which prefiling or similar publicity or promotion was involved. It then announced its position as to each. These 10 examples cover a wide variety of situations and deal in detail with the types and substance of publicity involved (brochures, reports, appearances before meetings of analysts, etc.) and the effect of the timing thereof. This release should be studied by all concerned with these phases of financial PR or publicity.[96]

35. Publicity vs. Independent Press Coverage.

The different treatment accorded to the newspaper man and the company's PR man presents some very real and practical problems. Not infrequently a member of the financial press may check rumors with corporate

officials. The corporate official—usually on advice from counsel—will refuse to discuss a forthcoming security issue. The resulting story may be
quite inaccurate and misleading. Even if it is labeled as "unconfirmed," its
effect on the market may be considerable.

Furthermore, with certain prospective issues from large and highly
regarded sources, it is almost impossible to prevent leaks. These leaks can
be blown up into news stories despite the honest efforts of the company to
avoid it. Probably the best example of this was the tremendous amount of
advance publicity when Ford Motor Company went public. As the SEC
investigation later proved, Ford and its public relations people were free
of any wrongdoing although it is understood that the SEC did censure
underwriters for their responsibility for "the resultant near-hysterical
rush to buy the Ford securities." [97]

Professor Loss has also commented upon this problem of "genesis" of
the news items: [98]

> It goes without saying that genuine news articles about securities
> and their issuers are in no sense prohibited by §5, since the news-
> paper is not selling any securities. By the same token, it seems
> [proper] . . . to permit the issuer or an underwriter or dealer to
> send to the newspapers copies of the "preliminary prospectus"
> whose use is permitted, and indeed encouraged, *after the filing of
> the registration statement.* The question is a more delicate one
> whether the issuer or underwriter may properly put out a press
> release containing a bare announcement of a filing. But this ques-
> tion is of no great consequence because the Commission itself
> issues a brief news release on each filing and these releases are
> picked up by the news services. In any event, the issuer or an
> underwriter or dealer should be slow to answer newspapermen's
> questions during the waiting period, whether those questions are
> the result of the distribution of the "preliminary prospectuses" or
> not. And, from the point of view of the newspaper, it seems clear
> that illegal advertisements or other items *paid for* by the issuer or
> an underwriter or dealer, directly or indirectly, would make the
> publisher an aider and abettor of any violation by the person
> making the payment.

E. MISCELLANEOUS FINANCIAL CONTROLS.

Some financial PR specialists also serve the PR, publicity, promotional
and advertising needs of various financial organizations or institutions—
in addition to publicly held "companies." See Section 1 above. For that
reason, Sections 36 to 40 below deal in broad strokes with certain governmental or exchange controls over such activities.

A preliminary caveat is in order. Some of the following materials speak
of "advertisements." They may not seem applicable to promotional

materials not clearly within the "paid advertising" category. However, the definitions of "advertisement" or "sales literature" may, in some cases, go beyond their normal meanings.

36. General Rule Against Deception.

Many of the requirements or restrictions discussed below deal with specifics. However, such detail is usually only a specific application of the statutory rule against deception. It may be generally accepted that the language of SEC Rule 10b-5 [99] is descriptive of the thrust against deception. See Section 9 above.

For example, as spelled out in the SEC's Statement of Policy [100] concerning sales literature used in the sale of investment company shares, literature is deemed materially misleading if it " (1) includes an untrue statement of a material fact or (2) omits to state a material fact necessary in order to make a statement made, in the light of the circumstances of its use, not misleading."

37. Investment Company Shares.

The advertising and "sales literature" of investment company shares is subject to the control of the SEC under the Securities Act and the Investment Company Act of 1940. In 1950 the SEC issued a Statement of Policy covering such advertising and sales literature.

The definition of "sales literature" includes "any communication (whether in writing, by radio or by television) used by an issuer, underwriter or dealer to induce the purchase of shares of any investment company" subject to certain exceptions.

The Statement, as amended November 5, 1957, appears below.

SECURITIES AND EXCHANGE COMMISSION
Washington, D. C.

STATEMENT OF POLICY
(As amended November 5, 1957)

The Securities and Exchange Commission with the assistance of the National Association of Securities Dealers, Inc., in 1950 reviewed samples of advertising and supplemental sales literature used in the sale of investment company shares, much of which was not filed with this Commission. This review revealed the existence of many practices in connection with the use, form and content of certain advertising and sales literature which, in the opinion of the Commission, might violate statutory standards, including provisions of the Securities Act of 1933 and the Investment Company Act of 1940.

The Commission, therefore, has issued the following Statement of Policy so that issuers, underwriters and dealers may understand certain of the types of advertising and sales literature which the Commission considers may be violative of the statutory standards.

It should be emphasized that the following Statement of Policy, as amended, does not attempt to cover all possible abuses, and that literature which complies with this Statement may not be used if it is in fact misleading. Conversely, nothing in this Statement of Policy is intended to prevent the use of factual statements, fairly presented, concerning fundamental investment policies and objectives, investment restrictions or other characteristics of a particular investment company.

> "Sales literature" as used hereafter shall be deemed to include any communication (whether in writing, by radio or by television) used by an issuer, underwriter, or dealer to induce the purchase of shares of an investment company. Reports of issuers to the extent they are transmitted to shareholders and do not contain an express offer are not deemed to be "sales literature" within the meaning of this definition but shall conform to this Statement of Policy. Communications between issuers, underwriters and dealers are included in this definition of "sales literature" only if such communications are passed on either orally or in writing or are shown to prospective investors or are designed to be employed in either written or oral form in the sale of securities.

For the purpose of interpreting this Statement of Policy, a piece of sales literature shall be deemed materially misleading by reason of an implication, as contemplated herein, if such sales literature (1) includes an untrue statement of a material fact or (2) omits to state a material fact necessary in order to make a statement made, in the light of the circumstances of its use, not misleading.

It will be considered materially misleading hereafter for sales literature—

Rates of Return

(a) To represent or imply a percentage return on an investment in the shares of an investment company unless based upon—

(1) Dividends from net investment income paid during a fiscal year related to the average monthly offering price for such fiscal year, provided that if any year prior to the most recent fiscal year is selected for this purpose, the rate of return for all subsequent fiscal years, similarly calculated, shall also be stated; or

(2) Dividends paid from net investment income during the twelve months ending not earlier than the close of the calendar month immediately preceding the date of publication related to an offering price current at said date of publication;

Show Asset Value Change

in either case the basis of the calculation shall be shown and adjustment made for capital gains distributions and any other factor necessary to make the presentation not misleading. "Net investment income" as used above shall include net accrued undivided earnings included in the price of capital shares issued and repurchased and shall be as required to be included in the issuer's prospectus. Every such statement of return shall be accompanied by a statement to the effect that such return is based upon dividends paid in the period covered and is not a representation of future results. Either in the same text, or by reference in the same text to an historical table elsewhere in the same piece of literature, there must be shown the per-share asset value at the beginning and end of the period, or the increase or decrease (stated in percentage) in asset value.

Capital vs. Income

(b) (1) To combine into any one amount distributions from net investment income and distributions from any other source.

(b) (2) To represent or imply an assurance that an investor will receive a stable, continuous, dependable, or liberal return or that he will receive any specified rate or rates of return.

Explain Risks

(c) To represent or imply an assurance that an investor's capital will increase or that purchase of investment company shares involves a preservation of original capital and a protection against loss in value. To discuss accumulation of capital, preservation of capital, accumulation of an estate, protection against loss of purchasing power, diversification of investments, financial independence or profit possibilities without pointing out or explaining the market risks inherently involved in the investment.

Government Regulation

(d) To make any reference to registration or regulation of any investment company under Federal or state authority without explaining that this does not involve supervision of management or investment practices or policies.

Custodial Services

(e) To represent or imply that services of banking institutions as custodian of securities, transfer agent, or dividend disbursing agent, provide protection for investors against possible depreciation of assets or that such institutions maintain any supervisory function over management in such matters as purchase and sale of portfolio securities or payment of dividends or provide any trusteeship protection, or to fail to state the extent of the limited role of the custodian whenever the advantages of custodial services are discussed.

Redemption

(f)   To state or discuss the redemption features of investment company shares without explaining in such statement that the value of the shares on redemption may be more or less than the investor's cost, depending upon the market value of the portfolio securities at the time of redemption.

Comparisons Generally

(g)   (1) To represent or imply that shares of an investment company are similar to or as safe as government bonds, insurance annuities, savings accounts or life insurance, or have the fixed income, principal, or any other features of a debt security.

(2) To represent or imply that the management of an investment company is under the same type of investment restrictions or is operated under limitations similar to or has fiduciary obligations such as those imposed by governmental authorities on savings banks and insurance companies, except to the extent that it is so restricted or limited by its statement of policy on file with this Commission.

Comparisons With Market Index or Other Security

(h)   To use any comparison of an investment company security with any other security or medium of investment or any security index or average without pointing out—

(1) that the particular security or index or average and period were selected; and,

(2) that the results disclosed should be considered in the light of the company's investment policy and objectives, the characteristics and quality of the company's investments, and the period selected; and,

(3) the material differences or similarities between the subjects of the comparisons; and,

(4) what the comparison is designed to show; and

(5) anything else that may be necessary to make the comparison fair.

New Capital

(i)   To represent or imply that investment companies in general are direct sources of new capital to industry or that a particular investment company is such a source unless the extent to which such investments are made is disclosed.

Performance Charts and Tables

(j)   To use any chart or table which is inaccurate in factual detail or tends to create a false or misleading impression as to any material aspect of the investment company's past performance or of an assumed investment of any investor in the investment company, or appears to represent that the investment company's past performance or investor experience will be repeated in the future. Charts or tables which conform to the "Approved Charts and Tables," described below and illustrated in the Appendix, will not be regarded by the Commission as materially false and misleading in the absence of facts or circumstances which make such charts or tables or their use in fact false and misleading in a particular use. Persons using other charts and tables must assume responsibility that they are not materially false or misleading. Any such chart or table may be submitted to the Commission for its views in advance of its use.

(1) Approved charts should conform with the following:
(i) The text, graphic detail and arrangement of any such chart should be substantially as shown on sample charts A, B, C, and D in the Appendix, whichever is applicable.

Drawn to Scale

(ii) Each chart should be drawn to scale which should be shown on the side of the chart and the same scale should be used for all segments of the chart. Appropriate shading or coloring should be added to distinguish between the different elements of the chart.
(iii) Charts A and B may not be used to show the reinvestment of dividend income.
(iv) The caption of sample chart B may, if desired, be changed to read as follows:
RECORD OF . . . . FUND IN TERMS OF NET ASSET VALUE PER SHARE, AND ILLUSTRATION OF AN ASSUMED INVESTMENT IN ONE SHARE WITH CAPITAL GAINS DISTRIBUTIONS ACCEPTED IN ADDITIONAL SHARES
(v) Chart C should be accompanied in the same piece of literature by Table 1 and Chart D should be so accompanied by Table 2. These tables should be prepared on the same assumption and cover the same period as the related chart, and should appear in a manner and location which permit easy reference from the chart to the corresponding table.

(2) Approved tables should conform with the following:
(i) The text, detail and arrangement of any table illustrating a dividend reinvestment or continuous investment program should be substantially as shown on Tables 1 and 2 in the Appendix, whichever is applicable. Tables prepared in accordance with the requirements for a table prescribed for use in the investment company's prospectus, or tables containing the same information as is shown on Charts A and B, may also be employed.

[Charts and Tables omitted.]

Contractual Plans

(ii) Any table designed to show any other investment program should contain comparable information. (*Contractual plan companies must use Sample Tables 3 and 4 on Pages 18 and 19*)

(iii) When Table 1 is used with Chart C or when Table 2 is used with Chart D in accordance with subparagraph (1)(v), above, such table need not contain any specific reference to the sales commission. When such table follows immediately after the chart, on the same page as the chart, the caption of the table and any notes thereto which are contained in the chart may be omitted from the table.

(3) Approved charts and tables should conform with the following:

Highest Sales Charge

(i) Charts and tables may be set up on a per share basis, or in amounts other than those shown on the attached samples, provided the charts and tables give effect to the maximum sales commission currently charged. The amounts used in constructing the chart or table should be amounts capable of being invested under the particular program being described. Any chart or table may be accompanied, in the same piece of literature, by a chart or table (which may be in summary form) illustrating investments in larger amounts at reduced sales commissions.

(ii) Any chart or table which reflects either the acceptance of capital gains distributions in additional shares or the reinvestment of dividends from investment income should not be captioned or characterized as the record of the fund, except as permitted in subparagraph (1)(iv).

Periods Covered

(iii) The period covered by such chart or table should be the most recent period ending with the latest available fiscal or calendar year and embracing:

A. The life of the company or the life of the issuer of the underlying investment company shares, or,

B. The duration of any plan or contract of the type referred to in Section 27(a) of the Investment Company Act of 1940, or,

C. The immediately preceding 10 years, or,

D. Periods longer than 10 years but less than the life of the company or the duration of such plan or contract, if such additional periods are multiples of five years;

provided that a portion of the current year may be added to the period ended with the last fiscal or calendar year. In no event should such chart or table relate to a period that exceeds the life of the company or the life of the issuer of the underlying shares.

Summary Results

(iv) Charts A, B, C, and D and Tables 1 and 2 may be accompanied in the same piece of literature by summary tables for the same period covered by the chart or table showing the end results which would have been obtained if alternative assumptions had been made as to the acceptance of capital gains distributions in shares or the reinvestment of dividends from investment income or both.

Use Same Basis

(v) Charts and tables may be accompanied in the same piece of literature by summary tables prepared on the same basis as the chart or table they accompany as follows:

A. A summary table showing the end results depicted in the chart or table.

Successive Summaries

B. Successive summary tables showing the end results over several periods of equal length, provided that the latest 10-year or longer period as well as every other such period within the total time span covered by the chart or table is included and that the chart or table and the summary tables are presented on the same page or on facing pages.

C. Successive summary tables showing the end results over several periods of unequal length, provided that such unequal periods start with each successive year and end with the last date shown on the chart or table, that every such period of unequal length within the total time span covered by the chart or table is included, and that the chart or table and the summary tables are presented on the same page or on facing pages.

Summary Content

(vi) In depicting the end results in any summary or successive summary tables provided for in (iv) and (v) above, the total of initial and periodic investments, total dividend reinvestment cost, total investment cost, total of capital gains distributions accepted in shares, and ending total asset value shall be shown separately to the extent applicable. The total capital gains distributions accepted in shares may be shown in a footnote. Summary tables need not contain any specific reference to sales commission.

May Need Added Facts

(vii) Any approved chart or table may be prepared on a basis which does not reflect the acceptance of capital gains distributions in shares or the reinvestment of dividends from investment income, or both, provided that no chart or table should reflect the reinvestment of dividends from investment income unless it also reflects the acceptance of capital gains distributions in shares.

(viii) Any chart or table should be preceded or accompanied by a prominent statement of any additional information or explanation of material significance to investors in appraising the figures shown, when necessary in a particular case to provide adequate and accurate disclosure of material facts.

(ix) Other relevant data in addition to that shown on the Approved Charts or Tables, such as the number of shares of stock acquired through assumed investments or the price of the shares so acquired, may be included, if the addition of such data does not result in a false and misleading presentation.

Management Claims

(k) To make any extravagant claims regarding management ability or competency.

(l) To represent or imply that investment companies are operated as, or are similar to, "co-operatives."

(m) To represent or imply that investment company shares generally have been selected by fiduciaries.

Continuous Investment Programs

(n) (1) To use the phrase "dollar averaging" or "averaging the dollar" (although the phrases "dollar cost averaging" or "cost averaging" are not objectionable) in referring to any plan of continuous investment in the shares of an investment company at stated intervals regardless of the price level of the shares.

Cost Averaging and Contractual Plans

(2) To discuss or portray the principles of dollar cost averaging, or cost averaging, or to discuss or portray any Periodic Payment Plan referred to in section 27(a) of the Investment Company Act of 1940, without making clear—

(i) that the investor will incur a loss under such plan if he discontinues the plan when the market value of his accumulated shares is less than his cost; and

(ii) that the investor is investing his funds primarily in securities subject to market fluctuations and that the method involves continuous investment in such shares at regular intervals regardless of price levels; and

(iii) that the investor must take into account his financial ability to continue such plan through periods of low price levels; and

(iv) that such plans do not protect against loss in value in declining markets.

(3) To discuss or portray any other type of continuous investment plan without making clear that such type of in-

vestment plan does not assure a profit and does not protect against depreciation in declining markets.

Sales Commissions

(o) To fail to include in any sales literature which does not state the amount or rate of the sales commission (except communications which deal only with routine business matters or which do not purport to discuss or describe any investment company or investment company security) a clear reference to the prospectus or prospectuses for information concerning the sales commission, and other information.

(p) To fail to include in any sales literature which is designed to encourage investors to switch from one investment company to another, or from one class of security of an investment company to another class, the substance of the following statement in a separate paragraph in type as large as that used generally in the body of the piece:

> "Switching from the securities of one investment company to another, or from one class of security of an investment company to another, involves a sales charge on each such transaction, for details of which see the prospectus. The prospective purchaser should measure these costs against the claimed advantage of the switch."

Industry Performance against Company Performance

(q) To represent or imply that the performance of any particular company may be measured by or compared with or related to the performance of a particular industry unless the extent and scope of the portfolio of the particular company is such that its performance will generally approximate that of the industry.

Reprints

(r) To employ material in whole or in part from published articles or documents descriptive of or relating to investment companies unless such material, or the literature including such material, complies with this Statement of Policy and in addition such material is not taken out of context in a manner which alters its intended meaning.

By agreement between the SEC and NASD, the latter organization administers the Statement of Policy.

All NASD members must file with the NASD all advertising and sales literature prepared by (or especially for) them, including all newspaper, radio or television advertising or scripts and all postal cards, form letters, and individually typed sales letters which repeat the theme of the same central idea. These must be filed with the Investment Companies Department, Executive Office of NASD, within three days after the first use of the publication. Also, members *may* submit such materials in advance of use or publication with a request for comment as to whether they seem to meet the requirements of the Statement of Policy.

NASD takes the position that news releases and other publicity intended to promote sales of shares of an investment company are within their jurisdiction and the coverage of the Statement of Policy.

NASD's "What You Should Know . . ." presents in detail the Statement of Policy, pertinent interpretations, a discussion of SEC policy on general or institutional literature and advertising and other NASD guides "to proper sales practices relating to investment company shares." It may be obtained from the Washington office of NASD, 888 17th Street, N.W.

The SEC also reacts to inquiries as to promotional practices in the sales of these shares. Typical is its August, 1963 letter ruling concerning the "practice of tendering to potential investors in mutual funds . . . a gift such as pen, wallet or a miniature bank." It ruled that this was prohibited by the Investment Company Act unless it is described in the prospectus since it would result in sales at a price other than "a current public offering price in the prospectus." [101]

The SEC has also stated its position in Securities Act Release No. 4709 as to permissible additional language or statements in tombstone advertising for "no-load" funds.

38. Securities Exchange Members.

Exchange members and member organizations are subject to strict exchange standards as to their advertising, market letters, research reports, sales literature, radio, television and writing and speaking activities, many of which fall within the PR periphery. These requirements are in addition to other—frequently similar—standards of the SEC or NASD.

Personnel charged with preparation of any of the above materials will find very useful the NYSE publication *Communications with the Public* which reprints the pertinent Exchange Rules and supplemental materials and explanations of the Rules. The Exchange's Public Relations and Market Development Circulars Nos. 2 and 3 and its Public Relations and Research Informational Circulars Nos. 4 to 7 contain additional interpretative guidelines for such activities and materials.

39. NASD Members.

The principal control over the activities of NASD members is the association's Rules of Fair Practice. By interpretation of the NASD Board of Governors, it is a violation of Article III, Section 1 thereof to publish or circulate any advertisement, sales literature or market letter which "the member knows or has reason to know contains any untrue statement of a material fact or is otherwise false or misleading." This generality is enlarged by "Advertising Interpretation (Advertising, Sales Literature, Market Letters and Recruiting of Sales Personnel)" issued by the NASD.[102]

The definition of "advertisements" includes "any material for use in any newspaper or magazine or other public media or by radio, telephone recording, motion picture or television."

Each advertisement must be filed for review with the Executive Office in Washington within five business days after initial use except that tombstone advertising or other excluded materials need not be so filed.

40. Savings and Loan Associations.

Accounts of most savings and loan associations are insured by the Federal Savings and Loan Insurance Corporation (FSLIC) whether the associations have federal or state charters. Accordingly they are subject to the rules of FSLIC. Rule 563.27 provides: [103]

> No insured institution shall use advertising (whether printed, radio display, or of any other nature) or *make any representation* which is inaccurate in any particular or which in any way misrepresents its services, contracts, investments or financial condition. (Emphasis added.)

Under this Rule, the Board's interest in deceptive communications or representations goes beyond paid advertising. However, no "formal proceedings" have been instituted for violations of such practices. "When practices have been subject to criticism, informal communications have been utilized with desired results." [104]

In December, 1966, the FHLBB, in conjunction with the Comptroller of the Currency, FDIC and the Board of Governors of the Federal Reserve System, issued a specific ruling as to "advertising for funds." The "minimum principles" were announced to be: [105]

> (1) Interest or dividend rates should be stated in terms of annual rates of simple interest, and the advertisement should state whether such earnings are compounded and, if so, the basis of compounding. Neither the total percentage return if held to final maturity nor the average annual rate achieved by compounding should be stated unless the annual rate of simple interest is presented with equal prominence.
> (2) No reference should be made to "profit" to the investor for use of his funds over a period of time.

(3) If an advertised rate is payable only on investments or deposits that meet fixed time or amount requirements, such requirements should be stated.

(4) No statement should be made implying that more than $15,000 of Federal insurance is provided for each depositor in a bank or each member in a savings and loan association.

The Securities and Exchange Commission has expressed the opinion that deposit and share accounts are subject to the antifraud provisions of the Securities Act of 1933 and the Securities Exchange Act of 1934 and that advertisements by financial institutions that are contrary to such principles may violate those antifraud provisions.

The FHLBB considers publicity or other efforts to obtain funds in the competitive money market as subject to these strictures.

The above reference to the SEC also applies to deposit and share accounts with FDIC-insured banks.[106]

Notes

1. P.R.S.A. Interpretation, reproduced at pages 745-7 of the text.
2. Gartley, *Financial Public Relations—Management's New Responsibility,* P.R.J., April, 1957, at 3.
3. BRANDEIS, OTHER PEOPLE'S MONEY, ch. 5 (1914).
4. S. Rep. No. 47, at 6–7 and H. R. Rep. No. 85, at 1–2, 73d Cong., 1st Sess. (1933).
5. Sec. Act Rel. No. 3844, Oct. 8, 1957.
6. N.Y. Stock Exchange, *Company Manual,* at A-19.
7. Rudick C. Lawrence, *Financial Public Relations and the NYSE,* remarks before the Public Relations Group of the Management Council of Southwestern Connecticut, Nov. 17, 1966, at 1.
8. Lawrence, *supra* note 7, at 3.
9. Lawrence, *supra* note 7, at 2.
10. Rudick C. Lawrence, *You, Your Company, and the Timely Disclosure Rules of The New York Stock Exchange,* remarks before the N.Y. Chapter, P.R.S.A., Nov. 23, 1965, at 2.
11. N.Y.S.E., M. F. Educational Circular No. 162, June 22, 1962.
12. H.R. Doc. No. 95, 88th Cong., 1st Sess., pts. 1–6 (1963).
13. *Id.* pt. 3, at 65–103, appendices IX-B, IX-C at 117-22. For a discussion of financial PR wrongdoing by a PR counselor, see Smith, *Financial Publicists and the S.E.C.'s Complaints,* Com. & Fin. Chronicle, May 3, 1962.
14. For a full discussion of securities regulation, see LOSS, SECURITIES REGULA-TION (2d ed. 1961; supp. 1962). This is generally considered the definitive text on the subject.
15. 48 Stat. 74, 15 U.S.C. §§77a–77aa, as amended.
16. 48 Stat. 881, 15 U.S.C. §§77b, etc., as amended.
17. 49 Stat. 803, 15 U.S.C. §§79–79X–6, as amended.
18. 53 Stat. 1149, 15 U.S.C. §§77aaa–77bbbb, as amended.
19. 54 Stat. 789, 11 U.S.C. §72,107, 15 U.S.C. §§80a–1 to 52, as amended.
20. 54 Stat. 847, 15 U.S.C. §§80b-1 to 21, as amended.
21. For a discussion of state securities controls and liability thereunder, see Loss, *supra* note 14, chs. 1B and 11C.
22. For an explanation of code enforcement and precedents established thereby for guidance of PR practitioners, see Decker, *PRSA's Code: How the Practitioner and Public Are Protected (A Review of Cases Brought Before Enforcement Bodies),* P.R.J., March, 1967, at 26. See also Goss, *Common Sense of the PRSA Financial Code,* P.R.J., April, 1964, at 6.
23. *Supra* note 16, at §10 (b).
24. 17 C.F.R. 240.10b-5.
25. Hooper v. Mountain States Sec. Corp., 282 F.2d 195 (5th Cir. 1960), *cert. denied,* 365 U.S. 814 (1961); Fischman v. Raytheon Mfg. Co., 188 F.2d 783 (2d Cir. 1951); Charles Hughes & Co. v. S.E.C., 139 F.2d 434 (2d Cir. 1943), *cert. denied,* 321 U.S. 786 (1944).

26. Equitable Co. v. Halsey, Stuart & Co., 312 U.S. 410 (1941); cf. RESTATE-MENT, TORTS §529 (1939).

27. List v. Fashion Park, Inc., 340 F.2d 457 (2d Cir. 1965), cert. denied, 382 U.S. 811 (1965); Kohler v. Kohler Co., 319 F.2d 634 (7th Cir. 1963); Cochran v. Channing Corp., 211 F. Supp. 239 (S.D.N.Y. 1962).

28. O'Neill v. Maytag, 339 F.2d 764 (2d Cir. 1964).

29. List v. Fashion Park, Inc., supra note 27.

30. See S.E.C. v. Capital Gains Bureau, 375 U.S. 180 (1963) as to similar provisions §206 of the Investment Advisers Act of 1940.

31. S.E.C. v. Texas Gulf Sulphur Co., 258 F. Supp. 262 (S.D.N.Y. 1966).

32. 40 S.E.C. 907, 913–14 (1961); see also 3 Loss, supra note 14, at 1454–55.

33. H. L. Green Co. v. Childree, 185 F. Supp. 95 (S.D.N.Y. 1960).

34. In re Cady, Roberts & Co., supra note 32.

35. S.E.C. v. Texas Gulf Sulphur Co., supra note 31.

36. For a discussion of these statutes, see 1 Loss, supra note 14, at 35–43.

37. N.Y. Gen. Bus. Law, §352-c, added by Laws, 1955, ch. 553, §2. See also Cal. Pen. Code, §§395, 523-a.

38. Special Study, supra note 13, pt. 3, at 96.

39. N.Y. Pen. Law, §§926, 952.

40. People v. Watson, 154 Misc. 667, 278 N.Y.S. 659, aff'd memo, 245 App. Div. 838, 282 N.Y.S. 235 (1935).

41. Saul, Timely Disclosure, The American Stock Exchange Experience, address before American Society of Corporate Secretaries, June 13, 1967, at 9.

42. S.E.C., Sec. Act Rel. No. 3844, Oct. 8, 1957.

43. S.E.C., Sec. Act Rel. No. 4697, May 28, 1964.

44. N.Y. Stock Exchange, Company Manual, at A-19.

45. AMEX, Listing Agreement, distributed in letter addressed to "Public Relations Counsellors," Jan. 14, 1965.

46. List v. Fashion Park, Inc., supra note 27, at 462.

47. RESTATEMENT, TORTS §538(2)(a) (1939).

48. Timely Disclosure: Ignore It at Your Peril, P.R.J., April, 1966, at 12–16; Timely Disclosure: The Need for Clarity, P.R.J., April, 1967, at 22–26.

49. Letter dated Dec. 21, 1965 to Dr. Frederick H. Teahan, Education Director, P.R.S.A.

50. N.Y. Stock Exchange, Company Manual, at A-20. See also N.Y. Stock Exchange letter and enclosures dated Feb., 1966, addressed to "Public Relations Executives and Counsellors of New York Stock Exchange Listed Companies."

51. Taft & Thompson, Timely Disclosure: The Need for Clarity, P.R.J., April, 1967, at 22.

52. Cohen, quoted in Loomis, Where Manny Cohen Is Leading The SEC, Fortune, Dec., 1966, 163, at 214.

53. N.Y.S.E. letter, supra note 50, at 5.

54. N.Y. Stock Exchange, Company Manual, at A-20.1.

55. Id. at A-39, 40 and 40.1.

56. AMEX, supra note 45, at 3.

57. N.Y. Stock Exchange letter, supra note 50, at 7, 10.

58. *Id.* at 5.

59. Burson, *Mere Disclosure Is Not Enough,* P.R.J., Nov., 1966, at 13.

60. Lawrence, *supra* note 7.

61. Burson, *supra* note 59, at 17.

62. S.E.C. brief on appeal, at 67–79; S.E.C. v. Texas Gulf Sulphur Co., *supra* note 31. See also Halloran, *Insider Trading in Stocks,* 21 Bus. Law. 1009, 20, 22 (1966).

63. S.E.C. brief, *supra* note 62, at 76–79.

64. S.E.C. v. Texas Gulf Sulphur Co. *et al.,* 37 L.W. 2126 (2d Cir. 1968). For a general discussion of the case, see Robards, *Texas Gulf Drama Is a Tragedy for Key Actors,* N. Y. Times, Aug. 18, 1968, p. 2F.

65. Smith, *"No Comment"—a Victim of Disclosure,* N. Y. Times, Aug. 25, 1968, p. F12.

66. Cohen, *supra* note 52, at 214.

67. N.Y. Stock Exchange letter, *supra* note 50, at 2.

68. See examples described in N.Y. Stock Exchange letter, *supra* note 50.

69. Conference of author with members of S.E.C. staff in Washington. Quotation permitted but without specific attribution.

70. See *In re* Cady, Roberts & Co., *supra* note 32.

71. For discussions of the "insider" trading problem, see Cary, *Insider Trading in Stocks,* 21 Bus. Law. 1009 (1966); Fleischer, *Securities Trading and Corporate Information Practices: The Implications of the Texas Gulf Sulphur Proceedings,* 51 Va. L. Rev. 1271 (1965); Fleischer, *Corporate Disclosure/Insider Trading,* Harv. Bus. Rev., Jan.–Feb., 1967, at 129–35 (discussing specific fact-situations).

72. Burson, *supra* note 59. See also P.R.N., Aug. 1, 1966, at 1.

73. As quoted in Smith, *supra* note 65.

74. For a discussion of this case, see Robards, *Insider vs. the Little Guy: Second Round Begins,* N. Y. Times, Sept. 1, 1968, at 1F.

75. S.E.C., Sec. Act Rel. No. 4885 and Sec. Exch. Act Rel. No. 8197, Nov. 29, 1967.

76. Hewens, *Annual Reports Reflect Corporate Good Sense,* P.R.J., April, 1967, at 32–3. See also *Public Relations and the Annual Report* (Case Study No. 1076), P.R.N., Sept. 26, 1966, at 3.

77. Krasny, *Let Me Send You an Annual Report,* P.R.J., April, 1967, at 17–19.

78. N.Y. Stock Exchange letter, *supra* note 50, at 5.

79. H. R. Rep. No. 85, 73d Cong., 1st Sess., at 24 (1933); for a discussion of the anti-touting cases, *see* 3 Loss, *supra* note 14, at 1518–19.

80. Bernays, Biography of an Idea, ch. 38 (1965).

81. Special Study, *supra* note 12, pt. 3, at 66.

82. Gadsby, *Public Relations Counsel and the Federal Securities Laws,* address to New York Chapter of P.R.S.A., April 8, 1958.

83. Beveridge, *How to Avoid Proxy Fights,* P.R.J., June, 1964, at 22, reprinted from Beveridge, Financial Public Relations (1963).

84. See, as to proxy solicitations generally, Exchange Act Rules 14a-1 to 12 and Schedules A, B and C attached thereto.

85. Beveridge, *supra* note 83, at 26.

86. For an explanation of the S.E.C. position, see Sec. Act Rel. No. 3844, *Publication of Information Prior to or After the Effective Date of Registration Statement,* October 8, 1957.

87. S.E.C. v. Arvida Corp., 169 F. Supp. 211 (D.C.S.D.N.Y. 1958), CCH FED. SEC. L. REP. ¶90,883, noted in (1959) DUKE B.J. 460, 54 NW. U. L. REV. 131 (1959). For a further discussion of this case, see Loss, *supra* note 14, at 219–21 and Byron D. Woodside, *Disclosures Under the Securities Act and the Financial Press,* address before the Society of American Business Writers, May 12, 1965.

88. Woodside, *supra* note 87, at 10.

89. First Maine Corp., S.E.C., Sec. Ex. Act Rel. No. 5898 (1959). See also Carl M. Loeb, Rhoades & Co., *infra* note 91.

90. Woodside, *supra* note 87, at 8.

91. In the matter of Loeb, Rhoades & Co. and Dominick & Dominick, 38 S.E.C. 843, 853; S.E.C., Sec. Act Rel. No. 5870 (1959).

92. *Investment Dealer's Digest,* Nov. 15, 1965, at 29–32.

93. Warnock, *SEC Regulations: How They Affect Your Company,* P.R.J., July, 1961, at 10–11; Eckhouse, *How Does It Look to the SEC?,* P.R.J., May, 1959, at 16–20.

94. S.E.C. v. Arvida, *supra* note 87, at 852.

95. Woodside, *supra* note 87, at 9.

96. For a discussion of these ten examples, see Sharp, *supra* note 92, at 31–32; Eckhouse, *supra* note 93, at 18, 20.

97. Special Study, *supra* note 12, at 82.

98. Loss, *supra* note 14, at 22.

99. *Supra* notes 23–24.

100. S.E.C., *Statement of Policy,* as amended Nov. 5, 1957, reprinted in full in *What You Should Know . . . ,* referred to in text.

101. S.E.C., letter to James M. Landis, Esq., dated Aug. 2, 1963.

102. For the full annotated text of this Advertising Interpretation and other provisions of the Rules of Fair Practice, see N.A.S.D., *Reprint of the Manual,* ¶2151, *et seq.*

103. F.S.L.I.C., *Rules and Regulations for Insurance of Accounts,* Ch. V (D), Title 12, C.F.R., §563.27.

104. F.S.L.I.C., letter to author, April 6, 1967.

105. F.H.L.B.B., Resolution and Notice No. 20,344, Dec. 14, 1966.

106. F.D.I.C., Letter dated Dec. 16, 1966 to the Presidents of All State Insured Banks Which Are Not Members of the Federal Reserve System.

Chapter 23

Lobbying

A. CONCEPTS AND CONTROLS

1. Definition of Lobbying
2. Propriety of Lobbying
3. Public Relations and Lobbying
4. The "Railroad/Truckers" Case
5. Congressional Control of Lobbying
6. Relation to the Federal Foreign Agents Registration Act
7. Relation to Federal Corrupt Practices Act
8. Federal Trade Commission and Lobbying
9. State Control of Lobbying
10. Lobbying Contracts

B. FEDERAL REGULATION OF LOBBYING ACT

11. Summary of the Act
12. Constitutionality
13. Applicability of the Act
14. Effect of Special Contributions
15. Exemptions From the Act
16. "Grass Roots" Lobbying
17. Administrative Agency and Other Governmental Contact
18. Registration and Report Forms and Filing
19. Enforcement of the Act

C. 1967 AMENDATORY BILL

20. The 1966 Joint Committee Report
21. Title V of The Legislative Reorganization Act of 1967

D. STATE CONTROLS OF LOBBYING

22. Variety and Ambiguity
23. Definitions

Chapter 23

Lobbying

A. CONCEPTS AND CONTROLS.

1. Definition of Lobbying.

President Kennedy—then a Senator—defined lobbying as "efforts by which various groups or individuals attempt to secure the passage or defeat of legislation." [1]

Commentators have pointed out that the meaning may vary with the period, the specific activity or purpose involved, the applicable statute, the branch of government in question—federal/state or legislative/executive—the propriety of the method used, etc.[2] It may well vary from the most arrant kind of bribery or corrupt practice to the most legitimate, constitutionally-protected pursuit of the right of petition by an individual citizen.

Probably the basic reason for this disparity of meaning is the fact that the various regulatory statutes do not, in most instances, define it specifically. The Federal Regulation of Lobbying Act, for example, does not define the term although it spells out the persons intended to be covered thereby. Another reason is the limited interpretation adopted by the Supreme Court in order to avoid difficult constitutional issues.[3]

Fortunately, these semantic differences are not overly important. Whatever the popular usages may be, the legal meaning of lobbying turns on the language, scope, applicability and interpretation of the relevant statute —state or federal. These are discussed below beginning at Section 11.

2. Propriety of Lobbying.

The word "lobbying" has unsavory and illicit implications. This is undoubtedly a residue from the days when lobbyists thought little of stooping to legislative bribery and all kinds of "influence peddling." [4] The investigations of the "five percenters" added to the murk.[5] This atmosphere has, in some quarters and under some circumstances, continued to taint even the most legitimate lobbying.

Honest lobbying is legitimate. Not only is it legally recognized but it is frequently necessary and highly desirable—even, on occasion, extremely moral. Legislators in all areas of government have frequently and publicly indicated that they welcome and need information and even partisan views from all sources.[6]

Lobbying is merely one method by which the citizen—either individually or as an organized subcommunity—exercises his right to petition the government for redress of his grievances under the protection of the First Amendment.[7] See Section 4 below. This constitutionally-protected unilateral basis for lobbying would be sufficient but there is also a bilateral necessity which is equally important—at least in the practical sense.

Legislation is rarely born in a vacuum. Once introduced, it does not come to fruition and final form under its own power. The individual legislator has neither the time nor, in some instances, the interest or capacity to explore and understand all of the hundreds or thousands of bills in legislative hoppers in Washington or a state capitol. See discussion of the *Harriss* case in Section 12 below.

To apply himself to this heterogeneous welter, to sort it out, to accord it proper priorities, to analyze and understand even a specific bill, eventually to vote on it intelligently—he must be urged and prodded, his attention directed and oriented, and information supplied to him. He must learn and appraise the needs and thinking of his constituents or of a substantial or significant fraction thereof.

Frequently, this is most capably performed by the organized and professional voice of the lobbyist. The intelligent and honest legislator has learned to recognize the not infrequently partisan interests in these appeals, approaches and explanations.

Lobbying also may help to resist political or party pressures on the legislator. Lobbyists may aid him in answering the pressures and demands of the executive.

It is the chore of the lawmaker to winnow from all of these frequently opposing representations and demands those which best advance and serve his constituency, making due allowance for the interests of minorities or others directly or incidentally affected by the legislation.

3. Public Relations and Lobbying.

Many of the fundamental and best-recognized methods and tools of public relations are essentially those of the lobbyist. By training and experience the public relations man is well-qualified to act as a lobbyist —more than that, to act as a successful lobbyist. Many of them do serve in that capacity, serving a wide variety of interests. We are here using "lobbyist" in its broadest meaning since many of the activities of the public relations man, in this context, do not come within the statutory definitions of lobbyists or lobbying activities.

Many of these activities are frequently and loosely called "lobbying." They are more aptly described as "government relations," a term which includes a considerable range of activity, some of which may, of course, be true lobbying. These aspects of government relations are discussed in Chapter 19, particularly Section 3 thereof.

Research has shown that the bulk of lobbyists come from the ranks of lawyers or "permanent group of corporation officials or representatives." The remainder is drawn from various sources including "public relations counsel or consultants." It has been knowledgeably suggested: [8]

> Of the [public relations counsel and consultants] particularly, there are relatively far fewer active and registered in the states than in Washington, although many state groups conduct activities that would come within any reasonably functional definition of "public relations."

The only requirement or limiting factor is that the public relations man, about to act as a lobbyist, must recognize promptly when he crosses the line from "straight PR" into "real" lobbying—especially of the sort which requires registration under the federal or appropriate state law. This line may not be too easy to recognize and legal counsel should be sought.

Having registered—if it be necessary—his activities are untrammeled and are limited only by anti-bribery or other laws affecting any citizen under similar circumstances.

The entire policy of federal—also most state—control of lobbying is based on registration and subsequent reporting, thereby announcing openly the sponsorship of the partisan activity. To some, the registered lobbyist may be more acceptable than the private-sector public relations practitioner. Those who think of the latter as a practitioner of "brainwashing" or of some kind of subliminal suasion, welcome the overt identification of the lobbyist as against the unproclaimed and allegedly devious machinations of the public relations man.[9]

4. The "Railroad/Truckers" Case.

One of the most important "lobbying cases" really involved alleged violations of the antitrust laws. We are here using "lobbying" in a broad sense—far beyond the limiting application given it by the Supreme Court in earlier cases.[10] This was the so-called "railroad/truckers case": *Noerr*

Motor Freight Co., Inc. et al. v. Eastern Railroad Presidents Conference et al.[11]

An action under the Sherman Act was brought in the Pennsylvania federal court by forty-one trucking operators and their state trade association against twenty-four eastern railroads, their trade association and their public relations counsel. The charge: conspiracy to prevent the Pennsylvania legislature and governor from adopting legislation favorable to the truckers and to damage the truckers' relations with their customers.

The campaign of the railroads was largely a public relations and publicity campaign involving, among other things, the so-called "third-party technique" or the "false front" method.[12] The trial court characterized this as "the technique of the 'Big Lie.'" The plaintiff's public relations practices were also in question. The court found for the truckers and enjoined the railroads from using, not only the third-party technique, but also any publicity activities against the truckers. It further enjoined against use of disparaging or misleading materials in any lobbying activities.

The federal circuit court affirmed this injunction by a two-to-one decision. On appeal, the Supreme Court unanimously reversed and found for the railroads, their association and their public relations firm.

The Supreme Court appears to have accepted the lower court's conclusion that the railroads had an anti-competitive purpose in their campaign although the record did not contain much evidence of this. Notwithstanding this, the Court reversed and premised its decision on the rights of the defendants under the First Amendment, saying:

> We do not see how this fact [the anti-competitive purpose] even if adequately supported in the record, could transform conduct otherwise lawful into a violation of the Sherman Act. All of the considerations which have lead us to the conclusion that the [Sherman] Act does not apply to mere group solicitation of governmental action are equally applicable in spite of the addition of this factor. The right of the people to inform their representatives in government of their desires with respect to the passage or enforcement of laws cannot properly be made to depend upon their intent in so doing.

The court referred to some of the publicity techniques as "deception of the public, . . . manufacture of bogus sources of information . . . [and] distortion of public sources of information. . . ." Yet the court went on to say:

> Insofar as the . . . Act sets up a code of ethics at all, it is a code that condemns trade restraints, not political activity, and as we

have already pointed out, a publicity campaign to influence governmental action falls clearly into the category of political activity.

As to the anti-competitive aspects of the activities of the two groups, the court pointed out:

> It is inevitable, whenever an attempt is made to influence legislation by a campaign of publicity, that an incidental effect of that campaign may be the infliction of some direct injury upon the interests of the party against whom the campaign is directed. And it seems equally inevitable that those conducting the campaign would be aware of, and possibly even pleased by, the prospect of such injury. To hold that the knowing infliction of such injury renders the campaign itself illegal would thus be tantamount to outlawing all such campaigns.

This was a situation in which the right of free speech and the right of petition met head-on with the anti-trust laws. Furthermore, some of the tactics of the parties were questionable. The Supreme Court found the constitutionally-protected rights so strong that it refused to derogate from them, even under these circumstances.

Many point to this case as a Magna Carta for public relations. The recognition of the right of business—even on an organized basis—to make its position clear is undoubtedly significant. This is especially true because of some of the methods used to that end. Cutlip and Center have said of this case: [13]

> The legal right of a [public relations] counselor to plead a cause in public is now clearly defined. The ethical problems posed by the malpractice of both PR agencies remain for solution.

There is no question that the public relations business might today be considerably different had this case been decided otherwise.

It should not be assumed that these constitutional rights are without limit in this competitive context. The Supreme Court pointed out there may be situations in which a publicity campaign "ostensibly directed toward influencing governmental action, is a mere sham to cover what is actually nothing more than an attempt to interfere directly with the business relationships of a competitor and the application of the Sherman Act would be justified." [14]

5. Congressional Control of Lobbying.

The federal controls over lobbying are premised upon the Federal Regulation of Lobbying Act adopted in 1946 by the Congress,[15] hereinafter referred to as the Act, and discussed in Sections 11 to 19 below.

It should be noted at the outset that, despite the title of the Act, it does not use the terms "lobby" or "lobbyist" in any way. The persons to whom it applies are essentially "statutory lobbyists" although included in the more general definitions of the term.

There had been scattered regulation prior to the adoption of the Act. Certain limited controls over utilities-lobbying were written into the Public Utility Holding Companies Act of 1935.[16] In 1936 the activities of the shipbuilders' and operators' lobby led to requirements for registration with the United States Maritime Commission.[17]

Also, to a limited extent, lobbying control at the federal level is exercised by the Federal Trade Commission. See Section 8 below.

6. Relation to the Federal Foreign Agents Registration Act.

Confusion has arisen in some sectors as to the relative application of the Act and the Foreign Agents Registration Act. The activities controlled by both acts seem—at least superficially and in part—similar. The theory of federal control is the same in both cases: open registration and repeated reporting thereafter.

There are, of course, significant differences. The lobbyist represents what might be called "domestic" principals exercising a constitutional right; the foreign agent represents foreign principals exercising a privilege by governmental grace. Furthermore, a much wider range of activities requires registration of a foreign agent. Among these, his "grass roots" activities are probably most distinctive. Under the Lobbying Act only direct approaches to the Congress are involved. See Section 13 below.

Since the registration, filing and reporting requirements under the two acts are substantively and procedurally quite different, this distinction between the two acts is of continuing importance. As a cautionary measure, a public relations firm operating under either act for the first time should study its obligations closely—especially if it represents an American company having foreign interests as well, or the American subsidiary or "associate" of a foreign concern or interests.

As to the Federal Foreign Agents Registration Act generally, see Chapter 24.

7. Relation to Federal Corrupt Practices Act.

The Lobbying Act has only an indirect relation to the Federal Corrupt Practices Act.[18] The latter deals essentially with political contributions and the reporting thereof. Its "bribery" provisions deal with candidates and promises of personal political appointments, rather than with passage or defeat of legislation.

The Lobbying Act, in §311 thereof, specifically provides that it shall "not apply to practices or activities regulated by the Federal Corrupt Practices Act nor be construed as repealing any portion . . . [thereof]."

8. Federal Trade Commission and Lobbying.

The truckers/railroads case—discussed in Section 4 above—arose under the Sherman Act. A parallel question arises under Section 5 of the Federal Trade Commission Act: whether lobbying or its associated public relations activities—again using the term in its broad context—is an unfair trade practice. There have been several such cases before the Commission although research does not indicate any court approval thereof.

In 1939 an FTC complaint was issued against an ice cream manufacturers' association charging lobbying for certain legislation affecting competition involved in the sale of freezers. The case was subsequently dismissed.[19] Some five years later, in 1944, the Commission actually did enter an order against a group of rock crusher manufacturers and their trade association preventing them and it from trying to have special, beneficial provisions inserted in government specifications.[20]

These cases do not appear to involve any First Amendment questions, but merely question whether the alleged lobbying activities were unfair trade practices under the FTC Act. It seems likely that the courts would —in FTC cases like this—upset such efforts and follow the doctrine of the Supreme Court in the *Noerr* case. See Section 4 above. It also seems significant that, to the best of our knowledge, the FTC has not instituted any other cases of this sort since 1944.

9. State Control of Lobbying.

Most of the several states have their own direct controls of lobbying. Others deal with the problem indirectly as a "corrupt practice" or otherwise. There is considerable variation in the basis, source, nature and extent of these controls which are discussed in Sections 22 to 28 below.

10. Lobbying Contracts.

Among the aspects of lobbying most often criticized in Congressional investigations and lobbying literature is the contingent fee arrangement between the lobbyist and his employer.[21] The public relations practitioner or lawyer who becomes a lobbyist has moved over into another area insofar as his right to compensation may be involved. This is particularly true of the contingent fee arrangement. See Sections 20, 21 and 26 below.

In the earlier cases recovery by the lobbyist was generally refused even if his compensation was a fixed amount and in no way contingent.[22] Some courts have since drawn a distinction between the fixed fee and the contingent fee contract, the latter being held to "suggest the use of sinister and corrupt means for the accomplishment of the end desired." [23]

Many of these contingent fee cases arose under state statutes which specifically outlawed the contingent fee claim on the ground of public policy. See Section 26 below.

B. FEDERAL REGULATION OF LOBBYING ACT.

11. Summary of the Act.

The Act deals with the registration and quarterly reporting by lobbyists although that term is not used in the Act. Subject to certain exceptions, registration and reporting are required of all who directly or indirectly receive any money or other "thing of value" to be used principally for, or whose principal purpose is, accomplishing or *influencing the passage or defeat of any Congressional legislation.*

Such persons are to maintain certain records and tender receipts. Registration is with both the Secretary of the Senate and the Clerk of the House and filing is with the Clerk of the House, both of whom publish a joint quarterly report in the *Congressional Record.* Violation is a misdemeanor subject to a fine of up to $5000 and/or up to twelve months' imprisonment.

12. Constitutionality.

The constitutionality of the Act has been attacked on the ground that it violates the right of petition guaranteed by the First Amendment. There is no doubt that Congress can take steps to stop corrupt practices. The more limited question is whether a registration requirement—as required by the Act—is constitutional. In the *Harriss* case [24] the Supreme Court held the Act to be constitutional.

The Court reconciled the Act with this alleged restraint on the right of petition by saying:

> Present-day legislative complexities are such that the individual member of Congress cannot be expected to explore the myriad pressures to which they are regularly subjected. Yet full realization of the American ideal of government by elected representatives depends to no small extent on their ability to properly evaluate such pressures. Otherwise the voice of the people may all too easily be drowned out by the voice of special interest groups seeking favored treatment . . .

Towards that end, Congress has not sought to prohibit these pressures. It has merely provided for a modicum of information from those who for hire attempt to influence legislation or who collect or spend funds for that purpose. It wants only to know who is being hired, who is putting up the money, and how much.

However, the Court, as it had in the earlier *Rumeley* case,[25] in a sense emasculated the Act by limiting its application as discussed in Section 13 below.

The Act's constitutionality had also been questioned successfully in an earlier lower court decision because of the vagueness of the expression "principal purpose." [26] In the *Harriss* opinion, the Supreme Court had no difficulty with this aspect, pointing out that it was clear from the legislative history of the Act that "principal" was used to exclude persons and contributions having only an "incidental" purpose of influencing legislation.

13. Applicability of the Act.

The cornerstone of the Act is §307 ("Persons To Whom Applicable"). Its pertinent provisions are:

[T]he provisions of this title shall apply to any person . . . [except certain political committees] who by himself, or through any agent or employee or other persons in any manner whatsoever, directly or indirectly, solicits, collects or receives money or any other thing of value to be used principally to aid, or the principal purpose of which person is to aid, in the accomplishment of any of the following purposes:

(a) The passage or defeat of any legislation by the Congress of the United States.

(b) To influence, directly or indirectly, the passage or defeat of any legislation by the Congress of the United States.

In the words of the Supreme Court,[27] the following three prerequisites must exist in order to bring a person within §307 of the Act:

(1) The person must have solicited, collected or received contributions;

(2) One of the main purposes of such person or one of the main purposes of such contributions must have been to influence the passage or defeat of legislation by Congress;

(3) The intended method of accomplishing this purpose must have been through direct communication with members of Congress.

The Supreme Court had earlier held in the *Rumeley* case [28] that "lobbying activities" means "lobbying in its commonly accepted sense."

This in turn means "representations made directly to the Congress, its members, or its committees." The Court then went on to say that "lobbying" does not cover attempts "to saturate the thinking of the community." In other words, the Act does not cover all activities which tend to influence, encourage, promote or retard legislation. It covers only specific activities—those directly addressed to Congress, its members or its committees.

This conclusion was reached after the Court had discussed at considerable length the well-respected and traditional obligation of the Court to construe a statute—if a fair alternative be available—so as to reach a conclusion "which will avoid serious doubt of . . . constitutionality." The Court then went on to point out that the broad meaning and application sought by the government would give the right "to inquire into all efforts of private individuals to influence public opinion through books and periodicals, however remote the radiations of influence which they may exert upon the ultimate legislative process . . ." The Court added that such interpretation "raises doubts of constitutionality in view of the prohibition of the First Amendment." See Section 16 below.

An employee of a trade association or other group may be required to register if his "principal" activity is lobbying. This is true even though the association itself need not register because lobbying is not its principal purpose.

14. Effect of Special Contributions.

There may be a serious question if a special fund is raised by a trade association, for example, by separate or special contributions—aside from general dues or assessments—which are to be used for lobbying. This may occur through "slush funds" or "war chests" collected to oppose or to seek directly some special piece of legislation. The "principal purpose" of such contributions would be clear.

This seems to follow from the *Harriss* opinion which pointed out that "the 'principal purpose' requirement does not exclude a contribution which in substantial part is to be used to influence legislation . . ."

15. Exemptions From the Act.

Under §307 of the Act, it does not apply to "a political committee as defined in the Federal Corrupt Practices Act, and duly organized State or local committees of a political party." This exemption is reinforced in §311 of the Act. See Section 7 above.

Section 308 of the Act specifically exempts the following:

(a) a person who merely appears before a committee of Congress in support of or opposition to legislation;

(b) a public official acting in his official capacity;

(c) a newspaper or any regularly published periodical (including any individual who owns, publishes, or is employed by any such newspaper or periodical) which in the ordinary course of business publishes news items, editorials or other comments or paid advertising, which directly or indirectly urge the passage or defeat of legislation, if they do nothing further in connection with the passage or defeat of such legislation, other than to appear before a committee of Congress in support of or in opposition to such legislation.

There appears to be no judicial construction of any of these exceptions except as to (a) above dealing with appearances before a Congressional committee. In the *Slaughter* case [29] it was held that this exemption protects any person who helps prepare a witness for his appearance before a Congressional committee. This would include meetings with the prospective witness, preparation of statements for such witness, research, accompanying the witness in his appearance as legal counsel, etc.

It is interesting to note the effect of the exemption and the *Slaughter* ruling upon certain of the reporting requirements under the same section. If a lobbyist "plants" a story in a newspaper or other publication, he would be required to list the publication in his quarterly report.

On the other hand, if the same material or argument is used by a witness appearing before a Congressional committee, it then becomes a matter of public record and the press may widely print it as such. Under such circumstances, the lobbyist need not mention the matter in the quarterly report nor need the witness register under the Act.

Another exception, discussed in Section 12 above, is lobbying which is only an "incidental" and not the "principal" purpose of the person, association or contribution. The legislative history of the Act, as supported by the *Harriss* case, supports this.

16. "Grass Roots" Lobbying.

According to the Congressional Reports accompanying the Act, one of the three classes of "so-called lobbyists" to which it was intended that the Act apply, were those who "initiate propaganda from all over the country in the form of letters and telegrams, . . ." [30] This is not to be taken as derogating from the right of the people to communicate their wishes to Congress. It refers to the individual or group which organizes a "grass roots" campaign for or against a Bill—perhaps even to the extent of supplying large numbers of identical postcards or letters to people scattered throughout the country.

Many trade associations which are not registered as lobbyists—nor are any of their employees—and which, in fact, should not be classified as such, are careful in reporting information from Washington. They advise their members only as to the facts and then suggest, for example, "make your wishes and interests known to your senators and congressmen." Perhaps a list of committee members is appended to the newsletter or other communication. No recommendation or request for specific kinds of communication is made. This is left up to the individual person.

This is done to avoid the strictures upon the lobbyist who does, in fact, "initiate propaganda from all over the country . . ."

17. Administrative Agency and Other Governmental Contact.

A person representing the interests of others in Washington may well be required to have contact—perhaps of a continuing nature—with many other elements of government besides Congress, its members and its committees. The various executive departments and the administrative agencies may, in some cases, be even more important than Congress in a particular situation.

Such contact does not technically qualify as lobbying under the Act. The Act—as do the *Rumeley* and *Harriss* decisions—limits its application to direct communications to Congress, its members and its committees and influencing legislation.

This may be an important factor in determining whether or not registration and reporting under the Act are necessary. If contact with Congress is merely "incidental" or sporadic but contact with the administrative agencies goes beyond this, registration may not be necessary.

18. Registration and Report Forms and Filing.

Both registrations and quarterly reports are incorporated into a single form, the face thereof being the "Preliminary" Report which is deemed the registration and supplies "identifying data." The reverse thereof deals with "financial data" and is used for quarterly reports. Only the face of the report need be filled out on the initial filing or registration. One copy is filed with the Secretary of the Senate and two copies with the Clerk of the House, from whom the blank forms may be obtained. The reports are filed under oath.

An "employee," if required to file, should not attempt to combine his reports with those of his employer. Employers, if required under the Act to file, are not relieved of that obligation merely because their agents or employees are also required to, and do, file. The latter's names are to be listed in the employer's own reports.

Employees should file as many reports as they have separate employers. Thus, an individual representing and lobbying for more than one company or association should file separate reports as to each such representation. This explains the multiple entries in the *Congressional Record* of the same individual or firm—particularly as to law firms and public relations firms.

19. Enforcement of the Act.

Enforcement of the Act has been conspicuously weak. It appears that there have been only five cases in which the Act was involved and only one conviction.[31] These five cases were a test case instituted by the *National Association of Manufacturers,* the *Harriss* case, the *Slaughter* case —all discussed heretofore—an indictment of the United States Savings and Loan League which was dismissed, and the so-called *Natural Gas* case which resulted in two attorneys pleading guilty for failing to register and being fined $2500 each with one year suspended sentences. The oil company which had retained the attorneys was fined $5000 on each of two counts of aiding and abetting the two men in violating the lobbying law. Bribery charges arising from the case were dropped.

In view of the general agreement that violations of the Act have been continuous over the years, this record of enforcement is not good. It has been emphatically stated: "Perhaps the most frequent criticism of the 1946 act is that it is simply not enforced." [32]

For this reason, the registration and reporting procedures would be materially altered under the 1967 amendments discussed in Section 20 below. While it was clear from the attitude of the joint Congressional committee that more vigorous enforcement was desired,[33] it is presently impossible to anticipate the degree of greater enforcement in the future.

C. 1967 AMENDATORY BILL.

20. The 1966 Joint Committee Report.

In July, 1966 the Joint Committee on The Organization of the Congress recommended changes in the organization of Congress. Among the subjects given extended attention was lobbying. The following five basic changes were recommended: [34]

> 1. The provision requiring registration by those who have as their "principal purpose" the influencing of the passage or defeat of legislation shall be amended to require registration by those having such activity as a "substantial purpose."
> 2. Organizations which contend that it is impossible for them to separate expenditures for lobbying purposes—and which have influencing of legislation as a substantial purpose—shall be required to file their total receipts and expenditures under oath and estimate the percentage properly allocable to lobbying activities.

3. Lobby registration information shall be filed with the General
Accounting Office [GAO] rather than the Clerk of the House of
Representatives and the Secretary of the Senate. It shall be the
responsibility of GAO to:

> (a) Maintain the registrations as public records for a
> five-year period.
> (b) Deliver to the Speaker of the House and the Presi-
> dent of the Senate quarterly records for publication in
> the Congressional Record.
> (c) Analyze registration information and deliver to
> Congress an annual report on lobbying activities.
> (d) Refer complaints of failure to register or false or
> improper registrations to the Department of Justice for
> appropriate action.

4. Individuals registering under the Act who are to receive contingent fees for lobbying activities shall be required to state the
terms of the fee in detail. This disclosure shall include a specific
description of the legislation on which the fee is contingent and
any other events which would affect the payment of all or any
portion of the fee.

5. The exemptions under the Act applicable to newspapers and
periodicals shall be extended to include the television and radio
media.

21. Title V of The Legislative Reorganization Act of 1967.

The Legislative Reorganization Act of 1967 was introduced in the 90th
Congress.[35] This Bill incorporates the recommendations contained in the
Report discussed in Section 20 above. Title V of the Bill deals with
regulation of lobbying by amending the Federal Regulation of Lobbying
Act of 1946.

    (a) Probably the most important of these recommendations is to
make the Act applicable to all having lobbying as a "substantial purpose." This changes the prior provision in which "principal purpose" was
the test for registration and reporting.

It still exempts those with whom lobbying activities are merely incidental to other functions and, of course, does not affect the right of the
individual to petition Congress. However, it "would put others on notice
that they should register if substantial sums were being spent on their
influencing of legislation."

    (b) The 1966 Report had said:

> Perhaps the most frequent criticism of the 1946 act is that it is
> simply not enforced. Convictions under the act had been obtained
> in only one case during the twenty years of its administration.

To remedy this, reports are now to be filed with the General Accounting Office (GAO) instead of with the Clerk of the House of Representatives and the Secretary of the Senate. The GAO is to refer complaints, failure to register or false or improper registrations to the Department of Justice for appropriate action.

(c) The third significant change is the requirement of detailed disclosure as to any contingent fee arrangements a lobbyist may have—including specific reference to the legislation upon which the contingency is based.

This legislation, toward the end of 1967, was stalled in the House Rules Committee despite President Johnson's earlier endorsement. On November 29, 1967 a separate Bill (H.R.14211) was introduced by Rep. Charles Bennett. This new Bill was essentially the same as Title V, referred to above. As this is written, Washington opinion appears to believe that this separate amendatory lobbying legislation may be passed sometime by 1970. In view of the important changes provided in this amendment, PR counsel should consult counsel as to the current status of such legislation.

D. STATE CONTROLS OF LOBBYING.

22. Variety and Ambiguity.

Any public relations practitioner contemplating any activity for his client in connection with state legislation must consult the specific laws of the state involved. A failure to do so tempts trouble—so varied are the controls and requirements from state to state.

Lobbying definitions vary. Methods of control vary. Need for prior registration and disclosure varies. For this reason—also others including the belief in the usefulness of "local connections"—the larger public relations firms are less frequently seen as state legislative lobbyists insofar as direct influence upon state legislators is concerned. See Section 3 above. In most instances, their activities are limited to "grass roots" techniques.

Historically, lobbying first became an "evil" at the state level. State controls antedate federal control by some seventy years, beginning with a Georgia constitutional provision in 1877. This was followed by a succession of constitutional and legislative enactments. Of particular interest is the Massachusetts law of 1890 which initiated the dual concept of "legislative counsel" and "legislative agent," discussed in Section 25 below.[36]

The variations which becloud a broad understanding of the state laws and controls involve approach, concept, language, definitions, exemptions, procedures and method and degree of enforcement.

23. Definitions.

Basic to the heterogeneity of state control measures are the disparity and ambiguity in defining lobbying and lobbyists. One commentator has said: [37]

> [T]he existing statutes either make no attempt at definition or . . . dispose of the question in such vague and meaningless phrases as to make them difficult, if not impossible, to interpret and enforce.

Lane suggests five different categories into which the state definitions of lobbying may fall: [38]

(a) Corrupt Solicitation.

This has been described as influencing legislation "by bribery, promise of reward, intimidation, or any other dishonest means" and activities by a person who "corruptly solicits, persuades, or influences, or attempts to influence any senator or representative to cast his vote. . . ."

(b) Claim of Improper Influence.

Lobbying, in this group of statutes, is defined as a claim of improper legislative influence by a person to obtain payment from another.

(c) Appeals to Other Than Judgment or Reason.

These definitions prohibit an approach to a legislator which is based on presumably illicit or immoral grounds—those which are not directed to his considered judgment or which are not based on reasoned argument. By implication these prohibited appeals include personal friendship, bribery, pressures of various kinds, etc.

(d) Pursuit of Private Interest.

This concept is based on the lobbyist's pursuit for pay of private— often pecuniary—interests, private interests being defined as "distinct from those of the whole people" in influencing legislation.

(e) Any Influence of Legislation.

This definition includes as lobbying "almost anything" which a person does for pay to influence legislation. Some laws speak of influencing legislation "in any manner," "in any way" or "directly or indirectly." This is the broadest base for the need for registration and disclosure of lobbying activities.

24. The Two General Methods of Control.

Twenty-seven states exercise lobbying control in the same manner as does the federal law—by the requirement that lobbyists publicly register and indicate their representation. See Section 27 below. All other states prohibit corrupt practices but do not require registration and the contemplated attendant publicity.[39] In Florida registration is not mandatory but may be required by legislative committees. As to corrupt practices, see Section 23 (a) above and as to registration requirements, see Section 27 below.

25. Legislative Counsel/Agents.

Ten states have set up two distinct classes of lobbyists: legislative counsel and legislative agents.[40] The Massachusetts statute—the pilot model of this dichotomy—is typical and defines "legislative counsel" as

> . . . any person who for compensation appears at any public hearing before any committee of the general court [the legislature] in regard to proposed legislation, and who does no other acts in regard to the same except such things as are necessarily incident to such appearance before such committee.

A "legislative agent" is defined as

> . . . any person who for hire or reward does any act to promote or oppose legislation except to appear at a public hearing before a committee of the general court [the legislature] as legislative counsel.

The legislative agent is therefore required to register if he performs any one of a wide variety of acts influencing legislation. The legislative counsel need register only if he appears before a legislative committee. It should be noted that appearance before a committee is an exempted activity under the federal statute as discussed in Section 15 above. Thus, both the federal law and these state statutes take notice of the special—perhaps more respectable—nature of a public appearance before a legislative committee.[41]

26. Contingent Fee Prohibition.

Except for the basic prohibition of bribery or other corrupt practices, state laws are not unduly restrictive. Among the few specific prohibitions are those outlawing contingent fee contracts between the lobbyist and his employer. All of the "registration states" except New Hampshire have such limitations.

There seems to be an historical fear of the probable conjunction between a lobbyist's contingent remuneration and secret or corrupt activity.[42] That this is a continuing attitude is clear from the 1967 amendment to the federal act which spells out special disclosure requirements if contingent fees are involved. See Section 21 above.

27. Registration Requirements.

Some twenty-seven states control lobbying by requiring registration of the lobbyist, his employer or both of them as the case may be. Registration is, variously, with the Secretary of State, the Attorney General or the Clerk of the legislature. Usually it should be filed before lobbying starts or within five days or a week thereafter. Registrations are open to the public.

The registration is under oath and commonly includes such information as the lobbyist's name and address, his employer's name and address, the term of his employment, by whom and how much he is paid for his services and expenses with an explanation of the included expenses, the legislation about which he will lobby and, in some states, a written authorization from the employer.[43]

A convenient tabulation of the registration requirements of all states will be found at pages 85–86 of volume 38 of *Notre Dame Lawyer* (1963). This tabulation details the states having only corrupt practices laws, those requiring registration, identity of the required registrants, time limits for registration, requirements as to financial reports and incidence of contingent fee laws (see page 819).

28. Financial Reports.

It is widely recognized that "money," if not the "root of all evil," is basic to lobbying. Accordingly, all but seven of the states having lobbyist registration laws also require the filing of financial reports. This may be required of the lobbyist, his employer or both, varying by state.[44]

There is some difference in the financial details which are to be revealed. Specific statutes should be examined both on this score and as to time of filing. Generally speaking, however, as in the New York statute, the required report covers

> in detail all expenses paid, incurred or promised directly or indirectly in connection with legislation . . . with the names of the payees and the amount paid to each, including all disbursements paid, incurred or promised to counsel or agents, and also specify-

---

Table on p. 819 reproduced by permission of the *Notre Dame Lawyer* and of Frank P. Maggio, the author thereof.

STATE	Limited to Corrupt Lobbying	Registration States; and, Place of Registration	Who Must Register	Registration Time Limit	Financial Report Required	Contingent Fees Illegal
Alabama	X					
Alaska		Director of Finance	Both Lobbyist and Employer		X	X
Arizona	X					
Arkansas	X					
California		Chief Clerk of the Assembly and Secretary of the Senate	Lobbyist		X	X
Colorado	X					
Connecticut		Secretary of State	Lobbyist	Before Service Rendered	X	X
Delaware	X					
Florida		X				
Georgia		Secretary of State	Lobbyist	Before Service Rendered	X	X
Hawaii	X					
Idaho	X					
Illinois		Secretary of State	Lobbyist	1 wk. after employment		X
Indiana		Secretary of State	Lobbyist	1 wk. after employment	X	X
Iowa	X					
Kansas		Secretary of State	Lobbyist	Before Service Rendered		X
Kentucky		Attorney General	Lobbyist	1 wk. after employment		X
Louisiana	X					
Maine		Secretary of State	Both	48 hrs. after employment		X
Maryland		Secretary of State	Both	1 wk. after employment	X	X
Massachusetts		Sergeant-at-Arms	Both	1 wk. after employment	X	X
Michigan		Secretary of State	Lobbyist	Before Service Rendered	X	X
Minnesota	X					
Mississippi		Secretary of State	Employer	5 days after employment	X	X
Missouri	X					
Montana	X					
Nebraska		Secretary of State	Lobbyist	Before Service Rendered	X	X
Nevada	X					
New Hampshire		Secretary of State	Lobbyist	Before Service Rendered	X	
New Jersey	X					
New Mexico	X					
New York		Secretary of State	Lobbyist	Before Service Rendered	X	X
North Carolina		Secretary of State	Lobbyist	1 wk. after employment	X	X
North Dakota		Secretary of State	Both	1 wk. after employment		X
Ohio		Secretary of State	Employer	1 wk. after employment	X	X
Oklahoma	X					
Oregon	X					
Pennsylvania	X					
Rhode Island		Secretary of State	Both	1 wk. after employment	X	X
South Carolina		Secretary of State	Both	1 wk. after employment	X	X
South Dakota		Secretary of State	Both	1 wk. after employment	X	X
Tennessee	X					
Texas		Clerk of the House of Representatives	Lobbyist	5 days after employment	X	X
Utah	X					
Vermont		Secretary of State	Both	48 hrs. after employment		X
Virginia		Secretary of State	Lobbyist	1 wk. after employment	X	X
Washington	X					
West Virginia	X					
Wisconsin		Secretary of State	Both	10 days after employment	X	X
Wyoming	X					

ing the nature of said legislation and the interest of the person
. . . therein.

Usually the reports are to be filed thirty or sixty days after the end of
the legislative session. Some few require monthly filing during the legislative sessions.[45]

Notes

1. Kennedy, *Congressional Lobbies: A Chronic Problem Reexamined,* 45 GEO. L.J. 535 (1957).
2. See, *e.g.,* LANE, LOBBYING AND THE LAW 3–12 (1964); Zeller, *The Federal Regulation of Lobbying Act,* 42 AM. POL. SCI. REV. 239 (1948).
3. United States v. Rumeley, 345 U.S. 41 (1952); United States v. Harriss, 347 U.S. 612 (1954).
4. For useful and informative background material on lobbying, see SCHRIFT-GIESSER, THE LOBBYISTS (1951); MILBRAITH, THE WASHINGTON LOBBYISTS (1963); DEAKEN, THE LOBBYISTS (1966); *Control of Lobbying,* 45 HARV. L. REV. 1242 (1932); *Improving the Legislative Process, Federal Regulation of Lobbying,* 56 YALE L.J. 316 (1947); J. Smith, *Regulation of National and State Legislative Lobbying,* 23 U. DET. L.J. 663 (1966).
5. Schriftgiesser, *supra* note 4, at 137.
6. See, *e.g.,* remarks to Senator Scott W. Lucas, *Getting Through to Congress,* CONG. REC. A4510 (June 10, 1957). For a further explanation of congressional attitudes about the propriety and necessity of lobbying, see Rosenbloom, *Effective Public Relations in Washington,* ch. 14 in PROFITABLE PUBLIC RELATIONS 191–93 (1968). For an earlier but consistent view, see 2 CHAFEE, GOVERNMENT AND MASS COMMUNICATIONS 784–85 (1947).
7. CORWIN, CONSTITUTION OF THE UNITED STATES OF AMERICA 810 (1953 ed.); Schriftgiesser, *supra* note 4, at 3.
8. Lane, *supra* note 2, at 124. See also PIMLOTT, PUBLIC RELATIONS AND AMERICAN DEMOCRACY 342–43 (1951).
9. See comments of Mark E. Richardson, Assistant Counsel of the National Association of Manufacturers, *Lobbying and Public Relations—Sensitive, Suspect, or Worse?,* 10 ANTITRUST BULL. 507 (1965).
10. See cases cited, *supra* note 3.
11. 155 F. Supp. 768 (E.D. Pa. 1957), *aff'd,* 273 F.2d 218 (3d Cir. 1959), *rev'd,* 365 U.S. 127 (1961).
12. For a discussion of the "false front" technique, see Hill, *The Making of a Public Relations Counselor,* P.R.J., June, 1964, at 24, where this subject is referred to as a "paper front." Also see PRSA Code, §9, dealing with a prohibition against such techniques, and discussed in the text hereof in Chapter 20, §9.
13. CUTLIP & CENTER, EFFECTIVE PUBLIC RELATIONS 478 (3d ed. 1964).
14. See also Harman v. Valley Nat'l Bank of Arizona *et al.,* 339 F.2d 564 (9th Cir. 1964).
15. Title III of The Legislative Reorganization Act of 1946, S. 2177, 79th Cong., 2d Sess., P.L. 610, 2 U.S.C. §§261–270 (1964).
16. 49 Stat. 823, 15 U.S.C. §79 (1) (i) (1958).
17. 66 Stat. 765, 46 U.S.C. §1225 (1958).

18. 43 Stat. 1070, as amended; 2 U.S.C. §256; 18 U.S.C. §599 (1952 ed. Supp. II 1955).

19. International Ass'n of Ice Cream Mfrs., F.T.C. Dkt. No. 2346, *dismissed,* 29 F.T.C. 1420 (1939).

20. Rock-Crushers Mfrs. Ass'n & Associated Equip. Distrib., F.T.C. Dkt. No. 5026, 38 F.T.C. 35 (1944).

21. Schriftgiesser, *supra* note 4, at 138–9.

22. *Id.*

23. *Supra* note 14. For a general discussion of the Act and its requirements, see LAMB & KITTELLE, TRADE ASSOCIATION LAW AND PRACTICE 155–160 (1956).

24. *Supra* note 3.

25. *Supra* note 3.

26. McGrath v. National Ass'n of Mfrs. of the United States, 103 F. Supp. 510 (D.D.C. 1952), *vacated as moot,* 344 U.S. 805 (1952).

27. Harriss, *supra* note 3, at 623.

28. *Supra* note 3.

29. United States v. Slaughter, 89 F. Supp. 875 (D.D.C. 1950).

30. S. Rep. No. 1400, 79th Cong., 2d Sess., at 27. See also statement of Senator La Follette, Chairman of the Joint Committee, 92 CONG. REC. 6367–68 (1946).

31. Hearings on S. Con. Res. 2 before the Joint Committee on the Reorganization of the Congress, 89th Cong., 1st Sess., pt. 6, at 1024–25 (1965). All five of the cases are discussed therein.

32. S. Rep. No. 1414, 89th Cong., 2d Sess. 53 (1966).

33. *Id.* at 54.

34. S. Rep. No. 1414, 89th Cong., 2d Sess. (1966).

35. S. 355, 90th Cong., 1st Sess. (1967). For comment upon the amendments, see P.R.J., Aug. 1967, at 22.

36. The most informative and complete discussion of state lobbying controls is E. LANE, LOBBYING AND THE LAW (1964). Also very useful is Note, *Lobbying —Multi-State Statutory Survey,* 38 NOTRE DAME LAW. 79 (1963).

    For a discussion of state constitutional convention lobbying, see Carol S. Greenwald, "Lobbyists' Perceptions of the 1967 New York State Constitutional Convention," unpublished dissertation submitted in partial fulfillment of the requirements of the degree of Ph.D. in Government, Department of Political Science, City University of New York.

37. Zeller, *Pressure Groups and Our State Legislatures,* XI STATE GOV'T 144 (Aug. 1938).

38. Lane, *supra* note 36, at 48–57. Citations to the various quotations in this section will be found in notes 2–36 of Lane.

39. See Note, *supra* note 37, as to identity of states falling into the two classifications, notes 59, 60.

40. Note, *supra* note 36, at 82.

41. Note, *The Federal Lobbying Act of 1946,* 47 COLUM. L. REV. 98 (1948).

42. Lane, *supra* note 36, at 73.

43. Note, *supra* note 36, at 81–82.

44. Lane, *supra* note 36, at 77–84.

45. *Id.* at 78.

Chapter 24

Activities and Control
of Foreign Agents

E. OTHER REQUIREMENTS

Chapter 24

Activities and Control
of Foreign Agents

A. INTRODUCTION.

1. Nature of Foreign Agents' Activities.

"Foreign agents" are merely the representatives of "foreign principals," a category running from foreign countries and their underground movements to some philatelic sources. Foreign agents are frequently the lobbyists, the PR men, or the advertising agencies for these foreign entities and perform, in many instances, no different functions.

With so many new and emerging countries coming into the international picture and with international trade and tourism burgeoning, a belief is growing that successful access to the eyes and ears of the American public or of the Congress, its committees and agencies, requires such representation. Foreign agents, in the last analysis, do not do anything different from "domestic agents"; they merely do it for different people. This is important to keep in mind since it is also the attitude of the lawmakers who recognize the need for such activities.

These activities may be biased and partisan—they frequently are and must be—but this makes little difference. It might even be said that a properly registered foreign agent can perform almost any service provided only that he violates no laws—the same strictures as apply to the "domestic agent." The importance of the Foreign Agents Registration Act of 1938 [1]—referred to herein and in the notes as the Act—lies partly in this freedom accorded the foreign agent who is properly registered and otherwise in compliance with the provisions of the Act.

2. Relation to "Lobbying."

The theories underlying foreign agent and lobbyist controls are similar. The fundamental premise is that both are "special pleaders" presenting a special—sometimes biased—point of view and that this fact should be disclosed so that it may be considered in the appraisal of their efforts and communications.[2] In a sense both the foreign agent and the lobbyist are similar to the lawyer pleading the case of his client. The lawyer's interest is disclosed of record and the judge or jury considers this in evaluating his plea or argument. This similarity to legal counsel was recognized by the 1966 amendments to the Act. The lawyer need register no longer provided he does not act "other than in the course of established agency proceedings, whether formal or informal." See Section 14 below.

The foreign agent's purpose and possible involvement with national security may create certain differences from "domestic lobbying." Lobbyist registration is required only if he seeks to influence legislation. The foreign agent's registration is required even if he communicates only with the public on behalf of the foreign principal or approaches the government for purposes other than legislation.

For a discussion of lobbying and the Federal Regulation of Lobbying Act, see Chapter 23.

3. Public Relations and the Act.

By the very nature of the public relations function, it is highly important in the "foreign agent picture." Public relations is among the few specific but significant activities singled out in the Act for special mention. This is no reflection on the PR man but rather a tribute to him as a skilled communicator. The Act pinpoints "public relations counsel, publicity agent, information-service employee . . ." in defining "agent of a foreign principal." See Section 10 below. Also, the exemption of a recognized foreign government official does not apply if he is "a public relations counsel, publicity agent, or information-service employee." See Section 12 below.

Quite apart from specific statutory reference, improved public relations is one of the prime targets of foreign principals and would naturally loom large in any foreign agent control. The investigations which led to the 1966 amendments of the Act dealt at length with many public relations activities—legitimate and otherwise—and served as specific foundation for certain of the statutory changes.

One of the problems facing the public relations counsel is his status under the Act. His activities on behalf of an apparent foreign principal may or may not require registration and other forms of compliance. It is therefore mandatory that public relations counsel, advertising agencies, etc., before entering upon such service, satisfy themselves as to whether registration, etc. is necessary. See Section 5 below.

4. Respectability of Foreign Agents.

The PR practitioner or any other non-diplomatic agent of a foreign principal should have no qualms of conscience about the legitimacy of his function. Such representation is legally recognized and the provisions of the Act merely provide for disclosure of certain facts. They do not imply in any way that there is any impropriety about such representation. The Attorney General has said: [3]

> Registration under the Act in no way places any limitation on the activities which may be engaged in by an agent of a foreign principal and places no stigma on any person registering. It may be assumed that persons who are legitimately engaged as agents of foreign principals have nothing to fear from public disclosure of their activities.

Many of the most reputable PR counsel, law firms, advertising agencies, etc. in the United States have registered, and their names appear year after year in the annual reports of the Attorney General to the Congress. As with lobbying generally, such representation is a legitimate and frequently necessary function—welcomed by members of Congress and by the Department of State.

5. Justice Department Advisory Opinions.

On occasion a PR man or firm will preliminarily not be certain of his statutory status and the need for registration. He should then ask for an advisory opinion from the Registration Section, Department of Justice, Internal Security Division. Such request should indicate the identity of the putative agent and foreign principal involved and the nature of the agent's activities for such principal. It should also include a copy (if written) of any existing or proposed agreement between the parties or a full description (if oral) of such agreement. [4]

This is a valuable avenue to explore in cases in which status is not clear. Registration involves considerable detail work and exposure, a continuing pattern of submission of materials to the Justice Department and the disclosure of the agent's status (if registered) on or in all published materials or other promotional efforts—a requirement which may diminish their effectiveness.

Advisory opinions may also be obtained to determine other questions such as the need for registration by certain of a firm's employees, results of a change in the nature of an agent's service, questions of termination of an agent's registration, etc.

6. Enforcement Policy and Activities.

Enforcement—especially during recent years—has been largely characterized by a cooperative Justice Department attitude, sometimes relying on "unofficial" procedures. About 30 indictments have been returned under the Act since it was enacted in 1938.[5]

Attorney General Katzenbach—then Deputy Attorney General—made it clear in his testimony before a Congressional subcommittee that the criminal sanctions were enforced only for "willful" violations and in "the clearest of cases." [6]

It was for this reason that the 1966 amendments permit the Attorney General to seek an injunction against the continuance of what might be considered a relatively minor or technical violation of the Act. Also, under the 1966 amendments, if a registration statement does not comply with the Act or its regulations, the Attorney General notifies the registrant, specifying the deficiency. The foreign agent then has ten days to comply fully with the Act and its regulations. This change gave statutory recognition to an informal procedure theretofore employed by the Attorney General as referred to above. See Section 21 below.

In his 1965 and 1966 reports to Congress, the Attorney General indicated that no criminal actions for willful violations of the Act were required during those years. At the same time, he pointed out that review of the filed statements in 1966 "generated many requests from the Department for further disclosure or other corrective action from registrants" and resulted "in the filing of 132 amended statements."

It may be anticipated that administrative enforcement under the injunction or notification procedures is likely to become more strict because of their statutory approval in the 1966 amendments. As before, indictment and criminal penalties will probably be reserved for willful and clear-cut violations.

7. Investigations of Agent Activities.

Beginning in 1962, the Senate Foreign Relations Committee began an investigation of the practical problems and developments under the Act as it then existed.[7] The inquiry was kicked off by the activities of lobbyists representing foreign sugar interests. The Committee had also become aware of efforts by American representatives to influence our foreign and domestic policies through "public relations campaigns, personal contacts, lavish entertaining, lobbying and other techniques outside of normal diplomatic channels." [8]

According to Senator Fulbright, Chairman of the Committee, there were two basic questions. The first was the need for identification of foreign government materials so that the reader might know their sources. At the same time, he recognized that it was the editors who had to cooperate in the disclosure of the source materials sent to them, and that control of such editing could not be legislated. His second concern dealt with the payment of money or other consideration to editors, etc. for publication of the foreign source material. Here were listed press junkets, entertainment and gifts.

The evidence developed in 1962 and thereafter indicated many violations of the law—or at least much skirting of the requirements to register and otherwise comply with the Act. One such example involved Igor Cassini, the newspaper columnist indicted in 1963 for failure to register as an agent for Rafael Trujillo, dictator of the Dominican Republic. Cassini operated through a public relations firm although he apparently took no part in its professional activities. Cassini pleaded "no contest" in 1964 and was fined $10,000 and placed on six months' probation. Other practices disclosed included the agreement by a major American network in 1959 to carry news and commentary not inconsistent with the Dominican Republic's best interests. For eighteen months of this service, the foreign government paid a network official $750,000. Another instance dealt with the distribution of films to television stations in the United States without charge. The films were produced for nationalist China, Mexico and Italy and carried no clear indication that foreign governments had paid for their production.

Throughout these investigations, no effort was made to challenge the right of a public relations firm or anyone else to represent a foreign principal. The demand was made that such public relations and other efforts should be clearly marked and labeled for what they are.

As a result of these investigations, amendatory legislation was introduced in 1963 and 1965 and eventually became law on July 4, 1966, effective ninety days thereafter. The Bill was S-693 of the 89th Congress and became Public Law 89-486.

B. PERSONS AFFECTED BY THE ACT.

8. Purpose of the Act.

The principal purpose of the Act in the words of the Attorney General is: [9]

> . . . To require public disclosure by persons engaging in propaganda activities or other activities for or on behalf of foreign governments, foreign political parties, and other foreign principals, so that the Government and the people of the United States may be informed of the identity of such persons and may appraise their

statements and actions in the light of other associations and activities.

Originally, in 1938, the Act was adopted as a national safety precaution during the critical period prior to World War II. It was aimed essentially toward Nazi and other subversive propaganda then entering and circulating throughout the country. The Nazi-orientation ended early in World War II when other, more specific legislation was adopted to cope with the wartime conditions. No better evidence of this reorientation of the Act and its enforcement need be cited than the fact that many of the current registrations thereunder stem from such innocuous representations as that of an advertising agency serving the tourist bureau of a friendly and closely-allied foreign nation.

9. Summary of the Act.

The Act requires all non-diplomatic agents of foreign principals (with certain exceptions) to file a detailed registration statement with the Department of Justice; to keep such registration current and supplemented; to give a full account of their activities and finances; to label all communications originating with them which are politically oriented; to file copies thereof with the Justice Department; to identify themselves when approaching Congress or other arms of government; to maintain certain books and records; to be subject to government inspection.

This summary is enlarged and the above terms defined in the following sections of this chapter.

10. Definitions.

The foregoing summary is not overly useful without "putting some meat on its bones" by defining several of the terms used therein. Most of the following definitions are taken from Section 1 of the Act and follow its language quite closely. Some, where so indicated, are taken from the regulations issued by the Attorney General to supplement the Act.

    (a) "Foreign principal" includes (1) the government of a foreign country (*de facto* or *de jure* or any insurgent group, whether or not recognized by the United States) and a foreign political party; (2) a person outside of the United States unless such person is an individual who is a citizen and domiciled within the United States, or, if not an individual, is organized under the laws of the United States or of a state and has its principal place of business in the United States; and (3) a partnership or corporation organized under the laws of, and having its principal place of business in, a foreign country.

    (b) "Agent of a foreign principal" means any person who acts as an agent, representative, employee, or servant, or in any other capacity at the order, request, or under the direction or control of a person, any of whose activities are directly or indirectly supervised, directed, controlled, financed or subsidized by a foreign principal, and who either directly or through any other person (1) engages within the United States in political activities in the interest of such foreign principal; (2) acts as a public relations counsel, publicity agent, information service employee or political consultant in the interests of such foreign principal; (3) within the United States, solicits, collects, disperses or dispenses contributions, loans, money, etc. in the interest of such foreign principal; (4) represents the interests of such foreign principal before any agency or official of the Government of the United States.

It also means any person who agrees or purports to act as, or holds himself out to be, whether or not pursuant to contractual relationship, an agent of a foreign principal as defined above.

The term does not include any news or press service organized under the law of the United States or any state thereof, or any newspaper, magazine, periodical or other publication which (1) files a sworn statement under the Act of 1912; [10] (2) is published in the United States solely by virtue of a bona fide news or journalistic activity; (3) is at least 80% beneficially owned by, and its officers and directors are, citizens of the United States; and (4) is not owned, directed, supervised, controlled, subsidized or financed nor its policies determined by any foreign principal or by the agent of any foreign principal.

See also Section 12 below as to exemptions from registration of certain agents of foreign principals.

(c) "Political propaganda" includes any communication or expression (oral, visual, graphic, written, pictorial) which is reasonably adapted to, or intended to indoctrinate, convert, induce or in any way influence the recipient or any section of the United States public with reference to the political or public interests, policies or relations of a foreign government or foreign political party or with reference to the foreign policies of the United States or to promote any racial, social or religious disorder or other conflict involving the use of force or violence in any American republic, this term referring to the signatories at Havana on July 30, 1940.

(d) "Political activities" means dissemination of political propaganda and any other activity which will, or is intended to, induce, persuade or influence any agency or official of the United States or any section of the public within the United States with reference to formulating, adopting or changing the domestic or foreign policies of the United States or with reference to the political or public interests, policies or relations of a foreign government or a foreign political party.

(e) "Political consultant" means one who informs or advises any other person with reference to the domestic or foreign policies of the United States or the political or public interest, etc. of a foreign country or a foreign political party.

(f) "Public relations counsel" includes any person who engages, directly or indirectly, in informing, advising or in any way representing a foreign principal on public relations matters pertaining to political or public interests, policies or relations of such principal.

(g) "Publicity agent" includes anyone who directly or indirectly publishes or disseminates oral, visual, graphic, written or pictorial matter of any kind including publication by advertising, books, periodicals, newspapers, lectures, broadcasts, motion pictures or otherwise. (See Subsection (f) above.)

(h) "Information service employee" includes anyone who furnishes, disseminates or publishes information or data relative to the political, industrial, employment, economic, social, cultural or other benefits of any foreign government, foreign political party or any group organized or having its principal place of business in a foreign country.

(i) "Prints" means newspapers and periodicals, books, pamphlets, sheet music, visiting and address cards, printing proofs, engravings, photographs, pictures, drawings, plans, maps, patterns to be cut out, catalogues, prospectuses, advertisements, and all reproductions on paper or similar materials by means of printing or other mechanical process except the copying press, stamps with movable or immovable type, and the typewriter.

C. REGISTRATION AND EXEMPTIONS.

11. In General.

Section 2 of the Act provides that "no person shall act as the agent of a foreign principal unless he has filed with the Attorney General a true and complete registration statement and supplements thereto . . . or unless he is exempt from registration under the . . . Act."

Before developing and discussing the registration requirements and procedures, the exemption provisions loom large; they are discussed in Section 12 immediately below.

12. Exemptions.

The registration requirements discussed in Sections 16 to 21 below do not apply to the following agents of foreign principals:

(a) Duly accredited diplomatic or consular officers.

(b) Any official of a foreign government recognized by the United States who is not a public relations counsel, publicity agent, information service employee or a citizen of the United States.

(c) Any member of the staff of a duly accredited diplomatic or consular officer if he is not a public relations counsel, publicity agent, information service employee or a citizen of the United States and if his activities are within his proper duties.

(d) Persons engaged only in private and non-political activities in furtherance of the bona fide trade or commerce of a foreign principal; or in other activities not serving predominantly a foreign interest; or collecting money to be used only for foreign aid and assistance or for food and clothing to relieve human suffering if such solicitation is in accordance with the Act of November 4, 1939 as amended.[11] See Section 13 below.

(e) Any person qualified to practice law insofar as he engages in legal representation of a disclosed foreign principal before any court of law or any United States government agency provided he does not attempt to influence or persuade agency personnel or officials other than in the course of established agency proceedings, whether formal or informal. See Section 14 below.

(f) Any person engaged only in furtherance of bona fide religious, scholastic, academic or scientific pursuits or of the fine arts.

(g) Provisionally, any person in the employ of a foreign country, the defense of which the President deems vital to the defense of the United States, while (1) engaged only in activities in furtherance of the national defense of both countries, which do not conflict with United States domestic or foreign policies; (2) his communications to the public are part of such activities, are truthful and accurate, and his identity as an agent of a foreign country is disclosed therein; and (3) such foreign country gives the Secretary of State such information as the Attorney General may require as to his identity, so that the Attorney General may, with due regard for national security, terminate the exemption.

Persons claiming benefit of the several exemptions have the burden of "establishing the availability" of the exemption. Further, they have the burden of proving that they have properly filed the required Notifications of their status or given the oral notifications sometimes required. Rules 300-06 should be carefully considered in this context—not only when service of the foreign principal is first undertaken but also annually thereafter and prior to *each* contact with Congress or a government agency.

These requirements apply to all exemptions including those discussed in Sections 13 and 14 below.

13. Special "Domestic Person" Commercial Exemption.

Under the 1966 amendments, activities in furtherance of a bona fide commercial, industrial or financial interest of a domestic person engaged in substantial commercial, etc. activities in the United States shall *not* be deemed to serve predominantly a foreign interest because such activities also benefit the interests of a foreign person engaged in bona fide trade or commerce which is owned or controlled by, or owns and controls, such domestic person, if (a) the foreign person is, or such activities are, not controlled, financed, subsidized by a foreign government or political party; (b) the identity of such foreign person is disclosed to the agency or official of the United States with whom such activities are conducted; and (c) whenever such foreign person owns or controls the domestic person, such activities are substantially a furtherance of the domestic person's bona fide commercial, etc. interests.

This exemption was added to cover the more and more common "commercial" situation in which an American company operates in one or more foreign countries and may be required by the laws of such countries to incorporate therein, perhaps even with majority control or ownership in the hands of foreign nationals. The purpose of such foreign activity and incorporation is really in furtherance of the American company's interests and not of those of the foreign nationals or country.

14. Status of Lawyers Under the Act.

Prior to the 1966 amendments, confusion had developed as to the need for lawyers to register as foreign agents when they were merely performing normal legal representation—either in or out of court—for foreign principals. The Bar took the position in many cases that such registration was not required. The question was finally resolved in the *Rabinowitz* case.[12] The Supreme Court here determined that legal counsel were not within the so-called commercial exemption of the Act as it then existed and therefore were required to register.

At the same time, some legal commentators believe this provision is still clouded by the broad definition of "political activities" (see Section 10 above) which is defined to include any activity designed to "persuade or in any other way influence any other person . . . with reference to the *domestic* or foreign policies of the United States." An attorney counseling foreign interests may find it difficult to advise his client unless he discusses domestic policies with his client. This is particularly true as to the attorney counseling a foreign individual not engaged in "bona fide trade or commerce." It is impossible to anticipate the direction and thrust of enforcement in this area.

15. Types of Activities Covered by the Act.

In addition to the more obvious activities likely to be engaged in by foreign agents—"politicking and buttonholing"—or the public relations and similar efforts specifically mentioned in the Act, a wide variety of activities or types of personnel have been the basis of registration under the Act. Among those appearing in the Attorney General's 1965 Report are:

> Acquisition of broadcast materials
> Administrative services
> Advertising agency
> Advertising services
> Advisor
> Broadcasting service
> Consultant
> Copy editor
> Correspondent
> Cultural advisor
> Distributor
> Economic consultant
> Editing service
> Film distribution
> Financial advisor
> Fund raising
> Honorary commercial agent
> Industrial promotion
> Information agency
> Investment promotion
> Journalist
> Legal services
> Literary agency
> Loan procurement
> News agency
> Nuclear materials representative
> Numismatic consultant
> Official representative
> Parcel forwarding service
> Patent application service
> Philatelic agency
> Political activity

Political movement
Political representative
Press officer
Procurement agency
Product promotion
Promotion of legislation
Proofreader
Publication distributor
Publicity
Public relations
Purchasing agent
Research
Resource consultant
Sales promotion
Selling agent
Style editor
Subscription agent
Ticket office
Tourist promotion
Trade bulletin preparation
Trade office
Travel promotion
World's Fair publicity agent
Writer

Some of these activities may not now require registration in view of the changes and added exemptions provided by the 1966 amendments. The advisory opinion procedure referred to in Section 5 above may be used to explore these possible changes with the Attorney General, in the event that current status under the amendments is not clear-cut.

D. REGISTRATION PROCEDURES.

Registration procedures under the Act are technical and require the disclosure of a great deal of information which the registrant may not personally believe necessary. Yet it is necessary to answer all questions completely and to fill in all items in the forms if they are pertinent. Whenever the item is inapplicable or the appropriate response to an item is "none," an express statement to that effect should be made.

Great care should be used in making up the statements since changes and formal amendments may be necessary if the Registration Section believes the registration to be incomplete or defective.

16. Registration Forms.

The various forms required for registration and subsequent filings are obtainable from the Registration Section, Internal Security Division, Department of Justice, Washington, D.C. 20530. Use of these forms is *required* except as explained under Section 17 below dealing with Exhibits.

The initial registration statement is to be filed on Form DJ-301 whether the registrant is an individual, a partnership, corporation or other group. It should be filed in duplicate with the Registration Section as above.

The so-called "short form" (Form DJ-305) should be filed by officers, directors, etc. of a registrant as discussed in Section 18 below.

Before making up these registration forms, applicants should carefully read both the Act and the Regulations thereunder. The forms themselves contain explanatory footnotes of pointed application.

17. Exhibits Required With Registration Statement.

Under Rule 201, the Initial Registration Statement (Form DJ-301) must be accompanied by exhibits which must be filed for *each* principal of the registrant.

Exhibit A, filed on Form DJ-306, discloses certain detailed information concerning the foreign principal.

Exhibit B, filed on Form DJ-304, sets forth the agreement between the agent and the foreign principal, whether a formal document, by correspondence or by oral understanding with either copies of the agreement or correspondence attached or the oral agreement completely described. Also included is a description of the nature and method of the agent's performance.

Exhibit C does not consist of a printed form. If the registrant is an association, corporation or other combination of individuals, it should submit a copy of its charter, articles of incorporation, constitution, by-laws and of any other document dealing with its organization, powers and purposes.

Exhibit D does not consist of a printed form and need be filed only if the registrant receives or collects contributions, money, etc. as part of a fund-raising campaign in the United States for a foreign principal. A statement captioned "Exhibit D" is filed, giving information about the fund-raising and its disposition.

Any change in Exhibit information is to be reported to the Registration Section within ten days of the change. A new Exhibit may then be required.

18. Registration and Liability of Officers, Partners, etc.

Under Rule 202, each partner, officer, director, associate, employee or subagent of a registrant must also file a registration unless

(a) he does not engage in activity on behalf of the foreign principal;

(b) his services are in a clerical, secretarial or similar capacity.

If the subagent of a registrant is itself a partnership or corporation, only those of its partners, officers, directors, etc. who engage in activity on behalf of the foreign principal must register.

Unless otherwise directed by the Registration Section, such registrations may be on the "short form" (Form DJ-305). The "ten-day rule" applies here as to changes in services rendered or compensation received. See Section 17 above. In such cases, new short form registrations shall be filed. There is no need to file exhibits or supplemental statements to a short form registration.

Under Section 7 of the Act, officers and directors of an agent of a foreign principal are under obligation to cause such agent to comply with the Act. If the agent fails to comply, each of its officers and directors is subject to prosecution therefor. Dissolution of an organization acting as an agent does not relieve the officers and directors of the obligation.

19. Time for Filing of Registration Statement.

Every person subject to the registration provision must file an original registration statement within ten days after the obligation to register arises. If this is impossible, or the requirements would impose undue hardship, the Chief of the Registration Section may extend the time in order reasonably to permit compliance with these requirements. Applications for extensions should set forth the reasons for the delay or the conditions which would create an undue hardship.

20. Supplemental Registrations.

Under Rule 203, every registrant (other than those who file a short form) must file in duplicate a supplemental statement within thirty days after the end of each six-month period succeeding such filing. Form DJ-302 should be used.

These supplemental statements must be filed even if the registrant did not engage in any activity on behalf of his foreign principal during the six-month period covered thereby—provided the agency relationship continued during such period. The time to file such statements may be extended upon sufficient cause shown.

21. Amendments.

An initial, supplemental or final statement deemed insufficient by the Registration Section must be amended upon a request or notice from the Section. Form DJ-307 is used therefor. Under Section 8 (g) of the Act—a new provision—a registrant may not continue to act unless the amendment is filed within ten days after receipt of such notice. If so filed within the ten-day period, the registrant may continue to act unless he receives a Notice of Non-Compliance from the Registration Section.

E. OTHER REQUIREMENTS.

22. Filing and Labeling of Propaganda.

Every foreign agent required to register who sends through the mails or by any other means, any political propaganda in the interests of a foreign principal in the form of "prints" or in any other form adapted or intended for circulation among two or more persons shall within forty-eight hours after the beginning of the transmittal thereof file two copies thereof with the Attorney General and a statement duly signed setting forth full information as to the places, times and extent of such transmittal. Such Dissemination Report shall be on Form DJ-310.

A Dissemination Report shall be complete in and of itself. Incorporation of information by reference to previously filed reports is not allowed. When propaganda is transmitted over a period of time, a Dissemination Report may be filed monthly as long as transmittals continue.

Also, in connection with such dissemination, the political propaganda shall be conspicuously marked at its beginning with, or accompanied by, a true statement setting forth that the transmitter is registered under the Act, together with his name and that of the foreign principal, and that his registration statement is available for inspection and that copies of the propaganda are being filed.

Political propaganda which is televised or in the form of a still or motion picture film sent through the mails shall be introduced by a statement reasonably intended to convey to viewers the information indicated above.

23. Deletions and Cuts by Media.

Even under the 1966 amendments, there is still a practical problem with which neither Congress nor the Attorney General seems to be able to cope. This results from uncontrolled deletions of the appropriate statutory labeling from materials submitted by or on behalf of the for-

eign principal. This difficulty was recognized by the Fulbright Committee
and also by the Attorney General's office. The Chief of the Registration
Section has said: [13]

> . . . there is a loophole in the law. It is this: that a film pro-
> ducer, for instance, is required to label political propaganda as
> coming from a foreign government, but the television station
> which chooses to show it can cut that identification from the film
> and often does. It is a weakness in the set-up. I don't know what
> you can do. We leave it to the good sense of the stations (not to
> show out-and-out propaganda). It would be an overwhelming job
> to keep track of labels. Just with television, you would have a
> couple of hundred people watching it around the clock. We pro-
> posed to the Senate committee to require keeping the label. But
> they saw right away it could not be done.

Thus the public relations counsel, acting on behalf of a foreign principal, would appear to have done all that the law requires of him if he
appropriately labels a news release, article or other material distributed
to the press on behalf of that foreign principal. If there is an understanding between the public relations counsel and a particular editor or commentator to delete the label, the public relations counsel would be liable
under the Act. The deletion by the editor would be attributable to the
public relations counsel, and, in effect, he would be guilty of distributing
unlabeled material.

24. Requirements for Government Contacts.

Before a foreign agent may transmit any political propaganda to, or
request any information from, any agency or official of the government
(including a member or committee of either House of Congress) he must
preface the propaganda or the request with a clear statement that he is
registered as an agent of such foreign principal under the Act.

Whenever a registered foreign agent appears or testifies before Congressional committees, he must furnish the committee with a copy of his
most recent registration statement, to be included in the record as part of
his testimony. These two provisions were added by the 1966 amendments
and now appear as part of Section 4 of the Act.

25. Maintenance of Books and Records.

Under Section 5 of the Act and Rule 500, every agent required to file
under the Act is also required to preserve in his possession, readily accessible for inspection, the following books and records:

(1) All correspondence, memoranda, cables, telegrams, teletype messages and other written communications to and from all foreign princi-

pals and all other persons relating to the registrant's activities on behalf of his foreign principals.

(2) All correspondence, memoranda, cables, telegrams, teletype messages and other written communications to and from all persons, other than foreign principals, relating to the registrant's political activity or relating to such activity on the part of any of the registrant's principals.

(3) Original copies of contracts between the registrant and any of his foreign principals.

(4) Records containing the names and addresses of persons to whom political propaganda has been transmitted.

(5) All bookkeeping and other financial records relating to registrant's activities on behalf of all foreign principals, including canceled checks, bank statements, and records of income and disbursements, showing names and addresses of all persons who paid money to, or received money from, the registrant, the specific amounts so paid or received, and the date on which each item was paid or received.

(6) If the registrant is a corporation, partnership, association, or other combination of individuals, all minute books.

(7) Such books or records as will disclose the names and addresses of all employees and agents of the registrant, including persons no longer acting as employees or agents.

(8) Such other books, records and documents as are necessary to reflect properly the activities for which registration is required.

These records may be destroyed after three years following termination of the registration or, upon permission from the Chief of the Registration Section, if they are more than five years old. All books and records may be inspected by officials of the Registration Section and the Federal Bureau of Investigation.

Notes

1. 22 U.S.C. §§611–621. The Regulations of the Attorney General appear in 28 C.F.R. ch. I, pt. 5, being A.G. Order 376–67 (April 17, 1967). Copies of the regulations are available upon request to the Assistant Attorney General in charge of the Internal Security Division, Washington, D.C. 20530.
2. Golden, *When Washington Investigates,* Sat. Rev., Dec. 8, 1962, at 70.
3. Introductory Statement to the Rules and Regulations Prescribed by The Attorney General, at 1 (1966).
4. Rule 5.2.
5. See Note, *Attorneys Under the Foreign Agents Registration Act of 1938,* 78 Harv. L. Rev. 619 at 623 (1965), which fixes the number at 31. Kennedy, *The Foreign Agents Registration Act,* P.R.Q., Fall, 1966, at 17, uses the figure of 29.
6. See Senate committee reports, *infra* note 7.
7. For a general discussion of these investigations and for further references to various comments and literature concerning the subject, see Cutlip & Center, Effective Public Relations 479–481 (3d ed. 1964). For specific examples of public relations activities considered improper under the Act, see the transcripts of testimony and reports of the Senate Committee on Foreign Relations relative to S.2136, 88th Cong. and S.693, 89th Cong.
8. Wilkins, *Amendments to Foreign Agents Registration Act Await 89th Congress,* P.R.J., Dec., 1964, at 19. For a discussion of the 1966 amendments, see Paul, *Foreign Agents Registration Act: The New Amendments,* 22 Bus. Law. 601 (1967); P.R.N., July 18, 1966, at 1.
9. Report of the Attorney General to Congress for the calendar year 1965, at 32.
10. Bourne Newspaper Act, 1912.
11. 54 Stat. 4 (1939).
12. Rabinowitz v. Kennedy, 376 U.S. 605 (1964).
13. Kennedy, *supra* note 5, at 20. See also O'Hara, *The Foreign Agen s Registration Act—the Spotlight of Pitiless Publicity,* 10 Vill. L. Rev. 435 (1965).

A Selective Bibliography

This is a "personal bibliography" based largely on the author's own library—works which have been useful in the study of the legal problems dealt with in this volume. There are undoubtedly other items which might have been included. This is a solid "working list"—not intended to be exhaustive.

The comments or notes appended to many of the entries were prepared by the author over the years as he worked with the material. They have been reviewed for purposes of this bibliography.

Some of the following items are not concerned solely or directly with public relations. All, however, are relevant to the larger concept of "communications" and its varied legal problems. The author has long felt that it is too limiting to confine research to purely PR questions and activities when dealing with the legal aspects of PR. Furthermore, purely PR legal materials are, thus far, scattered and minimal.

The large number of relevant articles in law reviews and industry journals have not been included. These will be found cited in the appropriate notes throughout the volume.

A

Advertising: Yesterday/Today/Tomorrow, Printers' Ink Books, Pleasantville, N.Y., 1962.
>   A survey of advertising and promotion, with chapters on governmental and other legal involvements written by this author and others.

Amdur, L. H., *Copyright Law and Practice*, Clark Boardman, New York, 1936.
>   A standard text on copyrights.

Amdur, L. H., *Trademark Law and Practice*, Lenham Act. ed., Clark Boardman, New York, 1948, 1959.

American Association of Advertising Agencies (A.A.A.A.), *Analysis and Criticism of a Study Entitled Advertising Agency Compensation, Law, Practice,* A.A.A.A., New York, 1935.

American Law Institute (A.L.I.), *Restatement of Agency,* A.L.I. Publishers, St. Paul, 2nd ed., 1958.

American Law Institute, *Restatement of Contracts,* A.L.I. Publishers, St. Paul, 1932.

American Law Institute, *Restatement of Torts,* A.L.I. Publishers, St. Paul, 2nd ed., 1965.

American Society of Composers, Authors and Publishers (A.S.C.A.P.), *Copyright Law Symposium,* Columbia Univ. Press, New York, 1939–67.
>   These volumes—fifteen in number through 1967—contain the winning essays in the Nathan Burkan Memorial Competition sponsored by A.S.C.A.P. Now published annually, most deal with current copyright developments. They have led to some very worthwhile and interesting promotional, publicity and advertising ideas.

Arthur, William R., and Crosman, Ralph L., *The Law of Newspapers,* McGraw-Hill, New York, 1940.

Probably the best rundown on various legal areas important to the press. While not current, what it says is valid, although further research is needed to bring it up to date.

Ashley, Paul P., *Say It Safely*, Seattle, Univ. of Washington Press, 3rd ed., 1966. An excellent brief course in libel law for the press and broadcaster. Full of examples. Used in journalism and communications schools.

Association of the Bar of the City of New York, *Radio, Television and the Administration of Justice.* Columbia Univ. Press, New York, 1965. A specialized but important documentation of the impact of broadcasting. Useful to all who deal with the public through the broadcast media. Good discussion of effect of adverse publicity. Broadly applicable by analogy, not just as to administration of justice.

B

Backman, Jules, *Advertising and Competition,* New York Univ. Press, New York, 1967. The A.N.A.-sponsored study in defense of advertising as a contribution to the American economy. Essential to an understanding of the relationship of advertising, public relations and other promotional methods and costs to product price.

Ball, Horace G., *Law of Copyright and Literary Property,* Bender, New York, 1944.

Barksdale, Hiram C., *The Use of Survey Research Findings as Legal Evidence,* Printers' Ink Books, Pleasantville, N.Y., 1957. Probably the best work devoted to this subject. Discusses both the cases and the research methodology necessary to judicial acceptance of surveys, polls and similar studies.

Bent, Silas, *Ballyhoo,* Liveright, New York, 1927. Vivid and critical description of the press agent and press in the "Roaring Twenties." Good historical material, whatever its relative importance.

Bently, Garth, *Editing the Company Publication,* Harper, New York, 2nd ed., 1953. Largely for the company editor but discusses in limited fashion some of his legal involvements.

Bernays, Edward L., *Biography of an Idea,* Simon & Schuster, New York, 1965. Despite its autobiographical approach, it gives good historical detail of PR, etc. Some portions deal with campaigns having legal implications, especially lobbying and government relations.

Better Journalism for a Better Tomorrow, John H. Drewry (ed.), Univ. of Georgia Press, Athens, 1963. One of the annual volumes from this press containing addresses and papers from various sources dealing with a wide variety of communications problems, some legal.

Bishop, Frank Patrick, *Advertising and the Law,* Benn, London, 1928. First book on English law applicable to advertising, PR, etc. Useful comparative source.

Bleyer, Willard G., *Main Currents in the History of American Journalism,* Houghton Mifflin, Boston, 1927.

> Essentially a history of the press and journalism. Good background and factual material.

British Labour Party, *Report of a Commission of Enquiry into Advertising,* The Labour Party, London, 1966.

> The famous "Reith Report." Critical of advertising and other promotion as a social force. Required reading in view of developments in Washington. See Firestone and Backman books.

C

California Continuing Education of the Bar, *Legal Aspects of Competitive Business Practices,* Univ. of California Printing Dept., Berkeley, 1961.

> Good panoramic legal view of wide variety of selling, advertising, promotional, etc., methods. Intended for "California consumption" but very useful generally.

Callmann, Rudolph, *Unfair Competition, Trademarks and Monopolies,* Callaghan, Chicago, 3rd ed., 1965.

> One of the best on the subject. Treats trademarks for what they really are: a monopoly. Integrates trademarks into unfair competition, a much broader subject and of ever-increasing importance.

Chafee, Zechariah, Jr., *Government and Mass Communications,* Univ. of Chicago Press, Chicago, 2 vols., 1947.

> Without a doubt the classic treatment of this subject. Thirty years have not dated it. "Must" reading—and interesting enough to take on a vacation.

Chernoff, George, and Sarbin, Hershel B., *Photography and the Law,* American Photographic Book Publ. Co., New York, 2nd ed., 1965.

> Apparently the only available book on this limited subject. Intended pretty much for the layman. Practical.

Communications Cartography, John H. Drewry (ed.), Univ. of Georgia Press, Athens, 1964.

> See comment under *Better Journalism for a Better Tomorrow.*

Copyright Institute of the Federal Bar Association, *Seven Copyright Problems Analyzed,* Commerce Clearing House, Inc., Chicago, 1952.

Cross, Harold L., *The People's Right to Know,* Columbia Univ. Press, New York, 1953; 2nd Supp., 1959.

> The standard work on legal access to public records and proceedings.

Cutlip, Scott M., *A Public Relations Bibliography,* Univ. of Wisconsin Press, Madison, 2nd ed., 1965.

> Should be "No. 1" in any PR or PR/legal library. Invaluable and indispensable. Well organized.

Cutlip, Scott M., and Center, Allen H., *Effective Public Relations,* Prentice-Hall, Englewood Cliffs, N.J., 3rd ed., 1964.

D

Derenberg, Walter J., *Trademarks,* Practicing Law Inst., New York, 1946.
Good text.

Developing the Corporate Image, Lee H. Bristol, Jr. (ed.), Scribner's, New York, 1960.
Thirty-one chapters, each dealing with a different segment of PR or publicity. Almost 31 different points of view. Legal issues—and some solutions—scattered through the book.

Diagnosis and Prognosis in Journalism, John H. Drewry (ed.), Univ. of Georgia Press, Athens, 1962.
See comment under *Better Journalism for a Better Tomorrow.*

Digges, I. W., *The Modern Law of Advertising and Marketing,* Funk & Wagnalls, New York, 1948.

Dover, C. J., *Effective Communication in Company Publications,* B.N.A., Inc., Washington, D.C., 1959.
A good do-it-yourself text on the company publication. Chapter 9 is called "It's Legal—and It's Necessary." Some case histories of company approaches to political and legal problems in employee publications.

Drinker, Henry S., *Legal Ethics,* Columbia Univ. Press, New York, 1953.
The standard reference on this important subject.

Drone, Eaton S., *Law of Property in Intellectual Productions in Great Britain and the United States,* Little, Brown, Boston, 1879.
One of the earliest books on the subject. Still sometimes quoted. Good starting point.

Duncan, Delbert J., *Trade Association Management,* Nat'l Inst. for Com. and Trade Org. Executives, New York, 1948.

E

Employee Patent and Secrecy Agreements, Nat'l Industrial Conf. Board, New York, 1965.
Good analysis and forms.

Engberg, Edward, *The Spy in the Corporate Structure,* World, New York, 1967.
A study in depth of personal privacy; includes industrial espionage and documents most of the reported cases, adding detail to the legal record. A serious defect is its lack of any index.

Ernst, Morris L., and Schwartz, Alan U., *Privacy,* Macmillan, New York, 1962.
Readable discussion of privacy law, using the case method. Excellent for the layman.

F

Federal Communications Commission (F.C.C.), *Annual Reports,* Govt. Printing Office, Washington, D.C., various years.
Good running history of broadcast controls.

Federal Communications Commission, *Broadcast Primer,* F.C.C., Washington, D.C., 1961.

Brief but instructive history and explanation of the functions of the F.C.C. A good starter and guide to the intricacies of broadcasting controls.

Federal Trade Commission, *Annual Reports,* Govt. Printing Office, Washington, D.C., various years.

Cumulatively they give a good picture of the changing emphasis of F.T.C. activity. Some contain good reviews of F.T.C./court activity.

Ferguson, Rowena, *Editing the Small Magazine,* Columbia Univ. Press, New York, 1958.

Some legal coverage.

Firestone, O. J., *The Economic Implications of Advertising,* Methuen, Toronto, 1967.

Commissioned by the Institute of Canadian Advertising, this is the Dominion equivalent of the Backman study.

Food and Drug Administration, *Compendium of Medical Advertising,* Govt. Printing Office, Washington, D.C., 1967.

Various materials dealing with advertising and labeling of drugs, etc., since the Kefauver Amendments of 1962. Good.

Freedom and Responsibility in Broadcasting, John E. Coons (ed.), Northwestern Univ. Press, 1961.

Papers by such men as Newton Minow, Lou Jaffe, Leroy Collins, and Roscoe Barrow, from a "neutral" seminar at Northwestern University. Good presentation of these authoritative sources. Joel Rosenbloom's 75-page documentation of legal authority of the F.C.C. is very good.

Freeman, William M., *The Big Name,* Printers' Ink Books, Pleasantville, N.Y., 1957.

An entertaining but solid analysis of the history and working of testimonial and endorsement promotions. Some discussion of legal problems. Urges self-regulation of testimonials and downgrades "phony" endorsements and methods.

Friedrich, C. J., *The Development of the Control of Advertising on the Air,* Harvard Univ. Press, Cambridge, 1940.

A good early study of this problem.

G

Gare, F. A., *Covenants in Restraint of Trade,* Solicitors Law Stationers Socy., London, 1935.

Apparently still a good English source.

Geller, Max A., *Advertising at the Crossroads,* Ronald, New York, 1952.

A working adman's views and concern about governmental dangers to advertising and communications. Prophetic in part, in view of its publication in 1952. Some excellent insights into government/communications relations.

H

Haase, Lockley, and Digges, I. W., *Advertising Agency Compensation in Theory, Law and Practice,* Assn. of Natl. Advertisers, New York, 1934.

Excellent study from company's side. See the 4A study for the contrary view. Legally postured.

Handbook of Public Relations, Howard Stevenson (ed.), New York, McGraw-Hill, 1960.

Standard readings by various practitioners.

Hiebert, Ray Eldon, *Courtier to the Crowd,* Iowa State Univ. Press, Iowa City, 1966.

A biography of Ivy Lee, which also details "the development of public relations." This and the Bernays and Hill autobiographies supply a substantial but not always consistent history of PR. Deals with government investigations of Lee in detail. Good background for modern Congressional investigations.

Higher Ground for Journalism, John H. Drewry (ed.), Univ. of Georgia Press, Athens, 1965.

See comment under *Better Journalism for a Better Tomorrow.*

Hill, John W., *The Making of a Public Relations Man,* McKay, New York, 1963.

Contains some good examples of PR and legal involvements, especially as to the influence of government. Interesting and informative background PR materials.

Hofstadter, Samuel H., and Horowitz, George, *The Right of Privacy,* Central Book Co., New York, 1964.

Excellent discussion of theory and cases. Organization a bit confusing. Limited index is a handicap.

Howell, Herbert A., *The Copyright Law,* Bureau of Natl. Affairs, Washington, D.C., 1962.

Hower, Ralph W., *The History of an Advertising Agency,* Harvard Univ. Press, Cambridge, 1939.

Remarkably detailed study of the history and operations of N. W. Ayer. Deals with Ayer's legal involvements with clients, government, etc. The best available in its field. "Must" reading.

Hudson, Frederic, *History of Journalism,* Harper, New York, 1873.

The first extended history of American journalism, preceded only by largely biographical works. Indispensable background material.

I

Institute of Social Ethics, Georgetown University, *Ethics, Advertising and Responsibility,* Francis X. Quinn (ed.), Canterbury Press, Westminster, Md., 1963.

Collection of essays by people in various segments of industry and the professions dealing with business ethics and responsibility in communications generally—not just advertising, despite the title.

Irwin, Will, *Propaganda and the News,* McGraw-Hill, New York, 1936.

J

Jacobs, Milton C., *Outline of Theatre Law,* Milton C. Jacobs, New York, 1949.

Jones, T. Artemus, *The Law Relating to Advertisements,* Butterworth, London, 1906.

Good early study, but now dated.

K

Kenner, H. J., *The Fight for Truth in Advertising,* Round Table, New York, 1936.
> Excellent history of the early development of self-regulation and the genesis of the Better Business Bureau movement.

Kuh, R. H., *Foolish Figleaves? Pornography in—and out of—Court,* Macmillan, New York, 1967.
> Interesting discussion of the Supreme Court's obscenity decisions by a county prosecutor who has lived with the problem and suggests some solutions.

Kursh, Harry, *The Franchise Boom,* Prentice-Hall, Englewood Cliffs, N.J., 1962.
> A good rundown on the booming franchise business with considerable attention to PR, advertising and promotion—also legal aspects involved, including franchise contracts.

L

Lamb, George P., and Kittelle, Sumner S., *Trade Association Law and Practice,* Little, Brown, Boston, 1956.
> Good discussion of antitrust limitations on trade association activities. Very useful as "screen" for such activities; generally cautionary and conservative. Best available.

Lamoreux, Stephen, *The Right of Privacy—A Bibliography—1890–1961,* Washington State Univ., 1961 (mimeographed).
> Excellent reference to privacy materials. Comments on each item are good. Brings Swindler's journalism bibliography down through 1961 as far as it concerns privacy.

Landmarks of Law, Ray D. Henson (ed.), Beacon Press, Boston, 1960.
> Excellent collection of seminal and definitive law review articles by outstanding scholars. Many articles are of considerable interest to the lay reader and deal with such subjects as privacy, publicity, ideas, literary property.

Lane, E., *Lobbying and the Law,* Univ. of California Press, Berkeley, 1964.

Leaper, W. J., *The Law of Advertising,* Butterworth, London, 1950.

Lindey, Alexander, *Plagiarism and Originality,* Harper, New York, 1952.

Ling-Mallison, E., *Law Relating to Advertising,* Isaac Pitman, London, 1931.

Linton, Bruce A., *Self-Regulation in Broadcasting,* Univ. of Kansas Press, Lawrence, 1967.
> A teaching outline, very useful and instructive. Apparently available also through N.A.B. in Washington.

Loss, Louis, *Securities Regulation,* Little, Brown, Boston, 3 vols., 1961, 1962.
> This is the generally accepted text on the subject. Because of the nature of securities regulation, much of the book applies somehow to PR and sales efforts.

M

Mason, Lowell, *The Language of Dissent,* World, New York, 1959.
> Fascinating and highly critical dissents of a former F.T.C. commissioner,

enlarged with further comments. Strikes at bureaucratic expansion of government control of business and communications. Like those of Holmes, some of Mason's dissents are now majority views. Despite F.T.C. orientation, excellent lay reading.

Mehling, Harold, *The Great Time-Killer,* World, New York, 1962.

A "rough" treatment and going-over of TV. Some useful injection of legal aspects. Well documented.

Miller, Justin P., *Unfair Competition—A Study in Criteria for the Control of Trade Practices,* Harvard Univ. Press, Cambridge, 1941.

N

National Association of Broadcasters (N.A.B.), *Broadcasting and the Bill of Rights,* N.A.B., Washington, D.C., 1947.

The statements before Congress of 25 witnesses from the broadcasting industry. States the industry's position on the F.C.C.'s limited rights over programing and other broadcasting functions. Mixture of legal and operational arguments. Good source material on subject. Analysis somewhat one-sided, as to be expected.

National Association of Broadcasters, *Broadcasting and the Lottery Laws,* N.A.B., Washington, D.C., current edition.

Very useful compendium on the position of broadcasters as to acceptable promotions using contest methods. Updated from time to time.

National Association of Broadcasters, *Broadcasting the News,* N.A.B., Washington, D.C., 1966.

National Association of Broadcasters, *The Challenge of Self-Regulation,* N.A.B., Washington, D.C., 1966.

A report on the workings and results of the TV Review Board.

National Association of Broadcasters, *Political Broadcast Catechism and the Fairness Doctrine,* N.A.B., Washington, D.C., 5th ed., 1966.

An invaluable collection of questions and answers covering this important broadcasting area. Probably the most complete work available.

National Association of Broadcasters, *The Television Code,* N.A.B., Washington, D.C., various years, current edition.

A frequently updated text of the Code. A "must" for all company communicators using the broadcast media in any way.

National Industrial Conference Board, Inc. (N.I.C.B.), *Patent Counsel in Industry,* N.I.C.B., New York, 1964.

National Industrial Conference Board, *New Product Development,* N.I.C.B., New York, 1963.

A good study of new product problems. Limited legal references.

New Products Marketing, Printers' Ink Books, Pleasantville, N.Y., 1964.

"A comprehensive exploration" of new product introduction by 87 "industry leaders and observers." Chapter 70 ("Call Your Lawyer—Before, Not After"), by the author of the present volume, deals with legal involvements.

Nimmer, Melville B., *The Law of Copyright,* Bender, New York, 1963.

A good text by an acknowledged authority. Also useful to the layman.

Nims, Harry D., *Unfair Competition and Trademarks*, Baker, Voorhis, New York, 4th ed., 1947.
A standard multi-volume text and source on this subject.

O

Onward and Upward with Communications, John E. Drewry (ed.), Univ. of Georgia Press, Athens, 1961.
See comment under *Better Journalism for a Better Tomorrow*.

P

Pilley, Charles, *Law for Journalists*, Isaac Pitman, London, 1932.
Pilpel, Harriet, and Zavin, Theodora, *Rights and Writers*, Dutton, New York, 1960.
Pimlott, J. A. R., *Public Relations and American Democracy*, Princeton Univ. Press, Princeton, 1951.
Excellent scholarly treatment, by a competent British observer, of public relations in the U.S., with considerable treatment of federal government publicity and PR methods and aims. Should be read along with Rourke's *Secrecy and Publicity*, written 10 years later.
Pollock, Sir Frederick, *Law of Torts*, Stevens, London, 1939.
Presbrey, Frank, *The History and Development of Advertising*, Doubleday, New York, 1929.
Prosser, William L., *Torts*, West Publishing, St. Paul, 1964.
The starting point for research into the law of torts. An outgrowth of Prosser's *Hornbook*. Follow up the footnote references for complete research. By an acknowledged authority.

R

Rhyne, Charles S., *Municipal Regulation, Taxation and Use of Radio and Television*, Natl. Inst. of Municipal Law Officers, Washington, D.C., 1955.
Ringer, Barbara A., and Gitlin, Paul, *Copyrights*, Practicing Law Inst., Philadelphia, 1965.
A relatively short text.
Roper, Burt W., *State Advertising Legislation*, Printers' Ink Books, Pleasantville, N.Y., 1945.
Best source of state law coverage through 1945.
Rourke, Francis E., *Secrecy and Publicity*, Johns Hopkins Press, Baltimore, 1961.
An excellent and relatively brief discussion of this "dilemma of democracy." Factual but also keyed to the applicable law.
Rowe, Frederick M., *Price Discrimination Under the Robinson-Patman Act*, Little, Brown, Boston, 1962.
Probably the best available text and explanation of this complex legal area and statute. Frequently quoted by the courts.

Rowell, George P., *Forty Years an Advertising Agent*, Printers' Ink Books, Pleasantville, N.Y., 1906.

A classic "personal history." Covers early history of advertising and the author's part therein. He was founder of *Printers' Ink*.

Ruder and Finn, various titles, published by Ruder and Finn, New York, various years.

A continuing series of brochures and pamphlets dealing with a wide variety of PR functions, methods and problems. Some deal with ethics, legal involvements, etc. Definitely worth reading. Very useful in many ways.

S

Sampson, Henry, *History of Advertising*, Chatto and Windus, London, 1874.

Fascinating "anecdotal" history of English advertising, with some coverage of American and colonial materials.

Schramm, Wilbur, *Mass Communications*, Univ. of Illinois Press, Urbana, 2nd ed., 1960.

"Readings" by leading scholars. Substantial sections on control of media, government, and media responsibilities fall into legal areas. Media and public opinion material good background.

Schriftgiesser, Karl, *The Lobbyists*, Little, Brown, Boston, 1951.

A good, frequently quoted discussion of the history and operations of lobbyists. Treats development of Lobbying Act at length.

Securities and Exchange Commission (S.E.C.), *Compilation of Releases Dealing with Matters Frequently Arising Under the Securities Act of 1933*, S.E.C., Washington, D.C., 1965.

Reprints important releases under the Act, including Nos. 3844, 4697 and 4709, discussed in the present text.

Securities and Exchange Commission, *General Rules and Regulations Under the Securities Exchange Act of 1934*, S.E.C., Washington, D.C., 1967.

Necessary for an understanding of the detailed operations and requirements of the S.E.C. under this Act.

Securities and Exchange Commission, *The Work of the Securities and Exchange Commission*, S.E.C., Washington, D.C., 1966.

A brief but very useful "primer" explaining the overall jurisdiction and activities of the S.E.C.

Seldes, Gilbert, *The Public Arts*, Simon & Schuster, New York, 1956.

Seldin, Joseph, *The Golden Fleece*, Macmillan, New York, 1963.

A highly critical but readable dissertation about the exploitation of the public by PR promotion and advertising. By means of a unilateral, highly selective choice of unsavory tactics, it makes its point. Good grist for the current governmental critic. Typical of the "anti-school," like Mehling's book.

Shafter, Alfred M., *Musical Copyright*, Callaghan, Chicago, 1939.

Simon, Morton J., *Advertising Truth Book*, Advertising Federation of America, New York, 1960, 1961, 1964.

Covers many F.T.C. *Guides* and guidelines for truthful and legally acceptable representations and claims.

Simon, Morton J., *The Law for Advertising and Marketing*, Norton, New York, 1956.
The most recent and complete coverage. By the author of the present volume.

Smead, Elmer E., *Freedom of Speech by Radio and Television*, Public Affairs Press, Washington, D.C., 1959.
One of the standard references on the subject. Very good for the history of the treatment of the problem. Quite inclusive references.

Socolow, A. W., *The Law of Radio Broadcasting*, Baker, Voorhis, New York, 1939.

Sovern, Michael I., *Legal Restraints on Racial Discrimination in Employment*, Twentieth Century Fund, New York, 1967.
A study in depth, including employment advertising, screening, and other employment practices. Goes into procedures and enforcement. Good.

Spring, Samuel, *Risks and Rights*, Norton, New York, 1952.
Good coverage of a variety of areas of interest to writers.

Steinberg, Charles S., *The Mass Communicators, Public Relations, Public Opinion and Mass Media*, Harper, New York, 1958.

Steinberg, Charles S., *Mass Media and Communications*, Hastings House, New York, 1966.
Series of essays by leading writers in communications. Little legal orientation, except incidentally, but presents a panoramic picture of the mass media, their impact and operation.

Swindler, William F., *A Bibliography of Law on Journalism*, Columbia Univ. Press, New York, 1947.
Excellent coverage through 1947. Refers to much seminal material in important journalistic/PR/advertising legal areas.

T

Taylor, Telford, *Grand Inquest, The Story of Congressional Investigations*, Simon & Schuster, New York, 1955.

Thayer, F., *Legal Control of the Press*, Foundation Press, Brooklyn, 4th ed., 1962.
Required reading for all concerned with almost any aspect of the press and its various functions.

Trade Regulation Reporter, Commerce Clearing House, Chicago, 1954.
Probably the best coverage of trade regulation matters. Weekly supplements and service, federal and state. Excellent for F.T.C. materials.

Turner, E. S., *The Shocking History of Advertising*, Dutton, New York, 1953.
Readable; good coverage.

U

U.S. Department of Commerce Advertising Advisory Committee, *Self-Regulation in Advertising*, Govt. Printing Office, Washington, D.C., 1964.

This is the closest that the federal government has come to admitting that advertising and selling are important, although Secretary Hodges denied any official imprimatur for it. A good rundown on the full scope of such regulation. Good historical source.

U.S. Department of Defense, *Clearance of Public Information Releases by Manufacturers* (Public Information Security Guidance No. 16), Washington, D.C., 1952.
Useful information as to permissible publicity activities by manufacturers holding government contracts.

U.S. Department of Defense, *Standards of Conduct* (Directive 5500.7), Washington, D.C., 1966.
Deals with such matters as PR use of military facilities and personnel by private sector and the community, cooperation of the services with business and state and local governments, etc.

U.S. Justice Department, *Attorney General's Memorandum on the Public Information Section of the Administrative Procedure Act,* Govt. Printing Office, Washington, D.C., 1967.
This is probably the best available explanation of the 1967 Freedom of Information Act. It explains the Act so that the administrative agencies may supplement it with their own regulations.

U.S. Navy, *Public Affairs Regulations,* Govt. Printing Office, Washington, D.C., 1965.
Extremely detailed instructions for Navy personnel in handling all forms of Navy "public affairs" and information. Very useful to the private sector which communicates with the Navy or seeks Navy cooperation in its own PR. Also a textbook on "practical PR."

U.S. Patent Office, *General Information Concerning Trademarks,* Govt. Printing Office, Washington, D.C., 1966.
A good, brief "primer" on trademarks.

U.S. Post Office Department, *The Law vs. Lotteries,* Govt. Printing Office, Washington, D.C., 1963.
Useful statement of this department's position as to acceptable and mailable materials dealing with contests. Contains frequent examples and discussions of precedents. Updated from time to time.

United States Trademark Association (U.S.T.A.), *"Honest" Truth or Unfair Competition?* U.S.T.A., New York, 1963.
This and the following U.S.T.A. materials are excellent sources for the layman. Very understandable, with many practical examples.

United States Trademark Association, *Notes from the Patent Office,* U.S.T.A., New York, 2 vols., various years.

United States Trademark Association, *Trademark Licensing, Domestic and Foreign,* U.S.T.A., New York, 1962.

United States Trademark Association, *Trademark Management,* U.S.T.A., New York, 1955.

United States Trademark Association, *Trademark Selection: The Management Team Method,* U.S.T.A., New York, 1960.

United States Trademark Association, *Trademarks in Advertising and Selling,* U.S.T.A., New York, 1966.

United States Trademark Association, *Trademarks in the Marketplace, Selection and Adoption, Proper Use and Protection,* U.S.T.A., New York, 1964.

W

Wade, Worth, *Industrial Espionage and Use of Trade Secrets,* Advance House, Ardmore, Pa., 1964.

Walls, Howard, *The Copyright Handbook for Fine and Applied Arts,* Watson-Guptill, New York, 1963.

Warner, Harry P., *Radio and Television Law,* Bender, New York, 1948.

Warner, Harry P., *Radio and Television Rights,* Bender, New York, 1954.

Webster, George D., *Federal Tax Aspects of Association Activities,* Chamber of Commerce of the U.S., Washington, D.C., 1959.

Good survey of trade association activities and their tax consequences. Now somewhat dated, but still a useful starting point.

Williston, Samuel, *Law of Contracts,* Baker, Voorhis, New York, 9 vols., 3rd ed., 1959–1967.

Wittenberg, P., *Dangerous Words,* Columbia Univ. Press, New York, 1948.

Y

Young, James W., *Advertising Agency Compensation,* Univ. of Chicago Press, Chicago, 1933.

One of the three "depression" studies. See the titles by the 4A's and by Haase.

Table of Cases

Index

(PR is used throughout this index as the abbreviation for Public relations.)